The Bulge Battlefields

A Fields of War Visitor's Guide to Historic Sites

Robert J Mueller

French Battlefields
Arlington Heights

French Battlefields
PO Box 4808
Buffalo Grove, Illinois 60089-4808
Fax: 1-224-735-3478
Email: contact@frenchbattlefields.com
Web address: http://www.frenchbattlefields.com

Copyright 2016 by Robert J Mueller
All rights reserved
Cover design by Vince Martinez
First Edition
Manufactured in the United States
Library of Congress Control Number: 2016916057
ISBN-13: 978-0-9823677-5-9
Unless otherwise indicated, all photographs and illustrations are the property of the author. No part of this book may be reproduced or transmitted without the written permission of the publisher.

Cover photographs:
Color: A section of the Mardasson Memorial to American forces engaged in the Battle of the Bulge, Bastogne, Belgium.
Time line: A patrol from the 101st Airborne Division moves out of Bastogne, left. NARA
One of twenty-six Farthest Advance Stones erected by the Touring Club of Belgium to mark the limits of the German assault during the Battle of the Bulge. This well-preserved example stands in Han-sur-Lesse, center.
Corporal James Gordon and Private LC Rainwater, 2nd Armored Division, pose with one of at least ten German Panthers destroyed near Grandmenil, Belgium, right. NARA
Spine: *Voie de la Liberté* Borne #1147 on Mardasson Hill

Abbreviations used for photographs:
NARA: US Army Signal Corps photograph preserved at the National Archives and Records Administration, College Park, Maryland

Dedicated to:
Riley, Madelyn, Sarah,
Heidi, and Alexander

We have only died in vain if you believe so;
You have to decide the wisdom of our choice,
By the world which you shall build upon our headstones,
And the everlasting truth, which have your voice.

Though dead, we are not heroes yet, nor can be,
'Til the living by their lives which are the tools,
Carve us the epitaph of wise men,
And give us not the epitaph of fools.

— Private David J Phillips Company G, 3rd Battalion,
506th Parachute Infantry Division, 101st Airborne Division
(used with the kind permission of John Phillips)

Contents

Introduction	viii
Chapter One	
The Battle of the Bulge (Overview)	1
Chapter Two	
Battle for Elsenborn Ridge	15
Battle of Monschau	21
Battle of Höfen	26
Battle of Wahlerscheid Crossroads	30
Defense of the Losheimergraben Crossroads	41
Defense of Lanzerath	44
Defense of Buchholz Station	47
Battle for Krinkelterwald	52
Battle for Lausdell Crossroads	56
Battle of Rocherath-Krinkelt	62
Defense of Dom Bütgenbach	70
Side Trip: Truschbaum Museum	77
Chapter Three	
Kampfgruppe Peiper	79
Side Trip: Peiper's Actual Route	83
Malmédy Massacre	84
Battle of Malmédy	89
Affair at Ligneuville	94
Battle for Stavelot	97
Battle for Trois-Ponts	103
Amblève Valley Trap	109
Side Trip: 82nd Airborne Division Park	114
Battle of Cheneux	115
Battle for Stoumont	119
Battle for the Stoumont Sanatorium	122
The End of Peiper	124
Side Trip: 82nd Airborne Division Counterattack	125
Chapter Four	
Battle for the Schnee Eifel, St-Vith, and Vielsalm	133
The Flanks Collapse	135
Destruction of the 106th Infantry Division	141
Side Trip: Wereth Massacre and Lt Eric Fisher Wood Memorials	154
Battle of St-Vith	156
Ambush at Poteau	164
Salm River Sector	167
Side Trip: Battle of Thier du Mont à Sart	170
Side Trip: 83rd Infantry Division Battlefield and Museum	173

Chapter Five
Battle of the Rivers — 175
- Battle for Parker's Crossroad — 177
- Battle for Manhay — 181
- Battle of Grandmenil — 186
- Battle for Haid-Hits — 190
- Battle for Hotton — 192
  - Side Trip: Battle for Dochamps — 197
  - Side Trip: Battle for Sandoz — 198
  - Side Trip: La Roche-en-Ardenne — 202
- Battle of the Verdenne Pocket — 209
  - Side Trip: Battle for Rochefort — 217
- Ardennes American Cemetery — 221
- Battle of the Celles Pocket — 223
  - Side Trip: Florennes Spitfire Museum — 229

Chapter Six
Skyline Drive — 230
- Battle of Lützkampen — 236
- Battle of the Ouren Bridges — 239
- Dasburg River Crossing — 243
- Battle of Marnach — 245
- Battle of Clervaux — 248
- Battle of Hosingen — 257
- Battle of Weiler and Hoscheid — 260
- Battle of Holzthum and Consthum — 265
- Battle for Wiltz — 267
- Affair at Schumann's Eck — 272
- Battle for Schumann's Eck — 273
  - Side Trip: Battle of Dahl and Nocher — 280
- Last Stand before Bastogne — 283

Chapter Seven
Defense of Bastogne — 288
- Battle of Longvilly — 302
- Battle for Mageret — 305
- Battle of Bizory — 308
- Battle for Neffe — 310
- Battle of Wardin — 313
- Battle of Marvie — 317
- Battle for Noville (1) — 321
- Battle of Foy (1) — 327
- Battle of Bois Jacques (1) — 329
- Affair at Barrère Hinck (Crossroads X) — 333
- Battle of Flamierge — 336
- Battle of Champs — 339

Contents

Battle of Chaumont	348
Battle of Assenois	353
Surrender Demand	359
Side Trip: Battle of Senonchamps	360
Side Trip: Battle of Lutrebois	362
Side Trip: Battle of Villers-la-Bonne-Eau	367
Battle of Longchamps	369
Battle of Bois Jacques (2)	372
Battle of Foy (2)	376
Battle of Noville (2)	379
Battle of Bastogne Ends	380

Chapter Eight
Battle of the Sûre and Sauer Rivers — 383

Battle of Fouhren	391
Wallendorf Trail and Hoesdorf–Bettendorf Promenade du Souvenir	393
Battle of Hoesdorf Plateau	397
Battle of Diekirch	400
Battle of Ettelbruck	403
Battle of Bettendorf	406
Battle of Ernz Noire	416
Battle of Berdorf	417
Crossing the Sauer River	421
Battle of Echternach	422
Side Trip: Westwallmuseum Panzerwerk Katzenkopf	425
Battle of Lauterborn (Lauterbur)	426
Luxembourg City	431

Acknowledgments — 435

Appendices — 436

Appendix A: Farthest Advance Stones	436
Appendix B: Comparison of Ranks	438
Appendix C: Unit compositions	439
Appendix D: German Military Units	441
Appendix E: Glossary of German Military Terms	443
Appendix F: Armor Comparison	445

Index — 447

Introduction

Ten years of touring European battlefields has brought a deep appreciation of how a commander's use of local terrain can significantly influence the outcome of military engagements. Defensive positions are strengthened by placement on high ground with clear lines of observation and fields of fire. Routes of advance are hidden by terrain or deception while attackers search for an enemy's weaknesses.

American forces' gallant refusals to surrender during the initial days of an immensely stronger German armored assault reinforces one's respect for those ordinary men, from ordinary backgrounds, who did extraordinary things.

The combat infantrymen's burden was indeed heavy. For example, by 1944, only 20 percent of American troops were in combat divisions and of those in combat divisions only 65 percent of the men were fighting soldiers. By war's end some rifle companies had suffered over 200 percent casualties; in other words, statistically, every man in the unit had become a casualty – and each of their replacements. Frequently a battalion's original combat soldiers that survived the entire war unscathed could be counted on one's fingers.

It is with this in mind that *The Bulge Battlefields* identifies and describes the actions of individual soldiers, enlisted men and officers, whose unflinching dedication to their fellow soldiers motivated heroic actions, frequently at the cost of their lives. The Fields of War series is in tribute to the soldiers of all nations who, willingly or not, suffered the cold, hunger, fear, and hurt of battle.

How to Use this Book

This guide brings battlefield visitors to specific sites of important battlefield events, describes what happened there, and offers opportunities to view commemorations, visit museums, or inspect surviving relics of the battle. Compromises to travel efficiency sometimes requires sacrifices to a purely chronological description of events.

Each chapter begins with a brief summary of the precipitating military events. A 'fact box' summarizes key information and a detailed battlefield map assists in following the action and locating selected sites. The 'Battle' section describes each commander's objectives and troop movements. An 'Aftermath' section notes results of the fighting and significant events which occurred after the engagement. The major section of each battle is devoted to the 'Battlefield Tour'. Each tour starts at an easy to locate town and has been designed to be taken in any order. Geographic coordinates (latitude, longitude), which can be entered into GPS locators, are given for each location allowing visitors to select only those sites of individual interest or to alter the order of visitation. Clear driving instructions, highlighted in boxes for easy reading, are designed to bring a visitor to various positions of importance on the battlefield. A brief explanation of the significance of the site includes descriptions of individual soldier's contributions to its eventual outcome. Footnotes provide insights into mentioned soldiers' post-battle lives.

The book has been written with the intent of touring battlefields by automobile without which visitation to Ardennes sites is difficult. For those unable or unwilling to provide their own transportation, a few tour companies offer a reasonable alternative Public transportation to battlefields is seldom a viable option.

The indicated positions of military units on the battlefield maps presented in this book are approximated for ease of viewing and do not necessarily indicate headquarters locations. The maps show modern roadways; but they should never be considered a substitute for current highway road maps. Farm or forest roads are generally not drivable without four-wheel drive vehicles.

    The appendices offer helpful comparisons of military ranks, unit sizes and their composition, German military terminology, and statistics on armored vehicles.

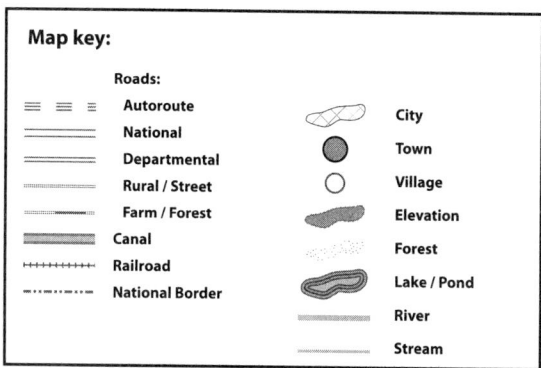

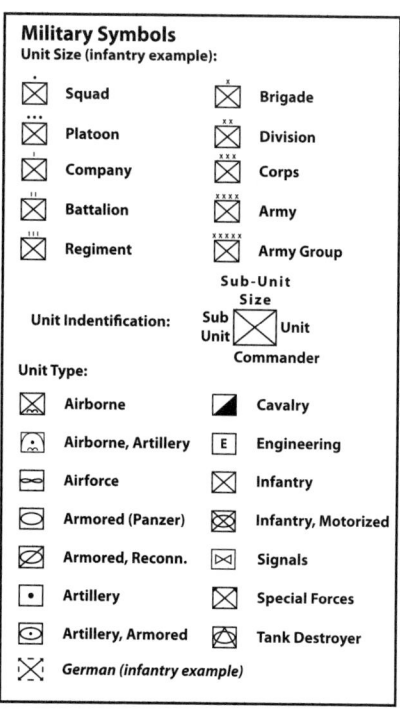

General Tourist Information

Tourist offices can provide helpful information regarding accommodations, cultural and historic sites, walking or cycling routes, and hours of operation for museums. The offices are not included in the tours, but their addresses and contact information are provided at the beginning of each town's description. The *Michelin Green Guide for Belgium and the Grand Duchy of Luxembourg* is highly recommended for its presentation of general tourist information. It makes an excellent accompaniment to this book and offers general touring advice in addition to listing historic and cultural locations, market days, festivals, and public holidays.

Twenty-four hour military time is in use in Europe; therefore operational hours in this book are so presented. Those sites open on weekends are frequently closed on Mondays or Tuesdays. Some variations exist, especially later closing hours during the summer tourist season. Few museums are handicap accessible; those that so advertise are indicated. The information contained herein is believed to be accurate at the time of printing, but museum hours are notoriously subject to change. If access to a certain site is of paramount importance, it is best to contact it in advance.

American military cemeteries are handicap accessible, but unlike British of German cemeteries, their hours are restricted from 9:00 to 17:00. An American representative is always on duty to assist relatives to locate graves of family members.

American visitors must accommodate the use of the metric system as it is the measure used on local road signs and maps. Each year roadways are improved or re-routed and intersections reconstructed. Therefore, up-to-date road maps or GPS locators are a necessity. The 1:50,000 scale maps prepared by the *Institut géographique national* (IGN) are available at many bookstores, automobile service areas, or over the internet from http://www.ngi.be/.

Local citizens are remarkably tolerant of battlefield visitors; however private property should be respected and never accessed without owner's permission. Crops are the farmer's livelihood and trampling planted fields should be avoided, although a field boundary often provides a useful walkpath. Forests may be the scene of the autumn shooting season and care should be exercised. Finally, an additional word of caution: abandoned bunkers or off-trail battlefield terrain frequently retain dangerous spikes, barbed wire, or even unexploded ordinance. Utmost caution must be exercised and independent exploration is discouraged.

Chapter One
The Battle of the Bulge (Overview)
16 December 1944 to 28 January 1945

Background

By autumn 1944, the Allies thought that Germany, though beaten, would just not admit it. The Soviet Red Army was marching across Poland; the German allies of Romania, Bulgaria, and Finland had switched sides or gone neutral. France, Belgium, Grand Duchy of Luxembourg, and half of both Italy and Holland had been liberated. Lack of gasoline and aircraft fuel strangled German transportation and a shortage of trained pilots limited air defenses. German ground units were losing 50,000 men each month, forcing a lowering of the draft age to sixteen. Rear areas and hospitals were being combed for front-line replacements.

The Allied armies on the northwest European Theater fielded sixty-nine divisions. The First Canadian, British Second, and US Ninth Armies formed Field Marshal Bernard Law Montgomery's 21st Army Group leading the main Allied attack north of the Ruhr industrial zone. The Belgian Ardennes forest split Lieutenant General Omar N Bradley's 12th Army Group, placing Major General Courtney H Hodges's First Army on its north and Lieutenant General George S Patton Jr's Third Army to its south. Lieutenant General Jacob L Dever's 6th Army Group's US Seventh Army and French Army B held the southern flank in Alsace.

However, few of the Allied units were at full strength. After five years of warfare, British units suffered serious manpower shortages. Two divisions were dissolved because the men were needed to refill the ranks of other units. US units were likewise savaged since, despite America's large manpower pool, occupational deferments driven by the requirements of critical industries forced the drafting of previously exempted fathers and the relaxation of physical and mental standards. By November, American casualties had reached 3,000 per day. Rifle companies, the point of any army's sword, were especially hard hit. Riflemen replacements received less and less training, some arriving on the battlefield barely able to load and fire their weapons. Moreover, the life expectancy of a junior officer in combat was twelve days.

After the rapid advance across France in August 1944, the disastrous failures of Operation Market Garden, the Scheldt estuary, and the Hürtgen Forest caused strife within the Allied High Command. Montgomery, with the consent of Chief of the Imperial General Staff, Field Marshall Alan Brooke, plotted to have Supreme Allied Commander General Dwight D Eisenhower removed and assume full operational control of all Allied ground forces. Meanwhile, Eisenhower refused the recommendations of American and some British commanders to relieve Montgomery.

Patton had stalled before Metz on his path to the industrial Saar region of Germany. The enemy held forces hostage to failed attempts to secure the Roer River dams. Between 1 November and 7 December, the British Second Army had advanced only 10 miles (16 kilometers) while V-2 rockets rained upon Antwerp and Liège with daily regularity.

The Soviet Summer Offensive in 1944 nearly destroyed German Army Group Center; to its south, the Soviets advanced through Romania and Bulgaria and into Yugoslavia. In Italy, British and American Armies had crossed the Arno River.

2 The Bulge Battlefields

The near-term Allied objective was to capture the Ruhr industrial district, thereby crippling Germany's armaments production and its ability to continue the war. Montgomery proposed that the Belgian Ardennes was a natural defensive barrier and that Allied operations should be divided into sectors north and south of the forest with him in command of all ground forces to the north. At a meeting on 7 December, Eisenhower made the decision to envelop the Ruhr from both north and south. The old 'broad front' versus 'narrow thrust' arguments continued while Allied intentions disregarded those of its enemy. No consideration was given to German potential for launching its own attacks.

From the officer-filled hotels of Paris, directions emanated for shipment of supplies to the front. Although the first cargo ships unloaded in Antwerp on 28 November, by mid-December Allied front-line troops still suffered from shortages of nearly everything. A thriving black market siphoned off coffee, gasoline, tires, soap, and morphine. Entire trucks loaded with consumer goods, which meant just about everything, had vanished. With what was to be the coldest winter in 50 years approaching, front-line troops were without winter coats, water-proof boots, extra blankets, and wool socks.

As early as September, Adolf Hitler ordered plans for an offensive on the western front that he claimed came to him in a flash of inspiration. The offensive would attempt to repeat the dramatic success of the 1940 German invasion of France with, this time, the extensive harbor and main Allied supply port of Antwerp as the ultimate objective. Such an advance, starting through the dense forest of the Ardennes, would split the British and American armies, create havoc in the Allied rear areas, and deny the shipment of winter supplies. Hitler envisioned another Dunkerque.

Despite the ruined status of his armies, the Führer's thirty divisions of varying strength and quality were devoted to Operation WACHT AM RHEIN (Watch on the Rhine), later renamed Operation HERBSTNEBEL (Autumn Mist). Two Panzer Armies would advance across Belgium toward the Meuse River bridges between Liège and Namur. The offensive would drive a wedge between British 21st Army Group and the American 12th Army Group in a winter attack across 125 miles (200 kilometers) despite too few men, too little gasoline, and limited air support. The planned destruction of one-third of all Allied divisions on the front would drive the Anglo-Americans into armistice negotiations — or so Hitler thought.

Allied plans called for a mid-December offensive with a three-pronged attack. British 21st Army Group would aim for the Ruhr, American First and Ninth American Armies toward Cologne, and US Third Army toward Frankfort. The area between the northern and southern American efforts, the Ardennes, would be held by VIII Corps whose positions were essentially unchanged from what they had been in September. On 9 December, VII Corps began operations to eliminate the German bridgehead west of the Roer River near Duren. By 15 December, they had successfully eliminated German forces west of that river barrier. On 13 December, V Corps attempted capture the Roer River dams, unknowingly disrupting German troop movements in support of its Ardennes Offensive.

The Ardennes region extends from the German Eifel west to the junction of the Meuse and Semois Rivers but does not constitute a solid forest. In fact, only one-

Chapter One The Ardennes Campaign

third of the land is wooded. However, the Amblève, Ourthe, and Salm Rivers, which flow in generally north-south directions, and numerous small streams in deep cut valleys cut the terrain force roadways to twist and wind, thereby slowing movement especially for large-tracked vehicles. The dense terrain, in places, limits defensive fields of fire and the paucity of roads limits maneuverability of reserve forces.

Three American divisions held an 85-mile (137-kilometer) front. Major General Walter E Lauer's 99th Infantry Division arrived in France on 3 November 1944, and proceeded immediately to occupy positions along the German frontier from Monschau, Germany to Lanzerath, Belgium. At the southern end of the German assault, Major General Norman Cota's 28th Infantry Division, after suffering 5,000 casualties in the Hürtgen Forest, held a 25-mile (40-kilometer) front along the Our River. In between, the 106th Infantry Division, also having only recently arrived from the United States on 6 December and full of 18-year-old draftees, was stationed across the Losheim Gap.

In mid-December, Montgomery had traveled to England for Christmas, Eisenhower was at his Paris headquarters celebrating the award of his fifth star, and much of the senior command was nowhere near the front. The exception, Major General Troy H Middleton, VIII Corps commander, was hosting a party at his command post in the Belgian crossroads city of Bastogne.

German Objective		To break through the allied line, capture the port of Antwerp, and trap the British 21st Army Group.
Force		
	American:	Four infantry divisions eventually growing to 26 divisions with 830,000 men and 1,580 tanks (Lieutenant General Omar Bradley)
	German:	24 divisions with 500,000 men, 1,400 armored vehicles, 2,600 artillery pieces, and 1,000 aircraft (Generalfeldmarschall Walter Model)
Result		The German army was stopped and driven back to its start line.
Casualties		
	American:	10,276 killed, 47,493 wounded, and 23,218 taken prisoner or missing; 733 tanks, 1,300 vehicles, and 592 planes lost
	German:	12,652 killed, 30,582 wounded, and 38,600 taken prisoner or missing; 324 tanks, 5,000 vehicles, and 320 planes lost
	British:	200 killed, 969 wounded, and 239 taken prisoner or missing
	Belgian:	2,500 civilians dead
Location		Liège is 370 km northeast of Paris; Malmédy is 60 km southeast of Liège; Bastogne is 330 km northeast of Paris

Battle Summary

The German plan envisioned three armies holding twenty-four divisions under German Field Marshal Walter Model's Army Group B attacking along a 100-

mile (160-kilometer) front. On the northern wing, the Sixth Panzer Army, commanded by General der Waffen-SS Joseph 'Sepp' Dietrich,[1] formed the main effort. Dietrich's nine divisions with 120,000 men, 1,000 guns, and 500 tanks or self-propelled guns planned to pass through the five-mile wide Losheim Gap. Their first objective was the Meuse River near Liège where they would veer northwest toward Antwerp. The Fifth Panzer Army, commanded by General der Panzertruppen Hasso von Manteuffel,[2] would move along Dietrich's left shielding it against counterattack from the south. The Fifth Panzer Army's seven divisions faced negotiating hilly terrain and icy roads while maintaining an exacting timetable. The southern-most Seventh Army, commanded by General der Panzertruppe Erich Brandenberger, fielded seven infantry divisions to protect the southern flank of the advancing forces. The German High Command held four additional first-rate units in reserve.

Both Model and his superior Generalfeldmarschall Gerd von Rundstedt, who had recently returned to command OB West, attempted to convince Hitler to adopt a less aggressive 'small solution' — capture the German city of Aachen, not Antwerp, and cut between the US First and Ninth Armies. Hitler refused to countenance any changes to his plan.

Terrain, commander's temperaments, and placement of American forces dictated differing approaches to the opening of the offensive. Dietrich's Sixth Panzer Army would employ a traditional heavy artillery-barrage preparation and attack at dawn. The American units facing Manteuffel's Fifth Panzer Army were widely spaced with undefended gaps between manned critical crossroads. Manteuffel refused a preliminary bombardment because it would warn the Americans of an impending attack. Instead, Fifth Panzer Army would infiltrate the thinly spread American positions during the night under artificial moonlight created by bouncing searchlight beams off the clouds. The tactic was not considered threatening to the secrecy of the attack because the procedure had been used many times in the past to detect American night patrols.

Security was paramount. Unit commanders were not informed of the assault until 11 December. No coded messages were sent, therefore no enigma decrypts were available to warn the allies. Positioned troops were not allowed open fires. All movement was conducted during the long northern European nights and any officer privy to the plan was prohibited from air travel to forestall inadvertently falling into Allied hands. Motor vehicles were held back 8 miles from the front.

---

1   General der Waffen-SS Joseph 'Sepp' Dietrich, a tank sergeant during the First World War and, afterwards, an early follower of Hitler becoming Der Führer's chauffeur and body guard. During the war, he commanded SS troops in France, Yugoslavia, Greece, and Russia. In 1946, the Dachau War Crimes Tribunal sentenced Dietrich to life imprisonment for ordering the execution of American prisoners of war, specifically in the Malmédy Massacre. He served 10 years in the same Bavaria prison where, in 1924, Adolf Hitler wrote *Mein Kampf*. Released, he was tried by German authorities for participation in the infamous Night of the Long Knives, the 1934 murder of Hitler's SA opponents, and received a nineteen-month sentence. He died in 1966 at age 73.

2   General der Panzertruppen Hasso-Eccard Freiherr von Manteuffel, a diminutive veteran of fighting in Africa and Russia, was considered by many to be the best German field commander of the war. Although briefly held after the surrender, he was released and eventually became a member of the West German legislature, the *Bundestag*. Manteuffel died in 1978 at age 81.

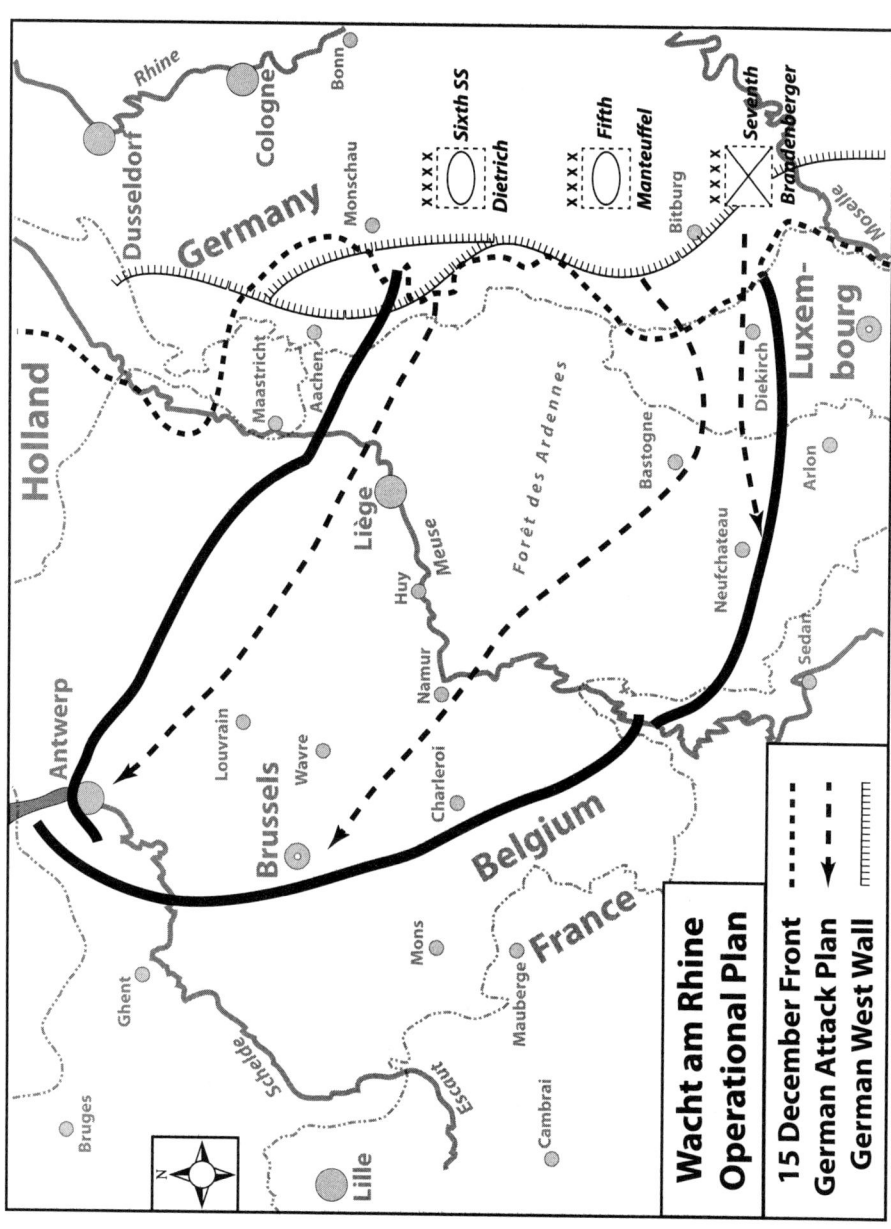

After two postponements to permit increasing fuel reserves and to position assault troops, the offensive was launched on 16 December 1944 — Ludwig van Beethoven's 174th birthday.

Sixth Panzer Army

The Sixth Panzer Army fielded four SS Panzer Divisions (1st, 2nd, 9th, and 12th) along with the first rate 12th Volksgrenadier Division (VGD) and the 3rd

Fallschirmjäger Division. The army also included newly-formed Volksgrenadier Divisions of unknown quality — the 246th, 277th, and 326th. The army's strength was its SS armored divisions that held 450 tanks and self-propelled guns.

Its mission was to drive 26 miles (42 kilometers) to the Meuse along a front ranging from Monschau in the north to Losheim in the south then to bypass Liège on both sides and continue on to Antwerp. The Sixth Panzer Army selected five routes, or *Rollbahnen* labeled A through E, for its armor to use in the attack. Most were narrow but paved roadways; however, some, like *Rollbahnen* A and B, were, at places, merely muddy forest trails. German infantry divisions were expected to breach the thin American lines within 24 hours. Although Hitler's plan called for the first forces to reach the Meuse River in two days, Dietrich's own calculations were more temperate at four days to reach the river and establish bridgeheads on the opposite shore.

The I SS Panzer Corps, commanded by General der Waffen-SS Hermann Priess, attacked north of the Losheim Gap with the 277th VGD followed by the 12th SS Panzer Division *Hitlerjugend*.[3] The penetration planned to attack between Hollerath and Losheim, cross the Höhes Venn to Stavelot, Malmédy, and Spa to reach the four northern Meuse bridges. The Losheim Gap, whose rolling terrain offered better opportunity for armored penetration, would be opened by the 3rd Fallschirmjäger Division on the left and the 12th VGD on the right. SS-Senior Colonel Wilhelm Mohnke's 1st SS Panzer Division *Leibstandarte SS Adolf Hitler* would follow the infantry penetration led by Kampfgruppe[4] Peiper and charge to the Meuse via Amblève, Trois-Ponts, and Vielsalm to bridges around Huy while ignoring all action along its flanks.

At the Sixth Army's northern limit, Generalleutnant Otto Hitzfeld's LXVII Corps would send its two infantry divisions (326th and 246th VGD) abreast to break through the front and wheel north to protect the army's right flank. The II SS Panzer Corps with 2nd and 9th SS Panzer divisions planned to exploit any success obtained by the two leading armored divisions.

Subsidiary operations in the north included 1,200 German paratroops, commanded by Oberstleutnant Friedrich August Freiherr von der Heydte, which were to land into the boggy Höhes Venn (Hautes Fagnes) to block American north-south support routes northwest of the Belgian–German frontier. In the event, the vast majority of the paratroopers missed drop zones or their planes were shot down, whereby only 100 men reached the combat zone. Their mission was a complete failure.

In addition, the German Panzer Brigade 150, 2,500 men commanded by Hitler favorite SS-Lieutenant Colonel Otto Skorzeny, had two missions. Operation GREIF was to race tanks and motorized infantry through American rear areas to seize Meuse River bridges at Engis, Amay, and Huy before they could be destroyed by a supposed retreating Allied Army. Skorzeny's men were to hold the bridges until the

---

3 The 12th SS Panzer Division possessed a checkered history having been responsible for the execution of 86 French civilians at Ascq in April 1944 and for murders of 156 British and Canadian PoWs at Ardenne Abbey near Caen during June 1944.

4 Kampfgruppe: a temporary combined-arms unit established for a specific purpose or task. The unit typically included infantry, armor, artillery, and other specialties as required. German kampfgruppe were usually named after its commanding officer.

Chapter One

The Ardennes Campaign

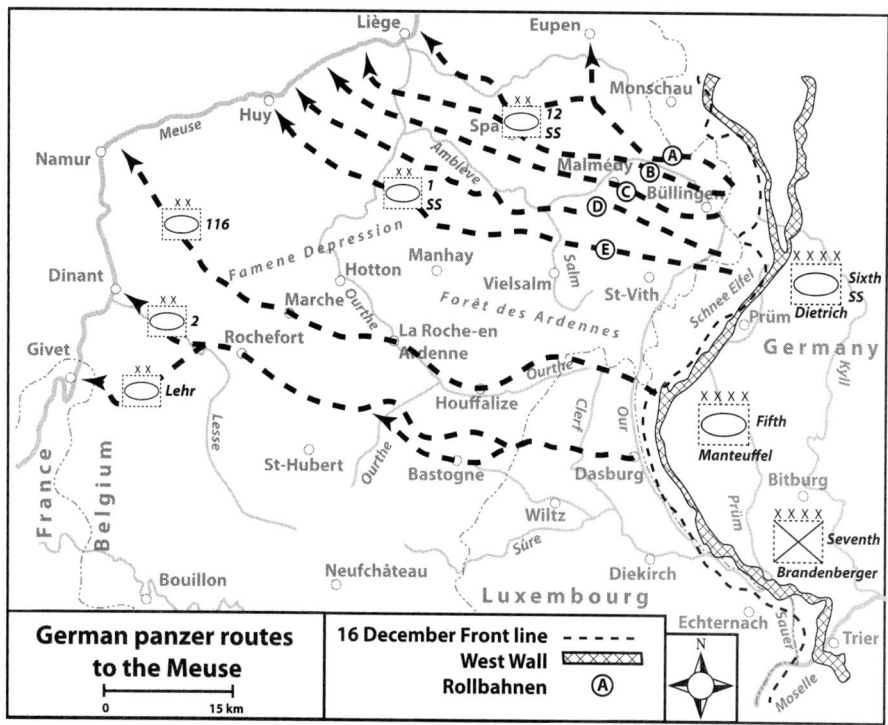

stronger armored spearheads could reach the river. Its smaller mission was to send a commando company of nine teams of officers and men to roam the American rear to spread rumors of disaster, destroy supply depots, and change roadway signs to create panic and confusion. Although Skorzeny's timetable on the northern shoulder was disrupted and its plans detected by Allied troops on the body of a dead German officer, stories of German infiltrators and saboteurs raced through American units. Military Police established checkpoints questioning all small-unit movements. One rumor to gain credibility was that Skorzeny would race across France to assassinate Eisenhower in Paris. The general was put under special guard and his movements restricted.

Skorzeny's mission ended on 17 December when it became obvious that the plan for rapid penetration of American positions had failed.[5] Many of his commandoes returned to German lines. His brigade was attached to I SS Panzer Corps, and Panzer Brigade 150 fought against the Ridge as infantry.

Fifth Panzer Army

The Fifth Panzer Army held four volksgrenadier and three panzer divisions supported by 350 tanks and self-propelled guns. The LVIII Panzer Corps, commanded by Generaloberst Walther Krüger and comprised of the 116th Panzer and 560th Volksgrenadier Divisions, was to cross the Our River near Lützkampen, Germany against the US 28th Infantry Division, seize Houffalize, Belgium, and pass over the Ourthe River to seize Meuse bridges between Namur and Andenne. The army's

---

5   Eventually seventeen of Skorzeny's men were captured; all were executed as spies.

XLVII Panzer Corps, commanded by General der Panzertruppen Heinrich Freiherr von Lüttwitz, had the longest and most difficult objective. His 2nd Panzer Division, Panzer Lehr, and 26th VGD were to cross the Our River near Dasburg, Germany, seize Clervaux and Bastogne, and continue to the Meuse bridges south of Namur. Meanwhile, the Fifth Panzer Army's LXVI Corps, commanded by General der Artillerie Walther Lucht, plotted to send its two infantry divisions (the 18th and 62nd VGDs) to bite off the US 106th Infantry Division's salient on the Schnee Eifel with a double envelopment and seize St-Vith, a transportation center with five roads and three rail lines emanating from the town.

Seventh Army

The German Seventh Army intended to send its LXXXV Corps, commanded by General der Infanterie Baptist Kniess, across the Our River near Vianden to then fan out south of Panzer Lehr and threaten capture of Luxembourg City if possible. The army's remaining LXXX Corps and LIII Corps sought to move west and form a defensive front facing south. Kniess fell against a variety of experienced American units. To the north was the 28th Division's 109th Infantry Regiment. In the middle was the new 60th Armored Infantry Battalion of 9th Armored Division, which, despite its lack of experience, defended a narrow front with an abundance of automatic weapons. The southern sector was defended by the 12th Infantry Regiment, 4th Infantry Division an experienced unit that fought since its Utah Beach landing.

Allied Intelligence Failure

In the days before the offensive, Allied intelligence received fragmented reports including a Japanese ambassador's report to Tokyo that Hitler amassed one-million men for combat in the west; that he had created Sixth Panzer Army with Sepp Dietrich as commander; that Ultra signals proved that he had ordered the Luftwaffe to stockpile fuel and to increase the number of aircraft north of Aachen. In addition, Allied air reconnaissance demonstrated increased levels of nighttime vehicular movements along the Rhine River, including hospital trains and tank-carrying flatcars moving west. Rationales and excuses disposed of all the evidence. Allied intelligence experts just could not believe that the German Army was capable of launching any offensives, let alone one during winter, although the first reports of elite German units being withdrawn from combat reached Allied intelligence as early as 1 October. By early December the intelligence had attracted the attention of Eisenhower's intelligence chief, Major General Kenneth WD Strong. In a meeting with Bradley at his headquarters in Luxembourg City, Strong presented his case for a large-scale attack through the Ardennes. He was ignored. Farther south, however, Third Army intelligence officer Brigadier General Oscar W Koch found an audience. He suggested that VIII Corps was especially vulnerable to an attack that could expose Third Army's left flank. Patton saw the offensive possibilities of at least fourteen German divisions facing the Ardennes and ordered the preparation of contingency plans to meet any such threat.

Chapter One

German Attack

After the early nightfall of Friday evening, 200,000 men in twenty-four divisions with 2,000 artillery pieces and 1,000 tanks and self-propelled guns moved toward assembly areas on straw-strewn roadways with rag-muffled wheels and horse hooves. The initial assault force crowded into a front 98 kilometers (61 miles) wide and 5 kilometers (3 miles) deep. Just before dawn at 0530 on 16 December, the eastern sky was illuminated by the muzzle flashes of over one-thousand cannon and rocket launchers unleashing explosives upon American front lines from Höfen to the Losheim Gap. The 35-minute barrage destroyed telephone lines and smashed tree tops. Ghostly, white-garbed images appeared from the fog and mist in probing attacks against outposts, foxholes, and company command posts. American infantry companies were driven back or surrounded in the dense forests in the north, but the German hoped-for breakthrough did not occur.

American Response

Bradley traveled to Paris by car on 16 December because weather had grounded his plane. By 1500, his meeting with Eisenhower in Versailles was interrupted by reports of strong attacks with an alarming number of different German divisions identified. The responses of commanders of the major Allied military units were remarkably varied: Eisenhower, after a few hours, responded with reinforcements and saw the opportunity to inflict a crushing defeat upon the Germans now that they had left the shelter of their defenses along the West Wall, whereas Bradley refused to accept the size of the offensive. Patton had already suspected something was afoot and prepared his unit commanders for an advance upon the enemy; headquartered at the Hotel Britannique in Spa, Lieutenant General Courtney Hodges, commander US First Army, was deeply shaken, fatigued, and ill. Incapacitated for two days, Hodges essentially put himself out of touch with his own troops.[6] His Chief of Staff, Major General William B Kean, ran the First Army.

By evening Eisenhower dispatched the 7th Armored Division to St-Vith, the 10th Armored Division toward Bastogne, and his only immediately available reserves, the 101st and 82nd Airborne Divisions, to hold the shoulders of the developing salient. Eisenhower's quick action led to rapid strengthening of Allied positions. Over 60,000 US troops arrived in the Ardennes on 17 December; within the week the number had risen to 250,000. North of the developing salient, Major General Leonard T Gerow, V Corps commander, ordered the 1st Infantry Division to the Belgian Army's Camp Elsenborn arriving on 17 December. The same day, fearful of a German move to the north around the western flank of Elsenborn defenses, Gerow sent the 30th Infantry Division to establish a line from Waimes–Malmédy–Stavelot. On 18 December, the 82nd Airborne Division took up positions west of the Salm River, and the VII Corps' 3rd Armored Division started to arrive between the Salm and Ourthe Rivers. By 20 December, the 84th Infantry Division defended Marche-en-Famenne.

General Cota's division penalized the German timetable. On the left, his 112th Regiment held off troops from LVIII Panzer Corps until withdrawing on 17 December

---

6 Then Lieutenant Colonel Courtney Hodges was awarded a Distinguished Service Cross for heroism in leading his regiment in an attack across the Marne River during the First World War.

toward St-Vith, where it established a position on the flank of the 106th Division. On the extreme right, 109th Regiment fought a three-day withdrawal to Diekirch, giving only four miles before establishing a defensive line along the Sûre River.

By 17 December, Manteuffel's Fifth Panzer Army had opened a gap of 10 miles (16 kilometers) despite American resistance in some insignificant road-junction villages. Manteuffel's only remaining obstacle to achieving the Meuse River was Bastogne. By 18 December, Bradley realized the possibility of Bastogne being cutoff, but he also understood the importance of the city's position astride major transportation routes. He approved Middleton's appropriation of 101st Airborne Division and Combat Command B of the 10th Armored Division for its defense.

By the end of 18 December, the 106th Infantry Division was all but lost while its two trapped regiments attempted to fight out of their encirclement. Kampfgruppe Peiper had penetrated the American front and moved among rear echelon troops with little difficulty approaching Stavelot. In the north, Rocherath-Krinkelt was near the end of its death throes while competing units littered its streets with burning armor carcasses.

On 19 December Eisenhower chaired a meeting with Bradley, Patton, and Devers in a dank stone room in the Verdun Citadel. After receiving reports on the battlefield situation, Eisenhower gave the orders. Dever's Sixth Army Group would hold Alsace; the high ground south of Liège near Elsenborn would be held; Patton would disengage from his front, pivot north, and attack the German left flank — exactly one of the multiple contingencies that Patton had expected.

That night, after recommendations from his staff, Eisenhower divided the command of Allied troops facing the Bulge. Montgomery took command of all troops north of the salient including Bradley's US First and Ninth Armies. Bradley retained command in the south although he was furious with the changes to the point of threatening to resign. Montgomery, the strutting peacock, was pleased no end.

The Battle Intensifies

By 20 December, the Sixth Panzer Army had failed to accomplish the planned breakthrough, but events in Fifth Panzer Army's sector proved more positive. The Führer Begleit Brigade was moving past St-Vith to the north, and the 116th Panzer Division had seized Samrée and was aiming to cross the Ourthe River at Hotton. The 2nd Panzer Division took Noville and was headed toward Dinant; Panzer Lehr was south of Bastogne driving west toward St-Hubert. The three German lines of march to the Meuse were cut by three rivers: the Amblève, Salm, and Ourthe, each of which saw a separate battle that ultimately resulted in German defeat.

The evacuation of St-Vith saved 15,000 American troops from encirclement, but it also freed the German 2nd and 9th SS Panzer Divisions, 18th and 62nd VGDs, 3rd Panzergrenadier Division, and Führer Begleit Brigade — a formidable force with the strength to still threaten Liège.

Strong American resistance fooled Manteuffel into believing LVIII Corps faced stronger opposition. He ordered the 116th Panzer Division to withdraw and cross the Ourthe at La Roche, then move northwest to cut the Hotton–Marche road.

Chapter One   The Ardennes Campaign   11

The 2nd Panzer Division headed northwest toward Namur via Marche. Manteuffel sent Panzer Lehr against Rochefort.

On 23 December, after a snowfall, a weather pattern known as a Russian High produced cold but clear skies and released Allied airpower from its cloud-

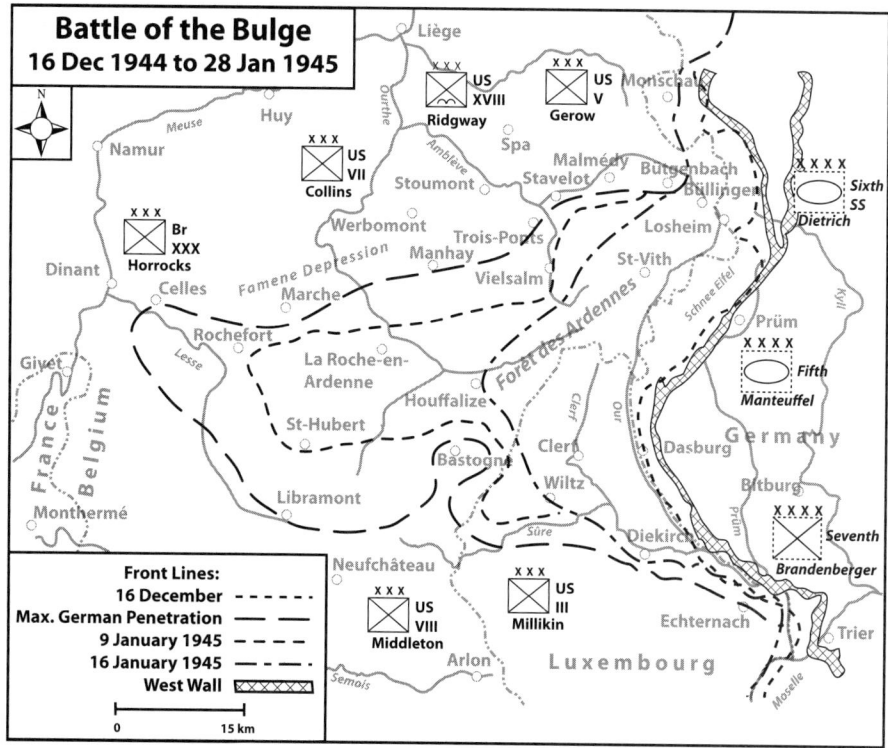

enforced silence. For the next two days, the heaviest air attacks of the war struck at battlefield highways, bridges, airfields, and the German transportation nexuses and supply centers at Koblenz, Trier, and Cologne. Air-dropped supplies into surrounded Bastogne included the usual medical supplies, food, and ammunition but also radio batteries and crystals necessary for observers to directly target P-47 squadrons onto German panzers or troop concentrations.

On 24 December, Montgomery ordered the 82nd Airborne Division to abandon the Salm River line in favor of a line Trois-Ponts–Manhay–Hotton to 'tidy up the battlefield.' General James Gavin hated the idea of giving up ground that would have to be recaptured later, but he obeyed orders.

By Christmas the tide had turned. German troops were forced to destroy their heavy weapons and flee La Gleize and Celles — the latter only 7.0 kilometers from the Meuse. Troops surrendered at Humain, and a panzer division was driven out of Manhay.

In one of the greatest maneuvers of the Second World War, one armored division (the 4th) and two infantry divisions (the 26th and 80th) disengaged from the enemy, changed direction, moved across 100 miles of winter roads, and attacked the enemy in three days. The main effort to relieve Bastogne centered upon Major General Hugh J Gaffey's 4th Armored Division attacking north on the Arlon road.[7] Patton's relief of Bastogne required his troops to face four German divisions (5th Fallschirmjäger Division, 212th, 276th, and 352nd VGD) through a screen of friendly troops, against uncertain enemy positions and units, over unfamiliar terrain, and in fog and snow. It was the stuff of legend and the maneuver solidified Patton's reputation.

The usual Allied differences of opinion held back an all-out counterattack by the armored units of First, Third, and Ninth Armies, which still fielded four thousand tanks. Patton argued for a drive to cut off the base of the salient with a drive toward Bitburg. Poor north-south roadways and the threat of German action against exposed flanks argued against such a bold move. The VII Corps commander Major General J Lawton 'Lightning Joe' Collins proposed driving on St-Vith from north and south. Montgomery hesitated fearing a second Rundstedt assault, but finally espoused pushing the enemy back at the middle of the Bulge at Houffalize — to be followed by his taking overall command. Bradley, for once, agreed with Montgomery but was somewhat influenced by his desire to regain command of his First Army. Montgomery won the day and his plan was adopted.

The Russian High ended on 28 December. 'Hitler weather', the overcast skies that limited aircraft, returned grounding much of the Allied air support. By the end of December, the German salient was 40 miles (64 kilometers) wide and 60 miles (100 kilometers) deep. American equipment losses to that point totaled 600 tanks, 700 trucks, 2,400 machine guns, and 1,700 bazookas.

Montgomery delayed the counterstrike, which Eisenhower believed would begin on 1 January, to 3 January, thereby leaving Patton to attack the Germans alone. A livid Eisenhower threatened to present the US Joint Chiefs of Staff with a 'him or me' ultimatum. Only the intercession of Montgomery's Chief of Staff, Major General Sir Francis de Guingand, salvaged Montgomery's job by encouraging Monty to sign an abject letter of support to Eisenhower.

Meanwhile, on 1 January a Luftwaffe air attack that later became known as the 'Hangover Raid' (formally Operation BODENPLATTE) sent 900 planes against 17 Allied airfields, catching most Allied planes on the ground. The attack destroyed 200 planes, but the Germans lost 300 planes and, more importantly, 237 irreplaceable pilots.

At 0830 on 3 January, the First US Army launched its attack toward Houffalize and the northern flank of the salient. Collin's VII Corps, led by the 3rd Armored Division, moved along the Manhay–Baraque-de-Fraiture–Houffalize axis. The severe weather limited air support, icy roads slowed tracked vehicles, and deep snow made infantry advance difficult. Days of fighting for every hamlet ensued. Meanwhile, Major General John Millikin's III Corps of Third Army expanded the supply tether to Bastogne by pushing northward to the west of Bastogne.

By 8 January even Hitler, always optimistic of success, had to admit defeat and authorize a withdrawal. For the next thirteen days, from 9 to 22 January, the German Sixth Panzer Army fought rearguard actions while it extricated itself from

---

7   Major General Hugh J Gaffey had been General Patton's Chief of Staff. He assumed command of 4th Armored Division only that December. He died in a B-25 bomber crash in 1946 at age 50.

the Ardennes salient. On 9 January, Patton struck on both sides of Bastogne with VIII Corps on its west and III Corps on its east. The 90th Infantry Division made the main effort and expanded the corridor to the southeast. The 101st Airborne and 4th Armored Division moved forward against Noville.

During the 2nd week of January, the Germans launched another thrust towards Bastogne. Patton now faced nine German divisions as his III and VIII Corps advanced only one mile per day. Collin's VII Corps did little better in its move toward Houffalize, fighting Germans as well as cold, snow, fog, and blown bridges while hampered by German artillery, mortar, and rocket fire. On 12 January, the Soviets launched their Winter Offensive. Within days they advanced as far as 200 miles (320 kilometers) against thin German lines. Within two days, Hitler ordered transfer of Sixth Panzer Army to the Eastern Front.

At 1140 on 16 January, the US First and Third Armies met outside Houffalize. The US 7th Armored Division re-entered St-Vith on 23 January, but the original battle line of 16 December was not recovered for another twelve days. Manteuffel's offensive expertise was matched by his skill in withdrawal. Thirteen divisions, although substantially reduced, withdrew across the Our River.

The Battle of the Bulge was over.

Aftermath

The American victory emerged thanks to the heroic efforts of small groups of soldiers who held their ground during the first days of the battle. Tank destroyers saved the crossroads at Domaine Bütgenbach; engineers stopped Peiper's tanks by destroying bridges at Trois-Ponts and Habiémont; and airborne troops refused to surrender Bastogne. Artillery support played a strong role in the victory, stopping infantry and armor attacks with a rain of shells. The grim hours of 16 December turned into the finest days of the American forces in Europe.

Once again Montgomery's after-action press interviews spread discord by suggesting that the British had come to the Americans' rescue. Relations between the field marshal and American commanders became as frosty as ever and never really thawed.

The German army suffered an enormous loss of matériel. The debilitating effect upon the *Wehrmacht,* although still capable of inflicting casualties upon the Allies, permanently weakened its defensive capabilities and contributed to its eventual collapse. The air battle over the Ardennes effectively destroyed the Luftwaffe. All pretense of victory, or even survival of the Nazi regime, was gone.

On the Western Front, the armies of Bradley and Montgomery had more bitter winter battles to fight, but the engagements resulted in hundreds of thousands of surrendering German soldiers. American forces crossed the Rhine at Remagen on 7 March 1945 and pincers closed upon the Ruhr Pocket on 4 April, trapping 430,000 German troops. By 11 April, allied armies halted at the Elbe River. Nineteen days later, with Berlin under a massive Red Army infantry and artillery attack, Hitler committed suicide in his underground bunker. The war in Europe was over eight days later.

Conclusion

The reasons for the German defeat lies in what the German Army could not control rather than in its failures. First on the list was the resourcefulness of the American soldier. Hitler and the German High Command underestimated the American soldiers' resourcefulness, stubbornness, and willingness to fight under adverse conditions and tenacity in resisting the advance despite being greatly outnumbered and knowing that they would eventually be overcome. Efforts at Lanzerath, Rocherath-Krinkelt, Parker's Crossroads, St-Vith, and Bastogne delayed the German timetable permitting reinforcements to seal the battlefield's flanks. The American resistance was assisted by the second factor – namely, that the nature of the ravine-ridden terrain that aided small American forces to withstand or to delay vastly larger German units. Finally, credit Eisenhower with rapid assessment of the developing situation on 16 December and his release of reserves that sent one-half million troops to contain the salient.

Hitler's plan of capturing Antwerp never had a chance of success, but with more fuel for his tanks, the capture of Liège could have been a distinct possibility. His hope to split the western alliance may seem far-fetched to modern observers, but the rancor generated by Montgomery against Eisenhower and Bradley was real. It is doubtful that US President Franklin Roosevelt or British Prime Minister Winston Churchill would have let the situation come down on Montgomery's behalf because the two leaders fully supported the Supreme Commander's decisions — and said so.

The battlefield heroes at senior levels are pitifully few. Brigadier Anthony McAuliffe, in command of the 101st Airborne Division at Bastogne by accident, was courageous and decisive. Credit Major General Walter Robertson with masterful extraction of the 2nd Infantry Division from a dangerously exposed salient. Major General Norman Cota, ordered to hold at all costs, did just that. With distinction, Lieutenant General George Patton displayed outstanding foresight and later ably faced the German Seventh Army, one-half of the Fifth Panzer Army, and elements of the Sixth Panzer Army. Still, the true heroes were the men: the junior officers, sergeants, and privates – men who refused to give ground or give up.

Chapter Two
Battle for Elsenborn Ridge
16 to 21 December 1944

As the place names so indicate, ethnic Germans inhabit the northeastern corner of Belgium. In fact, the province of Eupen-et-Malmédy transferred from Germany to Belgium as a result of the Treaty of Versailles that ended the First World War. The region is one of dense fir forests enclosing small farming communities and their pastures. The hilly terrain and paucity of reliable roads presented a challenge to German armor. In the north, the trackless moors of the Höhes Venn (Hautes Fagnes) provided little opportunity for rapid movement. The village of Elsenborn sits upon a 600-meter-high, crescent-shaped plateau riven by a series of parallel ridges sloping down to the Warche River valley. Camp Elsenborn[1], a Belgian military installation, stands 2.5 kilometers west of the town. Elsenborn Ridge does not appear on Belgian military maps, because it gained its name instead from American commanders.

Only the Losheim Gap, an eight-kilometer-wide corridor named after the German town at its eastern entrance, provided invaders with easy access across the border before encountering 4 kilometers of dense forest that barred the open country farther west. The route accommodated the Kaiser's horse cavalry in the early days of the First World War and the tanks of a then little-known General Erwin Rommel during the invasion of France in May 1940. The gap extends from around Losheim south to the northern end of a ridgeline known as the Schnee Eifel.

Much of the 1st SS Panzer Corps' attack fell upon the US 99th 'Checkerboard' Infantry Division that held a 32-kilometer front from Monschau, Germany to Lanzerath, Belgium. The 99th was an inexperienced unit that had arrived on the continent in early November. Only five weeks before the German Offensive, it assumed the positions of the 9th Infantry Division on the southern flank of V Corps. The extended front allowed the division commander, Major General Walter Lauer, only one reserve battalion. The division's 3rd Battalion, 395th Infantry Regiment held the northern flank in the German village of Höfen immediately south of the resort town of Monschau. The 1st and 3rd Battalions, 393rd Infantry Regiment, and the three battalions of 394th Infantry Regiment held positions straddling the International Highway (B265), so-named as it formed the German-Belgian border in this region of the Ardennes, although forward outposts were sited farther east in Germany.

GERMAN OBJECTIVE	To capture seven bridges over the Meuse River as the initial stage of the German drive to Antwerp.
FORCES	
American:	99th Infantry Division (Major General Walter Lauer) and 2nd Infantry Division (Major General Walter M Robertson)
German:	I SS Panzer Corps (SS-Major General Hermann Priess)
RESULT	German forces never achieved the Meuse River.

---

1 Camp Elsenborn was established by the Prussian Army in 1896 when the area was part of Germany.

16 The Bulge Battlefields

CASUALTIES	Period 16 to 23 December 1944:
American:	99th Infantry Division: 198 killed, 901 wounded, and 898 missing; in addition, 600 men reported weather-related, non-combat injuries
	2nd Infantry Division: 63 killed, 664 wounded, and 786 missing
German:	12th SS Panzer Division: 228 killed, 802 wounded, and 340 missing; 114 tanks, assault guns, and other armored vehicles destroyed
	12th, 277th, and 326th Volksgrenadier Divisions: 353 killed, 1,033 wounded, and 1,162 missing
LOCATION	Malmédy is 61 km southeast of Liège, Belgium

Battle Summary

The assault started at 0530 in the pre-dawn darkness of 16 December when 1,600 artillery pieces and thousands of mortars and rocket launchers began a 90-minute bombardment along the 99th Infantry Division's front. The initial German barrage severely disrupted telephone communications linking the various units. German jamming, the rugged terrain, and adverse weather conditions impacted radio transmissions.[2] Because of the construction of deep, log-covered dugouts, casualties were remarkably light. The following German infantry assault, aided by German searchlights positioned to the rear to create an artificial moonlight, was of overwhelming strength, however, frequently outnumbering and outgunning the defenders by 8-or-10-to-1.

As the barrage lifted, the 277th Volksgrenadier Division's Grenadier Regiments 989 and 991 struck the 393rd Regiment between its 1st and 3rd Battalions where adjoining Companies C and K were almost completely annihilated. The American regiment's refused right flank was seriously threatened when attacking grenadiers advanced over 900 meters toward the rear of the 3rd Battalion. By nightfall, much of the 393rd Regiment was surrounded. The 394th Regiment fared better because its foxholes were positioned on the very edge of the forest. Utilizing machine guns and clear fields of fire, its men inflicted heavy casualties upon the 12th Volksgrenadier Division.

The northern limit of the German assault attempted to envelop the Hôhes Venn from the north by attacking to the north and south of Monschau. The 38th Cavalry Squadron's line at Monschau was briefly penetrated. The 3rd Battalion, 395th Infantry Regiment, held firm in Höfen and easily repulsed infantry of the 326th Volksgrenadier Division.

In the afternoon of 16 December, after receiving an unusual request for support by towed tank destroyers, Major General Walter M Robertson, 2nd Infantry Division commander, traveled south to discuss the request at 99th Division headquarters. General Robertson found the command post in chaos with staff officers arguing and

---

2   American tactical radios were FM sets and, as such, their transmissions required line-of-sight. Signals were also deteriorated by fog and rain.

Chapter Two

Battle for Elsenborn Ridge

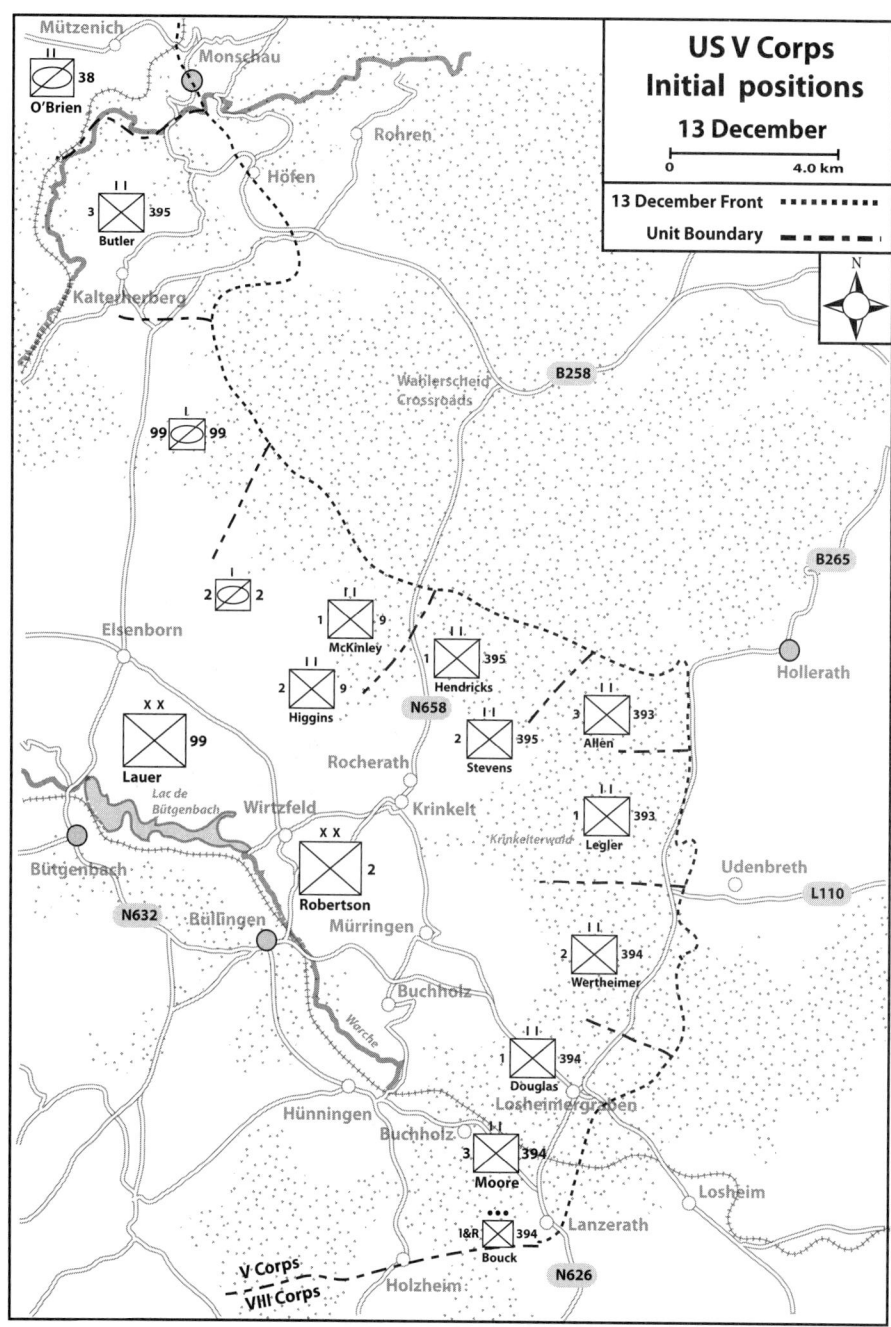

the division commander, Major General Walter E Lauer, calmly sitting in a corner playing a piano. Despite Lauer's assurances, Robertson sensed that all was not well on his southern flank. Later that day, V Corps detached Robertson's 3rd Battalion, 23rd

Infantry Regiment, to support the 393rd Infantry Regiment. Later still, the regiment's 1st Battalion was similarly detached and sent to Büllingen.

Events were also unclear to General Priess. His infantry had made progress, but less than planned. Nonetheless, he committed his two armored divisions, the 1st and 12th SS Panzer, to the battle. The 12th SS Panzer Division sent its Panther tanks and panzergrenadiers against Rocherath and Krinkelt while SS-Lieutenant Colonel Joachim Peiper led Kampfgruppe Peiper through Lanzerath on its way toward the Meuse River.

Originally Major General Leonard T Gerow, V Corps commander, underestimated the seriousness of the attack. On 17 December, however, he recognized the risks and cancelled the 2nd Infantry Division's attack toward Wahlerscheid and dictated that the American main line of resistance be formed along Elsenborn Ridge. About the same time, First Army reassigned the 1st 'Big Red One' Infantry Division to V Corps and dispatched the unit to Camp Elsenborn.

Elements of the 1st SS Panzer Division cut the road through Büllingen, leaving the route Rocherath–Krinkelt–Wirtzfeld as the only escape to Elsenborn for retreating front-line troops. The 2nd Division's 9th and 38th Infantry Regiments fought against superior armored forces to hold Rocherath and Krinkelt while 23rd Regiment and elements of 99th Division passed through to the rear. During the evening of 19 December, the remaining units also withdrew, leaving the two villages to German occupation. The 395th Regiment covered the withdrawal from Wahlerscheid area and then moved west passing north of Rocherath to the Höhes Venn while the 1st Division's 26th Infantry Regiment held firm at Dom Bütgenbach against repeated assaults.

Aftermath

By 21 December, hundreds of American artillery pieces on the Elsenborn Ridge threatened German movement to a depth of 20 kilometers along the northern shoulder. The US 9th Infantry Division strengthened the Monschau sector. Around its south the 99th and 2nd Divisions held limited fronts on the ridge. The 1st Infantry Division extended the line west from Bütgenbach to Waimes where it tied in with the 30th Infantry Division. In less than a week, an overextended, weak American line had been reformed by three of the most experienced divisions in the United States Army.

The American units repulsed repeated attacks upon Elsenborn Ridge by 3rd Panzergrenadier Division and 12th SS Panzer Division while Kampfgruppe Peiper was destroyed around La Gleize. Rundstedt and Model decided to shift the main effort to von Manteuffel's Fifth Panzer Army. (See Chapter Three for the full story of Kampfgruppe Peiper.)

Battlefield Tour Summary

The battlefield tour starts at Henri-Chapelle American Cemetery, where the battle ended for so many American servicemen. The tour continues along the northern shoulder of the Bulge battlefield reviewing the initial front-line engagements then proceeds west to the hotly contested farming communities.

Chapter Two — Battle for Elsenborn Ridge

Recommended Sites:
Henri Chapelle: Henri-Chapelle American Cemetery
Thimister-Clermont: Remember Museum 39-45
Hollerath: Start of Rollbahn A
Rocherath-Krinkelt: Ruppenvenn, Hasselpat Trail, village center, and Memorial Park
Bütgenbach: 1st Infantry Division Memorial

> The tour starts at the American military cemetery 38 km east of Liège, Belgium or 21 km southwest of Aachen, Germany. In either case follow highway N3 into the town of Henri-Chapelle. Turn toward Maastricht on Route d'Aubel (becomes rue du Mémorial Américain) and follow for 2.5 km to the American Cemetery. (50.696587, 5.899183)

The town of Henri-Chapelle was liberated on 12 September 1944 by troops of the US 1st Infantry Division. Near the site of the current cemetery, US Graves Registration established a temporary burial ground that held American and German war dead. From 1955 to 1956, German dead from numerous area locations were consolidated in a German Military Cemetery near Lommel, Belgium. Henri-Chapelle American Cemetery was established in 1960 with the dead re-interred in their present location.

Henri-Chapelle American Cemetery
rue du Mémorial Américain 159   4852 Hombourg, Belgium
Tel: +32 (0)87 68 71 73
Web: http://www.abmc.gov/cemeteries-memorials/europe/henri-chapelle-american-cemetery#

The rue du Mémorial Américain traverses a narrow ridge inviting picturesque views of the countryside. The highway enters the cemetery after passing between commemorative pylons. An observation platform to the left presents unobstructed views to the west. The Colonnade of the Missing on the right holds twelve pairs of pylons listing the names of 450 servicemen whose remains were never located. The left end of the colonnade houses a meditative, non-denominational chapel; the right end houses the visitor's office and small museum. An American member of the cemetery staff is always on duty at any time the cemetery is open.

Pass through the colonnade to the terrace overlooking the sweeping valley that holds the graves of 7,992 military dead, most of whom died as a result of fighting to penetrate the Westwall, the Battle of the Bulge, or the subsequent advance across Germany. The eight curved plots fan across the valley and are separated by broad grass pathways. Among the graves, thirty-three pairs of brothers rest side-by-side. Headstones inscribed 'Here rests in honored glory a comrade in arms known but to God' mark the graves of 94 unidentified servicemen.

Open daily from 09:00 to 17:00 except 25 December and 1 January.

20   The Bulge Battlefields

Although not strictly part of the Battle of the Bulge story, this area holds two commemorations of its liberation. Despite the following route requiring driving narrow country lanes, it does offer broad perspectives of attractive farming countryside and small villages. Although minimal traffic is the norm, beware overtaking slow farm vehicles. Please note the museum's very limited hours of operation.

> Leave the American Cemetery to the southeast and follow rue du Mémorial Américain for 900 m and then turn right on the country lane. After 850 m and immediately after passing a red brick house on the left roadside, turn left at the T-junction and continue downhill on Route de la Clouse (becomes Bach). Follow for 2.8 km, being especially careful to follow the curve to the left after the red brick tower. Turn left at the brown tourist sign for Remember Museum 39-45. Stop after 400 m among the farm buildings on the left housing the museum. (50.668717, 5.883893)

Remember Museum 39-45
Les Béolles 4   4890 Thimister-Clermont, Belgium
Tel: +32 (0)87 44 61 81   Web: http://remembermuseum.com/

This private museum sits in an old barn and is dedicated to the men of the US 1st Infantry Division who liberated this area in September 1944. Local fighting left most of the artifacts on the family farm augmented by contributions from visiting American soldiers after the war. Each of the museum's display items is accompanied by the story of the soldier to whom it is attached. Guided tours are available in five languages.

Open only on the first Sundays of each month from 09:00 to 18:00

> Return to the town of Henri Chapelle by continuing southeast from the Remember Museum 39–45. After 1.3 km, enter Clermont and turn left onto rue René Rutten. Follow the street for 650 m and then turn left onto highway N3. Continue for 2.3 km to the memorial obelisk on the right. (50.674104, 5.914274)

The **US 1st Infantry Division Memorial** obelisk is one of five such memorials that mark the battlefields where the unit fought during the Second World War. The memorial's surfaces record the inscribed names of 1,223 1st Division troops who died between 7 September and 15 December 1944. During that period, The Big Red One pushed through the Westwall to lay siege to the German city of Aachen, later capturing it by direct assault.

Other Points of Interest near Henri-Chapelle

> A smooth stone stele, erected in 2006, locates the site of the crashed **B-17 'Picklepuss'** from 418th Squadron, 100th Bomber Group, Eighth Airforce. A Luftwaffe Bf-110 nightfighter piloted by Hauptmann Hubertus von Bonin shot down the plane over Henri Chapelle on 17 August 1943 during a mission to bomb Regensburg, Germany.   Six of the ten crew members died in the crash. The four survivors were taken prisoner.

Chapter Two

Battle for Elsenborn Ridge 21

> Location: 3.6 km northeast of Henri-Chapelle on highway N3 (50.696471, 5.969072)[3]
>
> Leave the village of Henri-Chapelle to the northeast toward Aachen, Germany (N3). After 2 km, enter a roundabout and take the first exit toward Eupen (N67). Follow highways N67, N61, N68, again N67 (Eupenerstraße) through the streets of old Eupen always following signs toward Monschau. The road crosses the border into Germany and after 18.2 km becomes Beerenburg Str. After 800 m, take the 2nd exit onto Laufenstraße and follow for 1.4 km. Turn left onto Rurstraße, left onto Markt, and shortly right onto Austraße. After 190 m, enter the parking area on the left. (50.554714, 6.244500)

Battle of Monschau
16 to 17 December 1944

Monschau is a picturesque resort town located at the bottom of a deep pine-covered gorge formed by the Roer River. Sheer bluffs and hills offered unobserved routes of approach toward American positions in the town. Monschau's importance to the Germans lay in the highway that left the valley through Mützenich, Eupen, and on to Liège. Originally two full divisions planned to sweep north and south of Monschau under orders to avoid combat in the historic town. Transport difficulties left only Generalmajor Erwin Kaschner's 326th Volksgrenadier Division in attack position by 16 December. However, the weakened infantry division received artillery support from two whole Volksartillerie Corps and two Werfer Brigades.

The original German 326th Infantry Division was destroyed on 1 August 1944 while attacking Hill 309 in Normandy during British Operation BLUECOAT. A new 326th Volksgrenadier Division formed in September 1944 by re-naming a Volks unit assembling in Hungary. Less than fully mobile, the unit suffered from shortages of vehicles and horses causing some battalions to be late in arriving at their jump-off positions on 16 December. Armor support was provided by Sturmgeschütz Company 1326 fielding Jagdpanzer 38(t)s. The division resolved to capture the Monschau road network and established a fixed defensive front on a line through Eupen toward Liège.

The US 38th Cavalry Squadron, 102nd Cavalry Group defended Monschau with an 8,000-meter defensive line running from the train station on the north side of Konzen south parallel to the rail line along the Mützenich Ridge, then southeast to join the 395th Regiment's infantry at Höfen. Monschau was dominated by three hills: Monschau Hill to the east, Mützenich Hill to the northwest, and Höfen Hill to the southeast. Two deep draws ran between these hills and provided natural approaches to American lines. Although a platoon of Company[4] F's light Stuart tanks were stationed in Monschau, the strength of the defense was along the ridge lines that dominated Monschau and its eastern approaches. Artillery support was provided by elements of Colonel Oscar Axelson's 405th Field Artillery Group.

---

3   The plane's pilot, Captain Robert M Knox of Montgomery County, Pennsylvania is buried in Henri-Chapelle American Cemetery, Henri-Chapelle, Belgium.

4   Ironically, a reconnaissance unit was generally called a 'Troop'; however, a reconnaissance squadron's tank or assault gun unit was called a 'Company.'

22 The Bulge Battlefields

GERMAN OBJECTIVE	To capture the road network about Monschau and to establish a firm northern flank on the Höhes Venn
FORCES	
American:	38th Reconnaissance Cavalry Squadron (Lieutenant Colonel Robert O'Brien)
German:	Grenadier Regiment 751, 326th Volksgrenadier Division (Generalmajor Dr Erwin Kraschner)
RESULT	Repeated German attacks were repulsed
CASUALTIES	
American:	Reportedly 1 killed and 1 wounded
German:	198 killed, 62 wounded, and 50 taken prisoner
LOCATION	Monschau is 30 km northeast of Malmédy

Battle

On 16 December, the 38th Cavalry rode out the initial 35-minute Wehrmacht artillery barrage otherwise secure in its reinforced gun positions or in cellars. American positions were well-prepared and zones of fire well-established. German infantry moved forward in the Roer River gorge between Monschau and Höfen through an early morning mist and approached the American line before devastating fire brought its advance to a quick end. The grenadiers, targeting the high ground at Mützenich, renewed the attack north of Monschau on 17 December. Although achieving some minor penetrations of Troop B's positions, accurate fire from the 62nd Field Artillery Battalion eliminated the advance. On 18 December, General Kaschner shifted his attention south to the village of Höfen.[5]

Battlefield Tour

Start the Monschau tour at the Alter Schachthof parking area south of town on Ausstraße. (50.554714, 6.244500)

Monschau

Monschau-Touristik GmbH
Stadtstraße 16
Tel: +49 (0)2472 80480
Web: http://www.monschau.de/de/

52156 Monschau, Germany
Email: touristik@monschau.de

The town dates to the 12th century, and Monschau Schloß (Castle), the seat of the dukes of Jülich who ruled the area, was constructed 100 years later. The town was plundered in 1543 by Spanish Emperor Charles V and captured by French forces in 1795. After the defeat of Napoleon Bonaparte, the Congress of Vienna in 1815 assigned the area to the Kingdom of Prussia. In a curiosity of the Treaty of Versailles, the rail line to the west of the town, but not the territory, was assigned to Belgium. Thus, nearby Mützenich remains German territory completely surrounded

---

5 The 38th Cavalry Reconnaissance Squadron received the Presidential Unit Citation for its defense of Monschau. It was the only Mechanized Cavalry unit to be so honored in the Second World War.

by a narrow strip of Belgium. The city was captured by the US 9th Infantry Division on 15 September 1944.

The narrow streets of Monschau's historic town center are lined with numerous half-timbered houses which have seen little change for 300 years. The town was spared artillery bombardment by the direct order of Generalfeldmarschall Walter Model, the overall commander of Operation HERBSTNEBEL.

Monschau continues to be a German tourist favorite of those hiking the area's numerous forest trails. Therefore, the town center is very crowded and difficult for vehicular travel. Because most of the fighting for Monschau took place to the west in Mutzenich and to the south in Höfen, this tour specifically avoids entering old Monschau.

Walk 75 m west and north to the bridge over the Roer River. (50.555121, 6.244194)

As expected, the initial German artillery barrage was immediately followed by infantry of the I Battalion, Grenadier Regiment 751, attacking along the foggy Roer River valley. The light M5 'Stuart' tanks of 2nd Platoon, Company F were

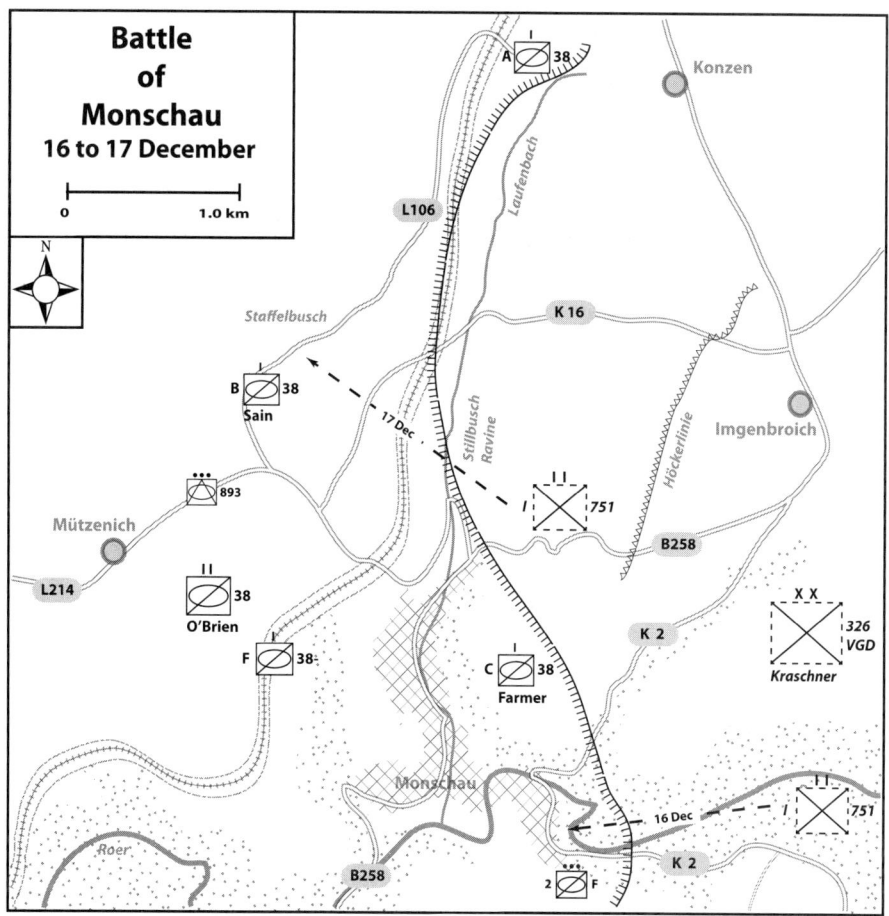

situated above the Roer River valley south of Monschau along Schleidener Straße. Their positions enfiladed the approach of Grenadier Regiment 751. Company F met the assault with machine-gun and 37-mm cannon canister fire at ranges as short as 50 meters. The effect upon the approaching infantry was devastating. While tank fire pinned down the German troops, 2nd Platoon Leader Staff Sergeant Bernard C Bielcki utilized the squadron's extensive communications network to call down artillery and mortar fire. German efforts to infiltrate the flanks of the tank platoon were stopped by dismounting the tanks' .30-caliber machine guns and bringing their fire upon the infiltrators. The German troops withdrew after two hours, leaving only a few snipers to keep Bielcki's men on edge.[6]

The bridge offers easy access to Monschau Altstadt to the west and the Roer Valley to the east. The mist-shrouded, twisting-river course offered the advancing German infantry shelter from observation. The valley is accessible by proceeding right after the bridge and right again onto Rosenthal, a narrow, steep roadway limited to resident's vehicles, but which promises a scenic walk.

> Retrieve your vehicle and proceed northwest to cross over the Roer River bridge. Turn right onto Eschbachstraße (becomes Alte Monschauerstraße) and follow for 2.2 km. Turn right onto B258 (Trier Straße) and then after 280 m left onto Bruchzaun. Follow for 500 m; turn left onto Kieselbacher Weg and enter a parking area. (50.571116, 6.258107)

Walk the hiking trail northwest for 500 meters to find a band of vegetation that crosses the trail. (50.568374, 6.252449) The zigzag Westwall *Höckerlinie*, or **dragon's teeth,** as they became known to American soldiers, formed an antitank barrier against invasion from the west. Dragon's teeth channeled attacking armored vehicles into well-mined paths or preregistered artillery targets. Attempts to cross over the concrete blocks would dangerously expose the vehicles unarmored underside to enemy hand-held antitank weapons, such as a *panzerfaust*.[7]

Most of these defensive structures were removed after the war, but a few examples remain. In this instance, the reinforced concrete blocks trace an 850-meter barrier across pastures to the right and left almost totally obscured by vegetation, thereby making them difficult to observe even up close. A one-meter-high concrete wall lines the west side of the barrier. The narrow wall held metal posts, since removed, every 2-to-3 meters that supported rolls of barbed wire. Walking on the wall is dangerous because it is only 0.5 meters wide and patches of slippery moss cover its surface. With care, one maneuvers to a bend in the wall where a bench offers enticing views across the valley almost directly west across the Laufenbach creek, a tributary of the Roer River.

---

6 Staff Sergeant Bernard C Bielcki from Albion, New York, died in 2014 at age 92.

7 Panzerfaust: a German single-use, antitank weapon manufactured in numerous calibers and designed to be fired by one soldier. The effective range varied with caliber but was usually less than 100 m requiring its user to approach dangerous close to his target.

> Reverse direction and return to highway B258. Turn right and follow for 1.6 km to a service road on the right. (50.565766, 6.245305)

A second grenadier attack on 16 December passed the Westwall dragon's teeth in Imgenbroich and hit Troop C's 2nd and 3rd Platoons along what the GIs called 'Snake Road' (highway B258). Still, the attackers met machine-gun and artillery fire directed by well-connected forward observers. Probing attacks resumed after nightfall with the strongest assault of the day again coming from Imgenbroich at 1700 that again met with concentrated artillery fire.

At 0800 on 17 December, Troop C's left flank repulsed feeble attacks at *Stillbusch* Ravine east of Mützenich. The assault was driven off by machine-gun fire and heavily punished by artillery fire while the enemy withdrew into the ravine. Renewed efforts to capture Monschau continued during the afternoon with four German assault guns making a brief appearance. Antitank gun and artillery fire destroyed three of the guns forcing the fourth to withdraw. The final German effort against Monschau at 2200 was again subjected to interlocking machine-gun fire and accurate artillery and mortar bursts.

True to its name, **Snake Road** curves right and left down into Laufenbach valley. The canyons and gullies are lined with trees making viewpoints difficult.

> Continue forward to the next roundabout, then take the 1st exit. The hairpin curve to the left allows brief views into *Stillbush* Ravine on the right, but no stopping point is convenient. The route follows Beerenburgstraße (becomes Eupenerstraße) back across the narrow strip of Belgium. After 1.8 km turn right onto Im Bruch. After 450 m, turn right onto highway L106 (Schiffenborn). Follow for 1.1 km and then turn right and park near a bicycle trail. (50.579865, 6.235151)

The hillside above the rail line was manned by Troops A and B of Colonel O'Brien's 38th Squadron. General Kaschner's second attack on 17 December targeted Mützenich and fell against the squadron in positions about this ridgeline. The assault hit Troop B's line north of Mützenich and managed to penetrate a gap between 1st and 2nd Platoons to threaten the squadron's rear area. Captain Joseph R Sain, Troop B Commander, requested and received reinforcements in the form of Company A, 146th Engineer Combat Battalion and two Company F tanks. Sain ordered a sharp counterattack led by Lieutenant Weldon J Yontz's 2nd Platoon toward *Staffelbusch* and drove the enemy back.

This location, where a bicycle path crosses the highway, is known as **Staffelbusch**. The sector downhill to the east came under attack on 17 December and marks where Troop B's line was penetrated despite mines, barbed wire, and trip flares on the slopes. Captain Sain's counterattack approached roughly along the bicycle trail from the west. Views of the Laufenbach valley and the German infantry attack are blocked by structures or trees that line most of highway L106; however, this site permits views down the hillside, a perspective of the terrain of the German attack, and the field of fire offered to the cavalry's dismounted machine guns.

> Reverse direction and follow highway L106 for 1.8 km. Turn right toward Eupen (Eupenerstraße). After 300 m, turn left onto Gustengasse, then left onto Reichensteiner Straße (becomes Messeweg) and follow for 6.6 km.

The route follows the ridge line that formed the defensive positions of Troops A and B, 38th Squadron. The road descends into the valley and across the Roer River near the Belgian rail line.

> Turn left onto highway B399 (Monschauerstraße) and follow for 3.1 km. Turn right toward Trier (B258, Umgehungsstraße) and, after 1.0 km, turn right onto Heimstraße. After 250 m, stop near the clinic complex on the right. (50.54234, 6.25374)

Battle of Höfen
16 to 18 December 1944

In 1944, Höfen was a long, narrow village stretching along a high hill surrounded by open fields cut by deep, wooded valleys. The 3rd Battalion, 395th Infantry Regiment, relieved CCB, 5th Armored Division in position around Höfen on 8 November 1944. The battalion manned a 6-kilometer front from Monschau through Höfen to Alzen, where the front swung to face south against German-held positions on the opposite side of the Fuhrstbach valley. The 99th Reconnaissance Platoon was to the southwest in Kalterherberg.

GERMAN OBJECTIVE	To capture the road network about Monschau and to establish a firm northern flank on the Höhes Venn
FORCES	
American:	3rd Battalion (Lieutenant Colonel McClernand Butler), 395th Infantry Regiment, 99th Infantry Division
German:	Grenadier Regiment 751, 326th Volksgrenadier Division (Generalmajor Dr Erwin Kraschner)
RESULT	Repeated German attacks were repulsed
CASUALTIES	
American:	3rd Battalion: 9 killed, 14 wounded, and 4 missing 612th Tank Destroyer Battalion: 1 killed, 2 wounded, and 6 missing
German:	308 killed, 160 wounded, and 61 taken prisoner
LOCATION	Höfen is 28 km northeast of Malmédy

Battle

At Höfen, the pre-dawn glow of 16 December was shattered by the sound of explosions of thousands of Nebelwerfer rockets and artillery shells. Lt Col Butler's 3rd Battalion had done a good job strengthening its dugouts with layers of logs whereby casualties were few. The village buildings were heavily damaged with rubble blocking the streets and telephone wires hanging limp and useless from their poles.

At 0600, two companies of Grenadier Regiment 751 crossed the open fields from Rohren under the artificial moonlight created by German antiaircraft searchlights to attack the battalion's left-most Company I. The defenders held fire until the last possible moment and then unleashed withering fire from automatic weapons, rifles, twelve 3-inch guns of Company A, 612th Tank Destroyer Battalion that fired anti-personnel canister shot, and eight 81-mm mortars positioned behind the foxhole line. Despite the concentrated American fire, the grenadiers' assault was determined and breached the foxhole line to enter Höfen. American artillery batteries responded by shredding the ravine and open ground toward Rohren. By 0700, the battle was over and with the front line restored, a brief period of quiet followed. At 1235, the right flank of Company K was attacked, but the enemy was beaten off with mortar and artillery fire.

After a relatively quiet 17 December, at 0330 the next day Kraschner added Grenadier Regiments 752 and 753 to a renewed attack upon Höfen with the main effort again against Company I. As at Mützenich, penetrations were made — at one point even to surround the battalion command post — but accurate American artillery support and the enemy's lack of armor support left the grenadiers too weak to retain the gains.

Aftermath

By 19 December the 326th Volksgrenadier Division's efforts shifted to

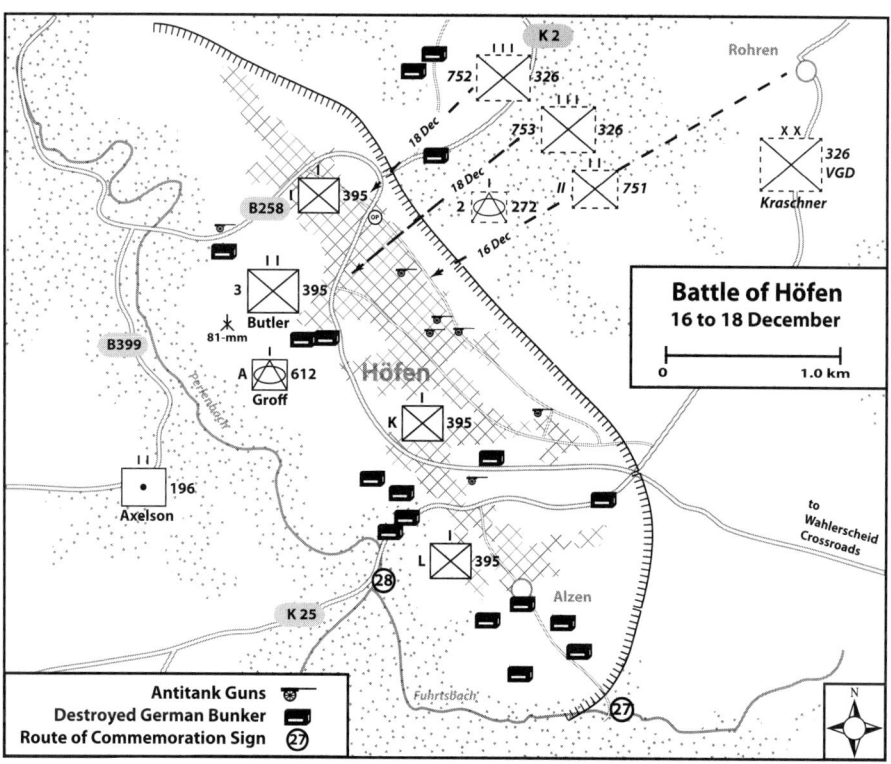

Wahlerscheid and Elsenborn Ridge. The 38th Cavalry Squadron and 3rd Battalion, 395th Infantry Regiment were the only units on the Battle of the Bulge front line that retained their original positions throughout the six-week battle.

Consequences
    A loss of Monschau and Höfen would have allowed the enemy to outflank the northern shoulder of the American positions. The efforts to deny the Höhes Venn to German troops played an important part in the American's ability to re-enforce and hold the Elsenborn Ridge.

Battlefield Tour
    Observation Post #6 (OP-6) was the tallest structure in Höfen and presented clear views across the snow-covered hills to the east. On 16 December, shelling ignited fires throughout the village. German infantry approached across the fields from the east only to be suddenly swept away by bursts of automatic weapons fire. Observers directed fire from the 105-mm guns of the 196th and 863rd Field Artillery Battalions and 3rd Battalion mortar teams. The observation post's lower floors held riflemen and machine gunners, and a towed 3-inch gun stood along an outside wall.
    The three-story observation post building still stands at the left of the St Joseph Haus rehabilitation clinic complex. The structures to the east were not present in 1944, providing defenders in the building clear viewpoints across the fields.

Continue 95 m on Heimstraße (becomes Wiesengrund) across highway B258 and stop at the shuttered café on the right. (50.541755, 6.254712)

    The 1st Platoon, Company I occupied **Gasthaus Schidden** and the surrounding gardens. In 1944, only cultivated fields cut by hedgerows rolled gently down into a shallow draw to the east toward the two grenadier regiments' attack.

Continue southeast on Wiesengrund for 800 m and stop briefly at the intersection with Neuestraße. (50.535883, 6.261106)

    The section of **Wiesengrund Straße** just traveled marked the foxhole line of Company I. The intersection set the junction with Company I's right flank and the left flank of Company K, which continued southeast along Neuestraße.
    During the first attack on 16 December, grenadiers penetrated the line at the boundary between Companies I and K and entered houses in Höfen. The area was quickly surrounded and put under shell fire from the tank destroyer battalion's .50-caliber machine guns. Outgunned, the enemy troops were forced into a building, surrounded, and soon thereafter forty surrendered.

Turn southwest on Neuestraße and after 220 m turn right on Triftstraße. Follow for 650 m and turn left onto B258 (Hauptstraße). The large building 90 m ahead and

> across from the church served as Col Butler's 3rd Battalion headquarters. (50.536671, 6.252081)

On 18 December, under heavy artillery and mortar fire and in pre-dawn darkness that made identification impossible, grenadiers infiltrated the left flank and much of the fighting became hand-to-hand. They surrounded the battalion observation post but were eventually driven back. The grenadiers repeated the attack twice again later that morning. At 0900, an attack supported by assault guns and self-propelled antiaircraft guns struck the left front against Company I. The pressure upon the defenders was so intense that Colonel Butler called down six five-minute artillery concentrations upon his own positions. The attacking infantry scattered and the armor withdrew. At 1000, the enemy occupied four stone houses, but point-blank fire from 57-mm antitank guns followed by white phosphorous grenades thrown through the windows forced their surrender.

Sergeant Thornton E Piersall of Company I occupied a position in the direct path of this assault. Accurate and intense fire from his BAR repulsed waves of enemy troops until his ammunition ran out. During the lull, the enemy moved a machine gun and rocket launcher into position to eliminate Piersall. The intrepid sergeant crawled from his protected position, secured a German grenade launcher and grenades from enemy dead, and returned to his post. Piersall fired two rounds with deadly accuracy to eliminate the enemy machine gun and rocket positions.[8]

> Continue south on highway B258 for 850 m. Turn right onto Im Sief then, after 450 m, right onto highway K25 (Mühlenweg). Park at the roadside after 550 m immediately before the road crosses the Perlenbach. (50.52666, 6.25621)

Route of Commemoration

The cities of Monschau, Bütgenbach, Büllingen, and Waimes, in conjunction with the European Union, created a 94-kilometer international hiking loop around the Belgian-German border area titled the Route of Commemoration to highlight sites pertaining to the Second World War. Many of the thirty sites are easily accessible by automobile and will be included in the tour route, albeit not all and not necessarily in their numbered order. Each site presents a four-language informational panel providing insight into the location. Maps indicating the route are available at local tourist offices, and panels on the tour route are indicated on maps with the symbol: (28).

Route of Commemoration information panel #28 describes the destruction the local area suffered during the Second World War. The nearby mill in the village of Höfen was completely destroyed as were seventy-seven percent of the village's buildings. Both the water supply system and electrical grid were destroyed, and almost

---

8   Sergeant Thornton E Piersall was awarded a Distinguished Service Cross for his heroic actions in defeating the enemy penetration of the company's positions. Piersall returned to his home in Oklahoma where he earned a Civil Engineering degree from Oklahoma A&M. He worked in Anaheim, California where he died in 2012 at age 87.

ninety-four percent of the area roadways suffered damage from bombs, grenades, mines, or tank traffic. Local forests suffered heavily as well.

After only 30 meters along the trail, a picnic table on the left side stands on a flat area where a destroyed Westwall bunker retains only two rear walls. Guns in the bunker protected approaches from the west along highway K25. (50.526245, 6.256353) The trail continues for 1.9 kilometers to sign #27, but it is more convenient to drive to the site.

> Reverse direction back toward Höfen. After 550 m, turn right onto Alzerstraße, then shortly left onto Kauferberg. Follow for 1.3 km to the bunker on the left immediately before Furthsbach. (50.51887, 6.27245)

The route passes through Alzen where the 395th Infantry Regiment's Company L was stationed. The area held numerous Westwall bunkers; however, new construction, camouflaging vegetation, and purposeful removal limit opportunities to view the structures.

The **Fuhrtsbachal bunker, or Bunker #121,** is a double machine-gun type 107 manned by twelve soldiers. The massive construction hides behind a thin veil of shrubbery. The walls are cracked and broken and sections of the roof have collapsed after being used for many years after the war to detonate excess ammunition. Iron gates block the entrance doorway to its dangerous interior. The large wing wall protected infantry troops entering or leaving the bunker from enemy fire.

Cross the bridge and to the right find **Route of Commemoration information panel #27**. The text notes the creation of Westwall structures that started in 1936 after German troops re-entered the demilitarized zone established after the First World War by the Treaty of Versailles. The work was stopped in 1940 after the German victory over France and the occupation of western European countries. Advancing Allied troops in September 1944 found most of the structures unmanned and stripped of their equipment. (50.51837, 6.27103)

Battle of Wahlerscheid Crossroads
14 to 17 December 1944

Although not part of the Battle of the Bulge, the attack of the US 2nd Infantry Division against the Wahlerscheid Crossroads was integral to the desperate struggle to defend Rocherath-Krinkelt.

The US 2nd 'Indianhead' Infantry Division was originally constituted in 1917 during the First World War. The unit fought with distinction in many of that war's major engagements. By December 1944, the division was a seasoned unit that had landed on Omaha Beach on D-Day +1. It immediately saw action crossing the Aure River and proceeding through Norman hedgerows to the Battle of St Lo. Later the division turned west to enter Brittany to capture the port of Brest after a 39-day battle.

In December 1944 Divisional Commander Major General Walter Robertson received instructions to launch an attack upon the Roer River dams — the stubbornly defended targets that resulted in so much American blood in the Hürtgen Forest. The plan required Robertson to approach the dams' defenses from the southern flank and

Chapter Two Battle for Elsenborn Ridge 31

rear while the 8th Infantry Division executed the second arm of the double envelopment by attacking from the north and the 78th Infantry Division beat upon the nose of the German salient from the west.

On 13 December, Robertson attacked German positions after passing through the middle of the 99th Division's sector.[9] The 1st and 2nd Battalions of the 99th Division's 395th Regiment and the 2nd Battalion, 393rd Regiment, formed the 395th Regimental Combat Team[10] supporting the 2nd Infantry Division's attack. Such an assault offered the 2nd Division only one supply route — a single, paved road from Büllingen through the farming villages of Rocherath and Krinkelt, and on to the front line that ran across a forested road intersection near a customs house named *Jägerhaus* Wahlerscheid.

German defenses in the Wahlerscheid sector included twenty-five concrete pillboxes situated on forward slopes and camouflaged in the densely-wooded terrain. Approaches to the pillboxes had been cleared of trees providing German gunners good fields of fire over mined terrain crossed by rows of barbed wire. The 277th VGD originally held the positions. The unit had been destroyed during the August fighting in Normandy and was reconstituted by ethnic Germans from captured Balkans territories and numerous Alsatians who, then considered being part of Germany, were conscripted into the German Army.

AMERICAN OBJECTIVE	To penetrate the Westwall and outflank its defenses by capturing Rohren
FORCES	
American:	2nd 'Indianhead' Infantry Division (Major General Walter M Robertson)
German:	277th Volksgrenadier Division (Generalmajor Wilhelm Viebig)
RESULT	The attack was halted because of the start of the Ardennes Offensive
CASUALTIES	
American:	1,200 killed, wounded, or missing
German:	Uncertain
LOCATION	Wahlerscheid Crossroads is 34 km northeast of Malmédy

Battle

Before daylight on 13 December, the leading 9th Infantry Regiment left the Belgian Army casern at Camp Elsenborn and by dawn was marching astride a trail through fir forests north of Rocherath. Deployment was straightforward: 1st Battalion on the left, 2nd Battalion on the right, and 3rd Battalion in reserve. In order to achieve

---

9 The 2nd Infantry Division's presence constituted a German intelligence failure, who believed the unit to be in reserve well to the rear.

10 Regimental Combat Team: a temporary fighting unit, usually consisting of an infantry regiment and supporting armor, artillery, engineering, supply, and other attached units, established for a specific mission..

secrecy, the attack was not preceded by artillery preparation and no patrolling was allowed in the attack area.

The column was within 100 meters of the Wahlerscheid intersection before enemy rifles and machine guns opened fire. The men faced barbed wire entanglements and antipersonnel mines hidden by the previous day's heavy, wet snowfall. Mortar and artillery shells crashed into the tree tops spraying the exposed ground troops with lethal metal shards and wood splinters. The 2nd Infantry Division had struck the Westwall.

Meanwhile to the south, battalions of the 99th Infantry Division launched eastward spoiling attacks up and down the ravines feeding Olef Creek to pin potential German reinforcements in place.

Late on the next day, a ten-man patrol from Company G, cloaked in the haze of approaching dusk, crawled and slid undetected under the rows of barbed wire before Wahlerscheid. Troops that followed cut an opening in the wire, but the patrols returned without engaging the enemy. On 15 December, a second patrol returned to the opening and surrounded a Westwall pillbox while Companies E and F exploited the widening gap. Regimental Commander Colonel Chester Hirschfelder dispatched his 2nd and 3rd Battalions to follow white engineer's tape through the gap in the wire.

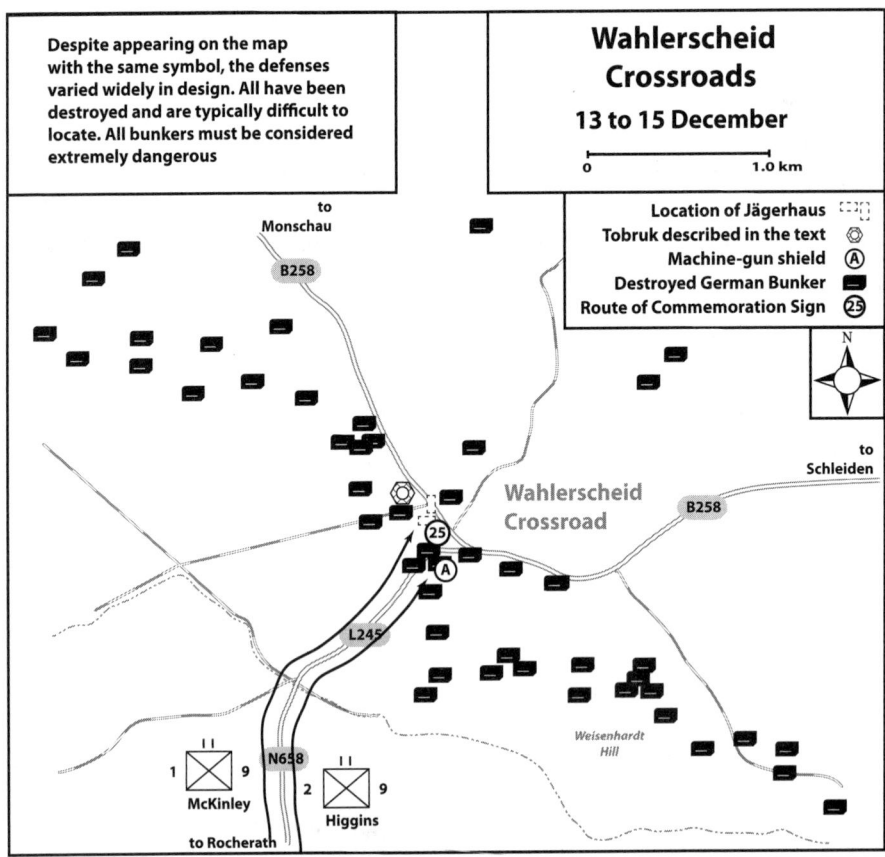

Explosive charges blew the metal doors off pillboxes while the defensive line erupted in gun fire. Fifteen pillboxes and the customs house eventually fell, with a total of 130 prisoners taken. The 38th Infantry Regiment moved forward to exploit the 1000-meter opening in the German front.

General Robertson was unfazed by pre-dawn artillery fire on 16 December. His men had achieved a penetration of the Westwall and a response of some sort seemed inevitable. Later in the day, he grew concerned about the strong attack upon 99th Infantry Division units on his right flank. His division depended upon supplies coming through Rocherath. If German forces advanced through the forests to cut that roadway, his men would be stranded. Robertson relocated his reserve 23rd Infantry Regiment to the roadside north of Rocherath and requested permission to halt the attack at Wahlerscheid (denied). Robertson's commander at US V Corps, Major General Leonard Gerow, ordered two 23rd Regiment battalions to reinforce the 393rd Infantry Regiment in the forest east of Krinkelt. Because Robertson knew what that meant, he temporarily halted the Wahlerscheid attack for the day. It was never to be resumed as events to the south became more pressing.

By the time the order to withdraw from the crossroads arrived, 1st Battalion, 9th Infantry Regiment had lost thirteen officers (including four company commanders) and 291 men. The order to relinquish the hard-fought ground was deeply resented by those not knowing the larger situation, and the label 'Heartbreak Crossroads' stuck to the lonely roadway intersection.

Battlefield Tour

> Follow highway B258 6.7 km east and south of Höfen into the heavily-forested border area. Stop in the parking area on the right (50.503272, 6.326468)

The parking area now occupies the location of the forestry and customs house known as *Jägerhaus* Wahlerscheid. **Route of Commemoration information panel #25** stands at the edge of the pavement and describes the events leading to the capture, abandonment, and recapture of the crossroads on 1 February 1945. During the 9th Infantry Regiment's nighttime assault, the attackers captured seventy-seven enemy troops in positions around this position.

Proceed on foot 70 m southeast of the parking area to the original intersection (50.502863, 6.326981) The Wahlerscheid Crossroad, a junction of a major north-south highway and one of the few east-west roads in the area, was stoutly defended and held with an impressive array of concrete gun positions, now hard to find and mostly ruined remnants. Nevertheless, a few are visible in the surrounding forests. Modern road reconstruction has modified the crossroads, moving the road junction 120 meters to the southeast.

Walk a short distance along the rough path on the right into the forest to find two reminders of the combat for Heartbreak Crossroads. (50.50262, 6.32678)

A concrete **machine-gun tobruk** is barely visible among the brush and broken branches to the left of the fire break. Slightly farther into the forest a metal cross held upright by an irregular block of cement presents a private memorial to PFC Marco L Jahr, a member of the 9th Infantry Regiment that attacked the Wahlerscheid area on 13 December 1944. He was killed at this location in the initial effort to penetrate the Westwall. His heroism in attacking a pillbox was recognized with a Silver Star. (50.5024, 6.32667)

Continue southeast on highway B258 to the new Wahlerscheid intersection. Turn right and walk 140 m along highway L245 toward Malmédy to a little used fire lane on the left. Follow the fire lane for approximately 140 m to a ruined concrete shelter on the left just barely inside the tree line. (50.50082, 6.32634)

In this regrown, dense forest, a patrol from 3rd Platoon, Company G commanded by T/Sergeant Clyde A Dugan of Canton, Ohio crawled through the fire zone of clear brush and trees and cut an opening in the barbed wire. The team toiled through the snow until they slid into a communications trench that ran behind the line of pillboxes. Meanwhile, a second group under S/Sgt James R Dunn expanded the wire gap and joined Dugan's men in the trench. Eventually detected, the combined group came under enemy fire. For five hours, Dugan and Dunn and their men fought off patrol after patrol until they slipped back across the clearing to safety.

Late on 15 December Dugan returned, this time armed with a telephone. Dugan reported no enemy activity as his men surrounded one of the pillboxes. Lieutenant Colonel Walter M Higgins, 2nd Battalion commander, hastily formulated an attack plan. Company F was sent through the gap and marked the path with white tape. Company E followed with the entire 3rd Battalion close behind. By the time the German troops were alerted to the growing American strength within their defense line, it was too late.

The remnants of a concrete **machine-gun shield** stand just within the line of trees with its gun opening aimed west. This construction was not a complete bunker but a concrete curtain to protect the gun team. As Americans lacked the explosives to destroy the positions after their capture in December 1944, German troops reoccupied the sites during the Ardennes offensive. The positions were eventually detonated in 1945 to prevent a repeat of that event.

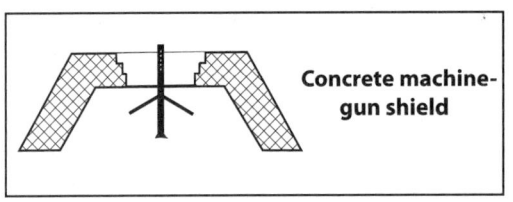

Concrete machine-gun shield

A good-sized crater is immediately in front of the shield and, to the rear, a trench line exits from the doorless entry to a T-junction with the communication trench line that runs 3 meters behind the bunker. Although blocked, covered and filled with forest debris, the connecting trench extends parallel with the fire lane connecting to other similarly destroyed German gun positions.

From the modern Wahlerscheid crossroads, proceed east toward Schleiden (B258) for 5.5 km. Turn right onto Hellenthaler Straße (becomes highway L159) for 5.1 km into Hellenthal. At the roundabout, take 1st exit onto highway B265 and follow for 5.3 km into Hollerath. The long route is required to pass around the reservoir created by the Oleftalsperre (Olef Dam).

Chapter Two   Battle for Elsenborn Ridge   35

Other Points of Interest near Hollerath

Hollerath

Hollerath, Germany was only 2.5 kilometers behind the front lines and held the headquarters for 12th SS Panzer Division during the course of the Northern Shoulder fighting.

The bell tower of St Bernard Parish Church is visible from the main highway. The **broken bell,** rescued from the ruins of the original church destroyed in the Ardennes fighting, stands on the church's southern side. Beside the bell, a memorial stone lists the village's victims of both world wars — soldiers and civilians alike.

Location: On Prethtalstraße in Hollerath. (50.456663, 6.405549)

A 12-meter by 22-meter, 16-room **regimental command post** stands in the forest north of Hollerath. Known as type *Regelbau* 117a, the bunker holds a reinforced observation tower, air lock, troop quarters, commander's quarters, and telephone exchange. The complex's massive walls have been damaged by post-war attempts to blow it up whereby a visitor's entry poses a certain danger. However, the original camouflage, gun embrasures, and exit doors are clearly visible under the encroaching vegetation.

Location: Automobile access is not possible because the gravel roads are restricted to residents and partially used as a cross-country ski trail in the winter. The site is not signed, and the many trails and paths in the area inhibit finding the location without GPS. Nevertheless, a hiking trail separates from a rural road opposite the Luxemburgerstraße bus stop west of the village. Follow the trail predominantly north for 1.2 km. Cross two branches of a creek to access a gravel road and continue for an additional 800 m. A short walk along a forest track on the left leads to the bunker. Total distance: 2.6 km (50.470505, 6.379591)

Leave Hollerath west on Luxemburgerstraße (B265); 850 m after the town limits, leave the highway to the right and then immediately turn left to proceed along a rural road that parallels the highway to a parking area. Continue forward on foot along the sweeping curve to the left and, after 530 m, turn right away from the roadway. Proceed 150 m and stop at the end of the pavement. (50.45209, 6.375534)

International Highway Sector
16 to 17 December 1944

Rollbahn A was the worst of the five routes assigned to German armor as passages west to the Meuse River. In 1944, it was (and, in places, still is) a muddy, logging road through a dense conifer forest. December weather had made it all but impassible. The road led directly to the twin villages of Rocherath and Krinkelt. The task of opening the route for the armor of the 12th SS Panzer Division '*Hitlerjugend*' fell to the infantry of the 277th Volksgrenadier Division.

This sector of the front was manned by Lieutenant Colonel Jack Allen's 3rd Battalion, 393rd Regiment. Allen's Company K held the terrain immediately west

36 The Bulge Battlefields

of the International Highway. The regiment's 1st Battalion and the 394th Infantry Regiment held the front along highway B265 south to Losheimergraben, Belgium.

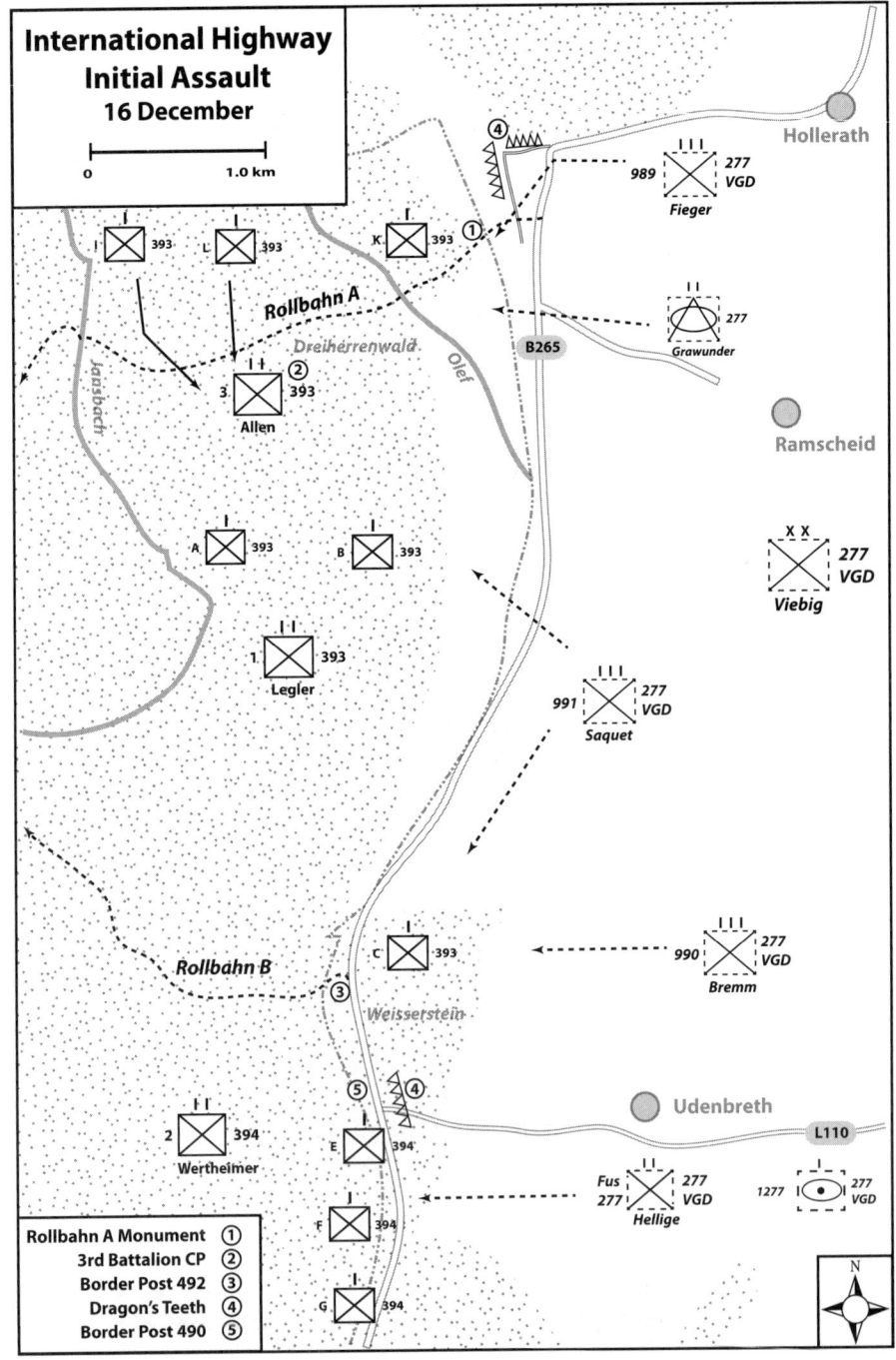

Chapter Two

Battle for Elsenborn Ridge

German Objective	To penetrate the American outpost line and open Rollbahn A and B to Rocherath-Krinkelt.
Forces	
American:	393rd Infantry Regiment (Lieutenant Colonel Jean D Scott)
German:	277th Volksgrenadier Division (Generalmajor Wilhelm Viebig) and Kampfgruppe Müller (SS-Major Siegfried Müller), 12th SS Panzer Division
Result	Despite the penetrations made, the expected breakthrough did not occur.
Casualties	
American:	At least 500 killed, wounded, or missing
German:	Heavy but non-specific
Location	Hollerath is 38 km east of Malmédy

Battle

Company K, 393rd Infantry Regiment held positions astride the forest track of Rollbahn A. Two platoons were overwhelmed before they could recover from the initial barrage and quickly became surrounded during an intense fire fight. The men ran out of ammunition and began an unauthorized withdrawal. Two hours later, Company K commander Captain Stephen B Plume surrendered what remained of his unit but not before inflicting heavy losses on the attackers.[11]

By 0855, Grenadier Regiment 989, supported by elements of the division's Panzerjäger Battalion, had penetrated 1.2 kilometers along Rollbahn A and approached the 3rd Battalion, 393rd Regiment command post (CP). Companies L and I established an all-around defense centered upon the CP and held off the advance. Phone contact was re-established with the regimental CP in Krinkelt, and Colonel Don Riley dispatched the 394th Regiment's Company I, from the division's reserve near Buchholz Station, as reinforcements. It arrived at the battalion CP around 1600. Despite the addition of German troops from I Battalion, SS Panzergrenadier Regiment 25, Pioneer Battalion 277, and towed howitzers to the attacking force, Colonel Allen's men held their positions through the day.

On the morning of 17 December, 3rd Battalion moved uphill and east of the battalion CP to re-establish its original line. The men almost immediately ran into a fresh battalion of General Viebig's grenadiers. Ninety minutes later II Battalion, SS Panzergrenadier Regiment 25, part of Kampfgruppe Müller,[12] joined the German attack led by five Jagdpanzer IVs [13] creeping forward, all the while aware of American

---

11 Captain Stephen B Plume was held at Oflag 13B in Hammelburg, Germany for the remainder of the war.

12 Kampfgruppe Müller consisted of SS Panzergrenadier Regiment 25; SS Flak Battalion 12; 1st Company, SS Panzer Pionier Battalion 12; 2nd Battalion, SS Panzer Artillery Regiment 12; and SS Panzerjäger Battalion 12 with 22 Jagdpanzer IVs.

13 The terminology is confusing. Panzer equates to armor or armored. A panzer may be any German armored vehicle. A Panzer Division is an Armored Division. A panzerjäger (literally 'armor hunter') was an individual, vehicle, or unit specifically tasked with destroying opposing armored vehicles.

bazooka teams sheltering in the roadside ditches. One such team disabled the leading vehicle which, nonetheless, provided covering fire for advancing Grenadiers with its machine gun.

By 1030, the remaining three jagdpanzers accompanied by panzergrenadiers moved around the flanks of the command post. The III Battalion, SS Panzergrenadier Regiment 25 and three more companies of jagdpanzers added to the assault. Thirty minutes later, with its wounded loaded onto the 3rd Battalion's few operational vehicles, the unit began a retreat toward Rocherath with Company L pulling back in stages as a rear guard. Jeep-mounted machine guns sprayed the woods on either side of the trail until the vehicles passed through the 23rd Infantry Regiment's lines.

Aftermath

On 17 December, desperate to put troops between the forest and the Wahlerscheid highway, General Lauer ordered the 3rd Battalion back into action. It established contact with Colonel McKinley's Company C near Lausdell and secured its left flank. (See Lausdell Crossroads, below).

The badly hit 1st Battalion, 393rd Regiment withdrew, as ordered, behind the 23rd Regiment and link to the right of Company L east of Rocherath. Communications difficulties left some isolated units unaware of the withdrawal order. The retromovement exposed the battalion to enemy troops to the east, south, and west. Low on ammunition and hard pressed by enemy shellfire, the battalion acted on recourse to move west through the forest and then north on the road toward Krinkelt. During the night of 17/18 December, the men proceeded along the draw east of the Mürringen–Krinkelt road until able to move cross-country to Wirtzfeld. Only 300 men Major Matthew Legler's 1st Battalion made the escape, leaving in their retreat hundreds of others stranded in the forests.

Battlefield Tour

The large curve in the highway is known as the Hollerather Knie. On the right, the rural road passes **dragon's teeth** on private property. The forest path is the beginning of **Rollbahn A** that followed the Schwarzenbruch Trail — one of only two routes through the forest. Continue approximately 40 meters after entering the forest to view an unusual **memorial stone** commemorating the attacking German 277th Volksgrenadier Division on one side and the defending US 99th Infantry Division on the opposite side. The accompanying wooden sign states, 'On this place began on the early morning of 16 December 1944 the German Ardennes Offensive. Soldiers of the 277th VG met the US 99th ID here in violent fighting.' (50.451831, 6.375162) **Trench lines** and **foxholes** of Company K, 393rd Infantry Regiment, are clearly visible in the undergrowth-free forest behind the memorial stone. These dark, dank forests are as fearsome today as they were in 1944.

To walk to Krinkelt is possible by adhering to the trail and passing through *Dreiherrenwald*, but it is a substantial distance. Olef creek, a surprisingly narrow,

---

A jagdpanzer refers to any specially built tank destroyer vehicle. A Jagdpanther was such a special tank destroyer built upon the chassis of the Panther (PzKpfw V) tank. Similarly, the Germans built a Jagdpanzer IV, Jagdtiger, and other variations.

shallow creek that did not inhibit vehicular passage, is 700 meters ahead and a walk to it provides a perspective of the initial combat zone. Be advised, however, that during fall and winter months, hunting is popular in these forests, and between 15 September and 31 December access is **absolutely prohibited** starting in late afternoon to the following morning (15:00 to 09:00). Jansbach is 1.8 kilometers from the Rollbahn A memorial, Ruppenvenn an additional 2.1 kilometers, and another 3.0 kilometers to Krinkelt for a total 7 kilometers. These sites are visited by automobile later in the tour.

> Return to the road and walk 550 m north on the gravel road that parallels the edge of the forest. (50.456276, 6.371899)

The **dragon's teeth** on the right are inside the barbed wire fence but are readily viewed. Their construction is visible because each row of four is connected at its base by a concrete slab. Those protected underneath the trees are in original condition and are noticeably taller than the exposed weather-worn stones. (50.453028, 6.374556) The straight, deep gully in the dark pine forest on the left is probably an **antitank ditch**. (50.453438, 6.373762)

> Retrieve your vehicle and continue south on the International Highway by turning right from the rural road. Proceed south 4.0 km on highway B265 and stop at the forest road on the right marked by border post 492 and blocked to traffic by red-striped concrete bollards. (50.419549, 6.366613)

The 3rd and 1st Battalions, 393rd Regiment held positions in the woods just passed on the right. Both battalions were hit by the initial Grenadier Regiment 991 assault. With telephone lines destroyed by the German artillery barrage, they could not request artillery support. The American foxhole line crossed the highway at the point where the highway enters into the forest. American front-line positions continued along the east edge of the forest.

Border Post 492 marked the forest road west of the International Highway where **Rollbahn B** followed the *Weisserstein* Trail as it passed through the dense forest to Krinkelt and on farther to Wirtzfeld. The road is restricted to forestry use and forbidden to motorists; however, one can walk the full 6.0 km to Krinkelt if so desired. More practically, the tour will review sites on the opposite side of the forest later.

Company C, 393rd Infantry Regiment, was the only unit in foxholes east of the International Highway. Grenadier Regiment 990 attacked its positions astride the *Weisserstein* Trail. The fighting became desperate when two platoons were overrun, but the company command post strengthened with the arrival of reinforcements in the form of the regiment's Antitank Platoon fighting as infantry. Lieutenant Harry C Parker ordered his men to fix bayonets and charge. The suddenness of the action drove off the attackers and led to perimeter defense established around the CP. Nowhere was the 1st Battalion, 393rd Regiment's line completely broken. In fact, by nightfall, the regiment, despite having suffered fifty percent casualties, still held some front-line foxholes in Company B's sector where the German initial attack weakened from accurate and intense mortar fire.

> Continue 650 m to Border Post 490 directly opposite highway L110 to Udenbreth. (50.413876, 6.368534)

In the 394th Regiment's sector, the initial German artillery bombardment struck Companies E and F, but the men suffered few casualties. Company G was also little affected in its covered foxholes. At 0735, Viebig's Fusilier Battalion 277 began to cross the open ground to the east to attack the northern platoons of Company E; however, well-coordinated American artillery fire drove it off. A short while later, the attackers returned under cover of smoke and with the added support of three 'Hetzer' armored vehicles.[14] American artillery repulsed their attack while Company G, 394th Regiment remained sheltered from the explosions in its log-covered bunkers. The Hetzers retreated and the fusiliers were driven off, suffering heavy casualties and thereby ending the attack upon 394th Regiment's 2nd Battalion. Unknown to the men, the front lines to its north and south were pushed back leaving 2nd Battalion in a dangerous, exposed salient.

The battalion later became trapped in the forests east of Mürringen along with elements of 1st Battalion, 394th Regiment that had found shelter in Hünningen after its escape from Losheimergraben. The next day, Captain Robert McGee, the 2nd Battalion's Operations Officer acting for the battalion's incoherent commander,[15] joined with lost members of the 1st Battalion. A makeshift combat team attempted to enter Mürringen to find it occupied by a battalion from Fusilier Regiment 89. Captain McGee's force skirted Mürringen to the north, eventually following the Holzwarche Valley into Wirtzfeld and successfully extracted 570 men to safety while making the Germans pay a dear price for the woodland trails.

The German highway (L110) from Neuhof lay adjacent to this position from the east and marked the start of **Rollbahn C** and roughly the boundary between 1st Battalion, 393rd Regiment, to the north and 2nd Battalion, 394th Regiment, to the south. The 2nd Battalion's positions straddled the roadway along the forest's edge. (50.413883, 6.368526) Rollbahn C did not enter the forest at this point but continued south on the International Highway to Losheimergraben, where it turned west on highway N632 towards Büllingen.[16]

The roadside shrubbery hides rows of **dragon's teeth** that roughly parallel International Highway 30-to-50 meters to the east. (50.414047, 6.369234)

---

14 Hetzer: officially Jagdpanzer 38 or Sd.Kfz 138/2, a light tank destroyer with a 75-mm Pak 39 gun mounted upon the chassis of a Czech 38(t) tank.

15 Lieutenant Colonel Philip Wertheimer failed to lead his troops and recommended surrender. Wertheimer was reduced in rank to major and discharged in December, 1945.

16 Post-war confusion lingers over this point. Some historians maintain that Rollbahn C entered the forest at this juncture and followed trails through Krinkelter Wald to Mürringen and on to Büllingen. Such a route would have put more armored forces on difficult forest trails rather than the highway through Losheimergraben and on to Büllingen. The presented version claims support from a captured German battle map.

Chapter Two   Battle for Elsenborn Ridge   41

> Continue south on highway B265 for 4.4 km to Losheimergraben.

Defense of the Losheimergraben Crossroads
16 to 17 December 1944

The 12th Volksgrenadier Division was responsible for capturing the crossroads at Losheimergraben to permit passage of troops approaching along Rollbahn C from the north on the International Highway and Rollbahn D from Losheim. The mission fell to Grenadier Regiment 48. The unit possessed experienced NCOs having seen action in Poland (1939), France (1940), and the Eastern Front (1941 - 44) but contained mostly green recruits since the division was destroyed during the Soviet summer offensive of July 1944.

The 1st Battalion, 394th Infantry Regiment, commanded by Lieutenant Colonel Robert H Douglas, held the cluster of border buildings known as Losheimergraben with forward positions in an arc to the southeast. The battalion's Company A, positioned on the slopes of *Eichelsberg*, overlooked the German town of Losheim. Company B straddled the road from Losheim, and Company C extended the front to the north to make contact with the 2nd Battalion's Company G. The machine guns of Company D (Heavy Weapons) were spread among Company A and B positions, and its 81-mm mortars occupied dug-in positions in an open field near buildings southwest of the crossroads. The slopes of Hill 664 held three 57-mm antitank guns of the battalion's Antitank Platoon.

OBJECTIVE	To capture the crossroads at the northern limit of the Losheim Gap.
FORCES	
American:	1st Battalion, 394th Infantry Regiment (Lieutenant Colonel Robert H Douglas)
German:	Grenadier Regiment 48 (Oberstleutnant Wilhelm Osterhold)
RESULT	The junction was taken after two days of fighting.
CASUALTIES	
American:	540 killed, wounded, or missing (some missing reappeared in their units later)
German:	Unknown
LOCATION	Losheimergraben is 12 km south of Hollerath, Germany; Hollerath is 38 km east of Malmédy

Battle

The German bombardment lifted at approximately 0715, but it was not until noon that Oberstleutnant Wilhelm Osterhold's Grenadier Regiment 48, 12th Volksgrenadier Division led by a captured American jeep and a StuG III self propelled (SP) assault gun,[17] approached along the highway from Losheim. When the gun passed

---

17   StuG III: abbreviation of Sturmgeschütz, a 75-mm cannon mounted upon the chassis of the PzKpfw III providing a self propelled artillery piece for close-infantry support. Numerous variations were manufactured during the war.

within 50 meters of the American antitank gun concealed among trees on the slopes of Hill 664, the American gun fired, knocking off a track. The American gun's third shot set the German self-propelled gun aflame. The men of Company B killed the jeep's occupants when the vehicle approached their line a short distance ahead.

Later that morning, the two battalions of enemy troops worked through thick woods to strike the junction of Companies B and C from the northeast. Suffering sixty casualties, Company B was driven back 400 meters. Survivors escaped by moving along a wooded draw and took up positions in the crossroads buildings. Company C attempted to re-establish the line but was unable to do so. The grenadiers achieved the edge of the forest by nightfall but were hesitant to advance without artillery support.

Meanwhile, about 175 men from Fusilier Regiment 27, repelled from an earlier attack upon Buchholz Station, outflanked Company A to the south. Company A successfully repulsed the assault and drove the German fusiliers toward Company D's mortar platoon. Staff Sergeant Delbert Stumpf's platoon, dug in around a farmhouse near the crossroads, swung its 81-mm mortars around and propped the bipod legs of its weapons on the edge of its foxholes to fire at almost a vertical 89 degrees against enemy only 15 meters away, repulsing several enemy attempts to advance. The Germans withdrew under an onslaught of tree bursts.

By early on 17 December, much of 1st Battalion had pulled back to positions north of Buchholz Station and later in the afternoon, farther back to high ground west of Mürringen. First Lieutenant Dewey Plankers led a small force of fifty riflemen, jeep drivers, and an antiaircraft gun crew as a rear guard still holding foxholes southeast of the crossroads. Fusilier Regiment 27 flanked the Losheimergraben positions on the west while Grenadier Regiment 48 continued its frontal attack from Losheim. Eventually, three StuG IIIs supported by a strong force of infantry drove Plankers lightly-armed force into three identical customs houses southeast of the crossroads.

Sturmgeschütz again led the German attack. The lead vehicle had been immobilized by a single bazooka round fired by Sergeant Mel Weidner and his loader, Private William P Kirkbride.[18] American small-arms fire drove off the accompanying German infantry, but that was a short reprieve. The force was too powerful for the men at the crossroads. When night fell, the Germans moved in, led by their commander. Osterhold arranged a parley during which he advised the Americans sheltering in the customs building cellars of an upcoming German grenade attack. Kirkbride and the others in the cellar waved a white flag of surrender while Plankers led twenty survivors through the forest to friendly lines. They had held the important crossroads for two days.[19]

---

18   Staff Sergeant Melvin J Weidner from Vanderburg County, Indiana and Private William P Kirkbride of Tulsa County, Oklahoma were captured and held at Stalag XIIIc in Hammelburg am Main, Bavaria until the end of the war. Weidner died in 2001 at age 86 and is buried in Evansville, Indiana. Kirkbride was liberated on 10 May 1945. He became an aeronautical engineer and worked for several aerospace companies. Kirkbride died in 2013 at age 90.

19   The 1st Battalion, 394th Infantry Regiment received a Presidential Unit Citation. Lt Dewey Plankers survived the war and died in 1973 at age 52.

Chapter Two

Battle for Elsenborn Ridge 43

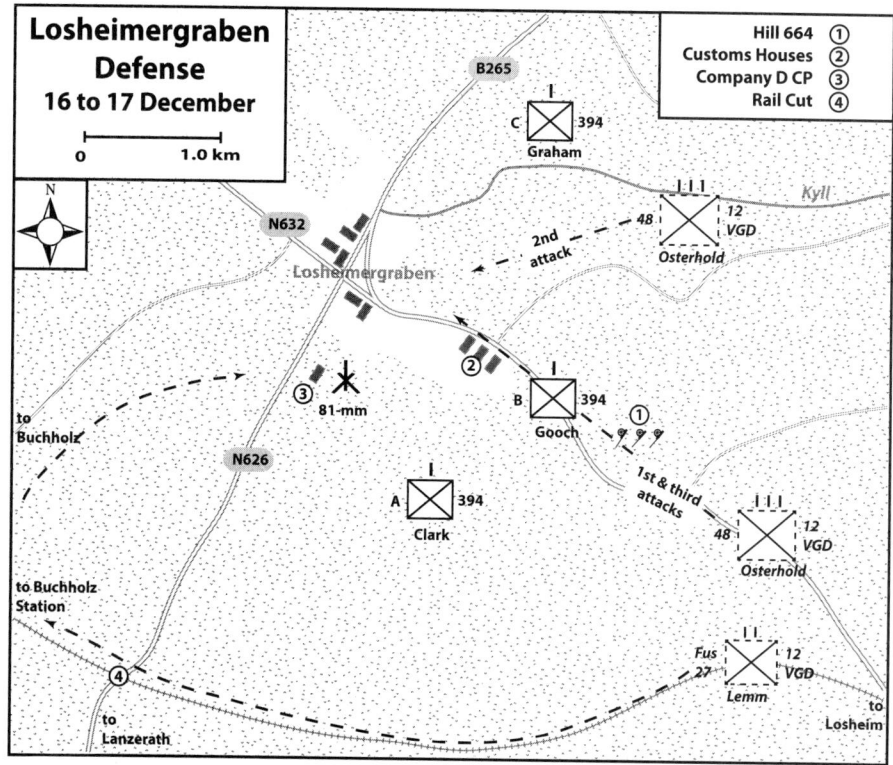

Battlefield Tour

The rural crossroad has been replaced with a roundabout, and the International Highway avoids even the roundabout with a sweeping curve, but many of the original structures remain. Continue straight through the roundabout (becomes highway N626 toward Lanzerath) and stop at the monument on the left side of the road 170 m past the roundabout. (50.378823, 6.342003)

The memorial stone, backed by an arc of shrubs, bears a plaque in English and German commemorating the defense of the crossroads by the **1st Battalion, 394th Infantry Regiment**, and attached units. The **farm house** behind the monument was the command post for Company D (Heavy Weapons) during the fighting. The company's mortars were initially positioned in a forest opening (now replanted) behind and to the right of the farmhouse. (50.377894, 6.343099) The mortar platoon later repositioned along the tree line to the northwest. (50.383231, 6.339001)

Walk back to the roundabout and turn right toward Losheim.

The **Kyll Creek** draw across the highway and behind the new structure on the corner witnessed the withdrawal of Company B survivors from the first day's grenadier attack. (50.380412, 6.346597) After darkness fell on 16 December, remnants of Companies B and C withdrew to the crossroads. The **house on the right** was occupied by 2nd and 3rd Platoons of Company C under the command of Sergeants John Hilliard and John Trent.[20] (50.379441, 6.343335) They were later joined by 20 survivors from Company B. The German assault of 17 December overran the position and most of the defenders were killed or taken prisoner.

Continue east 200 m to the three identical structures on the right. (50.37877, 6.346017)

The southern-most of the three **customs houses** held forward observers from Batteries A and C, 371st Field Artillery Battalion. The observers later fell back to rejoin their unit. Oberst Osterhold occupied the building during the evening of 17 December and made his surrender demands from there. The Sturmgeschütz knocked out by Sergeants Weidner and Kirkbride's bazooka eventually ground to a halt on the roadway between buildings one and two. Men of the Antitank Platoon and infantry survivors occupied the second and third customs buildings. These troops accepted Osterhold's surrender offer. (50.37888, 6.345481) [21]

The open field southeast of the customs houses once held the **temporary burial ground** for German and American casualties of the engagement. (50.378469, 6.346618)

> Return to your vehicle and continue south on highway N626. After 1.1 km, park on the right and walk 150 m to an overpass that crosses what once was the rail line from Losheim to Büllingen. (50.368634, 6.333607)

The highway passes over the **rail cut** used by Oberstleutnant Georg Lemm's Fusilier Regiment 27 to advance upon Buchholz Station 1.2 kilometers to the northwest. (See below.) This bridge was blown up by retreating German troops in September 1944, and the deep rail cut restricted German vehicular movement in the first days of the offensive. The rail line is now part of an area bicycle path.

> Continue a further 1.2 km into Lanzerath passing the wooded hill on the right. Turn right and, after 110 m, right again. Continue 300 m to the memorial on the right. (50.360348, 6.331199)

Defense of Lanzerath
16 December 1944

In 1944, Lanzerath was a farming hamlet of ten-or-so frame houses; it is not much more today. The town's location made it important because it was 300 meters south of a road junction that controlled routes to Buchholz Station to the west and Losheimergraben to the north. The road to Losheim was blocked by a demolished railway bridge; the road to Buchholz Station was its alternative. A knoll west of the

---

20 Staff Sergeant John W Hilliard and Technical Sergeant John C Trent were both captured and held at Stalag XIIIc in Hammelburg am Main, Germany.

21 Oberstleutnant Wilhelm Osterhold, a highly decorated German officer, fought in the Invasion of Poland, Battle of France, in the Soviet Union, and the Ardennes Offensive. Osterhold received the Knight's Cross of the Iron Cross with Oak Leaves in March 1944. He became an officer in the post-war German Bundeswehr. Osterhold died in 2002 at age 88.

Chapter Two Battle for Elsenborn Ridge 45

community gave occupying troops a dominant position over the road. Terrain gave observers on the knoll a view across a valley to the east and into Germany, providing an excellent position for observation of German troop movements. On 10 December, the Intelligence and Reconnaissance Platoon (I&R) of the 394th Infantry Regiment, well-armed with automatic weapons that included a jeep-mounted .50-caliber machine gun, two .30-caliber machineguns, several BARs, and one submachine gun, moved into wood-covered foxholes dug by the previous unit to occupy the position. The I&R Platoon's commander, 1st Lieutenant Lyle J Bouck, Jr, would in a week be 21 years old. Although the second youngest man in the platoon, Bouck was well respected by his men. The town also held a section of Company A, 820th Tank Destroyer Battalion, from the 14th Cavalry Group with four towed 3-inch (76.2-mm) guns.

OBJECTIVE		To open the road to Honsfeld and farther west
FORCES		
	American:	Intelligence and Reconnaissance Platoon (1st Lieutenant Lyle J Bouck), 394th Infantry Regiment
	German:	Fallschirmjäger Regiment 9 (Oberst Helmut von Hoffman), 3rd Fallschirmjäger Division
RESULT		The enemy advance was delayed for 12 hours.
CASUALTIES		
	American:	1 dead, 14 wounded
	German:	43 dead, 24 wounded
LOCATION		Lanzerath is 2.5 km south of Losheimergraben and 30 km east of Malmédy, Belgium

Battle

On 15 December, Bouck's senses told him something was just not right and, accordingly he kept his men on alert through the damp, cold night. Just before dawn, the eastern sky was lit by muzzle flashes of hundreds of artillery pieces. After an hour, the rolling barrage moved off the I&R Platoon. No one was injured under the protection of heavy timber roofs, but the tank destroyers had abandoned the hamlet and moved under orders south to Manderfeld.

Twenty minutes later, while conducting a patrol through Lanzerath, Bouck observed masses of German infantry apparently moving toward his right flank. The German troops marched in formation along both sides of the road from Losheim. While they approached, Bouck returned to his unit's positions after observing that they were not infantry but paratroopers. Bouck allowed about 100 men to pass awaiting an opportunity to ambush the unit's command staff. While he and his men prepared to fire upon the apparent commander, a young girl raced from a house and pointed up the hill at the I&R Platoon's position. Private William Tsakanikas had the girl in his sights, ready to shoot, but he hesitated. The young blonde reminded him of his sisters.

The surprise was lost when the German troops dove into roadside ditches. Bouck's jeep-mounted .50-caliber machine gun raked the ditches and swept the hillside while a firefight erupted. A barbed wire fence, hidden in the deep snow, thwarted the initial fallschirmjäger attack. Waves of German paratroopers came up the hill just to be cut down by interlocking automatic weapons fire. While the morning wore on, Bouck radioed for artillery support fire, but none came. Requesting instructions, he was told to 'hold at all cost' — and that is exactly what he did.

Shortly before noon, a white flag appeared and the Americans held their fire while German corpsmen cleared the hillside of the wounded. Then the assaults continued. A message sent at 1603 reported that they were still holding their positions but receiving enemy artillery fire. The early dusk of the northern European winter found Bouck's platoon nearly out of ammunition. Another white flag accompanied a surrender demand that met with rifle fire.

In darkness, while Bouck was planning a staggered retreat toward Buchholz Station, German Sergeant Vinz Kuhlbach[22] led fifty men against Bouck's flank and infiltrated among the foxholes. The platoon, most of whose members had wounds of varying severity, was captured. Bouck had taken a bullet in the calf and bled profusely. He was roused out of an entrenchment near a cabin with Private Tsakanikas, who had suffered several bullet wounds to his face during the final German assault. German medics treated the wounded before they were marched or carried into captivity.[23]

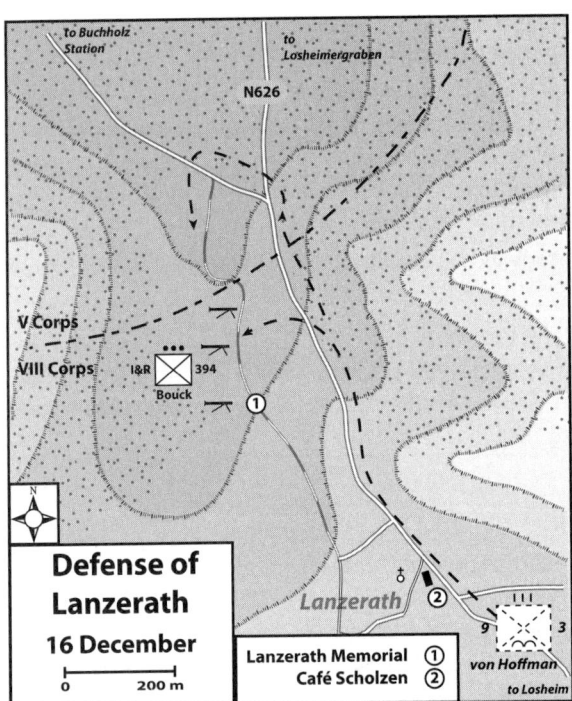

Defense of Lanzerath
16 December

Aftermath

Bouck, not aware of the contribution he and his men had made, believed himself to be a failure. However, their refusal to retreat delayed the spearhead of the entire German Sixth Panzer Army wherein its critical

---

22   Twenty-five-year-old Sergeant Vinz Kuhlbach was a veteran of fighting at Monte Cassino and Normandy. He survived the war and became an accountant.

23   Private William Tsakanikas changed his surname to James after the war but remained known by his nickname, 'Tsak'. His facial wounds were severe and eventually required thirty-seven operations, including three by German doctors when he was a PoW. He married a nurse that he met during rehabilitation, and they conceived four sons. Private 'Tsak' James suffered from his wounds for the remainder of his life. Tsak died in 1977 from an overdose of painkillers at age 52.

timetable fell hopelessly behind schedule. In a sense, although nobody knew it at the time, the German offensive was already beaten.[24]

Battlefield Tour

The farm track presents tremendous views to the south and east where the terrain descends in those directions. Any large troop movements in those directions would have been easily observable from this position. The forest edge that held Lt Bouck's positions has been altered by post-war harvesting and replanting of the trees. His position was slightly protected from enemy approach from the north by a slight pitch in the terrain.

An American flag flies next to a bench that overlooks the village. A beautifully inscribed small black and gray granite plaque rests on a stone near the bench dedicated to the **soldiers of all nations** that fought here. A hole drilled through the stone aims directly at the highway below, demonstrating the ideal firing position that Bouck's men had from this location.

> The farm track continues north, but at last view, it was barely drivable. Reverse direction and return to the main highway (N626). Turn right and proceed 100 m to the building on the right signed De Heksenketel (The Cauldron) above the door. (50.357595, 6.335152)

In 1944, this building was the **Café Scholzen**. After the Americans were captured, they marched at gunpoint down the hill to this building, which was the command post for Fallschirmjäger Regiment 9. While held captive here, Lt Bouck witnessed the arrival of the furious, and furiously impatient, SS-Lieutenant Colonel Joachim Peiper. The commander of Kampfgruppe Peiper stormed at Oberst von Hoffman for his delay in opening the road to Honsfeld that was re-assigned to Peiper's force as **Rollbahn D**. Peiper commandeered Hoffman's I Battalion to provide flank protection for his advance upon Honsfeld while the remainder of the Fallschirmjäger regiment followed behind.

> Reverse direction on highway N626 and, after 700 m, turn left toward Buchholz / Honsfeld. Proceed 1.5 km and turn right at Hotel Waldfrieden and continue to the open area bean the bicycle path. (50.374075, 6.319655)

Defense of Buchholz Station
16 December 1944

Buchholz Station headquartered the 3rd Battalion, 394th Infantry Regiment which acted as the 99th Division's 735-man reserve. The unit was left understrength after Colonel Riley sent Company I and a machine-gun detachment from its heavy

---

24 Only recognized for their efforts in 1983, the platoon become one of the most decorated American units of the war receiving a Presidential Unit Citation, four Distinguished Service Crosses, five Silver Stars, and ten Bronze Stars. Bouck was awarded a Silver Star and Distinguished Service Cross. Lyle Bouck survived his prison camp experiences to return to St Louis. He became a chiropractor, married, and raised five children. Two of his sons became Navy pilots.

weapons company to reinforce Company A, 393rd Regiment. Company L was positioned around the rail station, which was also the battalion CP. Companies K and M initially held positions along the road to the north. Using the rail line from Losheim through relatively open country, Fusilier Regiment 27, 12th Volksgrenadier Division advanced more quickly than the grenadiers from Losheimergraben.

German Objective	To push west along alternative Rollbahn D
Forces	
American:	3rd Battalion (Major Norman A Moore), 394th Infantry Regiment
German:	Fusilier Regiment 27 (Oberstleutnant Georg Lemm), 12th Volksgrenadier Division
Result	The rail station was captured after a day of fighting.
Casualties	
American:	Approximately 90 killed or wounded.
German:	75 dead, 30 taken prisoner
Location	Buchholz Station is 2.5 km northwest of Lanzerath and 27 km east of Malmédy

Battle

Company L was starting breakfast at 0705 when First Sergeant Elmer P Klug sighted Germans approaching out of the fog and marching two abreast along the rail tracks. Sergeant Klug grabbed his carbine and raced toward the approaching enemy column of 25 to 50 men. At 50 meters distance, Klug yelled an authoritative 'halt' and the column momentarily stopped. The unit's leader turned to shout orders and Klug shot him in the back. The enemy scattered while Klug ran back to the station house.[25]

Rifle fire forced the enemy to shelter behind boxcars while accurate German artillery fire swept through 3rd Battalion's command post. A jeep-towed antitank gun manned by Staff Sergeant Savino Travalini fired upon the fusiliers in the box cars and the artillery observer on the water tower.

By noon, Company K had moved to positions blocking the road to Honsfeld. Fusiliers again pressed forward at 1100, moving through the forest against Companies K and L. Sergeant Travalini's Antitank Platoon was pinned by a German machine gun positioned south of the station. The sergeant crawled along the roadside ditch until close enough to eliminate the gun with a fragmentation grenade. Then Travalini drove out enemy soldiers occupying the station roundhouse with bazooka fire. When

---

25 First Sergeant Elmer P Klug, from East Peoria, Illinois, had enlisted in the army during the depression. Klug broke his neck later in the battle when he drove into a foxhole to escape enemy artillery fire. A truck of wounded soldiers including Klug was machine gunned as it passed the outskirts of Krinkelt. Everyone in the vehicle was killed. Elmer P Klug is buried in Henri-Chapelle American Cemetery, Henri-Chapelle, Belgium.

Chapter Two

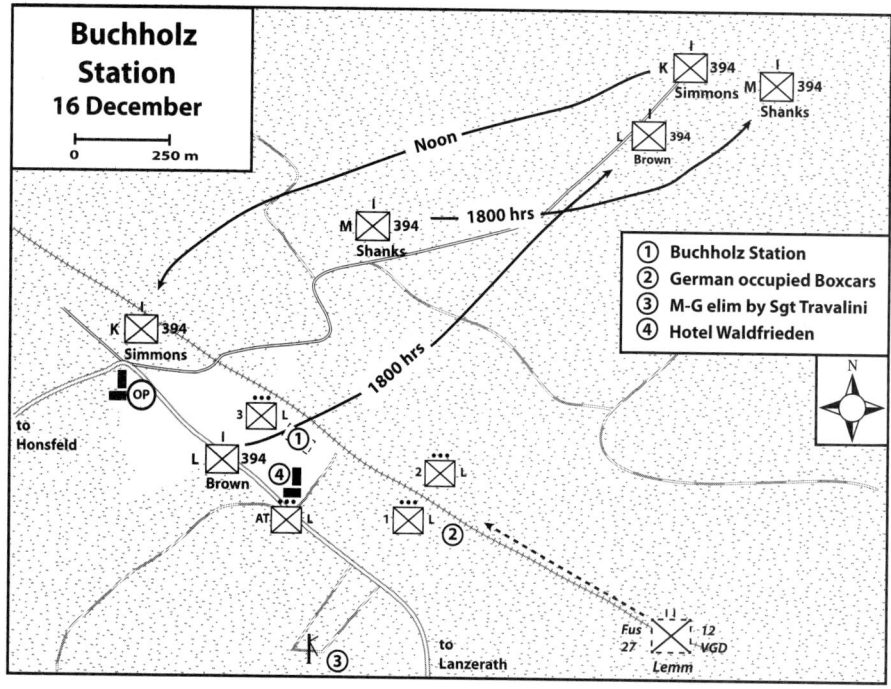

the troops fled the building, Travalini shot them with his M-1 carbine.[26] The German attack was finally repulsed with effective fire from 60-mm mortars.

Shortly after 1800, all of 3rd Battalion headed northeast to reinforce 1st Battalion, leaving only a rear guard of two rifle platoons of Company K. The next morning, Kampfgruppe Peiper passed through the sector towards Honsfeld, and his quad 20-mm flak guns sprayed Company K positions inflicting almost 100 percent casualties on the 60-man force while a Company K radio operator hid in the cellar of a nearby house reporting on German troop movements. He reported the passage of twenty-eight half-tracks and thirty tanks before going silent.

Battlefield Tour

The train station and buildings around it were demolished after the war, but **Buchholz Station** was located on the empty plot of ground along the rail line identified by the remaining paving stones. The round house and the boxcars occupied by German Fusiliers during the opening stages of the battle parked along the old roadway to the southeast.

The Hotel Waldfrieden was the **Antitank Company CP** on 16 December. The German machine gun that brought the CP under fire and was attacked by Sgt Tavalini was situated in the woods approximately 200 meters to the south.

---

26   Staff Sergeant Savino Travalini was awarded a Sliver Star and promoted to 2nd Lieutenant for his heroic actions that day.

The farmhouse occupied by the Company K radioman is 350 meters farther northwest past Hotel Waldfrieden. The complex now houses the regional Forestry Ministry. (50.375305, 6.314255)

The tour returns to the fighting along Rollbahns A and B by viewing sites on the west side of the Krinkelter Wald. Since Kampfgruppe Peiper passed through Buchholz, for convenience, sites relating to Peiper in Honsfeld and Büllingen may be reviewed at this time. See Chapter Three.

Other Points of Interest near the German border

Udenbreth
A second and more visible row of **dragon's teeth** runs through the edge of Udenbreth near the intersection of Auf dem Zollhof and Auf'm Klompertshof. However, the residential streets are *Anlieger Frei* (for residents only). To view this stunning example of dragon's teeth, park at end of Auf'm Klompertshof (50.414537, 6.386915) and walk west. Hidden by thickets of trees and shrubbery, the dragon's teeth continue across the road to the northeast. (50.414617, 6.383505)

Losheimergraben
One kilometer from the road junction toward Losheim, a side road on the left enters the *Schleiden* Forest, where Company C, 394th Infantry Regiment had manned **foxholes** south of Kyll Creek in advance of the Losheimergraben crossroads. Examples remain visible in the forest.
Location: Vehicles are prohibited, but the area is accessible on foot, 450 meters down a private road from the intersection with highway B265 at (50.380302, 6.353268) to a forest track to the left. After approximately 200 meters, foxholes loom in the forest on the left. (50.381493, 6.356381)

Losheim
Musée Ars Tecnica
Prümerstraße 55   D-53940 Losheim Germany
Tel: +49 (0)6557 920 640   Email: arstecnica@ardenner-center.de
Web: http://www.arstecnica.de/arstecnica/
The **Musée Ars Tecnica** displays almost 2,000 meters of miniature railways, many of which are scale models depicting battles and scenes from the Second World War. Artifacts are also on display. The musée is on the second floor and does charge an admission fee. The first floor store is cost-free and presents hundreds of cars, fixtures, landscape — everything necessary to construct a sophisticated miniature train environment in all various scales.
Open Tuesday to Friday from 12:00 to 18:00, Saturday, Sundays, and holidays from 10:00 to 18:00. Fee for museum only.
Location: In Losheim near the intersection of highways B265 and N634. (50.352945, 6.384428)

Hünningen

On 16 December, Hünningen held the 394th Infantry's Regimental Command Post. During that day, the growing strength of the German attacks to the regiment's front and the loss of contact with the 14th Cavalry Group on its southern flank forced General Robertson to reinforce the Krinkelt positions by detaching Lieutenant Colonel John M Hightower's 1st Battalion, 23rd Infantry Regiment — the 2nd Infantry Division's reserve unit — to occupy Hünningen. The first action did not occur until 1600 on 17 December when a short German artillery barrage hit the town followed by the assault by Fusilier Regiment 49 from woods to the southeast. First Lieutenant Charles W Stockell, forward observer for the 37th Field Artillery Battalion, climbed the church steeple to direct fire on the advancing fusiliers. The assault evaporated under punishing artillery fire and machine-gun fire from Company B. The Fusilier Regiment launched seven more attacks that afternoon and evening but was unable to push the Americans from the town. However, with American positions to the north and south being pushed back, Hightower's battalion was in an increasingly narrow salient and at threat of becoming surrounded. At 0200 on 18 December, he made the decision to withdraw, leaving 250 enemy dead in the surrounding fields.

Hünningen sits atop a long ridge between La Warche River and a tributary, the Tiefenbach. Old structures generally block lines of vision, but perspectives through gaps between houses prove the location's observational value. A small garden near the church holds a stone bearing the image of a Teutonic Knight. The field stone wall around the **war memorial** holds stones inscribed with the names of forty-seven soldiers and eight civilians killed in the two world wars.

Kulturroute #1 comprises of twelve informational signs that form a 2.5-kilometer trail around the village and that describe wartime and peacetime life in this small Belgian farming community. Informational sign #1 stands near the war memorial. Its text describes the life of a town resident named Otto. After conquering Belgium in 1940, this sector was incorporated into the Greater German Reich and Otto was conscripted into the German Army. He fought and was captured in Italy. Otto returned from imprisonment in 1946 to find nearly all of the cows, cattle, pigs, and chickens dead. Several houses had been burned down; water pipes and electricity network smashed. A graphic photograph of his classmates indicates that by war's end Otto was the only male survivor of seven childhood friends.
Location: At a three-way intersection in the center of Hünningen. (50.395996, 6.292119)

To continue the tour, from Buchholtz Station, reverse direction toward Lanzerath and return to highway N626; turn left toward Losheimergraben. From the roundabout in Losheimergraben, take the third exit toward Malmédy / Büllingen (N632). Follow the highway for 7.2 km into Büllingen and in the roundabout turn right on Bahnhofstraße toward Rocherath. After 300 m, turn right toward Rocherath (N658) and immediately pass under the disused rail line. Follow for 4.1 km into Krinkelt. Turn right onto Langergasse immediately before the church on the left and the memorial park on the right (the tour returns to this location later). After 260 m, turn left on Lütscheborren. After 1.1 km, turn right on the farm track, bear right at the next junction, and continue to the gate at the edge of the forest. For the past 1.3 km this road was Rollbahn B. (50.428031, 6.318744)

Battle for Krinkelterwald
16 to 17 December 1944

On 16 December, Lieutenant Colonel Paul V Tuttle's 3rd Battalion, 23rd Infantry Regiment, attached to 393rd Regiment, carried out orders to reposition in an area east of Rocherath known as Ruppenvenn (spelled Röppenvenn on area maps). The low-lying ground was the site where *Rollbahn* A exited from the forest. Captain Charles B MacDonald[27] led his Company I 1100 meters through the forest of the left side of *Rollbahn* A to establish a roadblock on the banks of the Jansbach. Company L moved into the forest south of the road junction while Company K established positions along the forest edge to its north.

On 17 December, Captain MacDonald could hear the trapped 3rd Battalion, 393rd Regiment, engaged in firefights. Shortly after noon, the retreating men of that unit passed through MacDonald's positions. Later the regiment's 1st Battalion, although less severely hit by German forces, was in danger of being cut off and similarly withdrew to establish a line south of Company L, 23rd Regiment. All that remained between the attackers and Rocherath was Captain MacDonald's Company I.

GERMAN OBJECTIVE	To push west along Rollbahn A to capture the Rocherath-Krinkelt road junction
FORCES	
American:	3rd Battalion (Lieutenant Colonel Paul V Tuttle Jr), 23rd Infantry Regiment
German:	Grenadier Regiment 989 (Oberst i.G. Fieger), Grenadier Regiment 990 (Oberstleutnant Bremm), and elements of Kampfgruppe Müller (SS-Major Siegfried Müller)
RESULT	The American battalion was routed in heavy fighting.
CASUALTIES	
American:	Uncertain but the 3rd Battalion was essentially destroyed
German:	Unknown
LOCATION	Ruppenvenn is 3 km east of Krinkelt; Krinkelt is 23 km east of Malmédy

Battle

At 1230, fifty German grenadiers, which had forced Colonel Allen's 3rd Battalion to retreat, attacked the right flank of Lieutenant Walter Eisler's Company

---

27 Charles B MacDonald later became Deputy Chief Historian for the United States Army and wrote several of the Army's official histories of the war. He wrote of his personal experiences as a junior officer in *Company Commander*.

L near the junction of two forest trails. Shortly thereafter, Captain MacDonald's Company I was attacked from across the Jansbach. During the day, Kampfgruppe Müller made six frontal attacks against Company I — all repulsed with hand grenades, intense small-arms fire, and 60-mm mortar shells. Repeated calls for artillery support and ammunition re-supply brought assurances that the battalion was 'doing all it can.' At 1430, five Jagdpanzer IVs carrying over 100 infantrymen approached Company I while firing directly into the shallow slit trenches and foxholes. His situation now hopeless against enemy armor and with 75-mm shells crashing through the fir-tree forest, MacDonald pulled his men back 200 meters behind a north-south firebreak, where they re-established positions among a dense growth of fir branches.

German infantry struck Company L's flanks and front, forcing it back 200 meters. Lt Eisler then received a message ordering him to continue his withdrawal all the way into Krinkelt. Company K was now isolated with fusiliers attacking its front and jagdpanzers with infantry hitting its left flank. With no answer to enemy armor, 1st Platoon was overrun while the other two platoons engaged in close-quarter combat. With three jagdpanzers approaching his left flank along the Schwarzenbruch Trail, 1st Lieutenant Lee Smith ordered a fighting withdrawal. Upon leaving the forest near Lausdell Crossroads, his unit was subjected to a Nebelwerfer barrage.

Aftermath

Despite the heavy losses, the efforts of 3rd Battalion delayed the German advance allowing American troops to pour into Rocherath-Krinkelt and, in particular, Lausdell Crossroads. The engagement was a difficult one for the panzergrenadiers as well: SS-Lieutenant Colonel Richard Schulze-Kossen, commander of II Battalion, SS Panzergrenadier Regiment 25 recalled after the war, that, within the first hours of the engagement, all of the unit's company commanders, the battalion adjutant, and all technical officers either killed or wounded. His unit was forced to pause to re-organize.

Battlefield Tour

The track follows **Rollbahn B** where it approached Krinkelt from *Gemeindewald Krinkelter*. An unlocked gate bars auto entry to a gravel road but permits foot traffic. After 100 meters from the gate, the gravel road crosses a crushed stone highway that comprises part of the blue diamond hiking path ('*Holzwarchtal*') and yellow column hiking trail ('*Zu den Nazissenweisen*'). The later 12-kilometer trail continues to the Jansbach viewed later in the tour. At the intersection, foxholes remain on the left behind a bench. (50.427589, 6.319945) The 1st Battalion, 393rd Infantry Regiment and Company L, 23rd Infantry Regiment both fought in this sector and a small German group led by SS-1st Lieutenant Zeiner passed through this intersection. A view back toward Rocherath-Krinkelt from the forest exit shows the water tower on the right and the church steeple on the left — much as it must have appeared to German soldiers when they exited the forest.

Reverse direction and in 550 m return to the intersection with Lütscheborren. Bear sharply right (east) on the road for an additional 1.7 km to the open space at edge of the forest where a gate again bars vehicle entry to the forest. (50.437172, 6.334795)

The road passed through **Ruppenvenn** where it approached the forest edge. The 23rd Infantry Regiment troops assembled in this boggy fen to delay the German advance while 393rd Regiment troops withdrew from the forest. The forest lane through this intersection was **Rollbahn A** that then continued northwest to Lausdell Crossroads.

The Germans identified the field near the corner of the forest as '**Sherman Ecke**,' the name referring to two Sherman tanks of Company C, 741st Tank Battalion that attacked German armor when it exited the forest. Although the Shermans were successful in destroying the Jagdpanzers, the Shermans in turn were also destroyed. During the engagement the tank company's commander, 1st Lieutenant Victor Miller, was killed.[28] The destroyed armor lay abandoned for the remainder of the battle and during German occupation of the twin villages.

Some Company I survivors joined Company K to establish a defensive position along the tree-line near the Ruppenvenn junction. Private First Class Jose M Lopez of Brownsville, Texas fixed his .30-caliber machine gun to fire upon German infantry that gathered around the two knocked out Sherman tanks. Lopez continued firing all the while under panzer, artillery, and small-arms fire. Lopez fell back to another position to buy time for the men of Companies I and K to withdraw into Krinkelt. He had single-handedly prevented the men from being overrun.[29]

As with the east end of Rollbahn A, only authorized vehicles are allowed to enter the forest; however, one might walk 1.8 kilometers to Jansbach by following the paved track into the forest. The forest road proceeds gradually uphill until the first curve, then starts going downhill into the shallow valley of the Jansbach. Immediately beyond the creek crossing lies a small religious shrine on the right, almost lost amidst the shrubbery. (50.446922, 6.350462)

The foxhole positions of Captain MacDonald's Company I, 23rd Infantry Regiment lay near the curve in the track immediately west of Jansbach. The 1st Platoon commanded by 1st Lieutenant Long H Goffigon took up positions in a previously dug foxhole line that straddled the roadway and formed the exposed left flank of the company. Two antitank guns originally supported the positions, but during the early morning darkness of 17 December, the gunners withdrew, leaving Lt Goffigon with only antitank mines and a few bazookas and rockets to face German armor. Two of Lt Miller's Sherman tanks took up positions behind 1st Platoon, but when the fighting started, they also withdrew to the edge of the forest at Sherman Ecke. Goffigon's men held off German infantry with their light machine guns for three hours, but they had no answer to approaching jagdpanzers that fired directly into his platoon's foxholes. Only Goffignon and his platoon runner escaped when the position collapsed; the remainder of his 35-man platoon was killed or captured.[30]

---

28 Oklahoma native Lieutenant Victor Miller is buried in Henri-Chapelle American Cemetery, Henri-Chapelle, Belgium.

29 Private First Class Jose M Lopez was promoted to sergeant and received his country's Medal of Honor for his gallant stand against a substantially superior force. Lopez died in 2005 at age 94.

30 A native of Cheriton, Virginia, 1st Lieutenant Long Goffigon remained with 23rd Infantry Regiment and survived the war. He died in 1997 at age 76.

Chapter Two Battle for Elsenborn Ridge 55

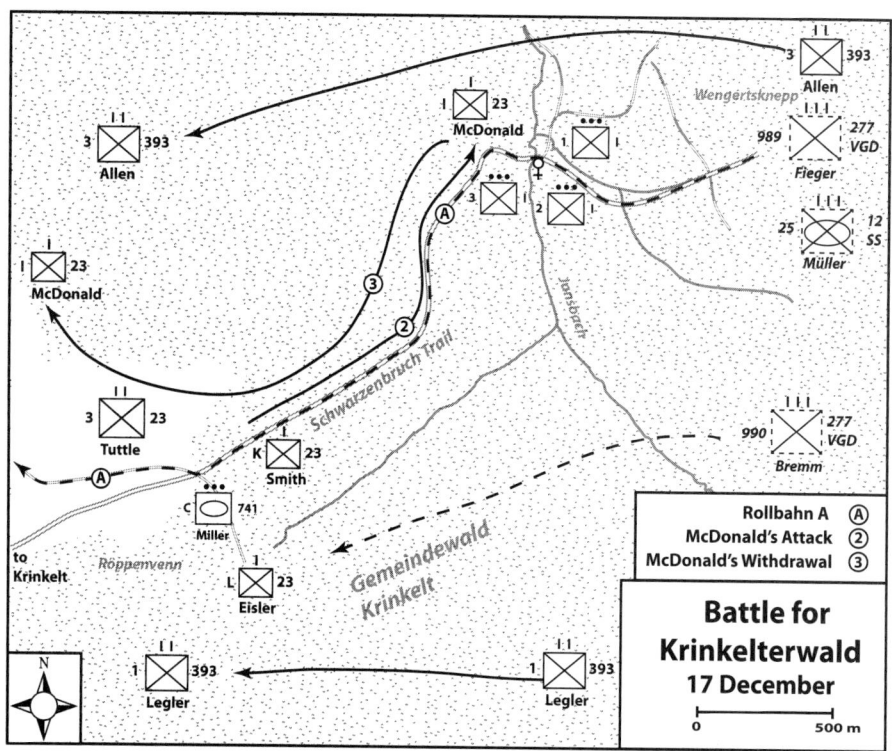

MacDonald attempted to reform his troops at a firebreak some meters behind their original position. Private First Class Richard Cowan of Wichita, Kansas positioned his light machine gun to fire into the low-hanging branches across the fire break. A German tank shell blew off the top of the small fir above Cowan's head, but he kept firing. Soon, Cowan was alone covering the retreat of the remaining men of Company I. With his ammunition exhausted and three enemy machine guns targeting his position, Cowan slung the gun over his shoulder and also beat a hasty retreat to Krinkelt.[31]

The **Jansbach Creek** crossing presents the intersection of multiple forestry trails. The logging road to the left enters a remote section of Camp Elsenborn, which, on occasion, is off limits to the public. The sign displays a paper schedule of closures and must be obeyed at all times. Near the Elsenborn sign the road forks with the level left fork continuing north along the Jansbach. The right fork meanders up the side of a hill to the positions of McDonald's 1st Platoon. Its positions, elevated 15- to-20 meters above the roadway, occupied a high ground above the approaches from Dreiherrenwald. Foxholes and battle positions still appear in this difficult terrain.

---

31 Private First Class Richard Cowan was credited with killing approximately one-hundred enemy troops during the engagement for which he was posthumously awarded the Medal of Honor. The 22-year old was killed the next day during the defense of Krinkelt.

Return to the Jansbach bridge and continue east along the asphalt road. The 1st Platoon defensive positions are visible on the left along a high-wooded ridge. The asphalt road runs along a swale formed by a tributary of the Jansbach and curves to the left going uphill.

Captain McDonald's 2nd Platoon occupied positions on the ridge directly to the south along a parallel ridge line. Obviously, McDonald was guarding against enemy infiltration along this shallow valley but lacked sufficient heavy weapons to stop German armor.

After 850 m, ascend to the crest of a hill where a sign identifies the beginning of the Stadt Wald Dreiherren. The muddy forest crossroads, on the broad, level ground around it known as **Wengertsknepp** (Hill), marks the approximate location of the 393rd Regiment Command Post. From there the road begins a gradual downhill slope to approach the Olef Creek 650 m ahead. Mature forest 30-to-40 meters deep line the roadway; farther away from the road the forest has been cleared within the past 20 years and densely replanted thereby blocking all entry. **Clusters of foxholes** scattered in the forest on the right adjoin the old growth timber, although the main command post was probably in the new growth section slightly to the southeast. (50.44703, 6.36122) Lumbering operations in the area require visitors to remain on the roadways and be aware of forestry vehicles.

On 17 December, Company L, 393rd Regiment squad leader Sergeant Vernon L McGarity, although wounded during the preliminary barrage the previous day, defended the battalion headquarters in these woods. McGarity maneuvered against enemy small-arms fire to ensure a better bazooka shot at an approaching Jagdpanzer. One shot was all it took. His squad's intense fire drove the panzergrenadiers from three remaining panzers that in turn withdrew avoiding the now-blocked trail by advancing along the area's array of tracks and firebreaks. McGarity continued his singular war by rescuing a wounded comrade and directing fire against an approaching 20-mm flak gun. The panzergrenadiers managed to position a machine gun to the rear of McGarity's squad, but he killed the team with rifle fire. Eventually, McGarity and his squad, by then surrounded, depleted their ammunition and were forced to surrender.[32]

> Reverse direction and return to the barred gate. By vehicle, proceed along the right fork. After 550 m at a junction of farm tracks, turn right and follow for 800 m. Stop at the intersection. The route is Rollbahn A, and the intersection is Lausdell Crossroads. (50.441067, 6.318875)

Battle for Lausdell Crossroads
17 to 18 December 1944

Twenty-eight-year-old Lieutenant Colonel William Dawes McKinley, grand-nephew of his namesake, the 25th President of the United States, commanded the 9th Regiment's 1st Battalion. A West Point graduate and career infantryman, he held no delusions regarding the perilous state of American defenses in the area. McKinley's

---

[32] Staff Sergeant Vernon L McGarity, from Bulloch County, Georgia was awarded a Medal of Honor after his release from a German PoW camp. He died in 2013 in Bartlett, Tennessee at age 91.

1st Battalion had already lost 304 men capturing the Wahlerscheid crossroads. By dusk on 17 December, McKinley took up positions and formed a broad arc along the ridge northeast of Krinkelt in front of Lausdell crossroads, a rural intersection amid pastures cut by hedgerows and farm tracks. The farmhouse and barn of dairy farmer Albert Palm stood nearby. The regiment's Company K, a section of machine guns from Company M, and a platoon of tank destroyers from Company C, 644th Tank Destroyer Battalion were also under McKinley's command. Shortly after nightfall the 600-man force heard the rattle of tank treads approaching from the east.

GERMAN OBJECTIVE	To open Rollbahn A to armored traffic.
FORCES	
American:	1st Battalion and Company K, 3rd Battalion, 9th Infantry Regiment with supporting units (Lieutenant Colonel William D McKinley)
German:	SS Panzergrenadier Regiment 25 (SS-Major Siegfried Müller)
RESULT	The crossroad was eventually captured after an intense battle.
CASUALTIES	
American:	31 killed, 206 wounded, and 146 taken prisoner
German:	Unknown casualties, 11 armored vehicles destroyed
LOCATION	Lausdell Crossroads is 1.3 km northwest of Ruppenvenn and 2.2 km northeast of Krinkelt

Battle

In the nighttime fog, mist, and blowing snow, twelve Jagdpanzer IVs of 1st Company, SS Panzerjäger Regiment 12 carrying 100 panzergrenadiers, crept down the Schwarzenbruch Trail toward Ruppenvenn to spearhead the assault upon Rocherath. The force became separated in the adverse weather at a trail junction. SS-1st Lt Helmut Zeiner led four Jagdpanzer IVs and one platoon of infantry through Ruppenvenn and on into Rocherath-Krinkelt, unaware that he had passed through American lines. The main force of eight Jagdpanzers and the remaining infantry approached McKinley's lines. The big vehicles surprised the men of Company B who anticipated stragglers from their own 393th Regiment, not German armor.

At 2230, the main body of Kampfgruppe Müller[33] (SS Panzergrenadier Regiment 25 and SS Panzerjäger Battalion 12) achieved the edge of the trees to the east in a column that stretched one kilometer along the road. The massed fire from divisional artillery battalions and three corps 155-mm howitzer battalions raked the column for roughly 10 minutes, causing heavy casualties to exposed German infantry retreating back into the forest.

At dawn on 18 December, twelve Panther tanks of I Battalion, SS Panzer Regiment 12 and a battalion of infantry approached Col McKinley's positions.

---

33 SS-Major Siegfried Müller was awarded the Knight's Cross of the Iron Cross for his efforts to capture Rocherath. Müller became an architect after the war under an assumed alias. He died in 1974 at age 59.

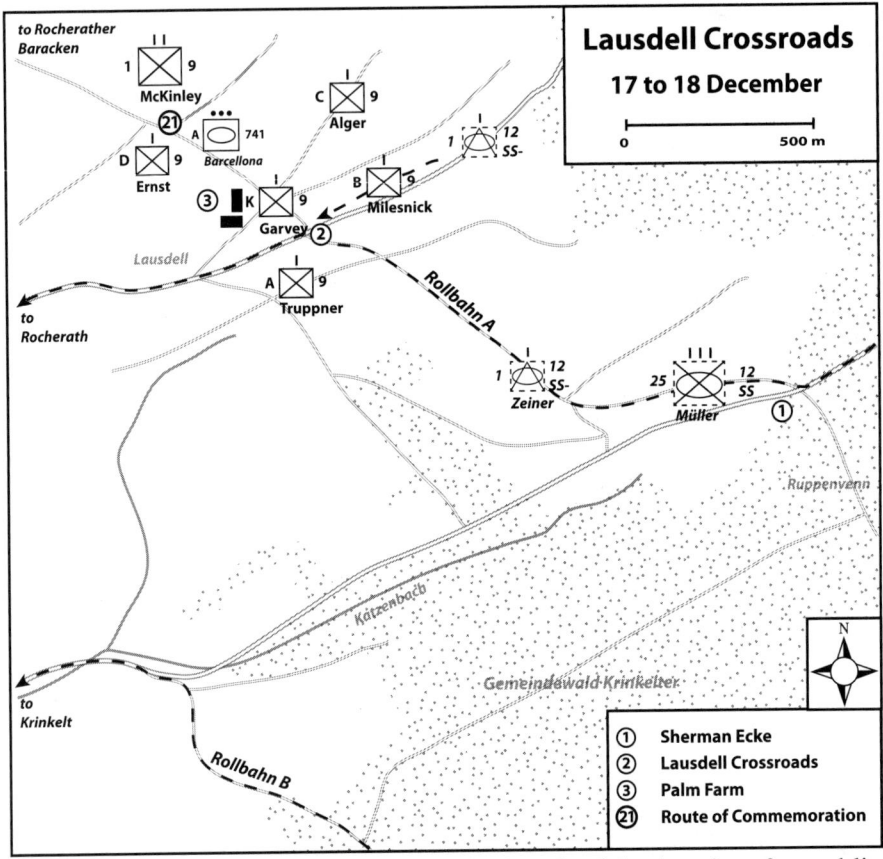

German tanks stopped within a couple hundred yards of the American forward line and fired their machine guns directly into Company A foxholes. Enemy tanks occupied Lausdell Crossroads while hand-to-hand fighting raged in the surrounding fields. By 0900, 1st Lieutenant Stephen Truppner's Company A was completely overrun. The situation was so hopeless that Truppner called American artillery fire onto his own positions. The assault was temporarily halted, but only twelve men from the company survived; the remainder were killed, wounded, or missing. Truppner himself was taken prisoner.[34]

By 1000, the 38th Infantry Regiment was firmly in place between Lausdell and Rocherath when McKinley received orders to withdraw, but his unit's close contact with the enemy precluded doing so. Four Sherman tanks from 2nd Platoon, Company A, 741st Tank Battalion, commanded by 1st Lieutenant Gaetano R Barcellona,[35] engaged

---

34   Lieutenant Stephen Truppner was held until 16 April 1945 at Oflag 73, the officers' section of Stalag XIIID in Nuremburg, Germany.

35   First Lieutenant Gaetano R Barcellona, from San Antonio, Texas had received the Distinguished Service Cross for his action on Omaha Beach in support of the 1st Infantry Division's landing on D-Day. He was wounded on 19 June 1944 in combat near St-Lô, evacuated to England, and returned to his unit in December. Barcellona was later captured and held in a PoW camp until April 1945. In

the Panthers and held the grenadiers at bay while the remnants of McKinley's battalion withdrew to the twin villages. Colonel McKinley was spotted near his command post grasping the hands of his soldiers while they passed, thanking them for their efforts to stop the enemy. Only 217 of his initial 600 men survived.[36]

Consequences

Lieutenant Colonel William McKinley and his infantrymen had delayed a strong enemy armored column from penetrating the American line for 18 hours. The defense of Lausdell Crossroads contributed to the successful withdrawal of both 2nd and 99th Infantry Divisions to the Elsenborn Ridge and the eventual defeat of the German Sixth Panzer Army.

Battlefield Tour

On 17 and 18 December the jagdpanzers of Lt Zeiner and the Panther tanks of Panzer Regiment 12 used the country lane from Ruppenvenn to the crossroads to attack American forces defending Lausdell.[37] Colonel McKinley's Company B held positions in the field to the north while Company A manned foxholes across the road directly ahead. In a blinding snow squall, Zeiner's small group became separated from the larger main body on 17 December and thus turned left to follow the road toward Rocherath. Although American troops in their foxholes detected his movements, they assumed that they were withdrawing American armored vehicles.

The Panther tanks of 1st and 3rd Companies approached late on 17 December (or before dawn on 18 December). The first Panther struck a mine that had been pulled across the roadway and blew a track. Its gunners continued to fire into McKinley's positions. Staff Sergeant Odis Bone of Company B and Sergeant Charles Roberts of Company D drained gasoline out of a wrecked American half-track, climbed atop the enemy tank, and – using the gasoline and a thermite grenade – ignited the tank.[38] American riflemen shot the German tankers when they fled the flaming vehicle.

The following Panther turned toward Rocherath, where Private First Class William Soderman of Company K manned a 3.2-inch bazooka near Palm's farmhouse. Although his loader had been wounded earlier, Private Soderman single-handedly fired at point-blank range to set it alight.

1946, he married his nurse in Birmingham, England and returned to San Antonio where the couple raised five children. Barcellona died in 1993 at age 77.

36   McKinley's unit's incredible defense of the critical crossroads earned it the Presidential Unit Citation; McKinley and eleven others received Silver Stars. Lieutenant Colonel McKinley died in 1957 at age 41.

37   American and German descriptions of the engagement do not agree on the timing of the arrival of the different armored vehicles. German reports indicate that the first Panther tanks did not arrive until the morning of 18 December. American troops frequently mistook one German armored vehicle for another.

38   Although Sergeant Charles Roberts was awarded a Silver Star, Sergeant Odis Bone never received the award promised to him. Sergeant Bone was wounded later in the Battle of the Bulge, but he survived the war and returned to San Antonio, where his family eventually included three grandchildren and numerous great-grandchildren. He died in 2011 at age 89.

Panzerjägers approached Company B. Two were immobilized by a daisy chain of mines dragged across the roadway. Two Panzerjägers left the roadway to bypass the burning hulks. While their treads churned the muddy pastures, bazooka teams hunted them down, eventually putting two more out of action. The remainder of the armored vehicles spread out across the fields. Assaulted by German armor from three directions, 1st Lieutenant John C Granville directed the fire of seven American artillery battalions onto the advancing enemy troops to arrest their progress. Combat quieted down after midnight while German armor withdrew back into the forest.

Before dawn on 18 December, American artillery again repelled an attack by two companies of Panther tanks supported by II Battalion, SS Panzergrenadier Regiment 25. After the eastern sky brightened, German troops renewed the assault. After spending the night under intense enemy mortar and machine-gun fire, Private Soderman leapt onto the roadway to disable another approaching Panther. Later he followed orders to withdraw but returned to engage a third enemy tank to allow elements of his company to escape. Although he disabled the tank with his last rocket, the tank's machine gun's bullets ripped into his right shoulder when he ran for cover. Soderman was successfully evacuated.[39]

The slightly elevated terrain of **Lausdell** offers views to the German approaches from the east and southeast and emphasizes the location's importance not only as a transportation route but also as an observation point.

The farm buildings to the northwest of the intersection comprised **Palm Farm**. Artillery and panzer fire paid special attention to the Palm farm buildings where a few survivors of Company I, 23rd Regiment, including Captain MacDonald, sheltered. The barn was set ablaze while its inhabitants sought refuge alongside a wall of the stone farmhouse.

The cellar of the sturdy stone farmhouse had served as command post for Company K. During the decisive German assault of 18 December, a tank approached the house, stopping with its cannon only meters away from the front door. To avoid complete destruction, Company K commander Captain Jack J Garvey surrendered his command.[40] (50.441227, 6.316876)

> Continue northwest from the crossroads. Colonel McKinley's command post lay in an abandoned artillery dugout in the field on the left immediately before the junction with the side road 450 m ahead. (50.443445, 6.313529) Continue 350 m to the sign on the left. (50.445211, 6.309408)

During McKinley's withdrawal, Company D machine gunner Technical Sergeant James L Bayliss carried a .30-caliber machine gun to an advantageous

---

39   Private First Class William A Soderman from Connecticut was awarded a Medal of Honor for his extreme heroism during the defense of Lausdell Crossroads. He died in 1980 at age 68.

40   Captain Jack Garvey, from Chicago, Illinois, was taken prisoner and held at the officer's section of Stalag XIIID in Nuremburg, Germany.

position and fired upon the advancing grenadiers. A Panther fired twice at Sgt Bayliss, missing its target both times. The third tank shell did not miss, and Bayliss was killed.[41]

The **Route of Commemoration Information Panel #21** stands beside the fences to the left. This panel describes the residual dangers presented to local civilians by mines placed in this sector after the arrival of American forces on 12 September 1944. The panel offers a brief description of the nine incidents that as a result killed thirteen individuals. The first three died on 20 September, and the final fatality occurred on 22 February 1954, despite extensive post-war mine clearing operations.

> Continue 350 m to the next intersection (N658). Turn right and, after 300 m, bear right where a sign indicates 'Erinnerungsstätte Hasselpat.' The intersection bears a large illuminated sign indicating closure dates of the highway into Camp Elsenborn. Continue for 1.3 km to the parking area on the right. (50.45869, 6.31095)

On 13 December, the 395th Regimental Combat Team (RCT) attacked through this forest to seize two remote hills that held Westwall defenses. This subsidiary flanking attack was part of the 2nd Infantry Division assault upon Wahlerscheid crossroads (see above). The attack lasted three days with casualties on both hills significant. Subsequently the two hills were dubbed '88 Hill,' named for the intense artillery fire from the dreaded German 88-mm cannon, and 'Purple Heart Hill.' **Route of Commemoration information panel #24** now stands upon 88 Hill and identifies the location where researchers discovered the hastily buried bodies of three members of the 395th Infantry Regiment in April 2001. All three were killed during the Wahlerscheid attack by enemy cannon or mortar fire.[42] The site is difficult to access and is a 6.6 kilometer hike from Hellenthal, Germany along forest roads. (50.481311, 6.351090)

By 18 December, the 395th RCT sat astride the Hasselpat Trail providing cover for the withdrawing 324th Engineer Combat Battalion and protecting the northern flank of the 2nd Division. At 1730 on 19 December, the RCT retired cross country to Elsenborn. The area was then occupied by I Battalion, Grenadier Regiment 989, that unsuccessfully attacked Elsenborn Ridge. The area was recaptured by American troops on 2 February 1945.

An infosign at the parking area identifies the **Hasselpat Woods** as a protected battleground '…as a place of remembrance and meditation; a symbol of peace and reconciliation beyond any frontier, any dugout, and any grave.' These woods had

---

41 T/Sergeant James L Bayliss was awarded a Distinguished Service Cross posthumously. He is buried in Baytown, Texas.

42 On 15 December, PFC David Read from Akron, Ohio was returning, on orders, to his company to obtain rations for his forward observation unit. On the way back, he was killed by a German mortar shell. Two days later, when the 39th Infantry was ordered to withdraw, Read along with Private First Class Saul Kokotovich from Gary, Indiana and Private First Class Jack C Beckwith from LaMoure, North Dakota were buried in shallow graves and abandoned. Their remains were eventually recovered by a team of American and Belgian volunteers on 1 March 2001. PFC David Read is buried in Arlington National Cemetery, Arlington, Virginia. He was 21 years old. Privates Kokotovich and Beckwith are reburied in Henri-Chapelle American Cemetery, Henri-Chapelle, Belgium.

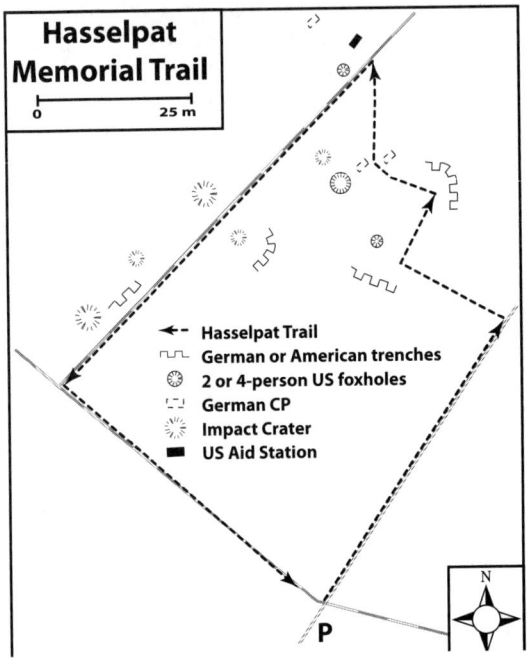

been occupied at times by American and German troops. Separate informational signs in four languages present the poignant stories of two soldiers who engaged in combat here: Unterfeldwebel Hans Hermann Paulsen, 2nd Company, Panzerjäger Battalion 277, 277th Volksgrenadier Division, the commander of a Hetzer assault gun, and PFC David A Read, Cannon Company, 395th Infantry Regiment, 99th Infantry Division, a forward radio observer. A metal grave marker carries photographs of the two soldiers.[43]

The road into the forest is closed to traffic, but the battlefield remnants are only 130 meters ahead in the woods on the left identified by a small white sign and and accessed via a board laid over the roadside ditch. **Trenches**, **foxholes**, **shell craters**, and an **aide station** remain in the forest. Information signs in Dutch, English, French, and German mark each site and explain its construction and use. The log-covered aide station, site of the casualties of the 13 December attack, has been reconstructed. The dead were buried in the surrounding forest. Because of the lack of undergrowth beneath the forest canopy and its proximity to roadways, this site is the easiest to access of any battlefield location in the Bulge battleground.

Reverse direction and return to highway N658. Turn left (south) and proceed 300 m to pass through Rocherather Baracken Crossroads. (50.445702, 6.304810) Continue south 1.0 km from Rocherather Baracken crossroads and then turn left. Proceed 350 m to the intersection of Wasserturmstraße — the water tower street — and Am Kornhof. Turn right and park. (50.439033, 6.304729)

Battle of Rocherath-Krinkelt
17 to 19 December 1944

The twin villages of Rocherath and Krinkelt straddled the only north-south highway west of the front lines. Supplies to troops facing the International Highway

---

43 On 15 January 1945, an enemy shell ended Hans Hermann Paulsen's life in section 536 of the Hasselpat Forest. Only recently married in September 1944, he never saw his unborn child. In a letter to his wife his company commander wrote, '…as a man, he had no enemies.' In 1947 his remains were brought back to his home town and reburied in Duisburg-Ruhort Cemetery. He was 24 years old.

Chapter Two   Battle for Elsenborn Ridge

and in support of the 2nd Infantry Division's attack upon Wahlerscheid had to pass through these two small farming communities. Most civilians were evacuated on 8 October, leaving only a small number to tend livestock. After the German assault of 16 December and the decision to withdraw the 2nd Infantry Division, holding Rocherath-Krinkelt became imperative because highway N658 was the only route by which the 2nd and 99th Divisions could retire to Elsenborn Ridge.

At 0800 on 17 December, the 3rd Battalion of Colonel Francis Boos's 38th Infantry Regiment left the Wahlerscheid area, passed through Baracken crossroad, and established positions south and east of Rocherath-Krinkelt despite interdictory German artillery fire. They joined elements of the 9th Regiment and several platoons of the 23rd Regiment. All available tanks and tank destroyers were assigned to the 3rd Battalion to block the roads approaching the village from the east.

At 1530, Lieutenant Colonel Frank Mildren led his 1st Battalion, 38th Infantry Regiment south from Wahlerscheid along the same route to link his men on the left flank of the 3rd Battalion along the east and northeast edges of the twin villages. Colonel Mildren's men occupied positions along the main highway from roughly the water tower in Rocherath south to the church in Krinkelt. Colonel Mildred established his CP in an abattoir across the road and south of the church while his men occupied houses or dug foxholes despite the foot-deep snow.

Later, Lieutenant Colonel Jack K Norris's 2nd Battalion, 38th Infantry Regiment ran the same gauntlet of enemy fire north of Baracken crossroads. Norris's Company F took up positions around the crossroads with Company E extending south of the crossroads and Company A, 741st Tank Battalion to its rear. Company G continued south to eventually establish a roadblock immediately north of the Krinkelt church.

German Objective		To open Rollbahn A and B to armored traffic.
Forces		
	American:	38th Infantry Regiment (Colonel Francis Boos)
	German:	277th Volksgrenadier Division (Oberst Wilhelm Viebig) and 12th SS Panzer Division *Hitlerjugend* (SS-Colonel Hugo Kraas)
Result		Rollbahn A and B were denied to German forces.
Casualties		
	American:	Uncertain
	German:	Unknown casualties; 67 tanks or tank destroyers lost
Location		Rocherath is 23 km east of Malmédy

Battle

During the confused fighting around Lausdell on the night of 17 December, SS-1st Lieutenant Zeiner led three Jagdpanzer IVs and a platoon of forty panzergrenadiers through Lausdell Crossroad and approached Rocherath from the east. An American fragmentation grenade scattered the German infantry, but a single shell from a

Jagdpanzer put a nearby antitank gun out of action. Having captured several prisoners, the German column turned toward the municipal water tower.

Stopping near the church, Zeiner's vehicles engaged and destroyed three Sherman tanks; however, American artillery, mortar, and small-arms fire, combined with a growing shortage of fuel and ammunition, drove the German force out of the village. Zeiner took up an 'all-around' defense 300 meters to the east. The fighting eventually subsided while both sides took stock and attempted to rest. The battle, however, had really just begun.

At 0800 on 18 December, eleven Panthers and PzKpfw IVs of SS-Major Arnold Jurgensen's I Battalion, SS Panzer Regiment 12, with a company of panzergrenadiers riding on their decks, drove through Company E, 38th Regiment, only to meet American Sherman tanks and tank destroyers. A large scale armored battle developed along the village streets with German Panthers, American Shermans, and tank destroyers of both sides firing at close range. The Sherman's firepower was no match for the heavily armored Panthers, but the experienced American tankers were skilled in establishing ambushes among the stone houses. The villages became an armor deathtrap as neither side gave quarter. Eventually, German troops withdrew by evening.

The assault renewed on 19 December, but the German commanders had changed their strategy and rerouted armored movements to Rollbahn C. The 3rd Panzergrenadier Division was assigned the task of clearing the villages supported by forty-one Sturmgeschütz of Panzerjäger Battalion 103. Because the 2nd Infantry Division had accomplished its withdrawal from its salient around Wahlerscheid Crossroads, the Americans decided that the twin villages had served their purpose. Troops withdrew that evening, thus allowing German forces to occupy both villages.

Aftermath

The last of 2nd Division troops left Wirtzfeld at 0200 on 20 December under enemy artillery fire to join units in forming a new defensive line upon the ridge. During the following days, 3rd Panzergrenadier Division launched several attacks against Elsenborn with negligible success.

On 29 January 1945, the 2nd Infantry Division left its positions on Elsenborn Ridge and, moving through two feet of snow, liberated Rocherath-Krinkelt the next day. The 99th Infantry Division attacked German positions in the forest to the north where they suffered more casualties for little gain. After three days they retired to Camp Elsenborn.

Consequences

American troops stubbornly defended their positions despite overwhelming German armored forces. Transportation routes critical to German success stalled against repeated armor attacks. The heroic stand of the 99th and 2nd Infantry Divisions allowed time for the critical military positions on the nearby Elsenborn Ridge to be extensively re-enforced. Rollbahns A and B were not open to German armor and never would be while American artillery on the ridge interdicted both roadways.

Chapter Two

Battle for Elsenborn Ridge   65

Major General Walter Robertson, given complete discretion in the mission to defend the Elsenborn Ridge, acquitted himself as an outstanding combat leader. During seven days of almost constant combat, Robertson's 2nd Division penetrated the Westwall at Wahlerscheid, executed a daylight withdrawal while in contact with the enemy, engaged a powerful enemy attack from a different direction, and held for two days before again withdrawing under fire.[44]

Battlefield Tour

The intersection marks the entry point of **Rollbahn A** into Rocherath. Three 57-mm antitank guns of the 3rd Platoon, of the 38th Infantry Regiment's Antitank Company, commanded by Captain James Love of Butte, Montana established positions around this intersection on 17 December. The regimental Service Company provided infantry protection for the roadblock. From this position, defenders overlooked terrain that dropped to the east providing excellent day-time observation of approaching enemy. In nighttime darkness and fog, Lt Zeiner approached from the east along Zum Sassevenn, easily pushed the defenders aside, and proceeded south toward the water tower. Unfortunately, current buildings and shrubbery now hide the views from the intersection.

Proceed right (south) 280 m to the water tower on the right. (50.436778, 6.303345)

When American troops entered the twin villages, the water tower immediately became an observation post to direct artillery fire against the German border area.

On 16 December, squad from 3rd Platoon, Company C occupied ditches on the eastern fringes of Krinkelt as listening posts near a 57-mm antitank gun. Only a short time elapsed before the creaks of tank treads crept nearer. One man threw a handgrenade. Zeiner's troops responded with an illumination flare. An armored round knocked out the antitank gun, and the squad withdrew back to the houses around the water tower. While advancing German infantry milled about the houses, a squad member dropped a grenade from an upper-floor window. A jagdpanzer fired point blank into the house forcing the surrender of seven Americans. After a brief questioning, all seven were shot, but one survived his injuries to relate the story.[45] German artillery observers eventually occupied the water tower, but ammunition shortages hampered German artillery fire.

The water tower parking area holds **Route of Commemoration information panel #20**. The sign presents striking photos of the armor-strewn streets of the twin villages, providing witness to the intensity of the armored conflict. The water tower allows observation of the whole area from the heights of Elsenborn to the west, across the twin villages and the eastern forests to the former Westwall.

---

44 Major General Robert Melville Robertson was awarded a Distinguished Service Cross for gallant leadership while repeatedly exposing himself to enemy fire. General Robertson, of Nelson County, Virginia died in 1954 and is buried in Arlington National Cemetery, Arlington, Virginia. He was 66 years old.

45 Private First Class John T Fisher was the lone survivor.

66 The Bulge Battlefields

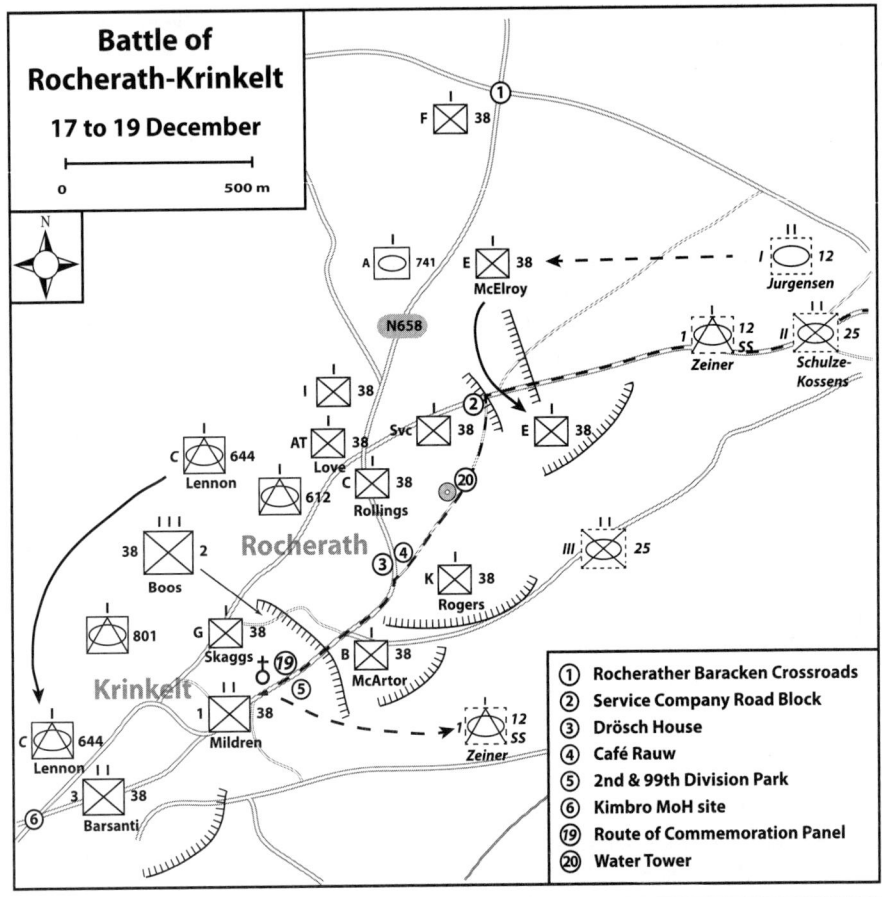

Continue to the road junction 270 m farther south. (50.434730, 6.301397)

Zeiner's force continued past the water tower toward the junction with highway N658 where Colonel Mildren's Company B engaged in digging slit trenches. Amid a concentration of German small-arms, mortar, and artillery fire, Company B fell back amid heavy casualties, including its company commander.[46]

This junction and the houses to the north on highway N658 became one of the most fiercely contested sectors of the Rocherath battlefield. Mildren's Company C occupied houses on both sides of the main street just north of the junction with Wasserturmstraße. Company C's 2nd Platoon, commanded by 1st Lieutenant George Adams, joined to Captain Love's command and stationed in the two houses overlooking the intersection — the **Rauw House**[47] to the east and the **Drösch House** to the west. Captain Love established his CP in a building 180 meters north of the intersection.

---

46 Captain William Stein McArtor was taken prisoner and held at Stalag XIII-D, Oflag 73 in Nuremburg, Germany. He was liberated on 16 April, 1945.

47 Address #61 (in 1944), known as Café Rauw, is now Hotel Restaurant Traiteur.

Adams and Love led their men in a confused two-day battle against German grenadiers and armor. Panthers and Jagdpanzer IVs drove past the water tower firing upon the defenders' positions while German infantry fought for control of the houses. At one point, Adams occupied the Drosch House while Germans held the Rauw House with both sides firing small-arms, rifle grenades, and hand-held rockets at the windows and doorways while civilians and prisoners sheltered in the cellars. The Americans ignored German surrender demands while the encounter, frequently hand-to-hand, raged through the night among the barns, streets, and houses of Rocherath.

On 18 December, Captain Love eyed eight German panzers racing past the water tower toward the road junction. Love led a Sherman tank into position to fire at the lead Panther's flank, and two perfect shots put it out of action. Soon another Panther approached. One of Love's men, Private Isabel Salazar, a cook's helper from Houston, Texas, grabbed a bazooka and ran up the stairs of the house[48] being used as a command post. From the upper window he destroyed the Panther with one shot.

The large scale tank battle drove Adams' small force to abandon the Drösch House, and move north. That afternoon they reoccupied the building and came under fire of a Jagdpanzer IV on the water tower road. Private Salazar repeated his earlier feat by knocking it out with a single bazooka round.

On 19 December, a panzerfaust rocket struck the attic and caved in the entire roof. Adams and his men continued to defend the house while German tanks fired against its stout stone walls interlaced with American machine-gun fire against nearby enemy infantry. Finally, tracer rounds ignited a thatched roof shed and, while the fire spread to the main building, the Drösch House was abandoned for the last time. Adams and his men withdrew to Wirtzfeld, soon to be followed by Love's Antitank Company. By 1830, the twin villages belonged to the Germans.[49]

> Continue 400 m south and stop at the large parking area on the right before the Krinkelt church. Walk to the information panel ahead. (50.43229, 6.29699)

Driven from a hastily prepared roadblock north of the church by Zeiner's force, Company B Weapons Platoon led by Sergeant Carl G Patterson sought shelter within the meter-thick walls of the **St John the Baptist Church**, by then an aide station, command post, and makeshift fortress. Sergeant Patterson directed an American tank-destroyer fire against Zeiner's vehicles before it was destroyed by a direct hit from a jagdpanzer. Three approaching Shermans from 741st Tank Battalion[50] were also destroyed, littering the church grounds with hulks that burned through the night. With their fire unable to penetrate the church walls, Zeiner's jagdpanzers briefly

---

48 Address #63 was known as the Radermacher House.

49 First Lieutenant George S Adams survived the battle but not the war. He died of wounds on 10 June 1945 and is buried in Lorraine American Cemetery, St-Avold, France.

50 The 741st Tank Battalion, commanded by Lieutenant Colonel Robert N Skaggs, accounted for twenty-seven German tanks, one SP assault gun, two armored cars, and two half-tracks. The unit received a Presidential Unit Citation for its actions in defending Rocherath and Krinkelt. Colonel Skaggs had led the unit since landing onto Omaha Beach when it was attached to the 1st Infantry Division on D-Day. His heroic leadership on that occasion earned him a Distinguished Service Cross.

turned their attention to Colonel Mildren's command post; however, probably fearing bazooka attack in their now-illuminated and exposed location, the jagdpanzers then withdrew.

Shortly after daybreak on 18 December, the 741st Tank Battalion and tank destroyers from Captain Harlow Lennon's Company C, 644th Tank Destroyer Battalion, sheltered in ambush among the villages' buildings. Near Colonel Boos's regimental CP, Captain Lennon's men knocked out the first three panzers while Colonel Boos's men fired every weapon at their disposal, killing or wounding most of the enemy infantry. First Lieutenant Robert A Parker of the tank destroyer's Reconnaissance Company singled-handedly destroyed or immobilized two Panthers with bazooka rockets.[51]

The roadway from the water tower to the church formed the main battlefield in the twin villages. **Route of Commemoration information panel #19**, unfortunately only in German, French, and Dutch, identifies the house across the street to be #14 Wahlerscheidstraße, with a striking 1944 photo of a destroyed German tank resting in front of the structure.[52] The photograph graphically displays the extent of the carnage inflicted upon the village. The Panther (PzKpfw V) shown in the image is from 3rd Company, SS Panzer Regiment 12. The **Faymonville House**, sited at the western end of the open ground to the north, had been Colonel Boos's regimental CP.

Walk along the street to the park across from the church. (50.431793, 6.296313)

Five Panthers from the force of eleven that passed the water tower on 18 December drove the length of the village to the church. Thus engaged, they failed to notice Shermans stationed to the east. The first two Panthers had been knocked out before two others continued southwest past the command post. One was eliminated by a Sherman that maneuvered around the church, another by a bazooka round. The final Panther escaped to the southwest where it was finally stopped on the road to Büllingen by three rounds from a tank destroyer.

Memorials to the 2nd and 99th Infantry Divisions now stand across the street from the rebuilt church to commemorate the fighting that completely destroyed the farming community. The fronts of both memorials carry dedications to those who died for freedom. The rear of the 99th Division's stone carries the traditional listing of units, battles, and decorations, including two Presidential Citations. The 2nd Division memorial is more poetic stating:

> May God help you to understand what the fighting here and in the area was like, for there was such a distance between those who suffered and those who observed suffering from afar.

Continue southwest 80 m to the butcher's shop along N658. (50.431457, 6.295357)

The headquarters of Lieutenant Colonel Frank Mildren's **1st Battalion, 38th Infantry Regiment** occupied an abattoir (slaughterhouse) on this site during the defense of Krinkelt. Late on 17 December, three German tanks accompanied by

---

51 First Lieutenant Robert A Parker was awarded a Distinguished Service Cross for his actions.

52 Address #14 Wahlerscheid Straße was known as the Kalpers House

panzergrenadiers riding on their decks approached the Krinkelt church from the east along Langergasse (the street between the HQ and the memorial park). Hearing the distinctive clank of approaching tanks, Mildren and his men rushed to the windows of this building and fired upon the panzergrenadiers. Private Grover C Farrell grabbed an unmounted machine gun and with the gun balanced upon his hip, marched along the road directly toward the tanks and fired at German troops riding on the tanks. Remarkably, the tanks pulled back behind the corner house, perhaps for the protection of the exposed infantry.

The next day, another German tank drove toward the battalion headquarters. Lieutenant Jesse Morrow, the battalion communications officer, fired a bazooka into its rear. The mortally-wounded tank brushed along a house and careened into a ditch, but the crew and its cannon were still operational. Morrow loaded a second rocket to finish off the tank, but the tank fired first. The shell missed Morrow, but he was knocked unconscious by the blast. Morrow was saved by an unidentified soldier who threw a thermite grenade into the tank's turret.[53]

> The next three sites interest those wishing to discover the history of a typical Belgian farming community. Proceed to the tourist office directly across from the church entrance to view the panel on its north exterior wall. (50.431858, 6.295636) Otherwise, return to your vehicle and continue south.
> **Route of Commemoration information panel #17** (Dutch, French, and German only) describes the pre-war parish church, its temporary replacement constructed immediately after the liberation, and the current third parish church completed in 1953.
> Walk past the front of the church to the T-junction.
> On the right the village cemetery displays an **octagonal memorial** to local citizens who died fighting in the Franco-Prussian War of 1870, when the area was part of Germany, and the two world wars. The interior of the gray-stone, peaked-roof building displays two plaques flanking the polished granite altar that list the names and death dates of military and civilian victims of all three wars. Of note, five members of the Hönen family died on 24 December 1944.(50.432101, 6.293333) Proceed 70 m southwest to the triangular park. (50.432115, 6.293329)
> **Route of Commemoration information panel #16** (Dutch, French, and German only) describes some of the older Krinkelt buildings that remain about this intersection.

> Leave information panel #19 south following highway N658. After 750 m observe the road on the right signed to Elsenborn / Wirtzfeld. (50.429601, 6.289383)

The rural road to the right goes to Wirtzfeld and on to Elsenborn Ridge. With German troops occupying Büllingen, it remained the only escape route for the

---

53 Lieutenant Jesse Morrow was awarded a Distinguished Service Cross. Earlier in the battle, Morrow and his sergeant, Hunziger, had been laying telephone wire when the sergeant was hit by German machine gun fire. Morrow dragged Hunziger into a barn and left to seek medical help. A German soldier entered the barn and fired his burp gun. Morrow rushed back to find Hunziger dead.

withdrawing 2nd and 99th Divisions. The narrow roadway was a bottleneck, one that combat engineers feverishly improved while fighting roared in Rocherath-Krinkelt.

On the night of 19 December, a rearguard of 2nd Engineer Combat Battalion, 741st Tank Battalion, and Company C, 644th Tank Destroyer Battalion laid mines and beat off advancing German troops. Near this intersection, Technician Fourth Grade Truman Kimbro, an engineer squad leader from Company C, crept forward with his squad to lay mines across the roadway. Kimbro found the intersection occupied by a German tank and approximately twenty enemy soldiers. After two futile attempts by his squad to reach the targeted intersection, Kimbro positioned his men in a protected area and, carrying the mines, moved forward alone. Despite being badly wounded by enemy fire, he continued forward and placed the mines. While returning to his men, Kimbro was killed by a burst of enemy machine-gun fire.[54]

> Continue south and follow highway N658 for 4.1 km to the center of Büllingen; bear left toward St Vith (N692) but not toward Bütgenbach because the Domaine Bütgenbach is not in the town of that name. Continue 2.1 km to a roundabout that now replaces the Morsheck Crossroads. Take the first exit toward Eupen / Bütgenbach (N658) and continue 1.0 km. Park in the entrance driveway to the plowed field on the left. (50.404569, 6.229656)

Defense of Dom Bütgenbach
18 to 22 December 1944

The veteran US 1st Infantry Division arrived at Camp Elsenborn on the morning on 17 December. Major General Clift Andrus had assumed command only one week earlier.[55] The unit was transported from rest areas after suffering a significant level of casualties in Hürtgen Forest fighting. The 26th Regiment was particularly hard hit during that engagement with its Companies E and F overrun and practically annihilated. Fully 60% of the 26th Regiment's men had been replacements whose companies mostly remained under-strength.

Later that day, the 26th Regiment sent its 2nd Battalion, led by the unlikely commander Lieutenant Colonel Derrill Daniel, a 39-year-old PhD entomologist, to dig in on two hills near a cluster of farm buildings known as Dom Bütgenbach. To impress upon the troops the importance of holding the position, Colonel Daniel adopted the motto, 'We fight and die here.' The position overlooked Belgian National Route 32

---

54   T/4 Truman Carol Kimbro of Madison Country, Texas was posthumously awarded the Medal of Honor for delaying the advance of enemy armor and preventing the withdrawing American columns from being attacked by the enemy. Kimbro is buried in Henri-Chapelle American Cemetery, Henri-Chapelle, Belgium. He was 25 years old. In 1947, the US Army transport ship Sgt Truman Kimbro was named in his honor. The vessel remained in service until 1973.

US Army historian Dr Hugh M Cole, in his account of the battle '*The Ardennes: The Battle of the Bulge*,' puts this action two days earlier near the Rocherath Baracken crossroads. His highly regarded and otherwise accurate account disagrees with the award citation.

55   An artillery expert, General Andrus focused time-on-target fire of 400 guns from 35 battalions from their positions on the ridge. The effect upon advancing and exposed German troops was devastating.

Chapter Two

(now, N632) that German planners had designated as Rollbahn C. Company C, 634th Tank Destroyer Battalion, platoons from the regiment's Antitank Company, and the 745th Tank Battalion were attached. Logs or planks covered most foxholes, the stout walls of the stone farmhouse offered protection to the battalion CP and aid station, and mines blocked the two roads approaching the manor. Forward patrols viewed masses of German vehicles from Kampfgruppe Peiper moving from Büllingen through the towards Amel.

GERMAN OBJECTIVE	To open Rollbahn C to armored traffic.
FORCES	
American:	2nd Battalion (Lieutenant Colonel Derrill Daniel), 26th Infantry Regiment, 1st Infantry Division
German:	SS Panzergrenadier Regiment 26 (SS-Lieutenant Colonel Bernard Krause), 12th SS Panzer Division *'Hitlerjugend'*
RESULT	The road junction was not captured and remained closed to German traffic for the remainder of the battle.
CASUALTIES	
American:	26th Regiment: 500 killed, wounded, or missing
German:	800 dead and 400 wounded or missing; 47 armored vehicles destroyed
LOCATION	Domaine Bütgenbach is 17 km east of Malmédy

Battle

At noon the next day, a scouting party of lightly armored SdKfz 251 halftracks from SS Reconnaissance Battalion 12 led a reconnaissance from Morsheck toward Bütgenbach. Three vehicles were knocked out by the 612th Tank Destroyer Battalion halfway between the two crossroads.[56]

During the night of 18/19 December, the 12th SS Panzer Division withdrew from Krinkelt via Losheimergraben to access Rollbahn C. At 0215, twenty halftracks of panzergrenadiers and twelve panzerjägers of Kampfgruppe Kühlmann[57], commanded by SS-Major Herbert Kühlmann, moved against Company F from the east and southeast across open ground from the Büllingen–Morsheck road (N692) in the second assault against Dom Bütgenbach. White phosphorus shells illuminated the battlefield and high explosive shells from American 155-mm guns dissipated the attack. Daybreak revealed 100 enemy dead among the wreckage of three tank destroyers and four trucks.

Later that morning, unsuccessful probing attacks from Morsheck and Büllingen by III Battalion, SS Panzergrenadier Regiment 26 against Companies F and

---

56   SdKfz 251 or Sonderkraftfahrzeug 251: an armored fighting vehicle designed to transport panzergrenadiers into combat. The open top mounted a MG-34 or MG-42 machine gun. Germany produced twenty-two variants, including several special-purpose models, during the war.

57   Kampfgruppe Kühlmann consisted of 1st Battalion, SS Panzer Regiment 12; SS Panzergrenadier Regiment 12; Heavy Panzerjäger Battalion 560; and 2nd Battalion, SS Panzer Artillery Regiment 12.

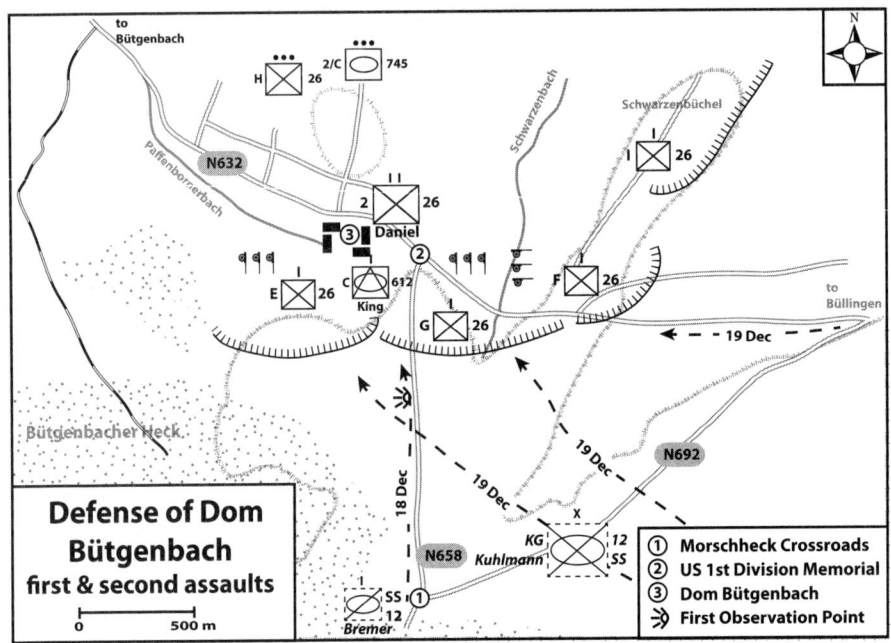

G followed an hour-long artillery bombardment. Those advances were, in time, beaten off by 57-mm antitank and 81-mm mortar fire.

In the early morning fog on 20 December, twenty jagdpanzers and two infantry battalions from Kampfgruppe Kühlmann led the fourth assault as they moved along both sides of the road, In der Reisbach, from Büllingen. Before reaching the American lines, the Kampfgruppe hit an American minefield and split into three columns. One moved north against a platoon from Company I on a ridge known as Schwarzenbüchel and captured most of the hill in a day-long battle. Further advance north was inadvisable due to the swampy nature of the terrain and Stausee Bütgenbach water barrier.

The main group continued west where it stalled in front of Company F's lines, unable to break through to the road junction at Dom Bütgenbach. The left-most column headed off the main road to attack cross-country and struck the boundary between Companies F and G. In the fog and smoke, American antitank guns withheld fire until the enemy armor advanced within 75 meters of the main line of resistance. Although three Jagdpanzers penetrated, German infantry became engaged in fierce combat. Jagdpanzers continued to the domaine area where, without their infantry protection, they attempted to withdraw. Two were hit by antitank guns while they passed back through the American line.

SS-Colonel Hugo Kraas re-organized and launched a second attack at 0545, striking from Büllingen and Morsheck with a battalion of grenadiers and twenty tanks of SS Panzer Regiment 12. American M10 Tank Destroyers destroyed ten tanks pressing along In der Reisbach while artillery and small-arms fire stopped the panzergrenadiers. The other ten tanks launched a savage attack against the rightmost

Chapter Two   Battle for Elsenborn Ridge   73

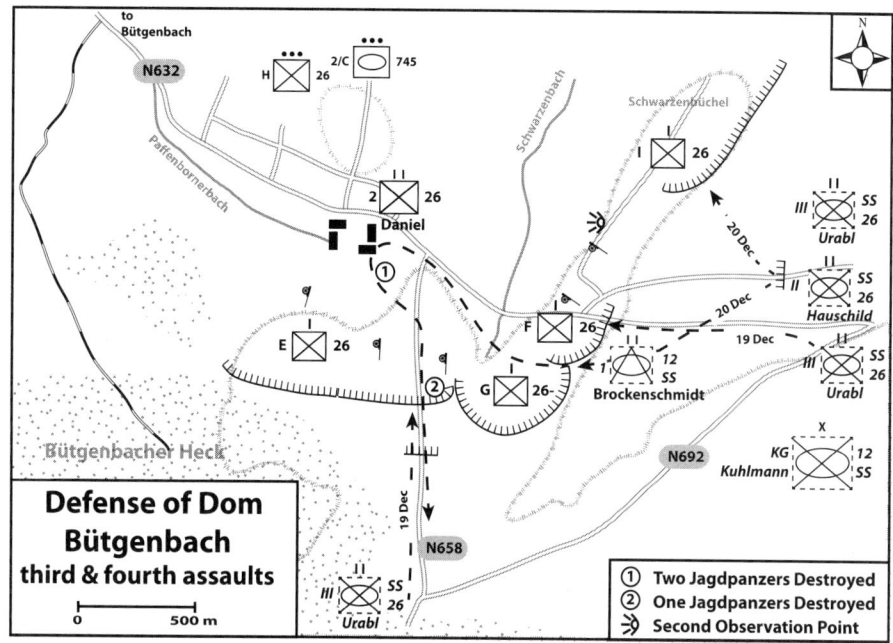

platoon of Company G. The American unit was destroyed, but American artillery fire blocked further forward movement.

Jagdpanzers from Heavy Panzerjäger Battalion 560[58] surged west of the Morsheck road approaching the main line of resistance. Two antitank guns engaged seven Jagdpanzers under illumination shells from Company E's 60-mm mortar team. After antitank guns destroyed three armored vehicles, the surviving guns and infantry withdrew.

The next day, starting at 0340, the sixth and final assault began with a three-hour barrage of artillery, mortar, and Nebelwerfer rocket fire that resulted in heavy American casualties, shredding its main line of resistance. All communications wires were severed, and two Shermans on the forward slope of Hill 600 were destroyed as was one M10 Tank Destroyer near the domaine barn. Three battalions of panzergrenadiers, supported by a company of PzKpfw IVs, attacked north from woods known as Bütgenbacher Heck. The massive German infantry assault approached within 75 yards from the regimental command post, despite massed salvos from at least ten American artillery battalions. By 0925, eight PzKpfw IVs passed the right flank of the battalion and charged along the north-south tree line toward the domaine buildings. Stripped of their infantry protection by the artillery fire, several of the tanks withdrew while Shermans ambushed two others among the farm buildings.

The battle raged throughout the day. To the east, Companies F and G held their ground against repeated enemy assaults. By noon, the battalion's entire main line of resistance from the Morsheck road to the west was completely open while three

---

58 Heavy Panzerjäger Battalion 560 fielded two companies of Jagdpanzer IVs and one company of Jagdpanthers.

enemy tanks held positions within the battalion command area under cover of the southern-most of the domaine's four barns. At 1250, Daniel requested tank destroyers to eliminate enemy tanks firing directly into the command posts of the battalion and Companies E and H. A platoon from 613th Tank Destroyer Battalion manning four M36 Tank Destroyers moved under cover of smoke from Bütgenbach to 2nd Battalion's CP. Their 90-mm guns fired through the south barn and quickly knocked out two tanks when they attempted to return to their own lines. The third was rooted out by high explosive and phosphorus shells from 81-mm mortars, but it escaped amid the smoke from burning vehicles.

At 0630 on 22 December, the panzers and III Battalion, SS Panzergrenadier Regiment 26 focused upon the 18th Infantry Regiment, now placed upon the 2nd Battalion's right flank. They penetrated American lines and overran the 18th Regiment's Companies A and G. German troops entered Bütgenbach to pressure the 2nd Battalion, 18th Regiment's command post, but the reserve 1st Battalion forced them to abandon the effort. German armor fell to the guns of the 613th Tank Destroyer Battalion, and the attack faltered. By 1900 the American lines were restored.

Aftermath

Later on 22 December, the 12th SS Panzer Division disengaged from the front lines for use in a different sector. In the end, it never did take the road junction.

The 26th Infantry Regiment held its positions against repeated enemy attacks through the period from 28 December to 15 January. During that period, the greatest single contributing factor to the successful defense of Domaine Bütgenbach was the support of artillery battalions sited upon Elsenborn Ridge. Repeatedly, enemy assembly area and troop concentrations were subjected to intense and timely artillery fire onto pre-arranged co-ordinates.

Consequences

Lt Col Daniel's defense of the Bütgenbach road junction prevented the 12th SS Panzer Division from outflanking Elsenborn Ridge, effectively denying three of the five routes assigned to the I SS Panzer Corps.

Battlefield Tour

Highway N658 leads directly from **Morsheck crossroads** to **Bütgenbach crossroads**. German attacks proceeded totally or partially along this highway. The thin line of spruce trees intersecting the highway marks the center of Colonel Daniel's defensive line. On 20 December, Company E formed the defense along the spruce trees to the west while Company F held positions on the opposite side of the highway in an arc back toward the Büllingen road and Schwarzenbüchel.

The second prong of the German assault on 20 December achieved the main line of resistance where three Jagdpanthers approached the position of Corporal Henry F Warner south of the 2nd Battalion command post. They fired cannon and machine guns when they came out of the early morning mist. When Warner fired his 57-mm AT gun, four shots each, two vehicles erupted in flames, but the antitank gun's breech had jammed. The third jagdpanther's commander opened his hatch to gain a view

Chapter Two   Battle for Elsenborn Ridge

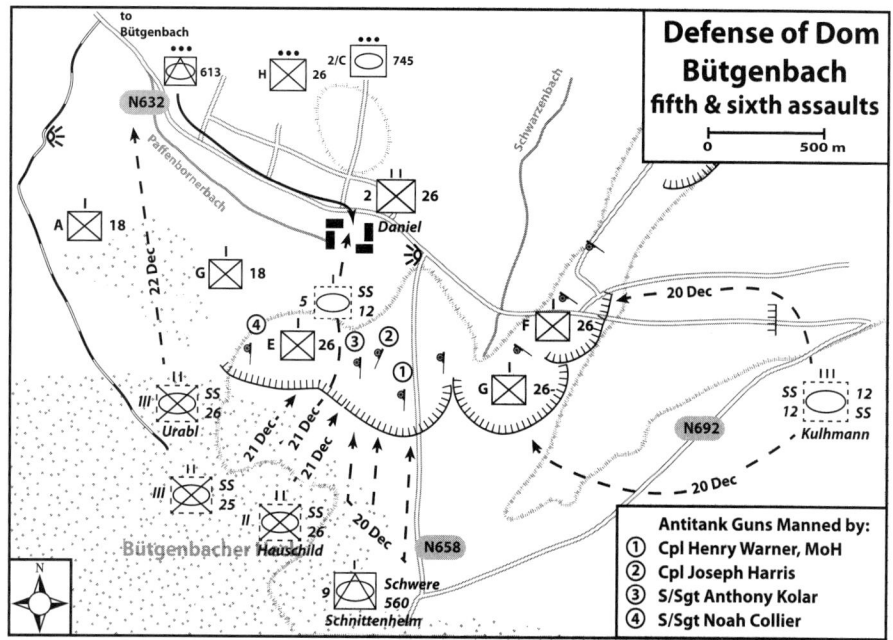

of the position. Warner drew his pistol and, standing five meters in front of the tank destroyer, shot him dead. The tank, with its commander's body hanging out of the turret hatch, withdrew along with the other operational vehicles. The German attack had failed to open the Dom Bütgenbach intersection.

On 21 December, 1st Platoon, Antitank Company, attached to Daniel's battalion only the prior afternoon, extended the antitank defenses to the west. Staff Sergeant Anthony Kolar's gun crew engaged two jagdpanzers that suddenly appeared out of the fog. Kolar's crew disabled one and then Kolar knocked out the second with a bazooka.[59] To the east, Corporal Joseph Harris fired his gun against a German Brummbär[60] firing high explosive rounds at the battalion command post. Harris fired four rounds to knock the huge gun out of action. Harris's gun was destroyed by a shell from a PzKpfw IV tank approaching on his left flank. In turn, that tank was damaged by the same Corporal Warner who had destroyed two tanks the day before. However, before Warner could fire a second round, he was cut down by the tank's machine gun.[61]

At the far western end of the American line, Staff Sergeant Noah Collier and the men of gun squad #5 fired their carbines and a BAR at the leading German infantry infiltrating from the woods of Bütgenbacher Heck. Corporal Irwin Schwartz manned the unit's 57-mm antitank gun against a following Jagdpanther. His first round damaged the vehicle's left drive sprocket. When the vehicle attempted to back up, it

---

59 Although wounded and captured during the engagement, Staff Sergeant Anthony Kolar survived the war.

60 Brummbär: a self-propelled 150-mm howitzer mounted upon a PzKpfw IV tank chassis.

61 Corporal Henry F Warner, a native of Troy, North Carolina, who had enlisted at age 19, received his Medal of Honor posthumously. He is buried in his hometown.

spun to the right, exposing its side to Schwartz, whose second round set it aflame. Schwartz grabbed his M-1 rifle to fire at advancing infantry when a PzKpfw IV appeared. He again manned the antitank gun and three shots later, the tank was in flames. A panzerfaust shell destroyed Schwartz's gun whereby his team resorted to small-arm fire until pushed back. During the confusion, Sgt Collier dashed out into the fog to rescue a wounded comrade. Neither, however, was ever seen again.[62]

The woods visible directly ahead to the west, known as Bütgenbacher Heck, sheltered German troops while they prepared for the 20 and 21 December attacks against American lines. Here the terrain slopes gently down Hill 613 toward Dom Bütgenbach; the slope increases farther to the west. Today the Domaine Bütgenbach is shrouded from view by a complete circle of trees and it is not visible from anyplace on the battlefield.

> Continue 400 m to the roundabout, taking the first exit (N632). Proceed 600 m toward Büllingen (N632) to the first junction on the right. (50.406138, 6.237772)

Highway N632, continuing into Büllingen, was often the route of attack by German forces from Büllingen against Domaine Bütgenbach. Company F held the highway at this spot against the attack by I Battalion, SS Panzergrenadier Regiment 26 on 21 December.

> Continue 60 m and turn onto to a rural road on the left (In der Reisbach) that continues into Büllingen; however, after 130 m, turn left again, follow for 800 m, and stop at a rural road crossing. (50.412663, 6.243610)

The American defenses in this sector lay along the top of this ridge, known as **Schwarzenbüchel**. Views from the ridge are generally obstructed by the large commercial buildings near the Dom, thus limiting the value of this location. Returning south on the crest road provides a view of the road to Morsheck, the forested hill of Bütgenbacher Heck, and the trees surrounding Dom Bütgenbach. The swampy area to the west of the Schwarzenbüchel inhibited a German armored flanking maneuver.

> Reverse direction, return to the Bütgenbach roundabout, and stop after passing through the circle at a poor but serviceable parking area on the left. (50.408732, 6.229722)

The best and safest view of the entire **Bütgenbach battlefield** owes to the grass verge to the left of the parking area. The trees on the right surround the Dom, Bütgenbacher Heck lies in the distance ahead on the right, and the line of spruce trees crosses the highway to the left. The noon attack on 18 December and early morning assault of 19 December occurred across the pasture to the southeast. Two Jagdpanzers were destroyed at this site during the pre-dawn attack on 20 December.

---

62 Staff Sergeant Noah G Collier posthumously received a Silver Star for his gallantry in action. He is buried in Ardennes American Cemetery, Neupré, Belgium.

Chapter Two　　　　　　　　　　Battle for Elsenborn Ridge　　77

A stone obelisk stands in the center of the roadway intersection; the second of five such memorials to the men of the **1st Infantry Division**. Inscriptions on its sides list the names of 458 1st Division men who died in the Ardennes. An enameled plaque briefly recounts in four languages the actions of the division and ends with the divisional motto, 'No mission too difficult, no sacrifice too great, duty first.' The 'Big Red One' emblem of the division is boldly embedded in the walkway approaches to the obelisk.

Heavily damaged during the battle, the **Domaine Bütgenbach** buildings remained mostly abandoned after the war. During the 1970s they became the property of a religious order that proceeded with repair and reconstruction. The Dom Bütgenbach farm buildings now hold the cloistered Congregation of the Franciscan Sisters of the Holy Family and are thus not open to the public.

> Leave the Dom Bütgenbach roundabout toward St-Vith (N632) and proceed 1.8 km to a narrow country lane on the left. Turn and continue 750 m to a curve in the roadway where the pavement widens to permit passing vehicles. (50.41315, 6.20991)

The country lane follows the western edge of the battlefield with a view of Bütgenbacher Heck on the right and the tree-shrouded Domaine to the front. During the decisive 21 December combat, German tanks spread across this field in front of the woods unobserved from the Dom because the terrain in the hayfield rises to the north before it drops back down to the Dom. German tank destroyers fired upon American positions from this location.

Side Trip: Truschbaum Museum

> Return to highway (N632) and continue west toward Bütgenbach. After 1.1 km, continue straight through the roundabout and follow highway N647 for 8.1 km. In the roundabout, take the first exit and proceed 750 m to the camp gate. (50.464074, 6.182563) The museum is 260 m ahead on the left. (50.464385, 6.184417)
> Total distance: 10.0 km

Truschbaum Museum

Camp d'Elsenborn　　　　　　　　　Lager Elsenborn Camp 1
4750 Bütgenbach, Belgium　　　　　Tel: +32 (0) 80 44 21 05
Web: http://www.camp-elsenborn.be

　　　The museum relates the history of Camp Elsenborn from its creation as a Prussian Army post in 1894 through both world wars to the camp's current function as an armored training ground. A few maps and displays, although not as elaborate or as professional as in other museums, relate the story. Dioramas cover the Ardennes Offensive showing the lives of American, British, and German soldiers during the battle. Guided tours may be available.

> Open weekdays except public holidays and certain military event days. Because the museum is located 100 meters within Camp Elsenborn, vehicles must park outside the entrance gate, and photographic identification must be presented to the guard. No Admission charge

Other Points of Interest near Elsenborn

Bôsfagne (Sourbrodt)

Route of Commemoration Information Panel #5 describes the camps for Russian PoWs located in fields to the south. The prison camp was created in March 1943 and abandoned in September 1944. Graves of two of its prisoners remain in the cemetery at Nidrum, next to twenty-six Russian compatriots who died in the army camp. A path across the gravel road opposite the sign leads into the field where a Russian Orthodox-style cross was erected in 1963 to honor the Russian prisoners of war held captive here during the Second World War.

Location: Rural lanes lead 2.1 kilometers north of the center of Bôsfagne to access two Route of Commemoration signs. The country lane ends at a parking area at the end of the drivable roadway. Continue on foot, bear right at the first gravel path, and continue to the small shelter on the left. (50.49442, 6.1335)

Route of Commemoration Information Panel #6, located upon a rise along the edge of a forested area, describes, in somewhat fractured English, the arrival of the first troops at Sourbrodt on 11 September 1944 and its subsequent occupation by the 99th Infantry Division. The town served as an important rail transportation hub and became a supply depot complete with hospital and airfield for light observation aircraft.

Location: Return to the parking area and continue in the opposite direction for 90 meters. Follow the trail on the right for 220 meters. (50.49088, 6.12761)

This completes the Elsenborn Ridge Tour.

Chapter Three
Kampfgruppe Peiper
17 December to 24 December 1944

The 1st SS Panzer Division *Leibstandarte Adolf Hitler*,[1] commanded by SS-Senior Colonel[2] Wilhelm Mohnke, formed the southern armored thrust of the I SS Panzer Corps. Though badly mauled during heavy fighting in Normandy, it managed to cross the Seine River after escaping encirclement at Falaise and spent the next two months refitting and receiving replacements. Although many of the soldiers were raw recruits, the NCOs and officers were experienced combat veterans.

The *schwerpunkt*, or spearhead, of the division was a 4000-man Kampfgruppe led by the ruthless twenty-nine-year-old SS-Lieutenant Colonel Joachim Peiper.[3] Although briefly on the staff of Reichsführer-SS Heinrich Himmler, Peiper had spent the last ten years with the *Leibstandarte* and much of the past three years on the brutal Eastern Front.

Peiper's battle group comprised a powerful, tank-heavy force fielding a mix of seventy-two PzKpfw IV and Panther tanks, a flak battalion of quad 20-mm guns, twenty-five assault guns and jagdpanzers, an artillery battalion with towed 105-mm howitzers, eighty half-tracks carrying III Battalion, SS Panzergrenadier Regiment 2, and two pionier [4] companies. Most ponderous of all, forty-five 68-ton PzKpfw VI, or King Tiger tanks of the Heavy Panzer Battalion 501, were attached.

The remainder of Mohnke's 1st SS Panzer Division divided into three Kampfgruppen, each named after their commanders: SS-Lieutenant Colonel Rudolf Sandig, SS-Colonel Max Hansen, and SS-Major Gustav Knittel. Sandig, with the remaining two battalions of SS Panzergrenadier Regiment 2, twenty tanks and twenty-two jagdpanzers, was to trail Peiper. Hansen, with SS Panzergrenadier Regiment 1 and a handful of jagdpanzers, was to proceed west along Rollbahn E. Knittel, commanding twelve-hundred men of the division's SS Reconnaissance Battalion 1 with an attached artillery battery of 105-mm guns and a pionier company, was to follow Peiper to deal with re-supply issues. Knittel had complete freedom of movement.

Kampfgruppe Peiper planned to drive through the northern edge of the Losheim Gap toward the Meuse River bridge at Huy. The plan called for him to reach the bridge by the end of the first day. Peiper's objective of the Meuse River was paramount. His instructions were to ignore his exposed flanks and by-pass opposition, if possible. The German High Command assigned Peiper to Rollbahn D, a route with fewer river crossings to contend with, but one that, in Peiper's own words, 'in some places was more fit for bicycles than tanks.'

---

1 The *Leibstandarte Adolf Hitler* was originally of regiment size and designated as Adolf Hitler's personal bodyguard. It grew to an elite division-sized unit and participated in the invasions of Poland, France, and Russia. It was one of only two units to bear the Fuhrer's name, the other being the 12th SS Panzer Division *Hitlerjugend*.

2 Senior Colonel, or Oberführer, was a Nazi Party rank without direct equivalent in the German Army. In importance it ranked between colonel and brigadier general.

3 Despite leaving school at an early age, Peiper hailed from a well-educated military family and spoke fluent English and French. Two of his brothers had already been killed in the war.

4 Pionier: German combat engineers

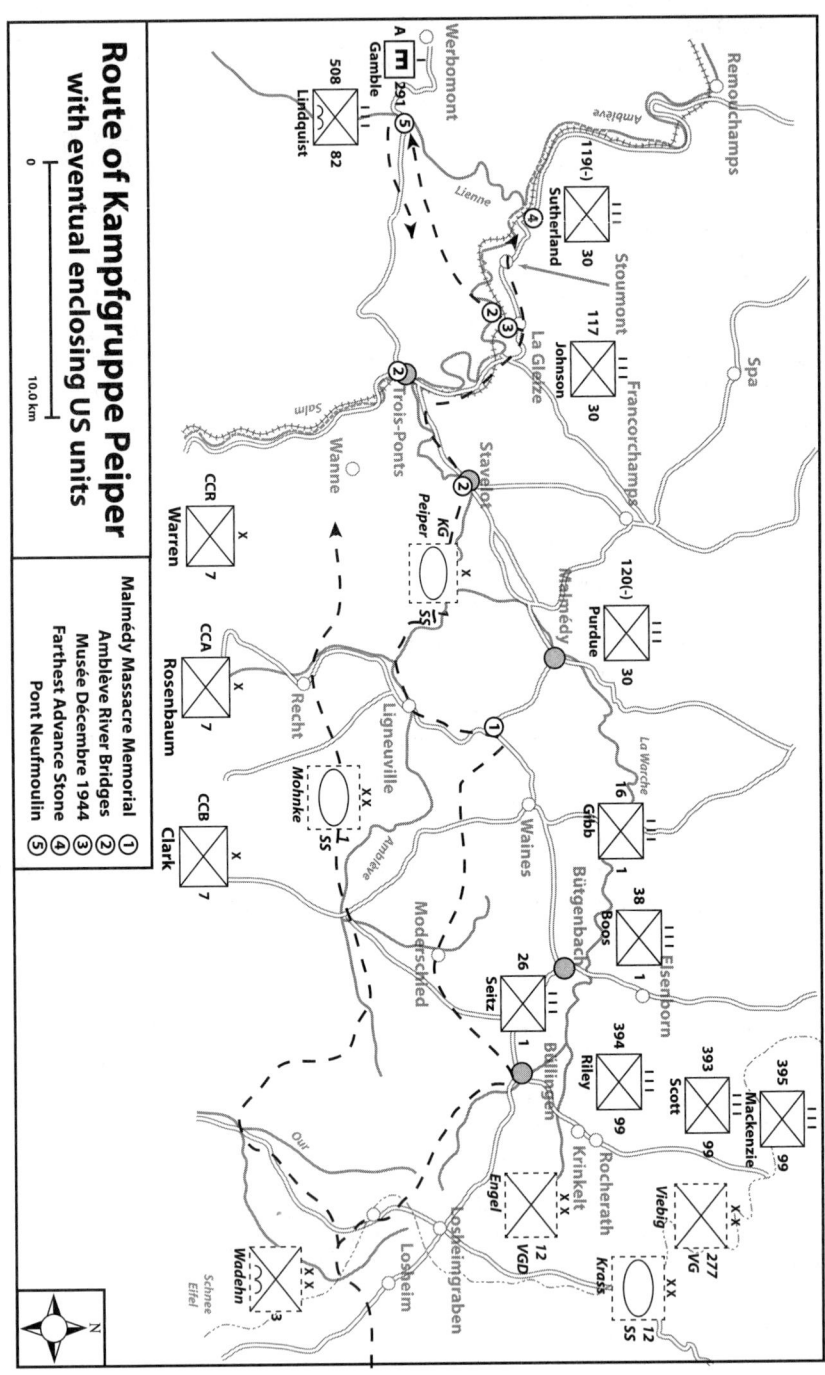

Chapter Three					Kampfgruppe Peiper	81

Kampfgruppe Peiper's beginning was as inauspicious as its end. Since late November, SS Panzergrenadier Regiment 2 had been on alert near Stadtkyll, Germany 10 kilometers east of Losheim. While the unit moved to its starting position on 16 December, Peiper's tanks stalled in traffic on highway B421 near Scheid behind the horse drawn artillery of 12th Volksgrenadier Division. A massive jam resulted from the slow repair of a rail bridge that was destroyed by retreating troops the past September.

With growing impatience, Peiper ordered his units to bypass the bridge by leaving the highway. The kampfgruppe's *Spitze*, or vanguard commanded by SS-1st Lieutenant Werner Sternebeck, hurried down the road embankment, crossed the track, and regained the highway south of Losheim. Since Peiper's original route from Losheim passed over a second rail bridge that had also not yet been repaired and then through Losheimergraben and Hünningen — both still held by the 394th Regiment, corps sent orders for Peiper to move west to Lanzerath via Hüllscheid and Merlscheid as an alternative to Rollbahn D. The new route had not been cleared and German-laid mines from the September retreat disabled three tanks. Peiper reached Lanzerath at midnight.

Peiper met with Oberst von Hoffmann in Lanzerath to arrange for the armored unit to past through the German paratroopers. The failure of Hoffmann's unit to rapidly punch through the American line had put Peiper irrecoverably behind schedule. Peiper started out from Lanzerath at 0400 on 17 December, already twenty-four hours behind schedule.

Battlefield Tour Summary
The battlefield tour follows the route of Kampfgruppe Peiper from its first action against American troops in Honsfeld to its ultimate destruction at La Gleize. The route is generally from east to west.

Recommended Sites
Malmédy: Malmédy Massacre Memorial and Baugnez 44 Historical Center
Trois-Ponts: Amblève River Bridge and 51st Engineer Combat Battalion Memorial
La Gleize: Musée Décembre 1944
Stoumont Station: Farthest Advance Stone
Habiémont: Pont Neufmoulin

> The tour starts at the Eifeler Hof in the center of Honsfeld. (50.381689, 6.281594)

Honsfeld operated as a rest center for the US 99th Infantry Division. In fact, a USO show featuring Hollywood actress Marlene Dietrich was scheduled in Honsfeld for the evening of 16 December. American troops from various units sheltered in the village's houses. Six 3-inch (76-mm) towed antitank guns from the 801st Tank Destroyer Battalion protected approaches to the town. During the night, towed guns from Company B, 612th Tank Destroyer Battalion, and A Troop, 32nd Calvary Reconnaissance Squadron, arrived to add to the defenses. With A Troop assigned the center of town, additional antitank guns defended the outskirts. The road from

Buchholz approached from the east and merged with a highway from Holzheim to the south.

On 17 December, Peiper's lead tank fell in line with the retreating American forces and followed into Honsfeld. In the dark night, it penetrated rag-tag American defenses before being recognized as German. However, the leading Panthers had some difficulty maneuvering past the sharp S-turn between the village's stone houses. An antitank gun knocked out two panzers and a mobile antiaircraft gun before being destroyed in turn by a third panzer. Upon reaching the center of town, German troops found American jeeps and armored vehicles parked along the roadway in front of the **Eifeler Hof**. A twenty-minute gun battle erupted between the few Americans and Lt Sternebeck's *Spitze*. The Americans — dramatically outgunned — then fled or surrendered. The Germans captured fifty vehicles, fifteen antitank guns, thirty trucks, and three hundred troops. About that time, the executions began.

> Continue west toward Büllingen for 200 m to the memorial on the left. (50.381785, 6.278816)

Eight exhausted GIs secluded themselves in an empty building until an SS officer uncovered the lot and machine-gunned all eight. Another five men attempted surrender; four were shot and the wounded fifth was run over by a tank — his flattened body lying in the street for days afterward. A tank's machine gun killed a final four while they attempted to surrender. The offensive was one-day old and already Peiper's force had committed its first atrocity in killing seventeen prisoners of war. The abuse continued while guards marched 250 prisoners down the road toward Lanzerath while passing grenadiers took random shots or performed purposeful executions. The death toll is uncertain but could have been an additional 25 to 35 prisoners, including two civilians.[5]

A horse trough became the pronounced feature from a photograph of the murdered American soldiers taken by a German soldier immediately after their execution. The photo shows German soldiers putting on boots removed from the dead Americans. A memorial stone stands above a modernized version of the 1944 horse trough. The stone bears a plaque commemorating the **612th and 801st Tank Destroyer Battalions** and attached units of the 99th Infantry Division.

Peiper left a detachment of Fallschirmjäger Regiment 9 in Honsfeld to clear up scattered resistance in the outlying farms. The regiment incurred fifty casualties in the process.

> Leave Honsfeld northwest toward Büllingen and continue for 3.5 km the junction with highway N632.

---

5   Some days later, five SS troopers insisted that pretty sixteen-year-old Erna Collas show them the way to Büllingen. The following spring, her bullet riddled body was found in a shallow grave alongside the roadway.

Peiper's assigned route ran along a marginal secondary road west from Honsfeld through Hepscheid–Möderscheid–Schoppen, but he purposely moved onto roadways assigned to the 12th SS Panzer Division to acquire gasoline in Büllingen.

Büllingen, the largest town yet encountered by Peiper, served as a supply center for 2nd Infantry Division's attack upon Wahlerscheid. On the morning of 17 December, only artillery service troops and a quartermaster company had quartered in the town. Airstrips to the south held light observation aircraft used by the 2nd and 99th Divisions. The 254th Engineer Combat Battalion was dispatched to Büllingen and the first companies to arrive took up positions to the east and south.

At approximately 0700, Sternebeck's *Spitze* received automatic weapons fire from a grass airfield two kilometers south of town. Peiper split his force and attacked from the south and east. A PzKpfw IV was destroyed entering the town. The remainder of Sternebeck's vehicles sped forward, firing their weapons indiscriminately. The defenders had no answer for German armor, and the defense quickly collapsed although pilots did manage to escape with a few of the planes. Peiper's men destroyed twelve light reconnaissance planes and captured 50,000 gallons of sorely-needed gasoline. They also sent approximately 200 more PoWs to the rear.

Although Peiper had turned the flank of the current American defenses at Elsenborn and was unknowingly only 750 meters from capturing General Robertson, his objective was the Meuse, and so he turned southwest to regain his assigned Rollbahn D. *Leibstandarte Adolf Hitler* had broken through American lines.

While it is possible to trace Peiper's next few steps, they offer little of interest. The suggested tour takes the most direct route to the next location of conflict.

> Leave Büllingen west towards Bütgenbach (N632). Follow for 12.0 km into Waimes, noting the junction with highway N676. After 3.2 km from the junction in Waimes, stop at the intersection with a country lane where a large stone building stands on the right. (50.407449, 6.073228) Total distance: 15.2 km.

Side Trip: Peiper's Actual Route

Peiper's exact route along Rollbahn D was indeed only fit for bicycles and even today provides drivers with challenges. In 1944, much of it was unpaved, resulting in the leading tracked vehicles churning the muddy route and making it almost impossible for the trailing vehicles. No wonder his 25-kilometer-long convoy of 800 vehicles encountered such difficulty. The more daring can follow Peiper's original Rollbahn D route; be forewarned, however, that some of the lanes are narrow.

> Leave Büllingen toward St-Vith / Amel (N692). The **American gasoline dump** captured by Peiper was located in the tree shaded park on the left immediately before exiting the town. (50.404869, 6.252810) From the Morscheck roundabout (intersection of highways N692 and N658), take the 2nd exit onto a minor road toward Möderscheid. In 1944, this was a dirt track. West of Möderscheid, cross the

Möderscheiderbach and start climbing up the opposite side of the valley. Pass through Schoppen toward Faymonville. Approximately 500 m before entering Faymonville, turn sharply left; the Chapel St-Hubert is aside the intersection. Follow the country lane through Am Stephanshof, Ondenval, and Thirimont. Leave Thirimont to the north and, after 2.6 km, enter the junction with highway N632 with the large stone building to the left front. (50.407449, 6.073228)
Total distance: 19.1 km

From the side road, Peiper achieved highway N632. Continue southwest 650 m toward Malmédy on highway N632 to the memorial on the left. The tree-shaded site, once open country, is unfortunately being encroached upon by commercial buildings and is easily missed on the busy highway. (50.403736, 6.066504)

Malmédy Massacre
17 December 1944

Peiper used narrow country lanes to avoid engagements in population centers such as Faymonville, Waimes, and Malmédy. He accepted the risk that this route presented. In fact, the leading tanks attempted to pass through Thirimont and continue west on a dirt road directly to highway N632 (N23 in 1944), but there Peiper's good fortune ended. The lead tank bogged down attempting to ford a small stream only 350 m short of the highway. The armored column turned north, then northwest, to pass through the wooded Grosbois.

Before the battle started, Lieutenant Colonel David Pergrin[6] commanded the 291st Engineer Combat Battalion, part of the 1111th Engineer Combat Group. The group's primary responsibility was to screen First Army headquarters in the ancient resort town of Spa, Belgium. Pergrin's battalion was assigned to cut lumber intended to provide sheltered winter quarters for units in the Ardennes. Thus, Pergrin's units happened to be spread across the route of Peiper's advance. The group headquarters was in Trois-Ponts; Pergrin's battalion headquarters was up the hill in Haute-Bodeux. Pergrin's Company A was in Werbomont, Company C in Château Froidecour near La Gleize, and Company B in Malmédy. Each location played a key role in the defeat of Kampfgruppe Peiper. Colonel Pergrin became a key figure in Peiper's story and reappears at several critical junctures.

Early that morning, Captain Leon T Scarborough[7] received orders to move his Battery B, 285th Field Artillery Observation Battalion, from the vicinity of Aachen to St-Vith in support of 7th Armored Division's CCR.[8] One-hundred-forty men in thirty-three vehicles stopped at 1145 outside of Malmédy for lunch. Colonel Pergrin flagged

---

6 Lieutenant Colonel David Pergrin was a degreed engineer, class president, and outstanding senior from Pennsylvania State University. From its ROTC program, Pergrin was called to active duty in April 1941 as a 2nd Lieutenant.

7 Captain Scarborough moved ahead of his unit to the 4th Division headquarters in Luxembourg. He was not at Baugnez at the time of the killings.

8 American armored divisions were divided into combat commands labeled CCA, CCB, and CCR (Reserve). Each unit was composed of an armored regiment of approximately 100 medium tanks, an

Chapter Three   Kampfgruppe Peiper   85

down the column while it left Malmédy. Most of the rear area troops in Malmédy had rushed west in the face of rumors of a German offensive. Pergrin decided to stay to defend the critical road center. Pergrin told Captain Roger Mills,[9] a 285th Battalion staff officer, and Lieutenant Virgil Lary, Battery B commander, that engineer patrols reported a German armored column approaching from the southeast. Nevertheless, not wanting to leave its assigned route, the convoy continued south to Baugnez.

OBJECTIVE	An engagement of encounter
FORCES	
American:	131 men from 285th Field Artillery Battalion (Captain Leon T Scarborough), medics, and an MP
German:	Disputed, but probably 9th SS Panzer Pionier Company (SS-Lieutenant Erich Rumpf)
RESULT	The American force was captured and prisoners executed
CASUALTIES	
American:	85 killed, 35 wounded, 1 missing, 7 taken prisoner
German:	None
LOCATION	Baugnez is 4 km southeast of Malmédy; Malmédy is 55 km southeast of Liège

Battle

At 1245, two PzKpfw IVs on the rural road from Thirimont crested a rise when they approached highway N632 and spotted an American convoy 800 meters to the west. They shelled the lead trucks, setting some on fire and causing others to crash, thereby effectively blocking the road. The lightly-armed Americans sought shelter in roadside ditches. Machine-gun fire from the approaching tanks quickly forced their surrender. Still, a few made for the shelter of the nearby woods. Three or four men found temporary safety in the shed behind the café across the road, but a Belgian civilian with German sympathies exposed them, and they were added to the other prisoners. Three trucks, still on the road from Malmédy, turned around and dashed back to safety.

The black uniformed SS troops herded 113 soldiers (eleven were killed in the initial engagement and seven PoWs were forced to drive the American vehicles) into a farm field 100 meters south of the crossroads. Peiper left to oversee the progress of the column toward Ligneuville. What followed was one of the Ardennes battle's most shameful episodes. Whereas events mire in controversy, apparently SS-Private George Fleps pulled out his pistol and fired at the assembled prisoners. With the first pistol shot, the prisoners began shouting, jostling, and some pushed their way to the rear. An officer, possibly Lt Lary, ordered the men to stand fast to preclude further

---

armored infantry regiment, and self-propelled howitzers as an artillery element. Combat commands were further divided into task forces of varying size, usually named after their commanding officer.

9   Captain Roger T Mills died in the massacre on 17 December 1944 at Malmédy. He is buried at Fort Gibson National Cemetery, Oklahoma. He was 26 years old.

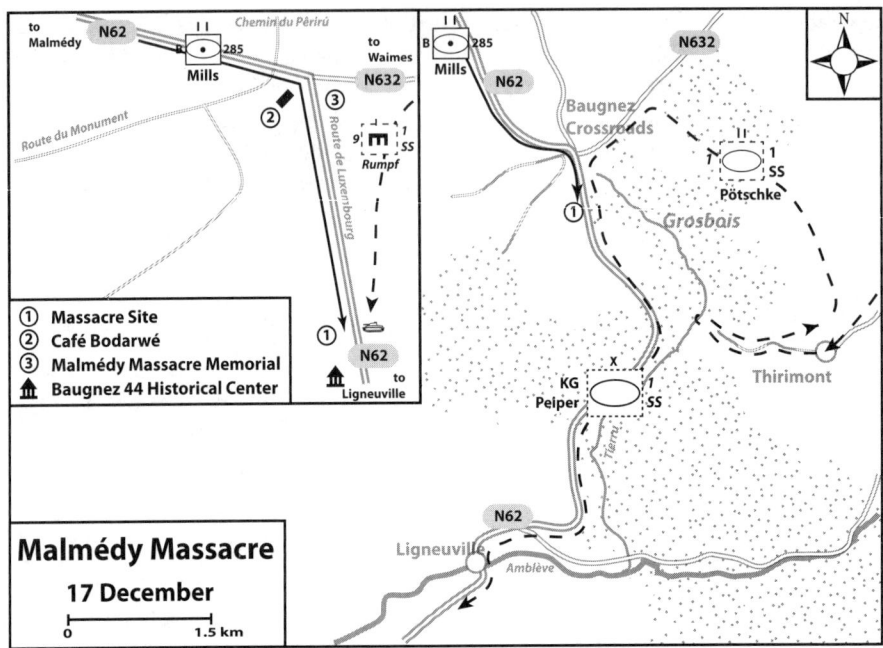

shooting. A second pistol shot killed medical officer 1st Lieutenant Carl R Guenther. As if on signal, someone shouted '*machen alle kaputt*' ('kill them all') whereby two tank machine guns fired into the eight rows of prisoners still standing with their hands raised. After the firing ceased, SS troops methodically walked among the wounded, executing each with a bullet to the head. Those perceived to be faking death were kicked in the groin, then shot. A medic tending a wounded soldier was shot along with his patient. Café owner Madame Adèle Bodarwé, who witnessed the crime, disappeared and was never seen again. A heavy snow later covered the bodies.

Twelve captives fled to shelter in the café across the road. As the building was set ablaze, the dozen were shot attempting to escape the flames. Three made their escape through the forest to the Malmédy road where Colonel Pergrin and his jeep driver picked them up. Twenty captives successfully feigned death to rise from the snow hours later. Survivors, mostly wounded, some not, sheltered in the forest, the burnt ruins of the café, or with courageous Belgium farmers. In all, forty-three, including Lt Lary,[10] escaped to tell the tale — although three died later of their wounds.

Aftermath

Word of the SS atrocity spread through American forces as what became known as the Malmédy Massacre. It was the worst such event in the American experience in the European war and was broadly publicized among allied troops. Subsequently, American troops took few SS prisoners.

---

10   Although wounded, Lieutenant Virgil Lary survived the encounter and achieved American lines with the help of a Belgian farmer. Lary made an unreliable witness at the war crimes trial by frequently changing his testimony. Lary died in 1981.

Chapter Three

Kampfgruppe Peiper 87

The true extent of the crime was not uncovered until 14 January 1945 when American forces reoccupied the crossroads. Graves Registration personnel retrieved the snow shrouded bodies of 71 servicemen and sent them to Malmédy for autopsy. Twenty-two were found to have been shot in the back of the head. Such brutality was a pattern that Peiper's Waffen-SS men brought from their experiences in Russia, where prisoners were routinely executed.

The individual responsible for giving the order has never been firmly established. At 1415 on 17 December, SS-Major Werner Pötschke, commander of SS Panzer Battalion 1, stopped two PzKpfw IVs and directed them to cover the prisoners. The fatal order may have been given by Pötschke to 1st Lieutenant Erich Rumpf, commander of the 9th SS Panzer Pionier Company. The engineering unit was considered little better than a penal squad with a reputation for brutality. Perhaps Pötschke[11] ordered tank commander SS-Sergeant Hans Siptrott to shoot the prisoners and Siptrott then relayed the order to his gunner, SS-Private George Fleps, or Fleps decided on his own to fire. In any case, the first shot seems to have been fired by Fleps.

Although Peiper was not present when the shooting began, some felt that his earlier comments regarding 'no time for prisoners' was an implied authorization for the executions. On the other hand, several instances of Kampfgruppe Peiper disarming large numbers of prisoners and leaving them for the trailing infantry surfaced. Peiper was a young, aggressive soldier who never joined the Nazi Party despite becoming one of Hitler's favorites. He was also well-educated, known to consider the war to have been lost, and disagreed with the Ardennes objectives.

What occurred on 17 December at Baugnez Crossroads has stirred controversy ever since, but, in any event, what seems certain is that SS men executed prisoners with single shots to the head.

In 1946, a US military court at the Dachau Concentration Camp arraigned Peiper and seventy-three men for war crimes – namely, for killing 350 captured American soldiers and over 100 civilians. All were convicted and forty-three sentenced to death, including Peiper, Sternebeck,[12] Rumpf, Siptrott, and Fleps. Twenty-two others received sentences of life imprisonment. However, torture, intimidation of witnesses, flawed evidence, and other trial abuses led to a judicial review that resulted in Peiper's sentence being commuted to time served after ten years. In fact, all of the death sentences were commuted and, by 1956, all of the guilty were released. Surprisingly, Peiper moved to France where, on Bastille Day in 1976, his house was burned down by unknown assailants, suspected to have been former members of the French Résistance, burned down his house. Peiper's body was found inside.

Battlefield Tour

The 285th Field Artillery Observation Battalion's convoy approached the then rural crossroads from Malmédy along the highway N62 from the northwest. The

---

11 Werner Pötschke became a convenient villain as he died fighting in Hungary in 1945. His reputation was one of an ardent and vicious Nazi. He was frequently described as a sadist brutalized by fighting on the Eastern Front.

12 After his release in 1956, Werner Sternebeck joined the German Bundeswehr, eventually becoming a lieutenant colonel of a training unit. He died in 1990.

88 The Bulge Battlefields

last truck had made the right turn to go south on the Route de Luxembourg when the German tank shells hit the leading vehicle.

The **Malmédy Massacre Memorial** consists of a curved fieldstone wall centered upon a rose garden and an American flag. Individual black stones mounted in the wall carry the eighty-four names of men killed in the massacre. Some are misspelled, and Private Louis Vairo's name was mistakenly deleted a few years ago. The open stone chapel on the left features a small altar and crucifix, where remembrances from individuals and military groups abound. A plaque bears the inscription in French and English:

>To the memory of the soldiers
>of the United States Army
>who while prisoners of war
>were massacred by Nazi troops
>on this spot on 17 December 1944

>'We here highly resolve that these dead
>shall not have died in vain.'
>— A. Lincoln

Despite the inscription on the stone, the memorial is not located upon the actual slaughter site, which was approximately 100 meters south of the intersection on the west side of the road toward Ligneuville in the field north of the museum parking area. (50.402694, 6.06608)

The Café Bodarwé was across the road to the west from the memorial. Burned down in 1944 to force hiding PoWs to exit the building, the site is now occupied by a private residence. (50.403764, 6.065986)

After the war, the *Touring Club de Belgique* erected small, rough-cut stones that identify the locations of the farthest penetration of German forces during the Ardennes Offensive. Twenty-six such **Farthest Advance Stones**, as they became known, carry an image of a tank and the words (in French) 'Here, the invader was stopped — winter 1944 - 45.' A complete list of locations of the stones appears in Appendix A.

The **Farthest Advance Stone** at Baugnez intersection marks the closest progress of Kampfgruppe Peiper toward Malmédy and stands to the west of the intersection. (50.403910, 6.065781)

Turn left on rue de Luxembourg (now N62 and E421) and continue 190 m south to the museum on the right. (50.401986, 6.066501)

Baugnez 44 Historical Center
Route de Luxembourg 10
Tel +32 (0)80 44 04 82
Web: http://www.baugnez44.be/

B-4960 Malmédy, Belgium
E-mail: info@baugnez44.be

The Baugnez 44 Historical Center opened in 2007 and is dedicated to presenting the Ardennes Offensive through two floors of displays and artifacts, a

Chapter Three   Kampfgruppe Peiper   89

25-minute multi-language film focusing upon Peiper's penetration and eventual prosecution for war crimes, and a diorama of the massacre. Sixteen specially designed displays each present a day in the life of an average soldier featuring American and German equipment discovered in the area.

Open Wednesday through Sunday from 10:00 to 18:00; closed Christmas and New Year's Day. Fee and handicap accessible.

> Reverse direction and return to Baugnez Crossroads. Turn left toward Malmédy (E421/N62) and continue to follow highway N62 for 4.2 km into Malmédy and along the narrow one-way streets of the city. Enter a parking area immediately past the church. (50.427485, 6.026918)

Battle of Malmédy
21 December 1944

On 17 December, Colonel Pergrin and the 159 men of Company B were all that held Malmédy. Its capture would open roads to Eupen to the north and Spa and Liège to the northeast. The only reinforcements available to First Army was the 99th Infantry Battalion (Separate) commanded by Lieutenant Colonel Harold D Hansen.

Hansen joined Pergrin in Malmédy on 18 December along with the 526th Armored Infantry Battalion and Company A, 825th Tank Destroyer Battalion. Random German artillery fire fell upon Malmédy for most of 18 December, accompanied by reconnaissance probes of its perimeter defenses. By 19 December, Colonel Branner Purdue's 120th Infantry Regiment had assumed responsibility for the defense of Malmédy from Colonel Pergrin. Overnight and undetected by the enemy, Malmédy exploded from lightly defended by a handful of engineers to strongly fortified.

The 120th Regiment's 1st Battalion tied into the 1st Infantry Division's positions west of Waimes, its 3rd Battalion protected the south and southeast approaches especially the highway from Stavelot, and its 2nd Battalion stood in reserve. Engineers manned roadblocks, laid minefields, wired the numerous river and railroad bridges for demolition, and established machine-gun positions along the U-shaped railroad embankment running along the southern outskirts of the town. Lt Col Hansen's Company B spread along the high railroad embankment to the south. The 526th Armored Infantry Battalion and the tank destroyers held the center by covering the small roads that approached from the south. The guns made effective use of the rail overpass as cover.

After the failure of Operation GREIF, one of SS-Colonel Otto Skorzeny's three large task forces of the Panzer Brigade 150 was attached to Kampfgruppe Peiper.

GERMAN OBJECTIVE	To move north of Malmédy and open the road network to further German advances.
FORCES	
American:	120th Infantry Regiment (Colonel Branner Purdue), 30th Infantry Division; elements of 291st Engineer Combat

	Battalion (Lieutenant Colonel David Pergrin); 99th Infantry Battalion (Separate) (Colonel Harold Hansen); elements of 526th Armored Infantry Battalion; one platoon from 825th Tank Destroyer Battalion
German:	Panzer Brigade 150 (SS-Colonel Otto Skorzeny)
RESULT	The German attack was repulsed
CASUALTIES	
American:	Unknown
German:	500 dead and numerous wounded
LOCATION	Malmédy is 55 km southeast of Liège

Battle

Before dawn on a foggy 21 December, men and tanks of Skorzeny's Brigade targeted Malmédy in a final effort to open Rollbahn C and expand the northern shoulder of the German penetration. Believing the town to be lightly defended, two groups attacked. A diversionary assault by 120 commandos supported by a few half-tracks charged from Baugnez toward eastern Malmédy, only to fall to an ambush prepared by 1st Battalion, 120th Regiment when the leading half-track struck a mine and exploded. The attack was easily repulsed by massed American artillery firing shells with the new 'pozit' proximity fuse.[13] Skorzeny's main effort approached along the east bank of the Warche River along the Route de Falize and not from Stavelot, as expected. The assault fell upon the 3rd Battalion, 120th Infantry Regiment and supporting artillery, engineer, and tank destroyer units in a blazing battle that extended well into the afternoon before also being repulsed.

Malmédy

Although Kampfgruppe Peiper never entered center Malmédy, the city offers a few simple memorials and a market town with better dining opportunities than the smaller surrounding villages.

Le Royal Syndicat d'Initiative de Malmédy
Place du Châtelet, 9   4960 Malmédy, Belgium
Tel: +32 (0)80 79 96 68   Email: tourisme@malmedy.be
Web: http://www.malmedy.be/fr/Tourisme/

Malmédy, founded in 648 as the site of a Benedictine Monastery, holds a pivotal location accounting for its history of its troubles, foremost having been invaded at least fifty times. In 1146 the area became part of the Germanic Holy Roman Empire and remained so until absorbed into France in 1795. King Louis XVI ordered its complete destruction in 1689. Rebuilt, the town became part of Prussia after the defeat of Napoleon Bonaparte but was little affected until after the Franco-Prussian

---

13   Pozit Fuse detonates artillery shells automatically at a preset distance from a target or the ground. The fuse enhanced the effectiveness of artillery shells by detonating them above ground level – dramatically increasing their kill radius and becoming one of the most important technological developments of land-based warfare. Thus, it was a closely guarded secret requiring SHAEP approval for its use.

War when the Prussian administration attempted to force Germanization. Although its citizens fought in the German Army in the First World War, the canton was annexed to Belgium by the Treaty of Versailles. Malmédy was briefly incorporated into the Third Reich during the war, its men forced to join the *Wehrmacht*. American troops liberated the town in September 1944.

Although Malmédy escaped damage from enemy troops, it was not so lucky with friendly forces. On 23 December, American bombers, targeting a German rail yard at Zulpich, missed their target by 51 kilometers and hit refugee-crowded Malmédy instead. The results were labeled 'excellent' after the bombs hit the center of town and ignited a massive fire. The next night, eighteen Liberator heavy bombers leveled what remained of the central core. On Christmas Day, four B-26s mistook Malmédy for St-Vith, again hitting the town. Altogether the bombings killed at least 125 civilians in addition to 37 soldiers killed and over 100 wounded.

The Place du Châtelet holds the **Cathédrale Saints-Pierre-Paul-et-Quirin**, built of local stone in the Renaissance style as an abbey church between 1776 and 1784. (50.426663, 6.027799)

A large sarcophagus-like memorial showcases the west side of the cathedral at the abbey cloister's main entrance. The large monument was erected in the memory of the victims of the War of 1914-1918 and is officially named the **Cenotaph de place de Châtelet**. An added plaque commemorates those killed in the war from 1939-1945 and lists the names of 230 dead soldiers. The cloister building now houses local administration offices and the tourist office. (50.426985, 6.027360)

Recent reconstruction of the area in front of the cathedral resulted in moving other memorials to the right rear behind the cathedral. A stone bears a plaque to the **US First Army** and lists the units that liberated the town in September 1944 and later defended it during the German offensive. A memorial commemorates local soldiers who died in the war. Five six-foot-high upright stone panels are inscribed with the names of the **civilian victims of the war** — many of whom died in the errant American bombings of 23, 24, and 25 December. Finally, a cave that sheltered three-hundred members of the civilian population during those raids still remain. (50.427415, 6.028428)

> Leave the place du Châtelet 100 m to the northwest on rue Devant to the intersection with highway N62. Turn left and, after 260 m, turn right (N68/N62). Continue for 600 m and then turn left onto rue Marie-Anne Libert. After 130 m, turn right onto Route de Falize. Follow for 1.2 km before stopping on the left side of the road at the junction with Ol'z-Eyôs. (50.414072, 6.007891)

At 0330 on 21 December, Skorzeny's main force of ten Panther tanks and accompanying commandos approached from the southwest along this road. At the nearby intersection, the column divided with a small force continuing straight upon the Route de Falize and the remainder turning left toward the Malmédy–Stavelot–Spa crossroads.

92   The Bulge Battlefields

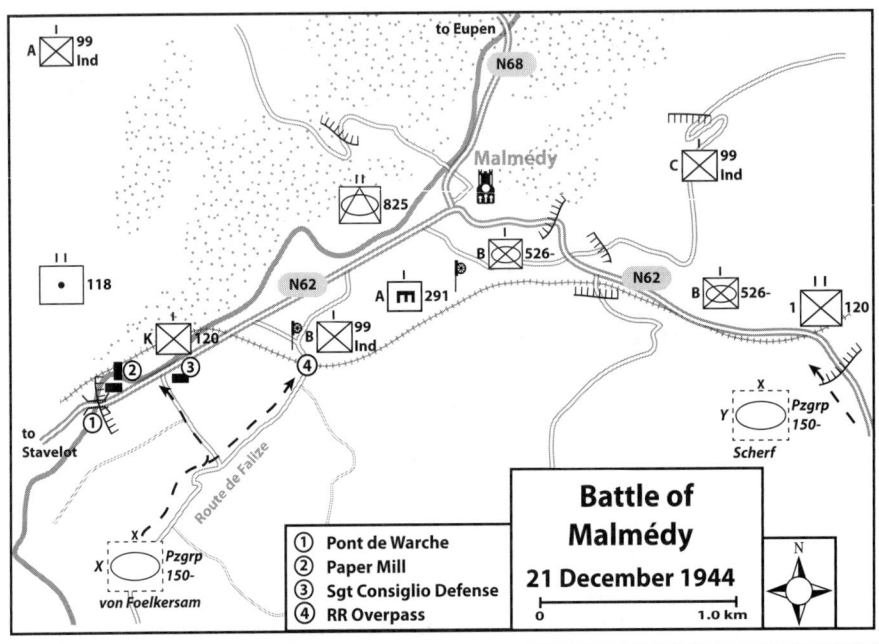

> Reverse direction and return 750 m to the railroad underpass (50.419037, 6.014534)

One Panther, disguised as an American Sherman, crept toward this underpass with commandos screaming 'Surrender or die.' The embankment was strongly defended by daisy chains of mines manned by Company A, 291st Engineers, and machine guns manned by Company B, 99th Infantry Battalion. The enemy succeeded in reaching the base of the embankment, but a gun from the 825th Tank Destroyer Battalion damaged the Panther. The devastating explosions of the new proximity fused shells and sweeping fire from the machine-gun-lined railroad embankment proved too deadly for German troops to overcome.

The rail line has been converted into a recreational walking and bicycle path. One can proceed left (northwest) to access a ramp that ascends the rail embankment to view the positions of the defenders against the attack of Skorzeny's right wing.

> Continue through the underpass (becomes rue Henri Bragard) and proceed 350 m before stopping at highway N62. The rail road viaduct is on the left. (50.420456, 6.009927)

Master Sergeant Ralph McCarty,[14] the 291st Engineers demolitions expert, took command at road blocks where the **rail viaduct** crossed highway N62 and at the rail crossing immediately south of the crossroads. His intention was to detonate

---

14   Master Sergeant Ralph McCarty received a battlefield commission to lieutenant for his leadership during the Malmédy battle. After the war, he returned to his farm in Turon, Kansas. McCarty died in 1988.

whichever bridge the Germans intended to use; however, someone had removed the detonators. Suddenly, the perimeter was brightly illuminated by hundreds of flares when tanks and infantry tripped wires in open fields south of the Pont de Warche. The leading Panther tank struck a mine and ignited, but others maneuvered around it to support the German infantry's charge. Guns all along the defense line opened fire upon the flare-lit enemy.

> Turn left onto highway N62 and proceed approximately 800 m and park in any one of the commercial areas near the Ahlstrom paper mill as identified by the tall chimney on the left. (50.417472, 6.001574)

    A large two-story house once stood across from the paper mill and became an American strongpoint backed by a platoon of 3-inch towed tank destroyers and several .50-caliber machine guns lodged in the windows of the house. When the warning flares fired, infantrymen and engineers instinctively sought shelter in the structure, eventually raising the number of defenders to thirty-three. The German attack found the strongpoint's gunners out of position inside the structure. Their sergeant rallied the men and led a charge out the door to man the guns.

    Sergeant Vincent Consiglio of Company B, 291st Engineer Combat Battalion, whose mission was to blow the Warche bridge, raced to a machine-gun bunker in the rear yard and fired at German infantrymen in the field to the south until the gun's barrel seized from the heat. Consiglio re-entered the house to find everyone on the first floor dead. He ran up to the second floor and joined Private Joe Spires firing their M-1s at targets to the south.

    The panzers crossed the timber trestle road bridge across the Warche unopposed and outflanked Company K, 120th Regiment stationed west of the Warche. They continued up the hillside where they encountered the fire of three 75-mm guns positioned upon the high ground overlooking the crossroads. Two Panthers exploded. Sergeant Francis A Currey, Company K, 120th Infantry Regiment watched while German armor advanced near his 3rd Platoon's position and forced the unit to withdraw into the mill. Sgt Currey located a bazooka, crossed the road under intense enemy fire, and knocked out a tank with one shot. Currey then proceeded to shoot enemy troops with his automatic rifle, drive the crews away from enemy tanks with rifle grenades, and mount a half-track to use its machine gun before moving to another location to use another machine gun whose team had been killed. Sgt Currey personally caused such heavy casualties that the German advance faltered and stopped.[15]

    At 1400 that afternoon, desperate fighting continued to swirl around the strongpoint and the paper mill. The strongpoint's thirty-three defenders were reduced to twelve men now hiding in the cellar. Sgt Consiglio made a mad dash for reinforcements. Despite being initially mistaken for one of Skorzeny's infiltrators,

---

15 Sergeant Francis A Currey was awarded the Medal of Honor for rescuing wounded comrades and inflicting heavy losses in men and material upon the enemy. Sgt Currey returned to New York and worked in the Albany Veterans Administration hospital before retiring to South Carolina where he still lives at age 90.

Consiglio convinced his captors of his identity and reported the desperate situation at the strongpoint.[16] The battle around the large house and paper mill slowly subsided by mid-afternoon. Skorzeny, faced with artillery fire for which he had no answer and with all his tanks destroyed, withdrew his men.

Unfortunately, the battlefield has been redeveloped into a commercial zone. The road bridge across the Warche is a non-descript replacement for the one built by American engineers in 1944. The construction of the A27 Autoroute had altered the bridges across the rail line. All in all, the site is an unsatisfying battleground to visit.

> Continue across the Warche bridge and after 120 meters, observe the road embankment on the right. (50.416881, 5.997979)

Panzer Brigade 150 made its closest approach to Malmédy along this highway. A **Farthest Advance Stone** once stood along the highway before its redevelopment; it is clearly visible now, having been incorporated into the roadside embankment.

> Reverse direction and turn right onto Ol'z-Eyôs. Stop at the monument on the right at the intersection with the avenue de Norvége. (50.416333, 6.005821)

A rough mountain stone at the corner of this intersection commemorates the actions of the **99th Infantry Battalion (Separate)**, known as 'the Norwegians,' for its actions in defending the city. The battalion was an independent unit originally organized in Minnesota as Ski Troopers comprised entirely of Norwegian Americans and Norwegian volunteers. For its service in the Normandy, Ardennes, Rhineland, Northern France, and Central European Campaigns the unit earned a Presidential Unit Citation and the French and Belgian Croix de Guerre.

> Reverse direction and return to highway N62 (avenue du Pont de Warche). Turn right follow highway N62 back through Malmédy to Baugnez Crossroad. Continue south toward Ligneuville / St-Vith (N62) for 4.2 km. The highway descends sharply into the Amblève River valley and retains several turnoffs of the original narrow and twisting roadway. After entering Ligneuville, stop before the memorial on the right. (50.375971, 6.054159)

Affair at Ligneuville
17 December 1944

Ligneuville was well behind the front lines on 16 December and held the headquarters for Brigadier General Edward W Timberlake's 49th Antiaircraft Brigade. Peiper was informed by a captured American officer of General Timberlake's presence, creating a target Peiper could not ignore. The town also held the Service Company for

---

16 Sergeant Vincent Consiglio received a Bronze Star for his mad dash for reinforcements. He died in 2013 at 90 years old.

the 9th Armored Division's 14th Tank Battalion. The unit was completing modifications on Sherman tanks to improve their traction on muddy ground.

Captain Seymour Green, commander of the Service Company, heard cannon fire somewhere to the north. A vehicle sped down the hill from the highway, its driver telling Captain Green of a German armored column approaching from Baugnez. Green sent word to headquarters and, while General Timberlake and his staff made their hurried escape, walked up the hill, rounded the curve, and came face-to-face with a Panther tank. Captain Seymour Green meekly surrendered.[17]

The Panther continued around the blind curve at the north entrance to the village where it was set on fire by a 76-mm shell from a disabled Sherman tank dozer up the street to the right of the memorial. The Panther chugged past the church and came to rest in front of the Hotel des Ardennes (the large beige building immediately past the church). An enraged Peiper grabbed a panzerfaust to personally hunt the offending Sherman, but a following Panther fired first. Other panzers also knocked out the remaining two Shermans undergoing modification and an antitank gun. Staff Sergeant Lincoln Abraham, a company mess sergeant, quickly manned the heavy machine gun of an assault gun under repair to provide protective cover to allow most of the personnel of the 14th Tank Battalion to escape. Panzergrenadiers quickly overpowered the remaining poorly-armed Americans and sent a column of prisoners marching up the hill. Peiper entered the headquarters and relished the American general's abandoned lunch.

After Peiper had left Ligneuville, SS-Staff Sergeant Paul Ochmann selected eight American PoWs from a group of twenty captives and ordered the digging of graves behind the Hôtel du Moulin for three German soldiers killed in the brief encounter. Afterwards, Ochmann marched the small group north along the road to the vicinity of the town cemetery. He had them stand on the south side of the road above a drop in the terrain where Ochmann methodically shot each in the head, prompting their bodies to fall down the slope. [18, 19] Miraculously, Corporal Joseph P Mass survived and feigned death until nightfall. He was recaptured attempting to reach St-Vith.[20]

The proprietor of the Hotel du Moulin, 69-year-old Peter Rupp, witnessed the executions. Fearful for the safety of fourteen other captured Americans including Captain Green, Rupp confronted Ochmann when the Nazi returned to the hotel. An SS officer told Ochmann to kill the other prisoners and the troublesome Rupp. A second officer countermanded the order and permitted Rupp to enter his cellar and return with an armful of bottles of wine and cognac. Unknown to all, Rupp was a member of the

---

17   Captain Seymour Green was held briefly at Hotel du Moulin before being transferred the notorious Mauthausen Concentration Camp. He survived the war and practiced law in Ardmore, Pennsylvania.

18   Staff Sergeant Lincoln Abraham was one of those executed. Abraham is buried in Minneapolis, Minnesota. He was 29 years old.

19   After the war, Ochmann confessed to the murder of the prisoners as a defendant in the Malmédy Massacre trial. He later retracted his statement but was nevertheless sentenced to death.

20   Corporal Joseph Mass spent the remainder of the war in various German PoW camps, including Stalag VIg in Bonn, Germany. He died in 1998 at age 86. He is buried in Holy Cross Cemetery, Brook Park, Ohio.

Belgian underground that smuggled downed allied fliers to safety in his hotel as a way station. The surviving PoWs were later moved rearward to captivity in Germany.

The **executed soldiers' memorial** presents two wings centered upon a tall central shaft. The shaft bears the emblem of the United States of America and a secondary stone plaque listing the names of the eight men. The wings bear the identical inscription, in English and in French: 'To the glorious American soldiers who were savagely murdered by German SS 17.12.1944.'

The **Hôtel du Moulin** survived the battle despite being used as 1st Panzer Division headquarters by SS-Senior Colonel Mohnke.

> Continue through Ligneuville and after 800 m on the opposite side of the village, bear right toward Pont (N660). Continue 2.1 km passing through Pont and under the Autoroute; turn right toward Beaumont / Stavelot and follow for 6.6 km into La Vaulx Richard. This scenic route rises high above the Amblève River and offers fine views of the valley and the opposite hillside. In La Vaulx Richard, observe the cement block residence sited close to the roadside. (50.385639, 5.964748)

This unnumbered rural road follows the exact route taken by Peiper when he approached Stavelot. Unlike most roadways on the tour, it remains essentially unchanged and provides a good example of the narrow passages and numerous sharp curves of the tree-lined 1944 roadway. Kampfgruppe Peiper exercised a technique he called 'reconnaissance by fire' whereby passing vehicles sprayed roadside buildings with machine-gun fire to discourage potential snipers or observant civilians. The eastern side of this particular house shows patched bullet holes in the cement blocks from that fire.

> Proceed 800 m and park on the side road to the left. Because of the blind curve and absence of roadside shoulder, view the next positions on foot. Walk ahead 100 m to view the building foundation below the road on the right. (50.388482, 5.953533)

By 17 December, Peiper was behind the American front lines and moving through territory defended only by American non-combat troops: supply and transport personnel, clerks, and cooks. His armored column was negotiating the ridgeline approaching the town of Stavelot when it first encountered men from Colonel Pergrin's combat engineers.

Platoon leader Lieutenant Warren Rombaugh led a twelve-man squad of engineers from Company C, 291st Engineer Combat Battalion. He sent Sergeant Charles Hensel of Lockport, New York to establish a roadblock. Hensel dispatched Private Bernie Goldstein to a stone shed once used as a guard station to warn him of the German troops' approach. Hensel's squad placed a 13-mine pattern across the road just below the curve and positioned his bazooka team and .30-calibre machine gun to the rear where they had a clear view of the curve. They then waited for the enemy.

At 2100, Goldstein heard the approach of armored vehicles, stepped into the middle of the road, and ordered, 'Halt!' The German response was to fire from numerous automatic weapons. Goldstein made his escape up the slope to his right and along a tree-lined dirt track back to Stavelot.[21]

Forewarned by Goldstein's rifle fire, Hensel's team fired a bazooka rocket at the leading Panther tank approaching the curve and inflicted marginal damage. Hensel and his team, expecting the enemy to advance, waited a long 20 minutes behind the roadblock. When they failed to appear, he ordered his team to board its truck, which coasted back to Stavelot.

Peiper, uncertain of the size force he was facing, called a halt, and his exhausted men took a few hours' rest in La Vaulx Richard before continuing. Hensel's small squad had done its job by delaying the panzer attack into Stavelot for one full night and unknowingly gave a company of the 526th Armored Infantry Battalion an opportunity to establish itself in the town.[22]

The foundation outlined on the ground to the right below the road marks the ruins of the stone shed used by Goldstein. The mined roadblock crossed the highway approximately 400 m ahead, and the bazooka team had waited in ambush above the road behind the roadblock. The terrain was an obvious choice for such an effort. The road clings to the side of the hill, dropping off sharply on the right into the Amblève River valley, and the sharp bend required tracked vehicles to maneuver slowly.

> Retrieve your vehicle and continue west, noting the cliff edge on the left side of the roadway. The roadblock and mines were positioned across the highway approximately 500 m ahead. (50.391128, 5.949720) After 120 m past the sharp curve, stop on a farm track on the left. (50.39115, 5.946825) The ground opens where the road approaches Stavelot, allowing tremendous views over the city and its 16th-century Benedictine Abbey. Proceed down the hill into Stavelot.

Battle for Stavelot
18 to 24 December

During the evening of 17/18 December, Company A, 526th Armored Infantry Battalion commanded by battalion Executive Officer Major Paul J Solis and 1st Platoon, Company A, 825th Tank Destroyer Battalion with five 3-inch towed antitank guns, detached in Stavelot while the bulk of the force continued on to support Pergrin in Malmédy. Solis established three gun positions around the town square.

GERMAN OBJECTIVE	To capture one of the few sturdy bridges crossing the Amblève River
FORCES	
American:	Company A, 526th Armored Infantry Battalion (Major Paul J Solis); later 1st Battalion (Lieutenant Colonel Robert

---

21 Private Bernie Goldstein later took three bullets in his hip and leg during the fighting in Stavelot. He suffered the effects of his wounds for the remainder of his life.

22 Sergeant Charles Hensel survived the war and, as of 2010, was still living in Lockport, New York.

German:	Frankland), 117th Infantry Regiment Kampfgruppe Peiper (SS-Lieutenant Colonel Joachim Peiper); later Kampfgruppe Knittel (SS-Major Gustav Knittel) and Kampfgruppe Sandig (SS-Lieutenant Colonel Rudolf Sandig)
Result	The town was briefly and partially occupied.
Casualties	
American:	526th Battalion: 33 killed, 58 wounded, and 24 missing 117th Regiment: 13 killed, 19 wounded, 10 missing 825th Tank Destroyer Battalion: 6 killed
German:	Kampfgruppe Peiper: 25 to 30 casualties Kampfgruppe Knittel: 300 casualties Kampfgruppe Sandig: 120 casualties
Civilian:	138 executed
Location	Stavelot is 8.5 km southwest of Malmédy

Battle

At dawn on 18 December, a company of paratroopers from Fallschirmjäger Regiment 9 led the charge down the road heading for the triple-arched stone bridge over the Amblève River. It met with shrapnel fire from Major Solis's antitank guns. The paratroopers took shelter in houses near the bridge to await the tanks. One panzer crashed through an antitank obstacle and two tank destroyers east of the river as the armored column continued down the hill.

Two towed antitank guns in commanding positions upon the hillside west of the town center engaged the Panthers leading a full assault upon Stavelot. Although antitank-gun fire destroyed four Panthers while they descended the roadway into town, others continued to surge forward. Panzergrenadiers stormed forward and captured the bridge when explosives failed to detonate. The Americans were driven back into the town center under a German mortar and artillery barrage.

A two-hour battle took place in the town square with antiaircraft half-tracks mounting quad .50-calibre machine guns and a company of 202nd Engineer Combat Battalion from 7th Armored Division's briefly joining the battle. The half-tracks and engineers responded to calls elsewhere and pulled out, leaving Major Solis's lone armored infantry company. At 0800, Solis ordered his men to disengage and withdraw to the north. Kampfgruppe Peiper turned left toward Trois-Ponts.

Although Peiper had moved on, the battle for the town and its important bridge was not yet over. Lieutenant Colonel Robert Frankland's 1st Battalion, 117th Infantry Regiment had replaced Major Solis and his positions along the road to Spa shortly after Peiper's tanks had left for Trois-Ponts. By nightfall, Frankland had retaken one-half of Stavelot against weak opposition. By noon the next day, Companies A and B of the 117th Infantry Regiment had cleared the town north of the river except for a stubborn Tiger tank on the western outskirts.

Peiper ordered a company of Knittel's SS Reconnaissance Battalion to return to re-open the route through Stavelot. With light armored cars augmented by three PzKpfw IVs, Knittel split his force to attack along the main road and from the heights

Chapter Three

Kampfgruppe Peiper 99

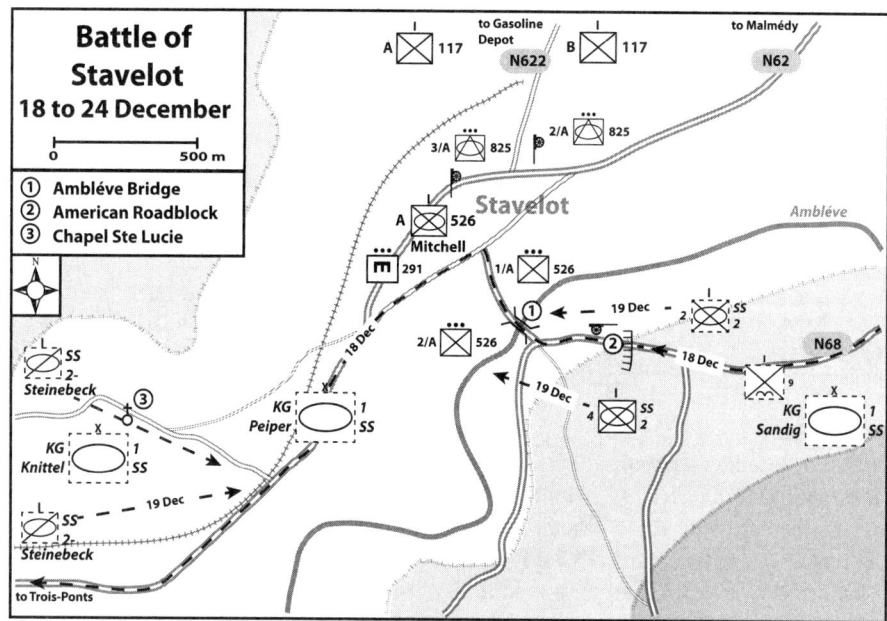

around Parfondruy. Bitter fighting to re-open the route continued until dusk on 24 December.

Also on 19 December, accurate fire from the towed tank destroyers repulsed counterattacks from south of the bridge by Kampfgruppe Sandig's SS Panzergrenadier Regiment 2. The threat from the south was sealed that night when American engineers blew the western ramp of the Amblève bridge.

Kampfgruppe Sandig[23] moved its bridging equipment forward and, before daylight on 20 December, its engineers attempted to ford the icy waters to establish a bridging point. American riflemen in the riverside buildings fired upon the men by light of flares, thereby ending the attack. Kampfgruppe Peiper was now cut off.

Aftermath

Civilians also paid the price of German defeat. At 2000 on 19 December, the SS ordered the removal of 26 civilians who had sheltered in the cellar below the house of the mayor. Gathered in the garden, Nazi troops began executing the women and children despite the pleas of Madame Regine Grégorie, who, as an outcome, was not harmed. The death toll of civilians murdered at Stavelot stood at 138.

Battlefield Tour

Stavelot
L'office du tourisme de la commune de Stavelot
Information desk: glass-window corridor of Stavelot Abbey
Mailing address: Place St-Remacle 32   B-4970 Stavelot, Belgium

---

23   SS-Lieutenant Colonel Rudolf Sandig was an early member of the Nazi Party, having joined in 1929. After the war Sandig became the director of an insurance company. He died in 1994 at age 82.

Tel. +32 (0)80 86 27 06 Email: infotourismestavelot@skynet.be
Web: http://www.stavelot.be/tourisme/

Stavelot lies in the Amblève River valley surrounded by high, sparsely-wooded hills. Most of the town, including the secularized remnants of its 16th-century abbey, stand north of the river. One bridge spans the river whose steep banks form a difficult-to-pass tank barrier. A highway (now, N622) leaving Stavelot to the north led 15.5 kilometers to Spa, headquarters of the US First Army and where, unknown to Peiper, an enormous fuel dump spread along 8 kilometers of the highway.

> Enter Stavelot along Chemin du Château and stop at the memorial on left. (50.391441, 5.934953)

Early on 18 December, four half-tracks of 2nd Platoon, Company A, 526th Armored Infantry Battalion and two half-track-towed, 3-inch antitank guns of Lieutenant Jack Doherty's 1st Platoon, Company A, 825th Tank Destroyer Battalion crossed the Amblève River bridge and took up positions to block Peiper's advance. The remainder of Company A's 1st Platoon and its 2nd Platoon guarded the north side of the bridge while 3rd Platoon was in reserve in place St-Remacle. The antitank guns proceeded up the hill toward this position only to encounter SS-Private First Class Eugen Zimmermann's leading panzer when it rounded the curve to the east. One shot later, the half-track towing one of the antitank guns was in flames. The men from the second gun scattered. Unable to establish positions, the towed guns never fired a single shot. All the half-tracks were in flames almost instantly and the infantry, under fire from paratroopers in the houses, scampered back across the bridge with about one-third becoming casualties. One survivor forded the ice-cold waters of the Amblève to safety. A few sheltered in houses or the nearby dairy where they were treated for their wounds and hidden by local civilians.

The rough stone memorial, erected by local citizens, commemorates the engineer, tank destroyer, and armored infantry units that defended Stavelot and marks the location of the attempted roadblock. Two large plaques record the names of those from the **825th Tank Destroyer Battalion**[24] and from the **526th Armored Infantry Battalion**[25] killed during the morning panzergrenadier attack. An additional plaque names those killed at the viaduct near Trois-Ponts. (See below.) A red brick house immediately opposite the memorial displays a number of repaired bullet marks from the engagement.

> Continue down the Chemin du Château for 160 m to the monument on the left. (50.391415, 5.932664)

---

24 Sgt John G Armstrong and PFC Douglas L Newman are buried in Henri-Chapelle American Cemetery, Henri-Chapelle, Belgium; Cpl Frank Richesin and Pvt Bernard F Gallagher are buried in Ardennes American Cemetery, Neupré, Belgium; also killed were Pvt Conley W Leach and Pvt Fowler H Williams.

25 Killed were Lt James J Evans, Sgt Jack W Ellery, Pvt Dale B Nelson, and Pvt Lloyd E Fisher. Fisher is buried in Henri-Chapelle American Cemetery, Henri-Chapelle, Belgium.

Chapter Three Kampfgruppe Peiper 101

The leading Panthers continued down the long, sloping roadway toward the bridge. Two M10 tank destroyers stationed almost 800 meters away on the hillside north of Stavelot waited until the panzers came within range. The first two were knocked out with one shell each, but the German column kept advancing. A third and fourth panzer fell to the M10s' fire, but by then German troops had reached the bridge.

The first of three **massacre memorials** in Stavelot consists of a large stone bearing a plaque stating, 'On these shores of the Amblève were massacred by the Germans 26 of our 138 Stavelot victims.' Each of the 26 victims is named; their ages run from 20 to 79 years.

> Continue 25 m into the Place du 18 Decembre 1944 before crossing the bridge. (50.391534, 5.932321)

At 0745, 9th Company, SS Panzer Regiment 1 occupied the square before the bridge after an intense firefight against two platoons of Company A stationed in the buildings north of the river. The 57-mm antitank gun crews from Company A's Antitank Platoon fired at the panzers crossing the bridge but, not powerful enough to penetrate the tank's frontal armor, carried little effect. The panzers rolled over the guns, and their crews fled.

The mid-16th century stone bridge, which still crosses the Amblève River and was rebuilt to resemble the original, remains 'guarded' by a US 30th Infantry Division **M3A1 half-track** stationed on the southeastern side of the place du 18 Décembre 1944.

> Continue to the west side of the bridge. (50.391775, 5.931729)

A rather inflammatory plaque on the west end of the bridge commemorates the civilian dead. The 1945 language emphasizes the emotions of the time:

> At this place, from December 18th, 1944 to January 13th, 1945, the Nazi hoards of von Rundstedt were driven back and contained by the forces of the First American Army. This plate was affixed by the town of Brussels, godmother of Stavelot, in memory of 131 executed martyrs.

A small bronze plaque mounted near the crucifix on the opposite side of the roadway commemorates the **596th Airborne (Parachute) Engineer Company**. The 137-man unit was usually attached to the 517th Parachute Infantry Regiment (PIR) although it experienced other attachments as well. The hand-picked volunteers were specially trained in demolition and explosive removal and fought in Italy before moving to the Northwest European Theater. Its significant contributions were the recapture of Manhay in December 1944 and the removal of an extensive minefield in the Hürtgen Forest in February 1945. (50.391813, 5.931737)

> Follow the rue Gustav Dewalque (becomes rue du Châtelet, then rue Général Jacques) for 350 m into place St-Remacle and park. (50.394778, 5.929935)

The highway N68 bypass around the old center of Stavelot did not exist in 1944. The main road wound through the old cobblestoned streets that still exist in the center of town and fed into place St-Remacle. Faced with one of Solis' 3-inch antitank guns and to avoid being trapped in the marketplace, the panzers turned left after crossing the bridge; emerged on rue Neuve, one of the wider streets to the southwest; joined the portion of the N68 that did exist at the time; and continued toward Trois-Ponts.

Shortly after midnight on 19 December, one of Peiper's trailing Tiger tanks clinked up the street from the bridge toward the square. A bazooka team from Company A, 117th Regiment knocked it out to block the narrow passage. Two following Tigers attempted to bypass the square using the side street. Slowed by the narrow passages between the stone houses and having to maneuver back and forth, they become easy targets for bazooka men. Both were destroyed.

The cobblestone place St-Remacle presents a wonderful image of a wartime Belgian town with its unused fountain in the center and a surround of commercial buildings and residences. Although reconstructed, for the most part the buildings retain their original appearance. A **Farthest Advance Stone** sits in the southwest corner of the square, marking the end point of the King Tiger tank that attempted to enter the square. (50.39458, 5.93009) The impassibly narrow streets exiting the square to the north demonstrate the impossibility of tanks maneuvering through the center of the town.

Walk 90 meters back toward the river on the rue du Châtelet to the town memorials beneath the trees on the left. A long wall bears numerous memorials including an inscribed plaque to the **Victims of 1940 to 1945**, which lists the names, ages, and locations of 133 victims to Nazi atrocities in December 1944. Included are 32 civilian victims of military operations — one as young as one year old — prisoners of war, deportees, and resistance fighters executed in the citadel in Liège. (50.393816, 5.930607)

The large excavation site behind the memorial marks the location of the abbey church destroyed during the French Revolution. Visitors may reach the Tourist Office by passing through the archway 80 meters south and entering the abbey grounds. The abbey courtyard held a temporary mass grave of inhabitants murdered by the SS in 1944. A plaque commemorates the event.

> Exit place St-Remacle to the north on the narrow rue Chaumont (how would a Tiger tank ever hope of navigating these streets?) and continue 90 m to the intersection with the highway bypass. Turn right toward Malmédy (N68) and then, after 250 m, left at the stoplight. One of the American tank destroyers positioned in this intersection fired upon German panzers descending the hill toward the bridge. Proceed up the hill. After 1.4 km, stop at the monument on the left. (50.407562, 5.929613)

North of Stavelot, a platoon of the 3rd Company, 5th Belgian Fusilier Battalion,[26] commanded by Lieutenant Albert Detroz, guarded 800,000 gallons of gasoline stored in 5-gallon jerricans along the road to Francorchamps. Major Solis, after his withdrawal from Stavelot, set up a defensive perimeter and ordered 134,000 gallons of the fuel to be set ablaze as a defensive barrier. Peiper's vehicles were unable to bypass the inferno due to the steeply-sloped sides of the road and turned back.

The thirteen-percent grade roadway approaching the monument speaks to the difficulty experienced by Peiper's armor in searching this road. The gray brick monument bears the insignias of the three units that defended to site: the **526th Armored Infantry Battalion, the 5th Belgian Fusiliers**, and the **825th Tank Destroyer Battalion**. The bronze plaque below bears witness to the events and locates the gas depot.

> Reverse direction, which may be difficult on the high speed highway, and return to the intersection with highway N68. Turn right toward Trois-Ponts.

Battle for Trois-Ponts
18 to 21 December 1944

From Stavelot, Peiper moved toward Trois-Ponts. As the name implies, Trois-Ponts was the location of three bridges – two over the Salm River and one over the Amblève River. The town also held a rail junction for lines going to Vielsalm, Aywaille, and Stavelot.

Peiper's plan was to cross the Amblève, then the Salm, and proceed along the main highway (N66) west toward Werbomont to finally escape the torturous Ardennes terrain. Peiper remained confident that he could still reach the Meuse River by the end of the day. He was only 60 kilometers away.

The 51st Engineer Combat Battalion spent 1 though 17 December cutting lumber to winterize command bunkers and build bridges. Its commander, Lieutenant Colonel Harvey R Fraser, had assumed command only three days previous. By 1730 on 17 December, the alert arrived ordering the engineers to occupy the area's bridges and delay the approaching enemy force. Captain Sam Scheuber's Company C proceeded from its base near Marche to Trois-Ponts to mine bridges at the confluence of the Amblève and Salm Rivers. At 2330, 140 men commanded by the 1111th Engineer Combat Battalion's executive officer, Major Robert B Yates, set up a command post in the train station and established roadblocks at entrances to the village. Earlier that day, Colonel Pergrin had sent a platoon from his Company A to mine the second Salm bridge south of the town.

By 0800 on 18 December, a 57-mm antitank gun and crew became separated from Company B, 526th Armored Infantry Battalion, when the half-track towing the gun threw a tread. While Scheuber's engineers worked to wire the bridge for demolition, the infantrymen positioned the gun near the Hotel Lifrange along the road

---

26 The 5th Belgian Fusilier Battalion was created after the country's liberation and staffed with underground resistance fighters. They were equipped with British uniforms and weapons but fought as part of the US First Army.

from Stavelot. It was a true suicide mission for the gun crew. It had only seven rounds of ammunition, yet the men knew that using them all was unlikely. They did not have long to wait.

AMERICAN OBJECTIVE	To defend the bridges at Trois-Ponts
FORCES	
American:	Company C, 51st Engineer Combat Battalion and elements 291st Engineer Combat Battalion (Major Robert B Yates); later 2nd Battalion (Lieutenant Colonel Benjamin H. Vandervoort), 505th Parachute Infantry Regiment
German:	Kampfgruppe Peiper; later III Battalion, SS Panzergrenadier Regiment 1 (SS-Captain Karl Böttcher), Kampfgruppe Hansen
RESULT	Trois-Ponts was held and the bridges destroyed
CASUALTIES	
American:	Approximately 50 killed and wounded
German:	Unknown
LOCATION	Trois-Ponts is 14 km southwest of Malmédy

Battle

At 1115, Kampfgruppe Peiper's vanguard of nineteen Panthers rounded the curve east of Hotel Lifrange. The American gun crew fired only one shot before a 75-mm tank shell destroyed the gun and killed four of its crew. The survivors fled. Nevertheless, that one shot disabled the lead tank that temporarily blocked the highway and signaled the engineers that the Germans were near. Within earshot of Peiper, the engineers blew the Amblève and northern Salm bridges. The southern Salm bridge was blown some hours later when a group of panzers threatened to cross.

German tanks continued through the two rail tunnels. Although the Amblève was not a wide or deep river and could be easily crossed by infantry, its steep banks were insurmountable to tanks and other vehicles. Peiper's only alternative was to turn north towards La Gleize. However, he was now enmeshed in the narrow Amblève valley. The twisting roadway and narrow passages between stone houses slowed his advance. Moreover, a shortage of gasoline forced him to conserve.

Trois-Ponts remained under threat from German positions on the hillside east of the train station. From 17 to 20 December, only the 51st Engineer Combat Battalion led by Major Yates manned its defenses. To give the Germans the impression that the town was held by a much larger force, Yates simulated the arrival of reinforcements by ordering his few trucks to leave town with their lights out and return with lights on. He ordered one truck to drive repeatedly through town dragging chains to simulate the sounds of a tank. The feign worked and the German troops delayed their attack.[27]

The 82nd Airborne Division left its bivouac at the French military barracks

---

27 Major Robert Yates was captured on 22 December doing reconnaissance along highway N4 southeast of Marche. Captain Scheuber and others escaped on foot, but Yates could not run due to

Chapter Three

Kampfgruppe Peiper 105

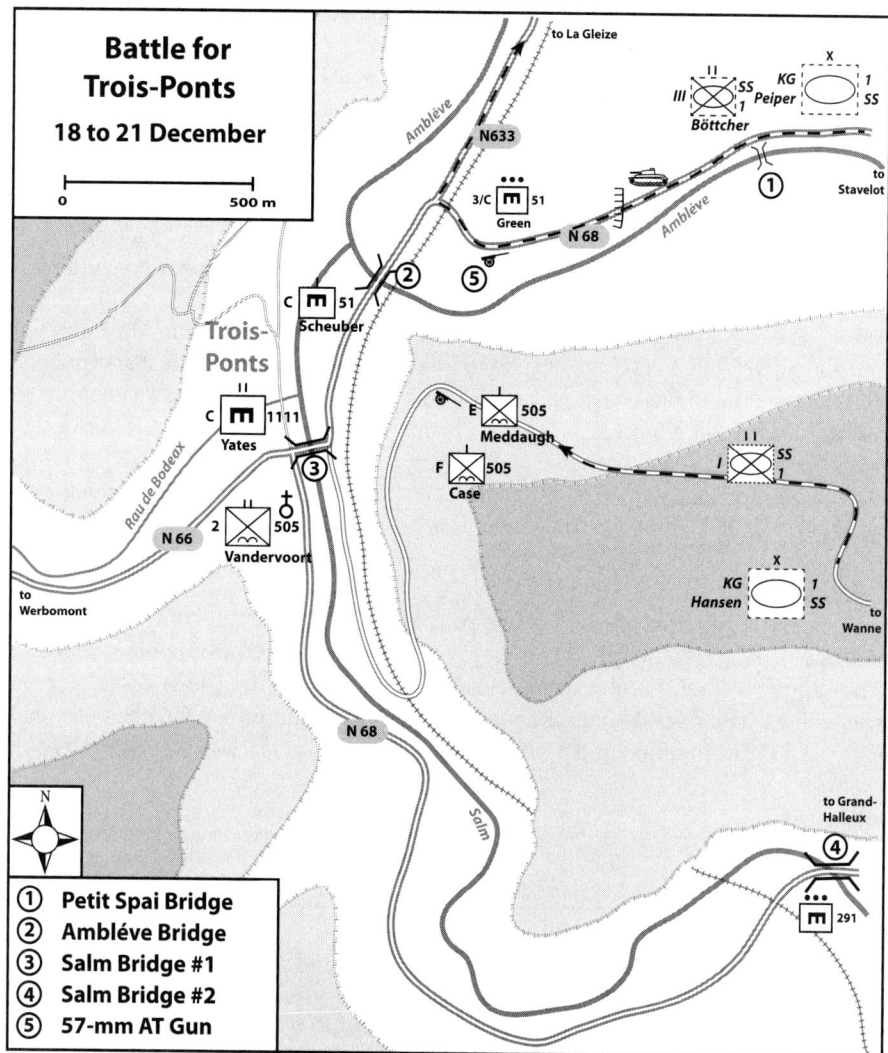

of Suippes. Although originally directed to Bastogne, the destination changed en route to Werbomont. On the morning of 19 December, 505th Parachute Infantry Regiment, commanded by Colonel William E Ekman, continued east to take up positions along the Salm River. Colonel Vandervoort's 2nd Battalion took up positions around Trois-Ponts. Little did the paratroopers know that Kampfgruppe Hansen was only four kilometers from their front line in Wanne.

Kampfgruppe Hansen struggled against muddy roads to move from near Recht toward Wanne in support of Peiper. On 21 December, while Kampfgruppe Peiper was trapped in La Gleize and after the bridge at Stavelot was destroyed,

---

a previous hospitalization for a leg injury. Yates escaped his guard two hours later by diving into a stream and swimming underwater amid a hail of small-arms fire. He was awarded a Silver Star.

Kampfgruppe Hansen moved out from Wanne to secure the east bank of the Salm River from Trois-Ponts to Grand Halleux and to use the remaining bridges to reinforce Peiper. Colonel Vandervoort sent Company E, commanded by Lieutenant William Meddaugh, to establish a blocking position on the only road on the hillside east of Trois-Ponts supported by Company F.

Armed with only bazookas, two 57-mm antitank guns, and the battalion's 81-mm mortar platoon, Lt Meddaugh's paratroopers held off SS-Captain Karl Böttcher's half-track-mounted panzergrenadiers and their supporting company of Jagdpanzer IVs for most of the day until casualties and increased pressure drove them down the hill and across the rail yard.

Protected by only combat engineers and the reduced and disorganized Company E, Headquarters Company, Trois-Ponts faced imminent capture. Paratroopers, however, occupied houses along the river and prevented the panzergrenadiers from crossing the open ground east of town. The temporarily repaired Salm River bridge south of town was blown for the second time by the 307th Airborne Engineer Battalion when panzergrenadiers attempted to flank its positions. The battle for Trois-Ponts was over. Kampfgruppe Peiper was beyond rescue.

Consequences

The destruction of the small highway bridge at Trois-Ponts completely altered the outcome of the battle. The main highway to the Meuse River was now denied to Kampfgruppe Peiper. Further delay to Peiper's advance allowed time for additional American units to rush to blunt the force of his advance. In effect, the engineers had guaranteed the destruction of the 1st SS Panzer Division *Leibstandarte Adolf Hitler*.

Battlefield Tour

> Leave Stavelot and continue for 4.5 km before turning into the side road where a small footbridge crosses the river. (50.377867, 5.88479)

Here in 1944, the **Petit Spai Bridge** crossed the Amblève and became the only avenue available to Kampfgruppe Hansen in its efforts to reinforce Peiper. The bridge collapsed on 21 December under the weight of a Jagdpanzer IV. During the evening, foot soldiers crossed over the wreckage, but vehicles could not follow. Intense American artillery fire met attempts by German engineers to rebuild the bridge.

The site now bears a pedestrian bridge across the Amblève. A roadway on the opposite shore approaches to within 200 meters of the bridge, but it is not accessible by vehicle.

> Continue 600 m to parking area on the left. (50.376096, 5.876683)

In 1944 the curve held the Hotel Lifrange, the site of a 57-mm antitank gun left after the breakdown of the half-track pulling the gun during the passage of the 526th Armored Infantry Battalion.[28] The gun crew came under the temporary command of Lieutenant Richard Green, commander of 3rd Platoon, Company C, 51st Engineer Combat Battalion. Ordered to defend the road east of the rail tunnels, Lt Green disposed the troops around the hotel position while Privates First Class Lillard McCullom, Donald Hollenbeck, Dallas Buchanan, and James L Higgins manned the gun and anxiously awaited the approach of German armor. Two men manned a .50-caliber machine gun mounted upon a truck near the rail underpass.

Shortly before noon on 18 December, the first Panther rounded the curve 130 meters to the east and stopped at a daisy-chain of mines spanning the highway. While the American gun crew hesitated to confirm that the vehicle was German, the panzer fired four rounds, but all missed. When the lead panzer exposed its flank to the gunners, they accurately fired one round striking the tank, which started smoking. The tank fired its 75-mm gun striking the base of the gun and killing the four-man crew.[29] With the antitank gun destroyed, the bridge blown, and with no reason for delay, the remaining engineers piled into the truck and repaired half-track to escape to Stoumont.

> Pass through the double railway tunnels and turn left toward Manhay (N68) after exiting the second tunnel; proceed 180 m to the nondescript highway bridge that crosses the Amblève River. (50.375613, 5.873511)

Trois-Ponts
Royal Syndicat d'Initiative de Trois-Ponts
Place Communale 1 Tel: +32 (0)80 68 40 45
4980 Trois-Ponts, Belgium

A 1944 wood bridge replaced the original stone Amblève River bridge destroyed by the Belgian Army during General Erwin Rommel's advance in 1940. A memorial on the left side of the highway remembers twenty civilian victims of the battle, many of whom were executed by SS troops during the fighting that raged against Kampfgruppe Hansen. The list of names includes one thirteen-year-old victim.

A small plaque on the bridge abutment to the left is dedicated to **Company C, 51st Engineer Combat Battalion** and states, 'The engineers at Trois-Ponts stopped elements of the German Sixth Panzer Army from breaking out to the Meuse River until reinforced by the 82nd Airborne Division.'[30] The high railway bridge behind the memorial existed in 1944 but was unusable by armored vehicles.

---

28 Controversy continues over the exact location of the antitank gun. Writers have placed it behind the two rail tunnels – highly unlikely because no direct fire could be placed from there onto approaching armor. Others have suggested the curve farther to the east. In any case, the results of the brief engagement remain the same.

29 Two of the gunners, Privates James Higgins and Donald Hollenbeck, are buried in Henri-Chapelle American Cemetery, Henri-Chapelle, Belgium.

30 Captain Samuel Scheuber was awarded a Silver Star. He survived the war. The 51st Engineer Combat Battalion was awarded a Presidential Unit Citation.

> Continue 400 m into Trois-Ponts and follow the curve of highway N68 to the right. Park at a convenient location near the bridge. (50.37229, 5.871648)

The **Salm River bridge** hides behind parked cars and between buildings. However, the rapidly flowing waters and steep bank made it an effective tank barrier. Captain Sam Scheuber's men blew this bridge 30 minutes after the Amblève River bridge was destroyed. The red brick building around the curve at 12 rue du Centre still displays its wartime bullet holes from machine-gun fire incurred during the battle. (50.372447, 5.871942)

> From the Salm River bridge, continue west on highway N66 (rue du Centre) for only 120 m. Turn left on rue des Hézalles and continue 75 m into place Communale in front of the church. (50.371416, 5.870486)

The park across the street from the church contains two prominent memorials to American airborne forces. A plaque commemorates the four men of the **80th Airborne Antiaircraft Battalion** who manned one of the 57-mm antitank guns guarding the approach through Noupré. All were killed when they refused to abandon their gun and continued firing upon the advancing German armor.[31]

The second memorial, written in French only, honors the entire **505th Parachute Infantry Regiment** for resisting a much stronger and better equipped enemy in defense of the town.

> Leave the place Communale to the northeast; turn left onto highway N62. After 40 m, continue straight onto rue des Villas. After 200 m, bear slight left onto Vieux Chemin de Brume and continue to the bunker on the left. (50.374162, 5.870402)

Between 1933 and 1936, the Belgian Army constructed between 332 and 375 shelters and small forts to protect the fortified zone of Liège against possible German invasion. Twenty-four such structures arose in area villages and valleys. They typically held a machine gun manned by four soldiers within reinforced concrete walls 40 to 60 centimeters thick.

The **Belgian Army bunker** in Trois-Ponts is a particularly fine example whose wooden staircase allows visitors to view the roof of the structure. The rear is built into the side of the hill and a small trench near the roof, which has been filled for the safety of visitors, provided the only access. The machine gun embrasure is aimed directly down the street toward highway N66 immediately west of the Salm River bridge.

---

31 The gun was manned by 1st Lieutenant Jake L Wertich, Corporal Stokes Taylor, Privates First Class Harry Robison and Gordon S Smithal. Lt Wertlich and Cpl Taylor were both awarded Distinguished Service Crosses for their gallant stand. Lt Wertich is buried in Henri-Chapelle American Cemetery, Henri-Chapelle, Belgium.

Other Points of Interest near Stavelot and Trois-Ponts

Parfondruy

Two memorials to civilians executed by German forces stand in Parfondruy outside of Stavelot. A Belgian flag along highway N68 locates a gray plaque on broken red granite slab marking the location where **38 of the 167 Civilian Victims** of Stavelot callously massacred by the SS in December 1944.
Location: 1.7 km southwest of Stavelot on highway N68. (50.38729, 5.921)
    Immediately to the left of the **chapel of Ste Lucie**, a gray stone mounted upon a free standing fieldstone wall is dedicated to the Civilian Martyrs of 19 December 1944 and bears the names of 26 individuals ranging in age from 9 months to 86 years.
Location: On Chemin de Parfondruy in Parfondruy. (50.38972, 5.91443)

Wanne

    A simple black and white placard presents a most unusual monument erected by the **517th Parachute Infantry Regiment**, which fought in this area against Kampfgruppe Hansen. Erected in 1988, the monument honors 'those brave Belgians who fought with us in the Ardennes during the Battle of the Bulge and those faithful Belgians who keep the memories of our joint fight for freedom and our friendship alive.'
Location: 6 km southeast of Trois-Ponts in the center of Wanne. (50.355412, 5.920469)

From the Salm River bridge in Trois-Ponts, proceed north toward La Gleize / Aywaille (N68, then N633) and follow for 7.1 km into La Gleize; turn left (rue de l'Église) and park in the small square behind the church. (50.410159, 5.84569)

Amblève Valley Trap
18 to 24 December 1944

At 1145 on 17 December, US First Army headquarters ordered Major General Leland Hobbs to move his 30th Infantry Division south to screen Spa from Peiper and to block the kampfgruppe from Liège — the German Army's assumed objective. The division was an experienced unit having fought in Normandy — especially distinguishing itself during the defense of Mortain, France during the German Operation LÜTTICH. The unit was motorized, and its leading 119th Infantry Regiment arrived in Eupen within twelve hours.

The road network west of Trois-Ponts presented two possible routes toward Liège. One followed the northern bank of the Amblève River through Stoumont and Remouchamps, the second south of the river through Werbomont and Aywaille. General Hobbs sent Colonel Edwin M Sutherland's 119th Infantry Regiment to block the north route while 82nd Airborne Division made for Trois-Ponts via the southern route.

On 19 December, 1st Battalion, 117th Infantry Regiment, US 30th Infantry Division advanced down the highway from Spa and recaptured Stavelot cutting

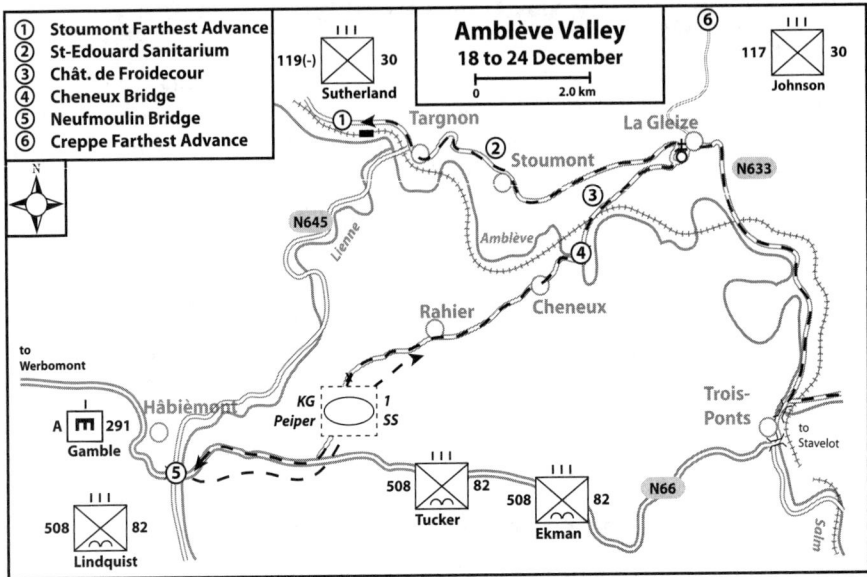

Peiper's supply line. The next day, Combat Command B (CCB) from 3rd Armored Division arrived from the north while units of the 82nd Airborne reached Werbomont and proceeded toward the Amblève valley at Trois-Ponts. Kampfgruppe Peiper was trapped.

AMERICAN OBJECTIVE	To halt Kampfgruppe Peiper's advance toward the Meuse River
FORCES	
American:	119th Infantry Regiment (Colonel Edwin M Sutherland), 30th Infantry Division and CCB (Brigadier General Truman E Boudinot), 3rd Armored Division
German:	Kampfgruppe Peiper (SS-Lieutenant Colonel Joachim Peiper)
RESULT	The German battle group was destroyed
CASUALTIES	
American:	30th Infantry Division: 65 killed, 260 wounded, and 422 missing
German:	5,000 killed, wounded, or missing
LOCATION	La Gleize is 20 km west of Malmédy

Battle

Kampfgruppe Peiper's next opportunity to cross the Amblève was a small rural road that led to a bridge near the village of Cheneux. However, the twists and turns of the road following along the rapidly flowing river frequently brought the tanks almost back upon themselves. Villages slowed the tanks' movements while they maneuvered between stone houses shouldering the roadway.

Chapter Three

Peiper passed through La Gleize and turned southwest, crossed the undefended Cheneux bridge, and continued on to regain the main east-west highway near Chaveheid. He had passed Trois-Ponts, but the effort had cost him an entire day. Peiper need to cross the Lienne Creek to reach flat 'tank country' only 16 kilometers to the west, but American troops were swarming into the area.

Like the bridges at Trois-Ponts, American engineers blew the Neufmoulin Bridge over the Lienne when Peiper's lead unit approached. Kampfgruppe Peiper, now cut off from reinforcements and running low on fuel for its gas-guzzling tanks, bivouacked that night between La Gleize and Stoumont on the grounds of Château Froidecour. The soldiers of Kampfgruppe Peiper became hunted men, trapped between the arriving 30th Infantry Division from the north and the 82nd Airborne Division from the south and west.

The next morning (19 December) Peiper tried to fight his way out of the valley by moving west from La Gleize through Stoumont, a less desirable but acceptable route. In the late afternoon haze and river fog, his lead panzers encountered an American tank that ambushed and destroyed two of the first three Panthers to round a bend in the road near a train stop named Stoumont Station. A tank destroyer knocked out a third Panther, effectively blocking the narrow passage.

By the time of Peiper's departure, many of La Gleize's buildings were reduced to roofless shells. Twenty-five abandoned German tanks and fifty-three half-tracks littered the small village's narrow streets and courtyards, left in the waking of the withdrawing Germans amid the structures where they had hidden.

Battlefield Tour

La Gleize has been rebuilt much to its 1944 appearance and size. Sturdy stone buildings still encroach upon its narrow roadways. After the battle, the short rue de l'Église was lined with four abandoned Panthers and an equal number of abandoned halftracks. The well-preserved **King Tiger (PzKpfw VI) #213**, one of six abandoned by the kampfgruppe, stands in the small square behind the church. During the battlefield clean up, this tank, once commanded by SS-1st Lieutenant Wilhelm Dollinger, was to be towed away for scrap. A few bottles of cognac supplied by a local resident convinced the salvagers to leave it, and the tank remains the only one to survive the salvager's torch. Its enormous bulk and nearly impenetrable 185-mm-thick armored turret still inspire amazement. This fearsome machine is the symbol of the museum, the village of La Gleize, and the Battle of the Bulge. (50.410137, 5.846177)

Behind the tank, a rough stone bears a plaque commemorating the forty million victims of the world war. (50.410069, 5.846144)

Musée Décembre 1944
Rue de l'Église, 7b   B-4987 La Gleize, Belgium
Tel: +32(0)80 78 51 91
Web: http://www.december44.com/en/info.htm

In 2013 new owners redesigned and expanded the museum. The various rooms tell the story of the local battle with information placards bearing photographs and information. The tour starts by going upstairs, where the initial rooms present predominantly German equipment before returning downstairs to American-themed exhibits. Display cases between the large placards contain only a few of the artifacts that once were the pride of the old museum. The artifacts are attractively and artistically presented but not carefully labeled — a serious flaw for a museum. A 30-minute film, in four languages using headsets, presents probably the most complete exposition of original wartime film currently available.

Plaques inside and outside the building commemorate the **505th Regimental Combat Team, 465th Parachute Field Artillery Battalion, 307th Engineer Combat Battalion, 80th Airborne Antiaircraft Battalion, 740th Tank Battalion**, and the **3rd Armored Division**. The quality of the materials justifies this as the best museum in this sector of the battlefield.

Open daily 1 March through 21 November from 10:00 to 18:00 and weekends and holidays during the remainder of the year. Fee. (50.41002, 5.846028)

> From the rear of the church, follow the rue de l'Église west and southwest for 2.7 km, leaving La Gleize toward Cheneux. Stop at the bridge over the Amblève River. (50.397999, 5.822454)

Although Peiper's men seized the undefended **Cheneux bridge**, an American reconnaissance plane spotted the first vehicles crossing the river. The skies cleared sufficiently to allow sixteen American P-47 Thunderbolts from the IX Tactical Air Command to locate and attack the German column fully exposed in the broad, open valley. The panzer crews and panzergrenadiers crawled under the armored vehicles while two *Wirbelwind* [32] fired their four-barreled guns in almost helpless defense. Three Panthers and seven other vehicles were destroyed. After dispersing into the woods, the panzers waited for darkness before continuing. Peiper, finally discovered by units in contact with American commanders, had lost the element of surprise.

> Proceed for 280 m to the bunker hidden among the vegetation on the left. (50.39606, 5.819664)

A **Belgian Army bunker**, whose gun embrasure faces directly towards the bridge crossing, was unmanned during the encounter. Peiper sheltered in the bunker during the American air attack where he was joined by SS-Major Knittel. After a discussion of the situation, Peiper sent Knittel to rejoin his kampfgruppe with instructions to reopen the route through Stavelot.

The first of a series of five informational panels, each in French, German, English, and Dutch, stands beside the bunker. The series, titled '*La Bataille de Cheneux, du 18 au 25 Décembre 44,*' describes the battle for that village and the battle's consequences for the civilian population. This panel presents a well-drawn artist's rendition of the bombing of the German convoy by American fighters. A

---

32 *Wirbelwind* or *Flakpanzer* IV: an armored weapon mounting four 20-mm antiaircraft guns upon the chassis of a PzKpfw IV.

Panther tank was brought to a standstill beside the **Dumont house** visible up the hill and across the road. The accidental bombing destroyed a section of the house where Maria Goffinet and Jules Dumont died while they were baking bread in the cellar. The destruction of the tank considerably slowed Peiper's column. The sign bears a small map specifying locations of the other signs in this series.

> Continue on the rural road for 6.7 km through Cheneux and Rahier to the intersection with the Trois-Ponts–Werbomont Road (N66). The tour will return to Cheneux later. Turn right toward Werbomont (N66) and proceed 2.6 km to the small highway bridge. Cross the bridge and park at the memorial on the left. (50.367279, 5.724076)

Near nightfall on 18 December, the first of Peiper's tanks approached a curve east of the Neufmoulin Bridge over the Lienne Creek. The hastily assembled headquarters of the 82nd Airborne Division lay only one mile ahead. However, once again, Colonel Pergrin's engineers were on the spot.[33] A 12-man platoon from Company A, 291st Engineer Combat Battalion, commanded by Lieutenant Alvin Edelstein, had orders to blow the bridge upon the approach of enemy troops. Staff Sergeant Edwin Pigg had already planted the explosives and wired the detonator.

At that time of year, the vegetation along the river was without leaves, so the American engineers could see the approaching vehicles 200 meters up the inclined road. At 1700, while the sun set on a cloudy winter's afternoon, a Panther tank[34] came around the curve in the highway 200 meters to the east firing its 75-mm main gun at the bridge defenders. The engineers dove for cover in every direction. Corporal Fred Chapin grabbed the detonator, which was left out in the open, and looked around for Lt Edelstein, who waved his arms frantically that Chapin interpreted as the signal to fire the explosives. Chapin twisted the key and detonated 2500 pounds of TNT. After a bright flash, the timber-trestle bridge collapsed into the river, and the kampfgruppe's advance was stopped. Peiper, who was close behind the lead vehicles, was observed to have pounded his knee and say 'Those damned engineers!' Peiper came to the river personally but observed that fording the stream near the bridge was not possible because the approach was too marshy for his heavy armor.[35]

The monument marks the location of the old Neufmoulin Bridge and the asphalt approaches on both sides of the river are remnants of the old highway. The inscription commemorates the '**291st Combat Engineer Battalion, 1111th Combat Engineer Group**, who stopped the advance of the tanks of the 1st SS Panzer Division on 18 December 1944.'

---

33   Colonel Pergrin's 291st Engineer Combat Battalion received a Presidential Unit Citation, and he personally received Belgian and French Croix de Guerre and Silver and Bronze Stars. He survived the war to become Vice-President of the Pennsylvania Railroad and raise five children. He died in 2012 at age 94.

34   Some sources state that it was a King Tiger tank hurriedly moved to the front of the column earlier that day.

35   Fred Chapin never received recognition for his feat, but he survived the war, dying in 1997 at age 77. He is buried in Riverside, California. Lieutenant Alvin Edelstein died in 1999 at age 82 and is buried in Fort Snelling National Cemetery, Minneapolis, Minnesota.

> Proceed 280 m toward Werbomont (N66) across the intersection with highway N645 to the white building on the right. (50.368188, 5.720346)

The rural road (now N645) that runs west of Lienne Creek would have provided German armor with a path around the destroyed Neufmoulin Bridge. Peiper, after returning to Rahier, sent two reconnaissance teams composed of 10th and 11th Companies, SS Panzergrenadier Regiment 2 to reconnoiter bridges capable of carrying the heavy King Tiger tanks. The 10th Company crossed the Lienne Creek over a small bridge to the north and approached Habiémont on the west side of the creek. However, traveling at night without lights, the group's half-tracks were unaware of the arrival at Habiémont of Captain Edward Arn's Company F, 2nd Battalion, 119th Infantry Regiment supported by four M10s from 823rd Tank Destroyer Battalion. The new troops quickly established defenses on the downhill slope from Werbomont. One M10 put three rounds into the leading German half-track setting it aflame. Captain Edward Arn's men, who had lined both sides of the road, fired on the remaining four half-tracks now illuminated by the burning vehicle. A second vehicle was knocked out and a third abandoned. Bazooka fire from the second floor window of the house stopped the remaining two half-tracks that managed a desperate U-turn to escape the trap. The engagement left only a handful of survivors.

The white house, used as a platoon station by Company F, bears a bronze plaque mounted toward its west end stating:

On December 18, 1944, from this house PFC Mason Armstrong, bazooka man of F Company, 119th Regiment, 30th US Division knocked out two German half tracks of SS Kampfgruppe Peiper and so stopped the forward spearhead of Hitler's great attack upon Antwerp. For this heroic action he was awarded the DSC [Distinguished Service Cross].

Immediately east of the white building, a cement **Belgian Army pillbox** guarded the Neufmoulin Bridge from German invasion. Corporal Chapin sheltered in the concrete structure when he energized the detonator that brought down the Neufmoulin Bridge.

The next morning Captain Arn was startled when a single jeep arrived carrying only a driver and Major General James Gavin, commander of the 82nd Airborne Division. General Gavin 'requested' the astonished captain's permission to scout ahead in preparation for moving troops into the area. Arn sheepishly agreed.[36]

A **Farthest Advance Stone** sits 40 meters farther up the road on the right marking the final advance of Kampfgruppe Peiper toward Werbomont. (50.368172, 5.719864)

---

36 Captain Edward Arn survived the war to write a book about his experiences titled '*Arn's War*.' He died in 2006 at age 97.

Side Trip: 82nd Airborne Division Park

> Continue toward Werbomont / Huy (N66) for 4.3 km.
> A gray stone memorial set into an alcove on the right side of the highway below the top of the hill is inscribed 'in recognition of the **heroes of the RAF** killed here 13 August 1944.' (50.379943, 5.688635)
> Continue to the plateau and stop at the small park on the right. (50.379931, 5.686564)
> The 82nd Airborne Division was one of the few reserve units available to Eisenhower when the German offensive struck the Ardennes. Committed on 17 December, the division left its bivouac area near Rheims, France, and arrived at Werbomont on 19 December.
> The park commemorates the arrival of the **US 82nd Airborne** Division and its subsequent actions in clearing Cheneux and the southern banks of the Amblève of the enemy. An inscribed stone set upon a star-shaped platform notes the event and asks that 'their sacrifice not be in vain.' Behind the stone is a **British 25-pounder** refitted with a 105-mm barrel.
> Reverse direction and return to Habiémont. Total distance: 8.8 km round trip

> Turn north toward Stoumont (N645) and continue 1.3 km to the side road on the right. Turn right and proceed 120 m to the bridge. (50.376155, 5.733126)

The 11th SS Panzergrenadier Company crossed the Lienne at this point in its search for a route around the destroyed Neufmoulin Bridge, but this 1944 stone bridge was not wide or strong enough to support Peiper's heavy panzers.

> Return to highway N645 and turn right. Continue 2.6 km to the second Lienne Creek bridge. (50.387933, 5.758145)

The 10th SS Panzergrenadier Company also searched for, and found, this Lienne Creek crossing before it turned south toward Habiémont and encountered Captain Arn's ambush.

> At the junction 60 m ahead, turn toward Xhierfomont and follow through Rahier toward Cheneux for 4.1 km. Park on the farm road on the left shortly after exiting the forest. (50.393624, 5.807588)

Battle of Cheneux
20 to 21 December 1944

Lieutenant Colonel Willard Harrison's 1st Battalion, 504th Parachute Infantry Regiment was ordered to block Peiper from moving south and to interdict any relief effort from the Trois-Ponts area. Company A moved to Brume west of Trois-Ponts and later relieved the 291st Engineer Combat Battalion troops there. Companies B and C were ordered to take Cheneux.

After the destruction of the Neufmoulin Bridge, Peiper left the reduced 11th

Company and SS Panzergrenadier Regiment 2 reinforced by the 84th Flak Assault Battalion with fourteen self-propelled 20-mm guns in Cheneux to guard his flank and the bridge.

AMERICAN OBJECTIVE	To capture Cheneux and cut possible German escape routes to the south and southeast
FORCES	
American:	1st Battalion (Lieutenant Colonel Willard E Harrison), 504th Parachute Infantry Regiment
German:	11th Company, SS Panzergrenadier Regiment 2 (SS-1st Lieutenant Heinz Tomhardt) and 84th Armored Flak Battalion (Major von Sacken)
RESULT	The town was taken.
CASUALTIES	
American:	23 killed and 202 wounded
German:	Precise number unknown, but five companies were virtually wiped out; fourteen Flak wagons, six half-tracks, and four 105-mm howitzers were destroyed
LOCATION	Cheneux is 25 km west of Malmédy

Battle

On 20 December, Companies B and C approached Cheneux in columns across open fields south of the village on either side of the road from Rahier. Heavy mist blinded American artillery, rendering it incapable to provide support. While the troops made first contact with a machine-gun outpost 500 meters outside of Rahier, German troops moved three half-tracks armed with single 20-mm guns, one half-track with an 80-mm mortar, and a towed 105-mm howitzer to positions along the road in front of the town. Their positions remained undetected until the advancing paratroopers crested the hill and exited the forest. Company B was on the road 500 meters from the village when the flak guns opened up. The 20-mm shells devastated the exposed paratroopers whose only defense was a quick dive into roadside ditches. A deep ravine prevented flanking movement to the right, and MG-42 machine-gun and 20-mm flak-cannon fire met attempts to flank the German guns on the left.

As night fell, Company C came forward in support, positioning the two companies at the forest's edge: Company B to the south of the road and Company C to the north. At 1930, the two companies fixed bayonets and began a nighttime attack across the fields. Slowed by barbed wire fences that crossed the fields every 20 or 30 meters and exposed to German machine-gun fire, the paratroopers suffered heavy losses but continued the charge across the open terrain. Hand-to-hand combat continued all night while the troopers gained a foothold in the village. Losses had so weakened the force that it was unable to push the panzergrenadiers out.[37]

---

37 During this fighting, Private First Class Daniel Del Grippo, although wounded, attacked and killed the crew of a self-propelled gun. Company B's Staff Sergeant William Walsh, also wounded,

Chapter Three   Kampfgruppe Peiper   117

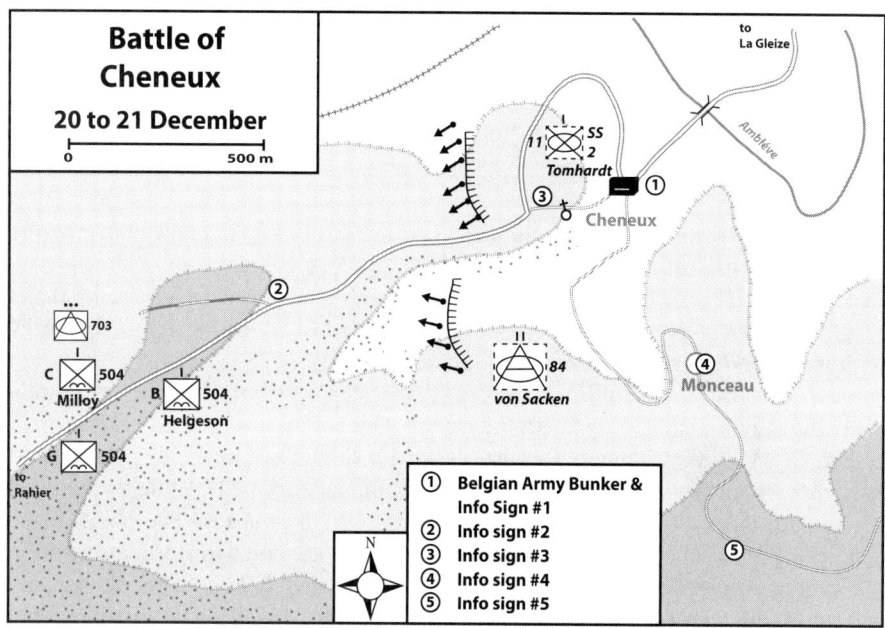

Reinforced by the 3rd Battalion's Company G, the attack resumed at 0200 but was met with a wall of machine-gun and 20-mm cannon fire. At 0745, after a 30-minute artillery barrage, the SS troops counterattacked, but the panzergrenadiers fell to fire from Colonel Harrison's 81-mm mortars. At 1700, an attached platoon of 703rd Tank Destroyer Battalion resumed the attack by systematically firing into each building in Cheneux. The paratroopers, strengthened by Companies H and I of 3rd Battalion attacking from the south, finally cleared the village.[38] About that time, Peiper ordered a consolidation of forces about La Gleize. The surviving German troops, after leaving their vehicles and heavy guns behind, withdrew by fording the Amblève.

Battlefield Tour

The paratroopers' approached Cheneux across the open terrain on both sides of the road. The second of the five '**La Bataille de Cheneux**' information panels portrays the civilians leaving the village after the battle carrying a few bundles of personal possessions while American troops advance in the opposite direction. The inhabitants of nearby Monceau and Beauloup passed through Cheneux on 25 December to discover the aftermath of the battle. When the weary civilians drew even with the last houses of the village on the road, they found the bodies of German and American troops killed during the hand-to-hand fighting. Two men, Lucien Piron and Honoré Quoilin, were compelled to move the bodies lying on the road to clear the way. The Bouchet House, mentioned on the panel, stands ahead on the right where the

---

saved his platoon from a flak gun when he rushed the position and eliminated it with a grenade. Both men were awarded the Distinguished Service Cross.

38 Companies B and C, 504th Parachute Infantry Regiment and the attached 1st Platoon, Company C, 307th Airborne Engineer Battalion received a Presidential Unit Citation.

Americans had set up a command post in the chicken coop next to the house during the fighting.

> Continue 700 m into Cheneux to the small monument on the right. (50.395605, 5.816381)

The old stone houses in the center of the farming community have hardly changed since the battle and present an image of 1944. A fieldstone with a plaque displaying the insignia of the All American (AA) Division stands beside the road and recognizes the bravery of the men of **Companies B and C, 504th Parachute Infantry Regiment, 82nd Airborne Division** in capturing the village.

The third '**La Bataille de Cheneux**' panel stands to the left toward the church. The painting portrays fighting about the church. German troops ordered civilians into the church where they sheltered in the chapel for three days in the coldest days of December without food or heat while deadly fighting raged outside. Bullets penetrated the building through the windows and whistled over their heads. The noise of the fighting was infernal. The 82nd Airborne paratroopers attempted to storm the position by climbing the embankment located to the rear of the church, only to be immediately targeted by German soldiers posted behind the graveyard walls. The fighting raged hand-to-hand with knives and pistols.

Locate the final two 'La Bataille de Cheneux' panels in Monceau and Beauloup by driving past the church and following the roadway. The Monceau panel lies in the center of the village (approximately 50.392380, 5.822014) and the Beauloup panel stands at the end of the paved road. (50.387952, 5.823185) Both panels speak to the sufferings of the civilian population. Innocent victims of the fighting, they were displaced from their homes, their livestock slaughtered, and possessions burned or looted. The Beauloup site is especially attractive by virtue of views across the Amblève Valley to Stoumont and La Gleize.

> Follow the road back over the Cheneux bridge and, after 1.6 km, turn left onto a narrow road. After 550 m, observe a farmhouse visible among the trees on the left. (50.409172, 5.826625)

The newly constructed forest home was originally a stone forester's lodge on the grounds of the Château de Froidcoeur used by Peiper as his command post during the battle for Stoumont.

> Continue another 240 m to highway N633. Turn left and proceed 5.5 km to Stoumont Station on the left. (50.417467, 5.77029)

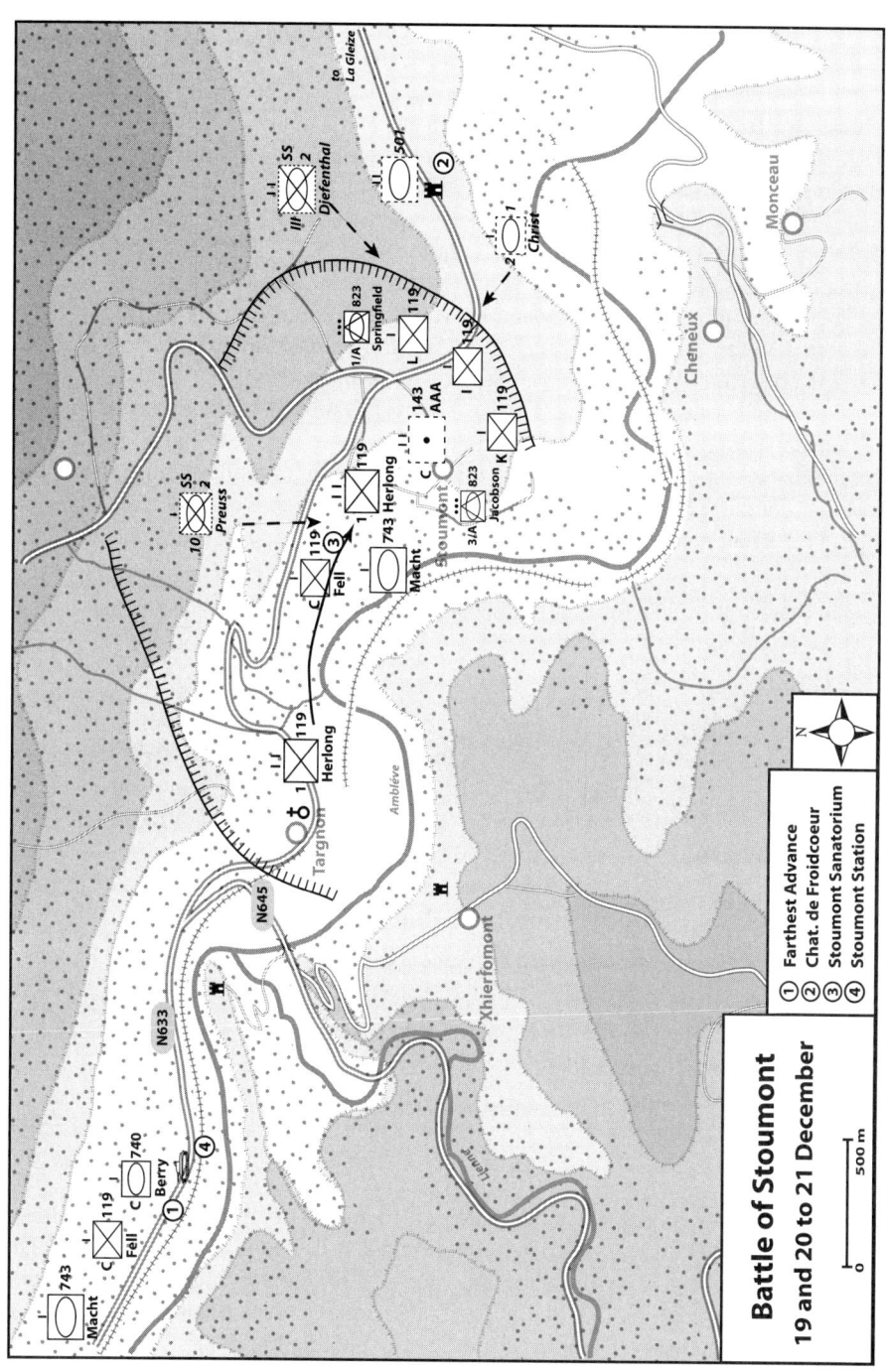

Battle for Stoumont
19 December 1944

As Peiper's armored units bivouacked in the fields between Stoumont and La Gleize, 3rd Battalion, 119th Infantry Regiment, 30th Infantry Division commanded by Lieutenant Colonel Roy G Fitzgerald Jr arrived from the west. Eight towed guns of Company A, 823rd Tank Destroyer Battalion took up firing positions covering the open fields along the road from La Gleize. Two powerful 90-mm antiaircraft guns of Battery C, 143rd Antiaircraft Artillery Battalion supported a roadblock by Company I near a farmhouse east of town. Company K and four of the tank destroyers protected the south side of Stoumont. Company L, with three 57-mm antitank guns, covered to the north. As ten Shermans of the 743rd Tank Battalion promised to arrive at dawn, German armor faced the task of staving off American artillery.

Peiper's new target was Chevron on the west bank of the Lienne Creek that he hoped to achieve by crossing the Amblève at a viable ford near Targnon. However, to use this crossing, Peiper had to push the Americans out of artillery range to the west past the Stoumont Station train depot. There the highway moved away from the river to provide a flat, marshy area on which the small rail yard and station stood.

GERMAN OBJECTIVE	To ford the Amblève River west of Targnon
FORCES	
American:	1st and 3rd Battalions, 119th Infantry Regiment (Colonel Edward M Sutherland) and attached 740th (Lieutenant Colonel George K Rubel) and 743rd (Lieutenant Colonel William D Duncan)Tank Battalions
German:	3rd Battalion (SS-Major Josef Diefenthal), SS Panzergrenadier Regiment 2 and 2nd Company (SS- Captain Friedrich Christ), SS Panzer Regiment 1
RESULT	The westward movement of Kampfgruppe Peiper was halted
CASUALTIES	
American:	8 killed, 30 wounded, 60 missing, and 143 taken prisoner
German:	Unknown
LOCATION	Stoumont Station is 27 km west of Malmédy

Battle

At 0830 on 19 December, Peiper attempted to escape from La Gleize by attacking west through Colonel Fitzgerald's 3rd Battalion at Stoumont. The morning mist rising from the river hid much of the approaching panzergrenadier battalion commanded by SS-Major Josef Diefenthal,[39] the remaining company of fallschirmjägers, and seven Panthers from SS-Captain Friedrich Christ's 2nd Company.

---

[39] SS-Major Josef Diefenthal was sentenced for war crimes at the Dachau Trails. After release from prison in 1956, he worked in a municipal tax office. He died in 2001 at age 85.

Chapter Three

Infantry at the roadblock knocked out two panzers with bazookas. One antiaircraft gun disabled a third before German fire set its ammunition exploding. The crew spiked the gun and fled. The second antiaircraft gun developed mechanical problems and never fired. The advancing panzers were hesitant — showing the fatigue of constant movement and battle for the past four days — but continued forward, rallied by threats from SS-Major Pötschke.

Two platoons of Sherman tanks from Company C, 743rd Tank Battalion under 1st Lieutenant Walter D Macht arrived while the roadblock defenses fell apart. German armor continued to work its way along the road against the slowly retreating infantry. After two hours of fighting, little remained of Company I, but it managed to destroy six more panzers. Lt Macht had not lost one tank while his men conducted a leap-frog fighting withdrawal. With the center pushed back, flanking Companies K and L also withdrew. Captain Donald Fell's Company C arrived and, along with Lt Macht's tanks, re-established a defense near Stoumont Station four kilometers west of Stoumont. They constituted the only force between Peiper and Liège. However, because Peiper's fuel situation was critical, he was forced to halt.

The 3rd Battalion, 119th Regiment was hit hard: Company I fielded only 24 men, companies K and L not many more. A company of fourteen tanks from 740th Tank Battalion, under Captain James D Berry, augmented by four self-propelled M36 tank destroyers mounting 90-mm guns, arrived to strengthen the pressured Americans. Much of Berry's equipment was recently cannibalized from a repair depot at Aywaille.

As Macht's tanks withdrew, now low on ammunition, Captain Berry's bastardized machines took their place at a curve west of Stoumont Station, where the road pinches between the river and the rising hillside. Companies A and B joined Company C while the three rifle companies established defensive positions on either side of the road. Lieutenant Colonel Robert Herlong, utilizing the newly arrived armor, organized his 1st Battalion for a tank-infantry attack on Stoumont. At 1600, amid the fog rolling up from the river, it ended Peiper's advance by knocking out three Panther tanks, thus blocking the road. His final hopes dashed, Peiper ordered a return to Stoumont.

His gasoline supply almost exhausted, Peiper radioed for permission to withdraw. Senior Colonel Mohnke refused and instead ordered Peiper to hold until the rest of the division broke through.

> Continue 450 m to a small stone marker on the left. (50.417265, 5.76418) Park on the forest road ahead on the right.

West of Stoumont Station, the valley is only 300-meters wide, with the road, river, and rail line running through it. In the rapidly darkening dusk, a Sherman tank commanded by 2nd Lieutenant Charles D Powers approached Stoumont. Hugging the left side of the roadway, Lt Powers spotted a grey shape approaching in the haze. It was a Panther. Powers fired, his shell penetrating the gun housing seam into the tank. Powers blasted a second shot against another Panther, but the shell bounced off the thick frontal armor. Powers, his gun now jammed, opened his hatch and from atop the turret signaled Staff Sergeant Charles Loopey to take on the Panther with his M36 Tank Destroyer. Sgt Loopey's first shell set the second Panther on fire. Powers's men worked frantically to clear their gun in time to fire on a third Panther. Their first shell hit the Panther's cannon barrel. Two more shells and the third Panther was also burning. The road out of Stoumont had been effectively blocked.[40]

This **Farthest Advance Stone** marks the location where the three panzers were disabled, thereby identifying the farthest advance of Kampfgruppe Peiper in its attempt to reach the Meuse at Huy. It fell 38 kilometers short.

> Reverse direction and 4.0 km east of the Farthest Advance stone stop in the driveway for Maison St-Edouard. (50.411689, 5.804984)

Battle for the Stoumont Sanatorium
20 to 21 December 1944

Over 250 patients and civilians sheltered in the St Edouard's Sanatorium for sick children and the elderly which lay roughly one kilometer northwest of Stoumont. During the attack of 19 December, German troops overcame a small American outpost established in the Catholic sanatorium. Staff and patients were herded into the large building's cellar while the Germans fortified the site overlooking the roadway into Stoumont.

The 119th Regiment facing Peiper was further strengthened by the attachment of CCB, 3rd Armored Division — a powerful force holding two medium tank battalions, a battalion of armored infantry, a battalion of self-propelled 105-mm howitzers, and a company of armored engineers.

AMERICAN OBJECTIVE		To capture the sanatorium building that dominated the road into Stoumont
FORCES		
	American:	1st and 2nd Battalions, 119th Infantry Regiment (Colonel Edward M Sutherland); elements of CCB (Brigadier General Truman E. Boudinot), 3rd Armored Division
	German:	10th Panzergrenadier Company (SS-Captain George Preuss), SS Panzergrenadier Regiment 2
RESULT		The building was captured.
CASUALTIES		
	American:	18 killed, 60 wounded, and 28 missing
	German:	Unknown
LOCATION		Stoumont is 23 km west of Malmédy

---

40 Both Powers and Lopez were awarded Silver Stars for their actions. Lt Powers was awarded his second Purple Heart for wounds received in battle on 25 February 1945 during a daylight assault on a German strongpoint when his tank was ignited by an 88-mm antitank gun. The wound ended his wartime service. Sergeant Lopez later received a battlefield commission to 2nd lieutenant. He also suffered a war-ending wound on 12 April 1945 when enemy shell fragments struck his face and neck.

Battle

In the swirling fog of the early hours of 20 December, an American counterattack on the sanatorium began. The 1st Battalion, 119th Regiment and a company from 740th Tank Battalion attacked from the northwest. However, progress was slowed by antitank mines set in the large S-curve east of Targnon covered by German infantry dug into the hillside. The American force advanced, nevertheless, to a point below the sanatorium. In the evening, hidden by fog rising from the river, American infantry climbed over the five-foot-high stone retaining wall at the base of the hill and successfully stormed the building. Companies B and C deployed north of the road and established command posts in the building.

While celebrating their liberation, a German tank and infantry counterattack from the hill above the sanatorium shocked the relieved inhabitants. Illuminated by flares, panzers knocked out two American tanks and a third fell to a panzerfaust. A horrific duel erupted inside the building, with men fighting from room to room and throwing hand grenades down hallways. German tanks fired into the building through its broken window frames. The German force retook most of the building, with the Americans holding isolated positions on the grounds. The annex building remained in American hands, and the two infantry companies established a line along the retaining wall.

Before dawn on 21 December, the Germans attacked down the road, setting three American tanks on fire with panzerfausts. The burning and exploding hulks effectively blocked the road. American tank destroyers brought fire onto the main building, blowing gaping holes in its façade. After noon, the two infantry battalions tried to overpower the sanatorium position after occupying two rooms, but the force was not strong enough to dislodge the panzergrenadiers. A Panther tank approached from the north and fired through the building at American troops.

Captain Berry's tankers and infantrymen from HQ Company finally built a ramp of felled trees and shell casings to maneuver their tanks over the stone-faced hedge line. Three Shermans and one tank destroyer moved around the right side of the building where Lt Powers knocked out the Panther that interdicted all movement in the vicinity of the building. The tanks then covered the escape of twenty-two infantrymen trapped in the building. The German troops withdrew during the night to consolidate around La Gleize.

Battlefield Tour

A row of shrubs blocks the view of the **Stoumont Sanatorium** from the highway. At the entrance driveway, however, a sign identifies the institution as the St-Rafael local school, although the St-Edouard home for the disabled remains on the grounds. A plaque on the wall of the old central building states the building once was the St-Edouard Sanatorium. Views from the grounds certify its dominant position overlooking the western and northern approaches to Stoumont and the Amblève valley.

Continue back toward La Gleize. Before re-entering the village, observe the **Château de Froidecour**, a 20th century replica of a medieval castle, in the vale on the right. The château grounds became the laager for Peiper's tanks after his defeat at Neufmoulin Bridge. Its cellars held the German casualty dressing station and 130 American PoWs.

The End of Peiper

On 21 December, after receiving word that contingents of 1st SS Panzer Division were attempting to break through to La Gleize, Peiper shortened his perimeter by abandoning Stoumont and Château de Froidecour. Peiper's much-reduced force spent the night in La Gleize's stone buildings. Mined approaches covered by direct fire from dug-in tanks and antitank guns defeated repeated American attempts to force passage into the village. By 22 December, American artillery had advanced to ring La Gleize and, with unobstructed views, pounded the village's buildings and the German troops sheltered in their deep cellars.

Surrounded and subjected to increasing American artillery fire using the 'pozit' fuse, Peiper's remaining force of approximately fifteen hundred men was desperately low on food, ammunition, and fuel. His armor, especially the King Tiger tanks, defeated American attempts to penetrate the village from west and north. From his headquarters in the stone building at #43 route d'Amblève, Peiper's repeated requests to Sixth Panzer Army for permission to attempt a breakout were denied. On 23 December, after the failure of Kampfgruppe Hansen[41] to secure a bridge over the Salm River, Peiper finally received approval to withdraw. Abandoning all heavy equipment, wounded, and prisoners, 770 men from Peiper's total force of almost six thousand left the village at 0200 on 24 December to make their way on foot through the woods to the south. The small force regained German lines the next day.

Aftermath

Kampfgruppe Peiper was disbanded on 26 December and the assigned units returned to their regiments. On 11 January 1945, Peiper was awarded Swords to his Knight's Cross of the Iron Cross for his performance during WACHT AM RHEIN.

Other Points of Interest

Creppe
A two-million gallon gasoline depot sat in the forest 9 kilometers north of La Gleize. Its presence was unknown to Peiper, but he sent a Panther along the road in search of the much-needed fuel. The German tank stopped short of the depot and returned to La Gleize. A **Farthest Advance Stone** marks the limit of Peiper's search for gasoline in this direction.
Location: 9 km north of La Gleize. (50.46334, 5.87209)

Targon
On its exterior side wall, the village church bears a simple plaque commemorating the liberation of Targnon by the **US 30th Infantry Division** on 20 December 1944.

---

41 SS-Major Max Hansen later fought in Hungary against the Soviet Red Army. After the war, Hansen ran a cleaning and laundry shop in the town of his birth where he died in 1990 at age 81.

Chapter Three

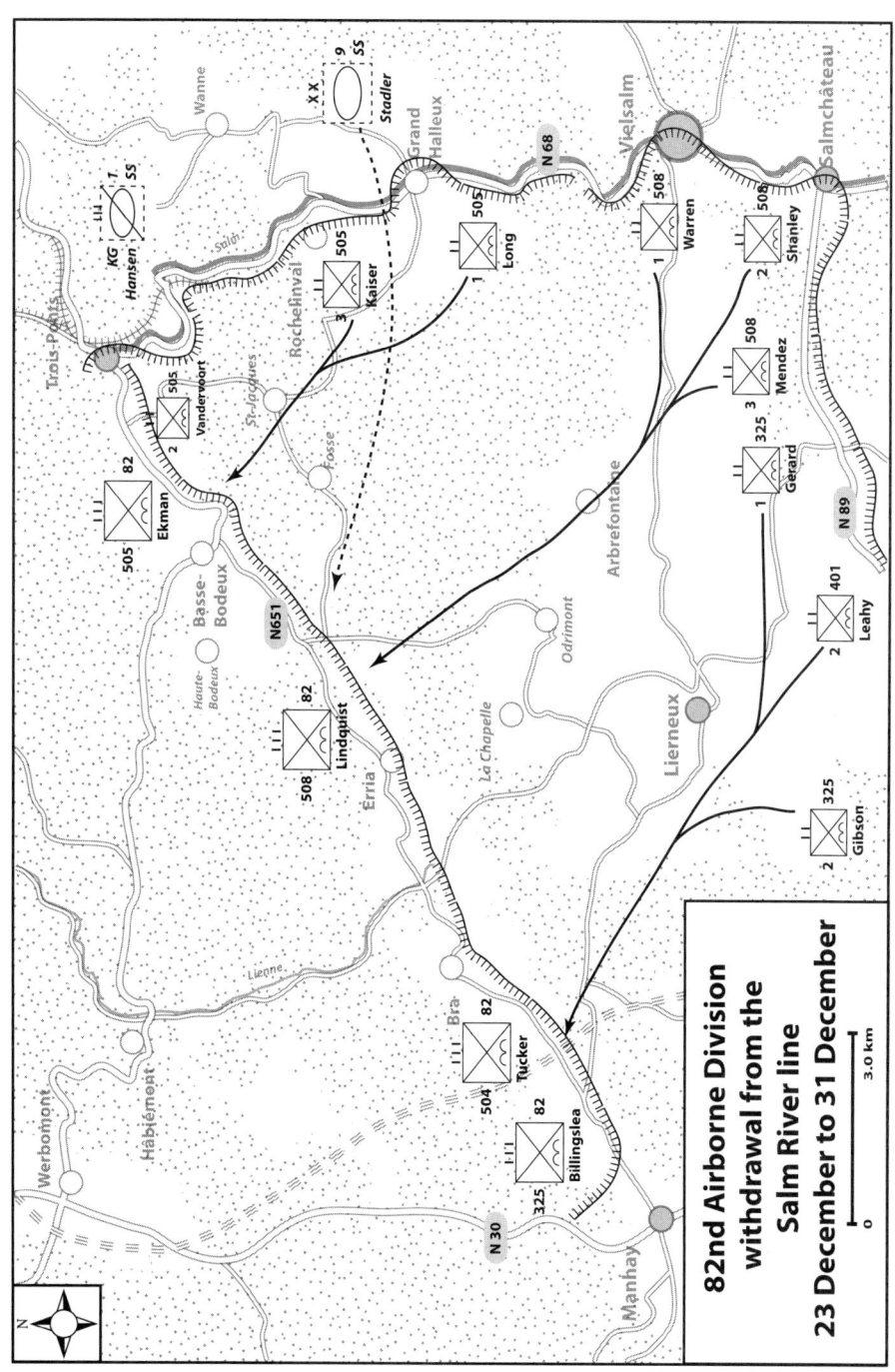

> Location: 6 km west of La Gleize on highway N633. (50.41223, 5.78303)

This completes the Kampfgruppe Peiper tour.

If desired, it is convenient from this point to review of the actions of the 82nd Airborne Division during the counteroffensive of early January that took place a few kilometers to the south. Although chronologically out of order and without the attractive memorials available in other sectors of the Bulge battlefield, the hilly, wooded terrain, narrow roads, and accounts of sacrifice by the paratroopers provide their own rewards. A signed 'Route du Panorama' indicates the picturesque nature of the surrounding countryside these hilltop villages offer. Driving instructions to these respective sites are not provided.

Side Trip: 82nd Airborne Division Counterattack
24 December 1944 and 3 to 9 January 1945

> On 20 December, General Eisenhower assigned British Field Marshal Montgomery control of US First and Ninth Armies north of the Bulge. The decision resulted from the communications difficulties presented between General Bradley's headquarters in Luxembourg City south of the Bulge and American forces north of the Bulge. The decision pleased almost no one — except General Montgomery. Consistent with his philosophy of a 'tidy battlefield,' Montgomery ordered the 82nd Airborne to withdraw to a line of hills roughly following the Trois-Ponts–Manhay highway (N651). The division's 505th PIR abandoned positions above the Salm River and Rochelinval; similarly, the 508th PIR left high ground near Their-du-Mont. Naturally, a unit that had never in its history withdrawn in the face of the enemy deeply resented the order. Both locations would be recaptured later at terrible costs.
>
> Also on that critical day, events elsewhere indicated the high water mark for the German Army in the Bulge. That night Kampfgruppe Peiper abandoned La Gleize, a 2nd SS Panzer Division thrust north toward Liège was stopped at Vaux-Chavanne north of Manhay, the 2nd Panzer Division was halted near Celles, and the 116th Panzer Division stalled at Verdenne. These important events and locations appear in later tours.

AMERICAN OBJECTIVE	To counterattack the limits of the German advance
FORCES	
American:	82nd Airborne Division (Major General James M Gavin)
German:	9th SS Panzer Division '*Hohenstaufen*' (SS-Generalmajor Sylvester Stadler), then 62nd Volksgrenadier Division (Oberst Friedrich Kittel)
RESULT	The German front line was pushed back to the Salm River

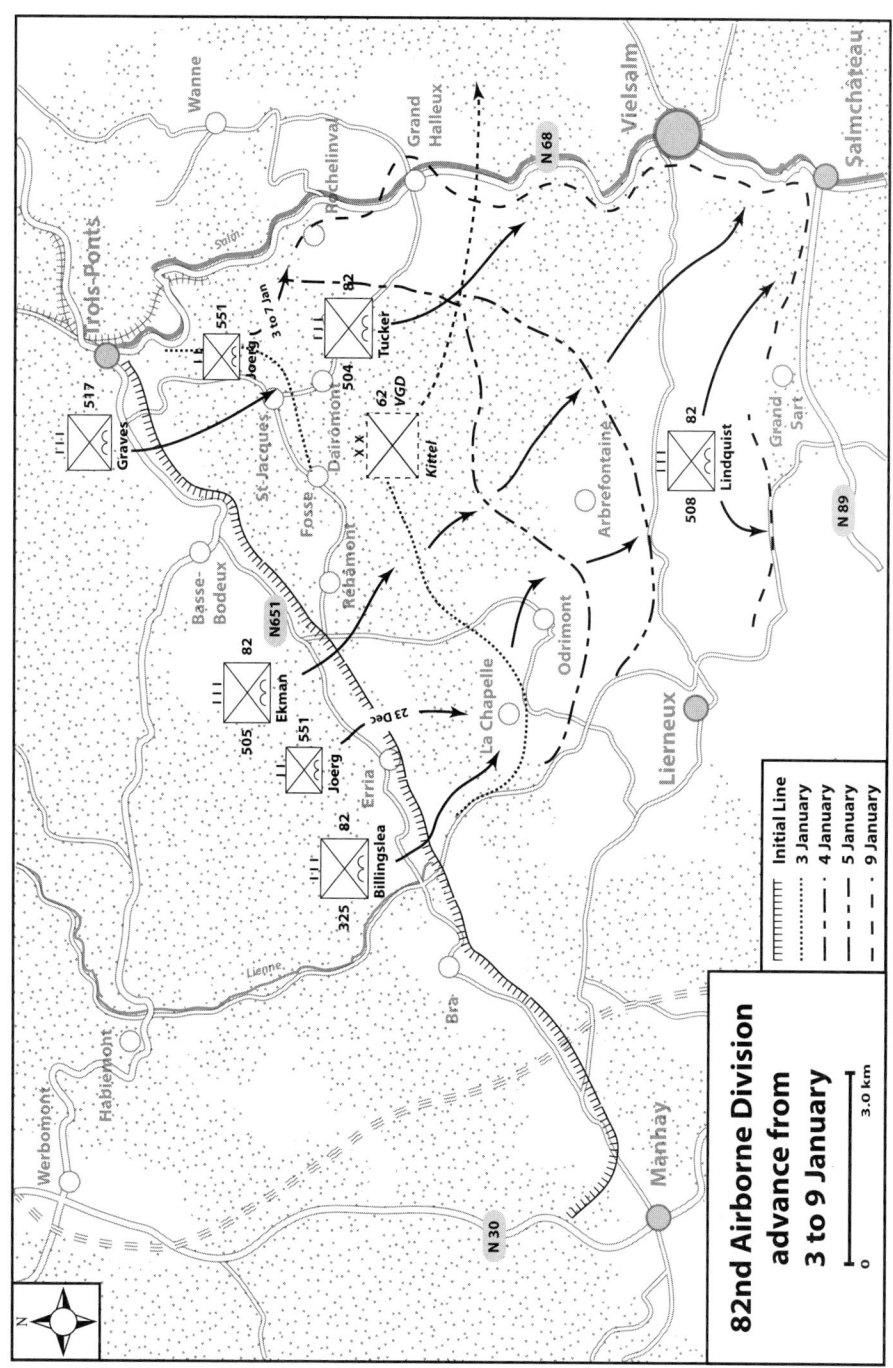

Casualties	
American:	174 killed, 853 wounded, and 76 missing
German:	252 killed, 719 wounded, and 685 missing
Location	Bra is 29 km southwest of Malmédy

Battle

The 3 January attack placed the 325th Glider Infantry Regiment on the right flank advancing along the east bank of Lienne Creek toward La Chapelle and Amcomont. In the center, 505th PIR forged through hilly terrain to capture Noirefontaine Ferme, Rèhârmont, and Fosse. The left flank found the 517th PIR with the attached 551st Parachute Infantry Battalion (Independent) advancing toward the Salm River from Trois-Ponts to Bergeval.

The attack began shortly after dawn with two feet of snow on the ground and temperatures well below zero. Fog and overcast skies limited aerial reconnaissance. Soon after leaving the Line of Departure, the assault companies faced strong resistance from the experienced grenadiers of the 62nd Volksgrenadier Division. Mortar fire, artillery tree bursts, and small-arm fire took a toll — especially among junior officers.

Combat engineers constructed bridges across the icy Rau de Bateur, often working under enemy fire in chest-deep water. Eventually, the arrival of tanks strengthened the impetus of the attack, but German resistance was overcome by mere brute force.

By 9 January, despite continuing snowfall, the division had achieved all of its objectives. Its units standing along the Salm River; however, the attack of 3 January was the most costly in the history of the division.

Battlefield Tour
Bra

The gatepost of the Château Naveau along highway N651 bears a memorial plaque to **Major General James M Gavin**, commander 82nd Airborne Division, who maintained his headquarters there during the critic days from 22 to 24 December 1944 when his division held the Salm River line. (50.323512, 5.733988)

The important crossroads (N651 and N645, a secondary route from Vielsalm to Stoumont) is protected by a Belgian Army pillbox barely inside the treeline south of the highway. (50.326265, 5.749630)

Erria

The 9th SS Panzer Division attacked Erria on 26/27 December from woods to the south only to be met in open fields by American 105-mm and 155-mm artillery fire. SS Panzergrenadier Regiment 19 pushed forward to drive defending Company G out of the village. Later that night, elements of Companies E, F, G, and I counterattacked to find overconfident German troops asleep in American bedrolls.

The force of the assault drove the grenadiers back across the fields and into the woods, leaving one hundred dead.

Highway N651 passes through the village upon the ridge defended by paratroopers behind mine fields and rolls of barbed wire. A bench located on the short frontage road, presents views down the slopes to the south showing the forested area used as an assembly point by the attackers. (50.331245, 5.776276)

La Chapelle

The independent **551st Parachute Infantry Battalion**, commanded by Lieutenant Colonel Wood Joerg, arrived in Werbomont on 21 December and attached to the 82nd Airborne Division on 25 December. Two days later, the unit started the XIII Airborne Corps' counteroffensive with an initial nighttime raid 6.4 kilometers within enemy lines against troops of the 62nd Volksgrenadier Division at a fortified farm complex named Noirefontaine. The paratroopers attacked under covering fire from their 81-mm mortars. Phosphorous rounds torched the wooden barns illuminating the scene.

Spotting a captured American half-track, the battalion destroyed the vehicle with bazooka fire; then a panzer met a similar fate. During the engagement, the paratroopers killed thirty enemy troops, including the German company commander, and took six prisoners while suffering two killed, two missing, and fifteen wounded. The bold action is commemorated with plaques in La Chapelle and Noirefontaine.

A relatively new-looking and beautifully-executed bronze plaque on the outside of the church wall states: (50.310703, 5.799001)

Mission Accomplie (Mission Accomplished)
551eme Bataillon d'Infanterie Parachutiste
On 27 December 1944 with ardor and courage, the battalion conducted the initial attack against enemy forces during the Battle of the Bulge. (Repeated in French)
Wood G. Joerg
Lieutenant Colonel Infantry Commanding (KIA)
551st Parachute Infantry Battalion

Noirefontaine

The plaque, sponsored by Company A veteran Joe Cicchinelli, emblazons the word 'Goya,' an acronym for Lt Col Joerg's favorite expression, 'Get off your a****.' The plaque recognizes the horror of wintertime warfare and promises that the grateful citizens of the region will always remember. (Approximate location: 50.332277, 5.802910)

The farm complex became the scene of fighting again on 3 January when Lieutenant Colonel Benjamin H Vandervoort's 2nd Battalion, 505th PIR approached along the roadway from the north. Company F rode tanks from the 740th Tank Battalion until heavy mortar fire and enemy SP guns knocked out two Shermans and sent the paratroopers into nearby woods where they met tree bursts and concentrated rifle fire. Company D, advancing to the east of the same road, fared somewhat better by passing safely through open fields west of Rèhârmont before meeting increased resistance in the woods.

Rèhârmont

After passing Manhay, the division bounced against the 82nd Airborne Division positions along highway N651. The Fifth Panzer Army went over to the defensive on 28 December along the line Trois-Ponts–Bra–Hotton. On 3 January the division was reassigned to the attack upon Bastogne.

The **Farthest Advance Stone** west of Rèhârmont identifies the farthest penetration of the 9th SS Panzer Division in this sector. (50.34053, 5.8073)

Fosse

The 505th Parachute Infantry Regiment held the Salm River line since its arrival in the Ardennes. On Christmas Eve, the unit fought against the retreating survivors of Joachim Peiper's 1st SS Panzer Division.

As part of General Montgomery's order to consolidate, the 505th abandoned its positions around Rochelinval, a decision that would prove costly for the 551st Parachute Battalion (see below).

At 0800 on 3 January 1945, Captain Archibald A McPheeters led Company I, 505th PIR from Basse-Bodeux through deep snow on a dirt trail up a hill to seize the town of Fosse. When the men exited the woods and began to crest the ridge, German machine guns opened fire, cutting a swathe through the American team now exposed in the open terrain.

Captain McPheeters and twelve of his company were killed. Despite continuing snowfall, freezing sleet, and increasing German artillery fire, squads flanked Fosse to the right. Later in the day, Company H approached from Rèhârmont and engaged the enemy in vicious house-to-house fighting. Company I suffered 50 casualties that day with every officer killed or wounded; German dead were uncounted, but an entire battalion was eliminated and 125 enemy troops captured.

A flag-flanked field stone plinth along a side road bears a bronze plaque dedicated **Company I, 505th PIR, 82nd Airborne Division** and the men who died during the 3 January attack. Headed by, 'May their sacrifices not have been in vain,' the memorial lists the thirteen men's names and their service numbers. The site provides good views down into the valley to the west — toward the American attack. (50.34324, 5.84052)

St-Jacques

On 1 January, the independent 517th Parachute Infantry Regiment, commanded by Colonel Rupert Graves, was attached to the 82nd Airborne. On the night of 3 January, Captain Dean D Robbins led Company B, through a thick fir forest, against Mont St Jacques. Exiting the forest, the company approached St Jacques across 400 meters of open ground to surprise German defenders who had expected a more sheltered approach. Paratroopers occupied the school and parish house across the road from the German-occupied church. Nine men stormed the church just before a panzer rolled along the village street to investigate the noise. The German tank absorbed two bazooka rounds before putting two shells through the church windows. It then reversed and withdrew. Shortly thereafter, General Gavin appeared and congratulated Captain Robbins on the capture of the village.

A rough field stone honoring the **517th PIR** and **505th PIR** stands inside the gated Église de St-Jacques churchyard. The inscription begins, (in English) 'The Belgian Ardennes to their liberators' followed by (in French) 'Neither the Nazi hordes nor the cold of winter in 1944-45 limited their courage – remember them.' A plaque to the victims of the bombardments of 1944 and 1945 on the wall near the entrance to the church heads a list of five local citizens who perished. (50.348513, 5.860473)

Dairomont

On 4 January paratroopers advanced from St-Jacques toward Dairomont. During a flanking assault, a section commanded by Lieutenant Durkee encountered a vastly superior number of enemy soldiers laying heavy fire on another assault section. Lieutenant Durkee ordered bayonets and, enraged by the high level of casualties suffered the previous day, the paratroopers ferociously attacked. Within minutes enemy resistance ended, and sixty-five enemy soldiers were dead.

An upright stone bears a bronze plaque commending **Company A, 551st Parachute Infantry Battalion** and Lieutenant Richard Durkee. The script describing the bayonet charge ends with, 'We will never forget their courage.' (50.341003, 5.863360)

Rochelinval

On 3 January 1945, 643 paratroopers (the plaque mistakenly states 790) of the 551st Parachute Infantry Battalion left their line of departure at Basse Bodeux to attack the 62nd VGD's Grenadier Regiment 183 in Rochelinval. A regiment of 88-mm guns and a battalion of 105-mm howitzers amply supported the grenadiers.

The Americans moved 6 kilometers cross-country while exposed to enemy artillery and mortar fire toward Rochelinval, a peaceful village of fifteen houses clinging to the hillside on the west bank of the Salm River. Often engaged in bayonet attacks and hand-to-hand fighting, by 7 January the substantially weakened unit charged uphill over open ground and captured the ridge-top village and closed the last exit for retreating German troops across a 16-kilometer stretch of the Salm River. During four days of bitter winter fighting against two German regiments, the unit reduced to 110 survivors, took 300 prisoners and killed an estimated 400 enemy. Its commander, Lieutenant Colonel Wood G Joerg, was killed in the final charge. The 551st Battalion was disbanded three weeks later, the survivors being absorbed into other units.

The hedge-surrounded **551st Battalion Memorial Park** on the hill overlooking the river crossing commemorates the battle that liberated the village. A stone-mounted plaque presents the bitter outcome of the battle. A smaller stone carries a plaque to Sergeant Robert H Hill (officially listed as a corporal), who was killed while attacking the village. A third plaque from the members of the 551st Battalion thanks the Belgian people for their courageous sacrifices and dedication to securing liberty. (50.341072, 5.897406)

On 10 May 1940, attempting to execute its instructions to delay the advance of the invading German Army, the 5th Company, 3rd Regiment Chasseurs Ardennais of the Belgian Army, held the west bank of the Salm River in this very same area. At 1400, cavalry from the German 8th Infantry Division approached from the village of Wanne. It launched a series of frontal attacks, each repulsed by chasseurs' fire. At 1530, the Germans attempted at advance on the right flank, which was also repulsed. At 1800, the Germans crossed the river downstream from the bridge and executed a broad flanking maneuver around the Belgian positions. During a brief lull, the Belgians, having delayed the enemy for four hours, withdrew.

The slate and field stone memorial to the 1940 fighting commemorates the brief **Battle for Rochelinval** and the deaths of the three Chasseurs Ardennes killed in the fighting: Corporal Marcel Royer and Privates Adrien Balaine and Urbain Streel. (50.33975, 5.900745)

A wayside park holds a memorial to those members of the **Chasseurs Ardennes,** who blew up the Rochelinval Bridge 200 meters to the north and delayed the advance of the German Army. The enemy crossed the river downstream and moved toward Rochelinval. (50.337732, 5.903123)

Ennal
Musée de la bataille de Salm et du Saillant (Dec 44 - Jan 45)

Ennal 24
Tel: +32 (0)477 20 78 09
Web: http://www.musee-ennal.com

B-6698 Ennal (Vielsalm)
or+32 (0)80 21 54 58

According to the museum's website, the small museum is in a barn that was an infirmary for the German soldiers injured in the fighting around Grand Halleux. Its three levels present several dioramas and artifacts including weapons, uniforms, and helmets. (50.32901, 5.924779)

Open from 1 July to 31 August on Friday, Saturday, and Sunday from 1400 to 1700.

On 15 January 1945, the 424th Infantry Regiment received orders to retake the town and the wooded high ground to its east. Heavy automatic weapons fire from enemy troops in the village's stone houses repulsed the initial daylight attacks. Company F took the town in house-to-house combat during a night assault.

The **424th Infantry Regiment Memorial** features two crossed M1 Garand rifles mounted upon a granite plinth. The plaque below relates the liberation of Ennal. (50.32886, 5.926611)

42

---

42 Sergeant Robert H Hill was awarded a Distinguished Service Cross for heroism. Caught with his platoon in the open and under a cross-fire from German machine-guns, Hill, despite several battle wounds, grabbed the BAR dropped by his dead scout and fired two magazines at the enemy. Hill is buried in Henri-Chapelle American Cemetery, Henri-Chapelle, Belgium.

The 551st Parachute Infantry Battalion's sacrifices were only recognized in 2001 with a Presidential Unit Citation. Douglas Dillard accepted the award on behalf of the paratroopers. Dillard had been a sergeant in Company A during the battle. Only eight men from that company survived. Dillard went on to fight in Korea and Vietnam, retiring as a colonel.

Chapter Four
Battle for the Schnee Eifel, St-Vith, and Vielsalm
16 to 23 December 1944

The Eifel, a low mountain range, extends from eastern Belgium into western Germany and runs from Aachen in the north to Trier in the south. The limits of the Ardennes forested area are the Moselle and Rhine Rivers on the east and the Meuse River on the west. The conifer-covered plateau is etched with twisting streams that fill deep gorges. The terrain-channeled transportation routes pass through road centers at Malmédy, St-Vith, and Bastogne. Each town loomed as a major early objective of WACHT AM RHEIN.

The heavily-wooded Schnee Eifel ridge stretches 15 kilometers from Ormont, Germany southwest to Brandscheid, Germany. Its reputation as a winter sports haven rests upon its severe weather with deep snow and cold temperatures. The highest point on the ridge, at an elevation of 697 meters (2,288 feet), is 'Schwarze Mann' or Black Man[1]. The western side of the ridge descends to large, rolling pastures dotted with small pine- and spruce-planted copses.

In September 1944, American infantry had penetrated a thinly fortified sector of the Westwall to occupy a section of the Schnee Eifel. On 10 December, the US 106th Infantry Division, fresh off the boats at Le Havre, began to occupy prepared positions to free the 2nd Infantry Division for its attack upon on the Roer River dams through Wahlerscheid.

The 106th Division was the last US infantry division to be activated during the Second World War. During its training at Fort Jackson, South Carolina it was frequently stripped to fill manpower shortages elsewhere. Replacements were frequently excess men from training programs, such as the Army Air Corps, and thus not fully trained as infantry. The division left Boston Harbor on 10 November 1944. Five weeks later it was under fire.

The 106th Infantry Division front ranged from the 14th Cavalry Group's outposts in the Losheim Gap south to near the Luxembourg border. In the north, 422nd Infantry Regiment held positions forward of the Westwall on the Schnee Eifel. On its right, the 423rd Infantry Regiment continued along the Schnee Eifel to where the ridge dropped into the Alfbach valley. Reconnaissance troops filled a gap where the line echeloned two kilometers to the west before tying into the 424th Infantry Regiment manning high ground east of the Our River, where it met the 28th Infantry Division near Großkampenberg. The total division front was over 40 kilometers (24 miles).

The existing road network offered General der Panzertruppen Hasso von Manteuffel[2] the opportunity to execute a double envelopment of the Schnee Eifel. A

---

1   The term originates from local lore that at a distance on foggy days in the forest people were transformed into dark shapes – the Schwartze Manner – or dark men.

2   General Hasso von Manteuffel belonged to one of the oldest German noble families. He began his military career at age 14 and served as an infantry officer in the First World War. Attracted to horsemanship, he transferred to the cavalry and later to armor after studying the principles of Heinz Guderian. Manteuffel was apolitical and never joined the Nazi Party. He fought extensively and with honor on the Eastern Front, rising to command the elite *Grossdeutschland* Panzer Division. By 1944, at 47 years of age, he was young for an Army commander. Manteuffel died in 1978 at age 81.

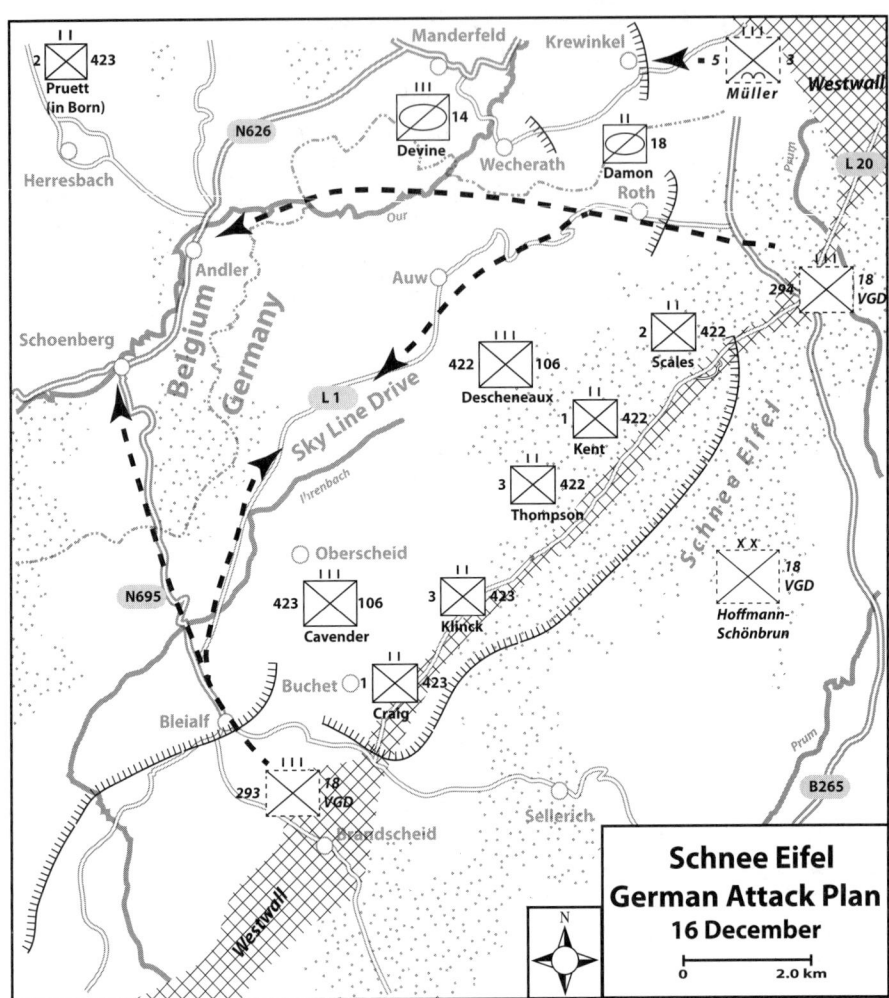

paved highway (L1), known to American soldiers as 'Skyline Drive,' because of its resemblance to the ridge-top road in Virginia's Blue Ridge Mountains, ran behind the ridge from the Losheim Gap village of Auw to the Alfbach valley village of Bleialf. A deeper envelopment was possible along highway N626 that followed the Our River from Andler to Schoenberg, where it junctioned with highway N695 from Bleialf.

Manteuffel assigned two infantry divisions of the LXVI Corps to penetrate American positions along the Schnee Eifel. He boldly decided to attack the US 106th Infantry Division with only six battalions of infantry from Oberst Günther Hoffmann-Schönbrun's 18th Volksgrenadier Division. The division had held the northern sector of the line since October and was familiar with the terrain. From the north, Grenadier Regiments 294 and 295 would use the two good roads through the Losheim Gap to swing around behind the Schnee Eifel. Meanwhile, that same division's Grenadier Regiment 293 would advance from Prüm along the Alf River northwest to Schoenberg, where it planned capture of a bridge over the Our River and, joining the other two

Chapter Four　　　　　　　　　　　　　　　　　　　　Schnee Eifel　　135

regiments approaching from the north, trapping the US 106th Infantry Division. Schönbrun's division was supported by a battalion of forty 75-mm assault guns and forty self-propelled tank destroyers. From Schoenberg, the road network branched out again towards St-Vith, only 10 kilometers distant. To the south, Oberst Frederick Kittel's inexperienced 62nd Volksgrenadier Division[3] was assigned to capture a bridge over the Our River at Steinebrück. Both divisions would then move against St-Vith, to be captured on the first day of the offensive.

Battlefield Tour Summary
　　　The tour starts near the German border before making a loop around sites in the Schnee Eifel. It then proceeds west to review the destruction and surrender of the 422nd and 423rd Infantry Regiments before continuing west to St-Vith and Vielsalm.

Highly Recommended Sites
Schnee Eifel: Westwall bunkers
St-Vith: 168th Engineering Combat Battalion Memorial and foxholes
Vielsalm: Rencheaux Airborne Memorial
Joubiéval: Bulge Relics Museum

The Flanks Collapse
16 to 17 December 1944
　　　Colonel Mark A Devine's 14th Cavalry Group drew an assignment to block three roadways that led from Germany into Belgium. The frontage was almost 10 kilometers, an impossible distance for so small a unit. Instead, Colonel Devine held his 32nd Cavalry Squadron in reserve near Vielsalm and established blocking forces from his 18th Cavalry Squadron in eight crossroad strongpoints. The squadron held three cavalry troops[4], an assault gun troop with eight 75-mm SP howitzers, and a light tank company with seventeen M3 Stuart tanks armed with 37-mm cannon. Troop A was divided between Kobscheid and Roth, and Troop C held Krewinkel and Afst. Company A, 820th Tank Destroyer Battalion added two platoons of armored cars and both self-propelled and towed 3-inch tank destroyers, spread across Lanzerath, Merlscheid, and Berterath. The assault gun troop and tank company held the squadron headquarters in Manderfeld while Troop B was detached to the south.
　　　Colonel Alexander D Reid's 424th Infantry Regiment held a 10-kilometer front from Heckhuscheid southwest to Großkampenberg with 2nd and 3rd Battalions forward and 1st Battalion in reserve at Steinebrück. The gap between it and the 423rd Regiment was thinly screened by the 106th Reconnaissance Troop and the regimental Cannon Company. The regiment gained artillery support from the 591st Field Artillery Battalion.

3　The 62nd Volksgrenadier Division had been rebuilt from remnants of a division destroyed in Eastern Front fighting.

4　A cavalry troop held 145 men, about one-quarter fewer that a rifle company, but significantly better armed. Each troop consisted of three platoons manning three M8 armored cars with 37-mm cannon and two machine guns and six jeeps. A cavalry troop was equipped for mobility and reconnaissance, not static defense.

German Objective	To penetrate the thin American outpost line with intention to trap two forward infantry regiments.
Forces	
American:	14th Cavalry Group (Colonel Mark A Devine Jr)
German:	18th Volksgrenadier Division (Oberst Günther Hoffmann-Schönbrun) and elements of 3rd Fallschirmjäger Division (Generalmajor Karl Wadehn)
Result	The weak line of American outposts was rapidly overcome
Casualties	
American:	2 killed, 20 wounded, and 154 missing
German:	600 dead and 1,200 wounded
Location	Krewinkel is 23 km east of St-Vith; St-Vith is 80 km southeast of Liège

Battle

While much of the 18th Cavalry Squadron experienced a bombardment from artillery, mortars, and Nebelwerfer rockets such as they had never seen before, some areas were spared. Instead, German troops infiltrated between and among the outposts. Earlier German patrols had discovered a 2-kilometer-wide undefended gap between Weckerath and Roth that became the main entry to Skyline Drive for a battalion of grenadiers.

The troopers were well supplied with .50-caliber machine guns and, despite the disparity in the size of the two forces, inflicted heavy casualties before succumbing to overwhelming force. Two platoons at Kobscheid held their fire until the grenadiers reached the barbed wire and then extracted a terrible price. Nevertheless, grenadiers fought into the village, control shifting back and forth for much of the morning. At Krewinkel, a platoon fought off two assaults and inflicted 150 casualties on troops of the 3rd Fallschirmjäger Division. Similarly at Afst, a platoon inflicted 30 dead. However, the small forces at Roth and Weckerath held no answer to the grenadiers' assault guns. Both positions were quickly overcome.

At 1100, Colonel Devine ordered the cavalrymen to withdraw to a ridge behind the Our River near Manderfeld. Five hours later, Devine ordered his troops to draw back another 3.5 kilometers to a line Andler–Holzheim. On the morning of 17 December, they pulled back again, eventually reaching Poteau; in the afternoon on the same day Devine, on a scouting mission, was ambushed near Recht. He returned to Poteau on foot and relieved himself from command.[5] Lieutenant Colonel William F Damon Jr, commanding officer of the 18th Cavalry Squadron, assumed command. Nevertheless, the men had done their job by alerting higher command to the German assault and in delaying the enemy advance.

---

5 Colonel Mark A Devine Jr went to bed and, on December 18, was evacuated through medical channels as a non-battle casualty. His military career was over. Devine died in 1950 at age 53 and is buried in Arlington National Cemetery, Arlington, Virginia.

Chapter Four   Schnee Eifel   137

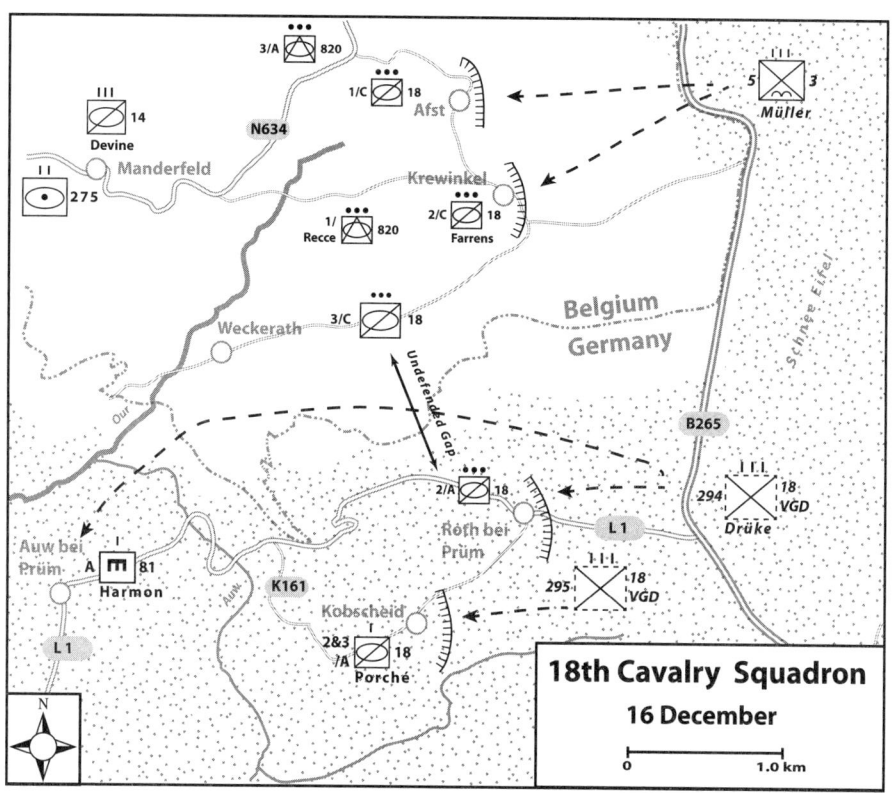

Battlefield Tour

The tour presents sites of the 18th Cavalry Squadron's defense and starts 4.2 km south of Losheim on the International Highway (B265). Turn southwest onto a minor road toward Krewinkel / Afst / Manderfeld. Upon entering Krewinkel, stop near the two side roads on the left. (50.328932, 6.385311)

Fallschirmjäger Regiment 5's attack against Krewinkel ranks as typical of the assaults that fell upon the 18th Cavalry Squadron outposts in the Losheim Gap. The 2nd Platoon, Troop C, 18th Cavalry Squadron, commanded by 1st Lieutenant Kenneth Farrens, was garrisoned in Krewinkel and supported by 1st Reconnaissance Platoon, 820th Tank Destroyer Battalion. Machine guns were positioned in log-fortified pits behind rolls of barbed concertina wire. Thirty minutes after the opening barrage ended, a Fallschirmjäger Assault Company came marching four abreast into the village from the east under searchlight-created artificial moonlight. Lt Farrens' positions in the houses overlooked the road whereby his men allowed the enemy to approach within 20 meters of their wire before the cavalrymen's automatic weapons opened up. The Germans scattered, but under fire support from a mortar team, 50 to 75 fallschirmjäger penetrated into the village. Fighting ensued at close quarters, but the troopers were firmly established behind the thick stone walls of the village's school and church.

By 0615, German troops were screaming for an American surrender. Fallschirmjäger attempted to breach the defenses by moving behind the eastern-facing guns from the north. The movement required crossing a snowy, open ridge where their silhouettes made easy targets for the light machine guns and riflemen in the buildings. The paratroopers' bodies slid down the hillside, leaving vivid bloody red streaks in the snow. The enemy withdrew before dawn yelling at Farrens's command post that it was only a ten-minute break. Farrens responded, 'And we will be waiting for you — you SOB.'

The furious firing depleted small-arms ammunition. The initial barrage broke communication lines with the troop's headquarters in Weckerath, but a line to the troop's 1st Platoon in nearby Afst remained. First Lieutenant Aubrey Mills, Executive Officer of Troop C, soon arrived from Afst with a half-track loaded with ammunition. Once distributed, Lt Mills returned toward Afst but was killed along the way by a single shot to the head.[6]

By 0700, a second artillery barrage fell on the cavalry positions augmented by self-propelled guns approaching from the southeast. The fallschirmjäger returned, but the resupplied troopers held them off. Quiet temporarily returned to Krewinkel. Later that morning, Lt Farrens received instructions to withdraw to Manderfeld. Joined by the defenders from Afst, the cavalrymen escaped while under fire of another fallschirmjäger attack. They left 150 to 200 enemy bodies around the northern and eastern approaches to the village. Americans casualties numbered two wounded and one dead (Lt Mills).

The roadway approaches Krewinkel from the southeast along the route used by the SP guns. When the white tower of the new village church comes into view ahead, the old gray-stucco house and barn visible on the right housed a **forward observation post** for the 275th Field Artillery Battalion. The structure still displays damage (especially on the gable) from the engagement when it received shell fire from the German assault guns approaching along this roadway. The hillside behind the building held one of five pit machine-gun positions contained within an arc of concertina wire. (50.329321, 6.384872)

> Continue 190 m to the new church on the left and stop. (50.330326, 6.383812)

The **command post** for the cavalry detachment and the tank destroyer reconnaissance platoon couched in the long, light-colored house and barn across the highway from the new church.

> Turn left and proceed 70 m to the chapel on the right. (50.330384, 6.382842)

The old **St Eligius Chapel** was well fortified by Lt Farrens. The 70-meter distance from the company command post to the old church indicates that fighting in Krewinkel took place on a tight battleground.

---

6   First Lieutenant Aubrey Mills was awarded a Distinguished Service Cross. He is buried in Henri-Chapelle American Cemetery, Henri-Chapelle, Belgium.

> Turn right past the old chapel and stop at the next intersection. (50.331110, 6.382063)

The final German attack from the north erupted down the side of a swale whose trees now lessen the impression of the height of the hillside. The defensive houses to the north of the church still bear their old appearance and hold broad views over the German approach route.

> Turn right and, after 90 m, stop at a convenient location. (50.331069, 6.383315)

A new house stands adjacent to the command post and occupies the corner of the intersection. The roadway entering Krewinkel from the east drops down five- to-seven meters before flattening. The initial German assault along this route drew support from German mortars located in the forest area to the northeast.

> Continue forward 1.7 km to return to the International Highway B265. Turn right and follow for 3.7 km, and then turn right toward Roth bei Prüm (Am Sportplatz becomes Hauptstraße). After 1.3 km, stop in the center of the village near the war memorial on the left. (50.307936, 6.385402)

The 18th Squadron's Troop A, commanded by Captain Stanley E Porché, did not suffer the initial bombardment that forewarned other units of impending attack. Per Manteuffel's orders, by 0500 on 16 December, troops of Grenadier Regiment 294 approaching along the road from highway B265 infiltrated and surrounded Porché's positions. While Lt Farrens was defending Krewinkel, Porché reported being attacked by 75-to-80 infantry and one tank (more probably a self-propelled assault gun). Against such a force, Troop A held its own, but the main body of the grenadier regiment simply bypassed the town by marching across the fields to the north.

One of the tank destroyers supporting Porché knocked out an enemy armored car but was then outflanked and destroyed. The second tank destroyer never managed a single shot. At 0830, Porché radioed that his command post was under direct fire from tanks only 75 meters away. Thereafter, Troop A was never heard from again. Of the 90-man force, three were killed and eighty-seven captured.[7] That night, the road through Roth carried heavy infantry weapons and artillery heading west.

The **Roth War Memorial** holds several plaques listing names of the dead from Roth and Kobscheid. The list is surprisingly long for such a small community and presents the human cost that the war exacted from small German communities. Of the fourteen First World War deaths, all but two were in France; of the thirty-four deaths in the Second World War, all but six were in Russia. Nineteen civilians died from bombs or mines — one being only 4 years old — and finally, thirteen civilians simply vanished. The family name of Schwahlen appears eight times on the several plaques.

---

7   Captain Stanley E Porché was held at German PoW camp Stalag XIIId in Nuremburg, Germany for the duration of the war.

> Leave Roth south on highway K161 (Kobscheider Straße). Follow for 1.6 km into Kobscheid. (50.29856, 6.371162)

The spruce forest passed on the left before entering the village sheltered II Battalion, Grenadier Regiment 295 before its assault on Kobscheid. As with Roth, Kobscheid received only cursory fire from one battery salvo since German infantry had already encircled the village before dawn. The attackers at Kobscheid actually drove inside the defensive perimeter before an alert sounded. The cavalrymen, supported by fire from the 275th Field Artillery Battalion, fought off the attack. Private Edward J Sklepkowski threw short-fused grenades through a slit in the command post wall, thus forcing the attackers to seek shelter in a barn. Forty grenadiers were taken prisoner. Later in the day, as artillery communications failed, the battle resumed. Kobscheid held out until dusk. After dark, platoon leader Lieutenant Lorenz Herdrick led sixty-one men across the snow-covered countryside arriving at St-Vith three days later.

Kobscheid sits atop a ridge explaining why the American Cavalry occupied the position. The village consists of only a few houses and a white chapel.

> Continue through Kobscheid (K161) and, after approximately 1.8 km, turn left on highway L1 and follow into Auw.

Auw sits astride the winding Skyline Drive. From it a side road leads northwest to the Our River Valley and Schoenberg. On 16 December, Company A, 81st Engineer Combat Battalion held Auw, a major target of Manteuffel's small envelopment since it marked the northern end of Skyline Drive. Being behind the front line, the village suffered from a heavy preliminary bombardment. By midmorning, Captain Harold M Harmon's small force was under increasing small-arms fire from I Battalion, Grenadier Regiment 294 and shelling from SP guns of the company-sized Sturmgeschütz Brigade 244. Harmon's men maintained a stand-off until German assault guns took each American position under direct fire. One platoon made an escape toward Andler. The remaining platoon (the third platoon had already left for a road-repair detail) could escape only across an open field. Corporal Edward S Withee, armed with only a submachine gun, distracted the enemy while the men of his platoon raced across open ground to safety. Withee then meekly surrendered.[8]

American 589th and 592nd Field Artillery Battalions brought fire onto advancing German troops throughout the sector and, from the German perspective, had to be eliminated. At noon, grenadiers began moving south from Auw against the batteries positioned in woods on either side of highway L1. Grenadiers brought the artillerymen under small-arms fire while mortars and assault guns attempted to destroy the guns. Battery A's Executive Officer Lieutenant Eric Fisher Wood Jr rushed to a hilltop and shouted commands for direct fire upon the leading panzer. Two hits and

---

8   Corporal Edward S Withee, a fireman from Portland, Maine, was awarded the Distinguished Service Cross. Withee spent the remainder of the war in Stalag XIIIc, Hammelburg-am-Main. At last report, he still lives in Connecticut at age 93.

Chapter Four Schnee Eifel 141

it was in flames. Wood then had his battery reduce shell fuses to a minimum whose intense detonations forced the German troops to withdraw. That evening, with infantry now covering the open left flank of the 422nd Regiment, the two artillery battalions displaced southward.[9]

Other Points of Interest (18th Cavalry Squadron Sector)

Ormont   The **Ormont Kriegsgräberstätte** rests behind a white chapel which hides the cemetery entrance. Inside the gateway, a long grass strip passes through a birch forest, ending at the cemetery plots enclosed within a sandstone wall. The groups of randomly placed stone crosses are commemorative. Individual grave markers line the sides of stone walkways. The cemetery holds 370 graves, of which 57 are unidentified German soldiers and 16 unnamed Polish soldiers. Most of dead were victims of the heavy fighting of January and February 1945, when American forces recaptured lost territory. Location: on Waldstraße in Ormont 200 m southeast of highway L20. (50.324547, 6.44636)

Auw   Upon entering Auw, note the civilian cemetery where sixty-two **German military graves** occupy the right rear with one or two burials per grave — all from December 1944 or very early 1945. Location: Beside highway L1 in Auw. (50.302143, 6.340270)

**Destruction of the 106th Infantry Division
16 to 21 December 1944**

Skyline Drive provided American artillery observers spectacular views across a broad shallow valley for a great distance into the enemy's camp. As any daytime troop movements would be subjected to heavy bombardment, the Germans need to capture the ridgeline.

GERMAN OBJECTIVE	To destroy the only major American unit between the German Westwall and the transportation hub of St-Vith
FORCES	
American:	106th Infantry Division (Major General Alan W Jones Sr)
German:	18th Volksgrenadier Division (Oberst Günther Hoffmann-Schönbrun) and 62nd Volksgrenadier Division (Oberst Frederich Kittel)
RESULT	Two American infantry regiments were surrounded and forced to surrender

---

9   Three members of the 18th Cavalry Reconnaissance Squadron were awarded the Distinguished Service Cross for gallantry in the battle at the villages: 1st Lieutenant AL Mills, Staff Sergeant Woodrow W Reeves, and Corporal CE Statler.

Casualties		
	American:	415 killed, 1,254 wounded, and 6,821 taken prisoner
	German:	unknown
Location		Bleialf is 18 km southeast of St-Vith; St-Vith is 80 km southeast of Liège

Battle

Despite the heavy bombardment on 16 December, the frontal German infantry attack on the 422nd and 423rd Infantry Regiments on the Schnee Eifel, of little more than patrol strength, was easily repulsed. However, by 0830, German troops approached Skyline Drive through the Roth–Weckerath gap, occupied Auw, and threatened the 589th and 592nd Field Artillery Battalions. The enemy had outflanked the northern battalion of 422nd Regiment and threatened its rear. Colonel George L Descheneaux, commanding the 422nd Regiment, sent his reserve Company L to retake Auw and block the highway. At 0830, General Jones, who had earlier ordered his reserve 2nd Battalion, 423rd Infantry Regiment to Schoenberg, re-routed it to the Andler–Auw road to relieve pressure on Descheneaux's left flank.

On the southern flank near Bleialf, the stronger attack fell against a weak American provisional battalion comprised of the Antitank Company, one platoon of Cannon Company, a rifle platoon, Company C, 820th Tank Destroyer Battalion, and Troop B, 18th Cavalry Squadron. Colonel Charles C Cavender, commanding the 423rd Infantry Regiment, organized a counterattack force of service troops and engineers and, in house-to-house fighting, re-took the town. On the southern flank, Troop B, 18th Cavalry Squadron, was hard hit and withdrew to Winterscheid.

Around midday, Lieutenant General Courtney Hodges, commander US First Army, released CCB, 9th Armored Division to reinforce the 106th Division. Later that evening, Hodges dispatched the entire 7th Armored Division from its bivouac in the Netherlands to St-Vith with intention to strengthen the beleaguered infantry. Events were looking up for General Jones' 106th Division, but neither unit would arrive in time.

Before dawn on 17 December, Grenadier Regiment 295, supported by assault guns, struck Bleialf. Colonel Cavender's provisional battalion evaporated, whereupon the road to Schoenberg lay open. At 0845, the Schoenberg bridge was captured, allowing no way out for the two infantry regiments, two divisional artillery battalions, and elements of three corps artillery battalions still on the east side of the Our River.

During the day, the two trapped regiments, the 422nd south of Schlausenbach and the 423rd around Oberlascheid and Buchet, prepared all-around defenses. The previous day's bombardment had destroyed telephone lines, and German radios had jammed American frequencies, thus making coordination between the regiments difficult and communication with division almost impossible. Messages were repeated and relayed, often not completed until hours after they had no relevance to the rapidly-changing situation. Colonels Cavender and Descheneaux believed that the 7th Armored Division was clearing an escape to the west — then it was not. Resupply by air was promised — but then it could not deliver.

Chapter Four Schnee Eifel 143

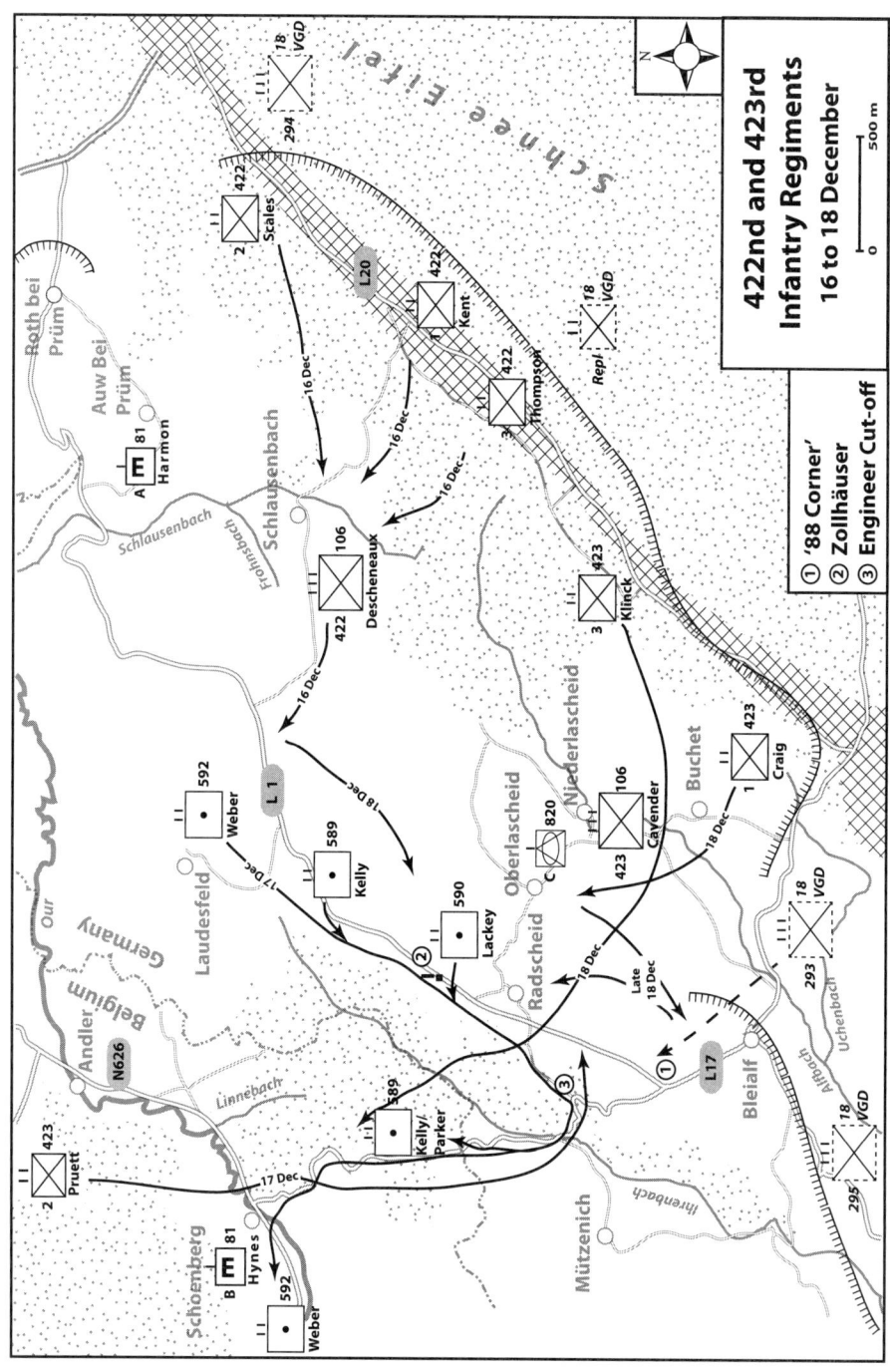

At 0040 on 18 December, Cavender and Descheneaux finally received orders to execute a fighting withdrawal to the southwest along the south side of the Bleialf–Schoenberg road. By then, however, the 18th Volksgrenadier Division lay firmly in place at the only viable crossing over the Our River at Schoenberg.

Unaware of events to its rear, the 423rd Regiment planned to move west via Oberlascheid–Radscheid–Engineer Cut-Off–Schoenberg in a column of battalions. Lieutenant Colonel Joseph F Pruett's 2nd Battalion led but received enemy fire south of Radschied. Colonel Pruett attacked south and advanced to the Bleialf–Schoenberg road where the battalion became pinned down. Lieutenant Colonel Earl F Klinck's 3rd Battalion bypassed the stopped 2nd Battalion and moved along a farm track across the Ihrenbach valley,[10] eventually consolidating on Hill 536. In the growing darkness, the 1st Battalion, the last unit to leave its Schnee Eifel positions, moved to occupy Hill 546 south of Oberlascheid. With the 2nd Battalion still pressured by troops coming from Bleialf, the 1st Battalion launched a night attack by moving south along the Durenbach valley on the 2nd Battalion's left flank. Machine-gun fire and shells from 88-mm guns hit the 1st Battalion, which disengaged, moved back up the Durenbach, and positioned to the right of 3rd Battalion. The 2nd Battalion followed and formed the regiment's right flank below Hill 536.

During the night, Colonel Cavender re-located his command post to the Skyline Drive near Hill 575. At 0900, an enemy artillery barrage struck the assembled troops. However, the attack upon Schoenberg began at 1000 as planned despite enemy artillery and antiaircraft gun fire to the front, tank fire to the rear, and an infantry company attacking from Bleialf. Two rifle companies of the 3rd Battalion achieved the southern limits of Schoenberg before being stopped by intense antiaircraft gun fire. By 1500, Colonel Klinck pulled his men back to Hill 504.

The 1st Battalion's attack, reduced to only Company B and Headquarters Company, achieved the Andler road on the northern slopes of Hill 504 only to come under fire by tanks. By 1400, the battalion was all but eliminated.

Colonel Pruett's 2nd Battalion arrived alongside 1st Battalion but on the opposite side of Linnebach. Pruett planned to attack Schoenberg from the northeast at 1430, but a friendly fire incident delayed the attack. Pruett put his force under 422nd Regiment command — still planning to carry out the attack.

At 1600, facing an approaching heavy enemy armored force firing artillery, mortars, and automatic weapons, Colonel Cavender, whose troops were fighting hunger and possessed only 5-to-10 rounds of M-1 ammunition per man, made the decision to surrender.[11]

---

10   The Ihrenbach, or Ihren Creek, forms the Belgian – German border in this area.

11   Colonel Charles C Cavender, a 1916 graduate of Texas A&M College, volunteered for the Army. He was a 5th Infantry Division private during the 1918 Battle of St-Mihiel. Later that year he received nomination to attend West Point Military Academy. After the surrender of his regiment, Colonel Cavender was held at Stalag IXb at Bad Orb, Hessen, Germany for five months, during which time he suffered injuries from an American bombing raid over Nuremberg, Germany. He served occupation duty in post-war Japan before retiring from the army. He died in 1995 at age 97 and is buried in Riverside National Cemetery, Riverside, California.

Chapter Four — Schnee Eifel — 145

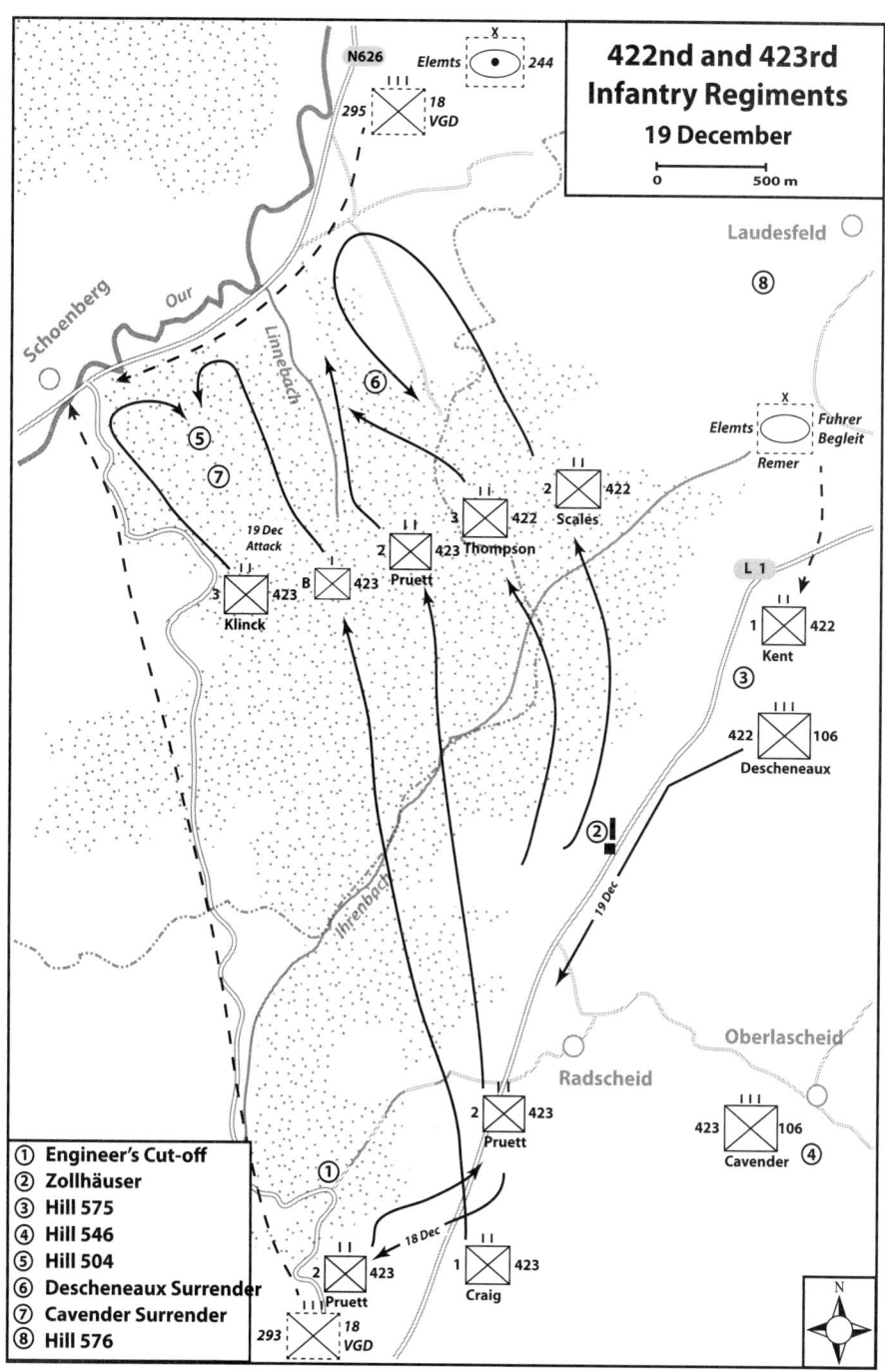

422nd and 423rd Infantry Regiments
19 December

1. Engineer's Cut-off
2. Zollhäuser
3. Hill 575
4. Hill 546
5. Hill 504
6. Descheneaux Surrender
7. Cavender Surrender
8. Hill 576

The original withdrawal plan called for Colonel Descheneaux's 422nd Regiment to follow the 423rd. During the night of 18 December, Descheneaux moved his troops from the Schnee Eifel to a cluster of small woods approximately 2.5 kilometers north of Oberlascheid. The assault on Schoenberg was to start the next morning, but Descheneaux's troops were not where they had planned.

On the morning of 19 December, Companies A and B of the 1st Battalion started forward, only to be hit in a narrow ravine by fire from assault guns of the Führer Begleit Brigade on the Auw road. They never left the assembly area, and only a few survivors scattered. Part of Company C crossed the highway, but only one platoon reached the high ground across the Ihrenbach.

The 2nd Battalion to the left crossed the Ihrenbach and achieved the sloped open ground above the Schoenberg–Andler road northeast of Schoenberg. Flak halftracks started a murderous fire between 1100 and 1120, and the three companies retreated over the crest of the hill to join Descheneaux. The 3rd Battalion crossed east of Hill 536 and into the woods of the Linnebach, where it came into a brief friendly-fire incident with Pruett's 2nd Battalion. Suddenly, panzers of the Führer Begleit Brigade appeared behind Descheneaux on Skyline Drive. The scene was fast becoming a slaughter.

Surrounded in a small depression with German artillery pouring in, Descheneaux surrendered despite the arguments of those objecting, 'We're being slaughtered,' he reasoned, '[and] I don't believe in fighting for glory if it won't accomplish anything. It looks like we'll have to pack it in.'[12] At 1430 on 19 December, Major William J Cody Garlow, Executive Officer of the 2nd Battalion, 423rd Infantry Regiment and grandson of Buffalo Bill Cody who, in the confusion of the friendly-fire incident, had joined with the 422nd Regiment, proceeded down the hillside frantically waving two white handkerchiefs. While Garlow parlayed with German officers to stop their artillery fire, word passed among the American troops to destroy their weapons. Only seventy men escaped. Approximately 7,000 men were taken into captivity, the largest American capitulation of the European war.[13]

Aftermath

Recriminations abound in seeking the causes of the 106th Division's collapse. Why had the front line units not sent out reconnaissance patrols in the days prior to the German offensive? Why had the bridge at Schoenberg not been prepared for demolition? Why had some unit commanders panicked and fled westward during the

---

12   Colonel George Louis Descheneaux Jr, from Newton, Massachusetts graduated from West Point in 1932. After the surrender, Colonel Descheneaux was initially held in Stalag XIIa before being transferred to Stalag IXb at Limburg an der Lahn, Germany where he contracted career-ending tuberculosis. Descheneaux died in 1984 at age 75 and is buried in the United States Military Academy Cemetery, West Point, New York.

Included in the capitulation was 22-year-old PFC Kurt Vonnegut, Jr whose 1969 novel, *Slaughterhouse-Five*, would describe his PoW experiences including the devastating fire-bombing of Dresden, Germany in February 1945.

13   On December 22, Division commander General Alan Jones was relieved; two days later, he suffered a heart attack. General Jones survived the war to die in 1969 at age 75. He is buried in Arlington National Cemetery, Arlington Virginia.

first hours of the assault? Certainly, the lack of combat experience and the recent occupation of new positions without adequate communications were mitigating factors.

Questions arose as to why Colonels Cavender and Descheneaux made no effort to attack or withdraw on 17 December while their positions were being encircled by the 18th Volksgrenadier Division. Had they done so, the outcome of the battle for the Schnee Eifel would have been quite different. On the other hand, both regiments lay within strong perimeters, but misunderstandings between division and corps commands led to confusion regarding permission to withdraw. Corps commanders promised re-enforcements that did not arrive.

Battlefield Tour

> From Auw continue south approximately 1.5 km. Turn left onto highway K158 and follow for 2.3 km into Schlausenbach on Hauptstraße. Stop at the Gasthaus on the right. (50.283811, 6.358031)

Only a few blown-up Westwall bunkers mark the Schnee Eifel battlefield, with no memorials to mark the 106th Division's disastrous defeat. The scarcity of memorials avows that much of the action took place in Germany and, perhaps, that America refused to commemorate defeat. However, those facts do not diminish the battlefield's importance, nor the sites where events occurred.

The roadway from Auw winds up and down the numerous ridges in the area, whose crests provide dramatic views of the countryside. Schlausenbach, named after the creek that flows through this area, crawls through a valley below. The Gasthaus 'Zum Kühlen Grunde' at Hauptstraße 6 is on the right, beyond a sharp curve and drop in elevation. The gasthaus held the **headquarters of the 422nd Infantry Regiment.** The small village holds only six-to-eight residences.

> Leave Schlausenbach east and, after 650 m, turn right and continue for 1.4 km to the forest track that crosses the roadway. (50.273945, 6.377939) The road from Schlausenbach meets highway L20 300 m ahead. Because highway L20 did not exist during the war, the main access to the ridge crest was slightly to the west along this parallel unimproved track, which connected the Westwall bunkers.

The **Westwall** (commonly called the **Siegfried Line** by the Allies) formed a defensive line stretching from Kleve, Germany in the Lower Rhine region to Basel, Switzerland. Along its 630-kilometer length, at times over 500,000 people working simultaneously erected 20,000 structures. Large quantities of material, including approximately 8 million tons of cement, 1.2 million tons of iron, and over 950,000 cubic meters of timber — almost twenty percent of the yearly production of iron and cement of the German Reich – abetted the labor.

The ruins of ten bunkers along this forest trail (signed *Bunkerweg*) that parallels the ridge slightly below its crest are readily visible. Understand that the bunkers often present little more than mangled blocks of steel-bar-reenforced concrete

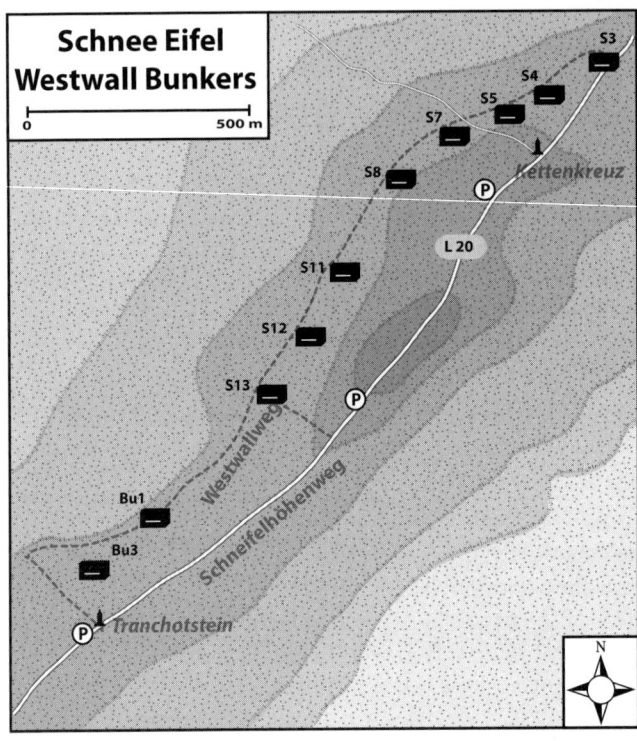

overgrown with trees and shrubs. In all cases they should be **considered to be extremely dangerous**. The walking distance to see all ten is 3.2 kilometers one-way, but two reasonable examples appear along the trail to the southwest.

Bunker S7 (standing for Schlausenbach #7) was a German type 105b machine-gun casemate and stands on the left, a short distance from the road to Schlausenbach. The ruins are covered with moss and trees, and shrubs grow through the cracks and holes behind a chain link fence.

After a further 310 meters, a footbridge over a drainage ditch provides access to **Bunker S8**, which was identical in design to S7 and is the best example on the *Bunkerweg*. The lack of forest vegetation allows easy viewing of the bunker ruins and the foxholes and shell craters that scar the surrounding terrain. Few of the West Wall bunkers were destroyed as a result of combat; instead, most were blown up by French engineers in 1949. The impressive pieces of concrete scattered about display the explosive forces used in the bunker's destruction. One, weighing approximately seven tons, rests 10 meters from the actual bunker site.

Return to the road from Schlausenbach.

The ruins of **Bunkers S5** and **S4** lie along the forest road on the opposite side of the road to Schlausenbach. They are typical squad shelters with ports for two machine guns. Both are heavily destroyed and surrounded by chain link fences because of the dangerous footing created by moss and dampness. Finally, **bunker S3** remains where the forest road meets highway L20. This bunker is completely covered in dirt and shrubs with none of it visible. S3 provides an example of how well these bunkers were hidden after the war and why, even with a bunker map, they are so difficult to locate.

Continue ahead 300 m, turn right, and follow highway (L20) along the Schnee Eifel, which parallels the initial positions of the 422nd and 423rd Infantry Regiments at

> the outbreak of the German offensive. After 6.4 km, turn right toward Bleialf (L17). After 3.4 km and upon entering Bleialf on Prümerstraße, follow the curve to the left (becomes Bahnhofstraße). After 1.4 km, stop at the old train station on the left. (50.232496, 6.270727)

At 0530 on 16 December, the 423rd Infantry Regiment's Antitank Company, commanded by Captain Charles B Reid, came under fire in Bleialf, three kilometers behind the front lines. After the 45-minute artillery bombardment lifted, Grenadier Regiment 293 struck Bleialf in force, driving the Antitank Company back through the village house-by-house. Simultaneously, another enemy group moved around the regiment's right flank along a railroad cut to insert itself between the Antitank Company and Cavalry Troop B that had been pushed back into the rail yards. As the right platoon of the Antitank Company was destroyed, the cavalry troops withdrew to Winterscheid 2.5 kilometers to the southwest. By 0800, the enemy held most of Bleialf.

Finally, at 0830, wire communication was re-established. Artillery fire from the 590th Field Artillery Battalion and commitment of Cannon Company troops fighting as infantry broke up the German attack. One hundred men from Service and Cannon Companies moved in by 0930. Seventy men of Company B, 81st Engineer Combat Battalion entrucked in Schoenberg and moved against the west shoulder of the penetration, but with only limited success. During the afternoon, thanks to fire support from Company C, 820th Tank Destroyer Battalion and field artillery, the village was cleared of enemy troops, with seventy-five taken prisoner.

German artillery fire again fell on Bleialf at 0300 on 17 December. The panzer-supported infantry attack began at 0530. The collapse of the defense along Bahnhofstraße enabled the enemy to attack from front and flank. Within one hour, the grenadiers had overrun defensive areas and the re-occupied town. Small teams fought as rear guard as others moved north toward the 423rd Regiment.

The disused rail line used by grenadiers to split the American defense approaches the **Bleialf train station** from the south. Ninety meters farther west a bicycle path heads north along a ridge following the rail cut and train tunnel of the original train line.

> Reverse direction and return east to Prümerstraße. Continue straight for 80 m before bearing right onto Oberstraße and continue to the cemetery on the left. (50.239413, 6.289760)

Because of its proximity to the Schwartze Mann cross-country skiing and hiking area, Bleialf has more than its fair share of restaurants providing a good stop for an afternoon lunch, especially when most villages in the area are rarely commercial.

Bleialf Communal Cemetery contains 244 German War Graves, indicative of the violence of the battle for the village. Surrounding tall yew bushes locate the plot in the center left. Quite possibly these are trench graves because of their narrow spacing — implying that they were not individual burials. Each grave is identified only by a small stone on the ground bearing whatever information may be known about the deceased. Many of the burials are dated 16 December 1944.

> Reverse direction and, after 180 m, turn right onto Auwer Straße (L1). Continue 1.1 km to the road junction locally known as *Justenschlag*. (50.248033, 6.280599)

North of Bleialf, the road splits with the left fork going to Schoenberg and the right fork to Auw. By capturing both ends of the Auw road, the Germans ensured that any American retrograde movement would be along forest trails. The choking mud and snow trapped vehicles forcing their abandonment. Thus, the displaced troops approached the Our River armed only with light automatic weapons and bazookas — at best.

During the quiet period of American occupation of this area, the *Justenschlag* intersection and much of Skyline Drive fell to German observation. The deadly accuracy of German fire against vehicles moving toward Bleialf earned the junction two nicknames: **88-corner** and **Purple Heart Corner**.

> From 88-corner, bear right onto highway L1 (Skyline Drive). After 1.6 km, the farm track on the left identifies the exit from the forest of Engineer's Cut-off (see below). (50.260986, 6.288727)

German armor used this route to pursue retreating American troops. The farm track in the wood visible to the left front was also the site of Lt Patton's encounter with that approaching armor (see below).

> Continue 1.1 km to the two houses on the left, then known as Zollhauser (50.269788, 6.294755).

The 590th Field Artillery Battalion used the two houses as a command post. On the evening of 18th December, the headquarters of the 423rd Regiment occupied the same structures. Colonel Cavender held his last battalion commander's conference here on the morning of 19 December.

American artillery was positioned of **Hill 575**, the high point across the highway that now holds a water reservoir for the city of Prüm. A service road offers parking and, from behind the water tanks, views of the Schnee Eifel ridgeline to the east are possible.

> Continue north on highway L1. After 1.4 km, a small copse stands on the left where the highway enters a curve to the right.

German guns in this small wood smashed the 422nd Infantry Regiment while it attempted to escape encirclement by crossing the highway to the west. (50.280906, 6.302952)

> Continue northeast for 1.1 km. Turn left toward Laudesfeld (K158) and stop after 700 m.

After the surrender of the two regiments, Second Lieutenant LR Walker, Company H, 422nd Regiment led a column of men away from the Andler road. He accumulated stragglers from fifteen different companies until the force numbered 199. Just before dark, they arrived at the 422nd Regiment's motor pool and supply base near Hill 576 southwest of Laudesfeld. Major Albert Ouellette,[14] 2nd Battalion Executive Officer, and Major William P Moon Jr,[15] commander 1st Battalion, 422nd Regiment joined the group that had by then grown to 355 and established a perimeter defense. Despite German artillery fire, the ad hoc group continued to present a stiff resistance but at one point escorted a column of captured American ambulances carrying German wounded through its lines. A German surrender demand led to negotiating terms, really more a delaying tactic to permit the exhausted men an opportunity to rest before entering captivity. At 0800 on 21 December, the last soldiers from the two ill-fated regiments surrendered.

A small pine copse not visible from highway K158 tops the hill. The side road is restricted to local residents and farm vehicles. Walk 280 meters up Hill 576 to a farm track on the right and follow to the copse. (50.288996, 6.302356) A fiber board nailed to a tree in the middle of the copse bears a fast-fading insignia of the 106th Infantry Division and the inscription:

> In proud memory of the '**Lost 500**' of the 106th Infantry Division who fought on this hill until 21 December 1944.

> Reverse direction and return southeast to highway L1. Turn right and, after 5.1 km, turn right at 88-corner toward Schoenberg (L17). Proceed 1.2 km to the hairpin curve where a forest trail enters the woods on the right. (50.25700, 6.27912)

At roughly 1500 on 16 December, Colonel Pruett's Company F arrived in Schoenberg from division reserve. Pruett ordered a young platoon leader, 2nd Lieutenant Oliver Patton, to move southeast to find the 590th and 589th Field Artillery Battalions. Patton selected three men and started off toward Bleialf in a jeep. About 1 kilometer north of Bleialf, he discovered a corduroy (log-covered) road that he believed led to the 590th. Taking the rough road, his jeep had not gone far before

---

14 Major Albert A Ouellette suffered two machine-gun-bullet wounds to his face shortly before his capture. He was stripped of his heavy overshoes and forced to trudge eastward in the snow. He survived his PoW experience to return to the United States in May 1945. Ouellette remained in the US Army, attaining the rank of lieutenant colonel. He died in 2007 at age 94.

15 Major William Perrow Moon Jr was held at Stalag IVb in Muhlberg, Saxony, Germany. Moon remained in the US Army after the war, attaining the rank of lieutenant colonel. He died in 1997 at age 85 and is buried in Fort Hill Memorial Park, Lynchburg, Virginia.

Patton heard the clanking racket and shouts of an approaching tracked vehicle and accompanying infantry. He realized that they could not be American. The jeep driver drove into a ditch, and the team dispersed into the woods. The German unit passed believing, as Patton had hoped, that the jeep was a long-abandoned wreck. Patton and his men then recovered the jeep and continued on their way. Patton found the two artillery battalions and delivered his message.[16] That night Pruett moved his battalion to the Skyline Drive and prepared to move north toward Auw.

American troops referred to the corduroy road as the **Engineer's Cut-Off** because it was constructed by men of the 168th Engineer Combat Battalion to avoid exposing troops to deadly German 88-mm artillery fire at 88-corner 900 meters to the south where the dangerously exposed hair-pin turn was always under interdiction fire from German gunners. The cut-off also shortened the route from Schoenberg to Radscheid by three kilometers.

The 423rd Regiment's I&R Platoon, commanded by Lieutenant Ivan H Long, had formed a roadblock south of Radscheid at the outlet of the Engineer Cut-Off to protect the regiment's left flank and rear. After Colonel Cavender's surrender, Lieutenant Long's men made their way north, crossed the Our, and achieved St-Vith. Long and his eighteen men formed the only organized escape in the two trapped regiments.

> Continue 2.6 km toward Schoenberg (L17, becomes highway N695 after crossing into Belgium). Stop at the side road on the right. (50.275254, 6.270928)

After the 589th Field Artillery Battalion displaced from its Skyline Drive positions, the remaining seven guns of Batteries A and B were situated east of this section of the highway. About 0700 on 17 December, German grenadiers overran the battalion command post where the battalion commander, Lieutenant Colonel Thomas P Kelley Jr was still trying to save Battery C's four howitzers. Battalion Executive Officer Major Arthur C Parker III assumed command of the remaining guns. With enemy troops approaching, Major Parker ordered the guns to displace again and to reassemble west of St-Vith.

First Lieutenant Eric Fisher Wood, executive officer of Battery A, maneuvered three of the unit's guns onto the road and across the Our River only minutes before grenadiers approached from Andler. Meanwhile, Lt Wood was still helping the crew extricate the fourth gun out of the mud. Under small-arms fire from approaching infantry, Wood jumped on a truck speeding through German troops in Schoenberg and crossed the bridge only to confront a tank blocking the highway west of town. The truck screeched to a halt. Wood dashed into the nearby forest despite fire from German infantry. The last American troops had crossed the Schoenberg bridge.

Battery B was cut off by a panzer. The artillerymen destroyed their guns and then attempted to follow Wood in their trucks. All were captured. As a result, Major

---

16 Second Lieutenant Oliver Patton was injured by his own handgrenade explosion two days later and shot in both legs later the same day. He was unable to withdraw with his battalion and was left in the care of an aidman in the basement command post at Zollhauser. Both men were captured. Lt Patton spent the remainder of the war in Stalag IXc, Bad Sulza, Saxony, Germany.

Parker had escaped with only three of the 589th Battalion's twelve howitzers. (See Chapter Five.)

> Continue 1.3 km to the curve to the right. (50.282919, 6.26774) With no safe parking, continue an additional 400 m onto Op der Schleef on the right, which ascends toward **Hill 504**. (50.286183, 6.266984)

Captain John B Huett's Company L led the 423rd Regiment's attack upon Schoenberg. Two platoons moved astride the road when a Sherman tank nosed around the hairpin curve in the road. Huett's joy subsided when the tank turret showed German helmets. Under assault by the tank and half-track-mounted flak guns to the front and grenadiers from the rear, Company L was trapped. Captain Huett pulled his men onto the lower slopes of Hill 504 and continued to resist. After ammunition ran out that afternoon, thirty-two survivors surrendered.

> Continue 400 m into Schoenberg; at the roundabout, take the 2nd exit to the front of the church. Park across the road from the church and walk to the Our River bridge. (50.289404, 6.263575)

On 17 December, the forward battalion of the Grenadier Regiment 294, supported by StuGs of Sturmgeschütz Brigade 244, attacked along the riverside road from Andler and pushed elements of the 32nd Cavalry Squadron out of Schoenberg to capture the bridge intact.

The **Schoenberg Bridge** has been demolished and rebuilt 50 meters downstream from the original in front of the new modern church in Koenig Baldwin Platz.

> Proceed back to the roundabout and take the 2nd exit toward Manderfeld / Andler (N626). Continue 1.0 km and turn right onto side road (Am Linebach). Stop at a convenient spot. (50.293091, 6.276869)

German half-tracks and assault vehicles lined this section of highway N626, pumping heavy fire into American troops on the high ground to the east. Colonel Pruett's 2nd Battalion, 423rd Regiment advanced toward highway N626 using a deep ravine as shelter, but it became separated from the remainder of the regiment in the rugged, wooded draw of the Linnebach, where it came under friendly fire from the neighboring 422nd Regiment. Pruett withdrew his men up the hillside to join Colonel Descheneaux.

> Return to the highway and turn right toward Manderfeld / Andler (N626, not signed). After 100 m, bear right and continue 290 m to the road junction; turn right and follow to the end of the road. Note: the road is narrow but paved; the turnaround at

> the end is difficult. (50.288971, 6.284732)

On the high ground to the right amid mixed woodlands and pastures, the 422nd and 423rd Infantry Regiments sheltered along the Linnebach before their surrender. Near that site, Major Garlow made contact with German troops to negotiate the surrender.

Side Trip: Wereth Massacre and Lt Eric Fisher Wood Memorials

> A convenient detour provides access to two sites of events in the Battle of the Bulge.

> Leave the Descheneaux surrender site by returning to highway N626. Turn right toward Manderfeld / Andler. After 1.4 km, turn left toward Amel / Herresbach (Auf Hoch). Continue 6.4 km through Wereth to the memorial on the hillside on the left. (50.348688, 6.231222)

The 333rd Field Artillery Battalion was manned by African-American soldiers under the command of a white commander and African-American junior officers. It fielded 155-mm towed howitzers. Starting in October 1944, the unit was stationed along the Andler–Schoenberg road as part of the US VIII Corps artillery. Although Batteries A and B displaced toward Bastogne at the beginning of the battle, Battery C participated in the early defense of Bleialf. The unit was overrun when it attempted to withdraw across the Our River on 17 December.

The **Wereth Massacre Memorial** was erected in honor of eleven soldiers captured, beaten, stabbed, and executed on this site by reconnaissance troops of Kampfgruppe Knittel's 3rd Company, SS Panzer Reconnaissance Battalion 1, 1st SS Panzer Division. The memorial consists of a small triangular park at the edge of a pasture backed by the flags of four Allied countries. Two plaques identify the event in English, German, Dutch, and French:

> On December 17, 1944 eleven African American soldiers with the 333rd FAB were captured and massacred here by the SS. This site is dedicated to all black soldiers of World War Two.

The eleven soldiers were Privates Curtis Adams, George Davis Jr, James Leatherwood, Nathaniel Moss, George Molten, and Due Turner; Corporals Mager Bradley and Robert Green; Sergeants Thomas Forte, William Pritchett, and James Stewart.

> Continue toward Halenfeld. After 1.1 km, turn left toward Meyerode and follow for 2.8 km in Meyerode. Turn left following Martinusstraße to the village school on the right. (50.328273, 6.188523)

Meyerode

A **German 75-mm Pak 40 antitank gun** stands in the village center in front of the school. The bar opposite the school briefly housed the headquarters of Generaloberst der Waffen-SS Josef 'Sepp' Dietrich, commander of the Sixth Panzer Army. (50.32817, 6.18868)

> Continue south on Martinusstraße and, after 450 m at a large curve to the right, turn left onto the country lane as indicated by a brown tourist sign 'Memorial Lt Eric Wood'. After 2.5 km, stop at the small stone cross on the right. (50.30289, 6.19484)

A few days after Lt Eric Wood made his escape west of Schoenberg, townspeople heard rifle fire coming from these woods. Civilians knew full well of German patrols hunting for American stranglers throughout the area. The Germans spread stories of resistance fighters in the woods. Such fighting continued for a month until mid January. On 23 January, the village of Meyerode was liberated when American troops pushed back the German lines. The townspeople re-entered the forest to find the frozen body of an American soldier on a hill outside the village. Around the dead American were the frozen corpses of seven German soldiers. The American was later identified as First Lieutenant Eric F Wood Jr.

After the war, German soldiers told of a band of Americans led by a young officer who roamed the forest attacking supply trucks and small-unit patrols. American Graves Registration carried over two-hundred dead Germans from the forest, most from shallow graves and stripped of their equipment. What really happened, we will never know.

The **Wood Memorial** identifies the site where the young officer's body was discovered. The forest renders it easy to miss, its only indication being a small sign 'US Memorial' on the left side. The dark grey stone cross mounted upon a large natural stone carries the inscription:

> In Jan 1945 died here in heroic struggles by the German Offensive
> Eric Fisher Wood
> Capt US Army
> [repeated in German]

The memorial certainly is not grandiose, but Wood's legacy remains.

> To regain the tour route, continue 2.0 km and then turn right toward St-Vith (N626, unsigned). Continue 3.1 km to the top of the rise and stop on the side road on the left. (50.284079, 6.152026) This completes the side trip. Total distance: 11 km

17,18

---

17   German 75-mm Pak 40 antitank gun, the mainstay of German forces later in the war, was capable of firing fourteen rounds per minute with a direct fire range of 1,800 meters (5,900 feet) for armor piercing shells and as far as 7,700 meters for high explosive rounds.

18   First Lieutenant Eric Fisher Wood Jr was the privileged son of Brigadier General Eric Fisher Wood Sr. He was the outstanding cadet at Valley Forge Military Academy and graduated from

> From the Descheneaux surrender site, return to the Schoenberg / Andler highway (N626). Turn left toward Schoenberg. At the roundabout, take the first exit and continue toward St-Vith for 9.4 km. At the top of the rise, stop on the side road on the right. (50.284079, 6.152026)

Battle of St-Vith
17 to 22 December 1944

Early in the morning of 17 December, Brigadier General William H Hoge's Combat Command B, 9th Armored Division rumbled through St-Vith on its way to Steinebrück. Although one of the unit's armored infantry battalions did cross the Our and drive on Winterspelt, events elsewhere convinced Hoge to recall the troops and establish a defense south of St-Vith. At 1600 that day, the first units of the CCB, 7th Armored Division arrived at St-Vith after fighting against the flow of retreating troops and vehicles on roadways to the west. Brigadier General Clarke, its commander, personally directed traffic west of St-Vith to establish priorities for his arriving units. General Clarke joined 106th divisional headquarters at St Josephs Kloster and took charge despite being junior in grade to both Generals Jones (106th Infantry Division) and Hoge (CCB, 9th Armored Division). The arrivals continued through the night as units built a defense in the shape of a large horseshoe based upon the hills to the east of the city stretching from Hünningen to Burg Reuland.

Von Manteuffel's plan called for the main German attack against St-Vith across the flat open ground from Wallerode. Subsidiary attacks occurred along the highway from Schoenberg and from Winterspelt via Steinebrück. However, German supply columns — many horse drawn — were ensnared in traffic jams in the Schnee Eifel and hampered operations. The Führer Begleit Brigade, the main German armored unit assigned to the assault, was partially occupied with containing the remnants of the two encircled American regiments. Thus, the first German efforts against St-Vith took the form of probing attacks while both sides accumulated additional forces.

GERMAN OBJECTIVE	To capture the road junction at St-Vith
FORCES	
American:	CCB, 7th Armored Division (Brigadier General Bruce C Clarke), CCB, 9th Armored Division (Brigadier General William M Hoge), and elements 424th Infantry Regiment
German:	18th Volksgrenadier Division (Oberst Günther Hoffmann-Schönbrun) and elements Führer Begleit Brigade (Oberst Otto Remer); later, elements of 62nd and 560th Volksgrenadier Divisions

---

Princeton University in 1942 while also being a member of the Pennsylvania National Guard.

Wood was posthumously awarded a Distinguished Service Cross. He is buried in Henri-Chapelle American Cemetery, Henri-Chapelle, Belgium. He never saw his only son born one a week before the battle began.

Chapter Four

Schnee Eifel

Result	American troops delayed the German advance for four days
Casualties	
American:	7th Armored Division: 228 killed, 642 wounded, and 162 missing and presumed PoW; 103 armored vehicles lost
German:	Estimated at 5,100 casualties
Location	St-Vith is 80 km southeast of Liège

Battle

The key to the defense of St-Vith was the Prümerberg Heights that overlooked a sharp curve in highway N676 1.2 kilometers east of St-Vith. Whoever occupied the ridgeline would dominate St-Vith. On the morning of 17 December and amid the wild confusion of military units and refugees pouring west, General Jones dispatched his engineers and the headquarters defense platoon to Prümerberg in an effort to block the German advance from Schoenberg. With an odd collection of antitank guns, a few bazookas, jeep-mounted machine guns, and a platoon of six tank destroyers from the 820th Tank Destroyer Battalion, Lieutenant Colonel Thomas J Riggs Jr, commander of the 81st Engineer Combat Battalion, joined 168th Engineer Combat Battalion troops and established a roadblock across the road to Schoenberg near the Prümerberg Heights. The weakly-armed force stopped the first German probes from the east.

Strong German units passed St-Vith to the north and south while the 7th Armored Division occupied the exposed salient. At 0200 on 18 December, troops from Panzergrenadier Regiment 2 threatened Clarke's left flank by capturing the crossroads at Recht. Enemy forces spent the day probing the American line striking the perimeter from the northeast (Wallerode at 0800), the north (Hünningen also at 0800), the east (Prümerberg at 0920, 1130, and in mid afternoon), the south (at midmorning), and the southeast (in the afternoon). After the surrender of 106th Division troops on 19 December, German forces focused their full strength upon St-Vith. Only the extreme road congestion in the German captured territory slowed their plans to attack the salient.

Throughout the night of 20 December, the defenders heard the roar of tank engines and the clank of tank treads. All American reserves had been committed. At 1100 on 21 December, after a short artillery bombardment, three regiments of grenadiers fortified by Panther tanks attacked along the entire line. Assault squads pressured the line despite incurring heavy casualties. Panzerfausts targeted machine-gun positions. By 2035, further attacks directed along three main roadways from Schonberg, Amblève, and Steinebrück all punctured the defensive line. At 2200 General Clarke ordered a withdrawal to high ground to the west. St-Vith was lost with twenty-thousand American troops running risk of capture.

By 22 December, Clarke's force showed signs of disintegrating. Command staffs had been killed or captured, patrols disappeared, fuel and ammunition supply levels were dire. Pressure on the flanks of the horseshoe forced American units westward to a defensive perimeter on high ground centered upon Commanster that became known as the Fortified Goose Egg because of its appearance on overlay maps. To General Hoge, it had more the appearance of Custer's Last Stand. Field Marshall

158 The Bulge Battlefields

Montgomery issued orders for the withdrawal of all forces east of the Salm River to positions behind the 82nd Airborne Division.

The evacuation began at 0600 the next morning with troops headed along three evacuation routes toward Salm River bridges at Salmchâteau and Vielsalm. Daylight withdrawal before the enemy, a most difficult military maneuver, operated like clockwork with units leapfrogging along the roadways while maintaining active rear guards. Much of the credit goes to General Clark. By dark, much of the surviving forces landed safely across the river. [19, 20]

Aftermath

Major German units, in particular, the 1st SS Panzer Division to the north and the 116th Panzer Division to the south, successfully bypassed St-Vith, although the inferior road network slowed their progress. By 20 December, the 560th Volksgrenadier Division and elements of 2nd Panzer Division also had moved far to the west.

On 25 December, with the town now firmly in German hands, American bombers dropped 1,700 tons of bombs and incendiaries that obliterated the town and killed unknown hundreds of Belgian civilians. On Sunday, 23 January 1945, CCB, 7th Armored Division, the heroic defenders of St-Vith, led the march back into the liberated city — by then little more than ruins.

Conclusion

The importance of the defense of St-Vith stands alongside that of Bastogne. The retention of St-Vith sent waves of disruption through the German supply situation. In the words of General der Panzertruppen Hasso von Manteuffel, 'You don't surround and bypass an armored division.'

Battlefield Tour

> The tour starts at the defensive line east of the city that Lieutenant Colonel Riggs established on 17 December. Riggs's main defense line ran on both sides of highway N626 along the ridge marked by the high point on the highway. (50.284079, 6.152026) Much of the four days' combat took place in the open fields to the north and east.

At 1030 on 17 December, 106th Division headquarters ordered Companies A and C, 168th Engineer Combat Battalion to establish defensive positions near Heuem, nine kilometers east of St-Vith. Learning that the objective was already in enemy hands, the two companies took up positions along the edge of the woods on the Prümerberg overlooking the highway. At 1155 Colonel Riggs arrived with 120 men of his HQ Company and Company A and one platoon of infantry from Company F, 423rd Infantry Regiment. The forces combined under Riggs's command. First contact occurred at 1225 when an enemy patrol encountered the 168th Battalion's foxhole line to exchange rifle and machine-gun fire.

---

19   Combat Command B, 7th Armored Division was awarded the Distinguished Unit Citation for its defense of St-Vith.

20   Major Wilhelm Druke, commander of Grenadier Regiment 294, received the Knight's Cross of the Iron Cross for capturing St-Vith.

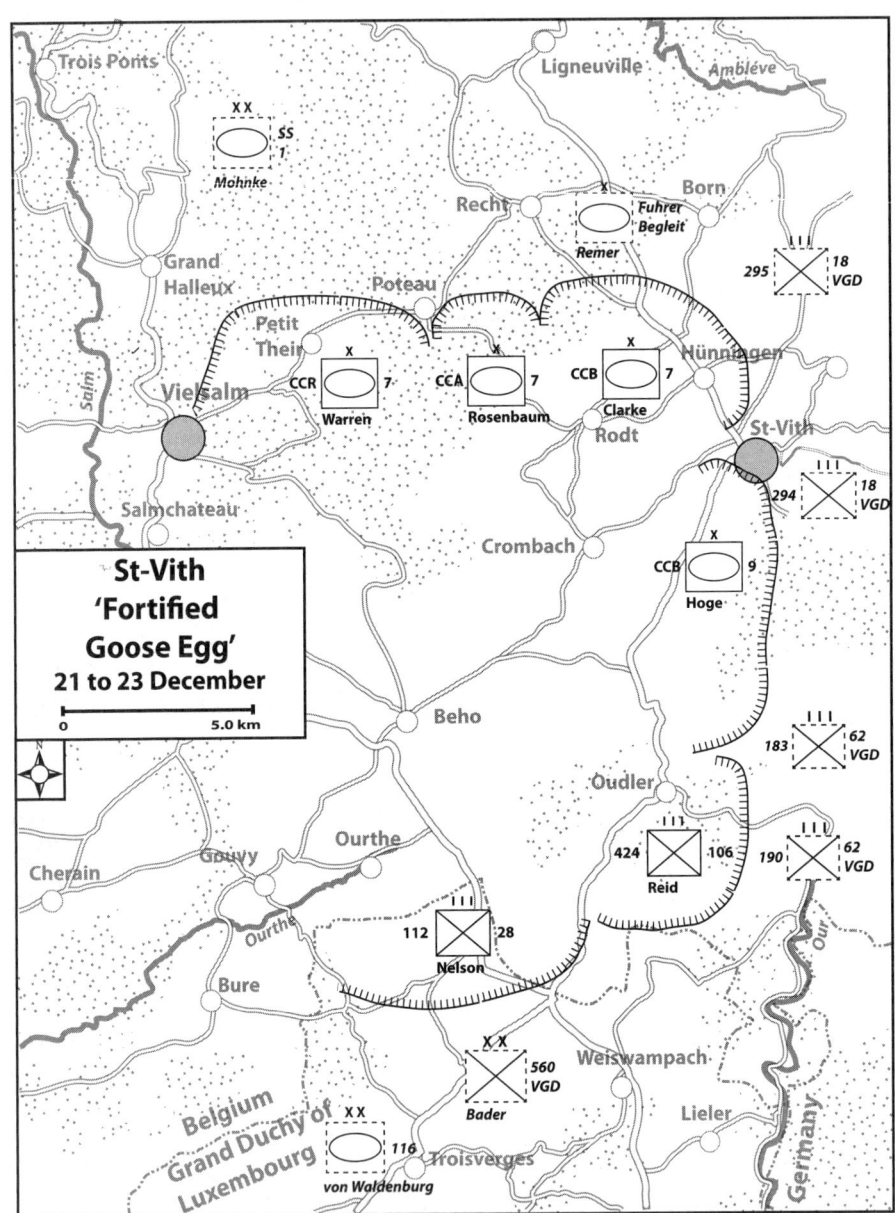

At 1430, a German column approached St-Vith with three assault guns accompanied by infantry. One gun crew dismounted almost in defiance of the American defenders. Lieutenant William E Holland, the commander of Company B, 168th Engineer Combat Battalion, killed them with a burst from a .50-caliber machine gun. A bazooka team took out a second SP gun. American tank destroyers, despite lacking gun sights and having to aim over the gun barrels, made the road hot enough that other approaching enemy armor was forced back. Colonel Riggs ordered the tank

Chapter Four Schnee Eifel 161

destroyers to reposition, but for some reason they left the scene entirely. A liaison officer then raised P-47 aircraft by radio. Fighter-bombers strafed the enemy troops and knocked out another assault gun.

Over the next few hours, General Clarke added men from Troop B, 87th Cavalry Reconnaissance Squadron, Company A, 31st Tank Battalion, and two companies of armored infantry. All troops east of St-Vith were placed under the command of Lieutenant Colonel William Fuller.

The German assault renewed, met this time by the recently arrived Sherman tanks of Company A, 31st Tank Battalion. Point-blank fire destroyed three panzers and killed 50 enemy infantry.

> Continue toward St-Vith. After 1.0 km where a sharp curve turns right, turn left onto Schlierbacher Weg, where brown and white tourist signs indicate 'US Memorial.' Follow for 1.1 km to the memorial of the left. (50.279146, 6.149016)

On 18 December, Fuller repulsed repeated attacks south of the highway. At 0800, four tanks, eight armored cars, and the Mobile Battalion of the 18th Volksgrenadier Division struck Company B, 38th Armored Infantry Battalion from Wallerode. Panzerfausts and artillery tree bursts wiped out a rifle squad, but Company B rallied with an immediate counterattack. At 0845, the enemy attack shifted to the right flank of Company B and the 168th engineers. A 200-man German force was driven back, leaving in its wake a burning PzKpfw IV and an assault gun. At 1130, a renewed attack quickly lost momentum when a lucky shot from a Sherman took out the leading tank.

In mid-afternoon, a battalion of infantry with support from four tanks and eight assault guns again hit the right-hand platoon of Company B and the engineers. Colonel Riggs personally led his 81st engineers up the hill against heavy automatic weapons fire to contain the penetration. Both tank companies added enfilade fire from the north. After three and one-half hours of sometimes hand-to-hand fighting, the reserve Troop B, 87th Cavalry Squadron restored the line.[21]

The final German assault started at 1600 on 21 December when waves of grenadiers, supported by artillery, mortars, and Nebelwerfer rockets, used panzerfausts against log-covered foxholes. After a brief pause around 1900, the tank-led assault renewed. A Panther tank was destroyed while approaching along a logging road while two more approached along the highway, firing directly into the foxholes. German grenadiers' bodies filled the roadside ditches, but waves kept coming. Fuller's machine-gun and bazooka teams were special targets. By 2000, when the 38th Battalion command post was overrun, eight Panther and Tiger tanks entered St-Vith.

Forty-five minutes later, the Prümerberg defenders received orders from General Clarke to withdraw behind the city. However, close contact with the enemy and twelve hours of continuous combat made such a move impossible. Survivors of the defense attempted to exfiltrate to the south along the forest track opposite the

---

21 The 81st Engineer Combat Battalion was awarded a Distinguished Unit Citation for gallantry and its determination to hold the position.

monument. They found the road in German hands. The Prümerberg force of 670 had been reduced to 187, of which only approximately one-half escaped capture. Colonel Riggs was taken prisoner.[22]

The memorial on the Prümerberg Heights is a large, smooth granite stone that displays the insignia of the **168th Engineering Combat Battalion** with the words 'assistance to all' and carries the inscription:

In Defense of St-Vith
December 17th – 23rd, 1944
By order of the Secretary of the Army in the name of the President of the United States of America
Awarded Distinguished Unit Citation
Cited in the order of the day by Charles Prince of Belgium, Regent of the Kingdom
Awarded Belgian Croix de Guerre
In Memory of those who paid the supreme sacrifice

Numerous **foxholes and shell craters** are evident along the logging trail across the roadway from the memorial. Trench lines and foxholes dug by Company B, 168th Engineer Combat Battalion punctuate the forest along the logging road behind the memorial, including some on the crest of the ridge that overlook highway N676. Unfortunately, forestry activity is slowly destroying artifacts of the battle. The defensive strength of the position is most evident 100 meters farther along the roadway where a view down the slope observes anything coming from the east.

Schlierbacher Weg continues east through the Sankt Vither Wald to Schlierbach. This alternative route of attack aided German armor in its efforts to dislodge the Prümerberg defenders.

Reverse direction and return to highway N626. Turn left toward St-Vith (N626) and follow for 1.2 km into the town. At the second roundabout, take the third exit onto Klosterstraße as indicated by a 'US Memorial' sign. Continue down Klosterstraße for 450 m to the four flag poles. (50.27515, 6.12669)

St-Vith

St-Vith (Sankt Vith) was named for St Vitus, a Sicilian martyr dating from the time of Roman Emperor Diocletian. The community's central location led to its being a major marketplace by the 12th century and also resulted in pillages in 1543, 1602, and 1689. The area was part of France until Napoleon's defeat in 1815. The Congress of Vienna gave the district to Prussia, hence the predominantly German geographic names. After the First World War, the Treaty of Versailles transferred it to Belgium.

---

22 Lieutenant Colonel Thomas J Riggs had been a midshipman at the US Naval Academy, then a star football player at the University of Illinois. After his capture, Colonel Riggs marched east. Riggs escaped captivity near the Polish border, sheltered with the Polish Underground for three days, joined an advancing Red Army tank unit, and was evacuated through Odessa, USSR to miraculously rejoin his unit in the spring of 1945.

Chapter Four

Schnee Eifel 163

St-Vith stands upon a low hill surrounded by higher elevations. The southern limit is defined by railway cuts. The city received occasional large caliber shellfire on 16 December, but it was the subsequent American bombing that destroyed the city. Today, St-Vith is a thriving town with a very active commercial district.

Office Du Tourisme Des Cantons De L'Est
Hauptstraße 54   4780 Sankt Vith, Belgium
Tel: +32 (0)80 22 76 64   Fax: +32 (0)80 22 65 39
E-mail: info@eastbelgium.com
Web: http://www.eastbelgium.com/home/ (German, French, and Dutch only)

Touristinfo St-Vith (located in the Rathaus with the civil government)
Hauptstraße 43   4780 St-Vith, Belgium
Tel: +32 (0)80 280 130   Fax: +32 (0)80 228 001
E-mail: touristinfo@st.vith.be   Web: https://www.st.vith.be

A large rock monument to the **106th Infantry Division** stands in front of 1950s school building. The divisional headquarters used the stone St Joseph Kloster building 70 meters to the south. The monument bears a plaque:
> In memory of the men of the 106th Infantry Division who fought and died for their country in the Ardennes Forest during the winter of 1944-45.

Reverse direction back to the large roundabout and take the 3rd exit onto Luxemburgerstraße (E421 & N62). After 230 m, turn left onto Büchelstraße and proceed 120 m to the tower on the left. (50.279607, 6.124805) Convenient parking extends along Pulverstraße, which is a short walk from shops and cafes in the central business district.

The **Buchel Tower** presents the sole remnant of the fortifications constructed by Johann von Valkenburg in 1350 that surrounded St-Vith prior to its destruction by French occupiers in 1689. The Christmas 1944 bombing by Allied warplanes partly destroyed the tower and buried a refugee family within its walls. The tower has become a symbol of the city's survival.

Several sign boards scattered throughout the central section of the city describe St-Vith's early history and its destruction during the battle. Accompanying photographs provide vivid comparison of St-Vith in the 1920s and 1930s with its current appearance. Most explanations are in four languages. Maps identifying their locations are available at the tourist office.

A plaque on the exterior wall of the St-Vith tourist office commemorates the **7th Armored Division**'s defense of the city and how '…preventing any advance and any exploitation of this main line, thus frustrating the German Offensive by its sacrifice permitting the launching of the Allied Counter-offensive.' (50.280593, 6.125888)

> Continue north along Pulverstraße. After 160 m, turn left onto Ortstraße and, after 80 m, take the 1st Roundabout exit onto Rodterstarsse (N675). Follow 300 m the roundabout intersection with Hauptstraße (E421 / N62). Take the 2nd exit and proceed 130 m to the monument on the right. (50.285368, 6.121359)

The **2nd Infantry Division Monument** is across the street from the town cemetery and is identified by the division's Indian Head insignia. The inscription, 'for those who fought and died for freedom,' is the same on both sides. The 2nd Infantry Division occupied positions on the Schnee Eifel until 11 December when the 106th Division replaced the 2nd. The 2nd Division then moved north for the attack on Wahlerscheid and the Roer Dams.

> Continue northwest toward Malmédy (E421 / N62) for 1.4 km. At the roundabout, take the 3rd exit toward Vielsalm (N670). Follow for 9.6 km while the highway crosses over the Autoroute and becomes highway N675. Stop at the Poteau crossroads. (50.312205, 6.011747)

Ambush at Poteau
18 December 1944

After withdrawing from Manderfeld, the 14th Cavalry Group established a command post in the stone building on the north side of the crossroads.

Objective	Engagement of opportunity
Forces	
American:	Task Force Mayes (Major James L Mayes)
German:	I Battalion, SS Panzergrenadier Regiment 1 (SS-Major Werner Pötschke) and SS Panzerjäger Battalion 1 (SS-Major Karl Rettlinger), Kampfgruppe Hansen
Result	Task Force Mayes withdrew toward Vielsalm
Casualties	
American:	A few wounded
German:	Uncertain
Location	Poteau is 11 km northwest of St-Vith

Battle

In the pre-dawn of 18 December, Task Force Mayes left Poteau with the assignment to re-occupy Born. Major James Mayes left Poteau toward Recht, unaware that it was in German hands. Only 600 meters from the Poteau Crossroads, panzerfausts struck and set aflame the leading M5 Stuart light tank and M8 armored car. The roadsides erupted in small-arms fire when the task force encountered I Battalion, SS Panzergrenadier Regiment 1 converging on Poteau from Recht.[23]

Mayes's men fought a delaying action while they withdrew their armored cars, half-tracks, and assault guns back toward the crossroads. They held the junction for the rest of the morning. At one point, Staff Sergeant Woodrow Reeves climbed upon the turret of his tank to man its antiaircraft machine gun against enemy infantry. He inflicted heavy casualties, even refusing an officer's order to seek shelter by replying, 'Can't, Lieutenant; too busy shooting Germans.' Sgt Reeves finally fell to enemy fire.[24] Pressured by the larger SS force, the 14th Cavalry Group's new commander, Lieutenant Colonel Augustine Dugan, ordered a withdrawal toward Vielsalm.[25]

The panzergrenadiers proceeded southwest and captured the crossroads at Poteau, thereby cutting behind St-Vith and establishing positions only 20 kilometers from Vielsalm. Brigadier General Robert W Hasbrouck, 7th Armored Division commander, reacted to this even more serious threat by sending Company C, 40th Tank Battalion, on a delaying mission while he assembled Colonel Dwight A Rosebaum's CCA to counterattack. The railway cut and open ground south of the crossroads exposed approaching vehicles to enemy guns sited upon the hillside to the north. The tank-infantry teams approaching from the south could not cross the 700 meters of open terrain against the intense automatic weapons and shell fire. At dusk, Lieutenant Gerald Reeves led his platoon of tanks against Poteau while the 48th Armored Infantry Battalion, courtesy of illumination by three burning enemy tanks, pressed into the village. The battle raged through the night. By morning, Americans held Poteau. The enemy retained possession of woods north of the village until CCA attacked to dislodge them in mid-morning. After five hours of brutal combat, CCA re-established contact with CCR on the left and CCB on the right.[26] Two days later, CCA abandoned Poteau and pulled back across the Salm River.

Battlefield Tour

Unfortunately, the privately owned **Ardennen Poteau '44 Museum** has been permanently closed.

Continue toward Recht (N659) for 650 m and stop on a forest track in a copse on the left. (50.315031, 6.018489)

The **German ambush** struck at this curve in the roadway. The terrain on the right drops two-to-three meters rather quickly into a field of scrub brush and lowlands

---

23   Task Force Mayes was composed in part of Troop C, 32nd Cavalry Squadron, survivors of 18th Cavalry Squadron, and a platoon of 3-inch towed guns from 820th Tank Destroyer Battalion.

24   Staff Sergeant Woodrow Reeves was awarded a Distinguished Service Cross. Sergeant Reeves is buried in Ramsey Springs, Michigan. He was 29 years old.

25   Despite his re-energizing the squadron, Colonel Dugan was relieved later in a general removal of senior officers of 14th Cavalry Group.

26   Lieutenant Gerald Reeves was wounded on December 19th.

that were snow and ice covered at the time of the engagement. The panzergrenadiers held positions on the hillside to the left and in the wooded area behind it.

> Proceed to Vielsalm by reversing direction and continuing toward Vielsalm (N675) at the Poteau crossroads. Follow the highway for 8 km into the city.

Other Points of Interest

> **Burtonville**
> The village has erected a number of small, plasticized cardboard posters on wooden posts around the village, probably for the 70th anniversary celebrations. The signs describe the story of 'Burtonville 1945' and bear photographs of wreckage of village buildings.
> On 23 December, the first civilian victims of the offensive against Burtonville were killed at **Chez Remacly** when a shell penetrated the building and killed Orphyse Remacly and Julie and Hortense Degeest. (50.28374, 5.96844)
> At 0800 on 24 December SS troops arrived and moved into this **presbytery**, driving Abbé Guillaume and his servant Clémence Paul into an unheated room in the building. After a few days, when the abbé died of cold, the SS threw his body into the snow. Clémence Paul was collected at Chez Gabriel and, after the return of American troops, she was taken to a Liège hospital. She died following the ill treatment and the state of shock at what she had suffered. (50.283263, 5.964741)
> The **Gabriel-Mathieu** farm complex was the site of a German radio system. After the reoccupation of the village, the Germans installed a radio truck in the courtyard of the farm half-hidden in the barn. American artillery quickly targeted the house, and the structure was completely destroyed. (50.283421, 5.965963)
> On the evening of 17 January, American troops launched an assault to recapture of the town. The **Lambert farm** was intentionally set afire with phosphorus bullets to illuminate the battlefield. As many as sixty refugees sheltered in the cellar ran in every direction to avoid the ricocheting bullets. (50.28448, 5.96301)
> An American fighter plane was shot down and crashed in the field behind the sign on 21 January 1945. American soldiers in the courtyard of a farmhouse at that time hurried to the rescue of the pilot. Unfortunately, his parachute had not opened, whereby the soldiers brought his body back into the barn. (50.28767, 5.96714)
> A stone memorial bears a plaque that states, 'In memory of the **290th Infantry Regiment, 75th Infantry Division** of the US Army. In gratitude for the liberation of Burtonville on the 17th and 18th January 1945.' An adjoining plaque lists the names of the ten civilians killed during the Battle of the Bulge. (50.285305, 5.971519)
> The final information sign stands to the right of the memorial and is titled **The German Aircraft**. In March 1945, village children discovered a downed German airplane in the Grand Bois barely one kilometer from the village. It contained the bodies of three crew members. The missing aircraft was later identified as a Junkers

Chapter Four

Schnee Eifel 167

> (JU88/G-1) piloted by Unteroffizier Günther Fengler and shot down by flak on 1 January 1945 after bombing Stavelot. The airplane presents an unsolved mystery as to the identity of a female member of the crew.
> The entire route around the village is 1.3 kilometers.

27

Salm River Sector
21 to 23 December 1944

On 21 December, while American defenses in front of St-Vith started to crumble, the US 82nd Airborne Division built a firm line along the Salm River from Trois-Ponts south through Salmchâteau. The withdrawal of the defenders of St-Vith from the Fortified Goose Egg on 23 December put the 82nd Airborne on the front line.

Vielsalm

Vielsalm is defined by the Salm River that runs along the western side of the city center where it flows in and out of the Lac de Doyards. The town was liberated on 17 January 1945.

Maison du Tourisme du Pays du Val de Salm et des Sources de l'Ourthe

avenue de la Salm 50　　　　　　　6690 Vielsalm, Belgium
Tel: +32 (0)80 21 50 52　　　　　　Fax: + 32 (0)80 21 74 62
Email: info@vielsalm-gouvy.be　　　Web: http://www.vielsalm-gouvy.be/en

> Upon the approach into Vielsalm on highway N675, stop opposite the tank on the left. (50.285877, 5.920161)

A **US M4A1 Sherman tank** from the 7th Armoured Division sits alongside the highway. The tank still guards the approach into Vielsalm with its turret gun aimed at a curve in the highway. The plaque identifies it as the 'Invincible' and dedicates it to the members of the armored division that held St-Vith, thereby delaying the German offensive.

> Continue on highway N675 into the city for 210 m and follow the curve to the left onto rue de l'Hôtel de Ville (N68), passing the Parc de Vielsalm as noted below and stopping after a total of 500 m in the place General Bruce C Clarke. (50.283927, 5.914706)

A statue of **Général Jules Marie Alphonse Jacques de Dixmuide**, a Belgian hero of the First World War who led the stubborn defense of the Flemish city of Dixmuide (Diksmuide) in 1914, faces the roadway. (50.284896, 5.91617)

27　The pilot, Captain James B Aageberg of Indiana and holder of the Distinguished Flying Cross, flying with the 390th Fighter Squadron, 366th Fighter Group, is buried in Henri-Chapelle American Cemetery, Henri-Chapelle, Belgium.

Sixty meters ahead, a memorial commemorates the officers and soldiers of the **3rd and 6th Regiment Chasseurs Ardennais** who died in the Second World War. Formed in 1933, the Chasseurs were stationed along the forested Ardennes borders with Germany and headquartered in Vielsalm. They briefly held the invading force in 10 May 1940 before being overwhelmed. The unit's emblem was the wild boar's head on a green beret. (50.284511, 5.915699)

The stone memorial bearing the emblem of the **7th Armored Division** commemorates the headquarters of the division in Vielsalm. The square has been renamed in honor of the commander of the division's Combat Command B and place Brigadier General Bruce C Clarke.

Reverse direction and proceed northeast on rue de l'Hôtel de Ville. After 280 m, turn left onto rue du Général Jacques (N68) and, after 250 m, turn right onto rue Jean Bertholet (still N68). After 110 m, park near the large church on the right. (50.288327, 5.914958)

Elements of the *Armée secrete,* the largest Belgian resistance organization during the Second World War, were former members of the Belgian Army. It claimed as many as 45,000 participants at its height, still only a fraction of that number was truly active. The organization participated in some military actions but was more effective in espionage and aiding escaping Allied airmen. Approximately 4,000 were killed before the country's liberation in 1944; over half died while in the hands of the German occupation force.

The church forecourt harbors a memorial to the Ardennes sector of the ***Armée secrete,*** featuring a black stone with inscribed white images depicting scenes of resistance action and execution. Numerous plaques adorn the lower section paying homage to the Allied fighters, civilian and military victims of the Ardennes, and all comrades who were victims of Nazism.

Leave the church parking area by turning right (northeast) onto rue Jean Bertholet (N68). Almost immediately turn left onto rue des Chasseurs Ardennais (N822). Continue for 240 m and then turn left into the parking area. Proceed to the memorial on the edge of the park. (50.287418, 5.91245)

On the night of 23 December, troops from the fortified goose egg crossed the Salm River to the west of Vielsalm. A detachment of airborne engineers protected by 1st Lieutenant George D Lamm's 2nd Platoon, Company A, 508th Parachute Infantry Regiment prepared the road and rail bridges for demolition. After the last stragglers crossed the bridges, Lt Lamm's men pulled the fuse lighters — but without result. With German troops at the edge of the river, the engineers re-wired both bridges. This time the rail bridge blew, but the highway bridge did not. Now under fire from a German tank, the engineers tried the third time — nothing. The platoon secured a box

Chapter Four   Schnee Eifel   169

of Composition C-2 [28] and placed it on the center of the bridge. A bazooka detonated the explosives but only managed to blow away the flooring. Finally, after an hour-long firefight, troops packed more explosives about the bridge piers. After a massive explosion that shook the earth, the joists blew into fragments.[29]

As the last covering force for the final withdrawal from Vielsalm, Lt Lamm established a command and observation post in the attic of a Rencheux house. Under cover of smoke, the Germans lined up tanks and half-tracks along the river bank and methodically blew the upper floors off the houses while German engineers attempted to construct a replacement wooden bridge. At 1245 on 24 December, grenadiers from the 9th SS Panzer Division began a full-scale assault. Moments later, they poured down the street of Rencheux while Lamm's 2nd Platoon exercised a fighting withdrawal.

The large memorial stone standing along the edge of the park holds five plaques. One plaque is 'In Tribute to the Defenders': **Companies A and B, 508th Parachute Infantry Regiment**; **Company D, 307th Airborne Engineer Battalion**, the engineers who set the explosives under enemy fire; and **Battery A, 319th Glider Field Artillery Battalion**, which provided artillery support. A second plaque is 'In Tribute to the Crossers': **7th Armored Division**; **106th Infantry Division**; **CCB, 9th Armored Division**; and **3rd Battalion, 112th Infantry Regiment, 28th Infantry Division**. Other plaques remember the contributions to victory by members of the **US Air Force** and the **Royal Air Force** of all nationalities serving in World War II in the skies over Belgium; the **SAS Belgium Special Air Service (Para Commando)**; and **320 Squadron Royal Air Force (Netherlands)**.

The terrain has been extensively reconstructed, and the rail bridges are long gone. A new highway bridge crosses the Salm River, but the original route still exists as Route de Rencheux.

Other Points of Interest south of Vielsalm

Salmchâteau

Salmchâteau's origins date to Celtic gold mining in the 5th century and, as the name implies, became the site of châteaux in the domain of the Count Henry IV of Salm starting in the 14th century. Over the next four hundred years, the castle was damaged, burned, restored, enlarged, and modified. During the French Revolution, the castle was sold for its stone. Two medieval towers remain despite efforts by US Army engineers to use the tower material to reconstruct rutted trails after the Battle of the Bulge.

At dusk on 23 December, while the remnants of General Jones's division streamed west, a lone company of Colonel Gustin M Nelson's 112th Regiment held the bridge at Salmchâteau. Paratroopers from the 82nd Airborne were stationed upon

---

28   Composition C refers to a family of plastic explosives developed during the 1940s and used extensively during the Second World War because they were more powerful than TNT.

29   Lieutenant George Lamm was awarded the Distinguished Service Cross for valor and leadership during this action. Lt Lamm had already received Silver Stars for his actions in Normandy and at the Waal River Bridge in Holland. Lamm died in 1992 at age 73 and is buried in Massachusetts National Cemetery, Bourne, Massachusetts.

a ridge west of town. The infantrymen asked the paratroopers to blow the bridge when the 2nd SS Panzer Division's Reconnaissance Battalion 2 occupied districts east of the river. That done, the units joined to form a defensive line.

The single arched span of the **Pont de Salm,** almost hidden by old stone buildings, crosses a shallow gorge that effectively blocked any vehicular movement through the town. The rail crossing and sharp blind turns between houses on the approach to the bridge would have forced attacking armor into a difficult approach. Wooded hills that overlook the valley to the west provided the attackers with observation sites for placement of artillery.

Location: In the center of the town at the intersection of highways N68 and N89. (50.266012, 5.904711)

Cierreux

During the American withdrawal behind the Salm River, the 112th Infantry Regiment provided the rear guard and was the last unit to cross the Salm. After Hoge's combat command passed, Nelson's force of one infantry battalion, attached engineers, and towed tank destroyers pulled back west from the village of Rogery, where a secondary road crossed the upper reaches of the river, which at this point is little more than a stream. Shortly after 1300, panzers and motorized infantry from Führer Begleit Brigade appeared at Rogery. A towed gun knocked out a German tank and a 90-mm tank destroyer another. The panzers fell back, but the German infantry left its vehicles and attacked by wading across the stream. Colonel Nelson sent his vehicles across the light bridge under cover of fire from his tank destroyers.

The full might of the Führer Begleit Brigade moved west of Rogery toward the bridge used by Colonel Nelson and his men. Only 1st Lieutenant Hugh T Bertruck Jr's platoon of the 814th Tank Destroyer Battalion barred the way. Under a brilliant moon, Lt Bertruck's tank destroyers opened up on the advancing enemy. The tank destroyer's' machine guns raked the infantry while the 90-mm guns knocked out seven German tanks. Eventually all of the tank destroyers were themselves destroyed, their surviving crew members retreating across the Salm before the engineers detonated the bridge. The destruction prevented the Führer Begleit Brigade from driving into the flank of a column of vehicles immobilized on the congested valley road.

The fact that the Führer Begleit Brigade was even temporarily stopped by the destruction of the **narrow road bridge** at Cierreux indicates the difficulty that armored units had traversing terrain crossed by steep-banked streams such as the Salm.

Location: 3.2 km south of Salmchâteau on highway N68. (50.243253, 5.921632)

Side Trip: Battle of Thier du Mont à Sart
7 January 1945

The 508th Parachute Infantry Regiment, 82nd Airborne Division occupied the Thier du Mont ridgeline on 21 December directly from its bivouac at Sissonne,

France. The 5.5-kilometer-long ridge extends from the Salm River south of Vielsalm directly west past Grand Sart and commands the Salmchâteau–La Roche-en-Ardenne highway (N89).

On Christmas Eve, the last remnants of 7th Armored Division and 106th Infantry Division cleared through the 82nd Airborne's lines at Vielsalm. As ordered, the paratroopers relinquished the hill and moved rearward.

In early January, as part of the Allied Army's counterattack, units of the 82nd Airborne Division left their accumulation point at Arbrefontaine to lead the attack toward the Salm River. Before they could attack Vielsalm, the 3-kilometer-long ridge at Thier du Mont had to be captured. To take the ridge, the 505th Parachute Regiment's 2nd Battalion moved to secure the village of Goronne. Oberst Arthur Jüttner, commander of German forces in the area, had placed a PzKpfw VI (King Tiger) hidden in the forest north of the road from Arbrefontaine. The monster tank knocked out two Shermans and two tank destroyers before succumbing to hits from the rear by a tank destroyer that had managed to circle around its position.

One of the wounded during the engagement was the battalion's commander, Lieutenant Colonel Benjamin Vandervoort. With the loss of the tank, the Germans retreated to Thier du Mont.

AMERICAN OBJECTIVE	To recapture high ground near Vielsalm
FORCES	
American:	3rd Battalion (Lieutenant Colonel Louis Mendez), 508th Parachute Infantry Regiment
German:	Grenadier Regiment 164 (Oberst Arthur Jüttner)
RESULT	The ridge was captured
CASUALTIES	
American:	14 killed, 44 wounded, and 2 missing
German:	unknown
LOCATION	Thier du Mont is 6 km west of Vielsalm

Battle

At first light on 7 January, Company G emerged from Thier del Preu woods north of Grand Sart and prepared to cross 800 meters of open ground to retake the hill that they had abandoned two weeks earlier. Four paratrooper platoons supported by five M-10 Tank Destroyers moved forward in a blinding combination of snow, fog, and American artillery-generated smoke while German rifle, mortar, and machine-gun fire opened up. The wooded summit held three well-camouflaged 88-mm guns. Almost instantly the 88s opened fire, whereby four of the M-10s exploded. Despite casualties, the paratroopers entered the woods to find the 88s protected by a ring of infantry foxholes and several machine-gun nests. A bazooka round killed the crew of one gun, but shrapnel from a second gun wounded Lieutenant William Call, who had headed the assault. Staff Sergeant Frank Sirovica signaled for the men to charge the German positions. The bold assault so surprised the enemy that first a few and then the remaining German troops began a full-scale retreat.

Battlefield Tour

> Leave Vielsalm west toward Hotton (N822) and follow through Goronne to a rural road on the western side of the town. Turn left toward Sart. Continue for 1.4 km to the memorial on the right. (50.278939, 5.853095)

A large memorial park stands in the saddle between Thier del Preu and Thier du Mont ridges — the open ground crossed by the attacking paratroopers. The memorial stone is mounted upon a fieldstone plinth and is situated upon a gravel bed in the shape of a five-pointed star. The bronze plaque commends the **508th Parachute Infantry Regiment** and expresses everlasting friendship with the Belgian people. The smaller plaque commends the leadership of 3rd Battalion commander, **Lieutenant Colonel Louis Mendez**. The wooded summit of the ridge that sheltered the German 88-mm guns lies to the east.

> Continue on the rural road to the T-junction immediately west of the Thier du Mont Memorial and turn left. Follow for 1.2 km through Grand Sart. Turn left toward Joubiéval (N645) and follow for 750 m. At the junction with highway N89, turn right and then left toward Ottré. Continue for 450 m to the museum in the old barn on the left. (50.25958, 5.848253)

Bulge Relics Museum
route d'Ottré 41 Joubiéval
B-6690 Vielsalm, Belgium Tel: +32 (0)496 31 61 74
Email: bulgerelics@hotmail.com
Web: http://www.bulge-relics-museum.be

Opened only since 2014 and housed in a typical old Ardennes barn, this privately-owned museum dramatically exhibits thousands of relics from Bulge battlefields collected over a lifetime. Most of the weapons emanating from the fields are therefore merely rusted shells of the original. Many of the items are of German origin including identification tags, field pay books, burial cards, and miniature cameras. A full-size diorama includes an American half-track, jeep with canvas shroud, and German Kubelwagen. One long wall features photographs of area villages taken during the battle. The quantity of military hardware left on a battlefield always amazes.

Open every Saturday and Sunday 1 June to 30 September and in December from 13:00 to 17:00.

---

30 Lieutenant Colonel Benjamin Vandervoort was the inspirational leader of the battalion during the defense of Ste-Mère Église, Normandy on D-Day. His wounds incurred at Goronne were severe and ended his military career. Vandervoort had received the Distinguished Service Cross with Oak

Side Trip: 83rd Infantry Division Battlefield and Museum

> At the junction immediately south of the Bulge Relics Museum, turn right. Carefully follow the road for 1.7 km through Ottré. Turn right after passing the church and cemetery on the right and follow 970 m to the memorial on the right. (50.243051, 5.836245)

The counteroffensive to regain territory lost during the German attack passed over this terrain during bitter cold weather in mid-January 1945. The 83rd Infantry Division took over from the 3rd Armored Division and in two days of combat recrossed the Salmchâteau–La Roche highway as far as the village of Bihain. The division spent another day fighting off German counterattacks.

On 11 January 1945, during its drive toward Petit-Langlire, two squads of Company F, 331st Infantry Regiment started a dawn attack in the forest. After progressing only 100 meters, they were pinned down by machine-gun crossfire. With most of the men dead or wounded, two SS soldiers approached the bodies and, if found alive, shot them. One of those killed was Private Henry I Tannenbaum of New York. Platoon Sergeant Harry Shoemaker was the only survivor and later told the story.

The **Memorial Tannenbaum** stands near the crest of a high ridge beside a minor rural road into the Bois des Roches. The stone bears a plaque commemorating Tannenbaum's sacrifice and that of all the members of the 83rd Infantry Division. The upright stone is backed by three flags and fronted by a five-pointed star.

> Turn right onto the country lane and follow southwest for 1.6 km. At the T-junction, turn right toward Bihain. After 800 m, turn sharp right and stop. (50.237932, 5.811265)

The **83rd 'Thunderbolt' Infantry Division**, a veteran unit, had seen fighting in Normandy, Brittany, and the Hürtgen Forest where it replaced the 4th Infantry Division before that unit moved to the 'quiet front' in Luxembourg.

On 9 January, the 83rd Division assumed the main assault role south of the Salmchâteau–La Roche-en-Ardennes highway. The unit fought through marshy ground and sub-zero temperatures for two days to liberate Bihain. The enemy struck back with a fearsome counterattack, but the Thunderbolt Division held firm — suffering 1,600 casualties in all. A stainless steel monolith stands before a Belgian Army bunker to commemorate the 83rd Infantry Division's liberation of Bihain.

Leaf Cluster and the Bronze Star among other awards. Vandervoort joined the Foreign Service serving in numerous military advisor roles. He died in 1990 at age 75 and is buried in Beaufort National Cemetery, Beaufort, South Carolina.

Staff Sergeant Frank Sirovica was awarded a Distinguished Service Cross for heroism and leadership for an assault upon a superior enemy position. Sergeant Sirovica died in 1973 at age 59.

Lieutenant Colonel Louis G Mendez, a 1940 graduate of West Point, commanded the 3rd Battalion, 508th PIR from its activation to occupation duty after the war. He received the Distinguished Service Cross for leading the attack upon Pretot, France in June 1944.

> Continue to the railroad box car on the right. (50.237929, 5.811466)

Henri Kichka, born in 1926, fled Belgium for France before the advancing German Army in 1940. The Vichy French regime imprisoned his entire Jewish family. Released, they made their way back to Brussels, but the entire family was recaptured, deported and all, except Henri, died in concentration camps.

This **vintage boxcar** was used during the Second World War to transport victims to the concentration camps. In 2006, it became a private memorial to Henri Kichka and all those who suffered deportation during the war. It contains a small exhibition regarding Kichka's life. Admission is obtained from the nearby 83rd Infantry Division Museum.

l'ASBL 83rd 'Thunderbolt Division' Museum
Bihain, 21A   B-6690 Vielsalm, Belgium
Tel: +32 (0)80 41 87 39   Email: auboisdesroches@skynet.be
Blog: http://11janvier45.skyrock.com/

Life-size dioramas brilliantly tell the story of the 83rd Infantry Division from its Normandy landing to its liberation of Langenstein, a sub-camp of Buchenwald concentration camp. The museum is as much a memorial to noted wartime photographer Tony Vaccaro as it is to the 83rd Infantry Division. Its walls carry numerous Vaccaro photographs, some enlarged to 4-foot by 5-foot dimensions. The museum, founded and operated by volunteers, continues to grow in presentation and labeling.

Generally open weekends from 14:00 to 17:00, but call for actual hours. (50.237928, 5.811807)

> Leave Bihain to the west and follow the road for 3.6 km through Petit-Tailles to the junction with highway N30. Turn right to return to Vielsalm.

31

This ends the Schnee Eifel tour.

---

31   Private Henry Tannenbaum is buried in Mount Hebron Cemetery, Flushing, New York. A photograph of Private Tannenbaum's body lying in the snow was taken by a fellow 83rd Division soldier, Tony Vaccaro, who went on to become a famous photojournalist. Vaccaro's photographs of battlefield life in the winter of 1944-45 were published in 2002 as *Shots of War*. The book's cover photograph, '*Death in White*,' features Private Tannenbaum's body partially covered in newly fallen snow.

Chapter Five
Battle of the Rivers
19 December 1944 to 7 January 1945

The Ourthe Occidentale River arises in a high plateau near Bastogne and flows northward. The Ourthe Orientale River starts near the village of Ourthe and flows southwest. The two branches join at a point west of Houffalize to form the main Ourthe River course, which continues northwest to flow into the Meuse River at Liège. For much of its length, shallow water twists and turns between forested banks. The banks are steep, however, and form the last militarily significant barrier before the terrain exits the forested Ardennes and enters the undulating pastures of the Condroz plateau forming the open country favored by tanks and continuing to the Meuse River and beyond.

By 19 December, General Hodge's First Army had re-allocated 208,000 men southward to stem the Nazi tide. Not every move was defensive. Hodges instructed Major General Joseph 'Lightning Joe' Lawton Collins to relocate his VII Corps to the west of Marche-en-Famenne. The corps, comprised of the vaunted 2nd and 3rd Armored Divisions,[1] the experienced 84th 'Railsplitters' Infantry Division,[2] and the untested 75th Infantry Division, shaped a plan to knock the German bulge back to the Fatherland. Collins preferred to cut-off the Bulge with a drive from Elsenborn to St-Vith, but he could not convince Montgomery that transportation routes were adequate to support such a move.

With the Sixth Panzer Army's main effort increasingly delayed in the north, the emphasis of the German Offensive shifted south, where General von Manteuffel's Fifth Panzer Army was making considerable progress, despite its originally subsidiary role. By 20 December, the area in front of Fifth Panzer Army subdivided into three sectors: between the Amblève and Salm Rivers, between the Salm and the Ourthe, and between the Ourthe and the Meuse. Because he was unable to combine his forces, Generalfeldmarschall Walter Model's armies fought three separate battles. Seven days later, his men had suffered defeat in all three.[3]

---

1   These two units were classified as 'heavy' armored divisions, meaning that they were structured differently than the fourteen other armored divisions in the US Army. At full complement, a heavy division contained two light and four medium tank battalions totaling 390 tanks (including 252 Sherman medium tanks) and one armored infantry regiment of three battalions. Total manpower was 14,000. A 'light' armored division fielded three mixed (light and medium) tank battalions and three separate armored infantry battalions for a total of 263 tanks (including 186 Shermans) and 10,500 personnel.

2   The 'Railsplitters' nickname and insignia originated from the unit's origins as an Illinois militia company in which a young Captain Abraham Lincoln served during the Black Hawk War of 1832.

3   Generalfeldmarschall Walter Model, who fought in the First World War, was known for his early aggressive style and later determined defense. Model led the assault upon Moscow in November 1941 and the northern assault upon Kursk in July 1943. His dedication to stubborn defense and ruthless Nazism earned the Führer's favor and the awarding of the Knight's Cross with Oak Leaves, Swords, and Diamonds. Trapped in the Ruhr Pocket with his Army Group B in April 1945, Model refused to surrender, but instead dissolved his command and, on 21 April 1945, committed suicide. He is buried in the Soldatenfriedhof Vossenack in the Hürtgen Forest.

On 20 December, Model released General der Waffen-SS Willi Bittrick's II SS Panzer Corps to the Fifth Panzer Army. The panzer corps held two experienced and well-equipped panzer divisions. The 9th SS Panzer Division '*Hohenstaufen*' negotiated the jammed roads of the Losheim Gap to make its appearance north of St-Vith. The 2nd SS Panzer Division '*Das Reich*'[4] circled south of St-Vith and passed through the defensive gap around Houffalize, following behind General der Panzertruppe Eugen Walter Krüger's LVIII Panzer Corps. The division, although already suffering from a shortage of gasoline, entered Houffalize and turned north to open the Salmchâteau–La Roche-en-Ardenne highway (N89).

After General Krüger's LVIII Corps pushed aside regiments of the US 28th Infantry Division (see Chapter Eight), only engineer combat troops and service personnel held the resulting gap. Generalmajor Siegfried von Waldenburg's 116th Panzer Division's reconnaissance troops bypassed Houffalize to the south only to find the highway bridge south of Ortho destroyed. The division reversed direction to cross the Ourthe Orientale at Houffalize and continue west along the branch's north bank. The maneuver cost the panzer division an entire day.

On 21 December the 116th Panzer Division used secondary roads to move between Task Force Orr and Task Force Hogan (see map page 199), then headed west along the Soy–Hotton road. That same day, the 2nd SS Panzer Division moved north of Houffalize intending to proceed to Liège through Manhay, but the stubborn defense of Baraque-de-Fraiture crossroads by mixed American units upset its timetable.

The 2nd SS Panzer Division drove the remnants of the exhausted CCA, 7th Armored Division from Manhay and turned west to Hotton. The 289th Infantry Regiment, 75th Infantry Division arrived along the road west of Manhay to stop the advance.

By 24 December, Kampfgruppe von Böhm,[5] 2nd Panzer Division, with a panzergrenadier regiment following, had advanced to within 6.5 kilometers of the Meuse. British tanks and a severe fuel shortage stopped the advance, whereby the Germans took up positions in Foy-Notre-Dame and near Celles, where they came under attack by American armored cavalry and later combat commands of the US 2nd Armored Division. The German advance was at an end.

Conclusion

By 26 December, losses in men and equipment limited the effectiveness of the 1st, 2nd, 9th, and 12th SS Panzer Divisions and the 2nd and 116th Panzer Divisions for the remainder of the Battle of the Bulge.

---

[4] The 2nd SS Panzer Division, under the command of SS-Brigadier General Heinz Lammerding, committed one of the worst atrocities of the war in destroying the French village of Oradour-sur-Glane on 10 June 1944. The division's I Battalion, *Der Führer* Regiment murdered 642 civilian inhabitants in a terrifying reprisal, leaving but five survivors.

[5] Kampfgruppe von Böhm consisted of Panzer Reconnaissance Battalion 2 with 12 armored cars, four companies of armored infantry, one Heavy Weapons Company, and one company of Panther tanks from Panzer Regiment 3 commanded by Hauptmann von Böhm.

Chapter Five					Battle of the Rivers 177

Battlefield Tour Summary
    The battlefield tour leaves Vielsalm and proceeds in a generally westward direction to the Meuse River through locations of the various encounters between American troops and the advancing *schwerpunkt* of the Fifth Panzer Army.

Highly Recommended Sites
Baraque-de-Fraiture: Parker's Crossroads
Grandmenil: Panther Ausf G (PzKpfw V)
Hotton: Sherman Firefly; 51st Engineer Combat Battalion Memorial; Farthest Advance Stone; Hotton War Cemetery
La Roche-en-Ardenne: M-10 Tank Destroyer; Musée de la Bataille des Ardennes
Neupré: Ardennes American Cemetery
Celles: Panther Ausf G (PzKpfw V)
Dinant: Rocher Bayard
Florennes: Musée Spitfire

Between the Salm and the Ourthe Sector
    The XVIII Airborne Corps, commanded by Major General Matthew Bunker Ridgway, bore responsibility for holding the 48-kilometer sector from Trois-Ponts to Hotton. Under its command at this time were the 82nd Airborne Division, 30th and 106th Infantry Divisions, and 3rd and 7th Armored Divisions. By 20 December the 82nd Airborne Division held an extended front along the Salm River from Trois-Pont to Vielsalm and then westward along the road from Salmchâteau to just east of Baraque-de-Fraiture crossroads. CCR, 3rd Armored attempted to plug holes between Vielsalm and the Ourthe. The 30th Infantry Division was holding fast against Kampfgruppe Peiper, and the surviving 424th Infantry Regiment of the 106th Infantry Division and 7th Armored Division still held St-Vith.

> Leave Vielsalm toward Salmchâteau (N68) then continue straight toward La Roche (N89) for 12.7 km and enter the parking area behind the memorial on the right. (50.249339, 5.737579)

Battle for Parker's Crossroad
19 to 23 December 1944
    Two serviceable highways cross the land west of Vielsalm: N89 travels southwest from Vielsalm to cross the Ourthe River at La Roche-en-Ardenne, and highway N30 (officially highway N15 in 1944) courses north from Bastogne, through Houffalize, Manhay, Aywaille and continues on to Liège. These two highways intersect on a high, wind-swept, marshy plateau at a barren crossroads known as Baraque-de-Fraiture. The intersection tops broad flat highlands that presented open fields of fire in every direction. The crossroads had originally been the objective of Task Force Orr, whose approach from Hotton, however, stalled at Dochamps. (See below.)
    Von Manteuffel reassigned the 2nd SS Panzer Division to move north from the vicinity of Bastogne and attack along this north-south highway toward Liege. The

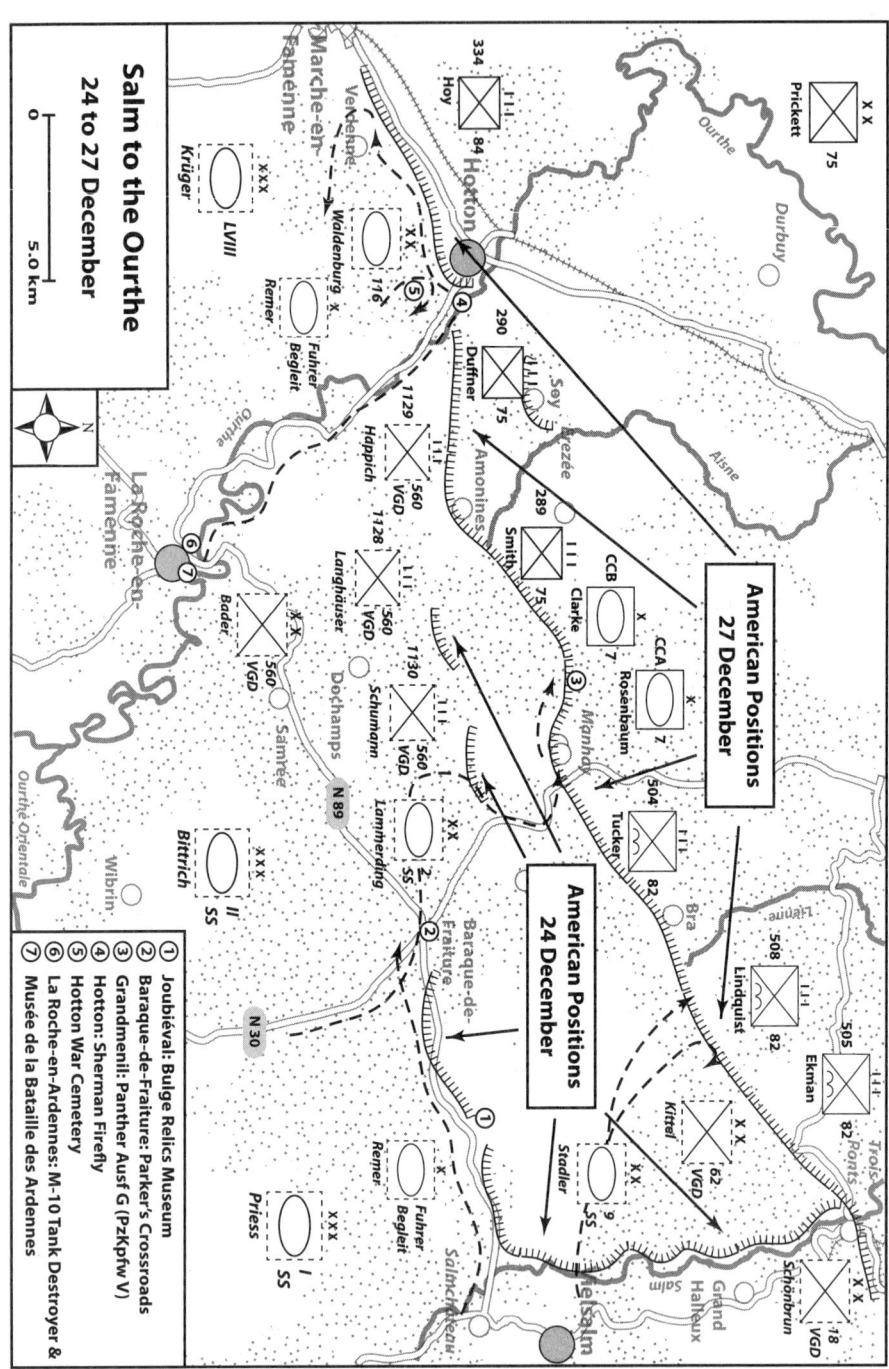

German commander did not realize, of course, that to use this road his troops would have to contend with one Major Arthur C Parker III and his 110 men.

Chapter Five   Battle of the Rivers   179

By 20 December, on his own initiative and recognizing the importance of the position, Major Parker firmly established his three 105-mm guns at the Baraque-de-Fraiture crossroads. He was joined by elements of an antiaircraft battalion with four half-tracks — three of which mounted quadruple .50-caliber machine guns, and the fourth a 37-mm gun. Parker told his small force, 'We will run no more. Here we will stand and fight, and here we will make a difference.' [6]

GERMAN OBJECTIVE	To open the road north from Houffalize toward Manhay
FORCES	
American:	Battery A, 589th Field Artillery Battalion (Major Arthur C Parker, later Major Elliot Goldstein); Battery D, 203rd Antiaircraft Artillery Battalion; Troop D, 87th Reconnaissance Squadron; Company F (Captain Junior R Woodruff), 325th Glider Infantry Regiment
German:	SS Panzergrenadier Regiment 4 *'Der Führer'* (SS-Lieutenant Colonel Otto Weidinger), 2nd SS Panzer Division *'Das Reich'*
RESULT	The Germans captured the road junction but suffered a significant delay
CASUALTIES	
American:	Company F, 325th GIR lost 72 of 116 men; other casualties are undetermined
German:	Unknown
LOCATION	Baraque-de-Fraiture is 15 km west of Vielsalm

Battle

Before dawn on 21 December, Parker's men beat off an 80-man patrol from the 560th Volksgrenadier Division. At 1100, eleven light tanks from Company D, 32nd Armored Regiment and a reconnaissance platoon moved forward to strengthen the roadblock. That afternoon, more help arrived from the 7th Armored Division with a troop from its reconnaissance squadron while commanders sent whatever units they could spare for the defense of the critical road junction. While late afternoon fog hid the enemy's movements, several patrols probed the defensive perimeter.

Both sides spent 22 December strengthening their positions. General Gavin was concerned about the threat to the 82nd Airborne Division's exposed right flank. He sent a company of glider infantry that moved to Baraque-de-Fraiture through a heavy snowfall. The effect was partially negated by the withdrawal of the tanks to stiffen the defense against the 560th Volksgrenadier Division at Dochamps. Parker's men repelled several more probing attacks, all the while subjected to miserable weather —

---

6   Major Parker was a graduate engineer who had seen active military duty in the 1930s. He assumed command of the 589th Field Artillery Battalion when its commanding officer became separated on the first day of the offensive. Parker's unit was mauled by the initial German assault when it was ambushed, cut off, and most of it captured. Only Parker and a three-gun battery of 105-mm howitzers escaped. See Chapter Four for the location of those events.

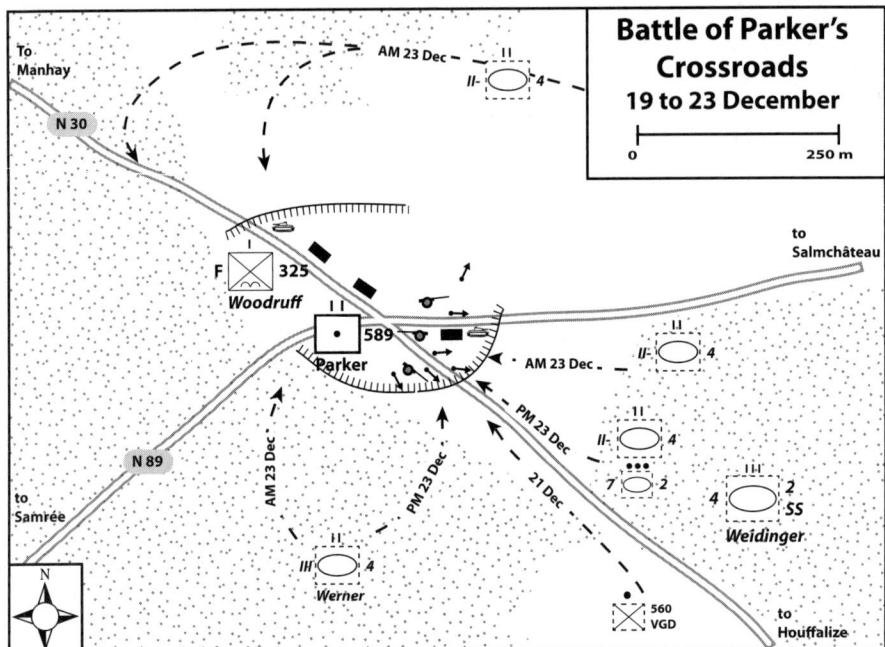

sleet, snow, and temperatures hovering near zero. Food was scarce, ammunition low, and re-supply impossible. A platoon of tank destroyers dispatched from Manhay by the 3rd Armored Division was surprised and captured by grenadiers who had circled to the north. That evening, Parker was severely wounded by mortar fragments and evacuated. A 29-year-old Major Elliot Goldstein, a graduate of Yale Law School, assumed command.

A gasoline shortage that had stalled the progress of the 2nd SS Panzer Division was partially alleviated, whereby II Battalion, SS Panzergrenadier Regiment 4 renewed the attack in the pre-dawn darkness of 23 December. Upon being repulsed, American positions were subjected to hours of unrelenting artillery fire. A relief force of recently arrived armored infantry and paratroopers dispatched from Manhay relieved some of the pressure. Although a German roadblock behind the crossroads denied passage to the infantry, five tanks barreled through and reached Baraque-de-Fraiture about 1300.

At 1600 the German bombardment from mortars and artillery reached a crescendo. The III Battalion, SS Panzergrenadier Regiment 4 attacked from the south and west while two platoons of PzKpfw IVs from 7th Company, SS Panzer Regiment 2, advanced on both sides of the highway from the southeast. The exposed Shermans lacked any cover on the flat open ground but nonetheless entered into a duel with the approaching panzers. Quickly flaming hulks raged on both sides. Suddenly, two Panthers appeared on the road from the east, and, by 1800, had overrun the crossroads. Small groups raced for the surrounding woods. Although some soldiers escaped, others were machine-gunned down.

Aftermath

Parker and Goldstein held the panzers for five days and four nights, days wherein 15,000 American troops escaped encirclement in St-Vith. The 2nd SS Panzer Division, damaged and unnerved by the engagement, never proceeded more than a few miles closer to its objective at Liège. Parker's determination to resist an overwhelming enemy force later became known as the Alamo Defense, and the Baraque-de-Fraiture crossroads has subsequently been renamed Parker's Crossroads.[7]

Battlefield Tour

A **US M2A1 105-mm howitzer**, mounted upon a stone base formed in the shape of a five-pointed star, is the same model used by Parker's artillery battalion to hold the road junction. Memorial plaques flank the gun. Moreover, a stone stele bears a plaque designating the intersection as **Parker's Crossroads** and recognizing the courage of soldiers of the 106th Infantry Division who stopped the enemy advance from 20 to 24 December. A second stone honors all American soldiers who fought for peace and freedom. A third plaque identifies the units involved in the action.

In 1944, the **Auberge du Carrefour**, then known as 'Laurent Jacquet,' became the 589th Battalion's command post. Although the name has changed, it is still owned by the same family. The building had been severely damaged during the battle by a German tank that ran straight into the building.

Battle for Manhay
24 to 27 December 1944

Manhay not only sat astride the Bastogne–Liège highway (then N15, now N30) but also across the main road from Trois-Ponts to Hotton (N807). Manhay was tactically untenable because surrounding wooded hills provided cover and observation for an attacking enemy. The area also suffered from organizational handicap. Highway N30 was designated as the boundary between Ridgway's XVIII Airborne Corps and Collins's VII Corps. As such, coordination and placement of units from each corps resulted in some confusion of responsibilities.

After the collapse of the defenses at Parker's Crossroads, General Rose sent Task Force Brewster[8] from the recently released 3rd Armored Division's CCA to hold the Houffalize–Manhay roadblock in an area known locally as Belle Haie, five kilometers south of Manhay. On 24 December, Colonel Rosenbaum's CCA, 7th Armored Division, just released from entrapment in St-Vith, withdrew to high ground north of Manhay, with Task Force Brewster providing a rear guard.

---

7   Major Arthur C Parker was awarded a Silver Star, and the French Government awarded his unit a Croix de Guerre. Parker survived the war and returned to his home in Alabama. General James Gavin, commander XVIII Airborne Corps, wrote to Parker in 1980 stating, 'The stand that your defenders made at the crossroads was one of the greatest actions of the war.'

Major Elliot Goldstein, who received a Bronze Star, also survived the war and returned to his hometown law practice in Atlanta, Georgia; he died in 2009 at age 94.

8   Task Force Brewster, commanded by Major Olin Brewster, was part of Task Force Richardson. It consisted of six tanks from Company H, 32nd Armored Regiment; the temporarily attached Company A, 509th Parachute Infantry Battalion; and Company C, 290th Infantry Regiment.

However, Lammerding planned to capture Manhay, Malempré, and Vaux-Chavanne before turning west through Grandmenil. Movement by the 2nd SS Panzer Division toward Manhay was restricted by dense forests that lined sections of the highway and clear weather that brought swarms of Allied fighter-bombers attacking anything that moved. General Lammerding sent his panzergrenadiers through the forests at night to attack Manhay from nearby woods.

German Objective	To capture the road junction at Manhay as a basis to move west toward the Meuse
Forces	
American:	CCA (Colonel Dwight A Rosenbaum), 7th Armored Division
German:	SS Panzergrenadier Regiment 3 *'Deutschland'* (SS-Lieutenant Colonel Günther Wisliceny); SS Panzergrenadier Regiment 4 *'Der Führer'* (SS-Lieutenant Colonel Otto Weidinger); SS Panzer Regiment 2 (SS-Lieutenant Colonel Rudolf Enseling)
Result	Manhay was easily captured
Casualties	
American:	24 December: 6 killed, 19 wounded, and 436 missing; 19 tanks destroyed; 27 December: 10 killed, 14 wounded
German:	24 December: negligible; 27 December: 66 killed, 46 wounded, 17 armored vehicles captured or destroyed
Location	Manhay is 20 km west of Vielsalm

Battle

At first light on 24 December, Grenadier Regiment 1130, 560th Volksgrenadier Division, moved against five light tanks from Task Force Kane and captured Odeigne. All that day, 2nd SS Panzer Division engineers improved the road into Odeigne from the south despite constant shell fire. By nightfall, SS Panzer Regiment 2 had positioned three companies of Panthers in the village.

At 2100, 4th Company, SS Panzer Regiment 2 with III Battalion, SS Panzergrenadier Regiment 4 *'Der Führer'* as infantry support left Odeigne toward highway N30 led by a captured American Sherman. A company of the 40th Tank Battalion with infantry from the 48th Armored Infantry Battalion manned a roadblock at a sharp curve north of Odeinge. American tankers hesitated to fire, confused by the appearance of the Sherman. The panzergrenadiers harbored no such uncertainty and opened fire with panzerfausts, knocking out four Shermans and damaging two others. Shorn of their armor, the American infantrymen broke and ran.

PzKpfw IVs and Panthers gained the main highway and continued toward Manhay. At a sweeping curve in the highway, nine partially dug-in Shermans awaited orders to withdraw as part of the re-organization of Allied lines. A column of Panthers, still led by the captured Sherman, blinded the American crews with high-intensity flares and proceeded to destroy most of them. The surviving crewmen and supporting infantry fled.

Chapter Five   Battle of the Rivers   183

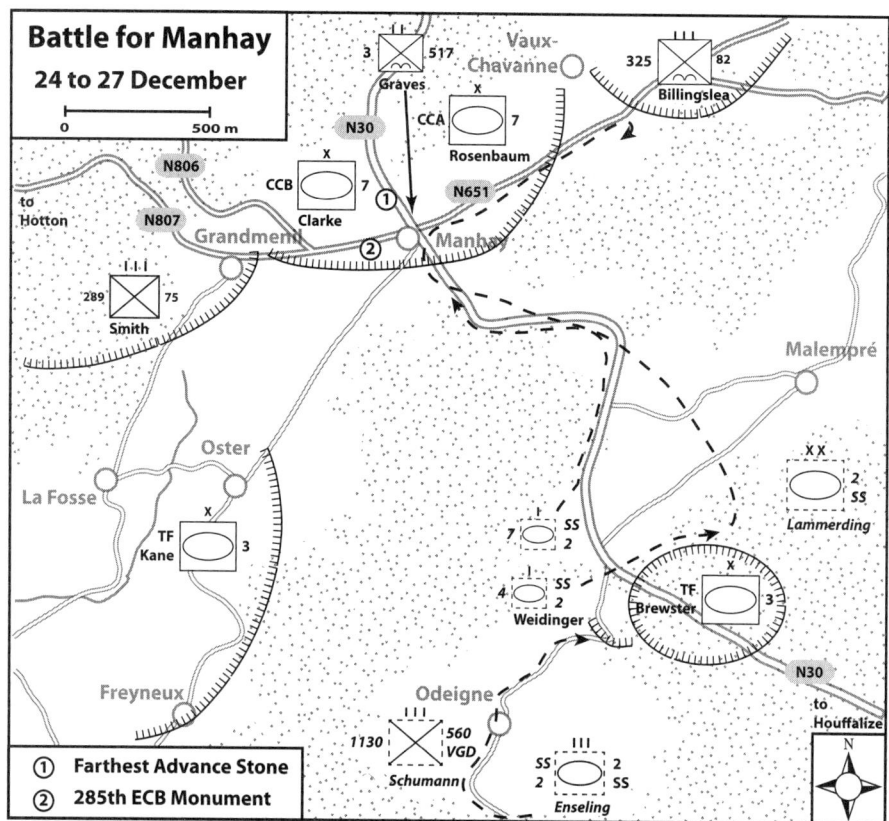

The panzers continued into Manhay, where two Shermans attempted to make a stand and even knocked out two panzers, but they were soon overcome along with three other Shermans parked along the highway to the north. Meanwhile, II Battalion, SS Panzergrenadier Regiment 4 *Der Führer* advanced through forests east of highway N30 to cut-off and attack Task Force Brewster. Forced to abandon his vehicles, Brewster escaped on foot to 82nd Airborne positions at Bra.[9]

By Christmas morning, the Allied situation at Manhay had improved. Units released from the St-Vith pocket, namely elements of the 7th Armored Division, the 424th Infantry Regiment, and the 112th Infantry Regiment, had arrived and formed a defensive line north of Manhay. During the day, Weidinger's panzergrenadiers soundly repulsed an effort to re-take the town. Lammerding, in turn, attempted to extend his right flank by sending SS Panzergrenadier Regiment 4 east from Manhay. The effort

---

9   General Rose was so upset with the unauthorized withdrawal that he brought court-martial charges against Major Brewster for cowardice before the enemy. Major Brewster's direct superiors, however, refused to endorse the charges. Major Brewster returned to duty until wounded at Sart, Belgium on 8 January 1945. He retired from the US Army in the 1990s.

General Rose died in March 1945 near Paderborn, Germany, when his jeep was machine-gunned by a Tiger tank. He is buried in Netherlands American Cemetery, Margraten, The Netherlands. He was 45 years old.

encountered the 325th Glider Infantry Regiment near Vaux-Chavanne and was driven back.

At 0200 on 27 December, Companies H and I, 517th Parachute Infantry Regiment moved into Manhay from the northeast after a 10-minute time-on-target artillery bombardment from eight artillery battalions.[10] A second barrage, intended to keep the enemy in shelters while the paratroopers approached, fell short, resulting in thirty-three friendly-fire casualties. Nonetheless, the attack continued. Bazooka teams targeted panzers that had survived the artillery fire. Troopers threw phosphorus grenades into the cellars where the enemy had sheltered, misled by the bazooka detonations into thinking that the artillery fire continued. Surprised by the fast and violent attack, the German troops retreated into woods to the south, and Manhay had been cleared of the enemy by 0330.

Battlefield Tour

Leave Parker's Crossroads to the southwest toward La Roche (N89) and, after 2.9 km, turn right on a rural road (Route de Poteau de Chabrehez) toward Odeigne. Follow for 4.7 km through Odeigne (staying on rue Saint-Donat) to a sharp curve where the road crosses the Fayi de la Folie creek. Stop on the right. (50.262345, 5.694458)

The SS Panzer Regiment 2 took the aforementioned route from Baraque-de-Fraiture toward Manhay, thus avoiding the blocking position of Task Force Brewster along highway N30 at Belle Haie. After easily overpowering a roadblock, the Panthers moved along logging roads east to regain highway N30 behind Brewster's position.

Continue 800 m and turn left toward Manhay (N30). After 1.9 km, enter a large sweeping curve in the highway. The American tank roadblock encountered by SS-Sergeant Barkmann (see below) was located in this area. (50.285215, 5.695812)
A 3-meter-high memorial stone 300 m ahead on the right commemorates Albert Lacroix, killed on this spot on 19 Sept 1943 as an agent of the *Armée Secrète*. (50.286071, 5.691943)
Continue 1.6 km into Manhay and turn left onto Voie de la Libération before the main highway junction. Stop at the park on the right. (50.291131, 5.675085)

During the battle for Parker's Crossroads and days later for Manhay, the 325th Glider Infantry Regiment held the village of Vaux-Chavanne, which represented the right flank of XVIII Corps' defensive line. The village was only two kilometers east of Manhay. A children's play yard across from the Community Hall in Manhay holds a memorial stone dedicated to the **325th Glider Infantry Regiment**. Nearby, the barrel

---

10   Time-on-target: a technique in which artillery guns of different calibers and at different distances from a target adjust their firing times so that all of the shells reach the target simultaneously for a devastating effect.

of a **German 75-mm Pak 40** (towed antitank gun) rests on a plinth as a victor's trophy.

> Return to highway N30 and continue north across the intersection to the mairie on the right.

A stone plaque affixed to the south wall on that building honors the soldiers of the **3rd Battalion, 517th Parachute Infantry Regiment**, who braved friendly artillery fire in a heroic battle to recover Manhay on the night of 26/27 December. (50.293503, 5.674734)

> Continue 350 m to the stone on the left. (50.296137, 5.672159)

During the advance upon Manhay, SS-Senior Sergeant Ernst Barkmann, commanding panzer #401, became separated from his unit. Assuming that he was trailing his comrades, Barkmann made a dash for Manhay to catch up. Instead, Barkmann was ahead of his unit and found himself facing the nine dug-in Shermans south of Manhay. With little alternative, he sped his way through the American position while nine Sherman turrets turned in his direction, but confused by Barkmann's sudden appearance, none fired. Barkmann continued into Manhay crossroads where he spotted three Shermans approaching from the west. He continued north passing several more Shermans parked along the side of the road. Barkmann dropped a smoke grenade and continued north. By now, the parked Shermans had reacted and started a pursuit. The Panther swung its turret around to be rear facing and fired. The shell set the leading American tank on fire. Barkman parked and awaited the arrival of his company. In all Barkmann is credited with destroying seven tanks, two tank destroyers, and three other vehicles.[11]

The **Farthest Advance Stone** on the west side of the highway presumably marks the limit of Barkmann's penetration.

> Reverse direction and return 500 m to the main highway intersection.

Other Points of Interest (Manhay Sector)

> **Malempré**
> A plaque on the wall fronting the church commemorates the 3rd Armored Division and lists the unit's battle locations from Normandy to Central Europe.
> A larger stone plaque to the right bears insignia of the **3rd, 7th,** and **9th Armored Divisions, 509th Parachute Infantry Regiment,** and **82nd Airborne Division** as the combatants of December 1944, then the insignia of the **83rd Infantry Division** and **3rd Armored Division** that liberated the village on 3 January 1945.

---

11 SS-Senior Sergeant Ernst Barkmann was awarded the Knight's Cross of the Iron Cross for his actions in Normandy's bocage. Although wounded in fighting near Vienna in April 1945, Barkmann survived the war and became the fire chief and later mayor of a small German village. He died in 2009 at age 89.

> The plaque ends with 'Malempré Remembers.'
> Location: In the center of Malempré 4.5 km east of Manhay. (50.281203, 5.715856)

> **Fanzel**
> The bronze plaque on the side of a building at the entrance to the village near the Aisne River is dedicated to the **750th Tank Battalion**. Although the site offers no farthest advance stone, it does mark the limit of the Bulge in this area.
> Location: 7 km north of Erezee along highway N876. (50.32278, 5.57293)

> Leave Manhay west toward Érezée (N807) and continue 800 m to the memorial stone on the left. (50.290971, 5.664214)

The 238th Engineer Combat Battalion took part in the fighting around Manhay in support of the 82nd Airborne Division. In particular, the engineers installed mine fields and other barriers to block the progress of the 2nd SS Panzer Division along the road from Manhay to Grandmenil and to interdict the road south toward La Fosse. A minefield stopped five 2nd SS Panzer Division Panthers and kept the enemy from occupying the center of Grandmenil.

Almost lost among the roadside grass, a weather-worn stone bears a plaque dedicated to the **238th Engineer Combat Battalion**. Highway N806, opposite the monument, leads around the north side of Grandmenil and continues toward Mormont.

> Continue 300 m and stop at a convenient location near the roundabout.

Battle of Grandmenil
25 to 27 December

After the capture of Manhay, General Lammerding had no interest in proceeding north. Liège was not his objective; he was to cross the Ourthe River and gain the Condroz Plateau. Lammerding turned west towards Érezée, where a road led northwest to an Ourthe-River crossing at Durbuy from where he could threaten the US VII Corps' left flank.

German Objective	To move west along the Manhay–Hotton road toward the Meuse River
Forces	
American:	289th Infantry Regiment (Colonel Douglas B Smith), 75th Infantry Division; Task Force McGeorge (Major Kenneth McGeorge)
German:	SS Panzergrenadier Regiment 3 '*Deutschland*' (SS-Lieutenant Colonel Günther Wisliceny); SS Panzer Regiment 2 (SS-Lieutenant Colonel Rudolf Enseling)

Result	Panzer movement to the west was stopped at Grandmenil
Casualties	
American:	137 killed
German:	100 killed, 180 PoWs, at least 18 tanks destroyed
Location	Grandmenil is 21.6 km west of Vielsalm

Battle

Three kilometers west of Grandmenil, the road passes through the Bois du Pays in an area known locally as Trou du Loup (Wolf Gap). The newly arrived and untested 3rd Battalion, 289th Infantry Regiment advanced east along both sides of the Manhay–Hotton road while elements of Task Force Richardson[12] passed to the west. Colonel Richardson advised the men that more Americans may be trailing his group, nevertheless warning that Germans were still active in Grandmenil.

At 0300 on Christmas morning, eight Panthers of 2nd Company, SS Panzer Regiment 2 approached the roadblock led by a captured Sherman tank that momentarily fooled the Americans into thinking that it was the last of Richardson's force. Orders shouted in German revealed the deception. The defenders fired several bazooka rockets at the enemy tanks, but in the excitement of their first battle, they had not removed the safety pins, thus leaving the rockets unarmed. The attacking Panthers machine-gunned the infantrymen who had sheltered behind rocks or in the ditches on either side of the road while the leading panzer ran over an American jeep. Finally, a lone bazooka man got behind the lead German tank and knocked it out with a rocket into its engine. The flaming Panther blocked a narrow spot in the road that ran along the side of a cliff. Unable to push the wreck to the side, without infantry protection, and with the approaching dawn sure to bring Allied air strikes, the remaining Panthers returned to Grandmenil.

At 1500 on Christmas Day, Grandmenil fell under attack from the 289th Infantry Regiment and 3rd Armored Division's Task Force McGeorge,[13] which had been recently released from the fight against Kampfgruppe Peiper.[14] At the same time, the Germans renewed their push west toward Érezée. Limited by the terrain to the highway, the action ran head-to-head, a conflict the Shermans could not win. The II SS Panzergrenadier Battalion and its accompanying Panthers repulsed the task force. All but two of the American tanks were immobilized. McGeorge received sixteen more Shermans from the 2nd Battalion, 33rd Armored Regiment, and troops from Company D, 36th Armored Infantry, and attacked again at 2000. After two hours of combat,

---

12 Task Force Richardson, commanded by Lieutenant Colonel Walter B Richardson, was part of CCA, 3rd Armored Division, and consisted of 3rd Battalion, 32nd Armored Regiment and Company I, 36th Armored Infantry Regiment.

13 Task Force McGeorge: Company F, 36th Armored Infantry Regiment; Company A, 33rd Reconnaissance Battalion (Stuart light tanks); Company F, 33rd Armored Regiment (Sherman medium tanks); 2nd Platoon, Company D, 23rd Engineer Combat Battalion.

14 While preparing to attack on 25 December, Task Force McGeorge fell under attack by eleven P-38 Lightnings from 430th Squadron, who ignored the orange recognition panels. Thirty-nine men were killed and the attack delayed.

he secured the western edge of the village but was forced to withdraw by a violent counterattack.

On 26 December, a separate German effort toward Érezée sent '*Deutschland*' Regiment's I Battalion northwest from Grandmenil through the forest toward Mormont. Company L, 289th Infantry Regiment had been working its way through the woods in the opposite direction when it received warning of the panzer force. They felled trees across the road and sited M10s from the 629th Tank Destroyer Battalion behind them. An M10 destroyed the lead Panther when the German column passed through a narrow gorge.[15] A bazooka-versus-tank battle ensued that forced the Panthers to return to Grandmenil.

Task Force McGeorge, strengthened once again by the addition of eight Shermans from Company H, 32nd Armored Regiment, renewed the attack on Grandmenil at 1425 after a heavy artillery concentration. Moving through the smoke-filled valley, tanks and bazookas eliminated machine-gun positions, prompting the Germans to retreat toward Manhay. The advance west of 2nd SS Panzer Division had ended.

Aftermath

General Lammerding realized that his weakened unit could no longer cope with the growing American strength. He ordered a fallback to positions south of Manhay. The threat to the XVIII Airborne Corps' right flank had been neutralized although a final German effort exploited a gap in the American line near Sadzot (see below).

Battlefield Tour

During the Christmas night attack by Task Force McGeorge, infantry crept past the first houses lining the highway. A German counterattack struck with shell fire, disabling three Shermans in fields south of the highway. Only the tank of Captain John Jordan, 1st Battalion, 33rd Tank Regiment, remained operational. Hard hit, American infantry sheltered in the foundation of a ruined house. With German infantry closing in, Jordan radioed for artillery fire upon his own location that stopped the assault. A withdrawal order mandated that the infantry pull back from the village, leaving Jordan and his tank in the path of thirteen approaching Panthers.

Captain Jordan and his crew spent the night playing possum in his tank, camouflaged among the other burned-out Shermans. In the morning, Jordan reported the Panther movements along the Mormont road to his headquarters before quietly returning to his lines.[16]

The **Panther Ausf G** (PzKpfw V) mounted upon a plinth on the edge of the roundabout comes from the 2nd SS Panzer Division. It was discovered, after the battle,

---

15   Sergeant Oscar M Mullins and Private First Class Edwin W Metz of Company A, 629th Tank Destroyer Battalion, were awarded Distinguished Service Crosses (both posthumously) for stopping this attack. Sgt Mullins and PFC Metz are memorialized on the Tablets of the Missing, Ardennes American Cemetery, Neupré, Belgium.

16   On 16 January 1945, Captain John W Jordan died of wounds incurred while fighting west of Vielsalm. Captain Jordan is buried in Pittsburgh, Pennsylvania. He was 32 years old.

Chapter Five Battle of the Rivers 189

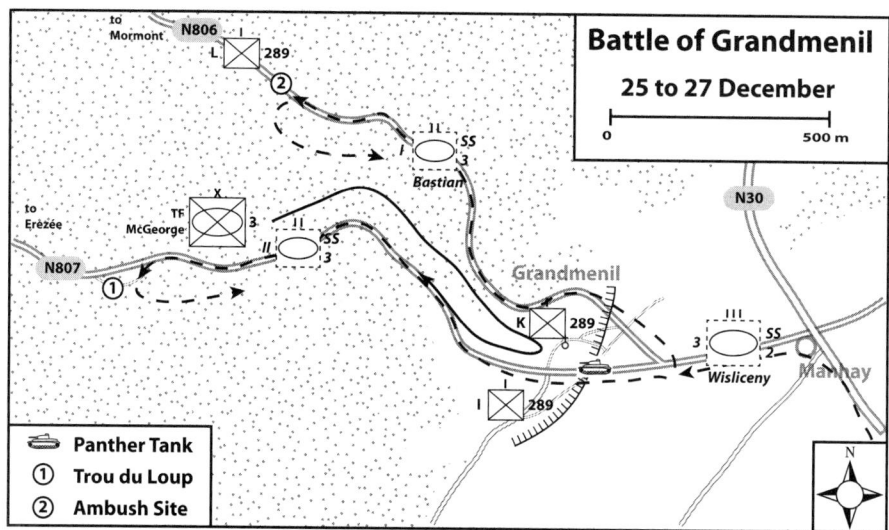

trapped in a minefield and abandoned south of the highway near the 238th Engineers monument. The beautifully-restored vehicle represents the German Panthers disabled during combat in the area. (50.290692, 5.660227)

On the opposite side of the roundabout (50.290163, 5.659706), an upright stone mounted on a star-shaped base backed by American, Belgian, British, and Walloon Province flags bears a slate plaque commemorating the **75th Infantry Division** and **3rd Armored Division** with the words:

> Valleys, hills, forests, and villages of the Ardennes, you have seen them pass, fight, suffer, and fall. Under the stars of their flag, liberty was marching.

To the left, a small stone bears a bronze plaque 'dedicated to the brave and gallant men of the **951st Field Artillery Battalion**, VII Corps, First Army.' The 951st manned towed, 155-mm howitzers and had fired thousands of rounds during the battle for Grandmenil and the later battle for Houffalize from positions around Érezée and La Fosse.

> Leave the roundabout to the west toward Erezee (N807) and, after 2.6 km, enter the forest track on the left. Continue for 230 m to the memorial. (50.294806, 5.627714)

At this curve in the original 1944 highway, a memorial commemorates **Corporal Richard F Wiegand**, Company K, 289th Infantry Regiment who, on this location on 25 December, managed to stop the German advance on Érezée with a bazooka. Cpl Wiegand was then killed by an enemy tank shell.[17] In 1944, there was

---

17 Corporal Richard F Wiegand was awarded a Silver Star. Wiegand, from Allegany County, Maryland, is buried in Henri-Chapelle American Cemetery, Henri-Chapelle, Belgium. He was 21 years old.

little opportunity for traffic on the then narrow winding road to pass a stopped vehicle — much less a flaming tank — forcing the German spearhead to withdraw.

> Continue on the rural road back to highway (N807) and turn left. Continue 2.6 km into Bristol and stop at the church on the left. (50.292929, 5.593172)

The **Farthest Advance Stone** identifies the limit of Kampfgruppe Krag's progress during the battle for Sadzot (see below) that occurred on 29 December when II SS Panzer Corps made its final and unsuccessful attempt to break through the American line along the Manhay–Hotton highway.

> Continue on highway N807 and carefully follow it through Érezée. After exiting Érezée, cross the l'Aisne River and enter a large roundabout. Take the 2nd exit toward Marche (N807). The road climbs up the side of a ridge and, 700 m after the roundabout at the tip of a sharp curve, notice the monument on the right. (50.29498, 5.544416) Stop, if desired, at a small layby ahead on the left.

The Maquis d'Érezée were Resistance fighters operating in this rugged terrain. On 9 September 1944, the Maquis fired upon retreating German soldiers from buildings in nearby Marcourt. The SS captured and executed ten villagers and burned thirty-five houses.

The dark grey stone memorial, almost lost in the dappled light of surrounding trees, commemorates **eight Maquis** from Érezée who were murdered by the SS. Down the hillside behind the stone, two smaller versions of the memorial mark the graves of two of the eight men.

> Continue on highway N807. In the village of Soy, 2.9 km west of the Maquis memorial, note the red brick house on the right.

Colonel Robert Howze Jr, commander CCR, 3rd Armored Division, used the structure as a headquarters during the fateful battles for Manhay and Hotton. The plaque recognizes Colonel Howze's quick action in stopping Germans advances at Amonines, Manhay, Hotton, and Marcouray. (50.285029, 5.507986)

> Continue 1.7 km and stop at monument on right immediately after the junction with a rural road. (50.278932, 5.486513)

Battle for Haid-Hits
22 to 24 December 1944

As part of its attack upon Hotton (see below), German infantry and SP guns constructed a roadblock on the Manhay–Hotton road at a crossroads known locally as *Quatre Bras* to cut-off the 3rd Armor Division force about Soy from its divisional

Chapter Five — Battle of the Rivers

headquarters in Hotton. After arriving in Soy by truck from Namur, Lieutenant Colonel William J Boyle's 1st Battalion, 517th Parachute Infantry Regiment moved out from Soy at 1715 on 22 December and almost immediately incurred intense automatic weapons fire.

AMERICAN OBJECTIVE	To eliminate German positions dominating the Manhay–Hotton road
FORCES	
American:	1st Battalion (Lieutenant Colonel William J Boyle), 517th Parachute Infantry Regiment
German:	Grenadier Regiment 1129 (Oberstleutnant Happich) 560th Volksgrenadier Division
RESULT	The enemy positions were captured
CASUALTIES	
American:	11 killed and 150 wounded
German:	Unknown
LOCATION	The road junction is 39 km west of Vielsalm and 12 km northeast of Marche-en-Famenne

Battle

Company A moved down the highway while Company B attempted encirclement from the south. By midnight the attack had faltered. With Major Donald Fraser in command, Company B formed a defensive line in front of German positions north of Melines. Colonel Boyle's Company A left Soy at 0200 on 23 December,

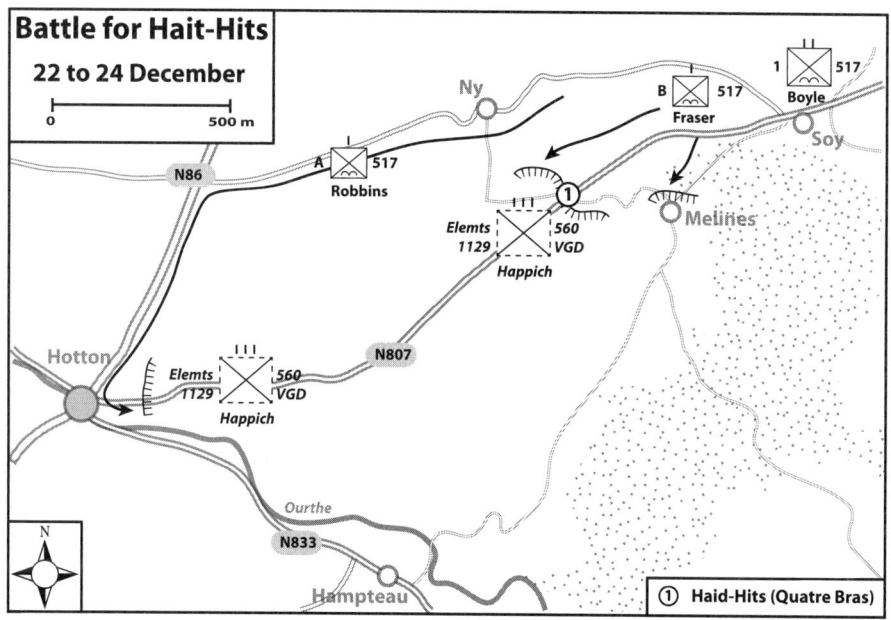

moving north of the German roadblock by way of Ny. At 0400 Boyle reported to 3rd Armored Division's command post in Hotton. Company A then attempted to circle around Hotton and return to Soy. German defenses set up in the houses on the outskirts of Hotton blocked the unit on its way back toward Soy.

Meanwhile, on 23 December, Major Fraser's force had failed in several attempts to capture the strongly fortified German positions at Haid-Hits crossroad. A dawn attack collapsed under heavy mortar and machine-gun fire. Later, when nine tanks arrived from Soy, the attack resumed at 1215. Within five minutes, four of the tanks were disabled, and again the attack had faltered. The remaining tanks returned to Soy.

At 2100 during a heavy snowfall that reduced visibility to a few meters, Major Fraser started a full frontal assault on the crossroad. The paratroopers slowly gained ground amid a battle of automatic weapons, hand grenades, and panzerfausts. A German counterattack failed and, in the resulting lull in fire, a platoon from Company C worked forward in small groups. In particular, over a 20-hour period, Private First Class Melvin Biddle of Company B scouted forward alone through thick underbrush, picking off enemy soldiers with rifle fire, and eliminating machine-gun nests with hand grenades. He was later credited with killing seventeen enemy soldiers.[18]

At 0200, enemy resistance at the crossroad ended. After a period of reorganization, Major Fraser led his force to Hotton, where it took the German position blocking Company A from the rear.

Battlefield Tour

Since 1992, the crossroads has been officially named Carrefour du 1.517th Parachute Infantry Regiment. The monument consists of two small stones flanking a larger stone that bears a bronze plaque honoring the **517th Parachute Infantry Regiment**. During the period, the unit suffered 139 casualties with 14 killed. The names of those killed are recorded on the plaque.[19]

> From Carrefour du 1.517th Parachute Infantry Regiment, continue west toward Hotton (N807). After 2.7 km, enter a roundabout. Take the 4th exit (N807) and stop at the park 210 m ahead on the left. (50.267718, 5.453304)

Battle for Hotton
21 to 26 December 1944

The Ourthe River widens where it flows northwest through Hotton before turning north. Three task forces from 3rd Armored Division left Hotton on 20/21

---

18 Private First Class Melvin Biddle was awarded the Medal of Honor for his intrepid action against the enemy. Biddle died on 16 December 2010, the 66th Anniversary of the start of the Battle of the Bulge. He was 87 years old and is buried in Anderson, Indiana.

19 The 1st Battalion, 517th Parachute Infantry Regiment was awarded a Presidential Unit Citation. Lieutenant Colonel William J Boyle was awarded a Distinguished Service Cross. He survived the war to return to combat in Korea and Vietnam. He died in 2009 at age 91 and is buried in Schuylerville, New York.

Chapter Five   Battle of the Rivers   193

December, leaving only 120 service troops with one 57-mm antitank gun along with a platoon from 51st Engineer Combat Battalion with two 40-mm antiaircraft guns. Engineers had erected a wooden replacement bridge for the one demolished by the retreating German Army the previous September.

GERMAN OBJECTIVE	To capture the crossing over the Ourthe River
FORCES	
American:	1st Platoon, Company A (Captain Preston C Hodges), 51st Engineer Combat Battalion; service detachments (Major Jack W Fickessen), 3rd Armored Division
German:	Kampfgruppe Bayer (Oberst Johannes Bayer); then 560th Volksgrenadier Division (Oberst Rudolf Langhäuser); then Führer Beliet Brigade (Oberst Otto Remer)
RESULT	The town and bridge were held against repeated German attacks
CASUALTIES	
American:	Unknown
German:	Unknown
LOCATION	Hotton is 9 km northeast of Marche-en-Famenne

Battle

At 0700 on 21 December, a reconnaissance force of twenty-five grenadiers crossed the Ourthe on the footbridge at Hampteau 2.5 kilometers upstream. The preliminary assault tested the platoon of 51st Engineers who defended the bridge with mortar and small-arms fire. Eight mortar rounds fell 30 minutes later near Headquarters Company in Hotton. Major Jack W Fickessen, Executive Officer of 23rd Armored Infantry Battalion, organized a defense of the town and radioed General Rose for help.

At roughly 0900, the first seven Panther tanks of the Kampfgruppe Bayer[20] approached the town from the east along highway N807 and charged for the bridge. An isolated Sherman, undergoing repairs in the town, got off a shot before being knocked out by the leading Panther. Bazooka men Sergeant Vern Sergent and Corporal Phillip Popp and their loaders, Private Hugh Lander and Private First Class Carl Nelson, took on the German panzers. Each team fired and scored damaging hits upon the enemy tanks, whose crews bailed out and escaped. Panzergrenadiers dug in on the ridge overlooking the town and the Manhay–Hotton road and occupied buildings on the east bank but did not reach the bridge. The small detachment of German infantry awaited reinforcements. The enemy remained behind the three 3rd Armored Division task forces and Colonel Howze's headquarters at Soy. The broad Condroz Plateau came into view across the river.

The 334th Infantry Regiment, 84th Infantry Division rushed troops from

---

20   Kampfgruppe Bayer, 116th Panzer Division proved a potent force consisting of Panzer Regiment 16 (43 Panthers and 26 PzKpfw IVs); one battalion from Panzergrenadier Regiment 60; I Battalion, Artillery Regiment 146 (SP guns); and 3rd Company, 675th Pioneer Battalion.

Marche accompanied by a platoon from the 638th Tank Destroyer Battalion. The platoon, manning its 90-mm antitank guns, moved among various positions on the left bank and achieved decisive success against German armor.

Rose ordered Colonel Howze to send a detachment to Hotton, but German possession of the ridge commanded the roadway. Two platoons of tanks, one medium and one light, and a platoon of Company B, 36th Armored Infantry Regiment, avoided the highway by using country lanes to finally arrive in Hotton after dark. Colonel Howze dispatched additional troops from Soy, but Panthers guarding the road south of Melines destroyed four Shermans on the morning of 22 December.

At 1900 on 22 December, German armor and II Battalion, Panzergrenadier Regiment 156, 116th Panzer Division launched an attack against Hotton from forests to the east, but with limited success. American patrols sent out the following morning found that the enemy had abandoned its positions. The arrival of a company from the 509th Parachute Infantry Regiment strengthened American positions.

General Krüger recognized that the American armored units at Hotton, Soy, Amonines, and Marcouray were too strong for his LVIII Corps. Learning that La Roche-en-Ardenne was abandoned, he ordered the 116th Panzer Division to again backtrack to cross the Ourthe at La Roche while his 560th Volksgrenadier Division maintained pressure against Hotton.

On Christmas Day, Colonel Remer's Führer Begleit Brigade resumed the effort to take Hotton after also crossing the Ourthe at La Roche. It gained the southern portion of the hamlet of Hampteau by attacking on the west side of the Ourthe River. It could advance no farther against the 334th Infantry Regiment and withdrew the next day to join the attack upon Bastogne.

Battlefield Tour
Hotton

A community has existed at this crossing of the Ourthe River since Roman times. The first mention of Hotton dates to 1187. The market town continues to thrive and offers most tourist amenities.

Royal Syndicat D'Initiative De Hotton-Sur-Ourthe
Rue Haute 4   6990 Hotton, Belgium
Tel: +32 (0)84 46 61 22
Web: http://www.si-hotton.be/tourism?set_language=en

The park presents a Sherman tank turret mounted upon a stone block plinth. The turret holds a 17-pounder gun — a modification to the Sherman tank by the British Army known as a **Sherman Firefly**. The upgraded gun gave the Firefly equality in firepower with 75-mm guns of the German PzKpfw IV and Panther. Of course, the turret of this tank points toward the German advance against the Hotton bridge. The text on the plaque reads:

> In tribute to the gallant soldiers of the **53rd (Welsh) Infantry Division** and their attached armoured regiments who liberated our towns and villages in January 1945 during the Ardennes Offensive.

Chapter Five

Battle of the Rivers 195

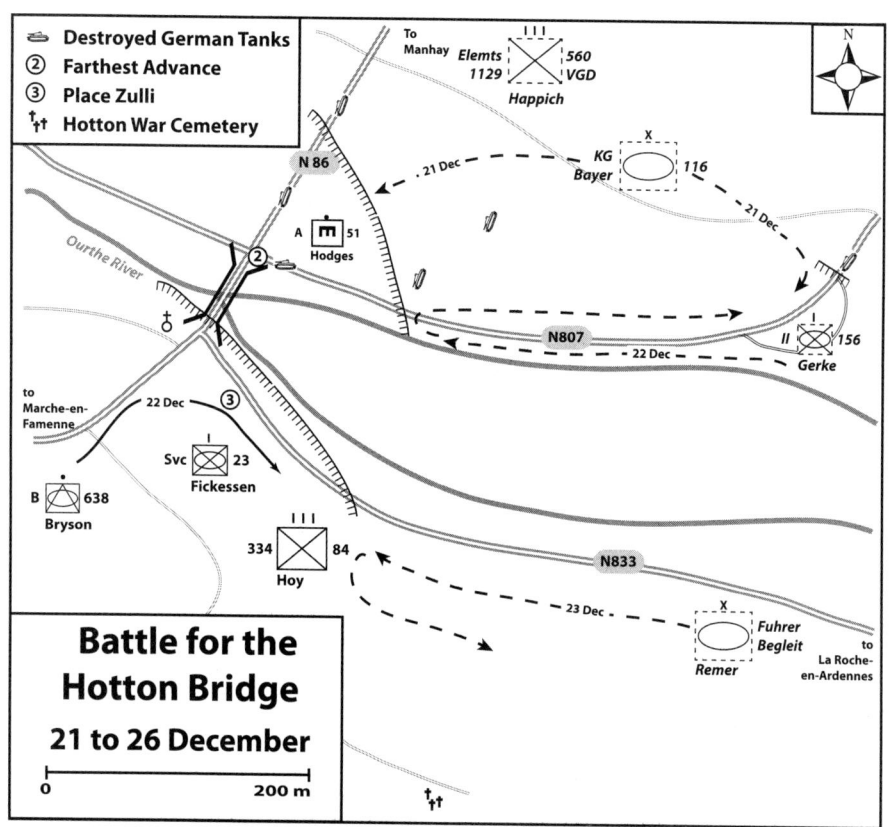

| Continue 450 m into the center of Hotton and the bridge over the Ourthe River. Park in a convenient location. (50.268279, 5.44746) |

The **Farthest Advance Stone**, attached to a railing support only feet away from the bridge roadway, presents how close the surprise attack of the 116th Panzer Division came to capturing the Hotton bridge.

A plaque affixed to the bridge railing immediately around the corner commemorates the actions of the **51st Engineer Combat Battalion**, commanded by Lieutenant Colonel Harvey R Fraser, during the period 17 to 21 December when it delayed and stopped elements of Fifth Panzer Army along the Ourthe River. The engineers defended and held the Hotton bridge during a seven-hour battle on 21 December. These actions significantly benefited the Allied efforts to reinforce defensive lines.[21] (50.268299, 5.447301)

---

21   The 51st Engineer Combat Battalion was awarded a Presidential Unit Citation and the French Legion of Merit with Silver Star for its actions during this period. Lt Col Harvey Fraser received a Bronze Star with Oak Leaf Clusters. The men of his command received numerous awards and commendations.

Cross the bridge to another plaque mounted on the bridge railing. The memorial pays homage to the American forces that fought here and in particular to **1st Lieutenant Charles K. Bryson**, commander 1st Platoon, Company B, **638th Tank Destroyer Battalion**. Bryson's four M18[22] guns entered into a duel with a Panther tank cross the river at 1000 on 22 December. Bryson's gun fired a series of three, two, and two rounds of armor piercing shells backing into a defilade position after each firing. Although three of the 76-mm shells scored direct hits on the Panther, the shells ricocheted off the tank's armor. The Panther fired five rounds but each landed long, passing over Bryson's positions. The platoon selected other firing positions just when four additional enemy tanks appeared. At a range of 800 to 900 meters, two tank destroyers fired on the leading panzer; one of the four hits ignited stored ammunition and the panzer burst into flames. Multiple hits upon the second, third, and fourth panzer induced the same effect. Four hits immobilized the fifth panzer, but it continued to fire until abandoned. (50.267805, 5.446931)

Almost directly south, a small square is named after twenty-eight-year-old **Lieutenant Philip Zulli** of the 36th Armored Infantry, 3rd Armored Division. Lt Zulli chatted calmly with friends when the German attack of 22 December started. Zulli's half-track had been hit and exploded, killing him instantly. (50.267564, 5.447024)

> Leave the bridge area to the southwest toward Rochefort / Marche (N86). Only 350 m from the bridge, turn left onto rue de la Libération and continue 600 m to the cemetery on the right. (50.262503, 5.447165)

The **Hotton War Cemetery** holds graves of 666 British Commonwealth soldiers who died during the Second World War. In addition to men killed during the German invasion of 1940 and the recapture of this area in 1944, the cemetery holds scores of airmen who were shot down or crashed while returning from missions in Germany or in support of ground fighting in Belgium. The Cross of Sacrifice, a feature of all Commonwealth War Graves Cemeteries, stands in front of the red-brick, gated entrance. The graves spread in twelve symmetrical plots on either side of a central grass plain.

> Reverse direction and return 600 m to highway N86. Turn right and, after 350 m, right again immediately before the bridge toward La Roche (N833). Continue 2.6 km along the west bank of the Ourthe River and stop at the rural road on the right. (50.255593, 5.476327)

On 23 December, Lt Bryson's unit was again is the midst of the fighting. At 1145, a house identified as holding a German observation post, fell to eight rounds of high explosives. During the day, Bryson's men killed the crew of a German antitank

---

22 The M18 'Hellcat' was a lightly-armored, tracked vehicle known for its speed and agility. The open turret carried the same 76-mm cannon as the Sherman but solved that gun's inability to penetrate German armor by utilizing high velocity armor-piercing ammunition. The turret also mounted a M2 Browning machine gun.

gun, captured the gun, and destroyed other German positions. Such actions continued for the next two days while German troops probed for a weak spot in the American defenses only to be met with high explosive fire from Bryson's guns. During the engagements, 638th Tank Destroyer Battalion suffered 12 killed, 14 wounded, and three missing. They claimed the destruction of 9 enemy tanks and the capture of 16 prisoners.[23]

A **Farthest Advance Stone** clustered among shrubs at the junction with a side road and identifies the limit of the Führer Beliet Brigade's advance upon Hotton.

Side Trip: Battle for Dochamps
20 to 27 December 1944

Major General Maurice Rose's CCR, 3rd Armored Division was defending a 21-kilometer segment of the Bastogne–Liège road from north of Houffalize to Manhay. General Rose created three task forces, each with a company of medium tanks, a battalion of self-propelled artillery, a few light tanks, and reconnaissance troops for a total of four-hundred men. A limited reserve of a company of medium tanks and a battalion of armored infantry remained near CCR headquarters in Soy. Task Force Hogan headed southeast to La Roche-en-Ardenne while Task Force Kane took up positions near Manhay. Task Force Orr headed toward positions between Kane and Hogan.

On 20 December at 1500, four PzKpfw IVs from 116th Panzer Division's Kampfgruppe Bayer bypassed Samrée to the west and fell upon the American flank to destroy eight tanks and capture 26,000 gallons of precious fuel. One hour later Samrée was captured.

GERMAN OBJECTIVE	To cut the Manhay–Hotton highway
FORCES American: German:	Task Force Orr (Lieutenant Colonel William R Orr) Kampfgruppe Bayer (Oberst Johannes Bayer), 116th Panzer Division
RESULT	Dochamps was captured and the Manhay–Hotton road reached near Soy, but the German force turned west toward Hotton, thereby saving American positions to the north.
CASUALTIES American: German:	7 killed, 48 wounded, and 12 missing; at least thirteen tanks destroyed 150 killed, 100 wounded, and 14 taken prisoner
LOCATION	Dochamps is 18 km southeast of Hotton

---

23   Lieutenant Charles K. Bryson was awarded a Bronze Star and survived the war. He died in 2006 at age 88 and is buried in Attleboro Falls, Massachusetts.

Battle

That evening Bayer encountered Task Force Orr at Dochamps while it moved toward Samrée. German troops occupied Dochamps before the leading reconnaissance battalion and Company H, 33rd Armored Regiment arrived to engage the enemy north of the village. The Americans pulled back when all but three tanks of the original two platoons had been knocked out by panzer and antitank gun fire. The surviving tanks and infantry fought a delaying action over the entire route to Amonines, where the main body of Task Force Orr joined the reconnaissance battalion. The action was only preliminary.

On 21 December, Task Force Orr established a roadblock 2.5 kilometers north of Dochamps at (50.243837, 5.605612). At 0700 it launched a strike force of the two armored infantry companies upon Dochamps, which almost immediately encountered small-arms fire from high ground to the right and from the tree line to the left. During the afternoon, the roadblock became untenable when enemy troops infiltrated the woods on both flanks. All the task force troops withdrew to Amonines.

On 22 December, Colonel Orr resumed the attack towards Dochamps with the final objective again being Samrée, because it straddled the Vielsalm–La Roche-en-Ardenne highway. Orr's force was again repulsed and spent the night behind a perimeter defense at Amonines, defeating no fewer than twelve enemy attempts to penetrate the positions. The German attack towards Érezée was re-directed and, on 27 December, the 75th Infantry Division relieved Task Force Orr. The 2nd Armored Division liberated Dochamps on 7 January.

Battlefield Tour

The **town war memorial** and a rather disappointing plaque to the town's liberation comprises the only remembrances of the battle. (50.234381, 5.622124)

[24]

Side Trip: Battle for Sandoz
28 to 29 December 1944

By 27 December, Manhay had been retaken while German troops stalled before Grandmenil. Surviving elements of SS Panzergrenadier Regiment 25, 2nd SS Panzer Division merged with Kampfgruppe Krag of the 12th SS Panzer Division that had survived the battles at Rocherath-Krinkelt and Bütgenbach. Together, they planned another effort to cross the Trois-Ponts–Hotton road. Their target was a 1 kilometer gap between 1st and 2nd Battalions of 289th Infantry Regiment that unknowingly resulted from a realignment of American forces.

---

[24] Task Force Orr consisted of Companies A and C, 36th Armored Infantry Regiment; Company H, 33rd Armored Regiment; Company B, 83rd Armored Reconnaissance Battalion; and Battery B, Armored Field Artillery Battalion.

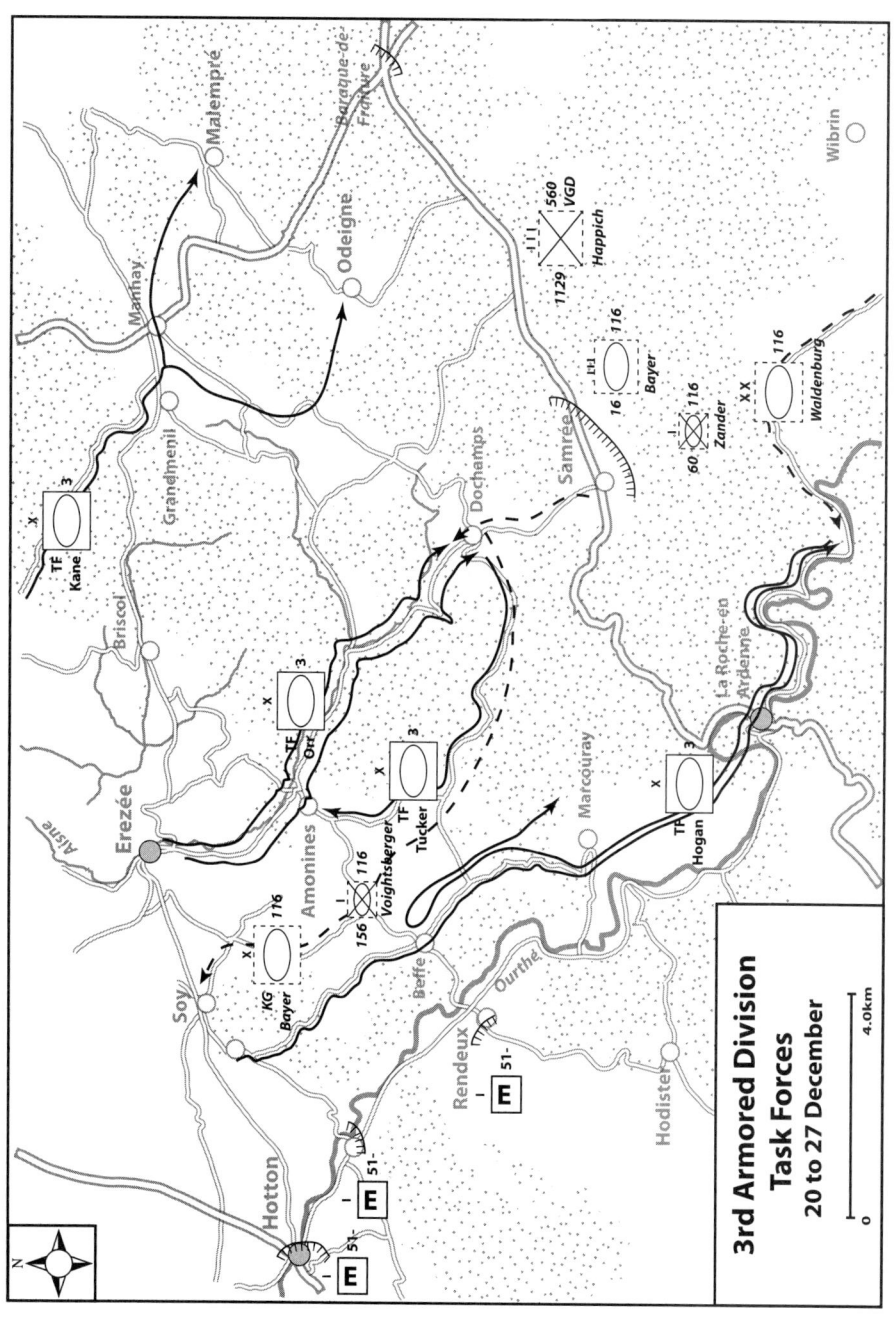

GERMAN OBJECTIVE	To cut the Manhay–Hotton highway
FORCES	
American:	Company B (Captain James J Marshall), 87th Chemical Mortar Battalion; 509th Parachute Infantry Battalion (Major Edmund J Tomasik)
German:	I and II Battalions, SS Panzergrenadier Regiment 25 (SS-Major Siegfried Müller), Kampfgruppe Krag (SS-Major Ernst-August Krag)
RESULT	The Sixth Panzer Army's last serious offensive effort was aborted.
CASUALTIES	
American:	87th Chemical Battalion: 2 killed, 15 wounded, and 26 missing 509th PIR: 120 killed or wounded
German:	289 killed and 49 taken prisoner
Civilians:	3 killed
LOCATION	Sadzot is 7.5 km west of Manhay

Battle

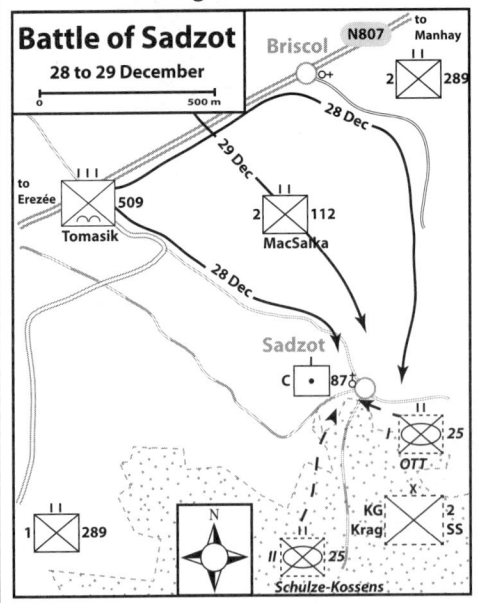

At midnight on 28 December, the German assault started through the deep woods south of Sandoz and Briscol. The pathless forest and broken ground disoriented units and negated originally good progress. Two of the panzergrenadier companies followed a creek bed into Sandoz and attacked at 0200. The village held a company from the 87th Chemical Mortal Battalion and a platoon of tank destroyers. The surprised Americans quickly recovered and established a defense in a few buildings on the north side of the village. Radio communication informed Brigadier General Doyle Hickey at CCA, 3rd Armored Division's headquarters, who dispatched the 509th Parachute Infantry Battalion from Érezée.

The paratroopers encountered Kampfgruppe Krag in the forest where a 'run-and-gun' battle ensued with both sides shooting at anything that moved

— sometimes even their own troops. With daylight, the paratroopers received artillery support and, by 1100, they had encircled the Germans in Sandoz. General Hickey also sent the 2nd Battalion, 112th Infantry Regiment to close the gap between the battalions of the 289th Regiment, but they became lost on the twisting forest trails. Early on 29 December, Hickey sent the 509th Regiment and six light tanks to attack to the southeast. The Germans similarly sent fresh battalions of infantry and Kampfgruppe Krag's panzerjäger company toward Sandoz. The two forces met in the forest. The Panzerjägers 75-mm guns quickly knocked out three tanks before both sides withdrew to reconsider. Finally that morning, the 2nd Battalion, 112th Infantry Regiment arrived at the scene. At twilight the paratroopers forced the Germans back. The 112th Regiment made a night assault and closed the gap. The Germans lost the opportunity to cut the roadway.

The failed effort to take advantage in the Érezée sector marked the last attempt by the Sixth Panzer Army. Although numerous spoiling raids and patrols occurred, the Sixth Panzer Army's armor repositioned to fight elsewhere. The initiative was now definitely all with the Americans.

Battlefield Tour

A tall mountain stone sited upon a slight rise bears a stone plaque describing the attack by 2nd and 12th SS Panzer Divisions against Sadzot on the night of 27/28 December as 'the desperate and savage.' The memorial pays homage to the courage of the defending units: **Company C, 87 Mortar Battalion**; **289th Infantry Regiment**; **509th Parachute Infantry Battalion**; and elements of the **3rd Armored Division**. (50.284104, 5.594041)

Sadzot Museum 44
Tel: 0492/84.19.38

A small private museum located in the third house in the village commemorates the Battle of Sadzot.

Open weekdays from 1800 to 2000 and weekends from 1000 to 2000.

25

Other Points of Interest near Hotton

Melines

On 3 January 1945, a column of medium tanks negotiated an icy slope toward Melines when a tank commanded by **Lieutenant George C Connealy** skidded off the edge of the pavement. The tank struck a daisy chain of mines and initiated a violent explosion that blew off the tank's turret, killed Connealy, his crew, and a group of infantry from the 84th Infantry Division that rode on the tank.

A local boy named Florent Lambert never forgot the young men who died

---

25 The 509th Parachute Infantry Battalion was awarded a Presidential Unit Citation. The battalion entered the battle at full strength of approximately 750 men, but when the unit was pulled from action in the end of January, only 48 enlisted men and 7 officers were still actively fighting. At that time the unit was disbanded and the men used as replacements in the 82nd Airborne Division.

liberating his country. Years later, Lambert built this memorial to honor them. The stone stele holds plaques dedicated to Lt Connealy and the **335th Infantry Regiment, 84th Division**. (50.27841, 5.49099)

On 20 December, local inhabitants reported the sound of German half-tracks in the area around Melines. Colonel Howze dispatched a platoon from Company C, 23rd Armored Engineer Battalion to investigate. The Americans fell into a German ambush launched from a forest lane leading into the Bois de Roumiere. Automatic weapons fire from eight half-tracks and a captured Sherman tank laced the engineers' vehicles.

Corporal John Shields stood up to hurl a grenade at the tank's open hatch when machine-gun fire cut him down. Only one of the thirty-three Americans survived the encounter.

This monument, also erected upon the initiative of Florent Lambert, commemorates American units that operated in the area at various times during later battles for Hotton and Soy. Identified on the memorial are units and commanders of **2nd** and **3rd Armored Divisions** (and attached 1st Battalion, 517th PIR), and the **75th** and **84th Infantry Divisions**. The portrait on the memorial is of **Corporal John Shields**, whose remains were discovered in 1947 by Lambert's father. (50.27827, 5.49729)

A stone cross 50 meters farther up the road marks the site of Cpl Shields death. (50.277671, 5.497643)

26, 27

Side Trip: La Roche-en-Ardenne

La Roche-en-Ardenne is somewhat distant from the main battlefield tour route, but the number and quality of the sites in the town make the side trip worthwhile. Alternatively, if visitors are planning to follow the described route from Dinant at the end of chapter five to the Skyline Drive locations at the beginning of chapter six, La Roche-en-Ardenne provides a good stop approximately halfway between those two locations.

Continue southeast from Hampteau toward La Roche-en-Ardenne (N833) for 13.4 km.

The attractive drive along the Ourthe River valley from Hotton towards La Roche-en-Ardenne follows a broad valley on a two-lane roadway through a number of small villages. The shoulders of the hills rise up steeply on both sides of the valley. Approaching La Roche, the road climbs up the rock face of a hill and passes

---

26 First Lieutenant George C Connealy is buried in Henri-Chapelle American Cemetery, Henri-Chapelle, Belgium. He left behind a wife and young son.

27 Corporal John Shields is buried in East Ripley, New York. He died three days shy of his 31st birthday.

the **British 51st Infantry Division Monument** on the left at the apex of a sharp curve. Two beautifully executed upright granite tablets bear Rolls of Honor listing fifty-four names of Scottish casualties incurred between 9 and 14 January 1945. (50.183312, 5.571862)

> Parking is not possible at the monument, but the road continues to an expansive overlook of La-Roche-en-Ardenne, where ample parking is available. (50.183822, 5.573636)

La Roche-en-Ardenne

The site was first settled during the Neolithic area. Celtic remains date to 850 BC and the Romans constructed a fort as part of their conquest of Gaul. John the Blind, King of Bohemia and Count of Luxembourg, granted permission to construct a wall town.

During the Second World War, the town was liberated in September 1944 but largely abandoned to German re-capture on the night of 22/23 December when the 116th Panzer Division passed through undefended La Roche and crossed the bridge to the west side of the Ourthe River.

On 5 January, British shell fire reverberated among the ruins of the air bombardments. Amid the destruction, the German SS set fire to the Hôtel Royale in reprisal for alleged aid to communist sympathizers. On 11 January, the British 51st (Highland) Division and the US 84th Infantry Division met to close the gap between allied forces.

The town is now a vibrant market center, and the street through the center of town that once was highway N89 (rue Chaumont) — a pedestrian zone with shops and restaurants.

Syndicat d'Initiative et du Tourisme de la Roche
place du Marché 15   6980 La Roche-en-Ardenne, Belgium
Tel: +32 (0)84 36 77 36   Fax: +32 (0)84 36 78 36
Email: info@la-roche-tourisme.com Web: http://www.la-roche-tourisme.com

The promenade provides a stunning view of the city and the ruins of a 9th century castle built upon a rocky outcrop that dominates the town and the bends in the Ourthe River. The **British 'Achilles' Tank Destroyer 'Northampton'** stands on the promenade. This tank was the first to enter La Roche and pays tribute to the **1st Northamptonshire Yeomanry**, which supported the 51st Highland Division during the counterattack.

> From the promenade, continue north past the tank destroyer on avenue du Hadja. After 400 m, turn right immediately after crossing the river onto quai du Gravier (N89), which becomes quai de l'Ourthe. After 100 m, enter the parking area on the left near the tank memorial. (50.183396, 5.57525)

The **US M4A1 Sherman tank 'Amboy'** occupies a place of honor along the Esplanade Quai de l'Ourthe. The tank is dedicated to the 'gallant soldiers of the 2nd and 3rd US Armored Divisions who liberated our town.' The plaque bears the emblems of both armored divisions and of the Belgian 1/3 Régiment de Lanciers (1st Battalion, 3rd Regiment), who restored and placed the tank. This particular Sherman suffered a direct hit that pierced the front glacis plate and killed all its crewmembers.

From the tank, walk away from the river on rue des Presbytère to rue Chamont (N89). Turn left to the entrance to the museum 30 m ahead. (50.183329, 5.575977)

Musée de la Bataille des Ardennes
rue Chamont 5 6980 La Roche-en-Ardenne, Belgium
Tel: +32 (0)84 41 17 25 Email: info@batarden.be
Web: http://www.batarden.be/

The museum presents its collection of military equipment in front of painted dioramas to present images of the nature of the fighting. The first display recounts the famous meeting of the American and British troops here in La Roche. Thematic wall displays separate the life-size diorama. Photographs show the region before the war and during the Nazi occupation and graphically depict the absolutely devastating damage incurred during the repeated bombings that the town suffered. The museum holds a collection of wartime propaganda posters hanging above various display cases. The second floor is dedicated to British and American troops and weapons while the third floor presents German equipment, more life-size dioramas, and vignettes with manikins in German uniforms. An ordinance room holds a collection of clearly identified weapons. Although on three floors, the museum offers an elevator. The labeling in French, Dutch, and English makes the museum very visitor friendly.

Open daily except Mondays April through December from 10:00 to 18:00; open every day in July and August; closed on school holidays and annual leave. Fee; handicap accessible.

A plaque on the left of the museum entrance commemorates the **114 civilian victims** killed in La Roche during the Ardennes Offensive.

From the museum, continue north 60 m on rue Chamont to the next intersection with rue du Hadja. (50.183866, 5.576522)

A slate plaque mounted into the building wall across the intersection commemorates the meeting between **US 84th Infantry Division** and the **British 51st Highland Division**, on 11 January 1945 that took place on this very site. The image recreates a photograph taken of the momentous closing of the gap between American and British forces.

Reverse direction and walk 280 m to the castle entrance way – a steep, narrow, stone staircase accessed beside 6, Place du Marché, across from the post office. (50.181539, 5.575373)

… Chapter Five   Battle of the Rivers   205

Château Féodal
rue du Vieux Château 4   6980 - La Roche-en-Ardenne
Tel: +32 (0)84 41 13 42   Email: info@chateaudelaroche.be
Web: http://www.chateaudelaroche.be/indexuk.php

The Lord of La Roche constructed the medieval chateau to control and tax river traffic on the Ourthe. Construction started in the 9th century and continued with additions and expansions to the 13th century. The forces of French King Louis XIV captured the castle in 1681, but by 1780 local inhabitants were using the abandoned structure as a source of building materials. Tours feature medieval activities, falconry, fireworks, the castle's own ghost, and other celebrations.

Open daily April through October from 11:00 to 17:00 (July and August to 18:00); November through March weekdays only from 13:00 to 16:00 (closed Fridays). Fee; limited access for people with reduced mobility.

From the riverside parking area, continue south on quai de l'Ourthe (N89) and follow the curve in the river. In 400 m, turn right onto rue du Pont and cross the river bridge. After 130 m, take the 1st roundabout exit onto rue du Chalet (N833) and follow along the west bank of the Ourthe for 10.7 km. In Rendeux, turn right toward Amonines on a rural road. Follow for 1.8 km into Beffe and the church on the left. (50.244967, 5.52333)

As Task Force Hogan's column moved north after abandoning La Roche-en-Ardenne on 21 December, a panzerfaust hit the lead tank while it traveled near the outskirts of Beffe. The task force found itself outflanked by Kampfgruppe Bayer (see Battle of Dochamps, above), forcing a withdrawal to a hill near Marcouray.

Although the entire unit became surrounded by the 116th Panzer Division, the Germans did not attack, preferring to expend their energies elsewhere. The bulk of the panzer division moved on leaving a contingent to keep Hogan's force captive. On 23 December, Hogan declined a surrender demand. An attempted re-supply by air was unsuccessful. On 26 December, Task Force Hogan destroyed its thirty vehicles – the men finding their way back to friendly lines on foot.

The wheelless and trackless **US M4A3 Sherman tank** is dedicated to the men of Task Force Hogan, 3rd Armored Division, who fought in this area until surrounded. The tank was abandoned along the side of the road to Magoster, where it had been disabled during the local fighting. After 40 years in the field, it was salvaged, restored, and mounted in Beffe in front of the rebuilt church as a memorial to the 33rd Tank Battalion, whose eight Sherman tanks formed the armored strength of Task Force Hogan.

To regain the tour route, reverse direction and, after 1.8 km, turn right toward Hotton (N833) and continue back to the Farthest Advance Stone in Hampteau.
Total distance: 32 km.

28

---

28 The British Achilles was a variant of the American M10 Tank Destroyer mounting a British 17-pounder gun instead of the standard 3-inch gun.

Other Points of Interest near La Roche-en-Ardenne

> **Bérismenil**
> **Museum 1944**
> Bérismenil 35
> Tel: +32 (0)4 77 59 53 79
> Web: www.history44.com
> 6982 Samrée, Belgium
> Email: history44@hotmail.be
>
> This private museum holds over 5,000 objects collected from the Bulge battlefields including displays of equipment, uniformed manikins, and vignettes covering the Battle of the Bulge, Belgian collaboration with the Nazi occupiers, and a B-17 bomber that crashed nearby. Many of the artifacts were collected from local citizens.
> Open 15 July to 15 August only on Saturdays from 10:00 to 18:00; and Sundays and holidays from 13:00 to 18:00. Fee.
> Location: In Bérismenil 10 km east of La Roche-en-Ardenne (50.178910, 5.667449)
>
> On 13 April 1944, an **American B-17 medium bomber**, nicknamed 'The Joker' from the 545th Bomber Squadron, came under attack by Luftwaffe fighters while returning from bombing the ball bearing factories at Schweinfurt, Germany. The airplane crashed in a ball of flames against the mountain known locally as 'Les Crestelles.' Fortunately, most of the 10-man crew had time to parachute to safety. The survivors took refuge with the Belgian resistance, but nonetheless German troops eventually captured seven of the nine and sent them to PoW camps. Two men successfully made their way to Switzerland.
> A rough concrete and stone base supports an upright aircraft propeller. The memorial is dedicated to the delivery of Belgium from German occupation by Allied forces. The view over the village of Maboge and the Ourthe valley is magnificent. The actual crash site remains along the country lane to the right of the monument.
> Location: along a rural road 1.5 km west of highway N860 north of Bérismenil. (50.174148, 5.644433)

29

> **Wibrin**
> An **US Sherman M4A3 tank** stands below the hilltop church. Although the tank looks complete from the street, the entire opposite side has been removed to expose its interior. Plaques on the nearby wall commemorate the civilian victims of the war and 50th anniversary of the town's liberation.
> Location: 15 km east of La Roche-en-Ardenne beside the church on rue de la Copette. (50.166120, 5.719443)

---

29   The lone victim was top turret gunner US Army Air Force Staff Sergeant James H Young, hit by the German fighter's machine-gun fire. Sgt Young is buried in Lorraine American Cemetery, St-Avold, France.

Cherain

A triangular park in front of the town's 11th century church holds a **German 150-mm sFH 18** (schwere Feldhaubitze 18 translates as heavy field howitzer, model 18) and the town's war memorial. This model was produced in fair numbers from 1933 by several manufacturers and was a standard heavy artillery piece used in divisional artillery batteries. The chassis suffered from solid rubber tires mounted upon iron wheels.
Location: 30 km east of La Roche-en-Ardenne beside highway N827. (50.180638, 5.864769)

Gouvy

Brown tourist signs in Gouvy lead three kilometers along an isolated country lane to the **Quatre Frères Léonard Memorial**, located only meters from the Luxembourg border. A 50-meter walkpath follows the edge of a pasture to an iron-fenced cemetery holding only one grave. An information panel explains that in January 1945 the four Léonard brothers — Amand, Herve, Aime, and Jose — reputedly members of the *Armée secrète*, were murdered by pro-German Belgians. Their bodies were discovered at this site on the evening of 6 March 1946.
Location: 35 km east of La Roche-en-Ardenne and 3 km southeast of Gouvy along rue de Wago (becomes rue de la Grotte). (50.168555, 5.962930)

Ourthe

The 84th Infantry Division pushed against the northern nose of the Bulge where it encountered the 116th Panzer Division on 15 January while the enemy force withdrew back across the Ourthe River. A memorial to the **84th Infantry Division** stands at the corner of the church in the center of the town. The stone, overgrown by aggressive rose bushes, depicts crossed Belgian and American flags and states, 'In memory of all of the GIs who died in January 1945 in the liberation of Ourthe.'
Location: 39 km east of La Roche-en-Ardenne near highway N815. (50.18854, 5.98066)

Between the Ourthe and the Meuse Sector

Highway N4 runs northwest from Bastogne through Marche-en-Flamenne to the Meuse River at Namur. The highway offered General von Manteuffel the most direct route to the Condroz Plateau, Brussels, and Antwerp. Other routes to the Meuse crossings such as Dinant were less desirable because those roads traversed an area called the Famenne Depression — rugged country of steep ridges and meandering streams.

Fearful of the loss of Marche, Brigadier General Alexander R Bolling sent his 84th Infantry Division's 334th Infantry Regiment to dig in south of the Hotton–Marche highway and his 335th Infantry Regiment to defend immediately in front of Marche with its 3rd Battalion sent farther on to Rochefort. The 3rd Armored Division's CCA joined the defenders of Marche to the south.

208   The Bulge Battlefields

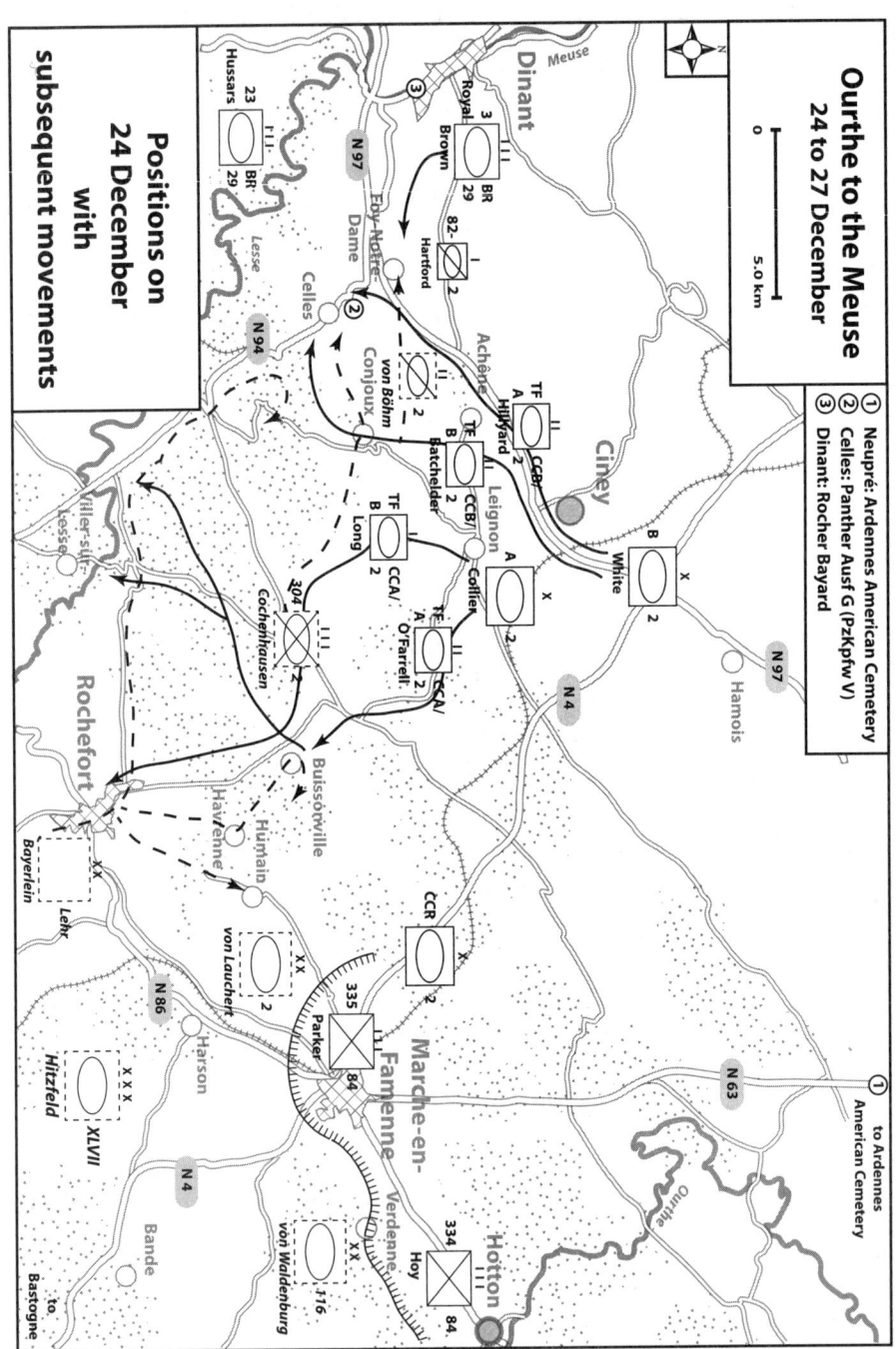

On 20 December, Oberst Meinrad von Lauchert's 2nd Panzer Division pushed aside weak engineer combat forces at Ourtheuville after explosives on the bridge twice failed to detonate. After losing two days due to fuel shortages, Lauchert's

Chapter Five   Battle of the Rivers   209

II Reconnaissance Battalion reached Buissonville, 8 kilometers past the Marche-Rochefort highway and on the 84th Division's open right flank. Alarmed at the news of German armor bypassing Marche, General Collins sent CCA, 2nd Armored Division to Ciney to await reports of German positions. While a kampfgruppe continued on toward Buissonville, Lauchert became equally alarmed about his northern flank becoming exposed to Bolling's 84th Infantry Division.

Meanwhile, also on 22 December, Panzer Lehr left one of its infantry regiments at Bastogne, passed through St-Hubert, and marched toward Rochefort. Two companies of the 335th Regiment in Rochefort were overcome in house-to-house fighting, where upon Panzer Lehr settled in for a day of rest.

By 24 December, five panzer divisions pushed forward to the eastern edge of the Bulge. The 2nd Panzer Division, with Panzer Lehr trailing, bypassed Marche to the south and was striving toward the Meuse. The 116th Panzer Division tried to cross the Hotton–Marche highway to gain the Condroz Plateau. The 2nd and 9th SS Panzer Divisions were still east of the Ourthe, but also moving toward the Condroz. The Führer Begleit Brigade across the Ourthe pressured Hotton from the south. As von Manteuffel's troops lay only 22 kilometers from the Meuse, he welcomed reinforcements in the form of 9th Panzer Division and 15th Panzergrenadier Division.

Battle of the Verdenne Pocket
24 to 26 December 1944

Generalmajor Siegfried von Waldenburg's 116th Panzer Division '*Windhund*' (Greyhound) was resurrected from the remnants of the 16th Panzergrenadier Division, destroyed at Stalingrad. In 1944, it fought in opposition to the Normandy landings but managed to escape the Falaise Pocket. The division participated in Hürtgen Forest fighting in November 1944, having inflicted heavy casualties upon the US 28th Infantry Division.

The division finally crossed the Ourthe at La Roche-en-Ardenne on 22 December with orders from General Krüger to cut the Hotton–Marche highway, the last major obstacle to accessing the Condroz. To von Waldenburg's discomfort, his division's units were scattered between La Roche and Marche as a result of the back-and-forth maneuvers required to find an Ourthe crossing and the clearing skies that exposed them to Allied aircraft. Consequently, his units entered the upcoming battle piecemeal when they arrived on the scene. On 23 December, Panzer Reconnaissance Battalion 116 entered Bois de Chardonne south of the small farming village of Verdenne.

The 84th Infantry Division was activated in October 1942 but did not enter combat until November 1944 when it attacked Geilenkirchen, Germany north of Aachen. On 18 December, the unit disengaged and relocated to Belgium to become the main infantry unit in VII Corps' counterattack. The German penetrations against Marche required the unit to be prematurely committed in a defensive role. The division's 334th Regiment held defensive positions from Hampteau on the Ourthe River near Hotton to Verdenne 7 kilometers to the southwest. A gap existed between its right flank and the 335th Regiment defending Marche.

German Objective	To cut the Hotton–Marche highway
Forces	
American:	3rd Battalion, 334th Infantry Regiment; later 3rd Battalion, 333rd Infantry Regiment, 84th Infantry Division (Brigadier General Alexander Bolling); and 771st Tank Battalion (Lieutenant Colonel Jack C Childers)
German:	116th Panzer Division (Generalmajor Siegfried von Waldenburg)
Result	The 116th Panzer Division was stopped with heavy losses of men and matériel
Casualties	
American:	112 killed and 348 wounded
German:	224 killed, 787 wounded, and 777 missing of which 591 were taken prisoner; also 41 tanks, 8 SP guns, and 190 other vehicles were destroyed
Location	Verdenne is 5 km southwest of Hotton

[30]

Battle

The 334th Infantry Regiment protected the Hotton–Marche road along a ridge from Hampteau to Verdenne, a hamlet roughly midway between Hotton and Marche. During the night of 23/24 December, two companies from Panzer Reconnaissance Battalion 116 infiltrated through the thin foxholes line on their right flank. One reconnaissance company held positions in a wood northwest of the village known locally as Grosse Haie and awaited the arrival of the bulk of 116th Panzer Division that advanced slowly under pressure from Allied aircraft.

Colonel Charles E Hoy, 334th Regiment commander, ordered a counterattack through the woods by Company K supported by a platoon of Company B, 771st Tank Battalion and Company A from the infantry regiment's reserve battalion.

At noon, I Battalion, Panzergrenadier Regiment 156, supported by five panzerjägers, moved to re-establish contact with the division's reconnaissance battalion. The attack captured Verdenne and continued 200 meters north of the village to the chateau. At 1500, they collided with Colonel Hoy's flanking counterattack and, upon reaching the southern edge of the woods, were repelled. Colonel Hoy reoccupied part of Verdenne and took 100 prisoners in the woods.

In the early evening the arrival of Kampfgruppe Bayer, which included the entire Panzergrenadier Regiment 60 supported by forty Panthers and PzKpfw IVs from Major Gerhard Tebbe's I Battalion, Panzer Regiment 16, strengthened the German

---

30 Generalmajor Siegfried von Waldenburg fought as an infantryman in the First World War, earning the Iron Cross First Class. During the Second World War, Waldenburg fought on the Eastern Front in various capacities from 1941 to 1944, during which he was awarded the Knight's Cross of the Iron Cross. As commander of the 116th Panzer Division, he led this division until the collapse of the Ruhr Pocket. Von Waldenburg surrendered to the US Ninth Army and after three years in captivity, he was released. Waldenburg died in 1973 at age 74.

Chapter Five — Battle of the Rivers

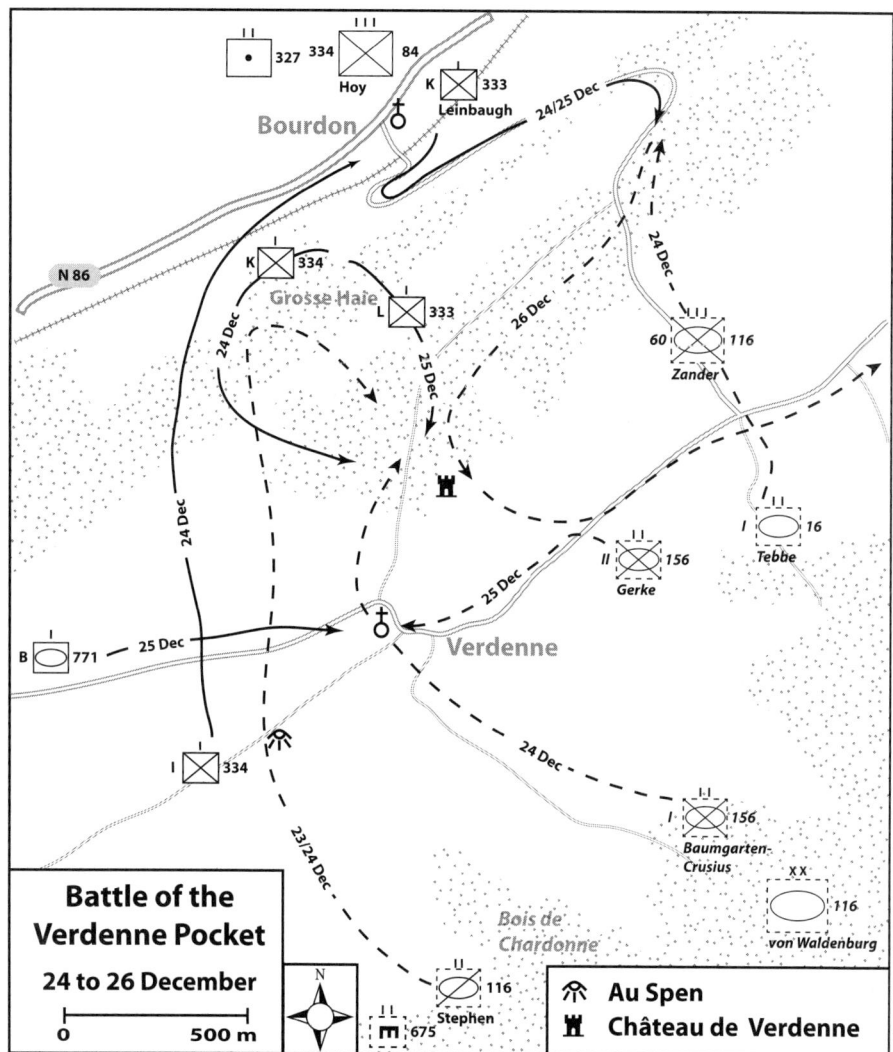

Battle of the Verdenne Pocket
24 to 26 December

force. They completed the capture of the village and pushed a deep salient into the forest between Verdenne and Bourdon, driving Companies I and K to a new line in front of the Hotton–Marche road. German patrols found the area farther north heavily mined, forcing Oberst Bayer to request artillery support to continue the advance the next morning. Instead he received orders to 'dig in.'

Colonel Timothy A Pedley Jr committed Companies K and L, 333rd Regiment, to launch a night counterattack from Bourdon. After crossing the twin railroad tracks, Company K began a gradual assent toward the ridgeline only to stop where the road forked. Unsure of the proper route and with map reading hampered by the cloudless nighttime darkness, Company K went left instead of right and walked away from the planned attack zone.

At 0100 on Christmas Day, Company L moved up a secondary road and joined forces with the much-reduced Company K, 334th Infantry Regiment. Together they fought into Verdenne behind a wall of artillery fire to recapture the village after grim house-to-house fighting. Kampfgruppe Bayer became trapped in a pocket between the 333rd Regiment's Company L in Verdenne, and the fortuitously misdirected Company K in Bourdon.

Von Waldenburg again attempted to consolidate his forces north of the village utilizing his last combat unit, II Battalion, Panzergrenadier Regiment 156, supported by nine recently repaired panzers. At noon, two panzer platoons assaulted Verdenne from the east only to be met by Company B, 771st Tank Battalion. The panzers were eventually all destroyed, but remnants of I Battalion and a reconnaissance platoon escaped. Kampfgruppe Bayer was still surrounded.

During the night and morning of 26 December, Kampfgruppe Bayer maintained its hedge-hog defense while engaging in repeated attacks and counterattacks. At 0330, Companies A and B, 333rd Regiment attacked the pocket, but strong tank fire repulsed the effort. At 0705, German artillery hit the Hotton–Marche road in Bourdon. At 1015, 334th Regiment, Company D, 87th Chemical Mortar Battalion, and divisional artillery units hit the pocket. The battle for the village resumed after dawn with a continued push west through Verdenne by the remaining grenadiers and elements of the Reconnaissance Battalion. German troops succeeded in reaching Hill 326 west of the village but were stopped by intense American artillery fire. Kampfgruppe Bayer joined this battle with an advance toward Verdenne, but it only reached as far as the chateau. After enduring a devastating afternoon artillery barrage, Bayer received permission to break out.

At 1730, the pocket survivors moved through Marenne led by seven Panthers and four assault guns. Upon reaching Menil-Favay, a Panther detonated an American mine and blocked the roadway between the narrowly-spaced houses. Major Tebbe ordered the combat group off-road only to find the field laced with antitank mines. The explosions brought American artillery fire onto the field where, after the battle, six burned-out tank wrecks remained. Nonetheless, surviving armor and grenadiers made their way south to escape through the forest.

Conclusion

The steadfast defense of 84th Infantry Division and the overwhelming superiority of American artillery and airpower essentially destroyed 116th Panzer Division as a cohesive fighting force. That defeat and the losses suffered by 2nd Panzer Division described below effectively ended Fifth Panzer Army's drive to the Meuse. The Germans were on the defensive with no hope of success. The initiative now fell to the Americans, and so it would remain.

Battlefield Tour

> From the Farthest Advance Stone in Hampteau, proceed north toward Hotton for 550 m and then turn left onto rue Chavée. Carefully follow this rural road for 6.9 km (becomes rue de la Chapelle, rue du Centre, rue Noël 1944, and finally Chemin de Verdenne; note the bear right and left curve in Menil-Favay and the right turn in

Chapter Five   Battle of the Rivers   213

> Verdenne). Stop at a convenient location near the slight hill west of Verdenne. (50.231613, 5.392839)

On the morning of 24 December, Private Eddie Korecki, Company I, 334th Infantry Regiment awoke and knew something was wrong. Korecki asked his foxhole partner Private Frank Carroll if he had heard troops moving through the line earlier that morning. Among company's foxholes, 50 meters apart and with mine-laying teams active during the night, such noise was not unusual. The two privates decided to check with their platoon sergeant only to find his foxhole empty. The adjoining foxhole was also empty, and footprints in the snow indicated that a large body of men had passed during the night. The trail led to a small fir forest on a ridge northwest of the village. Korecki and Carroll raised the alarm and a patrol investigated the footprints. Upon approaching the wood, the men met heavy small-arms fire.

The right flank of the 334th Regiment's line anchored in an area known locally as **Au Spen** (or Hill 336) The views south and southwest provide observation over the pastures to the Bois de Chardonne source of the German attack. The final German assault of 26 December unfolded against American forces on this hilltop.

> Reverse direction and return to Verdenne, stopping after 550 m at the crossroads. (50.234413, 5.39881)

On Christmas Day, a platoon of five PzKpfw IVs commanded by Leutnant Hans-Joachim Grzonka and a platoon of four Panthers commanded by Hauptmann Kuchenbach led the assault upon Verdenne. At 1130, the panzers rolled out of positions from the east and laid a barrage of tank shells upon the village. Heavy American artillery and tank fire destroyed Kuchenbach's four Panthers within minutes. Lt Grzonka's five PzKpfw IVs raced toward the center of the village. A Sherman shell destroyed the lead panzer, but the remaining four tanks reached the crossroads east of the church and dug in.

The next day, Grzonka's force joined the reconnaissance battalion in the attacks upon Hill 326. American artillery fire immobilized Grzonka's remaining four panzers before a machine-gun burst killed their leader.[31] German troops abandoned the last houses in the village and returned to their lines in Bois de Chardonne.

The three days of intense combat destroyed most of Verdenne's buildings. The main street of Verdenne was renamed rue Nöel 1944 in commemoration of the Christmas Day battle.

> Reverse direction and return 45 m before turning right onto rue du Gadeli (unsigned). Follow for 410 m (becomes rue du Calvaire) to the chateau entrance. (50.237858, 5.398252)

---

31   Leutnant Hans-Joachim Grzonka is buried in German War Cemetery in Lommel, Belgium. He was 19 years old.

Pass through the forest to the north, noting the shell craters in the woods, and pause briefly at the entrance to the **Château de Verdenne**. During the Christmas Day fighting, the combatants fought house-to-house with the chateau changing hands several times. The Belgian nobleman's home ended as a blood-stained shambles. The chateau and the surrounding property are now private.

> Continue 1.1 km (becomes Sentier de Verdenne) to the memorial in the center of the intersection. (50.245634, 5.406277)

Kampfgruppe Bayer's positions in the Verdenne Pocket laagered in the forest on either side of Sentier de Verdenne between the chateau and the memorial.

At almost exactly midnight on 24/25 December, after taking a wrong turn in nighttime darkness, 1st Lieutenant Harold P Leinbaugh led Company K, 333rd Regiment around a horseshoe curve in the uphill road and entered a dense forest. Just inside the forest line the huge bulk of a tank loomed ahead, nearly filling the narrow road. The men at the front of the column stopped several feet away and passed back word to hold up.

Believing the tank to be the unit's armored support, Sergeant Don Phelps pounded the side of the nearest tank to arouse a crewman who opened the hatch and inquired '*Was ist los*?' After an instant's hesitation, Phelps fired one round at the crewman and fled. Machine guns blazed while infantrymen dove for the roadside ditches, but the Panthers could not sufficiently depress their cannon to strike the ditches. Sgt Phelps grabbed a rocket launcher from his platoon's bazooka man and fired one round that exploded an armored personnel carrier. Phelps reloaded, but his second round bounced off the side of an armored vehicle. Shell fragments hit his hands and arm before he could fire again.[32] German infantry joined the confused engagement while Lt Leinbaugh and his men scrambled back and took up positions in a rock quarry below the bend in the road to block the road to Bourdon — only 200 meters from Bayer's panzers.

On the afternoon of 26 December, after several futile efforts to attack the pocket, Leinbaugh established radio contact with a field artillery battalion and directed ranging fire that set one Panther aflame. Those co-ordinates were transmitted to other batteries for a massive time-on-target firing from up to 150 barrels. The effect was devastating when shells from Corps artillery's 8-inch howitzers sent whole trees through the air and exploded the tanks. The massive barrage broke the back of Kampfgruppe Bayer.

The simple stele memorial identifies the nearby woods as the site of the **Verdenne Pocket**. The claim of '2,000 combatants lost their lives' is a considerable overstatement. Kampfgruppe Bayer sheltered in the slight depression northeast of the memorial. Sgt Phelps met his panzer at the edge of the forest 200 meters ahead along the road to the left toward Bourdon. The rock quarry where Lt Leinbaugh and his men

---

32   Sergeant Don Phelps survived the war to later complete his degree at Cornell University and enter into his family's business.

sheltered from German fire after their surprise meeting has been partially covered over with houses.[33]

> Leave the Verdenne Pocket Memorial to the north and descend the ridge line into Bourdon. Turn left toward Marche-en-Famenne (N86, Chaussée de l'Ourthe) and follow for 4.4 km to the roundabout in Marche-en-Famenne. (50.229886, 5.343972)

Other Points of Interest near Marche

> **Marche-en-Famenne**
> The left rear of the forecourt garden of Musée de la Famenne holds a stone wall backed by eight short flag poles displaying the flags of Britain, Canada, Belgium, and France. The wall bears several commemorative plaques. Most prominent is a bronze bust of **Brigadier General Alexander R Bolling**, commander 84th Infantry Division, and the praise, 'The city of Marché en Famenne recognizes the heroic 84th Division of the American Army, whose indomitable bravery broke the Ardennes Offensive during the last days of December 1944 before the gates of the city.' Other plaques are dedicated to '…the gallant English, Scots, Welsh, and Canadian combatants as well as the Belgian and French SAS of the British XXX Corps commanded by Lieutenant-General Brian C Horrocks, who liberated our towns and villages in January 1945 during the Ardennes Counteroffensive.'
> Location: In the center of Marche-en-Famenne on rue du Commerce (N856). (50.22682, 5.34384)
>
> A personal celebration of the **84th Infantry Division** takes the form of a private building where an external wall displays the unit's axe and log insignia. Location: northeast of the center of Marche-en-Famenne near the civilian cemetery beside Chaussée de l'Ourthe (N86). (50.23013, 5.34767)

> **Waha**
> The 9th Panzer Division formed in the winter of 1939/40 to participate in the Battle of France. It later demonstrated considerably capability in the Balkans, Ukraine, and Kursk battles. Badly reduced resisting the American advance from southern France, it was rebuilt near Aachen in the autumn. The division did not enter the Bulge fighting until 22 December. Its complement included seventy-six tanks and assault guns and a total of 14,000 men. This strong force assisted in driving the 24th Cavalry Squadron from Humain (see below).
> By 26 December, the division had replaced the badly damaged Panzer Lehr and struggled to hold the five-kilometer bridgehead at Rochefort against increased American attacks. By the next day, efforts of the German XLVII Panzer Corps, holding a line from the outskirts of Marche to Rochefort, and German LVIII Panzer

---

33   First Lieutenant Harold P Leinbaugh, along with John D Campbell, authored a history of his unit titled '*The Men of Company K.*' He became a special agent in the FBI and later Deputy Special Assistant to President Richard Nixon in the White House Press Office. Lt Leinbaugh died in 1990 at age 68 and he is buried in Arlington National Cemetery, Arlington, Virginia.

Corps, holding from Marche east to Amonines, stalled. The 9th Panzer Division's line extended when the shattered 2nd Panzer Division withdrew behind its front. Although the panzers had progressed west and northwest of Marche, General Bolling's 84th Infantry Division had repelled every effort to enter the city.

The **Farthest Advance Stone** of 9th Panzer Division stands at the intersection where highway N888 leads east to La Roche-en-Ardenne and highway N4 leads southeast to Bastogne.
Location: 3 km southeast of the center of Marche-en-Famenne. (50.209838, 5.367489)

Humain

After the defeat of the 2nd Panzer Division at the Battle of the Celles Pocket, Panzer Lehr attempted to maintain a corridor to allow for a successful withdrawal. Conversely, CCA, 2nd Armored Division was just as determined to close any escape route. In an attempt to break the 2nd Armored Division stranglehold upon 2nd Panzer Division, General Bayerlein divided his Panzer Lehr Panthers into two assault groups. A platoon of panzers supported by a rifle company was to seize Humain, and a company of panzers supported by a rifle battalion planned to drive through Havrenne to Buissonville.

Troop A, 24th Cavalry Squadron, attached to 2nd Armored Division, defended Humain. The German attack came at dawn and quickly drove the Americans from the village. Colonel John C MacDonald's 24th Cavalry Squadron attempted to retain Humain, but its light guns were no match for the Panthers, who sheltered from American artillery among the village buildings.

CCR took over the attack on the morning of 27 December with tanks circling south, east, and west and the 2nd Battalion, 67th Armored Infantry coming from the north. The Panthers had departed during the night, but it remained ten hours before the 150 grenadiers could be wedged out of the village's buildings. A stubborn detachment of 200 grenadiers held the large 18th-century Château de Humain. Flame-throwing British 'Crocodile' tanks persuaded the Germans to surrender.

To the left of the chateau's entrance gates, two polished stone steles recall the recapture of Havrenne and Humain by **General Harmon's 2nd Armored Division** and attached units against the forces of 2nd and 9th Panzer Divisions and Panzer Lehr. The plaques are replicated in French and English. (50.206773, 5.257165)

Across the road, a large stone with applied metallic lettering attests to the stoppage of the **German winter offensive** at the edges of the village.
Location: 8.5 km southwest of Marche-en-Famenne at the northern outskirts of Humain. (50.206822, 5.256904)

Havrenne

At the same time while the battle raged for Humain, a German column moved through an empty Havrenne only to be repulsed by CCA, 2nd Armored Division, that had reoccupied the village. During the night 25/26 December, the 9th

Panzer Division arrived on the scene and, at 0700 that morning, launched fifteen Panthers and a battalion from Panzergrenadier Regiment 101 against Havrenne. They were met by Companies H and I, 66th Armored Regiment, which pushed back three assaults that day.

An American **M1 57-mm antitank gun** rests upon one corner of the village's main intersection. Across from the gun and beside the village war memorial, a stone stele bears a plaque commemorating the Christmas Day 1944 heroic battle of **Companies H and I, 66th Armor Regiment** against the German 9th Panzer Division.
Location: 3 km west of Humain and 11 km southwest of Marche-en-Famenne in the center of the village. (50.202522, 5.223404)

Side Trip: Battle for Rochefort
23 to 24 December 1944

Highway N86 leads from Marche-en-Famenne directly into the center of Rochefort. After crossing the river, turn right on rue de Behogne to access the central square before the Hôtel de Ville. (50.15894, 5.22324) Total distance 13.9 km

GERMAN OBJECTIVE	To expand the penetration westward toward the Meuse River	
FORCES		
	American:	Companies I and K, 335th Infantry Regiment (Major Gordon A Bahe); 1st Platoon (Captain Robert R Kline), 638th Tank Destroyer Battalion; 1st Platoon (1st Lt Floyd Wright), Company A, 51st Engineer Combat Battalion
	German:	Panzergrenadier Regiment 902 (Oberstleutnant Joachim Ritter von Poschinger)
RESULT	German forces overwhelmed the much smaller American contingent	
CASUALTIES		
	American:	25 killed or captured and 15 wounded
	German:	unknown
LOCATION	Rochefort is 14 km southwest of Marche-en-Famenne	

Battle

General Fritz Bayerlein's Panzer Lehr trailed behind 2nd Panzer Division and reached Rochefort at 1640 on daylight-shortened 23 December. Shortly after midnight, the division began its attack upon the city. In house-to-house combat, the Germans pushed toward the crossroads in the center of town where the Americans had stationed 57-mm antitank guns encircling their headquarters in the Hôtel de Ville.

At 1300, General Bolling ordered a withdrawal, but close contact with the enemy made the maneuver difficult. Five hours later, the battalion, organized into separate groups and under cover of smoke grenades, made a dash for the town exits to the north and east. During the night, most of the men achieved friendly lines. Panzer Lehr, after a 10-hour march and 20 hours of combat, was exhausted and did not pursue the fleeing Americans. American troops re-entered Rochefort on 31 December.

Battlefield Tour

The **First World War memorial** stands in front of the red brick Hôtel de Ville featuring a copper life-sized Belgian soldier holding up a flag with one hand and his rifle with the other. The soldier displays a number of bullet holes, especially on the back side facing the Hôtel de Ville, and its stone plinth bears numerous chips and pits from small-arms fire incurred during the last stand defense by American troops.

Walk south on rue de Behogne 140 m.

Slightly below grade in front of a café under the shade of a spreading tree, a rough hewn stone dedicated to the 84th Infantry Division bears a rather faded metal plaque identifying this site where the **3rd Battalion, 335th Infantry Regiment, 84th Infantry Division**, commanded by Major Bahe, resisted the German troops. (50.1578, 5.2228)

Continue southwest 170m on rue de France (N86).

The 1st Canadian Parachute Battalion arrived at Ostend on 26 December 1944 and soon moved forward to Rochefort, where it prepared defensive positions and conducted active patrolling until 13 January. Even though combat was limited to only minor encounters with the enemy, the 1st Canadian Parachute Battalion earned the distinction of being the only Canadian combat unit to see action in the Ardennes.

The **1st Canadian Parachute Battalion Memorial** stands in square Crépin surrounded by once elegant houses. The upright plinth (50.15716, 5.22099) bears a slate plaque inscribed with the image of a lone soldier and the words:

1944-1994
50 years after
Rochefort remembers you

[34]

Other Points of Interest near Rochefort

Han-sur-Lesse

Panzer Lehr captured St-Hubert 24 kilometers to the southeast at 0100 on 22 December and continued through the night to approach Han-sur-Lesse via Bure and Tellin to drive opposing forces back across the Lesse River. Bayerlein's Panzergrenadier Regiment 902 pushed forward to capture Rochefort the next day.

---

[34] Major Gordon A Bahe, wounded later in the Battle of the Bulge, was awarded a Silver Star. Bahe remained in the US Army, retiring with the rank of lieutenant colonel. He died in 1992 at age 73 and is buried in Zachary Taylor National Cemetery, Louisville, Kentucky.

After the defeat of the 2nd Panzer Division on 24 December, Panzer Lehr returned to Han-sur-Lesse to establish a 38-kilometer defensive line to the southeast as far as Remagne.

American, Belgian, British, and French flags fly on Pont de la Liberté, where the Lesse was channelized to power an ancient mill. The cobblestone town center offers a number of restaurants, cafes, and hotels. The limestone Grottoes of Han attract over one-half million visitors each year. The **Farthest Advance Stone** along the N86 on the western edge of Han-sur-Lesse marks the limit of Panzer Lehr Division's westward penetration before it resumed its course northward. Location: 7 km southwest of Rochefort. (50.125744, 5.181893)

Bure

The British 6th Airborne Division arrived along the Meuse River between Dinant and Givet on Christmas Day. By early January, the paratroopers and the 29th Armoured Brigade faced the nose of the German salient southwest of Marche. British units participated in the general counteroffensive launched on 3 January (see Chapter Seven). That morning, its 13th Lancashire Battalion sheltered in woods west of Bure, awaiting the signal to launch its attack upon the bridge over the Homme River in Grupont 1.5 kilometers east of the village.

Company A led the attack across the 300 meters of open ground before being momentarily pinned down by machine guns along the roadway. Spurred on by Company Commander Major Jack Watson, the paras overcame the enemy line and started clearing the houses. Companies B and C followed against increasing mortar and SP-gun fire emanating from the far side of the village. By nightfall, the British held one half of the village up to the church and crossroads.

The next day Sherman tanks from the 29th Armoured Brigade arrived to assist clearing the village, but they were knocked out by the return of German Tigers (PzKpfw Vs). In all, the 2nd Battalion, Fife and Forfar Yeomanry lost 16 Shermans during the action. Under the protection of German infantry, the panzers methodically destroyed the village structures. British troops sheltered in cellars while artillery blasted advancing German troops. As was their custom, the German panzers left the village at nightfall and did not return the next morning when British forces occupied the remainder of the town. After three days and nights of tough fighting and heavy losses, the men of the 13th Lancashire Battalion, The Parachute Regiment had liberated the village of Bure.

St-Lambert church in Bure was first listed in 804. The current structure dates from 1738. The churchyard wall bears several plaques commemorating units that fought in the area. A **Belgian SAS** ceramic plaque names three parachutists killed during combat in Bure on 31 December 1944 — (Lt) Paul Renkin, Cpl Emile Lorphèvre, and Cpl Claude (Comte de) Villermont. A similar ceramic plaque honors the 110 men of the **Parachute Regiment, British 6th Airborne Division**, who fell during the Battle for Bure in December to January. Above the wall to the right of the church entrance, a gravestone commemorates:

Win or Die
13th Lancashire Battalion, The Parachute Regiment

61 officers and men of this battalion gave their lives for the village of Bure 3 to 5 January 1945 and here in this field were given temporary graves before being moved to their final resting place at the Hotton Military Cemetery. Remembered with gratitude. (50.08879, 5.25964)

The **Farthest Advance Stone** is 650 m west of Bure on highway N846. Bure is 10.5 km south of Rochefort. (50.08707, 5.2508)

Croix Renkin stands outside the town at the end of a farm lane. The route is well-signed from the center of Bure. A fieldstone wall bears the insignia of the Parachute Regiment and the plasticized photographs of the three Belgian SAS members named above killed at this location on 31 December. The three men were part of a Reconnaissance Squadron for the 13th Lancashire Battalion assembling in the woods to the north. Cpl Lorphèvre, having located a German antitank gun, destroyed it. Returning to its vehicle, his team discovered a newly-arrived German antitank battery. Lorphèvre opened fire with his machine gun. The enemy battery responded with a shell that hit the vehicle and killed the team.
Location: 1.4 km southwest of Bure. (50.08141, 5.24737)

Bande
In September 1944, members of the *Armée Secrète* attacked German troops in the forests outside Bande shortly before the arrival of American troops. On Christmas Eve, 2nd Panzer Division support troops were back in Bande and members of the *Sicherheitsdienst* (SD) took revenge for the earlier deaths. Under the guise of inspecting identity cards, the German security police arrested all males aged 17 to 30 years and brought them to a sawmill for interrogation. German guards then took the group of thirty-five men to the burned-out ruins of a house near the Café de la Poste on the outskirts of the village. One by one, they were led to an open door where they were executed, with a single shot to the back of the head, by an SD man positioned just inside the door. The bodies fell into the cellar. While the executions continued, Leon Praile, unwilling to go docilely to his death, punched a guard and made his escape into the woods. With bullets flying around him, he escaped into the woods and reported what had happened when the village was liberated by Allied forces.

At 0900 on 11 January 1945, soldiers of the 1st Canadian Parachute Battalion arrived to liberate Bande from the retreating German troops. With the village secured, a young boy took members of the battalion to the ruined house to show them the frozen bodies of the thirty-four murdered civilians. The Canadians were ordered to move on at 1100 after handing over Bande to the 9th Battalion of the 6th British Airborne Division.

After the distressing task of identification was completed, soldiers from the 9th Parachute Battalion placed the dead young men in coffins draped with the Belgian flag and acted as pallbearers to carry the coffins to the village cemetery.

The open-air courtyard accesses a shelter that holds a slate plaque bearing the names of the thirty-four victims. The rear wall bears a wooden plaque dedicated to the **1st Canadian Parachute Battalion** and the **9th Parachute Battalion**. The

Chapter Five   Battle of the Rivers   221

> damp, dark cellar remains, decorated with flowers, wreaths, fading photographs, and streamers. (50.16181, 5.40639)

[35]

> To continue the tour, regain highway N86 toward Marche. Return to the roundabout at the intersection of highways N86 and N63 in Marche-en-Famenne. Take the exit toward Liège (N63, Chaussée de Liège). Follow for 38.4 km to the Cimetière Américain entrance on the left. (50.541702, 5.469114) The one-way distance to the cemetery is 40 km.

Ardennes American Cemetery

Although not contained within the battlefield, the Ardennes American Cemetery is highly recommended. The most practical point on the tour to approach the cemetery begins in Marche-en-Famenne where highway N63 provides a high-speed route north for most of the 40 kilometers to the cemetery. All roads in the area pass through Marche-en-Famenne — the reason for its military importance — and the city provides a central point from that to tour other sites as presented below. The tour route proceeds from Marche to the Ardennes American Cemetery. (See below.)

Ardennes American Cemetery and Memorial
Route du Condroz 164   4121 Neupré, Belgium
Tel: +32 (0)4 371 42 87
Web: https://www.abmc.gov/cemeteries-memorials/europe/ardennes-american-cemetery

The cemetery does not hold as many burials of soldiers from the Battle of the Bulge as one would expect because the cemetery was founded in February 1945. By war's end, it contained only 300 graves from soldiers who had died in Liège hospitals. Because of its location near the excellent transportation routes around Liège, it became an accumulation cemetery and, when bodies were recovered from various battlefields, they were brought here. Thus, the cemetery holds burials from every campaign, including even North Africa — a rather unusual situation. Approximately 3,000 dead were members of the US Army Air Corps, whose planes were shot down during the battle or during bombing missions over Germany. In all, the cemetery's four symmetrical grave plots hold 5,311 burials, of which 792 are unidentified. Included among the burials are eleven pairs of brothers. In addition, the Tablets of the Missing include the names of 462 servicemen whose remains were never located.

The memorial holds a non-denominational chapel and is reserved for visitors looking for solitude to pause and reflect. The south façade bears an American eagle carved in high relief above three figures representing Justice, Liberty, and Truth. At the

---

35   Ernst Haldiman, a German-speaking Swiss national, was identified as being a member of the execution squad from No 8 SS Commando for Special Duties. Haldiman was picked up in Switzerland after the war and brought to trial before a Swiss Army Court. On 28 April 1948, he was sentenced to twenty years in prison. He was released on parole on 27 June 1960.

extreme right of the grave plots stands the Statue of Youth, reminding all who visit that those buried died in the prime of their lives.

Open daily from 09:00 to 17:00, except December 25 and January 1.

> Return south on highway N63. Follow for 23.9 km to a slip road exit to Route de Spa (N638). Turn right onto Route de Méan (N938) and follow for 19.8 km into Leignon. Turn left (rue de Custinne) at the train station to cross the tracks, and stop at the next intersection. (50.267853, 5.106496)

A **Farthest Advance Stone,** identifying the extent of the 2nd Panzer Division progress in this area, hides among the trimmed shrubs on the opposite side of the intersection on the left.

> Reverse direction, cross the rail line, and after 90 m, turn right again onto rue du Moulin (unsigned). After 270 m, turn left and continue 120 m to the church entrance on the right. (50.270093, 5.109704)

During the night 22/23 December, Private First Class Milo Huempfner of the 551st Parachute Infantry Regiment guarded a disabled ammunition truck near Leignon. Huempfner awaited the arrival of a recovery vehicle when a jeep with three soldiers arrived and asked if more American soldiers were in the village. After Huempfner answered in the negative, the jeep continued on. Huempfner, at that moment, did not realize that he had just spoken with members of SS-Colonel Otto Skorzeny's Panzer Brigade 150 dressed in American uniforms.

Later that afternoon, Huempfner was still at his post when he heard the clank of Kampfgruppe von Böhm approaching his position. Quickly reacting to the advancing enemy column, Huempfner poured gasoline on his truck and set it afire as a temporary roadblock. Although cut-off from friendly forces, the lone paratrooper started his own war. When the 2nd Armored Division reached Leignon two days later, they found the aggressive trooper with eighteen German prisoners.

A plaque on the wall outside the church commends **PFC Milo Huempfner**'s bravery and concern for the safety of local civilians. The townspeople feared German actions should they congregate for Christmas Eve services in the village church. Upon their request, Huempfner stood guard at the door of the church until services were concluded.[36]

> Reverse direction and, after 120 m, turn right onto rue du Moulin and after a further 270 m turn right toward Ciney / Dinant (Unsigned, N949). Enter a roundabout in 2.3 km and take the 2nd exit toward Philippeville / Dinant (Chaussée de Dinant also

---

36 Private First Class Milo Huempfner of Green Bay, Wisconsin, was awarded a Distinguished Service Cross. His harassing action resulted in the destruction of two enemy half-tracks, a machine-gun position, and three dead. Huempfner died in 1985 at age 67 and is buried in Allouez, Wisconsin.

Chapter Five   Battle of the Rivers   223

> known as Route de Charlemagne, N97). Continue 5.0 km and, after crossing highway E411, take the exit ramp toward Houyet / Dinant (N936). Turn left at the T-junction at the end of the ramp. Follow for 4.4 km (N936, becomes N910) and stop at the tank on the left. (50.232024, 5.004354)

Battle of the Celles Pocket
25 to 27 December 1944

The 2nd 'Hell on Wheels' Armored Division was activated in 1940 under its first commander, Major General George S Patton Jr. Under Major General Ernest N Harmon, the unit fought in Morocco and Sicily before transferring to northwest Europe, where it landed on Omaha Beach on 9 June. It participated in Operation COBRA, the race across France, and broke through the Siegfried Line near Aachen, Germany on 30 October.

On 21 December, the 2nd Armored Division left positions 18 kilometers north of Aachen and headed south under total blackout and radio silence. The unit formed General Collins's counterattack surprise. By midnight the next day, it established a command post at Havelange 115 kilometers southwest of Aachen. Unknown to either side, the leading elements of Oberst Meinrad von Lauchert's 2nd Panzer Division laagered only a few kilometers away.[37]

The 2nd Panzer Division had pushed forward 100 kilometers in eight days, farther than any other German unit during the Battle of the Bulge. In the process, it lost one-half of its armor and exhausted its fuel reserves. The division was strung out from Rochefort almost to Dinant. Kampfgruppe von Böhm sheltered in Foy-Notre-Dame only six kilometers from the Meuse. Kampfgruppe Cochenhausen[38] had formed a hedge-hog defense in the wooded hills between Celles and Conneux. The remainder of the division halted near Rochefort.

On 23 December, the US 2nd Division's Combat Command A moved south, encountering and destroying isolated detachments of panzers screening the German division's main body. CCA entered Buissonville, separating the leading kampfgruppe from the main body of the division.

AMERICAN OBJECTIVE	To encircle and destroy the 2nd Panzer Division approaching Dinant
FORCES	
American:	CCB (Brigadier General Isaac White), 2nd Armored Division

---

[37] Oberst Meinrad von Lauchert fought against the advancing Allied armies through March 1945. Backed up against the Rhine River, he authorized survivors to disband and escape. Lauchert swam the Rhine, quit the war, and walked to his home in Bamberg, Germany. Although imprisoned for war crimes, he was found innocent at the Nuremberg trials and released. He died in 1987 at age 82.

[38] Kampfgruppe von Cochenhausen consisted of Panzergrenadier Regiment 304; an unspecified number of tanks from I Battalion, Panzer Regiment 3; two battalions of self-propelled guns from Panzer Artillery Regiment 74; antiaircraft guns from Flak Battalion 273; and a company of Panzer Pionier Battalion 38.

German:	2nd Panzer Division (Oberst Meinrad von Lauchert)
Result	The 2nd Panzer Division was destroyed as a fighting force
Casualties	
American:	43 killed and 201 men wounded
German:	2,500 killed and 1,213 taken prisoner; 82 tanks, 83 artillery pieces, and 450 vehicles destroyed
Location	Celles is 34 km west of Marche-en-Famenne

Battle

After much confusion at Corps headquarters and with General Collins exercising the maximum discretion offered by Field Marshal Montgomery, on Christmas Day General White's CCB began a double-pronged encirclement of the German *schwerpunkt* by sending two task forces along each of the two ridgelines bordering Kampfgruppe Cochenhausen. Task Force A moved southwest through Achêne to cut off von Böhm in Foy-Notre-Dame (as described below) and to enter Celles from the northeast. Task Force B moved from Leignon through Conjoux down the southern ridgeline to converge with Task Force A at Celles. Kampfgruppe Cochenhausen was trapped in a pocket of woods southwest of Conneux.

All day long von Cochenhausen radioed reports of bitter fighting and heavy losses from Allied planes and tanks. Light observation aircraft flew over the German force at dangerously low levels, guiding British rocket-firing Typhoons and American P-38 Lightnings that strafed and bombed from tree-top levels.

A hastily organized kampfgruppe made a futile relief effort that also fell to Allied aircraft. A second attempt later in the afternoon met a similar fate. By evening, the German perimeter had been reduced to a section of Bois de Coreu northeast of Celles.

During the night 25/26 December, American artillery and mortars fired into the woods that sheltered the German force. With daylight, infantry supported by light tanks entered the woods to reduce German positions formed around any stalled armored vehicle.

The 2nd Panzer Division's advance was finished, whereby von Manteuffel authorized survivors to escape the cauldron as best they could. Shortly after midnight on 27 December, Major Ernst von Cochenhausen ordered the abandonment of the remaining heavy equipment and marched his men southeast. Major Cochenhausen and 600 men eventually rejoined the main body at Rochefort.[39]

Battlefield Tour

Before daylight on 24 December, 2nd Panzer Division's Reconnaissance Battalion 2 of Kampfgruppe von Böhm reached the village of Celles, where the leading Panther hit a mine at the main crossroads. Despite being deceived by a local

---

39 Major Ernst von Cochenhausen was captured by American forces later in the war. He was released in December 1945.

Chapter Five

Battle of the Rivers 225

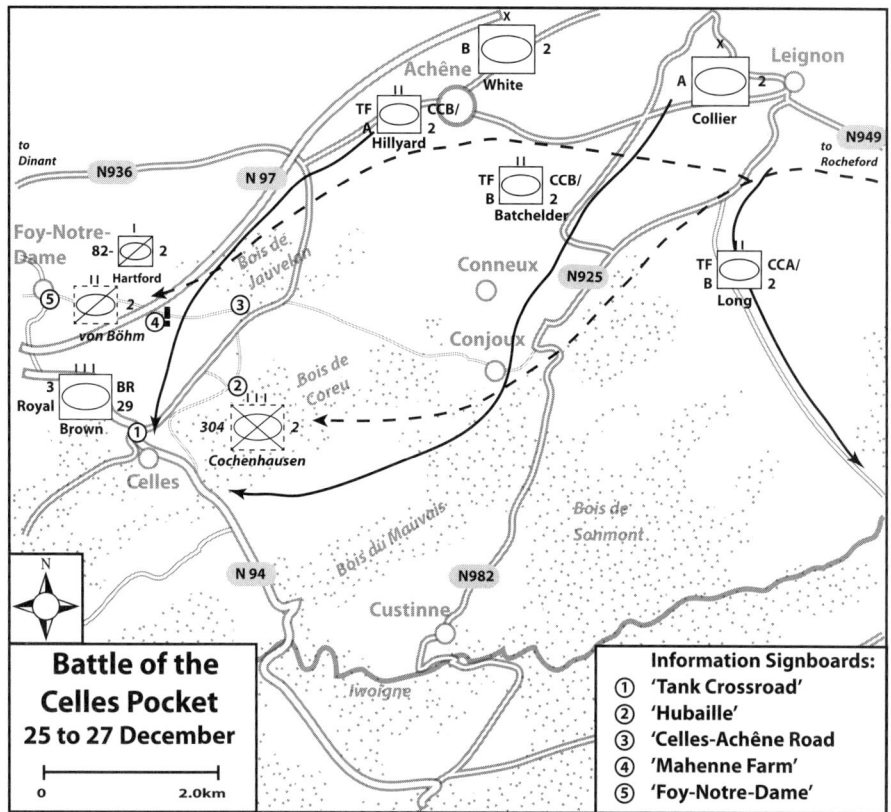

Battle of the Celles Pocket
25 to 27 December

Information Signboards:
① 'Tank Crossroad'
② 'Hubaille'
③ 'Celles-Achêne Road'
④ 'Mahenne Farm'
⑤ 'Foy-Notre-Dame'

resident into believing that the road to Dinant was mined, after some delay the force resumed its march toward the Meuse only 10 kilometers distant.

A **Panther Ausf G (PzKpfw V)** remains at the intersection. Immediately after the war, hatches, treads, and wheels were removed for their scrap value. The café owner placed the tank near the intersection as a monument to victory and, probably, to advertise the establishment. (50.232024, 5.004354)

A series of informational signboards established by the Commune of Houyet and the City of Dinant stands at various sites of importance in the battle against the 2nd Panzer Division. The first, titled **'Tank Crossroad,'** stands behind the Panther and describes the actions of Marthe Monrique, who misled enemy soldiers into believing that the roadway was heavily mined.

> Leave the parking area on Route d'Achêne toward Chiney (N910). After 1.1 km, toward right toward Hubaille and follow for 400 m to the signboard on the left. (50.236473, 5.018078)

Slightly east of the Celles crossroad, German troops occupied the small hamlet of Hubaille and its surrounding woods awaiting supplies from Buissonville.

With its attack on Buissonville, the 2nd Armored Division prevented these essential supplies from arriving. When the advanced elements of the 2nd Panzer Division arrived on the morning of 24 December, they installed their headquarters in a natural cave known as 'Le Trou Mairia' in Bois de Coreu.

Informational signboard #2 'Hubaille' describes the actions of local Baron Jacques de Villenfagne, an old Chasseur Ardennes from the Belgian Army who knew the forests and led a night reconnaissance for English troops. The baron guessed the probable location of the German headquarters correctly, permitting heavy Allied artillery fire onto the positions in the woods.

> Reverse direction and return to highway N910; turn right and, after 600 m, turn left onto a rural road (Route de Foy-Notre-Dame). Continue 110 m to the signboard on the right. (50.244206, 5.01952)

Advancing from Conjoux, the leading panzers of Kampfgruppe von Cochenhausen left the highway onto this road aiming to reinforce von Böhm at Foy-Notre-Dame. Unable to proceed further than the Ferme de Mahenne, visible across the fields to the left, the elements dispersed into these woods. After the 2nd Panzer Division's defeat, numerous vehicles were abandoned especially around Hubaille. The wreckage accumulated in the field across the road and made a dramatic presentation of a defeated German Army.

Informational signboard #3 'Celles–Achêne Road' describes the events and presents dramatic photographs of the wreckage that remained after the German defeat in the Celles Pocket.

> Continue 90 m and turn left. Proceed 800 m onto Ferme de Mahenne (public road) and note the signboard near the barn on the right. (50.245541, 5.007937)

The Ferme de Mahenne became a strategic defensive position of the now-trapped Kampfgruppe von Cochenhausen. Three Panther tanks positioned themselves around the stone farm buildings to fire in any direction against the expected Allied counterattack. They destroyed three half-tracks from Task Force A; however, air support from twelve P-38 Lightnings and Typhoons from 307th Fighter Group at Florennes bombed and strafed the German position until all three panzers were knocked out.

Informational signboard #4 'Mahenne Farm' near the restored stone barn describes the fighting around the farm and presents dramatic after-battle photographs of the damage to the buildings and the destroyed Panthers.

> Follow the rural road for 1.3 km into Foy-Notre-Dame; park at the signboard near the rear of the church. (50.24714, 4.990014)

1. US infantrymen from the 9th Infantry Regiment move silently through the snow-covered Krinkelter woods on their way to make contact with the enemy on 12 December. Less than one week later, the unit was defending the Lausdell Crossroads against the 12th SS Panzer Division. NARA

Dragon's teeth run across the field near Udenbreth.
The German machine-gun shield was part of the Westwall defense near Wahlerscheid crossroads, insert.

2. The mud track of Rollbahn A enters the forest east of the International Highway. The commemorative stone bears witness to the attacking German 277th Volksgrenadier Division on one side and the defending US 99th Infantry Division on the other.

A camouflaged pillbox serves as a regimental command post in the Krinkelter Forest, right. NARA

An American trench line passes among the trees in the fog-enshrouded, preserved Hasselpat Wood battlefield, below.

3. Two smouldering German Panthers stand before the Kalpers house across from the church in Krinkelt. A dead German crew member lies across the back of the first tank behind the turret. The panzer's barrel has been shot off. NARA
The repaired Kalpers house as it looks today, insert.

Monuments to the US 2nd and 99th Infantry Divisions occupy a memorial park across from the church in Krinkelt. The stones are dedicated to those who sacrificed for freedom.

4. Men of the 26th Infantry Regiment struggle to reposition an 57-mm antitank gun in the mud near Domaine Bütgenbach. NARA

The memorial obelisk of the US 1st Infantry Division now occupies the center of the Bütgenbach crossroads and bears the division's famous 'Big Red One' emblem, right.

One-half of the grave plots in the Henri-Chapelle American Cemetery are viewed from the memorial portico, below.

5. Photographic evidence of American soldiers massacred by Kampfgruppe Peiper in a field near Malmédy. Covered by snow while the area was under German control, the bodies have been uncovered and numbered for identification. The burned-out Bodarwé Café is seen in the background. NARA
Additional bodies were uncovered along the tree-lined road to Ligneuville, insert. NARA

The Wall of Remembrance at the Malmédy Massacre Memorial bears plaques listing the names of eighty-four servicemen killed.

6. A much-debated, staged photograph taken from a German propaganda film portrays members of Kampfgruppe Knittel, 1st SS Panzer Division Reconnaissance party in a Schwimmwagen checking directions at the Kaiserbaracke Crossroads. Despite earlier claims, the officer examining the signpost is not Lt Col Peiper. The crossroads today presents a fully industrialized intersection. NARA

German soldiers from the 3rd Fallschirmjäger Regiment, who had just murdered American Prisoners of War, try on the dead Americans' boots near a horse trough in Honsfeld, insert, left. NARA

A memorial to the murdered soldiers stands above a symbolic, modernized horse trough in Honsfeld, below.

7. The remains of an American gas dump on the Francorchamps road above Stavelot. US and Belgian troops set 124,000 gallons on fire to prevent the fuel from powering the Germans push into Belgium. NARA

A German PzKpfw VI (King Tiger) from schwere SS Panzer Battalion 501 ran up against a building in Stavelot where it became stuck and eventually knocked out of action. Two Soldiers from the 30th Infantry Division examine the vehicle after the town was recaptured, right. NARA

A different PzKpfw VI stands in front of the December '44 Museum in La Gleize. The vehicle was abandoned by Kampfgruppe Peiper when the unit began its retreat from the village, below.

8. As the battle progressed, the weather worsened. Here, soldiers of the 2nd Battalion, 289th Infantry Regiment, 75th Infantry Division march along the snow-covered road on their way to recover St Vith in January 1945. NARA

American troops, probably from the 99th Infantry Division, file to the German rear as the schwere SS Panzer Battalion 501 advances along Rollbahn D. The motorcyclists carry MP-40s (machine pistols) frequently misnamed 'Schmeissers', below. NARA

A 105-mm M2A1 howitzer forms the centerpiece of a memorial to Major Arthur C Parker III and his men who defended the Baraque-de-Fraiture Crossroads, below.

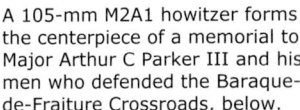

9. Troops of Headquarters Company, 340th Tank Battalion and 3rd Battalion, 504th Parachute Regiment, 82nd Airborne Division advance in a snowstorm behind a Sherman M4 tank to attack Herresbach, near the Our River in January 1945. The pack animal was not official US Army issue, but probably appropriated during the fighting. NARA

American foxholes remain in the woods near the memorial to the 168th Engineer Combat Battalion on the Prümerberg east of St-Vith.

10. An overturned US Sherman M4 tank and a damaged German Sturmgeschütz III remain on the edge of the Clervaux Cemetery after the battle. The tank, from Company A, 707th Tank Battalion, engaged German panzers during the enemy's approach to Clervaux. The German assault gun was abandoned during the German withdrawal in January 1945. NARA

The Sherman M4A3 tank, commanded by Sergeant Donald Fink from Company B, 2nd Tank Bn, 9th Armored Division and which defended the Château de Clervaux, stands in the castle's forecourt as a memorial to the city's defenders. The GI Statue in Clervaux stands near the bend in the Clerf River and is dedicated to all the American units that fought in the area, insert below.

11. Clervaux after the battle, top, and as it appears today, bottom, as viewed from slightly different angles. The gleaming white chateau stands out in the lower photograph while the roofless ruins are only identified by the round tower in the 1945 image. NARA

The twin towers of the local church and the Hotel du Parc on the hillside to the right are clearly visible in the modern photograph.

12. Vehicles of Team Cherry, CCB, 10th Armored Division lay along the Longvilly road after being destroyed defending the highway into Bastogne. Photograph taken after the front had moved on in January 1945, below left. NARA
Wreckage is strewn across Bastogne's central square, now known as place du général McAuliffe, a result of the Christmas Eve Luftwaffe bombardment, below,right. NARA

The renamed square forms the central memorial to Bastogne defenders with a Sherman tank, bust of General McAuliffe, and Circuit Historique informational sign #1. The heavy fog in this image is reminiscent of the early December 1944 fighting conditions, below.

13. This memorial, inaugurated on 14 December 2014, celebrates Major (later Lt Gen) William Desobry and the defenders of Noville. The site is across the street from the village church and the schoolhouse, which was used as the first command post.

Two weary infantrymen from 110th Infantry Regiment pause to exchange information and probably orders in front of an American military notice to the citizens of Bastogne on 19 December 1944, left. NARA

The park in Marvie is typical of the villages surrounding Bastogne. The memorial stone on the right celebrates the 327th Glider Infantry Regiment, which came to the village's rescue. One of the Sherman tank turrets that still 'defends' Bastogne along its approach roadways and Circuit Historique informational panel #6 are to the left, below.

14. The German PzKpfw IV knocked out during the 506th Parachute Infantry Regiment's attack upon Foy in January 1945 is passed by a 6th Armored Division half-track. NARA

Foxholes from Company E, 506th Parachute Infantry Regiment line the Foy – Bizory road. The road, barely visible through the tree-line on the right, formed the front between American and German forces in the infamous Bois Jacques, right.

The German War Cemetery in Recogne holds 6,807 dead, mostly from the local fighting, in a field originally occupied by a American and German temporary burial ground, below.

15. A memorial stone and flags identify the American Temporary Cemetery in Recogne. The central stone carries a poem written by Private David J Phillips and which appears as the epigram for this book.

A 'Screaming Eagle' drinks from an upturned soldier's helmet as a tribute to the 101st Airborne Division's defense of Bastogne, right.

The Mardasson Memorial is dedicated to the 80,987 American servicemen killed, wounded, or missing during the Battle of the Bulge, below.

16. The beautifully landscaped Square Patton in Ettelbruck holds a statue of the American Third Army commander (left), a sandstone plinth bearing the American eagle (center, rear), and a Sherman M4A1 tank, right, rear.

Luxembourg American Cemetery holds 5,076 burials including that of the famous general. This view displays the grave of Medal of Honor recipient Staff Sergeant Day Turner, foreground, and the Memorial Chapel flanked by two pylons bearing battle maps in the background. The pylons' exterior surfaces record the names of 371 servicemen whose remains were never located.

Chapter Five Battle of the Rivers 227

Information signboard #5 'Foy-Notre-Dame' completes the story of Kampfgruppe von Böhm: Each of five Sherman tanks of the British 3rd Royal Tank Regiment guarded separate approach roads into Dinant with orders to delay any approaching enemy before blowing the bridge over the river. Sergeant F 'Geordie' Probert, commanding the Sherman covering the highway from Celles (N94), and his crew had fallen asleep. At midnight of 23/24 December, they awoke with a start to the sound of approaching tanks. In the dim dawn glow, Probert saw a column of vehicles from Kampfgruppe von Böhm closing on his position. Probert's gunner fired — missing the leading vehicle but igniting an ammunition truck farther down the column. The exploding ammunition fired the gasoline truck behind it.

As gasoline supplies were low, the fuel shortage convinced von Böhm's reconnaissance battalion to seek shelter in the nearby village of Foy-Notre-Dame until it could be re-supplied. Böhm formed a hedge-hog defense around the farming community's 17th century church.

On Christmas Day, upon nearing Foy-Notre-Dame, Captain James Hartford, commanding 2nd Armored Division's Company A, 82nd Reconnaissance Battalion, saw German vehicles sheltering among the village buildings. The enemy fired upon the lead platoon whereupon Hartford sent his entire company against the enemy positions aided by the five British-manned Shermans and P-51 Mustang fighter-bombers. A charging American assault gun eliminated a troublesome antitank gun near the center of the village. British gunners took three Panthers, probably those already destroyed at Ferme de Mahenne, under fire. One-hundred-fifty Germans surrendered, including Hauptmann von Böhm.

The interior of **Notre-Dame de Foy** is worth a quick look. Built in 1623 (not 1723 as the signboard incorrectly states), the wood ceiling features 145 ornately framed religious images of Marian mysteries, saints, and doctors of the Catholic Church. The church was the handiwork of pilgrims designed to honor a small clay statue discovered inside a tree by a local woodcutter. The 25-centimeter-high statue stands near the side altar to the left. The dark wood pews and wall coverings attest to the church's age and careful preservation by the villagers. Under agreement by both sides, the church was not used or targeted during the battle and escaped major damage.

The **Farthest Advance Stone** lays 150 meters ahead around the curve in the road that passes before the front of the church. The stone identifies the nearest that any organized unit of the Germany Army approached the Meuse River stands next to a crucifix and is partially obscured by shrubs. (50.247857, 4.989193)

The **Ferme de Calande** mentioned on the signboard as the final resistance of the German troops is 300 meters west of the church parking area. The roadway ends shortly past the farm, trapping vehicles not capable of penetrating the thick forest. (50.246898, 4.985669)

From the Foy-Notre-Dame church parking area, turn right and then immediately left (unsigned) to pass under the structure built over the street. Follow for 1.2 km and then turn right at the T-junction toward Dinant (N94). Follow for 5.5 km, passing under the Route de Charlemagne. At the T-junction, turn right along the east bank of

> the Meuse (N95) and follow for 160 m to pass through the Rocher Bayard. Continue through the narrow opening and park immediately on the left. (50.244652, 4.921155)

During the night of 23/24 December, an American jeep carrying three men from Otto Skorzeny's Panzer Brigade 150, attempted to run a British roadblock. Soldiers of the 29th Armored Brigade manning the roadblock opened fire and killed all three. Hitler's march west to the Meuse River ended here. Three German soldiers had achieved the east bank of the river — but no farther.

The one-car wide northbound highway passes directly through the rock formation known as Rocher Bayard. Immediately north of the rock, a **Farthest Advance Stone** identifies the limit of the three-man force's progress. This is not one of the twenty-six Farthest Advance Stones erected by the Belgian Tourist Club, but carries a distinct construction appearing as a miniature of the Rocher Bayard. The inscription reads, 'Here came crashing the extreme advance of the Ardennes offensive.' (50.244783, 4.921091)

> Continue 2.0 km into the city of Dinant and park near the church on the right. (50.260987, 4.912041)

Dinant

Dinant sits in the upper Meuse valley where the river cuts into the Condroz Plateau. The location has been inhabited during Celtic and Roman times. The current settlement of Dinant was founded by a bishop in the 7th century. The strategic location caused the city to suffer repeated battles, sieges, and pillages during the Middle Ages by the French, Spanish, and Austrians. The city was ceded to France in 1795.

Battles for Dinant occurred during both world wars. On 15 August 1914, French and German troops fought for the river crossing. The bridge bears a plaque commemorating the wounding of **Lieutenant Charles de Gaulle** on 15 August 1914, when he defended the city against invading Germans.

On 13 May 1940, German General Erwin Rommel led his 7th Panzer Division across the Meuse River at an undefended island 4.3 kilometers to the north to start its race to trap the British Expeditionary Force at Dunkerque.

Maison du Tourisme de la Haute Meuse Dinantaise
avenue Cadoux, 8 5500 Dinant, Belgium
Tel: +32 (0)82 22 28 70 Fax: +32 (0)82 22 77 88
Web: http://www.dinant-tourisme.com/

Citadelle de Dinant
Place Reine Astrid 3
Tel: +32 (0)82 22 36 70 5500 Dinant, Belgium
Email: info@citadellededinant.be Fax: +32 (0)82 22 65 04
Web: http://www.citadellededinant.be/fr/contact?language=eng

Chapter Five   Battle of the Rivers   229

The Dinant **Citadel** emerged in the 11th century to control and tax river traffic. The citadel towers 100 meters above the onion-domed gothic **Cathedral of Notre-Dame de Dinant**. Views of the church and citadel are spectacular, especially from the opposite bank. The *Téléférique*, a cable car that climbs the side of the cliff from the south side of the cathedral, poses an ascent preferable to walking the 408 steps. Tours of the castle are guided, so arrivals must be timed accordingly. The open area in the courtyard does not provide the views of the Meuse valley that one might expect.

Open daily 1 April to 30 September from 10:00 to 18:00 (17:30 October to mid-November); mid-November to 31 March from 10:00 to 16:30, closed Fridays; January open weekends and school holidays only. Fee; handicap accessible only through the upper entrance.

Side Trip: Florennes Spitfire Museum

From the church in the center of Dinant, cross the Meuse bridge (N936) and, in the small roundabout on the west bank, take the 3rd exit toward Philippeville / Onhaye (N936). Follow for 5.3 km, then turn right onto the entrance ramp toward Philippeville / Givet (N97). Enter a roundabout after 18.9 km and take 1st exit onto highway N98. Proceed 4.8 km to a roundabout, and take 1st exit onto rue Henry de Rohan-Cabot. Continue 750 m to the *Aerodrome Militaire* entrance gate and stop at the guard post to present identification and receive directions to the museum. (50.244869, 4.623685)
Total one-way distance: 30 km

Originally constructed by the German Todt Organization in 1942, Florennes became known to the Allies as airbase A-78. It was the most forward airfield during the Battle of the Bulge and home to the US 370th and 474th Fighter Groups. P-38 Lightning aircraft, P-61 Black Widows, P-47 Thunderbolts, and B-26 Marauders all flew from its runways. The base is now home to the Belgian 2nd Tactical Wing.

Musée Spitfire
Rue de Rohan Chabot   Base J. Offenberg
5620 Florennes, Belgium   Tel: +32 (0)71 68 25 14
Email: museespitfire@hotmail.fr   Web: http://www.museespitfire.be/

The pride of the museum, a **Spitfire Mk XIV**, flew at the end of the war as part of the Belgian Air Force. The museum collection holds several older model jet fighters and a Tiger Moth biplane, used until 1956 to train future pilots. Wall displays and glass cases house the usual collection of flight memorabilia. Not all of the collection is labeled, with some identified in French only.

Open weekdays and the first Sunday of each month from 13:00 to 16:30. Because the museum is located on an operating military base, visitors must stop at gate #4 and present photographic identification (passport is ideal). Pre-registration is recommended. Fee.

This concludes the Battle of the Rivers tour.

Chapter Six
Skyline Drive
16 to 19 December 1944

Luxembourg Highway N7 (now E421) ran south from St-Vith, Belgium, and provided one of few serviceable north-south routes in eastern Luxembourg. To its east, the twisting Our River passes through narrow canyons and gorges to form the border between the Grand Duchy of Luxembourg and Germany. In December 1944, for the most part, the river also separated the American and German front lines. Any attempt by German troops to move westward had to contend with this natural defensive obstacle.

Major General Troy Middleton's US VIII Corps held 141 kilometers (88 miles) of front along the German border with the experienced 4th and 28th Infantry Divisions. Combat Command B, 10th Armored Division formed his only reserve. The corps headquarters at Heintz Barracks, meanwhile, lay on the northern outskirts of Bastogne.

The 28th 'Keystone,' or 'Bloody Bucket' Infantry Division, commanded by Major General Norman 'Dutch' Cota, who had led the 29th Infantry Division onto Omaha Beach as assistant division commander, rested in this 'quiet sector' of the Ardennes after having been brutally mauled while fighting in the Hürtgen Forest, where it suffered 6,184 casualties. The lengthy front line required General Cota to put all three of his regiments forward. The division's 112th Infantry Regiment held the northern sector deployed in Germany east of the Our River and along a line straddling the Belgium–Luxembourg border. To its south the 109th and 110th Infantry Regiments, west of the Our, extended the division's line to the the Sûre River.

Commanded by the well-regarded Generalmajor Siegfried von Waldenburg, the 116th Panzer Division *'Windhund'* (Greyhound) was one of the best, non-SS armored units in the German Army. The unit was created in March 1944 from the remnants of the 16th Panzergrenadier Division, virtually destroyed on the Eastern Front. The division participated in Normandy fighting and suffered a severe level of casualties holding open the Falaise Pocket while German troops escaped annihilation. It resisted American troops during the Battle of Aachen in October 1944. The 116th Panzer Division gave the US 28th Infantry Division the sobriquet 'Bloody Bucket' during the fighting in the Hürtgen Forest.

General der Panzertruppen Walter Krüger, commander of LVIII Panzer Corps, ordered General von Waldenburg to target the Our River crossings at Burg Reuland, Oberhausen, and Ouren. The first two stood in the 106th Infantry Division's sector, facing its 424th Infantry Regiment. After crossing the river, the Greyhound division's objectives included the Meuse River crossings between Namur and Dinant.

General Krüger's second unit, the 560th Volksgrenadier Division (VGD), formed in September 1944 having gathered troops from a previous 560th Infantry Division stationed in Norway. In December, it arrived in Denmark and later relocated to participate in Operation HERBSTNEBEL. Training was minimal, the new conscripts had no combat experience, and the division lacked antitank weapons. General Krüger assigned the division responsibility to capture two river crossings at Ouren defended by the 112th Infantry Regiment. In actual practice, German transportation difficulties delayed the appearance one of the division's three grenadier regiments onto the battlefield.

The challenging task on the left flank of the Fifth Panzer Army fell to General der Panzertruppen Heinrich Freiherr von Lüttwitz and his XLVII Panzer Corps. The 26th Volksgrenadier Division was to cross the Our River, breech the American line, and open the east-west roadways for the 2nd Panzer Division and Panzer Lehr, who were to capture Bastogne before moving on to the Meuse River.

The 26th VGD, an old-line infantry unit, formed in 1935 as the 26th Infantry Division. It participated in the invasion of the western countries in 1940 before moving east. On the Russian front the unit participated in important engagements along the Volga River, at Orel, in the Kursk counteroffensive, and the defense of Warsaw. Thousands of ex-sailors from the German navy, who were clearly not up to the previous Wehrmacht standards, replaced the heavy casualties incurred in these battles. By December 1944, the division fielded 17,000 men and was augmented by forty-two 75-mm towed antitank guns, the 1026th Assault Gun Company with fourteen Jagdpanzer 38(t) 'Hetzers', and four artillery battalions. Much of its equipment was horse-drawn. The 26th VGD manned Westwall defenses east of the Our that German troops also thought to be a 'quiet sector' to rest, refit, and absorb replacements. In reality the grenadiers were a screen for Panzer Lehr assembling to its east.

Created in 1935 under its original commander, the German armored-warfare expert Generaloberst Heinz Guderian, the 2nd Panzer Division was one of the oldest armored units in the German Army. The division participated in almost every major campaign on the Eastern and Western Fronts from the Invasion of Poland to the defense of the Rhine. In December 1944, the unit was ably commanded by Oberst Meinrad von Lauchert. Its Panzer Regiment 3 fielded 103 PzKpfw IV and V (Panther) tanks. The division looked to avoid becoming ensnared in urban combat by passing to the north of Bastogne. Its targets were Meuse River crossings in the Namur–Dinant sector.

The bridges across the Our River were destroyed during the German withdrawal behind the Westwall the previous September. To cross the rapidly flowing waters swollen by early winter rains, German engineers needed to transport and construct mobile bridges capable of supporting the heavy 45-ton Panther tanks at Dasburg, Gemünd, and Obereisenbach. The necessary delay in bringing forward armor and the widely-spaced American strongpoints led von Manteuffel to infiltrate 30- to 60-man assault teams across the river hours before the artillery bombardment. German reconnaissance revealed that American patrols withdrew into the fortified villages at night, thereby leaving the steep wooded slopes largely undefended.

GERMAN OBJECTIVE	To bypass American centers of resistance and capture the city of Bastogne before continuing to the Meuse River crossings
FORCES	
American:	112th and 110th Infantry Regiments, 28th Infantry Division (Major General Norman Cota)
German:	XLVII Panzer Corps (General der Panzertruppen Heinrich Freiherr von Lüttwitz) and elements of LVIII Panzer Corps

	(General der Panzertruppen Walter Krüger)
RESULT	The division was overwhelmed, but its stubborn defense delayed the enemy's approach to Bastogne for four days.
CASUALTIES American: German:	Period 16 to 31 December 1944: 50 killed, 1253 wounded, and 3900 missing 1054 taken prisoner
LOCATION	Großkampenberg, Germany is 41 km northeast of Wiltz, Luxembourg; Wiltz is 110 km south of Liège, Belgium

Battle Summary

Ninety minutes before the scheduled artillery barrage, the 26th Volksgrenadier Division's assault teams crossed the Our River in rubber boats hidden by a thick fog. The initial bombardment destroyed American wireline communications, and the terrain made radio contact unreliable. By early morning, American companies stationed in towns defending road junctions were all isolated. Platoons from the 707th Tank Battalion pressed forward, but were unable to contact the troops they intended to support.

The appearance of German armor altered the dynamics of the battle. American troops seldom possessed responses to the explosive force of the enemy's 75-mm guns. Despite the valiant efforts of tankers, antitank crews, and bazooka teams, the German infantry–armor combination was unstoppable. Town after town fell. The 110th Regiment's 1st Battalion headquarters was routed at Urspelt while its overwhelmed companies and the battalion ceased to function. Moments later the 2nd Battalion headquarters at Reuler fell when displaced American troops streamed westward, many heading for what they thought would be safety at regimental headquarters in Clervaux.

In general, the 28th Division was overrun, bypassed, and surrounded on 16 December, but isolated units fought on, adhering to Middleton's order to 'Hold at all cost.' By the next morning, Cota's 110th and 112th Infantry Regiments faced the combined might of Panzer Lehr, 2nd and 116th Panzer Divisions, and 26th and 560th Volksgrenadier Divisions. It was hardly an even fight, and General Cota knew that his division was in serious trouble.

Early on 17 December, General Middleton ordered Combat Command R (CCR),[1] 9th Armored Division, to establish roadblocks west of Clervaux as a backstop for the heavily pressured 110th Regiment. Cota committed his reserve 2nd Battalion, 110th Infantry Regiment, but German mortar and machine-gun fire stopped the battalion cold after an advance of only one kilometer. Seventeen light tanks of Company D, 707th Tank Battalion moved south on Skyline Drive only to encounter German antitank guns near Heinerscheid. Twelve of the M5 'Stuarts' were destroyed in a 10-minute engagement.

Meanwhile, as Hosingen fell, the 26th VGD established four bridgeheads across the Clerf River. After the fall of Clervaux, little stood between the 2nd Panzer

---

1   CCR, 9th Armored Division consisted of elements of 52nd Armored Infantry Battalion, 2nd Tank Battalion, 73rd Armored Field Artillery Battalion, and 811th Tank Destroyer Battalion.

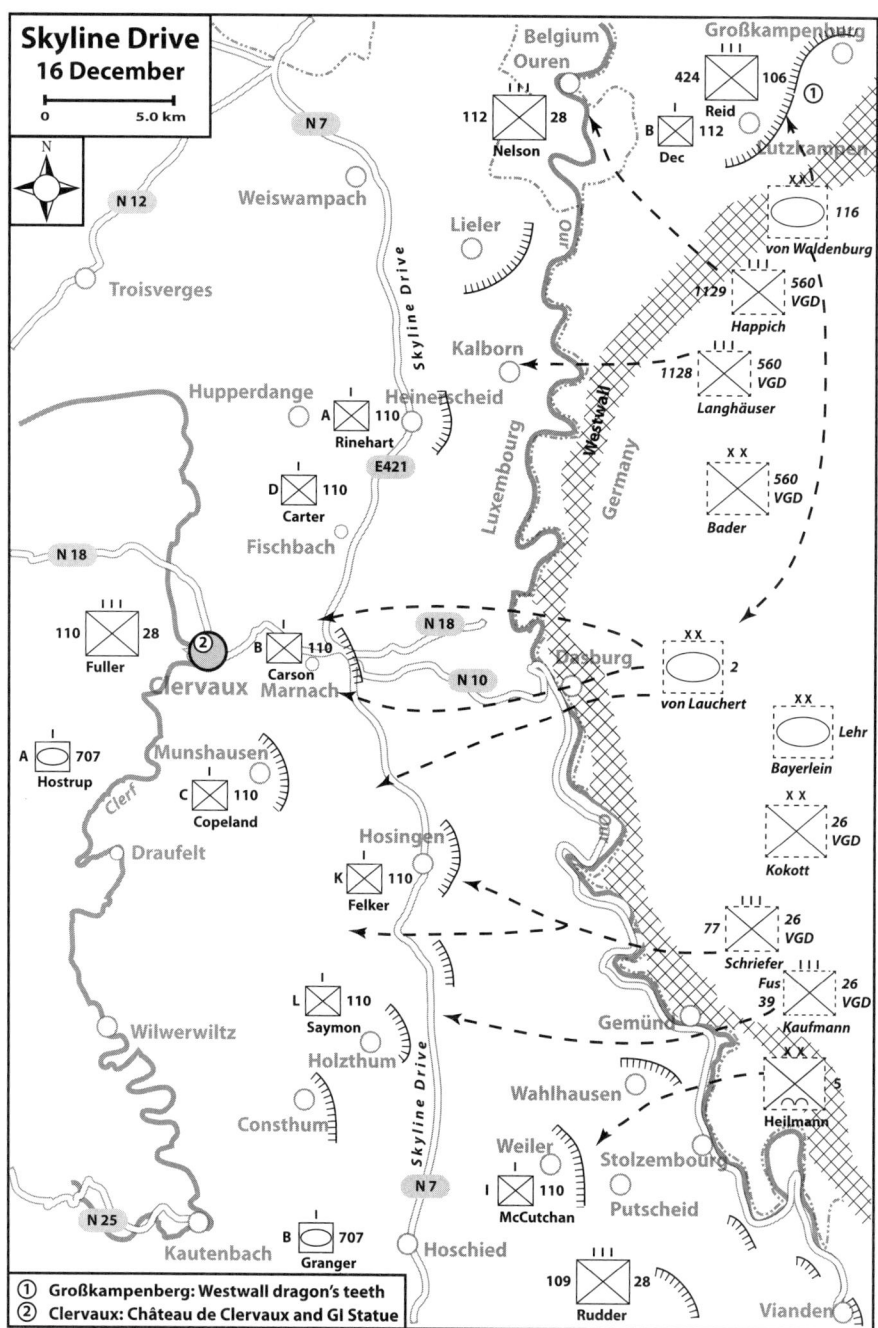

Division and Bastogne. German units advanced west in leaps and bounds, slowed only by a shortage of gasoline. On 19 December, General Cota relocated his divisional headquarters from Wiltz to Sibret, 20 kilometers to the west. The defense of Wiltz fell to a hodge-podge of 110th Regiment men, combat engineers, armor, and assorted stragglers. Hard pressed and fatigued after four days of almost continuous combat, the defense abandoned the town – and the road to Bastogne appeared open.

Aftermath

General Cota attempted to recollect his division at Sibret but came under continuing pressure from the 26th VGD while it moved south around Bastogne. Finally, with few troops remaining under his command, Cota relocated to Neufchâteau and disappeared from the Bulge picture. A reconstituted 28th Infantry Division under Cota's command participated in the reduction of the Colmar Pocket in February 1945.[2]

Consequences

The 28th Infantry Divisions' stubborn defense absorbed much of the shock of the Fifth Panzer Army assault and stymied German plans for a rapid advance and capture of Bastogne by delaying the enemy's advance for 36 to 48 hours.

Battlefield Tour Summary

The tour begins at German positions near the northern boundary of the 28th Infantry Division's sector and proceeds south along Skyline Drive to review the main American strongpoints.

Recommended Sites:
Großkampenberg: Westwall dragon's teeth
Dasburg: Our River crossing
Clervaux: Château de Clervaux, Museum of the Battle of the Bulge, and GI Statue
Wiltz: unit and individual memorials in the town's upper district, National Liberation Memorial, and Nothum Memorial Trail

112th Infantry Regiment Sector
16 to 17 December 1944

The 112th Infantry Regiment held the shortest sector of the front line running 5.5 kilometers from Lützkampen in the north along a ridge line south through Harspelt and Sevenig, then back across the Our to follow the western bank of the river to near Kalborn. The short distance permitted regimental commander Colonel Gustin Nelson to position his troops such that they maintained interlocking fields-of-fire — a luxury that the other two regiments of the division lacked the manpower to achieve. The regimental command post in Ouren, a resort town in a loop of the Our River, served as the site of two bridges over the border river. Additional support came from four batteries of the 229th Field Artillery Battalion, with observers stationed in forward outposts ahead of the main line of defense.

---

2   Then Brigadier General Norman Cota was awarded a Distinguished Service Cross for his daring leadership during the Normandy Invasion and for repeatedly exposing himself to enemy fire. Major General Cota died in 1971 at age 78 and is buried at the West Point Cemetery, United States Military Academy, West Point, New York.

Chapter Six

Skyline Drive

GERMAN OBJECTIVE	To bypass American centers of resistance and capture intact bridges over the Our River
FORCES	
American:	112th Infantry Regiment (Colonel Gustin M Nelson)
German:	Elements of 560th Volksgrenadier Division (Generalmajor Rudolf Bader) and 116th Panzer Division (Generalmajor Siegfried von Waldenburg)
RESULT	German armor was delayed for 48 hours
CASUALTIES	
American:	Uncertain, but considered moderate
German:	Estimated 400 to 600 killed or wounded and 186 taken prisoner; approximately 30 tanks knocked out
LOCATION	Ouren, Belgium is 31 km northeast of Wiltz, Luxembourg

Battle

Despite the 560th VGD's plans to infiltrate the 112th Regiment's front line shortly after midnight on 16 December and capture the two Ouren bridges, by dawn the grenadiers had overrun only two small field kitchens and briefly captured the small stone bridge south of Ouren before being driven back. They entered Lützkampen, 5 kilometers east of Ouren, but American positions on a hill west of the village extracted heavy casualties on the advancing grenadiers.

On 17 December, elements of 560th VGD captured the bridge at Ouren despite a counterattack hitting their flank near American-held Sevenig. However, the pressure of combined German infantry and armor could not be contained, and that night the regiment fell back to the Skyline Drive at Weiswampach.

Aftermath

From Weiswampach, the regiment engaged German troops in a fighting retreat to Huldange, where they joined the 106th Infantry Division's defensive line south of St-Vith. [3]

Battlefield Tour

The tour starts south of the German town of Großkampenberg at the intersection of highways L1 and K118. (50.151802, 6.217742)

American troops occupied Großkampenberg on 11 September 1944 despite being under sporadic German artillery bombardment. In the early morning of 16 December, the 424th Infantry Regiment defended the American line at Großkampenberg against the assault company of Panzergrenadier Regiment 60, 116th Panzer Division attacking from German-held Kesfeld only 1.5 kilometers to

---

[3] For its performance during December 1944, the 112th Infantry Regiment was awarded a Presidential Unit Citation.

the east. The panzergrenadiers had re-directed their movement after their repulse by 112th Regiment farther south and crossed in front of the Großkampenberg detachment diagonally, thus exposing their flank and absorbing terrible losses to Company I's small-arms and bazooka fire.

The rows of tank obstacles parallel to highway L1 wander across the pastures to the north from the rear of a roadside park that also holds picnic and parking areas. An informational panel explains the construction of the Westwall and the associated antitank defenses that included the cement blocks known as *Höckerlinie*. The **dragon's teeth** extend to the edge of the highway and are readily accessible.

> Proceed south on Hauptstraße (L1). After 1.3 km, turn right to remain on highway L1 and follow for 2.7 km through Lützkampen. Park on the wind turbine service road used to access Hill 539 and identified by a religious shrine at the intersection. (50.145675, 6.181500)

Battle of Lützkampen
16 December 1944

German Objective	To bypass American centers of resistance and capture intact bridges over the Our River
Forces	
American:	1st Battalion (Lieutenant Colonel William H Allen), 112th Infantry Regiment
German:	Grenadier Regiment 1130 (Oberstleutnant Schumann), 560th Volksgrenadier Division (Generalmajor Rudolf Bader), later Panzergrenadier Regiment 156 (Oberst Heinrich Voightsberger), 116th Panzer Division (Generalmajor Siegfried von Waldenburg)
Result	German armor was delayed for 12 hours
Casualties	
American:	Uncertain, but over 100 casualties
German:	at least 250 killed and 186 taken prisoner
Location	Lützkampen, Germany is 5 km east of Ouren, Belgium; Ouren is 31 km northeast of Wiltz, Luxembourg

Battle

Generalfeldmarschall von Manteuffel did not plan an artillery bombardment of any kind in the 112th Regiment's sector, relying instead upon stealth, infiltration, and surprise. American forward observers at Lützkampen detected German troops and armor movement coming from the east at 0500 on 16 December. Thus alerted, platoon officers and sergeants checked their men's positions and prepared for whatever was to come. Moments later German antiaircraft searchlights illuminated the sky. The eerie brightness was momentarily disconcerting but, when the confusion wore off, American riflemen opened fire on illuminated enemy troops moving across the open fields.

By early morning, the grenadiers had captured the town and started west. Unaware of two machine-gun nests near the last houses of the town, grenadiers carelessly strode down the roadway satisfied with their quick victory. Two American .30-caliber machine guns opened fire at a range of only 25 meters. A Browning Automatic Rifle (BAR) added its bark, and dead and dying grenadiers lined the roadway and its ditches.

A German MG-42 answered as other troops began a flanking action increasing the volume of return fire. Captain Stanley Dec, Company B commander, left the shelter of his dugout to redirect his men's fire. He did not make it; neither did the two medics who had rushed out to treat him. The three bodies painted the snow red.[4] Eventually the well-protected American positions prevailed, forcing forty-two grenadiers to surrender. As many as 250 dead German soldiers lay in the fields — some volunteers as young as 14 years old.

The real push for the Ouren bridges started at 1700 with the arrival in Lützkampen of German panzers. Seven of the black monsters emerged from the center of town led by one mounted with a flamethrower. In sequence, they took American-held buildings and foxholes under fire. Company B possessed no antitank weapons, and its calls for artillery support went unanswered. GIs burned when engulfed by the tongues of fire. An American 3-inch antitank gun crew from 3rd Platoon, Company B, 820th Tank Destroyer Battalion (attached to the neighboring 424th Infantry Regiment) witnessed the mayhem in the gathering darkness. PFC Paul Rosenthal's second shot from a range of 800 meters struck home, and the flamethrower became a German funeral pyre. In rapid succession, four more panzers exploded, and surviving armor tracked back among Lützkampen's buildings.[5]

On 17 December, Panzergrenadier Regiments 60 and 156 and Grenadier Regiment 1130, supported by eighteen Panther tanks from Panzer Regiment 3, drove through the 1st Battalion center and pushed American infantry northwest toward Welchenhausen while German infantry spread through the woods and along the draws between Lützkampen and Ouren, trapping the 1st Battalion. The order to withdraw found Company B on the extreme north flank forced rearward into 424th Infantry Regiment's area. The remainder of the battalion withdrew cross-country toward Ouren. An advance patrol found the by then captured bridge weakly defended by a small number of German troops. Approximately 235 Americans lined up in German formation and boldly marched across the bridge when a German-speaking American shouted commands in German.

Aftermath

The US 11th Armored Division reoccupied Lützkampen on 7 February 1945. The same unit pierced the Westwall at Großkampenberg ten days later.

---

4   Captain Stanley Dec, from Gary, Indiana, was awarded a Silver Star for bravery. He is buried in Calvary Cemetery, Portage, Indiana. He was 26 years old.

5   Private First Class Paul Rosenthal was awarded a Bronze Star for heroism. He was killed on 11 April 1945 during the Battle of the Ruhr Pocket. He is buried in Netherlands American Cemetery, Margraten, the Netherlands.

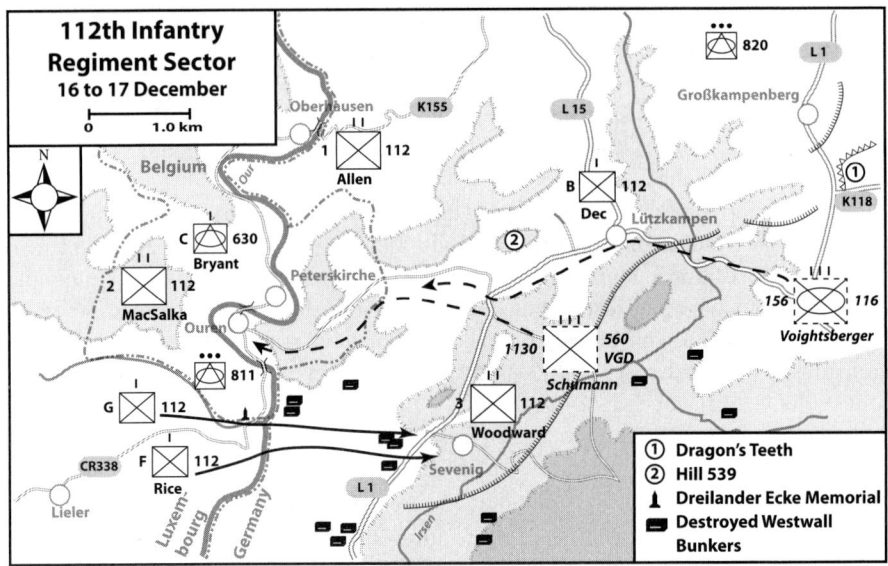

Battlefield Tour

At Hill 539 west of Lützkampen, one squad of Captain Dec's Company B with .30-caliber machine guns observed enemy troops ascending the hill. With German troops well within the kill zone, the light machine guns opened fire and drove the enemy into an area controlled by a .50-caliber heavy machine gun personally manned by the battalion commander. Lieutenant Colonel William Allen fired an extended burst into the clustered German soldiers. The effect was so devastating that forty enemy troops surrendered; however, a well-placed artillery barrage gave them cover to effect their escape toward Lützkampen. Under cover of the barrage, grenadiers made another push for the hill. Colonel Allen sent his reserve Company C to reinforce the position. Moving from its billets near the Our River, Company C trapped the German troops near the bottom of the hill and Company B's machine guns at the top. Enemy troops scattered while pockets of troops of both sides engaged in fluid combat in the draws and valleys around the hill.

The crest of **Hill 539** is to the left of the service road. The high ground provided American defenders unobstructed views of highway L1 that led to 1st Battalion headquarters in Harspelt to the southwest. American machine guns and BARs opened up at short range on unsuspecting German troops and destroyed the initial grenadier surge west.

Continue west on highway L1 toward Harspelt for 1.0 km. Turn right toward Ouren (Peterskirche) and stop. (50.141873, 6.169373)

The destruction of German tanks described above took place along highway L1 before the turn, where Company B sheltered in the cluster of farm buildings to the right. In 1944 Peterskirche was a mud road made worse by the churning of tank treads.

The muck severely hampered German vehicular movements and delayed the approach to Ouren.

> Continue on Peterskirche for 3.2 km into Ouren. Turn right and follow 350 m to the Ouren Bridge. (50.140515, 6.136057)

Battle of the Ouren Bridges
16 to 17 December 1944

In his command post in Ouren, Colonel Gustin Nelson realized that the town was likely the focus of the German assault even though the arched stone bridge was incapable of supporting armored vehicles' weight. Regimental Cannon Company, with its six towed 105-mm howitzers and .50-caliber machine guns, occupied the field north of the bridge.

GERMAN OBJECTIVE	To bypass American centers of resistance and capture intact bridges over the Clerf River
FORCES	
American:	112th Infantry Regiment (Colonel Gustin M Nelson)
German:	Grenadier Regiment 1130 (Oberstleutnant Schumann), 560th Volksgrenadier Division and 116th Panzer Division (Generalmajor Siegfried von Waldenburg)
RESULT	The bridge was eventually captured
CASUALTIES	
American:	Uncertain, but 200 taken prisoner
German:	560th Volksgrenadier Division: estimated 1,000 killed or wounded
116th Panzer Division: 42 killed and 31 taken prisoner; 13 tanks destroyed
LOCATION	Ouren, Belgium is 31 km northeast of Wiltz, Luxembourg

Battle

Colonel Nelson implemented one of several contingency plans that he and his staff had prepared for just such an emergency. Reserve Companies F and G moved forward along an east-west draw south of Ouren and drove the enemy as far back as Sevenig while inflicting hundreds of casualties. So far, so good.

On 17 December, a combined force of panzers and grenadiers overran American outposts, and then moved toward the Ouren bridges. A shell fired from a camouflaged antitank gun manned by a single, unknown American gunner engulfed in flames the first panzer to approach the stone bridge. The men of Cannon Company depressed the barrels of their 105-mm howitzers and fired with reduced powder charge, whereby several more panzers burst into flames. German tank shells destroyed one howitzer with a direct hit, and a near miss killed most of the crew of gun #3. The surviving gunner, Corporal Howard Minier, stayed by his weapon that he bore-sighted, loaded, and fired single-handedly for eight or ten rounds. German armor dispersed and returned fire against the howitzers while American bazooka teams circulated around the battlefield in hit-and-run fashion. With four panzers burning hulks and several more damaged, the tanks retreated.

At 1800 on 17 December, Colonel Nelson received instructions to withdraw, if necessary, after American units on both flanks had been driven back. The 112th Regiment relinquished control of the bridges and entered the dark forests to regroup around Weiswampach 4 kilometers to the west. Troops of the 560th VGD finally captured the bridges only to discover that they were too light to support heavy armor. The 116th Panzer Division rerouted south to the bridge at Dasburg.

Battlefield Tour

The **stone arched bridge** in the center of Ouren crossed the rain-fed and swollen Our River. German forces approaching from the east fell under the guns of Cannon Company positioned in the field behind the farm to the north.

The center of Ouren holds a few hotel and restaurants serving the local tourist trade and makes a pleasant midday stop. Several informational panels describe the history of the village. An aerial photograph clearly displays the bowl-like nature of the terrain and its excellent defensive possibilities as exercised by Colonel Nelson.

> Reverse direction, leave Ouren to the south, and proceed 1.0 km to the bridge. (50.134832, 6.137468)

At 0930 on 16 December, Captain William Cowan of the 1st Battalion staff organized the defense of the bridge just when a patrol of at least forty grenadiers armed with automatic weapons from Grenadier Regiment 1130 attempted to cross. Deadly .50-caliber bullets swept through the enemy ranks. Thirty were killed and the German-speaking captain convinced sixteen others to surrender. Despite the losses, German commanders received a report that the bridge had been taken and started to reroute units toward the crossing site. The southern Ouren bridge presents construction much like the northern bridge. Both are of post-war vintage. The support piers of the 1944 bridge are visible beside the current structure near the water's surface.

> Cross the southern Our River bridge and continue 600 m. (50.129975, 6.136167)

A ravine at the Europa Denkmal opens into the Our valley from the right. This natural avenue was used by Companies F and G in their counterattack of 17 December.

Other Points of Interest near Ouren

> The **Europa Denkmal** south of Ouren stands in an area known as Dreilandereck at the junction of three (Belgium, Luxembourg, and Germany) of the original six signatories of the Pact of Rome of 25 March 1957 (the other three being France, Netherlands, and Italy). The denkmal is a celebration of the creation of the

European Union with memorials to Paul-Henri Spaak, Robert Schumann, Conrad Adenauer, and Joseph Bech, honored for their leadership in creating the EU. Location 1.2 km south of Ouren. (50.130155, 6.136238)

Lieler
An upright granite stone commemorates the liberation of the village by the **712th Tank Battalion** and the **90th Infantry Division**. The inscribed slate plaque also remembers the 8th and 28th Infantry Divisions that garrisoned in the village prior to the Battle of the Bulge. The memorial is located in **place Griffin**, named after Lieutenant Ray Griffin, tank platoon leader who first entered Lieler on 26 January 1945. That evening, Company B, 357th Infantry Regiment, 90th Infantry Division occupied Leiler having marched four kilometers from Holler.
Location: 3.6 km southwest of Ouren along highway CR338. (50.124939, 6.110993)

Heinerscheid
Panzer Reconnaissance Battalion 116, commanded by Hauptmann Eberhard Stephen, surrounded Captain LeVoe Rinehardt's Company A in Heinerscheid by early afternoon of 17 December. Armor from the 116th Panzer Division, after having been re-routed over the Our River at Dasburg, approached from the south on Skyline Drive. The panzers and 75-mm antitank guns engaged an arriving platoon of Shermans from CCR, 9th Armored Division, destroyed two, and dispersed the other two. Hopelessly outnumbered and outgunned, Captain Rinehart ordered his men to retreat, but not everyone escaped. At least thirty-eight men were taken prisoner.
Heinerscheid extends along the Skyline Drive (highway N7/E421) upon a narrow ridgeline where the terrain slopes down on both sides of the road. A small park identified by American flags holds two partially destroyed stone walls flanking an iron artwork. The walls bear small plaques commending the **6th Armored Division** in English and French. A weather-worn cast concrete battle map outlining the route of the division rests on the ground between two artillery pieces. On the right, an American **105-mm howitzer** points toward the enemy advance. A considerably larger German **88-mm Pak 43/41 antitank gun** stands on the left. Repairs to the gun's solid rubber tire, using large square head bolts to attach a rubber patch directly to the wheel, demonstrate the state of German equipment at this late stage of the war.
Location: 8.4 km southwest of Ouren beside highway E421. (50.093794, 6.086714)

Continue south from the Ouren River, crossing into the Grand Duchy of Luxembourg on highway CR338. Follow CR338 for 4.6 km through Lieler (see below). Turn left toward Heinerscheid / Diekirch (E421) and follow for 8.0 km. In Marbourg, turn left toward Clervaux (N10) and follow for 5.7 km into the Our River valley and across the Dasburg Bridge. (50.049420, 6.126469)

110th Infantry Regiment Sector
16 to 19 December 1944

On 16 December, the 110th Infantry Division held a 24-kilometer front along a steep north-south ridgeline that ran parallel to and between the Our and Clerf Rivers. Although the regiment's main line of resistance protected only crossroad towns, it maintained a row of outposts generally along the line of the Our River. The stronger defenses at towns were chosen to block the four main east-west roadways that passed through the regimental sector. The 1st Battalion held positions from the junction with the 112th Infantry Regiment in the north near Kalborn to Munshausen south of Clervaux. The 3rd Battalion defended from Hosingen south to Hoscheid. The 2nd Battalion was held in reserve at Donnange, 10 kilometers west of the Skyline Drive. The regiment's commander, Colonel Hurley E Fuller, regularly sent patrols across the Our River to capture prisoners for interrogation.

Supporting the 110th Regiment were the 109th Field Artillery Battalion; Battery C, 687th Field Artillery Battalion; Battery A, 447th Antiaircraft Battalion; and Company B, 630th Tank Destroyer Battalion. The terrain and distance from the German front line required the various gun batteries into widely dispersed positions and closer to front line troops than would otherwise be desirable.

GERMAN OBJECTIVE	To bypass American centers of resistance, capture intact bridges over the Clerf River, and proceed to Bastogne
FORCES	
American:	110th Infantry Regiment (Colonel Hurley Edward Fuller) and attached units
German:	2nd SS Panzer Division (SS-Major General Heinz Lammerding), 26th Volksgrenadier Division (Oberst Heinz Kokott), and elements of 5th Fallschirmjäger Division (Oberst Ludwig Heilmann) totaling 27,000 men and 216 tanks
RESULT	American positions delayed the German advance but were eventually overrun
CASUALTIES	
American:	2,288 killed, wounded, or missing (including PoWs)
German:	2,100 dead
LOCATION	Clervaux is 16 km northeast of Wiltz

Battle Summary

The 110th Infantry Regiment's sector experienced a brief but intense artillery bombardment; however, the inexperienced grenadiers of the 560th VGD were slow in following the barrage, thus allowing American defenders an opportunity to prepare for the expected assault. Further south, Oberst Heinz Kokott's 26th VGD allowed no such

---

6 Oberst Ludwig Heilmann led paratrooper units in battles on the island of Crete, in Sicily, and at Monte Cassino, Italy. In May 1944 he received the extremely honored Swords to the Knight's Cross with Oak Leaves award. Heilmann died in 1959 and age 56.

Chapter Six

respite. Reinforced patrols crossed the Our and approached the Skyline Drive before the artillery fired. By 0530, Kokott's Grenadier Regiment 77 was in front of Hosingen and his Fusilier Regiment 39 had passed Wahlhausen. The difficulties in constructing the bridges necessary for armored vehicles to cross the Our River nullified much of the German advantage. Eventually, the completion of bridges at Dasburg and Gemünd allowed the panzers to move west.

The 110th Infantry Regiment sat astride the major routes toward Bastogne and therefore suffered the heaviest blow from the German attack. The regiment received orders to hold at all cost – exactly what it did. Division and regimental headquarters lost the ability to control the battle almost from its start, but isolated company strongpoints continued to offer stiff resistance until overwhelmed. At Clervaux, Marnach, Hosingen, Holzthum, and Weiler, the troops fought bravely and resisted until overwhelmed or out of ammunition.

By late on 17 December, the regiment existed only as isolated pockets or as stragglers moving west in search of friendly units. Colonel Fuller collected what troops he could and offered a brief defense of Clervaux. Weakly-defended Wiltz was evacuated while outgunned troops streamed west seeking shelter in Bastogne.

Aftermath

The collapse destroyed the 110th Regiment as an effective fighting force and opened the roads to Bastogne to the passage of German armor. Casualty levels for the regiment were extreme: out of 3,250 troops, 2,288 were killed, wounded, or taken prisoner with forty-eight tanks and eight field guns lost. American burial details estimated German losses at 2,100 dead.[7]

Battlefield Tour Summary

The 110th Infantry Regiment tour begins at the Dasburg bridge crossing point and continues west to Clervaux. The tour then returns to the Skyline Drive that today remains the major north-south highway in eastern Luxembourg. It reviews strongpoints held by the 110th Infantry Regiment before visiting sites in and around Wiltz.

Dasburg River Crossing
16 December 1944

At 0100 on 16 December, eight-man assault teams from Panzergrenadier Regiment 304 paddled rubber boats across the Our near Dasburg to begin infiltration of American lines. Hidden by darkness and fog, the men reached positions surrounding Marnach before the German artillery bombardment started at 0530.

Engineers of Panzer Pionier Battalion 600 finished a 62-ton heavy weapons bridge at 1300 on 16 December to allow German armor to move across. The first panzer to test the structure slipped through a span and crashed into the river. Repairs consumed three more hours of hurried work in the frigid waters.

The difficult hairpin curves of the approach road from Dasburg down to the river not only had to handle the assigned 2nd Panzer Division as originally planned but

---

7   For its performance during 16 to 23 December 1944, the 110th Infantry Regiment was awarded a Presidential Unit Citation.

also the re-routed 116th Panzer Division that found the bridges at Ouren inadequate. Dozens of PzKpfw IVs and Vs crossed the river and edged their way up the ridge to head west; however, obstacles built by German forces during their autumn retreat extensively blocked the Dasburg–Clervaux highway (N10). The slow movement of vehicles caused considerable congestion on the bridge and the approach road.

Dasburg

Tourist-Information Ourtal
Hauptstraße 3   D-54689 Dasburg, Germany
Email: info@dasburg.de   Web: http://www.dasburg.de/

Dasburg was a fief of the medieval Count of Prüm. Defensive works were constructed in 1222, but records indicate an earlier castle dating from 850. The town was eventually renamed after a contemporary of Geoffrey of Bouillon, leader of the First Crusade. The wartime bridge over the Our River dated from 1846. The current arched concrete road bridge was reconstructed in 1953. Fighting in 1944 to 1945 destroyed eighty per cent of the town's buildings.

A brass memorial plaque on the German side of the Dasburg bridge is dedicated to the valiant soldiers of the **249th Engineer Combat Battalion**, US Third Army, whose Company C constructed a Bailey Bridge on 28 February 1945 to replace the German pionier's bridge. The bridge provided armor passage across the river and into Germany.

A series of '**Remember US**' informational signs, sponsored by local and regional tourist boards and the Friends of US Veterans Organization, carry descriptive text in English, French, and German, interesting period photographs, and occasionally battlefield maps. They are recommended reading for military tourists and the locations of each sign are noted in this guide.

The **Remember US – Dasburg** panel relates the story of American efforts to bridge the Our River at Dasburg stating, in part, 'The town of Dasburg was under American control by 1700 on 21 February 1945. ... the 25th Armored Engineer Battalion of the 6th Armored Division started building a footbridge over the Our River, which reconnected Luxembourg to Germany. Because this bridge could not hold any heavy loads, it was replaced by a Bailey bridge on February 28, 1945 built by C Company of the 249th Engineer Combat Battalion.'

The highway climbs up toward the town with steep grades and sharp curves demonstrating the difficulties German bridging equipment and vehicles experienced approaching the crossing site at the beginning of the Bulge battle.

A Dasburg bridge **protection bunker**, constructed into the cliff faces, remains 40 meters to the east directly targeting the German side of the bridge. This defensive position is one of many Westwall features in the Dasburg area. The fortification line was disarmed and partially destroyed after the war. The ruins are now a habitat for rare animals and plants. The sign bears a German-only text description of the Westwall and a map of a 1.8 kilometer hiking trail of local remnants under the title *Bunkerwanderweg*. Although the bunkers' locations are indicated on the map, the installations are largely hidden under dirt mounds and vegetation and make poor visitor sites for all but the most ardent Westwall enthusiasts. (50.049170, 6.127217)

Dasburg has always been a border town and hosted a German Army base during the war despite the town's small size. Concrete entrance buildings once provided access to two tunnels cut into the hillside below the castle. The roadside entrance into the Dasburger **underground bunker system** lies 750 meters uphill from the bridge. The numerous tunnels driven into the hillside provided shelter for troops and equipment storage in the Westwall complex. Although used by the German Bundeswehr into the 1960s, the tunnels have been sealed and are no longer accessible. (50.047170, 6.133106)

Other Points of Interest east of Dasburg

> The **Daleiden German War Cemetery** holds 3,041 burials from the Second World War with single burial graves arranged in concentric circles about a central memorial. Grave stones sit at ground level and inscribe the soldiers' rank, name, birth date, and death date. As one would guess, many casualties date from December 1944 and January 1945. The memorial houses six metal tablets listing names of the missing.
> Location: 6.6 km east of the Dasburg Bridge. From Hauptstraße (B410) a *Kriegsgräberstätte* sign directs visitors to a parking area in a local park. Walk through the park and continue a strenuous 400 m to the top of the hill, then turn left for another 100 m to the entrance on the right. (50.068163, 6.186677)

> Leave the Dasburg bridge west on highway N10 and follow for 5.6 km. Turn right toward Marnach / Clervaux (N18) and continue 950 m into Marnach to the memorial across from the school on Schullstrooss. (50.054096, 6.062325)

Highway N10 from the Dasburg bridge to Marnach twists and turns through the forest where it continues uphill to the ridge crest. The forest would have sheltered the 2nd Panzer Division from air attack if the weather had permitted Allied aircraft over the battlefield. Hairpin turns were difficult for the large panzers. By the time the highway exits the forest, Marnach is only three kilometers distant near the summit of the ridge line.

Battle of Marnach
16 to 17 December 1944

Company B, 110th Infantry Regiment, with 76-mm towed guns from 630th Tank Destroyer Battalion, protected the vital crossroad east of Marnach where the Skyline Drive meets highway N10 from Dasburg, Germany. Company C and the regiment's Cannon Company with six howitzers were stationed at Munshausen 3 kilometers southwest of Marnach.

The 2nd Panzer Division's commander, Oberst Meinrad von Lauchert, had moved a battalion of Panzergrenadier Regiment 304 across the Our River by rubber boats while the engineer battalion labored to bring heavy bridging equipment down to the river to construct a bridge for its vehicles.

German Objective	To bypass American centers of resistance and capture intact bridges over the Clerf River
Forces	
American:	Company B (Lieutenant Kit Carson, later Captain James H Burns), 110th Infantry Regiment, and one platoon of 630th Tank Destroyer Battalion
German:	II Battalion, Panzergrenadier Regiment 304 (Major Ernst von Cochenhausen, acting), 2nd Panzer Division
Result	The town was captured after a determined resistance
Casualties	
American:	unknown
German:	unknown
Location	Marnach is 16 km northeast of Wiltz

Battle

The preliminary German artillery bombardment shattered buildings and set much of Marnach on fire. Infantrymen, asleep only a few moments earlier, scrambled from the warm billets into the freezing cold to man their foxholes. While the buildings burned, experienced NCOs knew that an assault was likely to follow.

Panzergrenadier Regiment 304 reached Marnach by 0800 on 16 December. Despite the morning fog, American riflemen and machine-gun teams zeroed in on numerous targets while enemy troops pushed forward in waves. Guns from the 109th Field Artillery Battalion and the regimental Cannon Company saturated the approaches, killing and wounding German troops in droves. Eventually, panzergrenadiers swept around Marnach to the north and south.

Later in the day, German armor raced across the rolling fields east of Marnach, lobbing shells into the already burning town. While enemy troops moved from house-to-house, an unidentified American corporal continued to radio target coordinates to his artillery battery. In desperation he called fire down upon his own building. In his last transmission he whispered, 'Hurry! Fire! They're coming up the steps.' He was never heard from again. By night enemy troops and vehicles swarmed the town.

By that afternoon Colonel Fuller's defensive positions became surrounded, thus they were slowly strangled for ammunition and reinforcements. Colonel Fuller repeatedly requested that General Cota release the reserve 2nd Battalion, but Cota was reluctant to commit his only reserve too early in the battle. While reports of overrun or surrounded positions continued to flood his headquarters at Wiltz, Cota constantly re-assessed the situation. Late on 16 December, Cota informed Fuller that he would send Companies E and F to Fuller. That measure would not be enough, but it was all he had.

On 17 December, Fuller's counterattacking Companies E and F approached Marnach from the west along the Clervaux road. The two infantry companies ran head on into advancing German armor and infantry, and the force of the German onslaught shattered American formations. Fuller's counterattack was over almost before it had begun.

Chapter Six

Skyline Drive

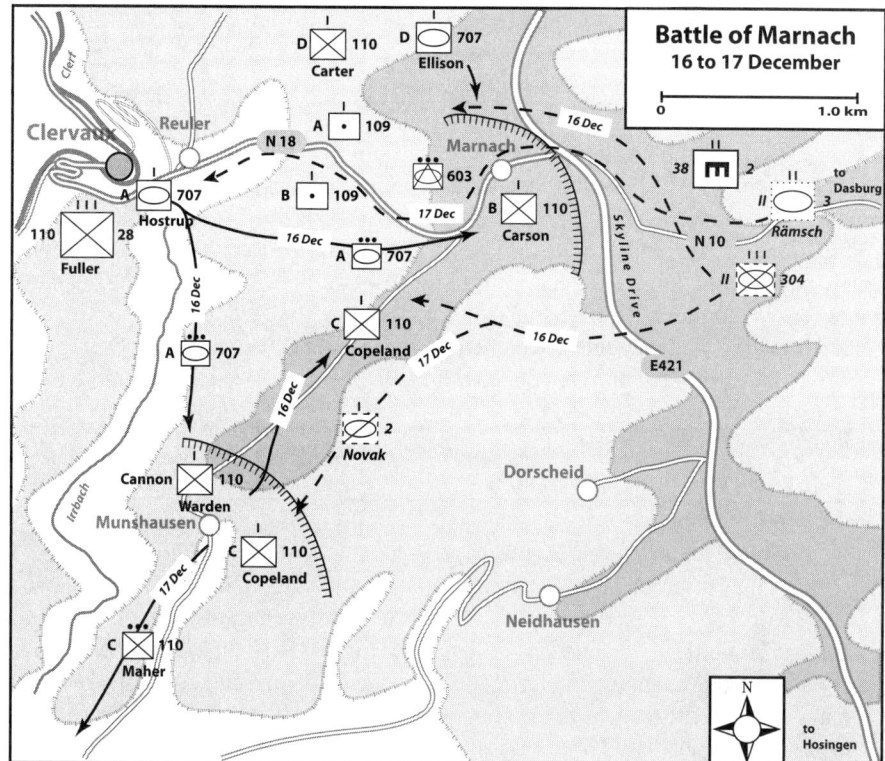

A third element of Fuller's response – Company D, 707th Tank Battalion – consisted of eighteen M5 'Stuart' tanks. German antitank guns and panzerfaust-bearing infantry ambushed Captain Herbert Ellison's company while approaching Fischbach along the elevated section of Skyline Drive from the north. With no room to maneuver, Captain Ellison's light tanks were picked off one by one. In ten minutes, eleven of the eighteen Stuarts were flaming wrecks. The survivors escaped to Heinerscheid or Urspelt.

German forces slowly and inexorably squeezed American troops out of Marnach during the night and the next morning by overcoming the small strongpoints. Finally, a German panzer crashed through the front door of Company B's command post in the hotel in central Marnach.

Battlefield Tour

A **28th Infantry Division Monument** rests in a small plaza on a side street in Marnach. It is not visible from the highway because of hedges, but three flags flying above the monument clearly identify the site. A concrete frame holds a red sandstone Keystone insignia in the center flanked by a plaque to the **707th Tank Battalion** 'for its gallantry in action and outstanding devotion to duty in this area during the Battle of the Ardennes, December 1944' and a plaque 'In honor to the 28th US Infantry 'Keystone' Division, liberator and defender of Marnach 1944.'

> Continue southwest on highway N18. After 500 m, turn left toward Munshausen (CR326). After 950 m, stop at the short side road half way between Marnach and Munshausen (50.044020, 6.050264).

Colonel Fuller dispatched Company C from Munshausen to reinforce the Marnach garrison. After waiting for tank support that never arrived, the infantry company commander, Captain Carrol Copeland, moved his force across rolling country on both sides of the road. About this point, the woods became alive with German small-arms fire whereby American troops spread out defensively. Captain Copeland was seriously wounded. While wounded troops fell to the ground, platoon leaders realized that they had encountered a much stronger force. Lieutenant Leo Seerey, the new commander, ordered an immediate withdrawal. Marnach was on its own.

> Continue on highway CR326 for 1.9 km into Munshausen and stop in front of the village church. (50.032419, 6.037069)

In 1944, Munshausen was little more than a few stone buildings clustered around the village church. By 17 December, Reconnaissance Battalion 2 supported by two PzKpfw Vs attacked Company C and the six 105-mm howitzers of Cannon Company from north, south, and east. The howitzer crews fired high-explosive rounds directly at charging German infantry while concealed riflemen sniped from windows, attics, and the church steeple. As the German troops closed on the village, their ranks thinned as one-by-one they fell to rifle shots. A Panther tank fired, causing the church steeple to collapse in a pile of dust-shrouded rubble.

The German commander, Hauptmann Heinz Novak, grew impatient for the town to be taken. Novak impetuously decided to reconnoiter the town on foot. When he approached the church, an American soldier leapt forward with his bayonet and slashed the German officer's throat. His own troops found his body later in the day.

The men of Company C were told to hold at all cost — and they did while combat became house-to-house. Surrounded, they were being slowly eliminated. That night, Platoon Leader Lieutenant John Maher and two-hundred men escaped from the tightening ring by moving southwest to safety through pitch-black darkness.

> Reverse direction and follow highway CR326 for 2.8 km back toward Marnach. Turn toward Clervaux (N18), enter the forest, and start a 3.0 km slow descent into the town. A memorial park occupies the first hairpin turn on the decent into Clervaux. Please do not block the driveway entrance to the St Francis Home for the Aged but continue to the next turn where a small cemetery parking area allows a safe stop. (50.053398, 6.026454)

Battle of Clervaux
17 to 18 December 1944

During the night of 15 December, a two-man German artillery observer team infiltrated Clervaux to establish an observation post in a building in the center of town.

Chapter Six

Skyline Drive

They radioed coordinates to take the Headquarters Company stationed in the chateau under fire. The next day, Colonel Hurley Fuller received his orders from General Cota: 'Hold, no retreat, nobody comes back.'

German Objective	To capture Clervaux and its bridges over the Clerf River
Forces	
American:	110th Regimental Headquarters (Lieutenant Colonel Hurley Fuller)
German:	'Monschau' Battalion, Panzergrenadier Regiment 2 (Oberst Joachim Guttmann) and II Battalion (Major Horst Rämsch), Panzer Regiment 3 (Oberstleutnant Carl von Wagner)
Result	Clervaux was captured despite stubborn resistance
Casualties	
American:	100 taken prisoner
German:	unknown
Location	Clervaux is 17 km northeast of Wiltz

Battle

As the sky brightened on 17 December, PzKpfw IVs and half-tracks filled with panzergrenadiers maneuvered the hair-pin turns on the road that entered Clervaux from the east. A platoon of Sherman tanks from Company A, 707th Tank Battalion moved from behind the castle and began its own slow trek up the winding road. The Shermans and PzKpfw IVs met at a range of 75 meters near the hillside cemetery. At that distance, the panzer's more powerful gun offered no advantage. Moments later, after the dust settled and a light breeze dissipated the smoke, the wrecks of four German and three American tanks blocked the narrow road.

While the two surviving Shermans returned to Clervaux and exited the town to the west, Captain Robert Lybarger from Black Lick, Indiana led Company B, 2nd Tank Battalion, from Colonel Gilbreth's CCR, 9th Armored Division into Clervaux from the north. The company's seventeen Shermans, which fielded the more powerful 76-mm gun, made a welcome addition to Fuller's defenses. Platoons of tanks hastened to Heinerscheid and Reuler while one remained in Clervaux.

The tank-versus-tank engagement made Oberst Wagner wary of encountering more American armor along the difficult roadway. The panzers held the top of the ridge with clear views of the town and fired at anything that moved while panzergrenadiers slowly infiltrated the town's buildings and alley ways.

German infantry surged passed the castle and took the town house-by-house. German armor approached Clervaux's northern bridge over the Clerf River from Reuler. The road crossed the train lines near the station only 220 meters from Colonel Fuller's headquarters at Hotel Claravallis, forcing him to escape while enemy tanks closed in. The final stand occurred within the stout walls of the Château de Clervaux where remnants of Headquarters Company continued to resist into the next afternoon.

Fuller's 110th Infantry Regiment ceased to exist. Later that day, the survivors started marching east to imprisonment.

Aftermath

On the morning of 18 December, Colonel Fuller and forty men paused on a wooded hill west of Eselborn after making his second escape from German encirclement. The small contingent of what was left of the 110th Infantry Regiment, aided by troops from the 630th Tank Destroyer Battalion, held off panzergrenadiers despite taking fire from German tanks. With ammunition nearly exhausted, Fuller ordered five-man groups to attempt exfiltrating west. His contingent managed only 1.6 kilometers before a German patrol captured his group. [8]

Battlefield Tour

A large memorial stone at the small park on the inside of the first hairpin turn displays the names of **civilian victims** of the German Gestapo that had assassinated six listed patriots, including three members of the Lamborelle family discussed below, in January 1945. Three additional individuals who were deported and disappeared are also named. Five metal human outlines stand erect on the ground scattered behind the memorial. Each bears a plasticized info sheet that speaks to biospheres, a misguided attempt to use the tragedy of the Second World War executions to promote a modern social and political policy. (50.053567, 6.024708)

The tank battle between defending Shermans and advancing panzers took place along this hillside on the road before the cemetery. A disabled Sherman blocked the highway preventing German panzers from continuing into town. The views over Clervaux are truly spectacular as are the white walls of the chateau.

Clervaux

In 1100 local nobility built a castle upon a rock spur that looped the Clerf River. Clervaux grew around this strong defensive position and became the ancestral home of John the Blind and the House of Burgundy. By the 20th Century, the town was a tourist haven supporting numerous hotels for guests exploring the surrounding woodlands and valleys.

Syndicat d'initiative et de tourisme de Clervaux Montée du Chateau
BP 53
Grand Duchy of Luxembourg
Email: info@tourisme-clervaux.lu
9712 Clervaux
Tel: +352 92 00 72
Web: http://www.tourisme-clervaux.lu

Continue the descent into Clervaux for 450 m. Turn left onto place de la Libération and left to park in the place du Marché. (50.054047, 6.029635)

---

8   Despite being slightly wounded during his capture, Colonel Hurley E Fuller and his fellow prisoners marched 200 kilometers (125 miles) east before being put on trains to Oflag 64 near Posen, Poland. Pressured by the advancing Red Army, German guards attempted to march the prisoners westward. As the Soviets neared, Allied officers in the group rebelled, and the guards fled. Colonel Fuller was liberated by the Red Army on 29 January in Wugarten, Germany (now Ogardy, Poland).

Chapter Six

A war memorial stands in the parking area below the castle dedicated to the men who died for local citizens' freedom. A special plaque remembers the **'Enrôlés de Force'** from the communes of Clervaux, Heinerscheid, Troisvierges, and Weiswampach who were Luxembourg men conscripted into the German Army.

A '**Remember US - Clervaux**' information panel describes the beginning minutes of the German offensive from the civilian point of view and its effect upon Luxembourg citizens forced once again to abandon their homes and farms. A second panel names the German *Sicherheitsdienst* and the Gestapo who followed close behind German combat troops looking for '*refractaires*' — young men who refused to join the German army — and their families and helpers who, if they were found, were deported or executed.

Walk to the right to the external elevator. Its intermediary level provides access to the tourist office. The upper level accesses the chateau's forecourt. (50.054263, 6.030509)

At 1100 on 17 December, a platoon of five Sherman tanks commanded by 1st Lieutenant Raymond E Fleig from Company B, 2nd Tank Battalion, 9th Armored Division, crept among the buildings clustered near the chateau. Suddenly the trailing tank was hit and burst into flames. The lead tank was hit and suffered the same fate. Then the second Sherman spotted the source — a German antitank gun across the valley to the north near the Parc Hotel. When two Sherman shells answered, the gun fell silent. More armor-piercing shells from the crest of the Marnach road hit the second and third tanks. The fourth tank, commanded by Sergeant Donald Fink, separately searched for an escape route. The crew positioned the tank behind a corner of Kratzenburg house such that they could move forward, fire its 76-mm main gun upon enemy vehicles approaching along the Marnach road, and then quickly reverse back into its hiding spot. At first the Germans had difficulty locating the source of the cannon fire. The Sherman's crew repeated the maneuver several times until eventually spotted. German armor responded and hit the Sherman twice forcing its crew to abandon the tank.[9]

One-hundred-two defenders from Captain Claude B Mackey's Headquarters Company barricaded the feudal castle and continued to resist. The narrow, arrow-slit windows of the medieval towers provided perfect firing positions for snipers. The thick walls resisted even the most powerful tank shells. Repeated assaults were beaten back with German dead and wounded littering the streets around the castle. However, the defenders were running out of ammunition while seventy-five civilians sheltered in the castle's dank cellar.

Finally on 18 December, German gunners targeted the castle's vulnerable thatched roof, setting it aflame. A Panther rammed the stout wooden gates and entered the courtyard firing its gun. The corridors filled with smoke and flaming debris dropping

---

9   Lieutenant Raymond Fleig and two enlisted men spent three days amid deep snow and freezing weather evading capture until they reached friendly forces at Bastogne. Lieutenant Fleig was awarded the Bronze Star for his action during the Battle of the Bulge. Earlier he received a Silver Star for his actions in the November 1944 Battle of Schmidt in the Hürtgen Forest. He later served in Korea as Commanding Officer of the 245th Tank Battalion and eventually became Executive Officer of Combat Command R, 4th Armored Division. Fleig retired from the military in 1962 as a Lieutenant Colonel to enjoy a second career as an associate professor at Ohio State Community College. He died in 2015 at 96 years of age.

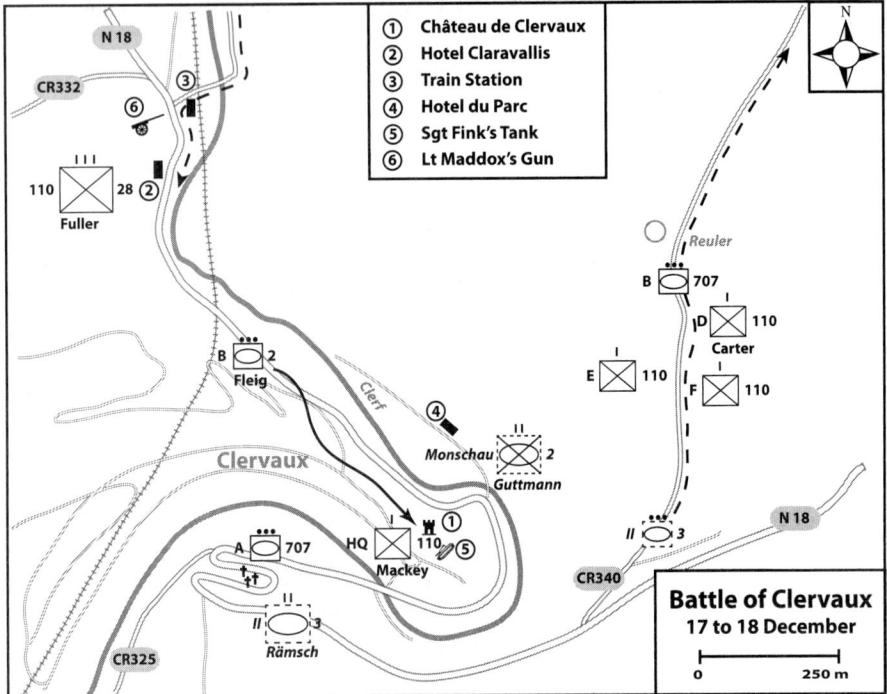

from above. Captain John Aiken, Regimental Communications Officer, desperately attempted to contact the no-longer existent headquarters in the Hotel Claravallis. At 1300 Captains Mackey and Aiken made the difficult decision and hoisted a white flag.[10]

The outer courtyard of the medieval chateau presents Sherman tank B-2 as a memorial to the **9th Armored Division**. The abandoned **Sherman M4A3 tank** remained in its location until 1956 when the Luxembourg Army repaired the damage and relocated the tank to its current position. The attached plaque claims that this vehicle is the only surviving combat vehicle of that division and that it was knocked out on 17 December defending the castle. A '**Remember US**' panel describes the battle for Clervaux and displays dramatic photographs of the destroyed town. Standing beside the American tank is an example of the deadly German **88-mm Pak 43/41 antitank gun**, that fired high-velocity, armor-piercing rounds capable of penetrating 132 mm of armor plate at a range of 2.0 kilometers. The weapon had a maximum range of 16 kilometers.

The **Hotel Commerce**, an American stronghold during the fighting, is visible from the forecourt to the south as is the **Hotel du Parc** on the hillside to the east, which German troops occupied early in the battle.

---

10 Captain Claude B Mackey was held in Stalag XIIIb, Weiden, Bavaria, Germany. The camp was liberated on 22 April 1945.

Captain John Aiken was held in Stalag IXb, Bad Orb, Germany. On 2 April 1945, 114th Regimental Combat Team drove 60 kilometers through enemy held territory to liberate approximately 4,700 US infantrymen captured during the Battle of the Bulge.

Chapter Six Skyline Drive 253

At the entrance to the chateau, a plaque honors the men of **Headquarters Company, 110th Infantry Regiment**, who held the castle from 16 to 18 December. (50.054321, 6.030397)

Enter the chateau's courtyard and proceed to the museum entrance on the left. (50.054430, 6.029852)

The 12th century feudal castle houses three museums: The Family of Man, a photo collection listed as a UNESCO World Heritage site; Museum of Models of Luxembourg Castles; and the Battle of the Bulge Museum.

Museum of the Battle of the Bulge (Musée de la Bataille des Ardennes or Museum der Ardennenoffensive)

Château de Clervaux
L-9712 Clervaux
Tel: (00352) 26 91 06 95
Email: secretariat@clervaux.lu

BP 35
Grand Duchy of Luxembourg
Fax: (00352) 92 91 80
Web: http://ceba.lu/museum.html

The chateau museum contains a multitude of battlefield relics, some labeled and many not. One area is devoted to ammunition cases, another to shells of all types and description. The museum follows a winding staircase into one of the castle towers where a good collection of uniforms are displayed on manikins. Much of the material has been contributed by returning veterans and includes personal photographs and other memorabilia.

Open daily except Monday, May through October from 1000 to 1800; weekends only, November through April from 1000 to 1800. Fee; the forecourt and courtyard are handicap accessible, but the museum is not.

Return to place du Marché and walk east through the commercial place Princess Maria-Teresa, where numerous hotels and restaurants offer the opportunity for a charming respite. (50.053153, 6.031238)

The **GI Statue** stands along the banks of the Clerf River in a commercial square in the heart of Clervaux. The image of a returning American soldier with his rifle slung upon his shoulder and a peaceful expression on his face celebrates the liberation of Luxembourg and the return to peace. The statue's plinth bears a glass plate bordered with the insignia of the units that had served in Clervaux. The central section carries an inscription, 'To our Liberators 1944 – 1945. They gave us back our freedom.' The statue was erected by CEBA, a group that continues to study the Battle of the Bulge. A plaque at the base of the statue expresses the appreciation of the **6th Armored Division** to the citizens of Clervaux. A '**Remember US**' Panel speaks to the statue and its dedication to 'The American Soldier.'

> Retrieve your vehicle and reverse direction back to highway N18. Turn left onto route de Bastogne (N18) and follow (becomes rue de la Gare) for 1.3 km to the Hotel Claravallis parking area on the right. (50.059521, 6.023748)

Officers and men inside the hotel engaged in hurried efforts to destroy intelligence documents and personnel records, to contact outlying units by radio, or to plan their escape. American infantrymen surrendered in the street in front of the hotel while six German panzers roamed back and forth, firing at any suspected resistance. One PzKpfw IV put several shells into the first floor of the hotel. Colonel Fuller knew that the time for withdrawal had come and that further 'hold-at-all-cost' efforts promised no benefit. He issued the order to regroup at Eselborn.

At 1800 an MP led Fuller and a few headquarters troops to a rear room on the third floor where an iron fire-escape ladder stretched across the 3-meter gap between the hotel and a solid rock cliff. Leading a man blinded by a rocket explosion moments before, Fuller brought the group to the cliff face and up the earthen steps to the top. The small group made its escape through the woods.

Although rebuilt and modernized, the rear of the **Hotel Claravallis** still abuts the rock cliff face to its rear and, although it no longer displays an iron fire escape, the nearness to the rock cliff suggests Colonel Fuller's escape route.

> Continue north on rue de la Gare (N18) for 250 m. Turn right to the rail line bridge and park at a convenient location. (50.061995, 6.025325)

German infantry largely bypassed Reuler early on 17 December, but by later in the day elements of the 2nd Panzer Division began pushing north through the town. The American defenders were a mix from heavy weapons Company D, riflemen from Companies E and F whose counterattack was so easily repelled earlier in the day, and armor support from a platoon of M18 Tank Destroyers and a platoon of Shermans from Company B, 2nd Tank Battalion. PzKpfw IVs drove up the main street blasting houses only to meet the Shermans approaching from the north. Both forces left the engagement with two vehicles in flames. Infantry combat continued while the more powerful German panzers slowly crept north.

Reuler is less than one kilometer east of Clervaux, but the intervening ridge-line forced vehicles onto a much longer highway route. Because destroyed armor blocked the snaking route down the hillside and into Clervaux. German tanks continued through Reuler, crossed over the ridge north of both towns, and after 4.3 kilometers entered Clervaux essentially via a rear door. They descended the ridgeline near Clervaux's train station and only a few hundred meters from the Hotel Claravallis. They needed to cross a bridge over the train tracks.

Lieutenant Kenneth Maddox from Headquarters Company, 2nd Battalion commanded the crew of a single 57-mm antitank gun near this north entry into the town. While Lt Maddox selected targets against enemy armor approaching the bridge, a German sergeant closed in on the gun crew with his burp gun at the ready. Maddox ran forward to protect his troops as both men fired, each mortally wounding the other. Moments later, a shell hit the antitank gun whose entire crew became casualties.[11]

The current rail bridge was built in 1993, but the roadway down the hillside on the opposite side of the rail line remains.

---

11   Lieutenant Kenneth G Maddox from Jefferson County, Kentucky, died of his wounds in a German field hospital on Christmas Day, 1944.

Other Points of Interest north of Clervaux

Maulusmühle

An elaborate memorial stands alongside the roadway dedicated to **1st Lieutenant Jesse P Sweat** and **Corporal Leonard A Deluga**. The two men were killed at this spot when they drove their jeep into a German ambush during the American advance into Luxembourg on 10 September 1944.

The memorial consists of two stones bearing the Keystone insignia of the 28th Infantry Division and the outline of the Grand Duchy of Luxembourg flanking a bronze plaque affixed to the sheer cliff face.

Location: 3.2 km north of Clervaux beside highway CR334. (50.085272, 6.027610)

A large irregularly shaped granite stone bears a plaque commemorating the **execution of four local civilians** by the German Gestapo on this spot in 1944. Ernest Lamborelle and his two sons, Michel and Georges, were arrested on 22 December. The men were accused of molesting a German collaborator during the September liberation. The sons were further charged as members of the Luxembourg Resistance. Jean Heck was innocently seized in the Gestapo raid that actually sought to apprehend his brother. Last seen on 25 December, the men's bodies were found the following February — each with a bullet hole in the neck.

Location: 3.5 km north of Clervaux beside highway CR334. (50.087500, 6.025608)

On 21 March 1945, US Air Force P-61 'Black Widow' night-fighter shot down a British Hudson transport plane from 161 Squadron, killing three of the four British crew members and three Belgian SOE operatives to be inserted into Germany near Leipzig. Only the pilot was able to parachute to safety. The American fighter pilot believed the plane to be German as, in keeping with the secrecy of the mission, RAF Bomber Command had not notified the Americans of the flight.

The crash site in deep forest 20 meters below the top of a ridge presents the most strenuous effort to achieve visitor site in our guide books. Despite the effort to follow the difficult uphill trail, it has been included as one of the few examples of a **crashed Second World War aircraft** remaining in its original crash location with associated aircrew graves. Unfortunately, the cockpit, instrument panel, and most of the fuselage were salvaged before preservation efforts began. The airplane's wings and two motors remain behind a wire fence. The dead are buried on the hillside immediately below the wreckage, their graves marked by six tombstones flanking a central granite stone cross.

Location: 6.2 km north of Clervaux; stairs to start up the hillside are beside a rural road 350 m from highway CR335. (50.094749, 6.022546) The crash site is at(50.092416, 6.021117)

12,13

---

12   First Lieutenant Jesse P Sweat from Georgia is buried at Epinal American Cemetery, Dinozé, France. Corporal Leonard Deluga is remembered on the Luzerne, Pennsylvania War Memorial

13   The victims were FO Henry Johnson RAFVR, Navigator; FO Forrest Thompson RNZAF, Air Gunner; Flt Lt Raymond Escreet RAF, Wireless Operator; Lt Guy Corbisier, SOE; Lt Jean Morel, SOE; and Lt Leon de Winter, SOE. The surviving pilot, Flt Lt Anthony Helfer, was awarded a Distinguished Flying Cross.

Cinqfontaines

German occupation forces seized over seven-hundred Jewish men, women, and children on the grounds of the religious Cloister de Cinqfontaines. From here the victims were deported to the Auschwitz concentration camp. Only forty-three survived.

A series of stone steps leads to five irregularly stacked blocks of rose granite taken from the quarry of Struthof concentration camp. The structure, designed by artist and former concentration camp prisoner Lucien Wercollier, symbolizes a bent but standing human. Several large glass-covered explanation tablets (German and French only) present a timeline of Jewish persecution in Nazi occupied territories and events at the cloister. The memorial is now known as **Monument Auschwitz**. The railway line used in the deportation lies a few meters ahead.

Location: 10.2 km north of Clervaux and 4.3 km northwest of the Maulusmühle train station. (50.107902, 6.006705)

Troisvierges

On 9 January 1945, the 6th Armored Division, reinforced by the 320th Infantry Regiment, 35th Infantry Division, pushed out from the Bastogne area astride the Longvilly-Bourcy highway and reoccupied Wardin, Mageret, Benonchamps, Longvilly, and Michamps. Advancing through deep snow, the division fought through desperate German rear-guard units to reach the Our River on 26 January, capturing 2,298 prisoners and 87 tanks in the process.

At a curve in highway CR337 on the southeast edge of town, a small strip of ground holds an upright quarry stone bearing two plaques recognizing the **6th Armoured Division** and the citizens of Troisvierges on the 50th Anniversary of the town's liberation on 23 January 1945. The opposite end of the space holds a **German 88-mm Pak 43 antitank gun** pointing east over the Luckeschbaach (creek).

Location: 12.5 km north of Clervaux beside highway CR337. (50.118212, 6.004782)

On 2 January 1945, despite the obvious pending defeat of the German Army in the Ardennes Offensive, the Gestapo launched an offensive of its own against civilian resistance members from Marnach and Munshausen. Five men were taken and trucked to a then-unknown destination. Four of the bodies were discovered at this site in February 1945. Each was murdered by gunshots from close range. A sixth victim, Aloyse Stelhems, was transported to Germany and, although later liberated by American troops, also died.

The rue Eichelsberg passes through a residential neighborhood before becoming a narrow but well-paved forest lane that continues to the hilltop. A slate stone set into a fieldstone wall commemorates the four Luxembourg and one Belgian patriots executed at this spot by the Gestapo in January 1945.

Location: 1.1 km south of central Troisverges and 500 m east of highway N12. (50.114145, 5.994699)

[14]

---

14 The five were JP Fischbach, Marcel Spaus, Aloyse Kaiser, JP Thelen, and Eudore Magonette.

Chapter Six   Skyline Drive   257

**Battle of Hosingen
16 to 18 December 1944**

Highway CR 324 led west from the Our River crossing at Obereisenbach south of Hosingen and on to the Clerf River crossing at Drauffelt. Two infantry platoons of Company K and two machine-gun sections from Company M (Heavy Weapons) were scattered among the village buildings that lined Skyline Drive. German spotlights reflected off the low clouds to illuminate the terrain to help the infiltrators navigate across the river and through the woods. Grenadiers from Regiment 77 climbed the ridgeline hidden by a heavy fog. They intended to bypass Hosingen, leaving its capture to the following armored forces. The regiment's objectives were the Clerf River crossings at Clervaux and Drauffelt.

GERMAN OBJECTIVE	To bypass American centers of resistance and capture intact bridges over the Clerf River
FORCES	
American:	Company K (Captain Frederick Feiker), 110th Infantry Regiment; one platoon of Antitank Company; and Company B (Captain WH Jarret), 103rd Engineer Combat Battalion
German:	Grenadier Regiment 77 (Oberstleutnant Martin Schriefer), 26th Volksgrenadier Division and Kampfgruppe von Fallois (Major Gerd von Fallois), Panzer Lehr
RESULT	The small force resisted German troops for two days.
CASUALTIES	
American:	7 killed, 12 wounded, and 289 taken prisoner
German:	300 killed
LOCATION	Hosingen is 19 km northeast of Wiltz

Battle

By the beginning of the 45-minute artillery bombardment at 0515, German grenadiers held positions in the woods near Hosingen and Wahlhausen. Well-aimed German artillery accurately targeted the fortified villages, command posts, and logistics areas. The first shells fell on Hosingen at 0525 but caused no casualties. Company K's commander, Captain Frederick Feiker, turned out his men who then occupied defensive positions about the town.

An outpost atop the town's water tower at the northern edge of Hosingen made first contact when it spotted enemy troops crossing Skyline Drive in small groups moving through a draw to the north. The outpost's machine gun and Company M's 81-mm mortars started to respond. South of town an initial rush of grenadiers overcame an outpost on Steinmauer Hill and cut-off the 3rd Platoon guarding the road junction. From the church steeple, Captain Jarrett [15]observed a large German force

---
15 Captain William H Jarrett was captured and sent to Stalag IVb in Mühlberg, Germany where 7,500 American soldiers captured during the Battle of the Bulge were incarcerated. Stalag IVb was

crossing the Skyline Drive south of town. By radio, he called down fire from the same 81-mm mortars, temporarily stopping enemy movement.

During the day, quiet generally shrouded Hosingen while German troops widened their berth around the town. General Cota ordered a counterattack to relieve Hosingen. Moving from Wilwerwiltz to Bockholtz, Sherman tanks from 1st Platoon, Company B, 707th Tank Battalion rescued Battery C, 109th Field Artillery Battalion that was under attack and continued to Skyline Drive. Inexplicably, they had made no contact with Captain Feiker in the town. Although German armor was still awaiting completion of an Our River bridge, grenadiers with panzerfausts attacked the Shermans. In confused tank actions probably caused by unreliable radio communications, the seven Company B Shermans headed south toward Hoscheid just as five Shermans from Company A entered Hosingen from the north. First Lieutenant Robert Payne sent three of his tanks to Steinmauer Hill to overlook the road from Obereisenbach, another near the water tower, and his command tank in town covering approaches from the south.

As the armored spearhead, Kampfgruppe von Fallois' original mission was to seize Bastogne.[16] Instead, General von Lüttwitz overrode Generalleutnant Fritz Bayerlein's objections and ordered von Fallois to reduce the American garrison at Hosingen. Oberst Kokott, also concerned about the American presence astride his 26th VGD's supply line, ordered II Battalion, Grenadier Regiment 78 to assault the town.

At 1700, three PzKpfw IVs chased the Shermans from Steinmauer Hill, but they returned to relative safely along the town's buildings. Meanwhile, Kokott's Replacement Training Battalion 26 struck against the outpost atop the water tower. Vicious hand-to-hand fighting spread among nearby houses until 2200, but the Americans denied penetrations of the perimeter.

By 0500 on 17 December, the full force of German armor moved along the repaired Obereisenbach road and against Hosingen. In frustration over the continued resistance, von Lüttwitz rerouted several Panther tanks from 2nd Panzer Division to help Kampfgruppe von Fallois. Under covering artillery fire, German panzers and infantry assaulted the American perimeter from several directions. After an hour and with numerous casualties falling to American machine-gun and tank fire, German troops drew back. Later the attack resumed and continued all afternoon while American ammunition supplies dwindled. By 1600, close-quarters fighting filled the center of the town while panzerfausts knocked out two Shermans. The Americans slowly shrank their perimeter, setting buildings on fire when they abandoned them. German advances cut the defenders into small, isolated groups.

By the morning of 18 December, the Hosingen garrison was tired, hungry, thirsty, and almost completely devoid of ammunition. The ever-tightening German

---

one of the largest camps in the German PoW system. He was liberated by the Soviet Red Army on 23 April 1945.

16 Kampfgruppe von Fallois was led by Major Gerd von Fallois and consisted of Reconnaissance Battalion 130; 8th Company, Panzer Regiment 130 (PzKpfw IVs); 3rd Company, Panzerjäger Battalion 130 (Jagdpanzer IVs); 4th Battery, Panzerartillery Battalion 130; and one company from Panzerpionier (Armored Engineer) Battalion 130.

Chapter Six　　　　　　　　　　　　　　　　　　　　　Skyline Drive　259

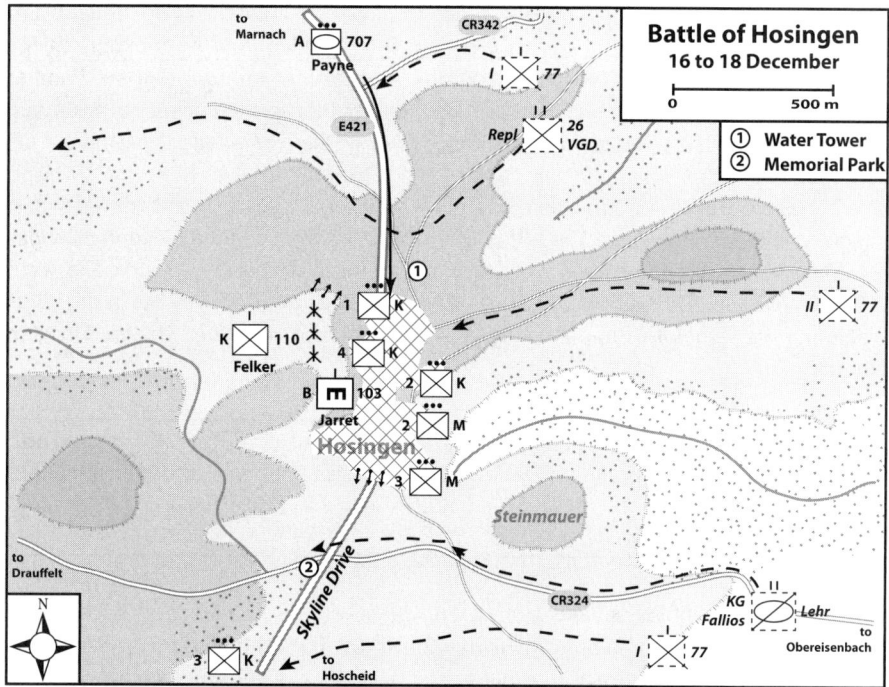

encirclement precluded escape. At 0830, Captain Feiker [17] raised a white cloth. The Germans immediately stopped firing. By 1000, the surviving members of the garrison marched eastward across that same Obereisenbach bridge. Remarkably, due largely only 19 casualties.

Conclusions
　　　　The soldiers at Hosingen had fought off elements of two German divisions for two whole days. Their gallant stand delayed the direct assault of Kampfgruppe von Fallois for one day — gaining the time required to rush reinforcements to Bastogne.

Battlefield Tour
The battlefield tour returns east to locations of German attacks upon American outposts.

> From Clervaux, exit the town to the south on highway N18 and follow back east to Marnach. Exit highway N18 toward Hosingen / Diekirch and merge onto highway E421. After 4.2 km, turn left onto Um Knupp and stop at the water tower 250 m ahead. (50.020499, 6.093152)

17　Captain Frederick Feiker was sent to the PoW camp at Hammelburg, Germany. After the failed rescue attempt by elements of General Patton's Third Army, the camp's prisoners were moved farther east. Captain Feiker was killed in Nürnberg during an American air raid on 5 April 1945. He is buried in Lorraine American Cemetery, St-Avold, France.

On 17 December, machine-gun fire from nearby houses and 60- and 81-mm mortar fire from the town cut down German infantry identified by lookouts in the water tower that had survived numerous hits from the 75-mm guns of six Panther tanks. A reward offered by the German tank commander to the crew who destroyed the outpost failed. The tower was abandoned later in the day when it became cut off from the town.

The water tower still stands just at the northern edge of Hosingen, which has expanded considerably since 1944. It is illuminated at night and the location provides generous views over the terrain especially to the north and east — where the wind turbines now identify German territory. The terrain drops down to the north, thus explaining the difficulties in observing German infiltrators crossing Skyline Drive in that direction.

> Continue south on Um Knupp for 180 m; turn right at the first cross street. Turn left onto E421 and continue for 750 m. Stop near the small park at the intersection of highway E421 and the cross road CR324 (also Boukelzerstroos / Eeberwée). (50.012360, 6.089374)

The park holds several stones with plaques to the defenders of Hosingen specifically commemorating the men of **Company K, 110th Infantry Regiment** surrounded here by German forces on 16 December 1944; the valiant men of **Company B, 103rd Engineer Combat Battalion** who gallantly defended Hosingen from 16 to 18 December 1944; and the **17th Parachute Infantry Division** (sic) that liberated Hosingen. A separate plaque remembers **Ralph R Wardle** and **John W Kelly**, members of the **702nd 'Red Devils' Tank Battalion**, who died on 27 January 1945 when antitank fire hit their tank while liberating the town. Their comrades and Tank Commander 2nd Lieutenant Milton Still erected the plaque to their memory.

Battle of Weiler and Hoscheid
16 December 1944

German Objective		To bypass American centers of resistance and capture intact bridges over the Clerf River
Forces		
	American:	Company I (Captain Floyd K McCutchan), 110th Infantry Regiment
	German:	Fallschirmjäger Regiment 14 (Oberst Arno Schimmel), 5th Fallschirmjäger Division
Result		The towns were captured
Casualties		
	American:	At least 28 taken prisoner
	German:	126 killed, wounded, or missing
Location		Hoscheid is 24 km east of Wiltz

Battle

A road junction known as Wäisse Wak north of Weiler held a 3rd Battalion observation post protected by 1st Platoon of Company I stationed along the road to Wahlhausen on the forward slope of the ridge. A mine field separated the remaining two platoons of Company I that were reinforced by a section of 81-mm mortars and a platoon of the regiment's Antitank Company. Sergeant Jacob Welc commanded the two 57-mm guns. Sgt Welc personally manned one of the guns and fired round after round of high-explosive shells into enemy formations of Fusilier Regiment 39 across the valley.[18] The deadly explosions broke up the German attack. Fallschirmjäger Regiment 14 attempted to clear the roadway with a flank attack, but the defenders at Weiler stood firm while they repelled wave after wave of attacking German infantry. Grenadiers entering the village were subjected to a fusillade of small-arms fire from doorways, windows, and rooftops. Unteroffizier Horst Helmus reported being fired upon from every direction. German medics requested and received a 30-minute cease fire to tend to the wounded. At 1330 the enemy ceased fire and sent forward a white flag, with a surrender offer that the Americans rejected.

By afternoon, it was obvious that Company I could not resist much longer. The mortar and artillery men had expended all of their ammunition and were fighting in the village as infantry. Machine-gun teams were forced to surrender when they completely ran out of ammunition. Then panzers arrived, taking position after position under direct short-range cannon fire. No structure offered protection from their powerful 75-mm guns.

About 1830, the battalion observation post reported enemy vehicles attacking with multiple 20-mm guns. Lieutenant Jack Fisher requested American artillery fire on his own position. Only one man escaped. In Weiler, small groups made their individual decisions to surrender while others made their escape as the town burned. That night, Captain McCutchan retreated with his troops to Consthum, 3rd Battalion's headquarters. The pursuing Germans eventually killed or imprisoned survivors.

Only a small force of regiment's Assault Gun Company with six Shermans carrying 105-mm howitzers and three tanks from Company B garrisoned Hoscheid despite its key position atop Skyline Drive. Attacked on the morning of 17 December by elements of the 5th Fallschirmjäger Division, the defenders of Hoscheid fought as infantry through the day, repelling three enemy assaults. By 1830, low ammunition levels forced the troops to board their vehicles and fall back to Wiltz.

Consequences

The stand at Weiler and Hoscheid delayed the progress of the German paratroopers for an entire day. However, the capture of the town separated the 110th Regiment from the 28th Division's 109th Regiment to the south. (The story of the 109th Infantry Regiment is related in Chapter Eight.)

---

18 In June 1945, Sergeant Welc, who had fought in Normandy hedgerows, Falaise, the Hürtgen Forest, Belgium, and Luxembourg, received a battlefield commission from Major General Norman Cota.

Battles for Weiler, Hoscheid, Holzthum and Consthum
16 to 18 December

① Wäisse Wak
② Schmuelen Farmhouse
③ Schinkert Crossroads

Elevations deleted for clarity

Battlefield Tour

Leave Hosingen south on highway E421. After 2.5 km, enter a roundabout and take the 3rd exit toward Vianden / Wahlhausen (CR322). Follow for 3.2 km to the water reservoirs beside the road at an area known as Wäisse Wak. (49.973753, 6.119417)

Two local water reservoirs mark the high point of the ridge overlooking Wahlhausen and the location of the 3rd Battalion observation team. The minor road that led to the river crossing at Obereisenbach only four kilometers distant magnified Wahlhausen's importance. First Platoon held field positions along the minor road.

Continue south 190 m to the Schmuelen Farmhouse. (49.975229, 6.118224)

The one-half strength 25-man 2nd Platoon maintained a CP in the farmhouse and outposts in the surrounding fields. Before the battle, patrols frequently approached the Our River at Gemünd only three kilometers to the east.

Continue southeast on CR322 and continue into Weiler. After 2.0 km, turn right onto rue Principale (CR320) and continue 450 m past the firehouse on the left. Turn left

Chapter Six Skyline Drive

> and proceed to the parking area. (49.961718, 6.124806)

Before the battle began, Private First Class Thomas Myers made acquaintance with local citizens in Weiler. When word came to withdraw toward Consthum, Myers' attempt to escape was thwarted when his small group became surrounded on a hillside west of Weiler. He was taken prisoner but escaped again when an artillery shell struck the PoW group and its guards. After regaining consciousness, Myers and another prisoner found most soldiers dead except for a German guard blinded by the blast. The two Americans sought shelter in the cellar of a nearby mill where they discovered a group of frightened civilians. One woman calmly spread jam on slices of bread and shared a meal with the Americans. Their liberty was brief because the structure also held a German headquarters that recaptured the two men.[19]

A memorial to the **110th Infantry Regiment** stands in **Tom Myers Square** near the rear of the fire station. The large mountain stone bears the bronze plaque of the 'Bloody Bucket' Division and a separate inscribed plaque dedicated, 'In memory of the brave American soldiers of Company I, 110th Regiment, 28th Infantry Division, who fought in Weiler in December 1944.' The final German attack advanced from the ravine behind the memorial.

A '**Remember US**' information panel stands to the left of the memorial stone. The panel recalls the events of the battle and describes the fighting at Wahlhausen and Weiler.

Other Points of Interest near Weiler

Putscheid
On 24 January 1945, Companies A and B, 10th Infantry Regiment, 5th Infantry Division attacked elements of Panzer Lehr defending the village. In spite of their strong artillery, mortar, and tank fire, the US troops were unable to liberate the village. On 27 January, the 3rd Battalion, 11th Regiment successfully occupied Weiler after a ten-hour fight. An artillery battery took up position in open fields west of Weiler. On 28 January, the American attack ran into a German counterattack composed of infantry, tanks, and self-propelled assault guns. A renewed attack by Companies A, B, C, and E, 10th Regiment, supported by 737th Tank Battalion, finally succeeded in driving away the defenders. Ruined Putscheid was finally liberated at 1340 on 28 January.

A '**Remember US**' information panel adorns the small village chapel. The text briefly summarizes the Battle of the Bulge and continues to describe the actions of the battle for Putscheid.
Location: 1.6 km east of Weiler beside highway CR320. (49.959464, 6.141610)

---

19 PFC Thomas R Myers lost 60 pounds in his forced march across Germany to Stalag IV-B south of Berlin. Forwarded to a labor camp in Czechoslovakia, Myers escaped in May 1945 as the Russian Army approached. An English-speaking Russian soldier who had grown up in Cleveland before returning to Russia assisted in returning eight survivors to American lines. Myers was awarded the Bronze Star. He lived to raise 4 children, 2 step-children, 12 grandchildren and 21 great-grandchildren lastly in Bend, Oregon where he died in 2011 at age 93.

Stolzembourg

A seven-man patrol from 2nd Platoon, Troop B, 85th Cavalry Reconnaissance Squadron, 5th Armored Division led by Staff Sergeant Warner W Holzinger, faced the opportunity to be the first American troops on German soil. With the bridge over the Our River demolished by retreating enemy forces, the patrol swam across the river at 1630 on 11 September 1944, despite spotting at least fifteen concrete pillboxes on the opposite bank. German-speaking Holzinger interrogated a local farmer and then scaled the riverside ridge to view further into Germany. The team reconnoitered the Westwall as far as Waldhof 2.2 kilometers northeast and found the vaunted bunkers unmanned before returning to report its findings.

American and Luxembourg flags identify a **memorial to the first allied soldiers to enter Germany**. The bronze plaque carrying the insignia of the 5th Armored Division crowns a German dragon's teeth tank barrier. The monument forms a neat little display in a beautiful location. An '**Remember US**' information panel identifies the men as Sergeant Warner W Holzinger, Corporal Ralph E Diven, T/5 Coy T Locke, PFC William McColligan, PFC George F McNeal, PFC Jesse Stevens, and French Lieutenant Lionel Delille.

On 16 December, Fallschirmjäger Regiment 14 re-crossed the river at the same location, hitting the boundary between the American 109th and 110th Regiments. Unit boundaries were frequently 'soft' spots in the American defense and allowed the fallschirmjäger to proceed against little opposition.
Location: 4 km east of Weiler beside highway N10 at the southern outskirts of Stolzembourg. (49.963081, 6.169996)

[20]

Hoscheid

In January 1945, the German Army grappled to maintain the river crossings open to retreating troops. During the nights of 22/23 and 23/24 January, the LVIII Panzer Corps and LIII Infantry Corps withdrew behind the Clerf River. However, on 25 January American troops executed a major breakthrough and by the next day drove up Skyline Drive and liberated Hoscheid.
Place de Liberation at the rear of the village church holds a monument to the **5th Infantry Division** and the thirty-eight soldiers killed while liberating the Hoscheid area.
Location: 4.8 km southwest of Weiler and 50 m west of highway CR320. (49.94591, 6.07979)

Schlindermanderscheid

During the last year of the war, seventeen young Luxembourgish conscientious objectors and deserters from the German Army found protection in an underground bunker located deep in the An der Dosbaach forest near Fridbësch. A 15-kilometer thematic trail called the *Schlindermanderscheid Bunkerwanderung*

---

[20] S/Sgt Warner W Holzinger, the first Allied soldier to set foot in Germany, was actually born in Germany. His family emigrated to the Unites States in 1921 and settled in the Fort Atkinson, Wisconsin area. After the war he returned to that state where he died in 1988 at age 72.

Chapter Six　　　　　　　　　　　　　　　　　Skyline Drive　265

visits their reconstructed, partly-hidden underground shelter used from late May until 10 September 1944. In December 2004, their refuge was rebuilt as it had appeared 60 years earlier, including the shelter's large bunk bed and complete stove.
Location: To find the bunker, follow the blue signs labeled 'BW' starting in the hamlet of Fridbësch along highway CR348 2.5 km north of Schlindermanderscheid (trail head: 49.951591, 6.055681; underground shelter: 49.950135, 6.046329)

Kautenbach
An existing **1944 Mark II Bailey Bridge** crosses the Clerf River in what are now the Kautenbach camping grounds. A long drive along the river bank approaches the bridge, still in use to cross the Clerf River to reach the reception office on the opposite bank. The gorgeous valley is enclosed by steep ridges covered in lush vegetation on both sides of the river.
Location: 11 km east of Wiltz and 1.4 km northeast of the bridge over the Wiltz River and the junction of highways CR332 and CR331. (49.955055, 6.030141)

Battle of Holzthum and Consthum
16 to 18 December 1944

Holzthum sits upon the downward slope of the ridgeline. The town offered shelter to the men of Company L manning the roadblock at the intersection of Skyline Drive and highway CR 322 from Gemünd, known locally as *Schinkert*. A battery of 687th Field Artillery Battalion supported by two half-tracks mounting quadruple .50-caliber machine guns from an antiaircraft battalion strengthened the defense.

Consthum, two kilometers to the southwest, held the 3rd Battalion Command Post in the schoolhouse on the western edge of town. Company M (Heavy Weapons) with battalion cooks, drivers, and clerks manned the defenses along with a battery from the 687th Field Artillery Battalion that dug in on the ridge on the right flank of the town.

GERMAN OBJECTIVE	To bypass American centers of resistance and capture intact bridges over the Clerf River
FORCES	
American:	Company L (Lieutenant Vert Saymon), 110th Infantry Regiment
German:	Kampfgruppe Kaufmann (Oberstleutnant Walter Kaufmann), 26th Volksgrenadier Division and Panzergrenadier Regiment 901 (Oberst Paul Freiherr von Hauser)
RESULT	The two villages were captured
CASUALTIES	
American:	100 killed, wounded, or missing
German:	At least 100 killed or wounded
LOCATION	Holzthum is 18 km east of Wiltz

Battle

Company-sized groups of Kampfgruppe Kaufmann[21] crossed Skyline Drive unimpeded and continued down the reverse slope of the ridge before being detected by Company L in Holzthum at 0615 and by battalion troops in Consthum slightly later. Heavy exchanges erupted. Proceeding cautiously in heavy fog, a large body of Kaufmann's troops approached an American half-track along the road to Holzthum. They assumed it was a captured vehicle under German control and waved it forward in a friendly manner. At 100 meters, the four .50-caliber barrels spewed bullets. Close to 100 German troops fell dead or wounded.

On 17 December, Holzthum felt the pressure of an entire infantry regiment and the light armor of Panzer Lehr's reconnaissance battalion. Two Panthers led the assault upon Lieutenant Vert Saymon's schoolhouse command post. Overwhelmed, the 140-man Company L was reduced to a platoon-sized forty survivors. Lt Saymon withdrew his men to 3rd Battalion headquarters at Consthum two kilometers to the southwest.

Concerned about the simultaneous German attacks on the Skyline Drive strongpoints at Marnach, Hosingen, and Hoscheid, General Cota sent regimental Executive Officer Lieutenant Colonel Daniel Strickler to Consthum to oversee the 3rd Battalion's defense. After two days of intense fighting, Consthum offered the only remaining resistance in the 3rd Battalion sector where a mixed group of headquarters troops, artillery men, and antiaircraft troops repelled five separate attacks by Panzergrenadier Regiment 901 from Bayerlein's Panzer Lehr. Even while they withdrew on 18 December, they continued to block the road to Wiltz 16 kilometers to the west.

Battlefield Tour

From Weiler, continue west on highway CR320 for 4.4 km, carefully noting the left turn in Merscheid. Turn right onto a long frontage road to join northbound highway E421. Continue 3.5 km to Schinckert roundabout. Take the 3rd exit toward Wiltz (N25/CR322) and stop at the parking area ahead. (49.991300, 6.088622)

Highway E421 does not provide the beautiful views into Germany that one might expect since summit of the ridge line is about 0.5 km to the east. The Schinckert intersection is now a large roundabout and holds no buildings.

Company L's 1st Platoon manned a roadblock at this key intersection of Skyline Drive and the road to the Gemünd river crossing, where a lone building once housed Café Schincker. Early on 16 December, an American jeep sped through the roadblock and disappeared into the fog. A few moments later, the soldiers heard small-arms fire; then they received tracer fire. Although the exchange was light, they observed grenadiers crossing Skyline Drive to the north and south effectively by-passing the roadblock. The platoon was ordered back to Holzthum but could not penetrate the enemy encirclement. It proceeded instead to Consthum.

---

21   Kampfgruppe Kaufmann consisted of Fusilier Regiment 39 and elements of Reconnaissance Battalion 130.

Chapter Six

The roundabout that has replaced the crossroads no longer supports a café or any other building in a wind-swept area of open farm fields. The terrain slopes away from the intersection in almost every direction, but offers little of interest.

> Continue on CR322 for 3.4 km passing through Holzthum. In Consthum, turn left onto rue Knapp to the memorial. (49.973949, 6.052751)

A stone monument surrounded by a stone retaining wall stands in a small clearing facing the front of the church. The stone bears a plaque with the 28th Division's 'Bloody Bucket' insignia in honor of **Colonel Daniel B Strickler** and the **110th Infantry Regiment** for its defense of the town.

Battle for Wiltz
18 to 19 December 1944

The old medieval district of Wiltz stands high upon a ridge line above the winding Wiltz River where the newer commercial district lines the banks of the river's curves where they swing from the southeast to the north and continue around to the southwest. Wiltz sits at the junction of three, albeit minor, roads – none of which carried any significance to German plans. However, the Germans could not permit an enemy garrison to remain to their rear threatening the important Ettelbruck–Bastogne highway to the south and the more distant Clervaux–Bastogne highway to the north. Nevertheless, General von Lüttwitz had no intention of attacking Wiltz. Instead, he assigned Grenadier Regiment 78 to contain the Americans while the bulk of his force attended to more important matters to the west.

By the morning of 18 December, the main highway from Holzthum to Wiltz had been cut in several places. Consthum, meanwhile, was isolated and under increasing pressure. German artillery began long-range fire on Wiltz, therefore forcing General Cota to move his headquarters from a comfortable building in the upper district to a cellar in a building in the lower section of the town.

Although most of the service personnel in Wiltz were unaccustomed to combat, the division headquarters organized Task Force Hoban[22] that included the last six partially serviceable Sherman tanks (out of original battalion strength of 25 medium and 17 light tanks) and five assault guns from the 707th Tank Battalion. The town's approaches held roadblocks formed around six antitank guns from 630th Tank Destroyer Battalion, quad .50-caliber and 40-mm Bofors antiaircraft guns from the 447th Antiaircraft Artillery Battalion, and the 44th Engineer Combat Battalion commanded by Lieutenant Colonel Clarion Kjeldseth. General Cota sent two companies of engineers to block approaches through Eschweiler and Erpeldange while retaining the third company to defend his headquarters. Thereafter, the 687th Field Artillery Battalion had the town within range of its guns.

---

22   The task force was under the command of Lieutenant Colonel Thomas L Hoban, commander of Headquarters troops, 28th Infantry Division.

GERMAN OBJECTIVE	To isolate Wiltz while major units continued west
FORCES	
American:	Task Force Hoban (Lieutenant Colonel Thomas L Hoban) and 44th Engineer Combat Battalion (Lieutenant Colonel Clarion J Kjeldseth)
German:	Reconnaissance Battalion 130 (Major Gerd von Fallois), Panzer Lehr; then Fusilier Regiment 39 (Oberstleutnant Walter Kaufmann), 26th Volksgrenadier Division and Fallschirmjäger Regiment 14 (Oberst Arno Schimmel), 5th Fallschirmjäger Division
RESULT	The town was captured
CASUALTIES	
American:	44th Engineer Combat Bn: 332 killed, wounded, or missing 707th Tank Bn: 146 killed, wounded, or missing
German:	unknown
LOCATION	Wiltz is 100 km south of Liège

Battle

On 18 December, General Cota and his headquarter's staff were still in their command post defended by Task Force Hoban when Cota received orders from Middleton to hold at all costs. General Cota expected CCB, 10th Armored Division to arrive shortly, unaware that Wiltz was not the unit's objective. (See Chapter Seven for the actions of CCB.)

By noon, German field guns that had advanced west of the Clerf River opened fire upon Wiltz. Shortly after 1400, troops of Panzer Lehr's Reconnaissance Battalion 130 attacked the Wiltz defensive perimeter from the northeast. The leading PzKpfw IVs blasted through engineer Company A. Reserve Company B rushed to reform the perimeter at Weidingen, only 3.5 kilometers from the city center. However, the German assault halted while the reconnaissance battalion rejoined its division in the race toward Bastogne. Fusilier Regiment 39 continued the attack upon Wiltz. While the fusiliers brought pressure from the north, Fallschirmjäger Regiment 14 drifted against the town from the south despite its orders to bypass the city.

Before dawn on 19 December, Cota sent much of his headquarters staff to establish a new headquarters at Sibret, Belgium. With the return of Lieutenant Colonel Strickler from Consthum, Cota appointed the colonel to command the remaining troops in Wiltz before leaving for Sibret.

The fusiliers attacked at 1400 and drove a provisional platoon composed of the divisional band from a hill to the northwest. The 44th Engineer Combat Companies fought off attacks from the northeast and east where the crossroads at Erpeldange changed hands four times during a three-hour fight. The engineers eventually blew the bridge and retreated into Wiltz. Meanwhile, that afternoon, Fallschirmjäger Regiment 15 moved through Roullingen to the southeast along with forty panzers to complete

Chapter Six   Skyline Drive   269

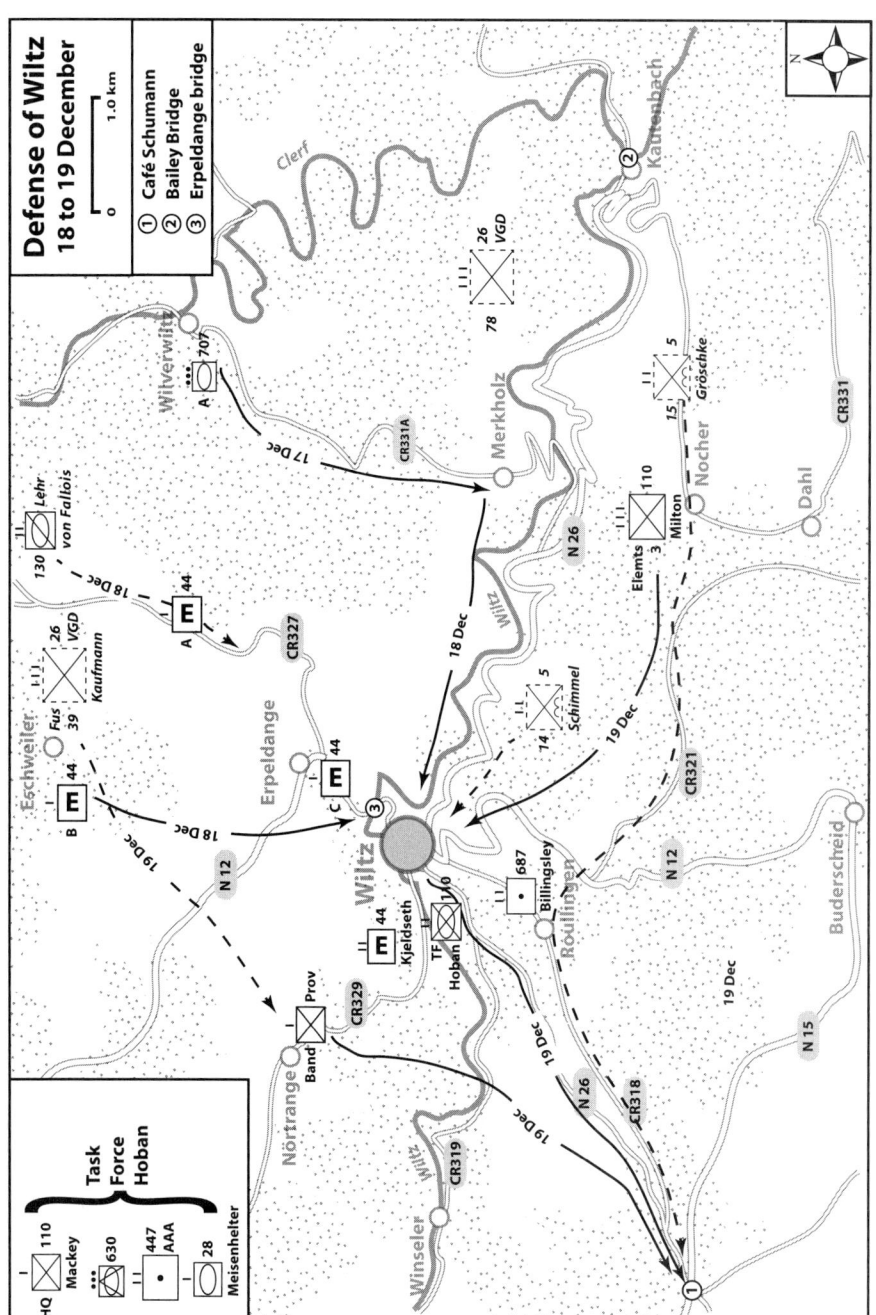

the encirclement of the town. That evening Fallschirmjäger Regiment 14 appeared on
the ridge east of Wiltz. The defending Shermans and assault guns were destroyed or
The defense of the town collapsed while individual groups made their escape to the
west.

Battlefield Tour

Leave Consthum west toward Wiltz (CR322). After 6.0 km, cross the Clerf and Wiltz Rivers in Kautenbach and turn left on N25. Follow for 9.9 km into Wiltz's upper district. Turn left onto rue du 31 Août 1942 and proceed 170 m to the chateau entrance. Recommended parking is available in the place de Château below the chateau to the west. Parking entry is via a steep ramp. (49.966646, 5.935956)

Wiltz

The nobility of Wiltz constitutes one of the oldest families in the Grand Duchy of Luxembourg, dating back twenty-one generations to the 12th century. The last Count of Wiltz fled his lands during the French Revolution in 1793 to die in exile in Germany. The picturesque upper-district is dominated by the town's 13th century chateau. The king of France destroyed the original chateau in 1388. Rebuilt, the Count of Nassau burned it down again in the early 15th century. The current Renaissance structure commenced construction in 1631, but the Thirty Years War, plagues, and famine delayed its completion until 1720. The US 26th Infantry Division and the US 6th Cavalry finally liberated Wiltz on 21 January 1945.

The tourist office and museum are located within the walls of the chateau:

Office Régional du Tourisme des Ardennes Luxembourgeoises
7 rue de l'Indépendance
Grand Duchy of Luxembourg
Email: info@ortal.lu

9532 Wiltz
Tel: +352 26 95 05 66
Web: http://www.ardennes-lux.lu/

Château de Wiltz
L-9516 Wiltz
Tel: +352 95 74 44 / Fax: +352 95 75 56
Web: http://www.touristinfowiltz.lu

Grand Duchy of Luxembourg
Email: siwiltz@pt.lu

Enter the courtyard of the chateau by crossing the stone bridge over a moat. The entrance to the small museum lies inside the courtyard on the right. (49.966331, 5.937435)

Museum of the Battle of the Bulge 1944/1945
35, rue du Château
Grand Duchy of Luxembourg
Web: http://www.amba.lu or http://www.touristinfowiltz.lu

L-9516 Wiltz
Tel: +352 26 95 00 32

The museum focuses on events that occurred in Wiltz and holds photographs of the labor strike (see below), destruction of the city by American and German bombardments, American GIs entering the town, and of Brookins playing St Nicolas. As such, it lacks the general interest of average battlefield tourists.

Open daily in July and August from 09:00 to 18:00; open every day except Sunday, September to June from 09:00 to 12:00 and from 14:00 to 17:00. Fee includes an audio guide.

A granite stone bearing the blood-red insignia of the **28th 'Bloody Bucket' Infantry Division** stands under a chestnut tree facing rue du Château. The associated plaque commemorates the division's liberation of Wiltz on 10 September 1944 and the subsequent defense of the town during the Battle of the Bulge. (49.966591, 5.937492)

To the left, a stone plaque celebrates the memory of **Corporal Richard Brookins**, a soldier of the 28th Infantry Division and, later, honorary citizen of Wiltz who, despite the hardships of military life in Wiltz, portrayed St Nicolas for the children of the town on 5 December 1944 (St Nicolas Eve). Corporal Brookins collected candy and chocolate from his fellow soldiers and encouraged the unit's field kitchen to prepare donuts and cakes. Brookins wore the robes and peaked hat of the local priest while he rode through the streets on the back of a jeep distributing sweets to the children — something that had not happened during the four year of occupation, also meaning that the younger children had never experienced the town's ancient ritual.[23] (49.966677, 5.937378)

Across the street, **Square Eisenhower** sits behind the Hôtel de Ville. General Dwight Eisenhower, Commander in Chief of Allied troops, stayed in Wiltz on 8 November 1944 to speak to General Cota. An upright stele behind a flower decked plot bears a brass plaque featuring the profile of General Dwight D Eisenhower. A second horizontal stone to the right carries brass letters of the general's name and, 'He stayed in Wiltz – 8.11.1944.' A barrel of a howitzer tops a cement base to the left. (49.966679, 5.936956)

Walk down hill to the west for 250 m along rue du Château (becomes rue du 31 Août 1942).

After the introduction of compulsory military service of Luxembourg's males into the German Army, local leaders proclaimed a general strike in protest on 31 August 1942. The strike movement began in the Wiltz leather factory and expanded to include all of Wiltz and other localities of the country. Nazi occupation forces shot twenty-one patriots, four teachers, and two community officials who protested German induction. Twenty-seven entire families suffered forced resettlement, fifteen men died in concentration camps, and 164 young men were forcibly recruited into German armed forces. Of those, forty-two were killed, fifteen went missing, and twenty-one came back wounded. An additional fifty civilians died during the local battles. Approximately eighty per cent of Wiltz houses were destroyed or damaged. Because of the heavy suffering in the Second World War (1940 - 1945), Wiltz received the honorary title 'Martyred City' from the Luxembourg government.

In tribute to the victims of this tragic and painful period of Luxembourg history, the city erected the **Monument National de la Grève (National Monument of Strike)**. The south side of the memorial tower depicts a symbolic David struggling against an overpowering colossus. The north-side relief presents featureless victims falling to the enemy's bullets. Every year on 31 August, concerned families as well as national and local authorities attend a solemn ceremony. The promenade around the rear of the tower offers spectacular views of lower Wiltz. (49.966601, 5.933967)

---

23 An Associated Press photographer happened to witness and film the celebration which appeared in newspapers across America. The event continues to be celebrated with Brookins returning to Wiltz several times to portray the 'American St Nicolas,' including in 2014 when he was 92 years old.

272   The Bulge Battlefields

> Retrieve your vehicle and proceed west on rue du 31 Août 1942. Turn right onto rue Michel Thilges (N12). After 500 m, turn left onto rue du Pont (CR329) and follow for 1.4 km out of the city and up the hillside toward Nötrange to the guns on the left. (49.970609, 5.915754)

The road toward Nörtrange holds a memorial to the 28th Infantry Division's band that participated as provisional platoon of infantrymen in the defense of Wiltz. Fusilier Regiment 39 drove the platoon off the high ground at 1400 on 19 December, thus exposing the flank of combat engineers manning perimeter defenses.

A brass plaque mounted upon the granite stele musically labels its actions the '**Bazooka Boogie.**' The location also holds German **88-mm Pak 43/41 antitank gun** and **105-mm FH18/40 light field cannon**. Both guns are in remarkably good repair (at last viewing) and provide excellent examples of German artillery pieces.

> Reverse direction and follow CR329 1.4 km back into the city. Turn right onto highway N12 (also highway N26A) and follow for 3.3 km to rue des Pêcheurs / Place des Martyrs. (49.962679, 5.934797)

An infosign explains the naming of the square and describes the labor strike protesting German Army conscription. A **Sherman M4A3** tank stands to the right. This particular vehicle was sent from Wiltz to Erpeldange on 18 December. However, it became stuck in deep mud and was abandoned by its crew. It has remained in this square since 1947.

> Reverse direction and leave Wiltz to the southwest following highway N12 for 1.7 km. Turn left onto highway N26 for 2.6 km, then turn into the parking area on the right. (49.949434, 5.888386)

Affair at Schumann's Eck
19 December 1944

During the day of 19 December, a series of confused orders, independent decisions, and lack of communication led to groups of American soldiers searching for escape route to the west.

AMERICAN OBJECTIVE	To withdraw from Wiltz to Bastogne
FORCES	
American:	Elements of 28th Infantry Division (Lieutenant Colonel Daniel Strickler)
German:	Fallschirmjäger Regiment 15 (Oberstleutnant Kurt Gröschke)
RESULT	The crossroads was captured
CASUALTIES	Unknown
LOCATION	Schumann's Eck is 5 km southwest of Wiltz

Battle

At the junction of two roads leading out of Wiltz (N26 and CR318), 3rd Battalion commander Major Harold F Milton mustered two-hundred men who planned to hold that intersection. While Milton drove back to Wiltz to clarify his orders from Colonel Strickler, 1st Company, Fallschirmjäger Regiment 15 marched toward the junction from Wiltz. Unsure of its identity amid the confused withdrawal in the inky darkness of a moonless night, the junction group dispersed into the woods and allowed the German troops to pass. The remnants of 3rd Battalion dissolved into small groups making their way west toward Bastogne. Confused combat continued while small parties of Americans seeking to move west intermingled with advancing fallschirmjäger.[24]

Battle for Schumann's Eck
27 December 1944 to 9 January 1945

At 0600 on 22 December, General George Patton's III Corps, commanded by Major General John Millikin, attacked the southern flank of the German bulge with three divisions abreast. On the left, the 4th Armored Division advanced north on the axis of the Arlon–Bastogne highway (see Chapter Seven). On the right, the 80th Infantry Division advanced north to the west of Ettelbruck toward Heiderscheid (see Chapter Eight for battles south of the Sûre River line). The 26th Infantry Division advanced north between the two flanking units.

Although the enemy vigorously defended critical road junctions and river crossings, by 25 December Ettelbruck was liberated. The next day, Millikin's troops crossed the Sûre River, opening the corridor into Bastogne. Schumann's Eck gained in importance because highway (N15) was the main German supply route between Wiltz and Bastogne for forces attacking that city.

AMERICAN OBJECTIVE	To cut off German troops southeast of Bastogne
FORCES	
American:	26th Infantry Division (Major General Willard S Paul), then 90th Infantry Division (Major General James van Fleet)
German:	9th Volksgrenadier Division (Oberst Werner Kolb) and elements of Führer Grenadier Brigade (Major von Courbière)
RESULT	The crossroads was recaptured
CASUALTIES	Period 24 December to 16 January
American:	26th Infantry Division: 209 killed, 1,951 wounded, and 357 missing

---

24   Colonel Strickler left Wiltz that night, passing north of Café Schumann on foot and gradually collecting stragglers. Two days later, tired, hungry, and nearly frozen, the group reached American lines in Vaux-les-Rosière. He was awarded a Silver Star. Strickler, a lawyer from Lancaster County, Pennsylvania who had fought in the Mexican Border Conflict and the First World War, became Lieutenant Governor of that state but later resigned his position to lead the 28th Infantry Division during the Korean War. He retired from active service as a major general and returned to his Lancaster law practice. Strickler died in 1992 at age 95.

German:	90th Infantry Division: 161 killed, 832 wounded, and 98 missing 9th VGD: 306 killed, 930 wounded, and 1,217 missing; Führer Grenadier Brigade: 235 killed, 540 wounded, and 733 missing
LOCATION	Schumann's Eck is 5 km southwest of Wiltz

Battle

On 27 December, 2nd Battalion, 101st Infantry Regiment, 26th Infantry Division attempted a night assault upon nearby Nothum. When the lead squad of Company F on the west side of the road from Mecher crested the ridge, its scout tripped a Teller mine. The blast killed the scout and alerted German troops in the nearby woods who proceeded to pour small-arms fire onto the company. Units became confused and intermixed in the darkness, and the assault floundered.

The attacked resumed at 0730 the next morning under an umbrella of artillery fire with 1st Battalion west of the Bavigne road, 2nd Battalion along the road from Mecher, and 3rd Battalion moving from Kaundorf. Grenadier Regiment 36, with support of Panzerjäger Battalion 9 and Sturmartillerie Brigade 911[25] from the Führer Grenadier Brigade, resisted all efforts to enter the town. In the waning light of that afternoon, Company E occupied Nothum, and Company F reached the cemetery only 300 meters from Schumann's Eck, but heavy fire coming from the ruins of Café Schumann repulsed Company G when it attempted to pass across open ground.

An expected German counterattack on 29 December did not materialize, but nevertheless the 101st Regiment pulled back to its starting positions along the ridge south of Nothum. When the exhausted German forces could not launch their assault, 2nd Battalion occupied Nothum without loss while the 3rd Battalion moved toward Wiltz. The next day, Company F captured Schumann's Eck and a large number of prisoners while 3rd Battalion moved between Grenadier Regiments 36 and 57.

As the new year started, the 328th Regiment gradually replaced the 101st Infantry Regiment. Fresh troops occupied the crossroads only to suffer counterattack by the 9th VGD's 'Hetzer' assault guns. American artillery intervened and saved the situation. On 2 January, the 2nd Battalion, 101st Regiment attacked toward Berlé attempting to capture Hill 490 but were repelled by German artillery, assault guns, and 20-mm antiaircraft fire.[26]

The American capture of Dahl to the southeast further weakened the German southern flank whose Führer Grenadier Brigade moved east to Nocher to fill the gap. The 90th Infantry Division took over for the exhausted 26th Division. On 9 January, its 357th Infantry Regiment captured Berlé — only 2.0 kilometers from the American positions of two weeks earlier.

---

25 A Sturmartillerie Brigade held antitank weapons also designed as self-propelled assault guns. A theoretical complement included thirty-three StuG III/IV (75mm L/48) assault guns and twelve Sturmhaubitze 42 (105mm L/28) assault howitzers, but these levels were seldom achieved.

26 Company F, commanded by Captain James R Creighton, had been surrounded and captured during November 1944 fighting in Lorraine and was reconstituted almost entirely with new recruits. The battle for Schumann's Eck was the first engagement for most of its members. From an original complement of 200 men, 27 marched out of the woods.

Chapter Six

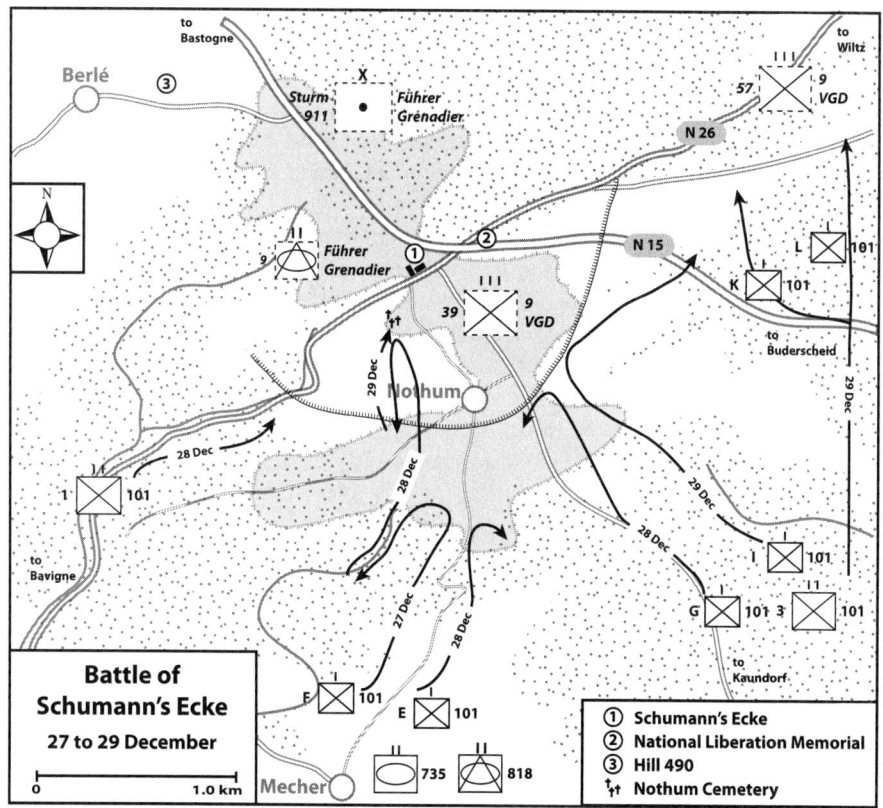

Battle of Schumann's Ecke
27 to 29 December

① Schumann's Ecke
② National Liberation Memorial
③ Hill 490
✝ Nothum Cemetery

Aftermath

Unexpectedly rapid American advances upon Doncols by the 90th Infantry Division from the south and the 6th Armored Division from the east trapped the 5th Fallschirmjäger Division's Regiments 13 and 15 in the Harlange Pocket. By 12 January, the paratrooper units had suffered fifty percent casualties and the loss of all heavy weapons. Survivors crept eastward at night through the still porous American lines. The 9th VGD, 1st SS Panzer Division and the Führer Grenadier Brigade continued to fiercely resist III Corps' advances. The attacks across the Sûre River by XX Corps on both sides of Diekirch sealed the German fate (see Chapter Eight). Individual units fought desperate rearguard actions while troops retreated into Germany.

Battlefield Tour

The forest to the north and east witnessed intense fighting from December 1944 to January 1945 while the 26th Infantry Division arrived on 30 December to engage the I Battalion, Grenadier Regiment 36, 9th Volksgrenadier Division that had occupied the forest after the fallschirmjäger had moved on. The second Battle for Schumann's Eck took place in these woods where a semblance of trench warfare saw the antagonists engage in close-quarters combat. The intensity of the fighting in the woods marks this area as the bloodiest battle ground in Luxembourg.

A memorial marks the location of a **mass grave** where 157 German and American soldiers were once buried before their removal to permanent cemeteries. The memorial consists of several large angular granite stones erected to form a stele, altar, and upright memorial. The road intersection near the parking area locates the junction of the two roads leaving Wiltz, where American troops established a roadblock on the night of 19 December only to permit passage of a German fallschirmjäger battalion as described above.

Four '**Remember US**' information panels recall the 'Hell at Schumann's Eck' and the deadly fighting in the forest. Two veterans of the battle — PFC Harry W Harvey from the 90th Infantry Division and Gefreiter Erhard Mitzinnek from the 9th Volksgrenadier Division — attended the inauguration of the Nothum Trail and the denkmal. The panel recalls the massive casualties of the Battle of the Bulge and the grisly task of Graves Registration personnel who recovered and identified the bodies.

The 2.8-kilometer **Nothum Memorial Trail (or Promenade du Souvenir Schumann's Eck)**, named after the village a few kilometers to the south, passes through German and American positions in this forest. The large parking area and nearby battle remnants offer a good alternative to walking the entire Nothum Trail. Two barred roads lead into the forest behind the denkmal; take the road to the left. Immediately upon entering into the woods, one senses that this is a different place. The density of trees limits visibility to 5 to 10 meters. All sound seems to disappear — even road noise from the nearby highway. Along the trail, signposts give detail to the map and provide exact locations of German gun emplacements, shelter trenches, foxholes, bomb craters, and shell holes. Because depressions in the forest floor are slowly being filled by leaves and pine needles washed in during the seventy seasons since the battle, visitors might have to invoke some imagination to recognize each example.

After less than 100 meters, the sentier enters the mixed wood forest on the right. A **German gun emplacement** had lain almost immediately ahead but it is now identified by only a slight depression. Continuing forward, a **trench** to the left of the trail is obvious — straight, still deep, and covered with vegetation. Several impressions by artist Fenand Zens have been erected in the woods and depict battle scenes as viewed by the participants at the exact location of the depicted incident. The first **artist signpost** is 500 meters ahead on the right. The depiction of winter fighting in deep woods borrows from a photograph of advancing German troops at just such a typical location. **Deep trench lines** lie 100 meters farther ahead on both sides of the trail.

The trail rejoins the forest road for a short distance until one achieves a Y-junction and turns right — signs facing in both directions indicate the proper route. The second **artist signpost** is achieved after a total 1.2 kilometers on the right side, approximately 100 meters before a forest road junction. The area around the sign holds clusters of **foxholes** on both sides of the track — just as in the artist's representation. (49.94885, 5.87934) An additional three signposts present differing images of combat.

This site does not present the accurate labeling of the Hasselpat Trail or the public's attention as in the Bois Jacques, but the suggested 1.2-kilometer walk to the second artist sign offers the solitude to contemplate the suffering of men of both armies.

Chapter Six

Skyline Drive

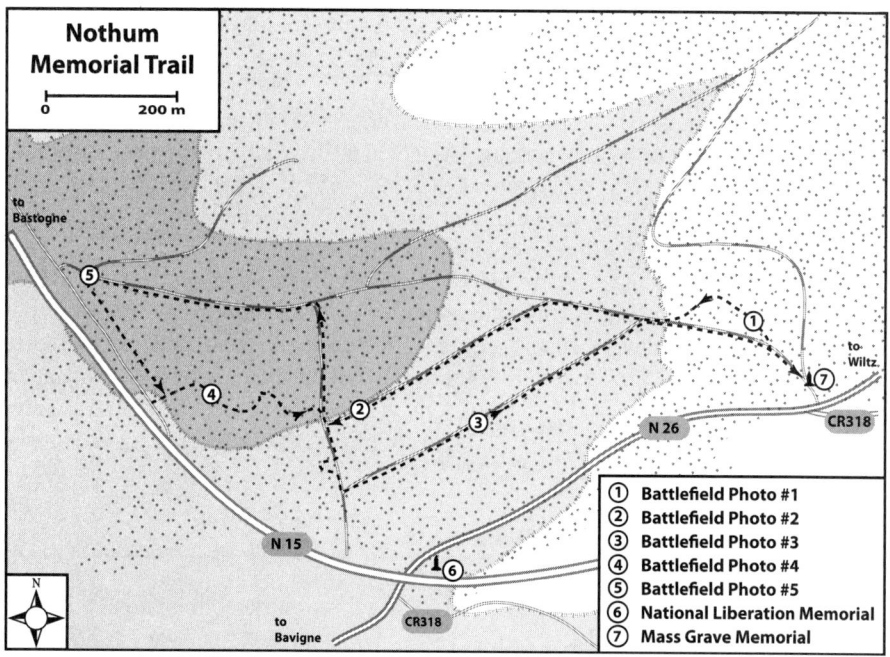

Leave the parking area and turn right onto highway N26. Stop at the memorial on the left 600 m ahead. (49.946767, 5.881253)

The **1944 - 1945 Liberation Memorial** near Schumann's Eck was constructed in celebration of the 50th Anniversary of the liberation of the Grand Duchy of Luxembourg. The memorial provides the appearance of a mostly destroyed building, as would have been the case for any number of the structures in Luxembourgish villages after the war. A central plaque honors the memory of the Allied liberators. Attached to the walls are plaques that display unit symbols and nicknames of the 28th, 26th, and 90th Infantry Divisions and the 6th Cavalry Group that fought in this particular sector. Public subscription funded the memorial.

An inlaid bronze **battle map** adorns a fieldstone wall that shows the local battle lines for 22 and 26 December 1944 and 2 January 1945, along with the movements of six American units. A '**Remember US – Schumann's Eck**' information panel presents a timeline for the Grand Duchy of Luxembourg, starting with its Independence in 1839 to the surrender of Japan to end the Second World War. The site also holds six additional '**Remember US**' information panels that describe local combat during the American evacuation, the start of Third Army's counterattack, renewed fighting at Nothum, Schumann's Eck, Doncols, and the final liberation of Luxembourg. The panels relate the actions of divisional units accompanied by battlefield maps. (49.946870, 5.881489)

The highway triangle holds a recently recovered **German 75-mm Pak 40 antitank gun**. (49.946539, 5.880692)

> Continue 150 m across highway N15 to Café Schumann on the right. (49.945997, 5.879602)

A lone country inn known as Café Schumann stood near the crossroads four kilometers southwest of Wiltz where highway N26 from Wiltz crossed the Ettelbruck–Bastogne highway (N15). The batteries of the 687th Field Artillery Battalion rendezvoused at the café before continuing on toward Poteau de Harlange. (See Other Points of Interest west of Wiltz, below.)

At 1030 on 9 January, Private Ted Long and his company attacked Nothum through deep snow and shrouded in heavy fog. Long was shot in the leg. He lay in the snow until 1630 that day when German soldiers administered aide and took their prisoner to a dugout. Long died during the night. A polished granite plaque hangs on the side of **Café Schumann** along the parking area dedicated to **Private Ted B Long** of Malakoff, Texas from Company L, 359th Regiment, 90th Division.[27] (49.945943, 5.879428)

Other Points of Interest west of Wiltz

> **Berlé**
> On 4 January 1945, German occupying forces ordered the parish priest of Berlé to leave the village that evening. Forty civilians made their way through the snow towards Doncols. They actually wanted to join the Americans at Bavigne, but were turned back by the Germans and forced to seek shelter in the forest.
> On 9 January 1945, the 357th Infantry Regiment, 90th Infantry Division moved to destroy the remaining pocket of enemy troops in the village. Armor from the 712th Tank Battalion and the 773rd Tank Destroyer Battalion led the assault along the road (Um Bierg) from Bavigne. After a 10-minute artillery preparation, the armor-infantry assault teams exited the woods and entered the village. The four-hour engagement netted eighty German prisoners from elements of the 36th Volksgrenadier Division. During the battle, every structure in Berlé, save one, was destroyed. An incomplete record of American losses included at least 4 killed and 14 wounded.
> A field stone near the church bears a plaque to the **90th Infantry Division** commemorating the liberation of the town by that unit. Adjacent, a larger red sandstone carving displays interwoven female figures in memory of the victims of the Second World War.
> Location: 6.8 km west of Wiltz near Duerfstrooss. (49.951467, 5.855042)

> **Poteau de Harlange**
> A rural cafe known as Poteau de Harlange became the temporary command post of the 687th Field Artillery Battalion. The artillerymen had repelled an assault by Fallschirmjäger Regiment 14 earlier in the day near Wiltz by lowering the barrels

---

27   Private Ted B Long is buried in Henderson County, Texas. He was 21 years old.

of their howitzers to engage direct fire upon enemy assault guns. The defense was temporarily successful, but consumed the last of their ammunition. The unit left Wiltz to save its guns and stopped here for a brief rest before continuing toward Bastogne.

About 2000, fallschirmjäger caught up to the artillerymen deployed in the nearby woods and fields and surrounded the battalion staff in the café. Small-arms fire arched to and from the café while the gunners made a stand with rifles and a few .50-caliber machine guns. Under the ghostly white of German flares, mortar fire showered pockets of American resistance.

Suddenly an American convoy carrying men from the 3rd Battalion appeared behind the German paratroopers. At first the Germans were stunned into silence; then they let half the vehicles pass before opening fire. A panzerfaust knocked out a half-track, blocking the road. Burp guns and MG-42s swept the trapped column. Americans jumped from their vehicles only to dive into ditches already occupied by German troops.

After nearly two hours and with most of the defenders down to their last rounds of ammunition, Major Edgar P German, Operations Officer for the artillery battalion who also spoke German, offered to surrender. The fallschirmjäger ceased fire and herded the 110-to-125 captured artillerymen toward the café while a few escaped unnoticed into the night. Battery A escaped capture by fleeing west at the beginning of the engagement followed later by Battery B. Their guns later took part in the defense of Bastogne.

Incredibly, after the prisoners were under guard in the nearby woods, a second American convoy approached from Wiltz. With German roadblocks now in position at the crossroads, few escapees successfully ran the gauntlet. Although a German NCO argued in favor of killing the captives, an arriving German officer decreed against the murder of prisoners.

The crossroads remains little changed. The destroyed café has been rebuilt. A small modern chapel has been built to commemorate the gallant stand of the **687th Field Artillery Battalion** against overwhelming strength and insurmountable firepower.

Location: 12 km southwest of Wiltz at the crossroads of highways CR309 and CR315 (49.908073, 5.808748)

28

---

28 Some controversy among survivors of the engagement exists over its actual location. Some feel that the 687th Field Artillery Battalion fought the fallschirmjäger at Café Schumann, 7.5 kilometers to the northeast, reported as fact in many official histories of the Battle of the Bulge. Recent investigations indicate that the engagement actually took place at Poteau de Harlange. The fact that such uncertainty exists underscores the confusion inherent in the disorganized American withdrawal from Wiltz. Nonetheless, considerable fighting abounded near Café Schumann.

Side Trip: Battle of Dahl and Nocher
6 to 9 January 1945

> Leave Château du Wiltz southwest on rue du Château (N25, becomes N26a). After 1.7 km, turn left toward Goesdorf / Nocher (N12). Follow for 3.5 km to a roundabout. Take the 3rd exit toward Nocher (CR321) and continue 3.7 km. Turn left onto CR331. After 950 m, turn left onto Am Aastert and stop at the memorial on the left. (49.935878, 5.979860) Total distance one-way: 12.1 km

Pushing the German Bulge back toward its starting point required days of arduous combat in increasingly difficult weather conditions. An example of that fighting occurred in the neighboring villages of Dahl and Nocher in early January.

The 319th Infantry Regiment seized Dahl on 6 January in a surprise attack from the south and west after crossing the Sûre River near Heidersheidgrund. Dahl sits upon a plateau whose heights command the terrain for kilometers in every direction. Nearby Nocher offered the same observation potential into the Wiltz River valley to its north. The resulting salient posed a serious threat to German forces in the vicinity of Bastogne, and the German Seventh Army was thus determined to re-establish the line along the Sûre River as far west as Esch-sur-Sûre.

AMERICAN OBJECTIVE	To cut off German troops southeast of Bastogne
FORCES	
American:	319th Infantry Regiment (Colonel William Taylor), 80th 'Blue Ridge' Infantry Division (Major General Horace L McBride)
German:	Führer Grenadier Brigade (Major von Courbière)
RESULT	The town was captured and held
CASUALTIES	
American:	Uncertain
German:	Included in totals for Schumann's Eck
LOCATION	Dahl is 10 km southeast of Wiltz

Battle

On the morning of 7 January, the Führer Grenadier Brigade and elements of the 276th Volksgrenadier Division attacked recently established positions of Company B, 319th Infantry Regiment, 80th Infantry Division under a barrage from 108 guns. Heavy American artillery fire beat back the assault.

At 0500 on 8 January, German artillery delivered a 45-minute barrage on the company's positions in Dahl before renewing the attack again assisted by elements of the 276th VGD. The assault collapsed against determined American resistance.

After the German attacks failed, their forces assumed a defensive posture, but battles for possession of Dahl and Nocher continued for 10 days with repeated assaults and counterattacks.

Chapter Six

Battlefield Tour

A 9-man squad commanded by Sergeant Day G Turner served as an outpost in foxholes dug in the frozen fields around an isolated farmhouse known as Am Aastert on the eastern outskirts of Dahl. The German assault started along a ravine that approached Dahl from neighboring Nocher and ended a short distance behind the farmhouse. Turner's squad withdrew under fire into the farmhouse. Repeated enemy attacks across an open field between the ravine and the town were repulsed with heavy losses. Supported by direct panzer fire, German infantry finally gained entrance to the farmhouse, but the intrepid Sgt Turner refused to surrender. Turner shot the first two attackers to crash through the door. His rifle empty, he boldly flung a flaming oil lamp at the next three who then ran out of the house into the snow to extinguish their burning clothing. Turner fought doggedly from room to room, closing with the enemy in fierce hand-to-hand encounters. He hurled handgrenade after handgrenade, bayoneted two Germans who had rushed a doorway he was defending, and, with his weapon useless, fought on with a captured German MP40 machine pistol. The savage fight raged for four hours, and finally, with only three men of the defending squad unwounded, the enemy surrendered. Twenty-five prisoners were taken, with eleven enemy dead and an unknown number of wounded.

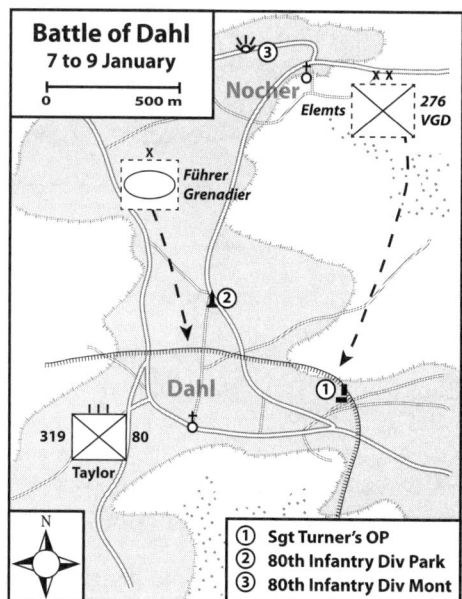

The house that Sgt Turner so vigorous defended sits near the edge of the village where a simple sign, 'S/Sgt Turner,' indicates the last turn onto a residential street. The rose garden beside the house holds a quarry-stone monument bearing the emblem of the **Unites States Medal of Honor**. Beneath, a plaque recognizes Turner's award. Americans are welcomed by the elderly Madame Leners, who has lived in the house all her life and witnessed the battle for the village. A **'Remember US'** information panel briefly describes the 5th and 80th Infantry Divisions drive against the Bulge. The text continues with Sergeant Turner's Medal of Honor citation that describes the defense his men waged around the then-isolated farmhouse.

> Reverse direction and after 160 m turn right onto Um Aale (CR331). Stop at the roadside park 600 m ahead on the left. (49.93892, 5.97266)

A small roadside park at a highway junction outside of Dahl holds a tree-shaded memorial stone honoring six local citizens who died as conscripted members of the German Army. An additional plaque is dedicated to the **80th Infantry Division** on the 50th Anniversary of the battle. The beautiful location provides sweeping views of Dahl and Nocher.

> Proceed north toward Nocher (CR331). After 1.0 km, turn left onto Um Knupp (CR321b) and continue 240 m to the memorial on the right. (49.94755, 5.97552)

Nocher commemorates local combat with a new memorial of unusual and graphic design located upon a ridge at a scenic overview of the Wiltz River valley to the north. A fieldstone plinth supports a curved stone arc bearing three plaques emblematic of Pennsylvania, Virginia and West Virginia, the states of the National Guard units that comprised the 80th Division. A separate stone displays the three-mountain-ridge insignia of the **80th 'Blue Ridge' Infantry Division**.

[29]

Other Points of Interest south of Wiltz

Kaundorf
The **Bomb Monument** stands at the southern edge of the village along highway CR 316 to Esch-sur Sûre. The bomb solemnizes the inhabitants and the allied troops who lived through the horror of the Battle of the Ardennes. It was dropped by a US aircraft during a flight on Christmas Day 1944 and later found in a wood near the monument. The memorial was inaugurated on 28 September 1980. Location: beside highway 316 at the southeastern outskirts of Kaundorf. (49.918320, 5.906960)

Other Points of Interest north of Wiltz

Eschweiler
At 0900 on 18 December, Panzer Lehr's Reconnaissance Battalion 130 followed by Panzergrenadier Regiment 902 crossed the Clerf River near Draufelt and continued southwest toward Eschweiler, personally led by General Bayerlein.

The 28th Division's 728th Reconnaissance Troop (Mechanized) that had been stationed in the town for the past month came under major attack. Artillery fire set parts of the village on fire. By 1300 enemy troops had bypassed the village, such that American unit commander Captain Lewis Meisenhelter ordered his sixty men to board the surviving six jeeps and proceed to Wiltz. The small convoy fell into a German ambush.

Private George Mergenthaler, a Princeton graduate of a wealthy Rye, New York family manned a machine gun mounted on the back of a jeep during the troop's attempted escape. Mergenthaler got off a few rounds before his gun jammed. While a German soldier crawled forward with his burp gun at the ready, Mergenthaler frantically worked to unjam his gun while calling to his buddies to make a run for it.

---

29   Sergeant Day G Turner, from Berwick, Pennsylvania, was killed one month after this engagement during an assault upon a Westwall bunker near Wallendorf. He was awarded the Medal of Honor posthumously and is buried in Luxembourg American Cemetery, Luxembourg City, Luxembourg. He was 23 years old.

Chapter Six

Skyline Drive 283

The private got off a few more rounds before the burp gun cut him down.

German troops temporarily buried Mergenthaler's body in a shallow grave that was discovered the following spring. Local townspeople remembered Mergenthaler as a well-liked young man who spoke both French and German. His family paid to rebuild the town church after the war. The villagers committed to never forget the sacrifice made for their liberation by someone from so far away.

South of Eschweiler on highway CR328, a sign with white and black lettering '**Memorial George Mergenthaler US GI 18.12.44**' indicates a forest road that sharply descends the hill. The forest road is not drivable in wet weather and, unfortunately, the highway provides no space to park. Continue 300 m towards Eschweiler, where a farm road allows safe parking. The monument is 60 meters down the hillside. (49.988184, 5.959849)

The moss-covered memorial stone states, in French, 'At this point on 18 December 1944 the valiant American soldier George O. Mergenthaler was killed for the liberty of the world. He was reburied by Curé A[ntoine] Bodson in the cemetery in Eschweiler until the day of his transfer to New York in 1947. In recognition by the Andre Wolf family of Luxembourg.' Below it states, 'My father do not fear; I will defend you.'

Location: 4.5 km northeast of Wiltz beside highway CR328. (49.988070, 5.959967)

A plaque in the village church also honors his memory with the words, 'This only son died that others' sons might live in love and peace.' A stained glass window and wall mural also commemorate Private Mergenthaler.

[30]

Pintsch

On 17 December, two tanks of 2nd Platoon, Company B occupied defensive positions around Pintsch but were overrun at 2130 during a strong enemy infantry and armor attack supported by artillery. Surviving personnel withdrew to Wilwerwiltz, where they were consolidated in the defense of headquarters. All combat vehicles at Pintsche were lost.

In January 1945, the 317th Infantry Regiment freed local villages from German occupation in a severe fight for the area. Five villages erected a monument in honor of the **317 Regiment, 80th Infantry Division**. The memorial plaque sits atop a granite stone outside the cemetery walls at the outskirts of the village.
Location: 11 km northeast of Wiltz 650 m down Op der Tomm from highway CR324. (49.992320, 6.006012)

Last Stand before Bastogne
18 December 1944

Colonel Joseph H Gilbreth, commander of CCR, 9th Armored Division divided his command into three task forces placing Task Force Rose[31] at Antoniushof,

---

30 Private George Ottmar Mergenthaler was 23 years old.

31 Task Force Rose was commanded by Captain Lawrence K Rose and consisted of Company A, 2nd Tank Battalion; Company C, 52nd Armored Infantry Battalion; and a platoon from Company C, 9th Armored Engineer Battalion.

Task Force Harper[32] at Féitsch, and Task Force Booth[33] as reserve in nearby Moinet. The established roadblocks became the last obstacle between the 2nd Panzer Division and Bastogne.

German Objective	To capture Bastogne.
Forces	
American:	Combat Command R (Colonel Joseph Gilbreth), 9th Armored Division
German:	Panzer Reconnaissance Battalion 2 (Hauptmann von Böhm) and Panzer Regiment 3 (Oberstleutnant Carl von Wagner), 2nd Panzer Division
Result	Efforts to stop the German advance were pushed aside
Casualties	Period 16 to 31 December:
American:	800 killed, wounded, or missing
German:	unknown
Location	Antoniushaff is 17 km north of Wiltz, Luxembourg and 20 km northeast of Bastogne, Belgium

Battle

At Antoniushaff (Antonuishof), Captain Rose spread his tanks across the flat, wind-swept fields that surrounded the crossroads with his infantry in foxholes 300 meters in front of the tanks. On the morning of 18 December, three PzKpfw IVs from 2nd Panzer Division's Reconnaissance Battalion 2 approached from the woods north of the Clervaux road. In an exchange of fire, one panzer was destroyed and the other two withdrew.

That afternoon panzers from Panzer Regiment 3 and armored infantry approached to within 800 meters under cover of a smoke screen. Shells from PzKpfw IVs and Vs rocked the infantry foxholes and buffeted the Shermans. The American 73rd Armored Field Artillery Battalion, positioned six kilometers away at Allerborn, answered in kind. For a short time the Shermans gave as good as they got, knocking out three PzKpfw IVs while losing two Shermans to enemy fire and a third to mechanical failure. However, as American infantry withdrew under direct fire from the German tanks, they left the Shermans without infantry support. One company of Shermans could not hold off two battalions of panzers.

---

32 Task Force Harper was commanded by Lieutenant Colonel Ralph Harper and consisted of Company C, 2nd Tank Battalion and Company B, 52nd Armored Infantry Battalion.

33 Task Force Booth was commanded by Lieutenant Colonel Robert M Booth and consisted of Headquarters Company and two platoons of Company A, 52nd Armored Infantry Battalion; a platoon of tank destroyers from 811th Tank Destroyer Battalion; and a platoon of light tanks from Company D, 2nd Tank Battalion.

Colonel Gilbreth, headquartered in nearby Longvilly and aware of the danger to Task Force Rose from radio reports, contacted General Middleton with a request to withdraw. Middleton, who had sent CCR forward as a sacrificial delay, refused.

By 1430, Task Force Rose was surrounded on three sides. German assault guns laced the American positions with white phosphorous shells driving the surviving Shermans to the rear slope behind the farmstead. In the early winter darkness, Company A commander Lieutenant John De Roche led the remaining five tanks and the assault gun platoon overland toward Houffalize, where they were later ambushed and destroyed. A few survivors made their way into Bastogne. However, the destruction of Task Force Rose cost the Germans seven daylight hours on their way to Bastogne.

After eliminating Task Force Rose at Antoniushaff, von Lauchert's 2nd Panzer Division continued southwest on highway N12 toward Allerborn. Lieutenant Colonel Harper had fashioned his blocking force at Féitsch, one kilometer to Allerborn's east, much like Captain Rose – tanks and half-tracks deployed in an arc on both sides of the junction and to the east. For the past few hours, the men heard the reports of rifles and guns coming from the fighting at Antoniushaff. American artillery positioned in Longvilly answered a sudden German artillery barrage. By 2000, panzergrenadiers began infiltrating American positions hidden from American observation by the engulfing darkness but aided by panzer-mounted infrared vision equipment.[34] Panzers fired and Shermans started to explode; then a Panther did the same from Sherman fire.

Within 15 minutes, the overwhelming German firepower annihilated Task Force Harper, destroying all of the task force's twenty-four tanks. Dispirited American troops disappeared into the night retreating west to Longvilly, where they would again meet German armor (see Chapter Seven). Lt Col Harper was killed near Houffalize during the attempted withdrawal when he dismounted his vehicle to view the terrain.[35]

Colonel Theodore Seeley, Colonel Fuller's predecessor as commander of 110th Regiment who was that day returning from the hospital from injuries suffered in the Hürtgen Forest, gathered 260 stragglers from his old regiment around Allerborn. His group constituted the last troops between 2nd Panzer Division and Bastogne but, without armor or even a bazooka, Seeley had few options. German panzers shelled Seeley's command post in the village school and the colonel was captured, although some of his men made an escape.[36]

---

34 The first military applications of night vision devices were introduced by the German Army in 1939. Nevertheless, by 1943, infrared searchlights and image converters with rangefinders had been mounted on no more than fifty Panther tanks.

35 Lieutenant Colonel Ralph S Harper was awarded the Bronze Star and is buried in Union Cemetery, Columbus, Ohio. He was 32 years old.

36 Colonel Theodore Seeley was the second senior officer captured that day. Both he and Colonel Fuller were recorded as regimental commanders. This brought no end of confusion to the German intelligence officers who believed that Seeley could be commander of a yet undiscovered infantry regiment. Seeley did nothing to disabuse his captors of the misconception.

Seeley was imprisoned at Oflag 113B in Hammelburg, Germany. After the failed attempt to liberate the officers at the camp, Seeley, along with numerous others, was marched southward. On 5 April they came under a nighttime Allied bombing at Nürnberg. Thirty American prisoners were killed in the raid, but Seeley survived although wounded by bomb fragments. He was liberated in May 1945.

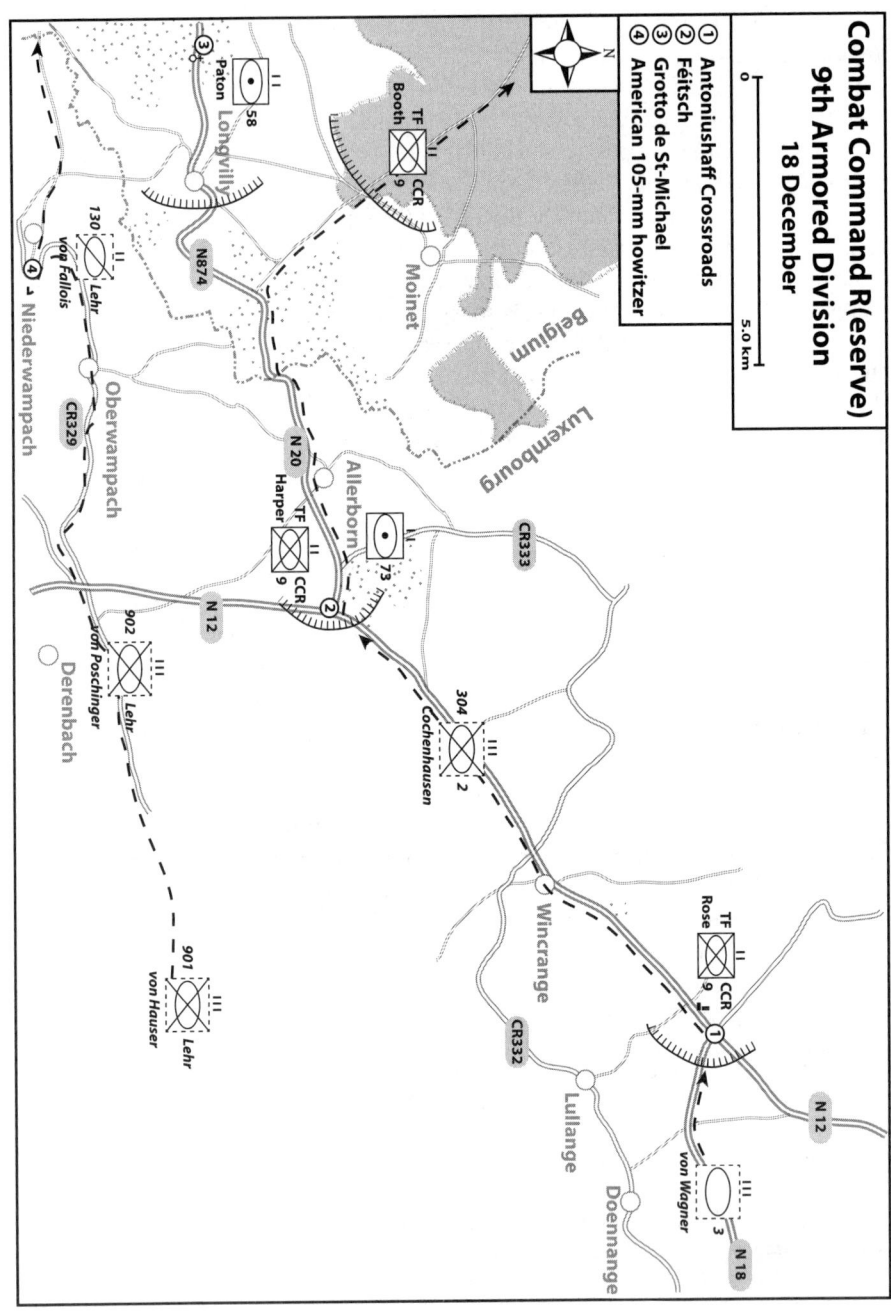

Task Force Booth deployed on a broad hilltop east of Moinet. Booth and his men dug in along both sides of the road backed by the tank destroyers. They held their positions while 2nd Panzer Division flanked the unit on its way to Bourcy. On 19 December, Colonel Booth led his men through Bourcy to Hardigny three kilometers northeast of Noville, where they became surrounded by that same division. The unit surrendered, although 225 men did manage to reach the Bastogne perimeter. Colonel Booth, injured during the withdrawal, was captured.[37]

Battlefield Tour

> Leave Wiltz northeast toward Clervaux (N12). Follow for 16.7 km before turning onto the minor road on the right. (50.067435, 5.933050)

The tour exits the deep forests of Luxembourg to enter an area of open fields, scattered tree plantations, and moderately level terrain — an area that permitted rapid advance and deployment favored by German armored tacticians.

The crossroad known as Antoniushaff was, as the saying goes, in the middle of nowhere. It held no town or village and lay near only one lonely structure in a nearby field. What it did have was roadways. The main east-west highway N18 from Clervaux ended there in a junction with highway N12 from St-Vith. The highway continued to the southwest before curving south at another lonely road junction at Féitsch, where highway N20 rolled west directly into Bastogne.

Antonuishaff crossroads, now a large, modern roundabout, is 220 meters to the northeast of the rural turn-off. German troops first appeared when they exited the copse visible across plowed fields to the east. Captain Rose's infantry held foxhole positions in an arc across highway N18, which crests at the corner of Lëlgerkamp woods and loses 11 meters of elevation descending into the road junction through a slight cut. The large farm that gave its name to the crossroad stands directly west and across the road. The terrain falls rather precipitously west of the farm buildings, precluding unobserved escape.

> Reverse direction (N12) and, after 4.8 km, turn into the parking area on the right (50.036882, 5.886514)

Féitsch intersection remains a rather barren location occupied only by a gas station and pizzeria restaurant. Draws to the northeast allowed German panzers and grenadiers to approach Harper's defenses undetected.

> Leave the parking area toward Bastogne (N20, becomes Belgian N874) and follow for 14.6 km into Bastogne.

This completes the Skyline Drive tour.

---

37   Lieutenant Colonel Robert M Booth was imprisoned in Oflag 79 near Braunschweig, Germany. The officers were housed in a large brick building that had once been the home of a German parachute regiment. The camp was liberated on 12 April 1945.

Chapter Seven
Defense of Bastogne
19 December 1944 to 16 January 1945

The German High Command agreed with Adolf Hitler that the capture of Bastogne was critical to the success of Operation HERBSTNEBEL — not that Hitler would have countenanced any disagreement. Von Manteuffel concurred and, since Bastogne lay almost 50 kilometers west of the German start line along the Our River, his plan to seize Bastogne employed a sudden surprise assault — a *coup de main*. General der Panzertruppe Heinrich Freiherr von Lüttwitz's XLVII Panzer Corps placed the 26th Volksgrenadier Division in the fore followed by Panzer Lehr along a route from Gemünd, Germany. The 2nd Panzer Division used a roughly parallel route passing to the north of Bastogne through Noville. In case of resistance, Panzer Lehr was to bypass to the south and leave Bastogne for capture by the grenadiers.

Bastogne was a minor city of only 3,500 inhabitants, but seven hard-surface routes radiated out from the city. In mid-December, the open fields around Bastogne were soft and muddy, and other approaches were too hilly or blocked by dense woods; therefore, German armor attack routes were limited to the seven roads.

The 82nd and 101st Airborne Divisions offered the Supreme Headquarters Allied Expeditionary Force's (SHAEF) only reserves. Eisenhower released the formations to Bradley, who assigned them to General Ridgway's XVIII Airborne Corps. The 82nd, further along in refitting after its Market Garden experience, departed on 18 December toward Bastogne. When word came down that Kampfgruppe Peiper was in La Gleize, the 82nd was redirected to Werbomont (see Chapter Three).

Expecting a quiet Christmas in France, the 101st Airborne Division's commander, Major General Maxwell Taylor, flew to Washington DC to discuss a reorganization of paratroop forces. The assistant commander, Brigadier General Gerald Higgins, traveled to England to deliver an after-action report on the Holland operations. Artillery commander Brigadier General Anthony C McAuliffe[1] operated as the unit's acting division commander. Each of the divisions three parachute infantry regiments rostered 2,330 men; a fourth glider infantry regiment held 2,940 men.

The division received orders to assemble and leave its camp near Reims, France at 0800 on 17 December. Open trucks transported the division 170 kilometers (107 miles) over eight hours through freezing sleet, cold rain, and occasional snow – arriving at a staging area west of Bastogne near Mande St-Etienne late on 18 December. The men left their trucks and marched east to the sound of the guns. General McAuliffe established his temporary headquarters in the Hotel de Commerce facing the train station. Thirty-six hours later, Lieutenant General Troy H Middleton, commander of VIII Corps then headquartered in Bastogne, left for new headquarters in Neufchâteau whereas McAuliffe moved his headquarters to Heintz Barracks.

---

1   Brigadier Anthony C McAuliffe, a native of Washington DC, was a career military officer and West Point graduate in 1918. Between the world wars, McAuliffe participated in the development of the bazooka and the jeep. He parachuted into Normandy, entered Holland by glider, and arrived in Bastogne by jeep. He died in 1975 at age 77 and is buried in Arlington National Cemetery, Arlington, Virginia.

Chapter Seven

Artillery was to play an important part in the defense of Bastogne and, in that arm of service, the defenders were well equipped. The 101st Division included its 377th and 463rd Parachute Field Artillery (PFA) Battalions manning light 75-mm Pack howitzers. Its 321st Parachute Field Artillery Battalion and the 907th Glider Field Artillery (GFA) Battalion manned snub-nosed 105-mm howitzers. The 333rd and 969th Field Artillery Battalions, part of Corps artillery, held 155-mm towed 'Long Tom' field guns. McAuliffe created an artillery park on the western outskirts of Bastogne where guns were stationed, limbered, and ready to respond to any enemy incursion of the defensive perimeter.[2]

Generalleutnant Fritz Hermann Bayerlein's Panzer Lehr led the attack toward Bastogne. This *Wehrmacht* division, sometimes referred to as 130th Panzer Lehr Division, was an elite command formed in 1943 as a training and demonstration unit. Therefore, it was generously equipped with tanks and half-tracks. The unit suffered near annihilation during Normandy's Operation COBRA and required extensive replenishment and refitting. During its advance toward Bastogne, Panzer Lehr became entangled with the horse-drawn units of the 26th Volksgrenadier Division, thus causing delays in launching its attack upon the city.

During the evening of 18 December, General Eisenhower realized that the German effort was not a local spoiling attack, but the beginning of a major offensive. The next morning he held a meeting of his senior American commanders in the dank, but bomb-proof, caverns of the ancient Verdun Citadel. Eisenhower dispelled the prevailing doom with the admonition that there should 'only be cheerful faces' in the room.

Eisenhower saw the opportunity for a major victory now that German forces had vacated their Westwall defenses. In response, he shifted the operational boundary between Lieutenant General Jacob Devers's 6th Army Group and Bradley's 21st Army Group which in turn released Lieutenant General George S Patton Jr's Third Army from responsibility for the front along the Saar River. Eisenhower ordered Patton to organize a counterattack against the already sizable bulge with at least six divisions. He asked his general 'When can you start?' Patton promised one of the most dazzling performances of the Second World War by committing to three divisions on the move within 48 hours. Eisenhower was incredulous, fearful of impetuous Patton committing troops piecemeal. The logistical and operational issues involved in relieving three divisions facing east and in contact with the enemy, turning them to the north, and moving them over 100 miles in winter weather over a meager road network for a major counterattack seemed too daunting to be accomplished in so short a timeframe.

What Ike did not know is that Patton had already ordered his staff to prepare three alternatives for how the Third Army might counter the Bulge. The transmission of a single code word launched execution of the selected operational program. With a telephone call back to his headquarters, the 4th Armored Division started to roll

---

2 The M116 75-mm Pack howitzer was a relatively light, towed gun developed to be horse-drawn before it underwent several evolutions and modifications. Its low weight made it well suited to parachute delivery or disassembly into six man-carried sections.

The M3 105-mm howitzer was a lighter, smaller version of the M2. The gun tube had been shortened by 27 inches, thus the 'snub-nosed' name.

toward Arlon, the 80th Infantry Division toward Luxembourg, and the 26th Infantry Division stood on alert.

German Objective	To capture the road junction city of Bastogne
Forces	
American:	101st Airborne Division (Brigadier General Anthony McAuliffe) and CCB, 10th Armored Division (Colonel William Roberts), including 40 Sherman tanks and 6 artillery battalions
German:	26th Volksgrenadier Division (Generalmajor Heintz Kokott) and Panzer Lehr (Generalleutnant Fritz Hermann Bayerlein)
Result	The city was held against attack by superior armored forces
Casualties	
American:	101st Airborne: 1,641 killed, wounded, injured, or missing CCB, 10th Armored Division: 503 total casualties Attached units: 205 total casualties
German:	3,000 killed, wounded, or missing
Civilians:	782 killed
Location	Bastogne is 92 km south of Liège

Battle Summary

After the collapse of Task Force Harper on the evening of 18 December, (see Chapter Six) the survivors of CCR, 9th Armored Division, withdrew to Longvilly where the unit's commander, Colonel Joseph H Gilbreth, gathered what forces he could. Nevertheless, his weak defensive line was temporarily saved when the 2nd Panzer Division turned northwest toward Bourcy and Noville instead of continuing straight into Bastogne, which was not its assigned objective.

Also on 18 December, the first elements of CCB, 10th Armored Division arrived in Bastogne. Middleton and the unit's commander, Colonel William Roberts, divided the unit into combat teams named for their commanders and assigned one for each of the three Bastogne roadways under threat. Team O'Hara moved southeast to Wardin; Team Cherry moved east to strengthen CCR, 9th Armored Division near Longvilly; and Team Desobry hastened north to Noville. CCB, 10th Armored Division added to the defensive artillery strength with its 420th Armored Field Artillery Battalion manning M7 'Priest' 105-mm self-propelled howitzers.

By 19 December, units of the 101st Airborne Division sought to establish a perimeter defense to the east and north of Bastogne. Lieutenant Colonel Julian J Ewell's 501st Parachute Infantry Regiment (PIR) marched east to Neffe, where it encountered panzers of Panzer Lehr. Colonel Ewell proceed to fan his three battalions in an arc from north of Bizory to west of Neffe and through Marvie to the Arlon highway.

Colonel Robert F Sink marched his 506th PIR north to reinforce Team Desobry in Noville, but their combined force fell under fire from a superior armored

Chapter Seven

The Defense of Bastogne 291

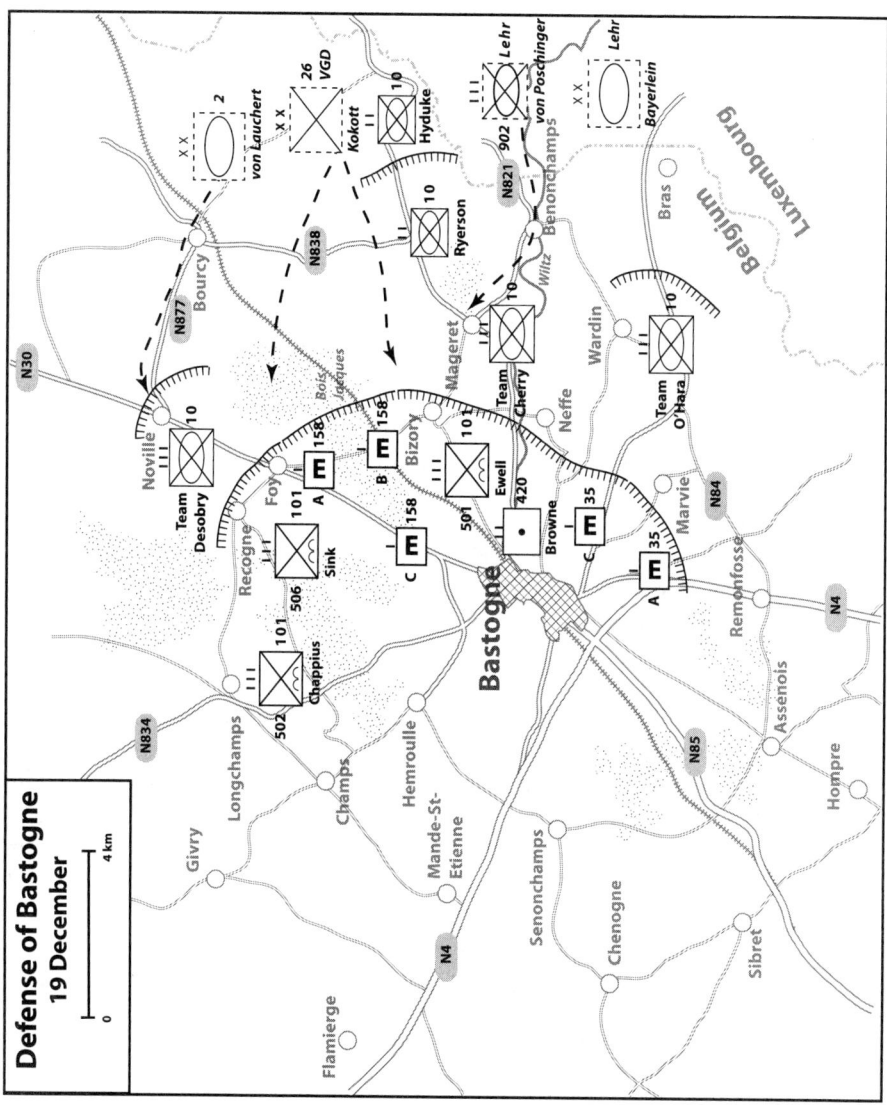

detachment of 2nd Panzer Division. On the afternoon of 20 December, the paratroopers and armor engaged in a scrambling withdrawal before establishing a perimeter arc from the junction with the 501st through Foy to Recogne. Colonel Steve Chappius's 502nd PIR extended the perimeter west from Recogne to Longchamps.

The 327th Glider Infantry Regiment (GIR), under command of Colonel Joseph H Harper,[3] took over defense of Marvie to the southeast when the 501st

---

[3] Not to be confused with Lieutenant Colonel Ralph S Harper of Task Force Harper, CCR, 9th Armored Division, who was killed on 18 December.

PIR shortened its line. The regiment's 3rd Battalion assumed responsibility of the Flamierge salient while the 502nd PIR extended its perimeter to meet it at Champs.[4]

McAuliffe, facing almost complete encirclement, realized that an attempt to evacuate his forces from Bastogne would probably result in their destruction. Although roads to Ourtheuville, Neufchâteau, and Arlon were still open, he decided to remain, as being surrounded did not intimidate airborne troops.

Late on 20 December, General von Lüttwitz realized that his XLVII Panzer Corps was not strong enough to capture the city by direct assault, even though 2nd Panzer Division had cut the roadway west to Marche while moving toward its fate at Celles (see Chapter Four). He requested use of 2nd Panzer Division to continue from Noville into Bastogne, but von Manteuffel refused by emphasizing its directive to achieve the Meuse. Oberst Heintz Kokott's 26th Volksgrenadier Division assumed the responsibility to isolate the city and accomplished the task on 20 December by cutting the road to Neufchâteau. The next day Kokott received an order from von Manteuffel. His infantry, strengthened by Panzergrenadier Regiment (PGR) 901 from Panzer Lehr, was to capture Bastogne.

By the morning of 21 December, the opposing forces in the battle for the city were set. McAuliffe fielded his four airborne regiments; seven artillery battalions; 40 tanks and an armored infantry battalion from CCB, 10th Armored Division; and the 705th Tank Destroyer Battalion.

On 22 December, while the first snow began to fall, General McAuliffe refused a German surrender demand with classic aplomb, while Kokott applied scattered pressure on Bastogne, hoping the shortage of supplies would eventually force McAuliffe to surrender.

After the snowfall, plunging temperatures solidified the previously muddy fields around the city. The paratroopers, ill-equipped for the cold, coped with the rigors of trench foot; armor and artillery troops' bare fingers froze to metal weapons, and night-time wind chill numbed faces. Now they faced two enemies — the Germans and the weather — and the weather was only to worsen.

The cold derived from a high pressure system known as a 'Russian High' also brought brilliant sunshine. The leaden skies that had dominated the Ardennes since the battle began finally broke. Starting at 1150 on 23 December, an armada of 241 C-47 'Dakota' transport planes dropped supplies into the encircled city. The color-coded parachutes identified the contents of the canisters — ammunition, water, rations, medical supplies, etc. They arrived none too early. P-47 fighters from the XIX Tactical Air Command came as well. Intended to act as escort for the lumbering transport planes, the fighter pilots could not resist the temptation of firing upon German positions.

Oberst Kokott's 26th Volksgrenadiers collapsed the Flamierge salient west of

---

4   Originally each of three glider infantry regiments fielded only two battalions. In March 1944, the 1st Battalion, 401st Glider Infantry Regiment became the 327th Glider Infantry Regiment's 3rd Battalion, and the 2nd Battalion, 401st Glider Infantry Regiment became the 325th Glider Infantry Regiment's 3rd Battalion. The original 401st retained the A, B, and C designations for its companies, whose designations also occurred in the 327th Regiment's 1st Battalion. For the purposes of clarity, we will retain the 1st Battalion, 401st GIR name.

Bastogne and drove back 1st Battalion, 401st GIR two miles while capturing Mande St-Etienne. Kokott, now fortified by a regimental combat team from Panzergrenadier Regiment 115, attacked from the northwest between Champs and Mande-St-Etienne on Christmas morning. Although Kokott's armor rolled through the lines of 1st Battalion, 401st GIR behind Mande St-Etienne, tank destroyers took their toll, machine gunners stripped the grenadiers from the sides of the panzers, and the 463rd PFAB finished off the enemy tanks. To the north, the 502nd PIR held firm in Champs as tank destroyers eliminated a second panzer column.

General Patton, good to his commitment, drove his 4th Armored Division's CCA along the Arlon road and the division's CCB from Habay to La Neuvre along secondary roads. However, both met increased resistance when they approached Bastogne. On 26 December, the division's CCR made the final breakthrough by-passing the heavily defended Neufchâteau road to enter the Bastogne perimeter along a secondary road through Assenois. The next day, Major General Maxwell Taylor entered Bastogne to resume command of his division.

Hitler accepted the analysis of his Armed Forces Operation Staff that his armies could not cross the Meuse. He decided to fight east of the river. To do that, he had to eliminate Bastogne, the ever-present threat to his lines of communication and supply. Hitler issued orders for an all-out effort to take Bastogne. Manteuffel re-routed divisions from all sectors of the Bulge for a concentrated attack. The Führer Begleit Brigade disengaged from its fight at Hotton and marched southwest. The Sixth Panzer Army's 1st, 9th, and 12th SS Panzer Divisions attacked the city from three directions. The Führer Begleit Brigade, 3rd Panzergrenadier Division, Führer Grenadier Brigade, 167th VGD, and 340th VGD were also en route. The realignment of German units provided a pause in their attacks from 27 to 29 December. By 1 January 1945, eight German divisions pressured the defenders.

American strength also grew. The supply problems, especially in artillery shells, medical supplies, and winter clothing, ended with their arrival by truck convoy, parachute, and gliders of the IX Troop-Carrier Command. On 28 December, entering from the Arlon Road, CCA, 4th Armored Division joined the division's CCR in the city. The 318th Infantry Regiment, 80th Infantry Division also arrived to attach to the 4th Armored. From Neufchâteau, CCA, 9th Armored Division and the remainder of 705th Tank Destroyer Battalion arrived.

With the corridor into Bastogne still tenuous, Eisenhower released the 87th Infantry Division and 11th Armored Division, both newly arrived from England, to Third Army and ordered them to expand Bastogne's lifeline by attacking northwards across ground 20 kilometers west of Bastogne. There, on 30 December, the two units hit the flank of an attack by the battle weary Panzer Lehr and 26th Volksgrenadier Division to cut the supply corridor. Meanwhile, the 26th and 35th Infantry Divisions and 4th Armored Division artillery defeated 1st SS Panzer Division and 167th Volksgrenadier Division efforts to cut the supply corridor through Assenois. These tough engagements continued through 4 January with substantial casualties to both sides. German attacks, seventeen in all, resumed against the Bastogne perimeter on 31 December. By 1 January, the 6th Armored Division had entered Bastogne and taken over the Bizory sector.

On New Year's Day, the Luftwaffe made its last major appearance over the American battlefields. Early that morning, 1,035 bombers and fighters appeared over Allied airfields catching American and British planes on the ground. Although hundreds of Allied planes were destroyed, it was a Pyrrhic victory. German losses of pilots were also heavy — and they could not be replaced.

American commanders agreed to cut off the German bulge by attacking from north and south toward Houffalize. General Collin's VII Corps attacked south from Manhay through Parker's Crossroads toward Houffalize along the axis of the Bastogne–Liège highway. General Gavin's 82nd Airborne recovered positions that it had abandoned between the Salm River and Baraque-de-Fraiture.

The re-supplied and re-invigorated 101st Airborne Division was also ready for offensive operations. On 2 January, American forces began their push against the German encirclement from the south. The 1st Battalion, 506th PIR fought through the lines of its 2nd Battalion in Bois Jacques. The 6th Armored Division, which had assumed the 501st PIR's positions south and east of the Bourcy rail line, moved against Arloncourt and liberated Bizory and Mageret. Team Cherry and a company from 327th GIR retook Senonchamps after CCA, 9th Armored Division had widened the corridor in that area the day before. On 3 January the pressure continued. The 6th Armored re-took Neffe and pushed to the outskirts of Wardin. The CCB, 11th Armored Division liberated Mande St-Etienne.

The worst enemy was again the weather, but the grinding success of the infantry forced Hitler to realize defeat. On 8 January, he authorized a withdrawal to a north-south line just west of the Bastogne–Liège highway. Fuel shortages and the sinking morale of troops who realized that the grand last gamble was a bust hampered Manteuffel's efforts to save his spearheads.

After three days of re-organizing the front line and assimilating fresh units (17th Airborne and 90th Infantry Divisions), Patton struck from the south with four infantry divisions, two airborne divisions, and two armored divisions. While 90th Infantry Division made the main effort against the eastern shoulder of the corridor, the 101st Airborne and 4th Armored Divisions moved north toward Noville against stubborn infantry resistance and heavy artillery, mortar, and Nebelwerfer fire.

On 12 January, the long-awaited Soviet winter offensive began, prompting the transfer of the Sixth Panzer Army to the Eastern Front. On 14 January north of Bastogne, amid counterpunches, enemy troops fought to hold open the Houffalize escape route for its withdrawing units. On 15 January, the pace quickened. The 101st finally took Noville, the division's objective for the past twelve days, and German troops abandoned Houffalize. At 1140 on 16 January, Company F, 41st Armored Infantry Battalion, 2nd Armored Division occupied a hillside south of Houffalize where a six-man patrol from the 41st Armored Reconnaissance Squadron, 11th Armored Division emerged from the woods. The Bulge was closed. Twelve days later, the battle lines of 16 December 1944 were restored, and the Battle of the Bulge was over.

Chapter Seven

The Defense of Bastogne

Battlefield Tour Summary
The battlefield tour starts in Bastogne with a review of locations made famous during this intensive engagement. Excursions then leave the city center to view battlefield sites where combat raged around the city's perimeter.

Highly Recommended Sites
Bastogne: Place McAuliffe, Museum le Mess, Heintz Barracks, Bastogne War Museum, Mardasson Memorial
Bras: Bastogne Ardennes 44 Museum
Noville: Desobry Memorial
Foy: Bois Jacques
Houffalize: Panther Ausf G (PzKpfw V)

Bastogne

Medieval Bastogne was a center of religious and economic development in ancient Luxembourg. Monasteries dotted the rolling hills among the farmsteads. In 1332, John the Blind, king of Bohemia, surrounded the town center with defensive walls. The town prospered until the end of the First World War. Nazis occupied Bastogne on 10 May 1940 at the beginning of their *Blitzkrieg* across Northern France. American forces liberated its citizens in September 1944.

At 1925 on Christmas Eve, formations of German Junker 88 aircraft dropped their payloads upon the center of Bastogne. The frigid winter night exploded in arrays of high-explosive, fragmentation, and incendiary bombs under bright magnesium flares. The only defense was to hide in deep cellars. The 10th Armored Division was especially hard hit with bombs falling upon its aid station and the Team Cherry command post. The .50-caliber machine guns of the 81st Antiaircraft Battalion could do little against the low-altitude planes that appeared and disappeared rapidly from view. The Americans had aimed their large caliber antiaircraft guns toward ground targets, and, by the time they re-adjusted, the enemy aircraft were gone.

The city of Bastogne takes immense pride in its historic defense. Nine Sherman tank gun turrets mounted upon fieldstone plinths symbolically guard the approaches to the city. The guns targeted the attacking German forces' approach. Many of the city's streets are named after heroes of the defense, marked by their distinctive identification signs.

Maison du Tourisme
Place McAuliffe 60
Tel: +32 (0)61 26 76 11
Web: http://www.bastogne-tourisme.be/

6600 Bastogne, Belgium
Email: info@bastogne-tourisme.be

> The tour begins in the heart of Bastogne in place du général McAuliffe. (50.000762, 5.715240)

Place du général McAuliffe (formerly place du Carré) in the heart of Bastogne is now a parking area surrounded by shops, cafés, restaurants, and the city's tourist office. The southern corner of the square, the center of the city's resistance during the Battle of the Bulge, beams with important memorials to the battle.

Most impressively, a **Sherman M4A3 tank 'Barracuda,'** complete with a German 75-mm shell hole in its left side and jagged panzerfaust damage to the stern, dominates a concrete platform. The Sherman tank, commanded by Staff Sergeant Wallace Alexander of Company B, 41st Tank Battalion, 11th Armored Division, participated in the 30 December drive to widen the western side of the relief corridor. After being separated from his company, Sgt Alexander proceeded toward Renaumont where he encountered the panzers of the Führer Begleit Brigade. In an attempt to escape from the more powerful enemy armor, the Sherman became mired in a snow-covered pond and was knocked out.[5] The vehicle's abandonment in that marshy pond permitted it to escape a post-war scrap-dealer's demolition. The tank was recovered, refurbished, and put on display at its current location in 1947. The memorial bears plaques from 10th Armored Division and the US Army Air Corps' 406th Fighter Group that frequently supported Bulge ground units.

A bronze bust of **Brigadier General Anthony McAuliffe** stands upon a cement plinth to the left of the tank. The bust clearly displays the general's decorations, most prominently his paratrooper's wings. The plinth bears the US 101st Airborne Division's Screaming Eagle insignia.[6]

The **Voie de la Liberté Borne #1145** lies to the right of the tank, indicating the 1,145 kilometers traveled by American armies from the landing beaches in Normandy to the famous square in Belgium to liberate Europe. The final bollard, number 1147, is located at the Mardasson Memorial.

A tourist route (***Circuit Historique***) has been established with distinctive information boards at fifteen selected locations around the city, ranging from Noville to the north, Champs to the west, and Villers-la-Bonne-Eau to the south. These well-executed signs provide multi-lingual descriptions of local events, historical photographs, sketches, and maps. The text is in four languages. The various tours described below locate all of these infosigns, but not in the numbered order. A complete list appears Appendix A.

Circuit Historique #1 provides sights about Bastogne, including the Sarma department store before and after the Christmas Eve bombing that killed wounded soldiers and staff at the improvised hospital. The results of the bombing of place McAuliffe are likewise depicted. (50.000779, 5.715130)

Leave place du général McAuliffe southwest toward Diekirch (rue Joseph-Renquin

---

5 Staff Sergeant Wallace R Alexander was wounded during the engagement and died the next day. Alexander was 22 years old and is buried at Golden Gate National Cemetery, San Bruno, California. The other four crew members were all captured and spent the remainder of the war in PoW camps.

6 Brigadier General Anthony McAuliffe, awarded the Distinguished Service Cross on 30 December 1944, was almost immediately promoted to major general and given command of the 103rd Infantry Division, which fought through southern Germany and into Austria capturing Innsbruck and the Brenner Pass where it met American units fighting the Italian Campaign. McAuliffe retired from the US Army in 1956 as a lieutenant general after having served as Commander of the US Army in Europe. He died in 1975 at age 77 and is buried in Arlington National Cemetery, Arlington, Virginia.

Chapter Seven				The Defense of Bastogne 297

> also N84 and N30). After 350 m, turn right into a large parking area and proceed to its west edge. (49.99811, 5.71555)

The **place du général Patton** is directly south of the place McAuliffe and along the Arlon highway. The recently relocated stone bas relief bust of the famous general stands upon a platform overlooking a parking area. **Circuit Historique #8** is nearby and describes General Patton's breaking of the siege of Bastogne by troops of his Third Army. (49.998474, 5.714663)

> Return to place du général McAuliffe and turn left onto rue de Neufchâteau (N85). Stop after 100 m to view the building on the right. (49.999887, 5.714301)

The Sarma Department store became the medical aid station for CCB, 10th Armored Division. Two nurses, Renée Lemaire, a Brussels-trained nurse from a local family, and Augusta Chiwy, an African from the Belgian Congo, assisted Doctor John Prior, 10th Armored Division Surgeon, in caring for 123 wounded men. On 24 December, the Luftwaffe struck beneath a brilliant moon and magnesium flares that turned night into a surreal day. A bomb hit the temporary hospital, causing the entire building to collapse into its cellar. Twenty patients were killed, as was Lemaire. The force of the blast threw Chiwy clear from the building. It was days before men dug all the bodies from the debris. John Prior wrapped Lemaire's body in a white silk parachute and carried her remains to her parents' home.

The reconstructed building site is now occupied by a restaurant, but the front wall bears a plaque identifying the location as the site of the **20th Armored Infantry Battalion's aid station** and recalls the death of thirty wounded soldiers (accounts vary as to the number actually killed by the bombing) and of nurse Renée Lemaire.

> Continue southwest on rue de Neufchâteau for 150 m and turn right onto avenue de la Gare. Stop at the museum 60 m ahead on the right. (49.999209, 5.712094)

Museum Le Mess
avenue de la Gare 11   6600 Bastogne, Belgium
Tel: +32 (0)61 50 12 00   +31 (0)64 790 43 47
Email: info@101airbornemuseumbastogne.com
Web: http://www.101airbornemuseumbastogne.com/

The Museum Le Mess is located in the former officers mess building of the Belgium Army. It is dedicated to the men of the 101st Airborne Division and presents authentic personal items of the men who fought at Bastogne. The walls are covered with mementos, photographs, hand written reports, and personal observations. The items are well documented with labels in French and English.

The basement presents a six-minute civilian experience of sheltering in the candlelit cellars during the Christmas Eve bombing. The event is replicated with sounds of approaching aircraft, flashes of bombs, and antiaircraft fire. A room displays a surgical hospital with wounded troops, equipment, bloodied dressings littering the floor, and manikin corpsmen and doctors.

Open daily except Mondays 1 April to 31 September from 10:00 to 17:00; open Wednesday through Sunday the remainder of the year. Fee.

> Continue west on rue de la Gare. After 120 m, turn right onto avenue Mathieu. Ahead 300 m, turn right onto place du général McAuliffe (N84), then left toward Liège (N30). Follow the one-way street for 800 m to a roundabout and take the 2nd exit toward La Roche / Houffalize (N30 and N874). At the next roundabout, take the 3rd exit onto rue de La Roche (N834) and continue 290 m to the entrance gates of Heintz Barracks. (50.008168, 5.718408)

Heintz Barracks
Route de la Roche 40
Tel: +32 (0)61 24 21 24
Website: none available
6600 Bastogne, Belgium
Email: bb.mra@skynet.be

The military barracks in Bastogne built in 1934 housed the 2nd Régiment de Chasseurs Ardennais and was named *Caserne Heintz*. The installation became a Hitler Youth training center during the German occupation, then later headquarters for General Troy Middleton's US VIII Corps. General McAuliffe established his headquarters in the basement of a barracks building on the southern side of the main courtyard shortly before midnight on 19 December. A towed antitank gun covered the main gate in case a panzer arrived unexpectedly. The re-supply drop zone lay beyond the cemetery across the street, and the glider landing zone was located north of the barracks.

In that basement room General McAuliffe made the most important decisions of his military career. Pressed by an apparently superior enemy force and with only inadequate supply route along a single road to the southwest, McAuliffe decided not to attempt a risky withdrawal but to stay and fight. In the damp cellar McAuliffe also made his famous written reply to the German surrender ultimatum.

In 2010 the barracks became part of the Royal Museum of the Armed Forces and of Military History. All of the red brick buildings in the camp are original to the barracks. The tour features large poster-sized photos placed around the camp to compare 1944 conditions with current views. The 101st Airborne headquarters with McAuliffe's office is complete with dioramas of the famous response and a not too cheery Christmas dinner. The site houses an extensive vehicle restoration facility with an impressive collection of armored vehicles.

Open daily, except Monday, by guided tour only starting at 09:00, 10:00, 13:00, and 14:00. No admission charge.

The cemetery holds the honored graves of Renée Lemaire and Augusta Chiwy.[7] Lemaire's tombstone is the second tallest in the cemetery. Chiwy is buried slightly farther distant toward the rear of the cemetery.

---

7 Augusta Chiwy died on 23 August 2015 at age 94.

Chapter Seven The Defense of Bastogne 299

> Continue northwest on highway N834 for 140 m. (50.009138, 5.717070)

    Circuit Historique #15 describes the origin and utilization of nearby Heintz Barracks by General McAuliffe.
    Only 200 meters to the northwest, a **Sherman tank turret** guarding the highway to Bertogne rests incongruously at the end of a parking space before a relatively new home. The turret carries the older 75-mm gun of a Sherman model M34A1. During the various tours around Bastogne, one notes the major and sometime very slight differences between the various Sherman turrets, as design modifications continued during the war. (50.010655, 5.715711)

> Reverse direction and, in the roundabout after 600 m, take the 2nd exit and continue to the next roundabout to the 1st exit toward Clervaux (N874). After 500 m, turn left onto the frontage road and stop. (50.008633, 5.729224)

    The Clervaux highway **Sherman tank turret** bears the insignia of the 10th Armored Division and stands between the original roadway and the modern highway. Many turrets bear the damage that ended their participation in the battle. This turret displays an almost perfectly round antitank projectile hole on its left side.
    A new (2011) plaque sits at the base of the field stone plinth commemorating **Combat Command B, 10th Armored Division** for its early and continued defense of Bastogne.[8]

> Continue to regain highway N874. After only 110 m, turn left onto rue de Clervaux and note the memorial and pillbox on the left. Unfortunately, access to the memorial is difficult because of high curbs and road improvements to speed traffic to the Mardasson Memorial and nearby museum. (50.009051, 5.731349)

    The corner holds a memorial to the **Belgian Chasseurs Ardennais**. This Belgian Army group was specially trained as a rapid movement command to hold the country's borders from enemy invasion until stronger forces could be mobilized. The units were equipped with light tanks and self-propelled guns. The Chasseurs Ardennais harassed and delayed the German *Blitzkrieg* of 10 May 1940 with minefields, road obstacles, and destruction of bridges. The Boar's Head insignia of the Chasseurs prominently fronts the memorial.
    The monument is constructed to the left of a **Belgian Army bunker** that held a 47-mm antitank gun. On 10 May 1940, the gun resisted German armor, knocking out five panzers approaching along the Clervaux highway before being overwhelmed. A post-war reconfiguration of the intersection has somewhat altered the embrasure's orientation. Belgian Corporal Emile Cady died during the engagement in the defense of Bastogne and a plaque commemorates his death. (50.009073, 5.731454)

---

8   The plaque also notes that CCB, 10th Armored Division was awarded the Presidential Unit Citation in recognition of its actions in delaying the German advance.

> Continue northeast 400 m and then bear slightly right and note the Borne on the right. (50.010794, 5.736578)

Near the memorial entrance is the final **Borne #1147,** marking the end of the *Voie de la Liberté* and US Third Army's race across France and Belgium.

> Proceed forward 280 m before turning left into the museum parking area. (50.010607, 5.739192)

Bastogne War Museum (recently renamed from Bastogne Historique Centre)
Colline du Mardasson 5   6600 Bastogne, Belgium
Tel: +32 (0)61 21 02 20   Email: info@bastognewarmuseum.be
Web: http://www.bastognewarmuseum.be/home.html

At the cost of ten million Euros, the museum was expanded and completely redesigned for the 70th Anniversary celebrations. A significant quantity of the original relics and equipment has been removed in favor of a more interpretative approach emphasizing the horrors of war. Utilizing numerous multimedia projectors, monitors, and hidden speakers, the museum tells the wartime story. An audio guide puts the visitor into the personality of German Hans Wegmüller, a 21-year-old Wehrmacht Leutnant, and American Robert King, a 20-year-old parachutist from 101st Airborne Division. The headsets automatically change topic while one moves through the museum. Labeling is in four languages.

The tour starts with the Sherman tank 'Blockbuster' then proceeds to tell the story of the European Crisis at the end of the First World War when the victorious powers tried to resolve territorial boundary disputes. A 3-D projection of old news film presents the war until 5 June 1944. One exits the theater back into the exhibit area where the Normandy Invasion, Belgian Resistance, and Nazi collaboration come under review. Stairs and an elevator access a lower level where the Battle of the Ardennes, starting with the display of a German Hetzer, conjures up powerful and disturbing images. A second Sherman tank named 'Absentee' dramatically displays a shell hole in one side and a small exit hole on the opposite side.

The museum caters to visitors unfamiliar with the course of the war or the Ardennes battle. It explains the events with a large series of graphics, limited weaponry, and film clips, but it is not the place to view equipment or battlefield relics.

Generally open daily from 09:30 to 18:00 (19:00 during summer); closed Mondays during fall; closed for Christmas holidays and in January. For complete schedule of open days and hours, see the museum's website. Fee; handicap accessible.

The **101st Airborne Division Memorial** is located between the Bastogne War Museum and the Mardasson Memorial. The city of Bastogne and its inhabitants donated the stone 'Screaming Eagle' drinking from an up-turned soldier's helmet. The plaque states, 'May this eagle symbolize the sacrifices and heroism of the 101st Airborne Division and all its attached units.' (50.010079, 5.739563)

Walk south to the memorial. (50.009349, 5.739012)

Chapter Seven   The Defense of Bastogne

The **Mémorial Mardasson,** constructed by the people of Belgium in gratitude to the Americans killed or missing in the battle to liberate their country, rises over a slight incline from the museum. Legend has it that a German patrol crossed the hill on 19 December in the enemy's nearest approach to the city. The memorial's columns form a five-pointed star around a central open gallery. Across the top of the memorial are the names of the forty-eight American states. The walls list the names and insignia of units that participated in the fighting and a description of the battle that ends with the memorial's seminal sentence, 'Seldom has more American blood been spilt in the course of a single battle.' A sixty-step staircase ascends 12 meters to provide access to the rooftop-viewing platform, where each point of the star holds a table of orientation to battlefield locations. The memorial stands on a hill above the city of Bastogne, and the panoramic view from it provides an understanding of the military advantages of the site. Always open; no admission charge.

Other Points of Interest in Bastogne

> Framed by ivy covered pillars, the **Bastogne War Memorial** records the names of all the fallen soldiers, members of the Resistance, and political prisoners who died in the two World Wars. A statue represents an austerely clothed, battered woman who is counting the beads on her rosary while she searches for eternal peace through prayer. Nearby stands **Voie de la Liberté Borne #1146,** one kilometer closer to the end of the trek from Normandy to Mardasson Hill.
> Location: beside highway N30 in the place St-Pierre northeast of the city center. (50.005528, 5.721902)
>
> The **501st PIR regimental aid station** occupied the stone church of Le Petit Seminaire, where the wounded lay in rows upon the cold stone floor with only enough space for aid men to walk between them. The alcove devoted to the Blessed Virgin to one side of the altar became an operating theater where surgeons worked almost until they dropped from fatigue.
> An **iron cross** imbedded into the stone wall in a public courtyard remembers the deaths of thirteen 501st PIR men who died in a violent explosion while loading land mines onto trucks in the courtyard.
> Location: off the roundabout north of the city center on highway N30. (50.006708, 5.721338)
>
> The grateful town of Bastogne erected a fieldstone memorial flanked by American and Belgian flags to honor the memory of **Ernest Glessener,** the first American soldier to fall liberating Bastogne, killed on this spot on 10 September 1944 after having destroyed a German tank. A **Sherman tank turret** stands beside the memorial with its long barreled 76-mm gun aimed along the Neufchâteau highway (N85).
> Location: southwest of city center near the intersection of highways N85 and N4. (49.994591, 5.705492)

> The tour of the perimeter battlefields starts to the east — toward initial German assault. Leave place du général McAuliffe to the northeast toward Liège (N30). Follow the one-way street for 800 m to a roundabout and take the 1st exit toward Clervaux (N874) and follow for 9.5 km into Longvilly. Leave Longvilly toward Bastogne (N874) and, after 1.2 km, slow at the curve to the left to note the Grotto of St-Michael. (50.024705, 5.822941)

Eastern Sector
Battle of Longvilly
18 to 19 December 1944

By 18 December, von Lüttwitz's two panzer divisions were poised to follow their assigned routes. In the north, 2nd Panzer Division passed east of Longvilly and turned northwest toward Bourcy. To the south, the forward elements of Panzer Lehr entered Niederwampach.

Longvilly held the headquarters of Colonel Joseph Gilbreth's CCR, 9th Armored Division. Stragglers from the 28th Infantry Division and the crippled Task Force Harper (see Chapter Six) filtered through town. On the third day of the offensive, Gilbreth and the remnants of Task Force Harper were all that stood between the enemy and Bastogne.

German Objective		To eliminate American armored troops standing before Bastogne
Forces	American:	CCR, 9th Armored Division (Colonel Joseph H Gilbreth)
	German:	Panzergrenadier Regiment 901 (Oberst Paul Freiherr von Hauser); Grenadier Regiment 77 (Oberstleutnant Martin Schriefer)
Result		The American forces were destroyed but not without inflicting a delay upon the German advance
Casualties	American:	Over 100 taken prisoner; 23 Sherman tanks, 15 self-propelled guns, 14 armored cars, and 55 other vehicles captured or destroyed
	German:	52 killed or wounded; 8 panzers destroyed
Location		Longvilly is 10 km northeast of Bastogne

Battle

On the evening of 18 December, Colonel William L Roberts, commander of CCB, 10th Armored Division, ordered Team Cherry[9] to move east on the Clervaux

---

[9] Team Cherry was commanded by Lieutenant Colonel Henry T Cherry and consisted of 3rd Tank Battalion (less Co B and 2nd Platoon, Co D); Co C, 20th Armored Infantry Battalion; 3rd Platoon, Co C, 55th Armored Engineer Battalion; 2nd Platoon, Troop B, 90th Cavalry Squadron; and one platoon from Co C, 609th Tank Destroyer Battalion.

Chapter Seven

The Defense of Bastogne   303

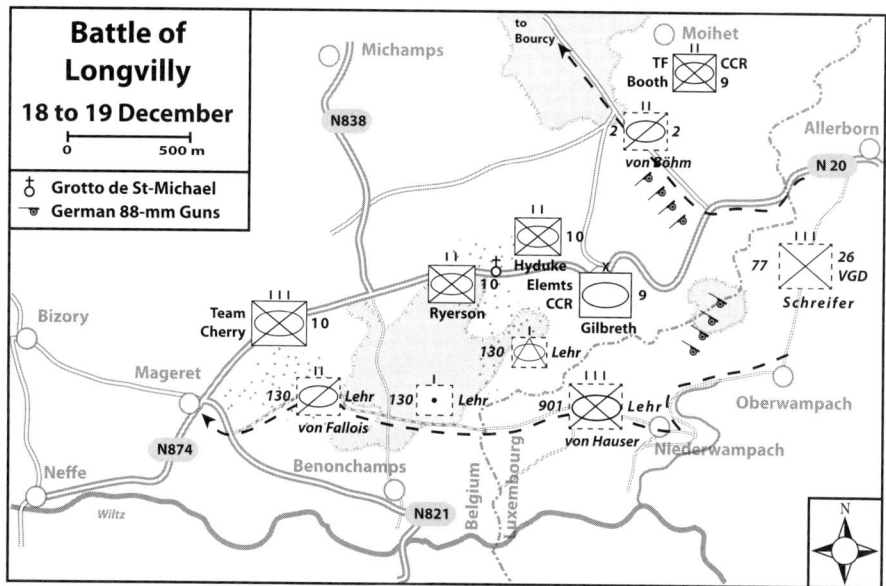

road to join elements of CCR, 9th Armored Division in the vicinity of Longvilly. It became the first of Bastogne's defenders to encounter the advancing enemy.

The advance guard of Company A, commanded by 1st Lt Edward P Hyduke, met CCR just west of Longvilly at 1920 while the rear guard of Team Cherry, under Captain William Ryerson, was still finding its way out of Bastogne. With no radio communications, Colonel Cherry returned to Bastogne to report. He found the road thick with 9th Armored vehicles moving west. Once in Bastogne, Colonel Roberts told Colonel Cherry to hold Longvilly – no matter what.

At midnight, Colonel Gilbreth decided to withdraw his battered command from Longvilly, thus leaving Team Cherry to defend the approach to Bastogne. The withdrawal became a desperate panic when all semblance of order disappeared in the darkness and confusion amid clinging fog punctuated by the chatter of burp guns from German patrols. Vehicles enmeshed with those of Team Cherry while both units became bottled up on the road. A degree of order followed once daylight arrived, but the head of the column was stopped by elements of Panzer Lehr that had arrived in Mageret and Neffe during the night from the south.

By afternoon of 19 December, Bayerlein posted PGR 901, twenty tank destroyers of Panzerjäger Battalion 130, and an artillery battalion near Benonchamps to break the American block at Longvilly. He ordered an attack from the woods going east. The assault force of infantry and five tank destroyers reached the top of Hill 490 shortly after 1400. Observing the tangle of American armor strung out along the Clervaux highway, fifteen additional tank destroyers came forward, and all twenty opened fire at a range of 1.5 to 2.0 kilometers. In addition, elements of Oberstleutnant Schriefer's Grenadier Regiment 77 struck from the southeast. The two forces hit almost at the same time. Von Lauchert responded to American fire received from Longvilly by positioning five or six 88-mm guns to add their fire to the rout.

With precision, German gunners knocked out the first and last vehicles, thereby trapping the entire column. Antitank artillery and mortars exploded self-propelled artillery, armored cars, and tanks; ammunition trailers burst into fireballs. Shells and bullets pierced the thin skins of trucks, half-tracks, and ambulances while their infantry cargo scattered for shelter.

Artillerymen of the 58th Armored Field Artillery Battalion fought back with their SP-guns. The quad .50-caliber machine guns of the 482nd Antiaircraft Artillery Battalion attempted to keep German infantry at bay. Nonetheless, Gilbreth's command was swiftly annihilated;[10] he and his headquarters troops found back roads into Bastogne. Hundreds of stragglers found their way to Bastogne as well — adding to the chaos already present in the city's streets.

Battlefield Tour

Artillery Regiment 130 occupied the partially-forested hilltop visible on the left that was an excellent position for Bayerlein's force to bombard Team Cherry. Troops on the highway had no opportunity to attack the grenadier-protected artillery. (50.020952, 5.828458)

Lt Hyduke, unwilling to entangle his advance guard with the withdrawing combat command, chose to position his force on high ground along the highway near a religious grotto. During the late morning of 19 December, Hyduke's Company A took Schriefer's Grenadier Regiment 77 under fire while the enemy passed through Longvilly. Hyduke's armored infantry in its armored cars and light tanks held for little more than one hour. A platoon from 811th Tank Destroyer Battalion added some firepower and even knocked out eight panzers. When the order to withdraw came from Colonel Cherry, the highway was so blocked with wreckage that Hyduke ordered his remaining vehicles destroyed before the men headed cross-country on foot.

American armor strewn between the crosses and statues of the religious grottoes lined both sides of the highway. Note the bullet and shell fragment damage to the iron gates at the entrance to the **Grotto of St-Michael**. The steep roadside shoulders provided some temporary shelter from German artillery but also trapped American vehicles by preventing them from leaving the highway.

Other Points of Interest

Niederwampach

After leaving Wiltz, narrow, winding, and muddy roads compounded by congestion from the infantry, wagons, and horse-drawn guns of the 26th Volksgrenadier Division slowed Panzer Lehr. The advance guard under Major Gerd

---

10 Colonel Joseph Gilbreth was born to a military family at Fort Sheridan, Illinois. Gilbreth graduated from West Point in 1927 and became an infantry officer, later transferring to the armored branch. After the end of the Battle of Bastogne, Major General Maxwell Taylor recommended that CCR receive a unit citation for delaying the enemy advance. The recognition was never processed because the unit was on a secret list with no public recognition of its existence allowed. Gilbreth continued to serve after the war, mainly in German occupation forces. He died in 1962 at age 57 and is buried in Fort Sam Houston National Cemetery, San Antonio, Texas.

Chapter Seven

> von Fallois did not reach Niederwampach — a distance of just 11 kilometers — until 1700 on 18 December.
>
> A signboard compares the German 150-mm heavy infantry gun to the lighter **American 105-mm M2A1 howitzer**. The German 150-mm gun was the basic division-level heavy howitzer in the German Army with a range of 13 kilometers. An example abandoned here during the German withdrawal from the Bulge is now in the National Museum of Military History in Diekirch. The American 105-mm was the workhorse of American parachute field artillery units during the war. With full charge, the gun ranged 11 kilometers.
> Location: 14 km east of Bastogne beside highway CR329. (50.01082 5.84693)

Bayerlein's route from Niederwampach to Mageret flows over hills and along ridgelines in this unforested sector and would have exposed Bayerlein's vehicles to observation and aerial attack. Fortunately for the Germans, Hitler welcomed the weather that his armies needed for this stage of the offensive. Rising fog and lowering clouds grounded Allied aircraft and concealed the troops' movements. Unfortunately for Bayerlein, the road became a dirt track where it approached the Benonchamps–Mageret road, and the wet winter weather had churned it into almost impassable mud, further delaying the German advance.

> Continue west toward Bastogne for 2.1 km; stop at the farm road on the right. (50.020285, 5.794281)

Battle for Mageret
18 to 19 December 1944

Bayerlein, on the advice of some Luxembourg civilians, chose to reach the Clervaux road into Bastogne by taking a side road through Benonchamps to Mageret. The route, however, was not in as a good condition as the civilians had stated. The narrow road appeared driveable before deteriorating into a muddy farm track. However, three hours after leaving Niederwampach, Bayerlein's vanguard of Kampfgruppe von Fallois with fifteen PzKpfw IVs reached the Benonchamps–Mageret road at 2100. Another hour and they were in Mageret, shortly after Team Cherry had passed through the village on its way east to Longvilly. Fallois easily overwhelmed a small roadblock maintained by a platoon from Company B, 158th Engineer Combat Battalion.

Local civilian Emile Frere told Bayerlein that, only hours earlier, a strong American armored force of fifty tanks and forty half-tracks had passed through Mageret heading for Longvilly, inflating the size of Team Cherry to a whole armored regiment. Why Bayerlein relied on questionable civilian intelligence remains unexplained, but the information supported Bayerlein's concern that an American armored unit could be to his rear. Bayerlein ordered a roadblock east of Mageret consisting of a minefield, three panzers, and grenadiers while other troops established defensive positions on both sides of the road to the west. Bayerlein decided to sit tight and await events.

American Objective		To counter the German presence in Mageret and open the road back to Bastogne
Forces		
	American:	Team Ryerson (Captain William H Ryerson)
	German:	Panzergrenadier Regiment 902 (Oberstleutnant Joachim von Poschinger)
Result		The German troops held, but Ryerson managed to escape
Casualties		
	American:	175 killed or missing; 18 tanks and 23 half-tracks destroyed
	German:	unknown
Location		Mageret is 5 km east of Bastogne

Battle

When Colonel Cherry attempted to return to his command at Longvilly, he found the intersection at Mageret occupied by German panzers. He established a headquarters in a chateau south of Neffe and contacted Colonel Roberts for orders. Colonel Roberts decided to abandon Longvilly and ordered Team Cherry to return to Bastogne.

As a result of the order to withdraw, Hyduke's advance guard became the team's rear guard, and Ryerson's rear guard became the advance guard. Thus, Ryerson led the column back towards Bastogne. Captain Ryerson's lead tank rounded a curve in a cut 300 meters east of Mageret when an enemy antitank gun knocked it out. The burning wreckage plugged the roadway that ran through a deep cut at that point. Heavy automatic weapons and mortar fire fell upon Ryerson's half-track-mounted infantry from a tree line to the north. For the remainder of the day, efforts to outflank the German position were generally unsuccessful because of constant and accurate shelling by Panzer Lehr elements to the south.[11]

Shortly after dark, Captain Ryerson's armored infantrymen gained three houses at the northwest edge of Mageret and hung on for the remainder of the night. Just before dawn, Ryerson's tanks shoved aside the wreckage blocking the cut and gained a dirt track to bypass Mageret by moving north to Bizory, where they entered the lines of the 501st PIR.[12]

Consequences

For the German Army, the Battle for Bastogne was lost at Mageret. Even though Team Cherry had suffered severe losses in men and equipment, the German advance was delayed for several hours allowing American forces valuable time to establish a defensive line east and southeast of Bastogne. Bayerlein's willingness

---

[11] Team Ryerson formed the bulk of Team Cherry and was built around Company C, 20th Armored Infantry Battalion and Companies A and C, 3rd Tank Battalion.

[12] Captain William Ryerson was killed during the Christmas Eve Luftwaffe raid on Bastogne when a German bomb hit the Team Cherry command post. He is buried in Luxembourg American Cemetery, Luxembourg City, Luxembourg.

Chapter Seven — The Defense of Bastogne

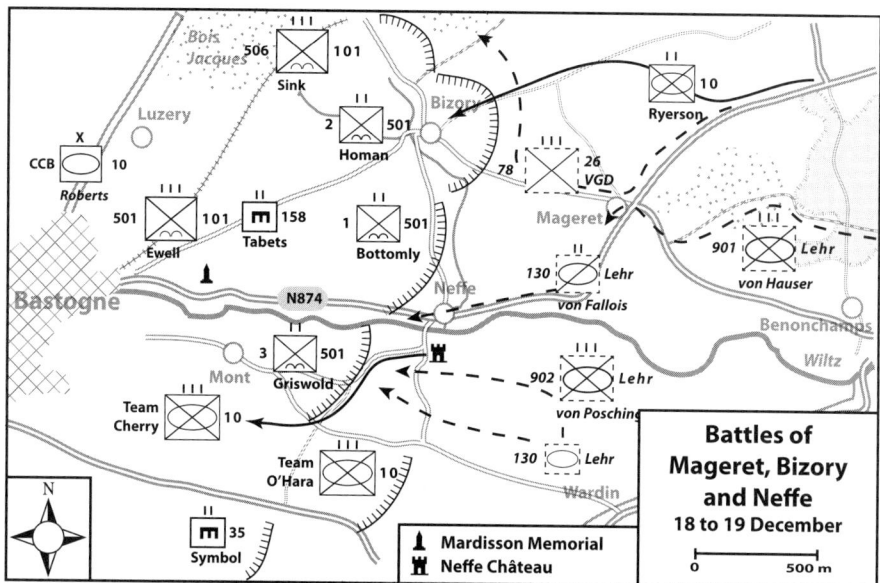

Battles of Mageret, Bizory and Neffe
18 to 19 December

to accept civilian intelligence and his misunderstanding of the size and nature of American opposition slowed Panzer Lehr's approach toward Bastogne and probably relinquished the opportunity to seize the city while it was still weakly defended.

Battlefield Tour

All official reports of the confused fighting between Longvilly and Mageret clearly state that a destroyed Sherman tank in a road cut at a curve 300 yards from Mageret blocked Ryerson's progress. Still, the curve on the road to Longvilly is neither in a cut nor 300 yards from the village. The mystery remains unexplained. However, the farm road at the curve provides an opportunity to view the exposed terrain in this sector of the battlefield. German armored units observed movement along the highway and brought it under annihilating firepower.

> Continue 900 m toward Bastogne before turning right into Mageret. Continue into the church parking area on the right. (50.014442, 5.784964)

Circuit Historique #4 provides dramatic wartime photographs of the extent of destroyed American armor trapped west of Longvilly. Adjacent to the infosign, the Mageret **Sherman tank turret** (turret model T23), with its 76-mm gun, stands some distance away from the current Clervaux highway. (50.014456, 5.784913)

> Return to the intersection with highway N874 and turn right (south). Continue 1.4 km and stop along the roadside. (50.007670, 5.773491)

During his personal reconnaissance of the approaches to Bastogne, Bayerlein reached this location when he heard the fire of guns from the ridgeline visible to the left front. Battery B, 907th Glider Field Artillery Battalion (GFAB) had occupied positions 500 meters northwest of Bastogne approximately 1000 meters behind a paratrooper skirmish line. Bayerlein, who had never faced the 'snub-nosed' M3 howitzer, may have concluded that the fire was from approaching American armor. Fearful of becoming trapped between armor approaching from Bastogne and Team Cherry to his rear, Bayerlein paused to consolidate his spread out forces. That hesitation might have lost the Battle of Bastogne for the German Army.

> Turn right onto the unmarked side road 350 m ahead. Follow the roadway around to the right for 1.0 km and stop at a convenient location. (50.013738, 5.776457)

Battle of Bizory
19 to 20 December 1944

The 35th Engineer Combat Battalion was part of the 35th Combat Engineer Regiment that constructed the famous Alaskan-Canadian (Alcan) Highway in 1942 to provide an overland route to Alaskan airbases, then believed to be threatened by Japanese invasion. In December 1944, the unit established the initial defensive perimeter around Bastogne by placing nearly 1,000 antitank mines on the roadways from Noville to Neffe. On 18 December, the 158th Engineer Combat Battalion arrived and assumed responsibility for that same sector.

Troops of the 158th Engineer Combat Battalion held Bizory when the 2nd Battalion, 501st PIR arrived at 1000 on 19 December. The paratroop battalion established a command post in the Château Remy in the center of the village and began to feel its way toward Mageret. On 20 December, the 26th VGD's Grenadier Regiment 78, under the temporary command of General Bayerlein, targeted Luzery, a northern suburb of Bastogne.

AMERICAN OBJECTIVE	To establish a defensive perimeter northeast of Bastogne
FORCES	
American:	2nd Battalion (Major Sammie Homan), 501st Parachute Infantry Regiment
German:	Grenadier Regiment 78, 26th Volksgrenadier Division (Oberst Heinz Kokott)
RESULT	The attack upon Bastogne was stopped
CASUALTIES	
American:	4 killed and at least 6 wounded
German:	unknown, but substantial
LOCATION	Bizory is 4 km northeast of Bastogne

Battle

Major Sammie Homan's 2nd Battalion, 501st PIR entered Bizory only to find a massive traffic jam of engineering vehicles. Major Homan sent Company E on the road toward Mageret. At a curve 700 meters outside of Bizory, Captain Frank Gregg, Company E's commander, observed enemy troops moving across the hillside to his left. Grenadier Regiment 78's Reconnaissance Platoon spotted Captain Gregg at that time, and it started flanking maneuvers to Gregg's left and rear. Company E deployed into the fields. Firefights erupted along Gregg's line but were tempered somewhat by swirling fog that blinded the paratroopers to enemy movements. One group of enemy troops attempted to infiltrate along a slight depression nearer to Bizory. The fog lifted to reveal its presence to the 2nd Platoon. The enemy troops were all killed.

Meanwhile, Company F moved northeast along a dirt track to the left. Although the two companies could not see each other through the dense fog, Company F heard the gunfire from Company E and proceeded cautiously. Airborne artillery laid down a wall of fire onto the German half-tracks observed through the fog on the hillside that drove German infantry into the waiting guns of the two companies. The enemy held the rounded height against an American advance with automatic weapons, whereby any movement against it met with sweeping fire. The fighting continued until 1600, when the winter gloom settled over the strung-out positions of Companies E and F. The battalion fell back to form a defensive perimeter on the east and northeast edges of Bizory.

Early the next morning, the paratroopers heard the clank of tank treads coming out of the fog to the east. They had only a few bazookas and Molotov cocktails to fight German armor. While the men anxiously looked for targets, the Sherman tanks of Captain Ryerson's team emerged from the fog. The relief was apparent on the faces of everyone.

Later that morning, an intense German artillery barrage hit the men in Bizory followed by infantry and five panzers from II Battalion, Grenadier Regiment 78 attacking Company F from the east. The 101st artillery units replied with hundreds of rounds, and by 1400 the attack was over.

Aftermath

The stubborn defense of Company F defeated the German attempt to enter Bastogne by swinging around Bizory and moving across open ground to east of Luzery. After receiving flanking fire, Grenadier Regiment 78 instead swung wider to the north behind cover of large forested area northeast of Bizory. Masked by the wood, it proceeded west to the Bastogne–Bourcy rail line where the 506th PIR halted its advance (see below).

Although Homan's men defeated the enemy attack aimed at Bastogne through Bizory, they remained in a precarious position because Bizory was situated in a bowl and overlooked by enemy positions on the surrounding hills. During the night of 21/22 December, they withdrew from the village to establish positions on the broad hill to the west. The 2nd Battalion, 501st PIR held that line until 29 December.

Bayerlein ordered the 26th VGD's Reconnaissance Battalion to disengage and swing along a wide arc south of Bastogne to severe American lines of communications along the Neufchâteau highway.

Battlefield Tour
   Hill 510, where Company E resisted the enemy advance toward Bizory, is not where most battlefield maps place it. The hill lies west of Mageret, where it overlooks both villages and provided excellent artillery observation, thus the reason for 2nd Battalion's eventual withdrawal from the village. (50.014103, 5.772872)

> Turn left at the next intersection and continue 1.1 km into the center of Bizory (50.019621, 5.763302)

The Musée Animaliane now occupies **Château Remy**, Major Homan's command post during the occupation of Bizory. The old white barn across the road locates the site of the **battalion aid station** during the engagement.

> Reverse direction and, after 80 m, turn left and then left again after 60 m. Stop at the white house 60 m ahead on the right. (50.020227, 5.764780)

The small white farmhouse at the crook of the curve in the road leaving Bizory was the site of a forward **command post**. Company F's front was immediately before this post and facing north during the night of 19 December.

> Reverse direction and continue back through the small farming community. After 70 m, turn left at the first side road and follow south for 1.5 km into Neffe and the junction with highway N874. Cross the intersection to the chapel opposite. (50.005709, 5.763951)

Battle for Neffe
19 December 1944

An ever-cautious Bayerlein waited an hour before resuming his advance at 0800 on 19 December. He was less than 4 kilometers from Bastogne. In post-war interviews, Generalfeldmarschall von Manteuffel criticized Bayerlein's decisions at this point of the battle, describing his actions as indicating '… a breach in the leadership of the Panzer Division. Independent maneuvering was an essential part of the speed and mobility of this arm.'

AMERICAN OBJECTIVE	To defend the eastern approach to Bastogne
FORCES	
American:	1st Battalion (Major Raymond V Bottomly Jr), 501st Parachute Infantry Regiment
German:	Kampfgruppe von Fallois (Major Gerd von Fallois)
RESULT	The German advance was stopped

Chapter Seven

The Defense of Bastogne 311

CASUALTIES	
American:	50 taken prisoner; 6 tanks destroyed
German:	unknown
LOCATION	Neffe is 4 km east of Bastogne

Battle

Enemy panzers and infantry from the east hit Team Cherry's Reconnaissance Platoon posted at the road junction at Neffe. While the men exchanged small-arms fire, German engineers disarmed the roadblock's mines to allow the panzers to continue forward. The overwhelmed unit fell back under a storm of rifle and machine-gun fire. Three German PzKpfw IVs occupied positions close to a hillside on the road to Bizory from where they fired north. A ridgeline gave them defilade to fire from the west.

Two hours later, the 1st Battalion of Lieutenant Colonel Julian J Ewell's 501st PIR moved out of Bastogne with orders to clear up the situation at Longvilly. At Neffe the battalion's Reconnaissance Platoon met Kampfgruppe von Fallois while enemy forces resumed their move toward Bastogne. Predictably, heavy fog limited visibility. The lead paratroopers rounded a curve and entered a straight roadway toward Neffe when a German machine gun opened fire. Unable to position his only heavy weapons, seven 57-mm antitank guns, 1st Battalion Commander Major Raymond V Bottomly Jr pulled his men back and called for assistance from the 907th Glider Field Artillery Battalion that had established its Battery B 1000 meters west of Bastogne, and brought fire from its M3 light 105-mm howitzers down upon German panzers and small groups of German infantry. The lead panzer cautiously continued around the curve when a two-man bazooka team fired. The rocket hit the pavement short of the tank, but the vehicle stopped and then retreated. The ground south of the road descended sharply into Wiltz Creek, therefore affording a natural tank barrier. Bottomly deployed his men to the north of the road and fought the enemy force to a stalemate.

Colonel Ewell also sent Lieutenant Colonel George M Griswold's 3rd Battalion to Mont, a small village east of Neffe on a side road that ran parallel to the Clervaux road. Griswold sent one company farther south to link with the 10th Armored Division's Team O'Hara in Wardin.

Consequences

Ewell's aggressive attack further convinced Bayerlein that he was facing strong opposition. Accordingly, Bayerlein started to move his main force to the south to slip around Bastogne. Once again during the Battle of the Bulge, American troops suddenly arrived at exactly the right place — and none too soon.

Battlefield Tour

In the pre-dawn darkness of 19 December, two companies of panzergrenadiers with twelve panzers left Mageret and moved east along the Clervaux road toward Neffe. Immediately east of the first houses in the village and near the chapel, Private Bernard Michin, Company B, 158th Engineer Combat Battalion, sheltered in a roadside ditch. Michin did not see the approaching panzer through the fog until it was nearly on top of him. At a range of ten meters, he quickly pointed his bazooka and fired. The panzer exploded, showering Michin with flaming debris. Machine-gun tracer bullets then searched for Michin's position, but he silenced the gun with a handgrenade. Badly burned and temporarily blinded, he made his way back to Bastogne.[13]

The stone block chapel in Neffe witnessed some of the intense local fighting on 19 December. **Circuit Historique #5** describes the fighting for the village and displays photographs of destroyed German armor near the chapel and a PzKpfw IV knocked out between Neffe and Bastogne.

> Proceed west on highway N874 for 1.3 km. (50.007311, 5.746388)

The Neffe **Farthest Advance Stone** identifies the location where a bazooka rocket hit the pavement stopping the lead panzer and where Bottomly established his first defensive line. The location is only 2.4 kilometers from place McAuliffe.

> Reverse direction and return 1.3 km to turn right onto the road to the Neffe chapel. Follow for 190 m and then turn left and proceed 200 m to the farm buildings on the left. (50.003346, 5.762715)

Later that morning, the arrival from Mageret of four more panzers, an armored car, and 97 grenadiers strengthened the German force at the Neffe road junction. While much of this force repulsed Bottomly's battalion west of Neffe, a company of panzergrenadiers moved across the open ground to attack the chateau. Colonel Cherry's headquarters troops moved .50-caliber machine guns, which they had removed from their vehicles, from window to doorway while the attack shifted around the chateau's solidly constructed stone walls. Reinforcements of one platoon from 3rd Battalion, 501st PIR managed to fight its way to the chateau from Mont. At nightfall, German high-explosive shells ignited the chateau's roof. Colonel Cherry knew he could hold no longer. He sent a message to Colonel Roberts: 'We're not driven out… we were burned out. We're not withdrawing…we are moving.' He then led his men into 501st lines near Mont.

The current farm buildings stand upon the site of the destroyed **Château de Neffe**. The white section is only a minor portion of the original chateau that was originally much larger.

> Continue south to the first right turn and proceed 650 m to the driveway on top of the hill on the left. (50.001760, 5.748825)

At 1900 on 20 December, after a day of minor exchanges, a wall of American artillery fire destroyed three panzers leading a move against Major Bottomly's 1st Battalion in Neffe. At 1930, enemy SP guns moved along the rail line towards Mont accompanied by infantry of PGR 901 and under covering fire of panzers in a small

---

13 Private Bernard Michin survived his wounds. He died in 1996 at age 72 and he is buried in the Rhode Island Veterans Cemetery, Exeter, Rhode Island.

Chapter Seven   The Defense of Bastogne   313

woodlot west of Neffe Château. The paratroopers fell back but rallied around the tank destroyer of Sergeant George Schmidt from Company B, 705th Tank Destroyer Battalion. Schmidt's crew fought as infantry while Schmidt manned the vehicle's .50-caliber machine gun. Over a short few minutes, he threw 2,000 rounds into the advancing enemy.[14] The three other tank destroyers of the platoon took on the SP guns along the rail line. By the time the fighting had died down four hours later, the SP guns were knocked out and the ground littered with dead grenadiers, many of whom were trapped among the barbed wire fences of cattle feed pens.

Two of the four tank destroyers defended the north edge of Mont with a fourth tank destroyer behind Schmidt's on the road. The farm offers compelling sightlines back toward the Clervaux–Bastogne road and the intersection at Neffe.

> Continue west 150 m into Mont. Turn left toward Wardin.

Although a narrow country lane, the road is better than maps indicate and, where it climbs the hill leaving Mont to follow a slight ridge, it presents the terrain where the early fighting took place. The road also marks the probable route of Company I, 501st PIR to Wardin.

> Continue 3.1 km to the junction with highway N821. After 270 m, turn right and park at the side of the church. (49.990909, 5.788734)

Battle of Wardin
19 December 1944

On the night of 18 December, five-hundred men and thirty tanks of Team O'Hara,[15] commanded by Lieutenant Colonel James O'Hara, occupied high ground south of Wardin on the edge of a huge forest. Early the next morning, O'Hara sent his I & R platoon forward toward Bras to search out the enemy. At 1140, the patrol observed two PzKpfw IVs approaching through the fog along the Wiltz road. By noon, Team O'Hara's tanks took hits from high-velocity guns and direct artillery fire from the north. Colonel Ewell dispatched Company I, led by Captain Claude D Wallace Jr to strengthen Wardin's defenses. The paratroopers entered the town from the northwest while seven tanks and a battalion of infantry from Panzer Lehr's PGR 901 entered from the northeast.

| AMERICAN OBJECTIVE | To hold the advance position along the Wiltz highway |

---

14   Sergeant Schmidt's story is continued during the Battle of Champs (see below).

15   Team O'Hara consisted of Co B, 54th Armored Infantry Battalion; Co C, 21st Tank Battalion; one platoon from Co C, 55th Armored Engineer Battalion; one platoon from Co D, 3rd Tank Battalion; and one platoon from Troop D, 90th Reconnaissance Squadron.

Forces	
American:	Company I (Captain Claude D Wallace), 501st Parachute Infantry Regiment
German:	One Battalion, Panzergrenadier Regiment 901 (Oberst Paul von Hauser)
Result	The paratroopers were routed and Wardin captured
Casualties	
American:	57 killed or missing of an original 140 men
German:	Unknown casualties; three panzers destroyed
Location	Wardin is 7 km southeast of Bastogne

Battle

Captain Wallace established his command post in a stone house before sending Lieutenant Howard Gielow's 1st Platoon on the main road toward the eastern edge of town. Lieutenant Robert Harrison's 2nd Platoon headed for the church. Staff Sergeant Robert Houston[16] held the middle with a command post at the crossroads near Wallace's CP.

The first German tank shell smashed through the stone façade of the house holding the company CP and continued through the house and adjoining barn.

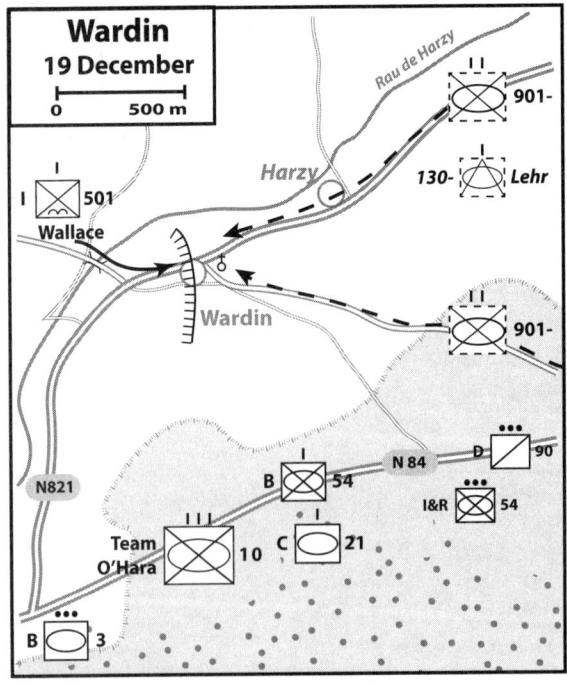

Company I became involve in close-quarters, house-to-house fighting against panzer-supported grenadiers. A bazooka team led by Sgt Houston hit a panzer's thick frontal armor with its first shot — doing no damage. After repositioning, its second shot holed the lower side. Paratroopers shot the tankers when they tumbled out of the burning wreck. A second panzer pushed through the wreckage. A bazooka man from Lt Harrison's 2nd Platoon crawled to within meters of the PzKpfw IV before firing. The resulting explosion blew him down the hill.

Von Hauser's panzergrenadiers eventually

---

16   S/Sgt Robert Houston was a combat veteran who had received the Distinguish Service Cross in Normandy for actions during the attack upon Hill 30 on 12 June 1944.

Chapter Seven

The Defense of Bastogne

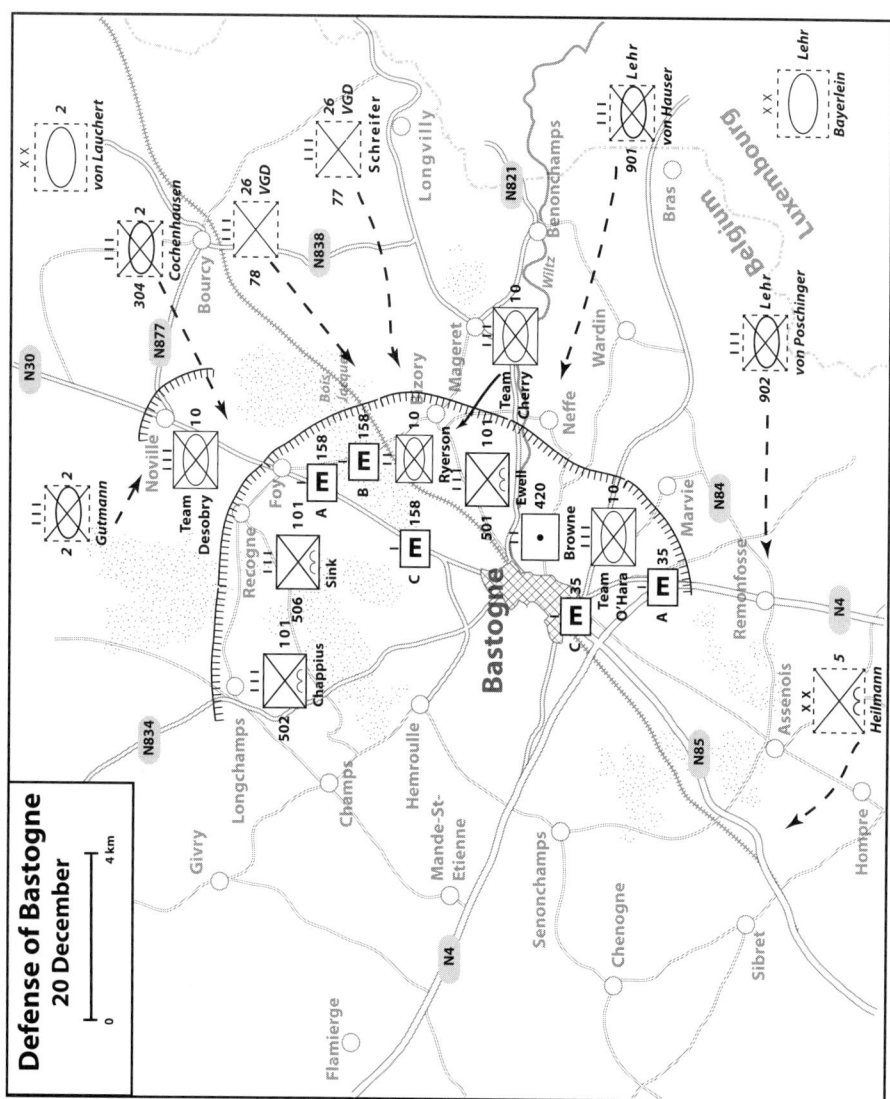

overran Wardin one house at a time while their panzers' MG-34 machine guns fired at any observed movement. The paratroopers were unable to stop the advancing panzers and were slowly overcome. Company I troopers trudged back to Bastogne through the day and following night. Team O'Hara did not participate in the battle while it engaged enemy troops along its front. With a strong force then occupying his flank, O'Hara received approval to withdraw.

Aftermath

Colonel Ewell realized that the offensive phase of his efforts was over. McAuliffe approved Ewell's request to go over to defense. By that evening the three battalions of the 501st PIR formed a solid line on a ridge west of Neffe extending north through Bizory to the Bastogne–Bourcy rail line and south to the Wiltz highway near Marvie. The 1st Battalion, 327th Glider Infantry Regiment (GIR) was inserted at Marvie between Team O'Hara and the 501st. The defensive perimeter on the southeast sector of Bastogne had formed.

Battlefield Tour

One battalion from Panzer-grenadier Regiment 901 approached Wardin in two prongs – one along highway N821 from Benonchamps and the second from the southeast from Bras. The prongs met in Harzy and proceeded into Wardin. Fighting raged along the main street progressing toward the company command post on the western edge of the village. The enemy was on the verge of capturing the company CP when Captain Wallace announced a withdrawal with, 'Every man for himself.' Captain Wallace, his executive officer, 2nd Lieutenant William Schumaker, and the headquarters group ran through the barn behind the CP and toward the stream to the east, hoping to shelter in the stream bed while making their way back to Bastogne. The two officers never made it.[17]

Near the now abandoned CP, Private Wilbrod Gauthier stood upright in the middle of the street to take on another panzer. His bazooka rocket destroyed its target, but machine-gun fire sliced through Gauthier, killing him instantly.

Continue southeast through Wardin for 1.1 km. Turn left toward Bras (unsigned, but N84) and continue 2.4 km into Bras to the museum on the left. (49.983491, 5.833379)

Bastogne Ardennes 44 Museum
Bras (Bastogne) N84, 635　　　　　　6600 Bastogne, Belgium
Tel: +32 (0)61 217 895
Email: info@bastogneardennes44museum.com
Web: http://www.bastogneardennes44.com/EN/index.html

The museum presents life-size vignettes of battle conditions that are better than average and not behind glass. Video displays show events recorded in 1944. Signage, intended to explain the various vehicles on display, appears in English, Dutch, and French. The cellar is the true highlight of the museum presenting the sights and sounds of the battle while one walks through a battlefield landscape strewn with wreckage and weapons. The noise of battle and the low-light level replicate forest fighting in all its terror. A small shop offers equipment for sale. A well-preserved Hetzer is on display outside of the museum.

Open daily July and August from 10:00 to 18:00; open April through December on weekends from 10:00 to 18:00 and Wednesday through Friday from 13:30 to 18:00. Fee.

17　Captain Claude D Wallace Jr of Tuscaloosa, Alabama, was the recipient of the Bronze Star with two Oak leaf Clusters. He was 23 years old and is buried in Henri-Chapelle American Cemetery, Henri-Chapelle, Belgium.

Chapter Seven

The Defense of Bastogne 317

Battle of Marvie
20 and 23 to 24 December 1944

Lt Col O'Hara relocated his force on high ground overlooking Marvie late on 19 December. His team established daisy-chains of mines across the side road that led to the Wiltz highway and dug in along the road sides. Tanks sheltered behind the hedges while armored engineers built a large road block of interlaced trees and mines at the junction of the Wiltz highway and a farm road that approached Marvie from the southeast.

AMERICAN OBJECTIVE	To block the enemy advance to Bastogne along the Wiltz highway
FORCES	
American:	2nd Battalion (Lieutenant Colonel Roy Inman, later Major RB Galbraieth), 327th Glider Infantry Regiment
German:	Panzergrenadier Regiment 901 (Oberst Paul Freiherr von Hauser); two companies of Panzer Regiment 130 (Oberst Rudolph Gerhardt)
RESULT	The defensive perimeter held
CASUALTIES	
American:	20 December only: 5 killed and 15 wounded
German:	20 December only: 30 killed and 20 taken prisoner
LOCATION	Marvie is 3.5 km southeast of Bastogne

Battle

At 0645 on 20 December, enemy armor shelled Team O'Hara's roadblock on the Wiltz road. At about that same time, newly-arrived companies of 327th GIR supported by O'Hara's five light tanks established fields of fire to the south and east along the edge of Marvie in a rough arc from the village southeast to the Remoifosse road.

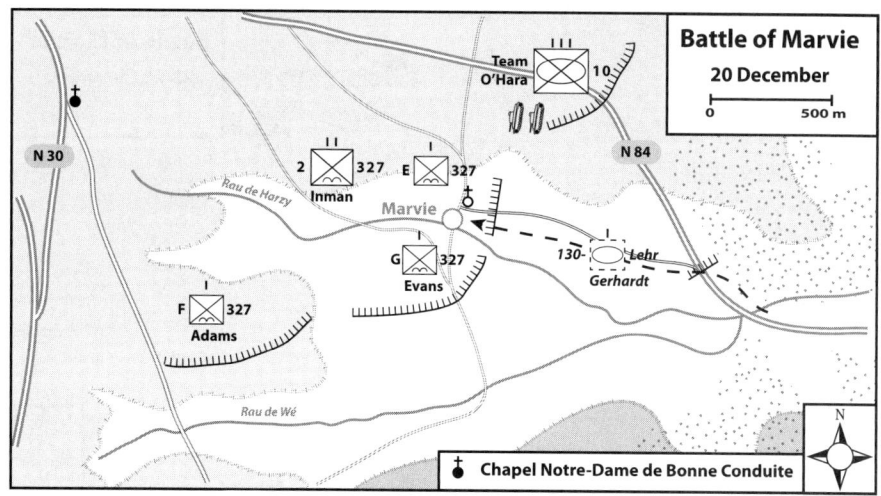

At 1125, the battalion received shell fire from one StuG, four PzKpfw IVs, and six half-tracks that emerged from the woods southeast of the village. German armor also fired at Team O'Hara's light tanks moving among the village buildings. The over-matched tanks withdrew to the north and left for Bastogne. German armor pressed the attack. In minutes, two Shermans up the hill on the approaching enemy's right flank destroyed two panzers and a half-track. A panzer and the StuG III raced toward the village and overran the troopers' foxholes on the northern flank to enter the village only to be met and destroyed by bazooka fire. The fighting became house-to-house.

A PzKpfw IV approached the glider battalion command post where a shell had wounded Colonel Inman, the battalion commander, and Captain Hugh Evans, Company G commander. The fourth PzKpfw IV made a hasty retreat. The remaining half-tracks continued through Marvie while grenadiers engaged Companies E and G in an hours-long gun battle that saw all of the enemy troops killed or captured.

The battle for Marvie renewed on the night of 23/24 December. At 1725 amid a light snowfall, panzergrenadiers and tanks attacked 2nd Battalion, 327th GIR from the south. A platoon of Company G stationed upon Hill 500 became surrounded and lost. The fighting spread through Marvie, causing Major Galbraieth's line to break. The back door into Bastogne was thus wide open.

American commanders were quick to respond. A platoon from Company F extended its line east from the Arlon highway. Batteries D and E, 81st Airborne Antiaircraft Battalion, and remnants of Team Cherry filled in on high ground between the Arlon and Wiltz highways. The 327th GIR Executive Officer Lieutenant Colonel Thomas Rouzie collected sixty-four men from Company F and formed a line in front of the gun batteries. Colonel Harper, despite lacking authority to do so, ordered O'Hara to send two Shermans into the village to counter German armor. The town's buildings changed hands several times in vicious close-quarters fighting while the panzergrenadiers gained a foothold in the south and west portions of the village.

German armor lashed at the right flank on the Arlon highway twice again after

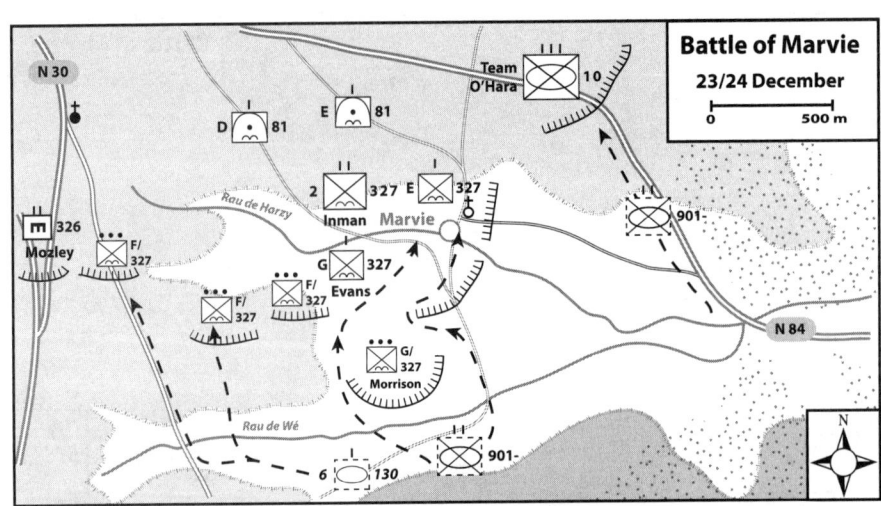

midnight, but they were pushed back by bazooka fire and Shermans from a detachment from Team O'Hara known as Force Charlie 16. Lieutenant Leslie E Smith, Weapons Platoon, and Technical Sergeant Oswald Butler — the same men who had received the German surrender parliamentarians the day before (see below) — held their post despite enemy tanks pumping fifteen rounds into the house and setting it on fire. By dawn the German troops held a few houses in southern Marvie, but later tanks from Team O'Hara later drove them out. During the afternoon, P-47s struck setting much of Marvie aflame.

Battlefield Tour

| Leave Bras west toward Bastogne and follow for 5.4 km. (49.982016, 5.761817) |

Armored engineers constructed a roadblock at this point on the Wiltz highway on 19 December. At 0900 on 20 December, enemy panzers and infantry exited the forest from the south, broke through the roadblock, and proceeded along the Marenwez road on the left to attack Marvie.

| Continue on highway N84 for 1.1 km. (49.989862, 5.752968) |

Lt Col James O'Hara had established minefields across the highway at both ends of this curve and positioned his tanks along the hedge across the roadway. O'Hara's command post had been in a farmhouse farther along the road. The positions offered excellent views from the ridgeline down into the village of Marvie.

| Continue for 400 m and then turn left (south) toward Marvie. |

O'Hara's light tanks were no match for the attacking assault gun and panzers. They exited Marvie along this road in the opposite direction and turned toward Bastogne. The two Sherman tanks that caught German armor in enfilade had embedded in the fields to the east behind the roadside houses. The observation of Marvie from their elevated position is visible from the roadway.

| Proceed 450 m south to the memorials on the right. (49.987032, 5.746730) |

The historical markers in Marvie sit near the north flank of Company E's defensive positions which faced east behind the houses on the left. The gray boulder bears several memorial plaques. On the face, the inscribed stone records the names of twenty-nine civilian victims of the winter offensive, including six members of the Abinet family. The left side bears a recently-inaugurated memorial to the men of the **327th Glider Infantry Regiment** who died in the defense of Marvie.

Circuit Historique #6 briefly describes the two German assaults upon Marvie. The depicted cartoon of Glider Infantry arriving by truck is amusing but inaccurate. The glider troopers marched from Bastogne to Marvie. The Marvie **Sherman tank turret** sits along the main street into Marvie and displays the killing shot by a German armor-piercing shell on the left front quarter. Usually the turret hatch is open allowing a view inside; however, most of the equipment was stripped away long ago.

> Proceed on the left fork in the roadway for 200 m to the church on the left. (49.985361, 5.746767)

On 23 December, German panzers advanced into Marvie from the south as far as the church where they saw the road ahead blocked by a destroyed American half-track. Paratrooper Dennis Parsons machine gunned the rear vents of a PzKpfw IV from his position near the church before a second trooper hit the enemy panzer with a bazooka rocket to finish it off.

The brick house across from the church still belongs to the Nisen family. The Circuit Historique panel describes the miraculous survival of Leo LeBlanc, an American veteran who spent Christmas Eve in the barn at Nisen's farm. LeBlanc recalled a bomb that traversed the thick wall, without exploding, but rendered him deaf for a few moments. In 1999 he met the American aviators who had bombarded the village and faced the men who had nearly killed him.

> Continue 980 m through the village to the road junction passing Hill 500, a broad and weakly-defined high ground at the south end of the village on the right. (49.976919, 5.748187)

The 23 December German attack debouched from the woods to the south from where German panzers maintained an artillery bombardment upon American forces. Lieutenant Harold E Young, commanding an engineer platoon from Company C, 326th Airborne Engineer Battalion, had occupied the hill since 19 December. German panzers took the engineers' machine-gun foxholes under direct fire. Young attempted to reach his forward positions along the road to the east, but panzergrenadiers in white camouflage who moved among the American positions firing their MP40 machine pistols forced him back.[18] Grenadiers and half-tracks moving among the houses at the base of the hill defeated attempts to consolidate. Young led his survivors through patches of woods and eventually into Bastogne.

Lieutenant Stanley Morrison, commanding the 98 men holding Hill 500, responded to Colonel Harper's radioed status request with, 'Now they are all around me. I see tanks just outside my window.' Harper called back three minutes later and Morrison replied, 'We're still holding on.' Morrison and his men were never heard from again.[19]

---

18   The MP40, a German submachine gun produced in large quantities during the war, was capable of firing 500 rounds per minute. The weapon usually was fed from a 32-round detachable magazine. It was frequently, and erroneously, referred to as a 'Schmeisser' after Hugo Schmeisser, who did develop the MP18 submachine gun but had nothing to do with the design of the MP40.

19   Lieutenant Stanley Morrison and many of his men were captured. Morrison spent the remainder of the war in German PoW camp Stalag XIIIb in Weiden, Bavaria.

Chapter Seven   The Defense of Bastogne   321

> Reverse direction and, after 750 m, turn left and then, after 350 m, turn right. Follow for 1.5 km to the junction with highway N84.

The Wiltz highway **Sherman tank turret** sits across the highway slightly to the right. This particular turret drew from a later model M4 tank that carried the more powerful 76-mm gun. (49.994167, 5.729589)

> Turn left to return to Bastogne.

Northern Sector
Battle for Noville (1)
19 to 20 December 1944

Noville straddles the Houffalize highway upon relatively high ground. Large open fields in every direction afforded defenders good fields of fire: however, the terrain is dominated by ridges to the southeast toward Bourcy and a long narrow height that swept from north to northwest of the town. The village church likewise dominated the main intersection. The stucco-covered walls of the village school building stood on the opposing corner.

Team Desobry[20] assembled around the village at 2300 on 18 December. Despite the total darkness and thick fog, Captain Omar Billet's Company B, 20th Armored Infantry Battalion established roadblocks, each consisting of two infantry squads and a tank section[21] on the three roads toward Bourcy, Houffalize, and Vaux. Tank sections and assault guns formed an inner perimeter covering each of the five roads emanating from the village. Infantry squads dug foxholes to protect the tanks and fill in the gaps between the roadblocks. Stragglers from CCR, 9th Armored Division and 28th Infantry Division filtered past the roadblocks before seeking shelter in the village's cellars. It was a long, sleepless night. By 0430, the approach of groups of discouraged GIs had stopped. The next troops to approach would be German.

AMERICAN OBJECTIVE	To defend the northern route into Bastogne
FORCES	
American:	797 men from Team Desobry (Major William Desobry, later Major Charles Hustead) and 1st Battalion (Lieutenant Colonel James L LaPrade, later Major Robert Harwick), 506th Parachute Infantry Regiment
German:	Panzer Regiment 3 and one battalion Panzergrenadier Regiment 2, 2nd Panzer Division (Oberst Meinrad von Lauchert)

---

20 Team Desobry consisted of 20th Armored Infantry Battalion (less Companies A & C); Company B, 3rd Tank Battalion; one platoon, Company C, 609th Tank Destroyer Battalion; 2nd Platoon, Company D, 3rd Tank Battalion (light tanks); one platoon, Company C, 55th Armored Engineer Battalion; one platoon, Troop D, 90th Reconnaissance Squadron.

21 An American tank section usually consisted of two tanks.

Result	American forces were pushed back to Foy
Casualties	
American:	275 killed, wounded, or missing; 11 of 15 tanks destroyed
German:	Over 600 killed or wounded; 31 tanks destroyed
Location	Noville is 8 km north of Bastogne

Battle

At 0530 on 19 December, half-tracks approached the Bourcy roadblock where the lead vehicle stopped a few yards away. When its passengers were heard speaking German, Sergeant Leon D Gantt and his infantry squad showered them with handgrenades. The other vehicles quickly emptied and deployed in the roadside ditches for a 20-minute exchange of automatic weapons fire and handgrenades, during which interlude the Sherman tanks supporting the roadblock were surprisingly quiet. Both sides then slowly disengaged — the Americans returned to Noville.[22]

At 0610, three panzers approached from Houffalize. Staff Sergeant Major I Jones yelled, 'Halt!' and fired a quick burst from his BAR from his foxhole some 75 meters in front of the roadblock. The lead panzer's .50-caliber pinned Jones to the ground while his support Sherman got off one wildly errant shot. The panzer answered with six rounds taking out both Shermans, but the wreckage blocked the roadway. American half-tracks answered with their .50-caliber machine guns while both sides continued firing into the swirling fog. Bazookamen stalked the panzers, but could not secure a firing position. At 0730, the men withdrew to Noville when enemy infantry worked around their flank.

At 1030, the usual morning fog curtain lifted to reveal thirty-two PzKpfw IVs and Vs along the ridgeline that straddled the Vaux road. A platoon from the attached 609th Tank Destroyer Battalion, guns of the 420th Airborne Field Artillery Battalion, and the 3rd Tank Battalion's Shermans opened fire against enemy armor neatly silhouetted atop the ridge. Nine panzers were destroyed and their scattering crews slain by American machine guns while advancing German infantry hit a wall of machine-gun fire. After an hour, the enemy withdrew.

Now knowing that he faced a much larger force, Colonel Desobry radioed Colonel Roberts for assistance. Fortunately, at that precise moment Colonel Robert F Sink's 506th PIR moved north through Bastogne. Sink ordered Lieutenant Colonel James L LaPrade's 1st Battalion to head to Noville. Because of their hasty departure from their French bivouac, the paratroopers were short of almost everything, but especially weapons and ammunition. While they marched north toward Noville, jeeps and trucks distributed handgrenades, mortar bombs, bazooka rockets, and ammunition to the troops. More matériel was piled along the roadside so the men could grab what they needed when they passed.

Both LaPrade and Desobry knew that the town could not be held with enemy armor occupying the surrounding ridges. At 1430, the paratroopers sprinted up the hillsides into a descending fog to take the high ground to the north and east. They

---

22 Staff Sergeant Leon D Gantt was killed in February 1945.

Chapter Seven The Defense of Bastogne 323

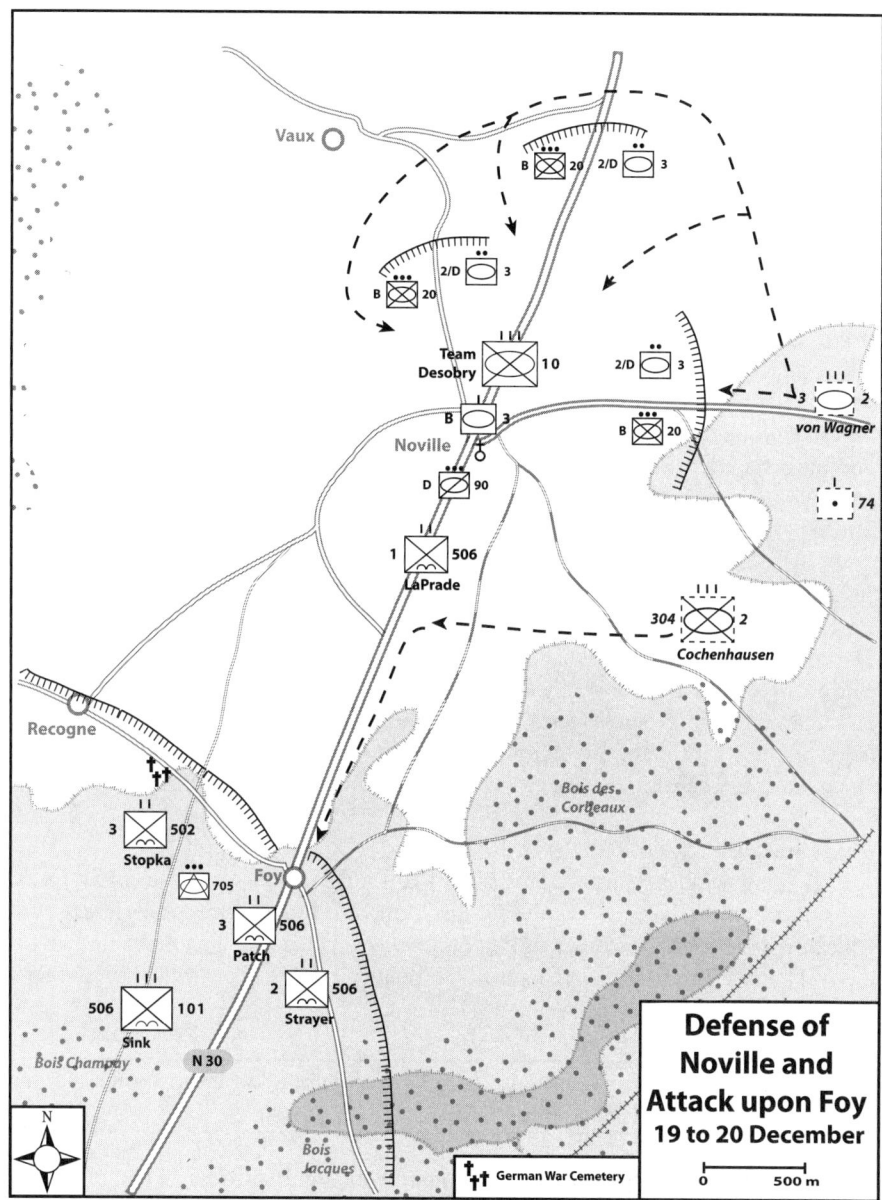

Defense of Noville and Attack upon Foy
19 to 20 December

struck a developing German armored attack of one battalion of grenadiers and sixteen panzers, which fired into the exposed paratroopers while artillery bombarded the town. The Americans scampered back to Noville through fields littered with dead and dying comrades under the cover of American tank-destroyer fire. By 1700, the German assault was halted. German guns and panzers positioned on reverse slopes continued to shell Noville at will. Panzer-led probing attacks and desultory fire continued during the night, looking for a weak spot in the American line.

At 0730 on 20 December, after a two-hour artillery barrage that destroyed what was left of the town, German armor attempted to force its way into Noville along the Houffalize road. One panzer shot its way along the main street, only to be knocked out by a combination of bazooka and tank fire. Small probing actions against Desobry's shrunken perimeter continued all morning. Shortly after dawn, when the battlefield was still shrouded in an all-enveloping fog, Company A's Sergeant Ted Vetland left the Company's foxhole line to hunt the panzers that had shelled and machine-gunned the paratroopers the previous day and night. Vetland possessed a bazooka and carry-bag with three rockets. He could not see the panzers in the gloom, but he could hear the low whine of their idling engines. Vetland crept forward until he could touch the damp armor. He pointed the bazooka at the panzer's midsection and slowly backed away a safe distance while the target faded into the fog. With the bazooka still aimed at its now invisible target, Vetland fired and the panzer exploded in flames. Vetland, unnoticed in the same gloom that hid his enemy, repeated the process and another panzer exploded. The third rocket missed a vulnerable spot but inflicted enough damage to force the crippled panzer to reverse back over the hill.[23] A sudden lifting of the fog revealed fifteen panzers moving around Noville to the south.

At 1300 the Noville commanders received orders to withdraw while the 502nd and 506th PIRs launched diversionary attacks north toward Foy. Medics evacuated the wounded on half-tracks or jeeps, the fighting men on tanks or on foot. The column came under fire when it passed an enemy-occupied roadside house. Enemy panzers fired upon tanks and blocked the roadway with the wreckage of four destroyed Shermans. Men and vehicles farther back in the column left the road to continue across fields on the west side of the highway and on into Foy. Those that attempted to move along the east side were met by German panzers and killed or captured.

Consequences:

The suddenly-thrown together team of tankers, armored infantry, and paratroopers in Noville held against a much larger armored force for 48 hours during which time the overall defenses of Bastogne were organized and strengthened. In turn, the 2nd Panzer Division suffered a two-day delay in its drive toward the Meuse River.

Battlefield Tour

Leave Bastogne northeast on highway N30. Continue 8 km into Noville and park before the church. (50.063409, 5.760659)

The town's **First World War memorial** stands in front of the church and retains the damage suffered during the battle for Noville. Unable to transport unused ordinance from the town, Team Desobry's men piled shells, rockets, and demolitions into the town church. As the last act before leaving Noville, they detonated the ammunition and in the process dropped the church tower into the intersection, where

---

23 Technical Sergeant Theodore Vetland, a native of Norway, was awarded a Silver Star for the destruction of the two German tanks. He was one of a very few original members of Company A, 506th PIR to survive the war.

it formed an effective roadblock and prevented the tower from being used for artillery observation by the Germans. (50.063430, 5.760761)

Walk north along highway N30 and cross to the opposite side of highway N877 that is now re-named rue du général Desobry. (50.063786, 5.761135)

A café that stood on this site was converted to an aid station. Dr John Prior tended to seriously-wounded patients when he received the order to abandon Noville. Prior and his medics did not have transportation for all of the wounded who filled the building's cellar. Prior announced his intention to remain with his patients and become a prisoner of war. At that, the unit's first sergeant enlisted the help of tankers to strip the tavern of its doors and strap a patient to each. The wounded were then placed upon a tank or half-track and evacuated — all while under enemy fire. Dr Prior stewarded his wounded through the German ambush and established the 20th Armored Infantry Battalion's aid station on rue Neufchâteau in Bastogne — the same aid station bombed on Christmas Eve. [24]

Below the street sign, a polished plaque from the Commune of Bastogne records the dedication in English and French, '**General US William R Desobry** (1918 – 1996) 10th Armored Division defended Noville in December 1944 with outstanding courage.'

An attending boulder reads, 'Never Forget,' flanked by images of a tank and an advancing paratrooper. A polished granite plaque on the field stone wall succinctly tells the story of the battle for Noville:

Thanks Boys
Never forget the courage and the sacrifice of the young GIs in the Battle around Noville
-On the 19th and 20th of December 1944 in Noville: 412 losses in the Team Desobry and the 1st BN, 506th PIR (101st Airborne Div) reinforced with a platoon of the 609th Tank Destroyer: the 2nd Panzer Division was stopped; 30 of their tanks were destroyed.
-On 20th of December, the 3rd Bn, 502 PIR and the 3rd Bn, 506 PIR made their withdrawal to Foy possible.
-On the 13th and 14th of January, the 327th Glider Regiment (101st Airborne Div), took action in Bois Jacques.
-On the 14th and 15th of January, the 101st Airborne Div, a Task Force of the 705th Tank Destroyer and the 11th Armored Div of General Patton liberated the region of Noville after heavy losses.
Let us also remember all the civilian victims of this terrible battle.

The Noville elementary school remains across highway N30. The building housed the first **headquarters** of Colonel Desobry and Major LaPrade during the defense of Noville. (50.063722, 5.760613)

---

24 With bullets and shells flying overhead, Dr John Prior frequently risked his life treating wounded on the battlefield. During his military career, Dr Prior received the Silver Star, Bronze Star, French Legion of Merit, and Belgian Croix de Guerre, eventually retiring with the rank of colonel. He survived the war to become a Professor of Pathology in Syracuse, New York. He died in 2007 at age 90, leaving a wife of 59 years, six children, and nineteen grandchildren.

Continue a few meters to the north to a side road on the left.

From this intersection, Sherman tank gunner PFC Delmer Hildoer fired four armor-piercing shells to stop a panzer on the ridge. Four more shots accredited Hildoer with two more panzers. Finally, Hildoer's high-explosive shell destroyed an infantry-loaded half-track approaching on the Houffalize road. The next day, Hildoer spotted enemy troops coming over a slight rise. Hildoer and loader PFC Jerry Goolkasian fired the tank's .50-caliber machine gun into the approaching ranks. Despite the casualties, and as the enemy continued to advance, Hildoer continued to fire until he exhausted his ammunition and heat distorted the machine-gun barrel. While Hildoer and Goolkasian changed the replaceable barrel and searched for more ammo, a mortar shell hit the back deck of the tank. At that moment, the fog lifted to reveal an enemy panzer less than 100 meters distant. The panzer fired and a shell exploded before the Sherman. Goolkasian nearly had an arm torn off, and Hildoer received multiple shrapnel wounds and had an ear severed. Medics brought both men to the aid station in the café. [25] (50.063917, 5.760832)

Return to the church and continue on foot south along highway N30.

Circuit Historique #2 describes the initial liberation of Noville in September 1944, the battle in December, and the subsequent German occupation. When American troops liberated Noville on 10 September, local citizens celebrated their liberation and photographed the occasion. When German SS troops reoccupied Noville on 21 December, they found the photographs. After forcing twenty-three residents to clear away the roadblock formed by the fallen church tower, Gestapo agents took eight of the men behind the Café Louis and executed them. (50.062845, 5.760347)

A fieldstone wall to the rear of the information panel surrounds the '*Enclos des Fusillés*,' where the Gestapo shot seven residents, including the schoolmaster and village priest, Abbé Louis Delvaux. The eighth victim was a refugee from Luxembourg who had evaded conscription into the German Army. (50.062848, 5.760623)

Continue south to address 448 (house 15a in 1944) across the highway.

During the battle, the joint command post moved to this then-vacant building. During the engagement, an American tank recovery vehicle stopped outside the building to report to the commanders. German gunners observed the activity and aimed artillery fire onto the building. One shell, exploding in the street but missing the building, blew fragments into a meeting room occupied by Colonel Desobry and Major LaPrade, among others. Desobry was severely wounded and LaPrade was killed.[26] The executive officers of each unit assumed command. (50.062838, 5.760090)

---

25 Private First Class Delmer David Hildoer survived the war to later fight in Korea and Vietnam. He died in 1979 at age 64 and is buried in Puerto Rico National Cemetery.

Private First Class Jerry Goolkasian, from Dorchester, Massachusetts, kept his left arm, but it was almost totally disabled. He survived the war.

26 Lieutenant Colonel Desobry was taken to the 326th Airborne Medical Company field hospital stationed at Barrère Hinck. A few hours later, German troops overran the hospital, and he was taken prisoner. Desobry spent his captivity in Stalag XIb in Fallingbostel, Germany. He remained in the army after the war, eventually fighting in Vietnam and retiring as a lieutenant general. Desobry is buried in Fort Sam Houston National Cemetery, San Antonio, Texas. He was 77 years old.

Chapter Seven

The Defense of Bastogne 327

> Return to your vehicle and proceed 1.9 km southwest on highway N30 to the parking area on the right. (50.047956, 5.750861)

An M8 armored car, four half-tracks, and five Sherman tanks led the Noville evacuation followed by half-tracks and trucks carrying a mix of wounded and healthy, but dispirited, troops. A platoon of M18 tank destroyers formed the rear guard to keep the panzers at bay. At 1315, when a fortuitous fog again descended upon the town, the column moved south.

North of Foy, a sudden stop by the lead half-track initiated a chain-reaction crash. German small-arms fire then erupted from the roadside ditches and the small red brick farmhouse to the east. While the column behind started and stopped its way forward, three German tanks crossed open fields to the east and established ambush positions just north of Foy. Two Shermans eliminated the threat from the roadside house and then resumed toward Foy, only to fall into the German ambush. The three panzers knocked out the two Shermans and then took the column of vehicles under fire. Grenadiers from PGR 304 strafed American troops who had bailed out of the stalled trucks and half-tracks. German mortar and artillery fire searched out soldiers sheltering in the roadside ditches.

Major Hustead and Captain Billet realized that the only escape into Foy was through the fields to the west. Without order or plan, vehicles that still functioned bounced and rocked over the rough ground. Eventually the survivors entered the 506th PIR's perimeter when darkness fell.

Battle of Foy (1)
20 December 1944

Lieutenant Colonel Lloyd E Patch's 3rd Battalion, 506th PIR entered Foy early in the evening of 19 December after the regiment's 1st Battalion had passed through on its way to Noville. Situated atop a ridgeline facing north, the hamlet afforded a better defensive position than Noville. By 0800 on 20 December, Colonel Patch's force had established back stop positions for Team Desobry along the northwest-southeast running ridge. Patch's men encountered German patrols and occasional enemy artillery fire.

American Objective	To re-establish the northern defensive perimeter	
Forces		
American:	3rd Battalion (Lieutenant Colonel Lloyd E Patch), 506th Parachute Infantry Regiment	
German:	Panzergrenadier Regiment 304 (Major Ernst von Cochenhausen)	
Result	Foy was lost, but further enemy movement was blocked	

Casualties	
American:	Uncertain
German:	80 taken prisoner; 2 tanks and 7 SP-guns destroyed
Location	Foy is 5 km north of Bastogne

Battle

Von Lauchert's 2nd Panzer Division attacked Foy on 20 December. Three platoons of M18 tank destroyers from 705th Tank Destroyer Battalion initially repelled von Lauchert's efforts. By midday, PGR 304 had pushed the paratroopers south of the town and cut the road behind the units still occupying Noville. General McAuliffe ordered Colonel Sink to re-take Foy and Colonel Steve Chappius to drive northeast from Longchamps with his 502nd PIR. The combined efforts were not successful, but they did exert sufficient pressure to give von Lauchert pause. The German panzer commander then requested permission from Lüttwitz to continue into Bastogne — an effort that probably would have been successful at that time. Lüttwitz, however, reminded the division commander that his objective was the Meuse. Accordingly, the Germans lost another opportunity to capture Bastogne.

Aftermath

After the capture of Foy by the 2nd Panzer Division, the armored unit left a security detachment and turned west to cross the Ourthe River via an undamaged bridge at Ourtheuville. Fuel shortages severely hampered further progress, costing the panzer division days of delay in its efforts to reach the Meuse.

Battlefield Tour

Continue southwest 350 m into Foy. Turn right toward Recogne and proceed to the German cemetery 170 m ahead. (50.049233, 5.741334)

On 20 December, the 502nd Parachute Infantry Regiment positioned southwest of Noville in support of Team Desobry to prevent penetration of the Bastogne perimeter. The 3rd Battalion commanded by Lieutenant Colonel John P Stopka fought in and around Recogne all day with support from Company C, 705th Tank Destroyer Battalion. Although they took the village by noon and dug in along the woods to the south, Colonel Stopka decided to abandon Recogne in favor of higher ground to the southwest from where the battalion could retain observation of the village.[27] Recogne was finally re-taken on 9 January only to be lost again the next day.

Circuit Historique #3 describes how the village of Recogne sat between the two armies for much of the battle. (50.049214, 5.741350)

---

27 Lieutenant Colonel [then major] John P Stopka was awarded the Distinguished Service Cross for continuously exposing himself to heavy enemy fire during the paratrooper attack upon Carentan, France on 11 June 1944. Colonel Stopka was killed mistakenly on 14 January 1945 when American aircraft bombed the 3rd Battalion positions. He is buried in Luxembourg American Cemetery, Luxembourg City, Luxembourg.

Access to the **German War Cemetery** in Recogne is provided through a red sandstone chapel set in the corner of the wall enclosure. Gray granite crosses mark each grave and generally recognize three names on each side, totaling six burials per grave. The cemetery holds 6,807 soldiers killed as early as 1940 through to the defeat of the Ardennes Offensive and recovered from the surrounding battlefields. Many of the dead remain listed as *unbekannt* — unidentified. (50.049541, 5.740831)

> Reverse direction and, after 170 m, turn left. Continue 100 m to the memorial on the left. (50.049188, 5.743924)

A monument marks the original location of the **American Temporary Cemetery**, across the highway from the German Cemetery, although the placement of the memorial disguises that fact. In 1948, 2,701 American war dead were reinterred at Henri-Chapelle, Ardennes, or Luxembourg American Cemeteries, and Germany received Belgium permission to utilize the vacated ground for their own war cemetery. Private David J Phillips Company G, 3rd Battalion, 506th Parachute Infantry Division, 101st Airborne Division wrote the quotation on the memorial.[28] It captures the emotions of the one million combatants in eight lines.

> We have only died in vain if you believe so;
> You have to decide the wisdom of our choice,
> By the world which you shall build upon our headstones,
> And the everlasting truth, which have your voice.
>
> Though dead, we are not heroes yet, nor can be,
> 'Til the living by their lives which are the tools,
> Carve us the epitaph of wise men,
> And give us not the epitaph of fools.

> Reverse direction and, after 100 m, turn left back toward Foy. Pass through the village following the road toward Mageret for 800 m to the parking area on the right. (50.033607, 5.752707)

Battle of Bois Jacques (1)
20 to 21 December 1944

A now-abandoned rail line ran from Bastogne to Bourcy and formed the boundary between the 501st and 506th PIRs but the confusion of battle had prevented the two companies from making contact. Oberst Kokott, recognizing the opportunity, dispatched a battalion of grenadiers supported by seven StuGs along the rail line toward Bastogne.

Company A, 501st, in reserve in a quarry near Luzery, came under attack by a 30-man German patrol at 2300 on 19 December. The patrol was repulsed, but its

---

28 Private David J Phillips edited the divisional history of the 101st Airborne Division before returning to Nebraska and enjoying a long career in newspaper writing and public relations. He died in 2009 at age 83 and is buried in Sacramento Valley National Cemetery, California.

appearance brought Colonel Ewell's attention to the vulnerability of this sector of the front.

AMERICAN OBJECTIVE	To block the enemy advance into Bastogne from the northeast
FORCES	
American:	Company A (Lieutenant Joseph B Schweiker), 501st Parachute Infantry Regiment; Company D (Captain Richard G Snodgrass), 501st PIR; and Company D (Captain Joe F McMillan), 506th Parachute Infantry Regiment
German:	A battalion of Grenadier Regiment 77 (Oberstleutnant Martin Schriefer)
RESULT	A firm defensive line was established in the Bois Jacques
CASUALTIES	
American:	Approximately 6 killed or wounded
German:	55 killed, 100 taken prisoner, and 80 unspecified casualties
LOCATION	Bois Jacques is 4 km north of Bastogne

Battle

On 20 December, patrols from Company D, 501st PIR tried four times to move north toward Foy, but enemy fire emanating from the Bois Jacques in the vicinity of a rural train stop at the intersection of the rail line and the Foy–Bizory road thwarted each attempt.[29] Meanwhile, Company D, 506th PIR also pushed toward the rail line from Foy but was otherwise occupied fending off small groups in the Bois Jacques and along the Foy–Bizory road several hundred meters west of Halt.

Around 1600 on 20 December, Company A, 501st PIR, led by the company's Executive Officer Lieutenant Joseph B Schweiker, pulled out of its positions near Neffe and advanced northeast along the rail line to close the gap between the two 'D' Companies. The patrol entered the fir plantation south of the tracks and west of the Foy–Bizory road. Approximately 300 meters to the west of the Foy–Bizory road and at the edge of the wood, German-speaking Private First Class William C Michel heard the approach of German troops. The 3rd Platoon deployed along the wood north of the rail line and prepared an ambush. In the deepening gloom of approaching nightfall and intensifying fog, the lead German platoon fell to a surprise volley. The enemy force of two companies unloaded mortar, grenade, and automatic weapons fire onto 1st and 2nd Platoons from south of the tracks. The engagement continued in darkness with each force firing at enemy rifle flashes. At risk of being outflanked from the north, 3rd Platoon pulled westward to protect the rear of Company A. At 2230, Lt Schweiker ordered his men to fall back to a plantation south of the rail line. The German force also withdrew.

---

29   The train stop became incorrectly known as the 'Halt' station to GIs, named after the German language 'Stop' sign at the rail crossing.

Chapter Seven — The Defense of Bastogne

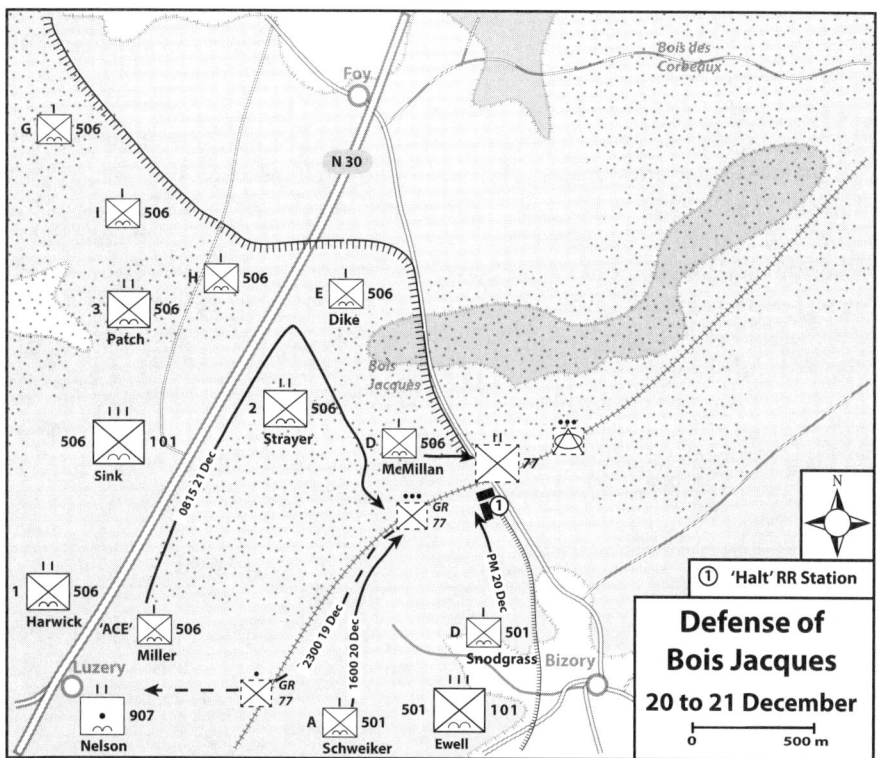

The 1st Battalion, 506th PIR, even though badly depleted from the fighting and its escape from Noville, sent its Companies A and C forward from Luzery. On the morning of 21 December, paratroopers moved against the German force at Halt station from the northeast, north, east, southwest, and south amid heavy morning fog that hid their movement from enemy observation. By 1100, the enemy force was completely enveloped. For the remainder of the day, the companies rooted out enemy troops from the woods.

Aftermath

The enemy's best chance to drive into Bastogne from the northeast was lost. The 501st and 506th sectors became relatively quiet until 1 January 1945.

Battlefield Tour

The 2nd Battalion, 506th PIR held the front from south of Foy to the rail line with Company E on the left and Company D on the right. The period of quiet came, however, not without its risks. Besides the cold and eerie nighttime silence, American and German units dispatched frequent patrols to search out the opposition's outposts or main line of resistance and to bring back prisoners for questioning. Sporadic machine-gun fire or mortar attacks kept everyone on edge.

A **Bois Jacques Monument** inaugurated in 2015 pays homage to the men who engaged in violent combat in the Bois Jacques during the bitter winter of 1944-

1945. The fieldstone plinth carries the carved images of a soldier cradling his rifle while attempting to keep his hands warm, a single soldier in reflection inside a church, and an American Sherman tank.

A well-established path leads from the rear of the monument to the remains of shell craters and the foxholes of the men of Company E, 506th PIR hidden in the dark and foreboding **Bois Jacques,** where the sun rarely penetrates and undergrowth is absent. The rectangular and gradually disappearing depressions originated as two-man foxholes in which the paratroopers attempted to shelter from the numbing cold, fearsomely quiet nights, and the air bursts of German artillery shells. Just inside the tree line overlooking the Bizory–Foy road is a particularly strong line of eight-to-ten foxholes facing the enemy, who at times were as near as the opposite side of the road. (50.03461, 5.75259)

The forested area holds numerous other foxholes scattered among the trees. Positions facing Foy at the northern end of the forest, found at (50.03609, 5.74998), and a row of five foxhole depressions located along the edge of the forest at (50.03346, 5.7511), are indicative of the density of American paratrooper positions.

> Continue south for 600 m to the memorial on the right. (50.028871, 5.756397)

The memorial commemorates the actions of **Company E, 2nd Battalion, 506th PIR, 101st Airborne Division**, and records the names of fourteen Company E men killed during the defense of Bastogne (the *Band of Brothers* television miniseries depicted the company's actions). The center pier proudly displays the Screaming Eagle emblem of the 101st, but the engraved scene below is more emblematic of the fight for Bastogne: cold, weary soldiers with glazed eyes, passing the upturned rifle of a dead comrade. In the distance behind the memorial is the Bois Jacques, where the 101st Airborne fought off German attempts to penetrate the Bastogne perimeter. The center panel is titled 'May the world never forget,' followed by a description of the fighting in the Bois Jacques. The inscription ends with 'Airborne Always, Men of E Company.'

Walk 30 m south to the rail crossing (now a hiking and bicycle path. (50.028613, 5.756564)

The occupied house was once the so-called **'Halt' train station** — a rural stop on the Bourcy to Bastogne rail line. The intersection and surrounding forests saw intense fighting during German attempts to penetrate the perimeter and later while American troops fought to regain the ground. Lt Schweiker and his company engaged, and defeated a much larger force from 26th VGD approximately 350 meters to the southwest.

> From the Easy Company memorial, reverse direction and return to Foy. Turn southwest to return to Bastogne (N30). Only 500 m after the Foy intersection, note the white-and-gray home on the right before continuing into Bastogne. (50.04069 5.74633)

Chapter Seven The Defense of Bastogne

The stone indicating the **Farthest Advance** of German forces south of Foy is now all but lost behind the driveway wall of a newly-constructed home. The stone marks the limit of the German advance on 20 December. It also indicates the location of the start of the attack by 3rd Battalion, 506th PIR to recover the hamlet the following January. The tour returns to this area later to review the conclusion of the fighting for Foy, Noville, and the Bois Jacques.

Other Memorial or Relics (northern Sector)

> **Bizory**
> Four thousand trees arranged in the mother and child symbol of UNICEF within a circular ring fill the **Bois de la Paix**. The designed plantation is dedicated to American and Belgian veterans of the battle and the servicemen and civilians who died during the fighting. Individual trees bear a plaque carrying the name of returning veterans. Sign posts spaced around the circular ring speak to various European cities, describing their history and involvement in the Second World War (in French, German, and English). The site, whose signs provide explanations of the purpose of the memorial, is always open. No admission charge; entrance path at (50.027547, 5.770759); parking at (50.026743, 5.769271).

Northwestern Sector
Affair at Barrère Hinck (Crossroads X)
19 to 21 December 1944

NO OBJECTIVE	An accidental encounter when a German reconnaissance patrol advanced west seeking a crossing of the Ourthe River
FORCES	
American:	326th Airborne Medical Company (Lieutenant Colonel David Gold)
German:	Panzer Reconnaissance Battalion 2 (Hauptmann von Böhm)
RESULT	The American unit was captured
CASUALTIES	
American:	At least 3 killed and 142 taken prisoner
German:	unknown
LOCATION	Barrère Hinck is 12 km northwest of Bastogne

Battle

At approximately 2230 on 19 December, a reconnaissance detachment from the 2nd Panzer Division, estimated at one-hundred infantry soldiers supported by six armored half-tracks, proceeded southwest on the Houffalize–St-Hubert road to a rural crossroads known locally as Barrère Hinck, nicknamed 'Crossroads X' by American troops. Two nights earlier, 326th Airborne Medical Company had established the 101st Division's Clearing Hospital in the adjoining fields. The half-tracks sprayed the undefended medical tents with machine-gun fire. During the attack, a convoy of twelve trucks approached from Bastogne on its way back to Reims. The German

334   The Bulge Battlefields

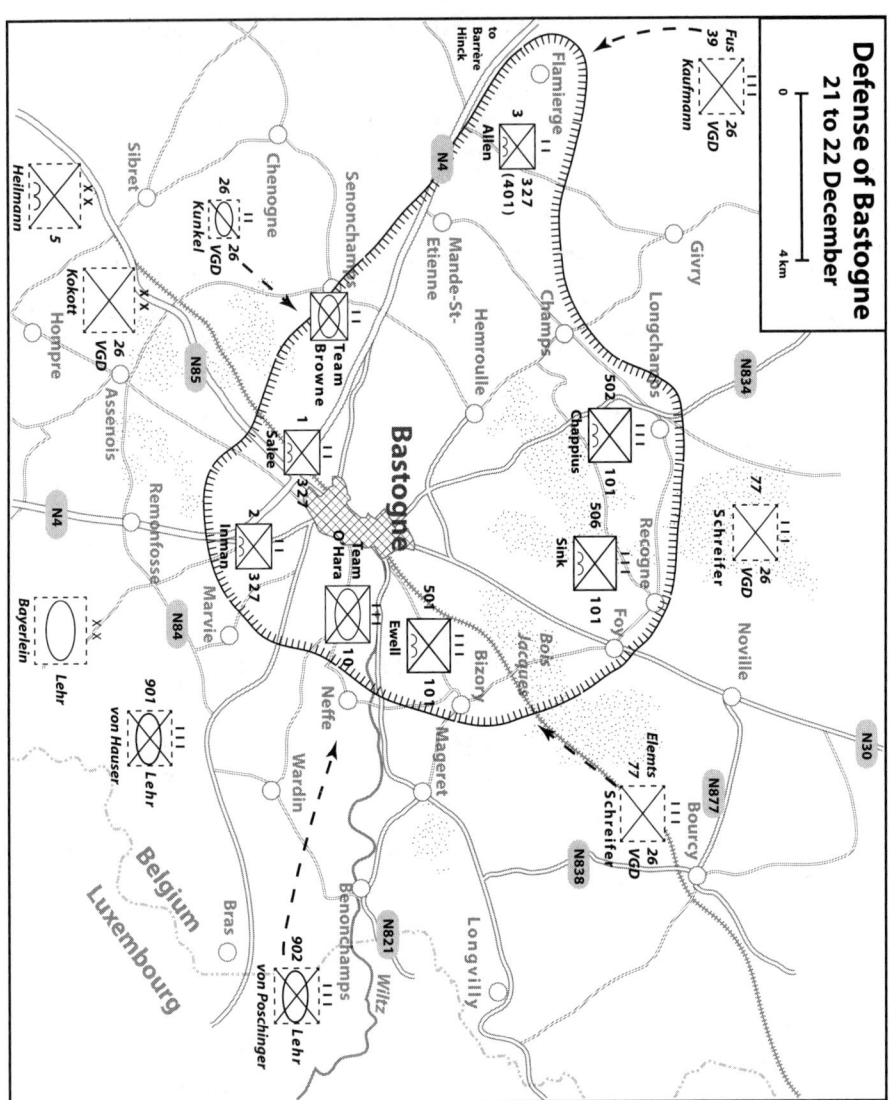

gunners set each truck on fire despite desperate resistance by the trucks' drivers using their cab mounted .50-caliber machine guns.

After a discussion with the enemy commander, Division Surgeon Lieutenant Colonel David Gold surrendered the medical company to the enemy. The German troops allowed the medics thirty minutes to load equipment and personnel onto vehicles and then escorted them back to German lines.[30]

---

30   Lieutenant Colonel David Gold was imprisoned in Oflag 64, a German PoW camp in the old Polish Corridor. In late January 1945, the approaching Soviet Red Army forced the abandonment of the camp and nearly 2,000 officers (Oflag camps held captured officers only) marched westward in temperatures as low as sixteen degrees below zero and snow drifts three meters deep. The group traveled 234 miles in 60 days to a camp west of Berlin where Colonel Gold was eventually liberated.

Chapter Seven The Defense of Bastogne

The American command was shocked that enemy troops had managed to maneuver behind the defensive perimeter so quickly, and as Captain Robert J MacDonald and his Company B, 401st Glider Infantry Regiment approached the road junction shortly after midnight on 20 December. Scouts observed sixteen burning trucks and a few German soldiers milling among the bullet-riddled tents of the abandoned field hospital. MacDonald sited his 2nd and 3rd Platoons to occupy blocking positions near the road. The 1st Platoon and Weapons Platoon blocked the middle along the Marche-en-Famenne road. At the scouts' signal, the troopers' machine guns and BARs opened fire, killing or scattering the enemy. Only a few managed to escape into the Bois de Herbiamont. At 0445, MacDonald repositioned his men to defend the crossroads.

At daybreak on 21 December, bazookamen positioned north of the crossroads beside the Marche road heard the clank of approaching armor. Twenty-year-old Private George Karpac, from Allegheny County, Pennsylvania, lay on the road with his armed bazooka. Suddenly he spied two PzKpfw IVs coming out of the haze directly down the roadway. Karpac's first shot missed. The panzer fired its main gun at a second bazooka team, who had also missed. While the panzer reloaded, Karpac dashed back into the roadway. His shot hit, and the iron monster started to slowly brew-up. The second panzer slowly reversed back into the fog.

At 0900, Sergeant Mike Campana's 3rd Platoon ambushed and destroyed nine vehicles from a 2nd Panzer Division column traveling south from Houffalize. American control of the crossroads by a lone company of glider infantrymen forced German units west of Bastogne to make a long detour, further worsening their supply problems.

Determined to eliminate the threat to his supply lines, von Lauchert sent a weak kampfgruppe against the lone company later that afternoon. MacDonald held his position until 1600 when, under threat of being cut off by enemy troops approaching from Sibret, he received orders to withdraw back to Flamizoulle. For almost thirty-six hours, one rifle company had disrupted the supply line to an entire panzer division.

> Leave Bastogne toward Bruxelles / Marche on highway N84, then merge onto highway N4. After 10.1 km, exit the limited access highway toward Barrière Hinck At the end of the ramp, turn right (N826) and then execute a U-turn 500 m ahead to return under highway N4. Stop at the memorial on the left 210 m ahead. (50.04661, 5.56973).

The once-isolated crossroads has been extensively redeveloped to accommodate traffic on the important Arlon–Namur highway (N4). Regardless, a memorial to **326th Airborne Medical Company** stands nearby. Under the insignia of the 101st Airborne, the inscription describes the capture of the medics and ends with, 'This site is to memorize (sic) all the victims and to honor the 326th Airborne Medical Company and all other medical units who served during WW2. They had their rendezvous with destiny. May this monument be a symbol of honor for those brave men and women who were willing to give their lives while saving others, some came home but so many didn't.' Unfortunately, thick roadside vegetation prevents views into the field behind the memorial where the aide station stood in 1944.

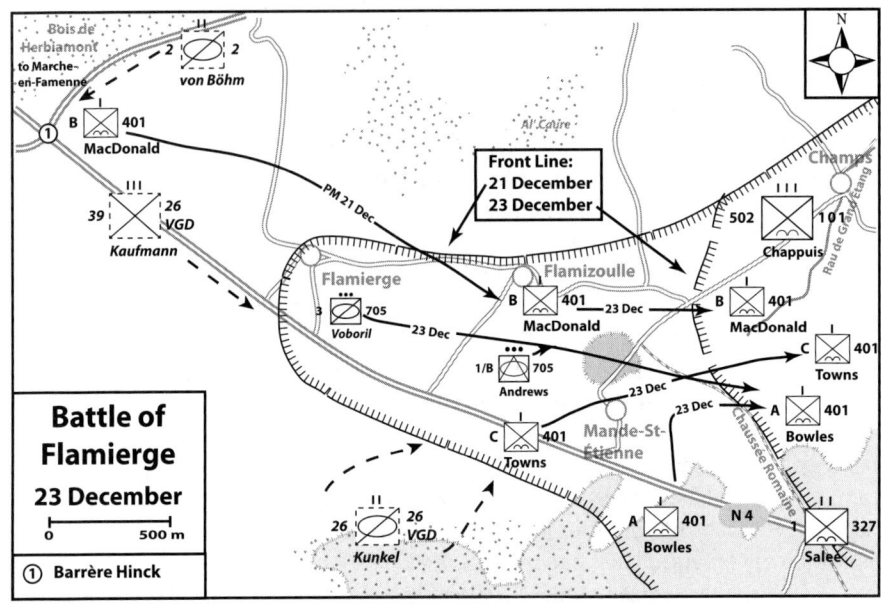

Reverse direction and return toward Bastogne (N4). After approximately 3.0 km, exit the highway toward Flamierge. Continue 850 m into Flamierge. Turn right at the T-junction and follow the roadway for 320 m where it curves broadly to the right and stop at the memorial on the left. (50.033092, 5.603668)

Battle of Flamierge
23 December 1944

German Objective	To push against the American perimeter from the northwest
Forces	
American:	1st Battalion, 401st Glider Infantry Regiment (Lieutenant Colonel Ray C Allen) and 3rd Platoon (Lieutenant Rudolph Voboril), Reconnaissance Company, 705th Tank Destroyer Battalion
German:	Fusilier Regiment 39 (Oberstleutnant Walter Kaufmann), 26th Volksgrenadier Division and Reconnaissance Battalion 26 (Major Rolf Kunkel), 26th Volksgrenadier Division
Result	The American salient was eliminated
Casualties	
American:	unknown
German:	unknown
Location	Flamierge is 9.5 km northwest of Bastogne

Battle

At 0950 on 23 December, Lieutenant Rudolph Voboril's platoon, with a squad of Company B, 502nd PIR attached, moved against German troops who had easily occupied Flamierge earlier that morning. Transported by jeeps, two M8 armored cars, and strengthened by one Stuart tank converted to hold a 75-mm howitzer, the unit stopped along the road from Flamizoulle during an ammunition-limited American artillery bombardment. German machine guns fired down the road from houses on the eastern edge of the village. While the troopers sheltered in roadside ditches, the modified Stuart gun fired into every house while it moved along the highway. The dismounted troopers following behind the Stuart threw fragmentation grenades into each house while they advanced. Within one hour the village was taken along with twenty prisoners.

By noon, the grenadiers were back at Flamierge moving in from the west behind a wall of mortar fire. Lt Voboril's armored cars ferried in reinforcements while a growing melée of automatic-weapons fire ricocheted through the village streets. At 1600, threatened with being cut-off by a German flanking action, Voboril's force fell back to Flamisoul (Flamizoulle).

On 23 December, about the same time that the enemy counterattacked Flamierge, Kampfgruppe Kunkel, backed by five panzers, hit Captain Preston Towns's Company C near Mande St-Etienne from the west. A re-enforcement platoon of six M18 tank destroyers sent to repel the German PzKpfw IVs was ambushed on the Marché-en-Famenne highway, where it exited a cut east of Cochelonval. After two M18s were knocked out, the four survivors made a dash back to Mande that was now under assault by panzergrenadiers and a dozen more PzKpfw IVs and Panthers.[31]

The timely airdrop of artillery ammunition earlier that day saved Colonel Allen's 1st Battalion, 401st GIR from encirclement. The 75-mm rounds from 463rd PFA Battalion fell on a cluster of ten panzers. Nonetheless, the pressure of German fire against Mande continued and, at 1840, Colonel Allen ordered his companies to execute a leapfrog withdrawal to a new defensive line west of Hemroulle.

Aftermath

General McAuliffe ordered a general shortening of Bastogne's defensive perimeter abandoning Flamierge, Flamizoulle, and Mande St-Etienne to growing enemy pressure.

Battlefield Tour

No memorial to the defense of Flamierge exists, but a stone commemorates the village's liberation. On 7 January, the **513th PIR, 17th Airborne Division** crossed 1.6 kilometers of knee-deep snow to seize Flamierge. Major Morris Anderson's 3rd Battalion led the way down the gradual slope to the edge of the village. The open fields offered no cover, whereby German panzers, artillery, and mortars met the advance. The battalion halted 150 meters from the village when American artillery laid down

---

31 Captain Preston Towns was killed on 26 December during bombing by an American P-47. Towns is buried in the Luxembourg American Cemetery, Luxembourg City, Luxembourg.

a heavy barrage in support. Bazookas knocked out two panzers while paratroopers cleared the houses with handgrenades.

Unfortunately, the 193rd Glider Infantry Regiment on the right flank had not kept pace, thus prompting enemy troops to infiltrate behind Anderson's position in the village. At 0600 the next day, fifteen to twenty panzers converged upon Flamierge from the Al' Caure Woods to the north. Several more panzers with infantry and six SP-guns attacked through heavy morning fog from the east. Artillery fire was random because of the lack of visibility and intermittent radio contact. Bazooka fire held the panzers at bay, but their shells fell upon paratrooper foxholes. The fighting continued until 2100 when the last two panzers withdrew.

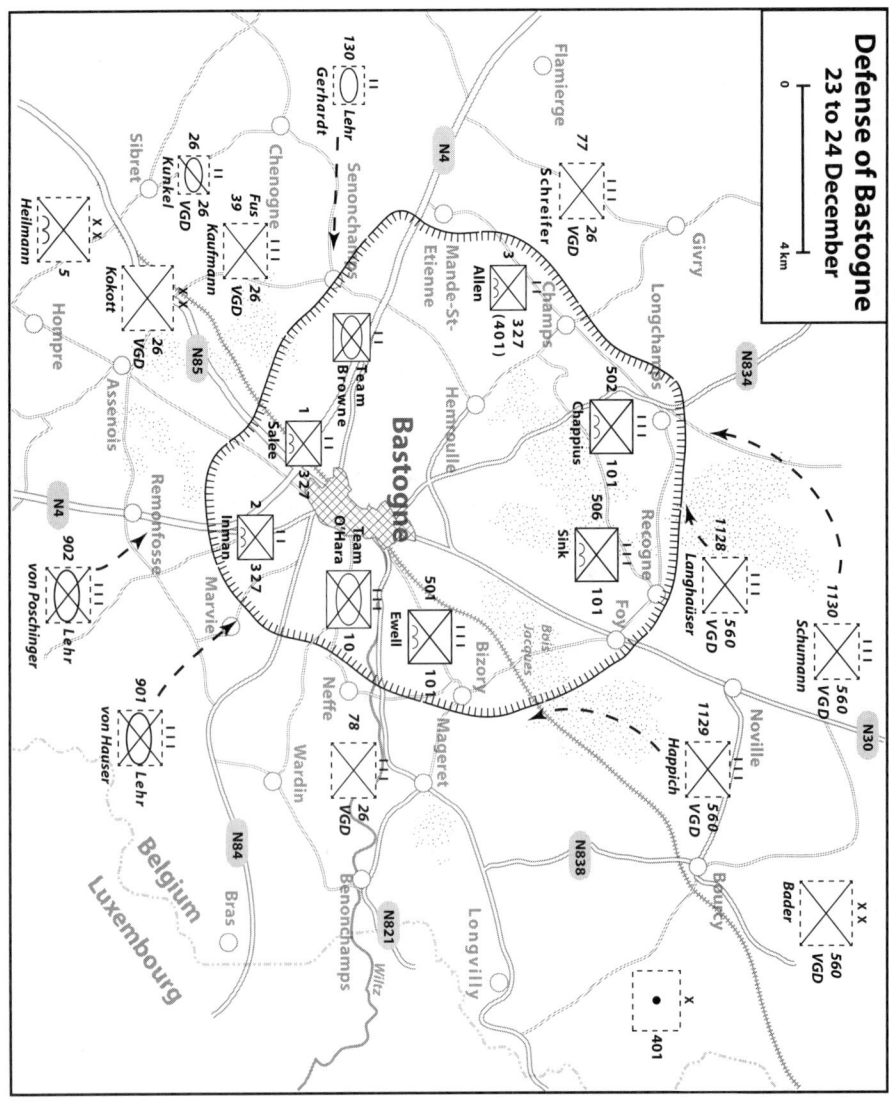

Chapter Seven   The Defense of Bastogne   339

Major Anderson's men had been battered without rest for two days. Early on 9 January, they withdrew. The battalion had been reduced by one-half. After a short rest and hot food, the men were back on the frontline.

Battle of Champs
25 December 1944

Terrain west of the Bastogne–Givry road between Champs and Hemroulle consisted of gently rolling hills broken by only a few isolated woodlots. The ground was quite different east of the road. Several small streams and frozen ponds cut larger forests and sloping hills. Therefore, the west was tank country whereas the east favored infantry movement. Champs lay in a valley overlooked by hills to north and south.

The encirclement of Bastogne and the news of the evacuation of St-Vith led Oberst Kokott to believe that American forces in Bastogne were also looking for a way out of the city. Activity along the roadways to Neufchâteau and Marche-en-Famenne convinced Kokott that the Americans were feeling out his troops. Of course, Kokott was wrong, but his mistaken belief led him to tighten the noose. His Grenadier Regiment 77 relieved the 2nd Panzer Division units of responsibility for the northwest sector.

The temporary attachment of the mechanized 15th Panzergrenadier Division gave Kokott the armored power he felt that he needed to punch into Bastogne. For his final assault, Kokott chose the ground around Champs toward Hemroulle, where open fields, now-frozen soil, and few wooded areas provided his troops the terrain that they needed for a successful assault against the already worn 401st GIR. Kokott planned to spend Christmas Day in Bastogne.

GERMAN OBJECTIVE	To drive along the Marche and Champs highways directly into Bastogne
FORCES	
American:	Mande St-Etienne: Company A (Captain Howard G Bowles), 401st Glider Infantry Regiment; Champs: Company A (Captain Wallace Swanson), 502nd Parachute Infantry Regiment and Company C (Captain George R Cody), 502nd Parachute Infantry Regiment Hemroulle: 463rd Parachute Field Artillery Battalion (Lieutenant Colonel John Cooper)
German:	Mande St-Etienne: Panzergrenadier Regiment 115 (Oberst Wolfgang Maucke) Champs: Grenadier Regiment 77 (Oberstleutnant Martin Schriefer)
RESULT	The German attack was repulsed with significant losses

Casualties	
American:	9 killed, 16 wounded, and 6 missing
German:	166 killed, over 100 wounded, and 127 taken prisoner
Location	Champs is 6.5 km northwest of Bastogne

Battle

Two battalions of Panzergrenadier Regiment 115, supported by the PzKpfw IVs of Hauptman Schmidt's Panzer Battalion 115, led the Christmas Day assault upon Bastogne. Fourteen PzKpfw IVs and three StuG IIIs formed up in Al' Caure Woods before dividing into two columns. The I Battalion attacked along the Marche-en-Famenne road through Mande St-Etienne against the 401st GIR's 1st Battalion. The German III Battalion provided flank protection to the north. Heavy fog, especially in the lower valleys, shrouded white camouflaged attackers while they moved along the Rau de Flamizoulle valley and through Flamizoulle. At the same time, Grenadier Regiment 77 supported by four 'Hetzer' SP-guns attacked Champs from the north, intending to continue through Hemroulle into Bastogne. German artillery batteries started their preliminary bombardment at 0330 on 25 December. In addition to 105-mm shells, the Americans at Champs felt the tremble of German bombers. It was the beginning of the final assault upon Bastogne that they had all been expecting.

The infantry and armored assault moved directly toward the center of Company A's 75-man line. A patrol from Captain Howard G Bowles's Company A, 401st PIR detected the panzer approach although his men held only a few bazookas. Captain Bowles let the German armor pass followed by the white-clad panzergrenadiers. Four tank destroyers from Company A, 705th Tank Destroyer Battalion — the same unit whose two vehicles were destroyed attacking Flamierge two days earlier — supported Captain Bowles with overlapping fields of fire.

The 75-mm Pack howitzers of Colonel John T Cooper's 463rd PFA Battalion sent 123 rounds of high-explosives into the enemy clusters, but they continued to follow the advancing armor only to have the survivors fall to massed .50-caliber machine-gun fire from Captain Bowles' by-passed force.

To the north, German armor passed through reserve Company C's lines where the column split with seven PzKpfw IVs and three StuG's turning north toward Champs and four PzKpfw IVs, pulling sled-loads of panzergrenadiers, turning southeast. The armor moving north aimed directly for Colonel Allen's battalion headquarters along the Champs–Hemroulle road. Allen, his staff, and Company C, 502nd PIR moving forward to support Company A at Champs, all dashed for the woods while 75-mm tank shells smashed the two-story farmhouse. Panzergrenadiers captured those who did not move fast enough. The German tanks, by then outpacing their infantry support and upon unreconnoitered ground, hesitated to move forward. They clustered around the farm house headquarters awaiting orders and for the infantry to catch up. The infantry, however, did not show – it had been slaughtered by the glider infantry's machine guns.

German armor eventually moved north toward Champs approaching the 502nd regimental headquarters at Château Rolle, manned by only headquarters personnel — radio operators, cooks, clerks, engineers, and twenty walking wounded.

Chapter Seven   The Defense of Bastogne   341

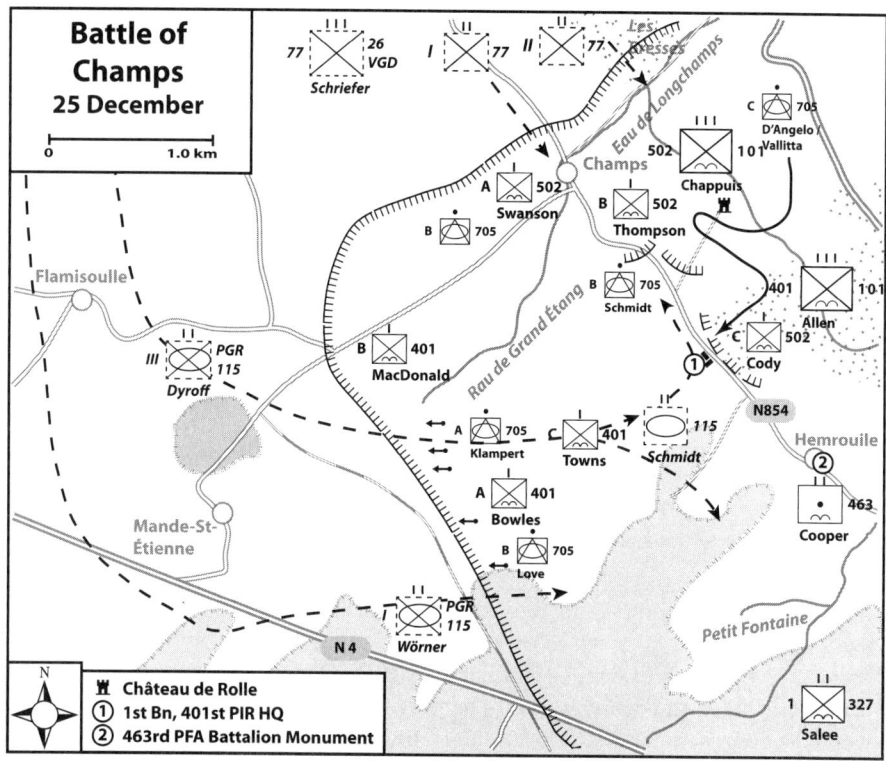

Tank destroyers intercepted the column and set four panzers aflame from enfilade positions in the forest. Only two PzKpfw IVs remained to approach the chateau. A bazooka rocket disabled one, and the final vehicle escaped. The four PzKpfw IVs that proceeded southeast fell into an armor-killing zone established by the 463rd PFAB. Caught in deadly artillery crossfire, all four were destroyed.

Meanwhile, I Battalion, Grenadier Regiment 77 at Champs penetrated between Company A's 1st and 3rd Platoons, and set the 2nd Platoon command post on fire. The Americans continued to fight even while moving rearwards. Burning haystacks and German flares silhouetted the grenadiers, making them easy targets for the tank destroyer's machine guns. By 0330, hand-to-hand fighting occurred in Champs. Grenadiers backed by Hetzer SP guns fought down the Givry–Champs road to occupy the chapel and most of the houses on the right side of the highway to the northwest. For a moment, the Germans sensed that they might win the battle for Champs while the paratroopers hid from the Hetzers' guns. While the morning progressed, German fire grew weaker under the assault of two tank destroyers until it ceased altogether. By 0530 the battle had turned in the American's favor. By 0600 the battle was over.

Aftermath

None of the armor in either German attack survived. By 0900, the extended battlefield had claimed fourteen German armored vehicles destroyed and all of the infantry killed or captured. Hasso von Manteuffel stated after the war that the losses were so severe that the attacking divisions were no longer able to launch large scale operations.

On 31 December, I Battalion, Grenadier Regiment 77 launched a diversionary dawn attack against the 1st Battalion, 502nd PIR holding Champs. The shrunken force, although supported by artillery, attempted to capture and hold the three northernmost buildings while the II Battalion targeted the hilltop observation site to the west. Although initially successful, the enemy was destroyed after two hours of snow-shrouded fighting. German casualties amounted to 55 killed and 37 taken prisoner while Americans suffered 3 killed, 4 wounded, and 9 taken prisoner (all later released).

Battlefield Tour

> Leave Flamierge to the east toward Flamisoul by turning right (signed toward Champs on a small street sign on the right).

The German attack started from the woods to the left and crossed the fields and creek valleys to achieve the Bastogne–Marche highway (N4) highway.

> In Flamisoul, follow the large curve around to the right and then to the left to exit the village after a total distance of 1.9 km. Turn right and stop anywhere along the highway. Mande St-Etienne is straight ahead. The American foxholes were in the pastures in the distance to the left. The gravel road to the left does approach the woodlots described below (at 50.011056, 5.661088), but it is not worth the effort to continue.

At 0710, the southern column of I Battalion, Panzergrenadier Regiment 115 passed along the Marche road (N4) through Mande St-Etienne. An M18 commanded by Sergeant Clyde J Love of Sugar Grove, North Carolina sheltered in a small woodlot behind the foxholes of Company A, 401st GIR. The last two of four PzKpfw IVs moved up the draw, heading east. Love fired his 76-mm gun and one panzer brewed up. Love turned his attention to the second PzKpfw IV lumbering up the incline pulling a sled of panzergrenadiers. Love's gunner fired at the rear of the panzer and it started to burn while the lead two panzers escaped over the rise toward Hemroulle.

> Reverse direction and proceed approximately 2.4 km toward Champs. Turn right at the end of the road onto highway N854 (unsigned, but a memorial stands above the road on the right). Follow highway N854 for 1.0 km before turning right onto the well-sunken, gravel farm track sandwiched between mature trees and continue (or walk) 120 m to the first gentle curve to the right for overviews to the south and southwest. (50.031122, 5.676536)

Hemroulle was a small village of a dozen farmhouses and less than one-hundred inhabitants who rode out the battle in their cellars. Companies B and C, 502nd

PIR were stationed as a reserve around Hemroulle with their headquarters in a two-story farmhouse along highway N854. (50.027295, 5.682262)

PzKpfw IVs attacked Allen's headquarters from the right across the field to the south. The M18 tank destroyer of Sergeant George Schmidt hid in ambush behind haystacks. At 0800 Schmidt squinted through the pre-dawn fog to see the source of the tank noise coming from the south. Schmidt rolled forward 100 meters to see six PzKpfw IVs and three StuGs crossing the field before him. After firing several rounds at the vague shadows, Schmidt ordered a rapid reverse to again hide.

Sgt Schmidt noticed the first two StuGs heading for Champs. He waited until they crested the ridge before firing — knocking out two in rapid succession. However, the fire revealed his positions to a trailing PzKpfw IV. After firing one 75-mm armor-piercing shell, Schmidt's vehicle was a burning wreck. Sgt Schmidt and crew member Private Manuel Rivas were killed.[32]

After the German panzers captured the battalion CP, Captain George R Cody reorganized his scattered Company C in the woods across the Champs–Hemroulle highway (N854). At 0400, Company A commander Captain Wallace Swanson ordered forward two M18 tank destroyers commanded by Sergeants Anthony D'Angelo and Lawrence Valletta. The latter's tank destroyer cleared the houses of the enemy by slowly inching his lightly-armored vehicle along the road and putting German positions under fire as identified by the paratroopers. The force of one shell from its powerful 76-mm gun could collapse an entire building.

D'Angelo's and Valletta's tank destroyers then sheltered along the northern edge of the woods, visible in the distance across the highway to the left. Their gray shapes were well-camouflaged in the dark forest, only 200 meters from the four PzKpfw IVs in the farmhouse courtyard. Their positions provided perfect sightlines along the Champs–Hemroulle road — and all but invisible to the enemy.

German armor moved from the farmhouse northwest toward Champs with the apparent intention to link up with Grenadier Regiment 77. With everything at their disposal, Captain Cody's men opened fire upon the panzers and a few accompanying German infantry. When the panzers turned north, they exposed their flanks to D'Angelo and Valletta's tank destroyers.[33] D'Angelo shouted to his gunner to take the last tank in the line while Valletta took the lead tank under fire. Firing fast and accurately from an optimum range, both tank destroyers' first shots hit their targets, destroying two panzers. When Valletta's gun jammed, D'Angelo took on the remaining enemy armor. All together, a total of six shots silenced four PzKpfw IVs. D'Angelo's final shot hit its victim in the rear, causing its ammunition to ignite in white-hot flames.

The two leading PzKpfw IVs escaped D'Angelo's death grip and continued on toward Champs. Combat engineer Sergeant Schuyler Jackson, hiding behind the

---

32 Sergeant George Schmidt, from Pardeeville, Wisconsin, was awarded a posthumous Silver Star. He had previously held off the German attack upon Mont on 20 December with the tank destroyer's .50-caliber machine gun.

Private Manuel Rivas, from Tombstone, Arizona, is buried in Luxembourg American Cemetery, Luxembourg City, Luxembourg.

33 One panzer turned south at the farmhouse and went toward Hemroulle. It was destroyed by 463rd PFA Battalion. That panzer was the one that had knocked out Schmidt's tank destroyer.

trees lining the approach road to Château Rolle on the east side on N854, readied a hastily-commandeered bazooka. He let the first of the two escaping panzers pass before he put a rocket into the trailing vehicle's engine compartment. His excited ad hoc loader had forgotten to pull the safety pin from the second rocket and, although Jackson scored a perfect hit upon the panzers turret base, the rocket did not ignite. One lucky panzer that escaped over the crest of the roadway to the north was found days later, the victim of some unknown weapon.[34]

The 17th century stone **Château Rolle** [35] sits along a straight lane across the highway once-lined with elm and pine trees and nearly surrounded by trout ponds. The ancient ruins of an earlier 10th century castle stood nearby. The building held Col Chappuis's headquarters. The chateau is private and should not be approached. (50.032191, 5.677609)

> Return to highway N854, is best done by driving to the first curve of the farm track where a wide flat area allows turning. Turn left to regain highway N854 toward Champs. Continue 1.0 km to the memorial on the left. Turn left and park in the area behind the memorial. (50.038277, 5.669762)

The memorial at the intersection is titled '**Bertogne Remembers**,' referring to the local municipality to which Champs belongs. The white cross and gray stone commemorate the 60th anniversary of the Battle of the Bulge.

> Continue 190 m into Champs to the intersection with the road to Longchamps, where an information board appears on the right. (50.039793, 5.668832)

Captain Swanson's Company A established a roadblock across this intersection as a last fall-back position. His command post operated in a large structure near the intersection.

Circuit Historique #12, dedicated to Col Chappius and the men of the 502nd Parachute Infantry Regiment, stands near the intersection. It also presents several photographs of Château Rolle during the encirclement of the colonel's headquarters. A **Sherman tank turret** sits behind the information panel. The version carries the longer and more powerful 76-mm gun aimed toward Champs. (50.039804, 5.668904)

> Continue north on highway N854 for 1.1 km to a roadway picnic area on the left (50.047836, 5.659767)

When the Christmas attack upon Champs started at 0300, Corporal Willis Fowler manned a .30-caliber machine gun in a pit to the west of the Givry–Champs road. Fowler had personally cleaned the gun the night before as a precaution against jamming from accumulated moisture, dirt, and lubricant. For almost three hours,

---

34 Sergeant Schuyler Jackson was awarded a Silver Star.
35 The family Rolle name was changed to Rolley after the war, as it now appears on modern maps.

Fowler poured belt-after-belt of machine-gun rounds into the white camouflaged grenadiers approaching down the road or across the open fields to the northwest. Across the road, American machine guns had failed to operate in the below-freezing temperatures, whereby outpost positions fell to the advancing grenadiers who moved along the road capturing house after house. Fowler's foresight in meticulously maintaining his weapon and his courage in engaging a large enemy force saved the left flank of the company. Fire from a 'Hetzer' that appeared over the ridge to the left damaged Corporal Fowler's machine gun and put a tank destroyer out of action.[36]

Forward artillery observer Lieutenant James Robinson used a lull in the fighting to occupy an observation position that he had identified days before. While the paratroopers in Champs sheltered without an answer for the Hetzers, Robinson called in the hillside's co-ordinates. Under pressure from 75-mm high explosive rounds, the Hetzers withdrew behind the ridgeline. Later that morning, four P-47s bombed and strafed the reverse hillside, permanently eliminating the Hetzer threat.

The high ridge line over which German troops had advanced and that Fowler had defended with his machine gun is evident to the left. The wooded position of Lt Robinson's observation post lies some distance on the opposite side of that ridge, marked today by an electricity pylon.

> Reverse direction and, after 1.1 km, turn left toward Longchamps. After 950 m, stop at the logging road on the left just past the stone house on the right. (50.045669, 5.677858)

Les Bresses Woods lies on the left. The II Battalion, Grenadier Regiment 77 crept along two forest lanes flanking the Rau Routte, using the thick forest and foggy early morning darkness to hide their approach toward Château Rolle in the forest to the east. The grenadiers infiltrated, surprised, and routed the outpost line west of the Champs–Longchamps road. However, they were observed by alerted American troops where the terrain sloped down to the roadway and the woods thinned. Just yards apart, both lines erupted in gunfire while the 377th Parachute Field Artillery Battalion fired round after round of 75-mm high explosive shells into the wood, covering it with metal shards and wood splinters. German survivors of the devastating tree bursts retreated. The threat to Château Rolle had ended.

> Again, reverse direction and return to Champs. Turn left toward Bastogne (N854) and continue 2.6 km to the church in Hemroulle on the left. (50.022491, 5.688893)

During the fighting, Major John Hanlon, commander 1st Battalion, 502nd PIR borrowed forty-eight bed sheets from the villagers of Hemroulle to camouflage his troops amid the new-fallen snow. Thus began a practice widely exercised during

---

36   Corporal Willis Fowler, a former peanut farmer from Cordele, Georgia, was awarded a Silver Star.

346   The Bulge Battlefields

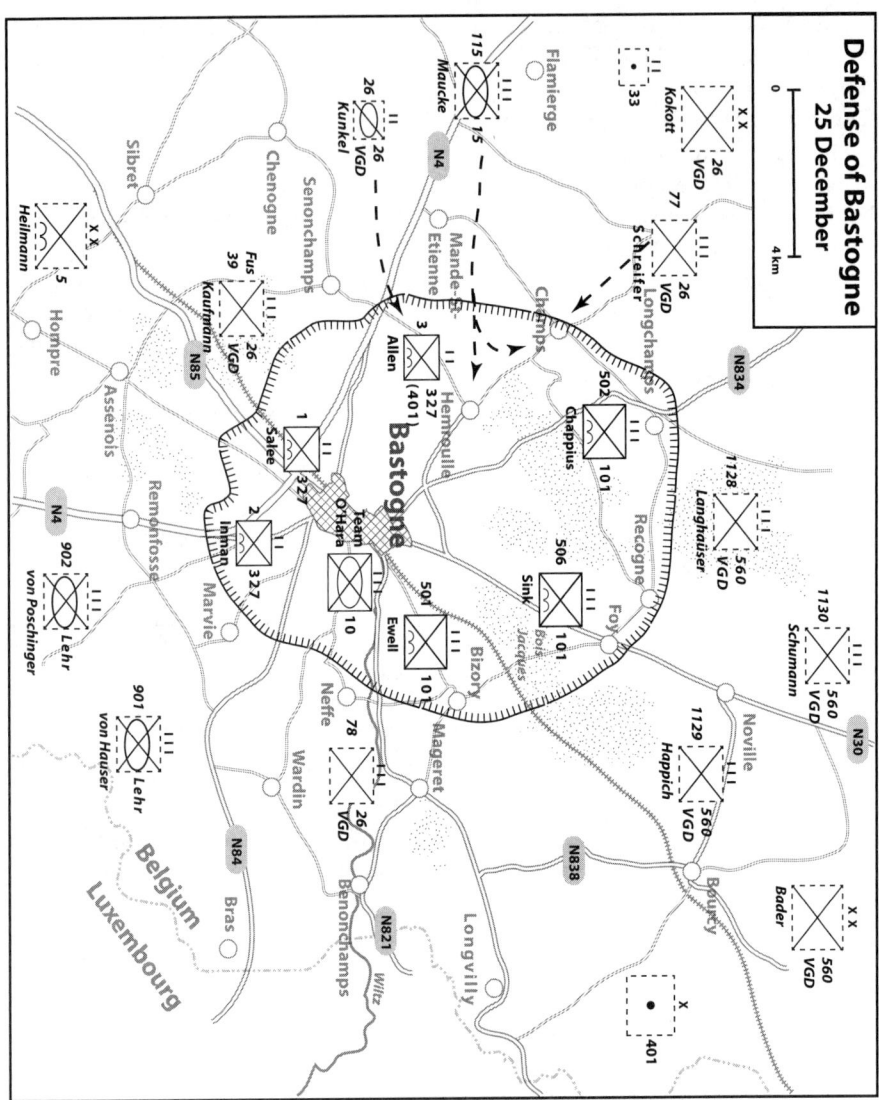

the Bastogne fighting. Soldiers would borrow or liberate white bed sheets to hide their dark appearance against the pure white snowy backdrops.[37]

Oberst Wolfgang Maucke's southern armored column achieved the hills above Hemroulle — only 1.5 kilometers from Bastogne. Lieutenant Colonel John Cooper, commanding 463rd PFA Battalion, headquartered in a farm house across the road from the church. He felt the possibility of a German tank assault and planned

---

[37] Major Hanlon returned to civilian life in Winchester, Massachusetts, but never forgot the kindness of the villagers. In 1948, he put out a call to replace the bed linen that was lent to his soldiers and destroyed. The people of Winchester responded with 740 bed sheets. Hanlon delivered the replacements personally during a much-celebrated return to Hemroulle.

accordingly, positioning his M1A1 75-mm Pack howitzers in an arc to the east along the still-visible tree line that marks the Rau de Petit Fontaine.

Shortly after dawn at 0830, the remaining four PzKpfw IVs unknowingly moved forward into the artillery trap. Batteries B and D fired their guns almost simultaneously and continued firing while shells slammed into the frozen hillside or the panzer's frontal armor. Machine guns stripped panzergrenadiers from the sides of the armor. After artillery fire destroyed the leading three tanks and the supporting infantry vanquished, the attack on Bastogne was over.

Circuit Historique #14, almost totally obscured by massive arborvitae shrubs, displays photographs of the battle for Hemroulle and the story of John Hanlon collecting bed sheets from his home town for the local citizens.

The church wall behind the Circuit Historique bears a small but really quite attractive and heartfelt memorial dedicated to the American paratroopers of the **463rd Parachute Field Artillery Battalion**.

Continue to follow highway N854 back into Bastogne.

Other Points of Interest near Champs

Bertogne

The busy and high-speed highway N826 between Bertogne and Givry holds **Monument des Fusillés** dedicated to four inhabitants of Givry killed by the occupying forces on 23 December 1944 for acts of resistance. A laborer discovered their bodies on 16 March 1945. The victims were extracted from two shallow trenches with their hands still bound. The memorial is fronted by a small parking area for 1 or 2 vehicles. The memorial consists of a large rough hewn rock with an inscribed cross bearing the names of the individuals.[38] Location: 12 km northwest of Bastogne beside highway N826. (50.074564, 5.651855)

Opening the Corridor
21 to 26 December 1944

During a meeting on 20 December, Generals Patton and Middleton decided to break the anticipated Bastogne encirclement by sending Major General Hugh Gaffey's 4th Armored Division north on the Arlon highway and the 26th and 80th Infantry Divisions through the Luxembourg countryside east of that road to protect the 4th Division's right flank.

The 4th Armored Division began its advance in two columns with CCB along the Arlon highway and CCA along secondary roads to the west. During the afternoon of 22 December, CCA approached Martelange, 20 kilometers south of Bastogne, and its two demolished bridges across the deep gorge of the Sûre River. A brief skirmish with a company from the 5th Fallschirmjäger Division occurred, and the construction

---

[38] They were Achille Choffray, Fernand Pierson, Cyrille Wenkin, and Maurice LaForge.

of a Bailey bridge over the river delayed the combat command until the next afternoon. Meanwhile, Brigadier General Holmes Dager's CCB moved north toward Hompré.

> Leave Bastogne south toward Martelange / Arlon on highway N4. After 9.7 km, exit toward Hollange and follow rue de la Chapelle (becomes rue du Tilleul) through Hollange for 5.2 km. At the T-junction, turn left onto rue des Neufs Prés and continue 550 m to cross the Pont de Menufontaine (49.886046, 5.658762) and stop at the farm track on the left 40 m south of the bridge. Total one-way distance: 19.5 km.

Battle of Chaumont
23 to 25 December 1944

The leading 8th Tank Battalion, commanded by Major Albin Irzyk, approached Burnon on 22 December while receiving harassing fire from weakly-defended German positions. The small bridge over the Sûre River, destroyed during the American withdrawal, had to be replaced. The reconstruction effort completed, the task force continued forward all night. Chaumont, the next village on the road toward Bastogne, lay in swampy lowlands drained by the Grandru Creek and surrounded by connected ridge lines.

AMERICAN OBJECTIVE		To break the German encirclement of Bastogne
FORCES		
	American:	CCB (Brigadier General Holmes Dager), 4th Armored Division
	German:	One company of Fallschirmjäger Regiment 14 (Oberst Arno Schimmel), 5th Fallschirmjäger Division; later Assault Gun Brigade 11 and Fusilier Regiment 39, 26th Volksgrenadier Division (Oberst Heinz Kokott)
RESULT		CCB's progress toward Bastogne was delayed for two days
CASUALTIES		
	American:	318th Regiment: 100 casualties 10th Armored Infantry: 65 casualties 8th Tank Battalion: 24 tanks knocked out
	German:	Uncertain
LOCATION		Chaumont is 11 km south of Bastogne

Battle

Shortly after midnight on 23 December, light Stuart tanks and jeeps from the 25th Armored Reconnaissance Battalion crept forward over the frozen ground to encounter light small-arms fire while the force approached Chaumont. Antitank guns knocked out one of the tanks. The main force deployed upon a partially-wooded ridge south of the village.

Shortly after dawn, the 22nd Armored Field Artillery Battalion pounded the houses of Chaumont followed by the fighter-bombers of the XIX Tactical Air

Chapter Seven

The Defense of Bastogne 349

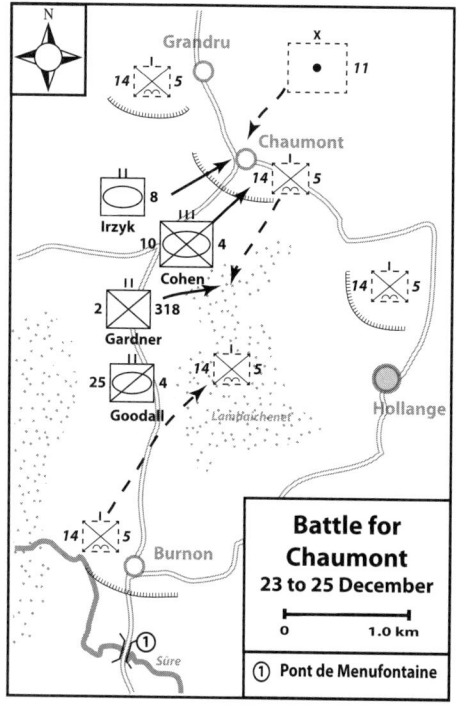

Battle for Chaumont
23 to 25 December

① Pont de Menufontaine

Command. A ground assault by Major Irzyk's tanks and Lieutenant Colonel Harold Cohen's 10th Armored Infantry Battalion began at 1330 with Company B tanks in the center and Company's A and C on the right and left flank, respectively.

An entire platoon of five Company C tanks bogged down in the thawing fields bordering a flowing creek while the infantry fought through the village against a company of fallschirmjäger. General Kokott had dispatched his Assault Gun Brigade 11 to move along a wooded trail from Hompré to the north and down the ridge into Chaumont. Ten StuG III assault guns mounting 75-mm guns and five Jagdtigers[39] from Heavy Panzerjäger Battalion 653 arrived to extract a heavy toll on American tanks moving along the valley roadway. The panzers rained armor-piercing and high-explosive shells upon American forces from the ridge while German infantry approached behind a smoke screen. Eleven Shermans were knocked out and 65 men lost when the heavy firepower drove back American infantry. First Lieutenant Charles R Gniot, the sole surviving officer from Company A, remained behind to cover the withdrawal back up the hillside with his BAR until he too was killed.[40]

CCB had only two platoons of medium tanks still operational and thus spent most of 24 December awaiting replacements and repairs. Reinforced by the 2nd Battalion, 318th Infantry Regiment, detached from the neighboring 80th Infantry Division, General Dager made another push against Chaumont on 25 December. By then enemy troops were well dug in throughout the woods south of the village, but the fearsome Jagdtigers had departed for Alsace. While Major Irzyk's tanks fired indiscriminately into the pine-wood lots, Lieutenant Colonel Glenn Gardner's infantry overcame strong rifle and automatic weapons fire to clear the enemy positions. By dark, the enemy had withdrawn farther north.

Battlefield Tour

On 22 December the tanks of leading Company A of Major Irzyk's task force received German fire and deployed west of the roadway. The Sûre's boggy ground

---

39   The Panzerjäger Tiger Ausf B, or *Jagdtiger*, was a 72-ton behemoth carrying a deadly 128-mm Pak 44 L/55 gun. Only 88 such vehicles were built, and only three remain in existence.

40   First Lieutenant Charles R Gniot was awarded the Distinguished Service Cross posthumously. He is buried in Luxembourg American Cemetery, Luxembourg City.

running parallel to the roadway prevented deployment to the east. The tanks continued to fire across the Sûre while they approached the destroyed Pont de Menufontaine. The 22nd Armored Artillery Battalion deployed and started to drop shells around the bridge site and the area across from it. The 24th Armored Engineer Battalion spent two hours constructing a 36-foot treadway bridge across the rain swollen stream. Armored infantry swarmed across followed by Company A tanks to establish and widen a bridgehead. By 2100, the troops achieved open ground north of Burnon.

The rebuilt bridge over the narrow Sûre River today does not appear to present a significant obstacle. However, the road twists down to the bridge and back up again out of the valley with some very sharp turns. The difficulty of maneuvering these roadways in winter ice is obvious. Terrain prevented overland movement.

> Leave the Menufontaine bridge to the north and follow for 2.9 km, stopping at a farm track on the right. (49.909815, 5.660930)

Under orders from General Patton to move all night, Irzyk encountered enemy infantry at 2300 firing upon the mobile force from the Bois de Lambaichenet east of the highway. German artillery, panzerfaust, and small-arms fire erupted against the 25th Cavalry Squadron reconnaissance troops when they reached this point. In the cold and darkness of that December night, Major Irzyk had met the edge of German defenses.

Days later, the woods became a staging area for continued raiding attacks upon CCB after Dager's force had been displaced from Chaumont. Irzyk turned his artillery upon the woods along with eight P-47s. Infantry moved in and cleared the forest of enemy. By 25 December, after the enemy had re-infiltrated the woods, it had to be cleared again by 2nd Battalion, 318th Regiment, with the support of the eight remaining tanks of Company A, 8th Tank Battalion. The short but difficult action completed, the 2nd Battalion continued forward.

> Continue 1.0 km to the memorial on the right. (49.917297, 5.667310)

During the advance of 23 December, panzerfaust fire, or perhaps a mine at this spot, hit one of the reconnaissance squadron's jeeps, completely destroying the vehicle and killing all four occupants. The impact was so severe that the body of one of its occupants was blown into the branches of the tree. A Signal Corp photographer captured the scene, that image became a symbol of CCB's attack upon Chaumont and the intensity of winter combat in the Ardennes.

Beneath that very same tree, a memorial to the 4th Armored Division takes the form of a metal plaque attached to a rough stone bearing the unit insignia and a dedication (in French only), 'To the American combatants and civilian victims killed at Chaumont during the Battle of the Ardennes December 1944 – January 1945.' An adjacent information board describes the battle in graphic detail.

Fallschirmjägers pressured the woods to the southeast on 25 December when Private Paul Wiedorfer's platoon became pinned down by fire from emplaced machine guns. Slipping and sliding across the snow-covered open ground, Wiedorfer single-handedly charged two enemy machine-gun positions. He eliminated the first team with a hand grenade. After wounding a member of the second German gun team with rifle fire, the remaining six enemy troops surrendered.[41]

> Continue 350 m to the small park at the road fork. (49.919122, 5.670783)

During the German counterattack in Chaumont, Irzyk was wounded when his tank was hit by a German 128-mm Jagdtiger shell while it attempted to escape back out of town to the southwest. Irzyk and the tank crew's lives were saved by a 6-inch thick armor plate mounted upon the rear of his turret that deflected the armor piercing shell up and over the Sherman tank.

The **place du général Irzyk** is a small park with a heartfelt memorial to him and his men. The polished granite plaque commemorates (later) Brigadier General Irzyk and his men who executed a 161-mile non-stop, drive from Lorraine, France to Bastogne. An information panel describes events before the final assault upon Chaumont and Grandru on 25 December.

> Continue into Chaumont for 160 m to the rue du Colonel H Cohen (49.920217, 5.672241)

The memorial to Colonel Cohen, an inscribed plaque mounted upon a simple wood stele, remembers Colonel Harold Cohen, commander of the 10th Armored Infantry Battalion, and his troops as part of the task force that captured and liberated Chaumont and Grandru on 25 December 1944 while undergoing the loss of over 65 of their men.

Other Points of Interest near Martelange

Perlé
The 385th Bombardment Group (Heavy), part of the US Eighth Air Force, performed strategic bombing missions during the war flying B-17 medium bombers. On 12 July 1944, two B-17 'Flying Fortresses' collided over Perlé while on a mission to bomb Munich, Germany. The aircraft flown by Captain Richard B White caught the prop wash of a preceding plane, nosed up, and hit the aircraft flown by 1st Lieutenant Robert L McDonald. Both aircraft plummeted to earth while only two crew members parachuted to safety. One survivor was quickly captured by German occupation authorities while the other escaped across the border with the help of local Belgian Maquis. Burning wreckage and exploding ordinance spread around the village, with only a few charred bodies found and carried to the village schoolhouse — now the home of the museum.

---

41 Sergeant Paul J Wiedorfer received the Medal of Honor.

WW II 385th Bombardment Group (Heavy) Memorial Museum
6 rue de l'Église
Grand Duchy of Luxembourg
Email: museum385bg@yahoo.com
L-8826 Perlé
Tel: +352 23 64 94 65
Web: http://www.385bg.com

The private museum displays an antiaircraft gun standing in front of the building. Interior displays include radio equipment, relics of crashed aircraft, models, and photographs of aircrews. The museum started as a collection of debris from the two crashed planes, but over the years donations, including some from the families of the victims, have expanded the collection.
Open only on request, no admission fee.
Location: 25 km south of Bastogne or 5 km south of Martelange beside rue de l'Église (CR312). (49.810084, 5.763984)

A memorial in front of the village church salutes the **eighteen airmen** who died. Their names inscribed on the plinth, the monument in the form of a window frame holds a bent aircraft propeller in its center, and its base forms a short watercourse.
Location: in Perlé 120 m south of the museum. (49.809395, 5.764917)

[42]

Boulaide
On 27 December 1944, the 35th Infantry Division's 137th Infantry Regiment liberated nearby Surre after overcoming stubborn resistance. Meanwhile, the division's 320th Infantry Regiment waded the icy Sûre River to liberate Boulaide and Bashleiden against Panzergrenadier Regiment 104, 15th Panzergrenadier Division.
A memorial stands in a shrub-enclosed garden where a tall mountain rock bears an inscribed slate tablet that states, 'In memory of the valiant soldiers of the **35th Division of Infantry** US 1944-1945.' (French only)
Location: 17 km southeast of Bastogne beside highway CR310 at the southwestern outskirts of the village. (49.882826, 5.808884)

Hochfels Park looks down from bluff high above the Sûre River. The park's panoramic view over the river valley provided siting for German field guns, and two examples remain. A German **88-mm Pak43** antitank gun and a **German 155-mm sFH18 heavy field howitzer** stand at the forest edge. Large wooden panels describe each gun's performance characteristics.
Location: at the extreme end of an 800-meter-long narrow country lane that junctions with highway CR310 750 m south of the memorial park. (49.871938, 5.808089)

---

[42] Captain Richard B White and 1st Lieutenant Robert L McDonald are buried in Henri-Chapelle American Cemetery, Henri-Chapelle, Belgium.

Chapter Seven

The Defense of Bastogne 353

> **Bigonville**
> On 22 December 1944, the advance guard of the Führer Grenadier Brigade looked to cut the Arlon–Bastogne highway. The 4th Armored Division's Major General Hugh Gaffey ordered his division's Combat Command Reserve to intercept the enemy force by moving toward Bigonville. Slowed by icy highways, the 53rd Armored Infantry Battalion and 37th Tank Battalion struggled cautiously ahead until they came under fire from troops of Fallschirmjäger Regiment 13 from a wood 1.5 kilometers south of Bigonville. During the night, the enemy force withdrew to the stone houses of the village.
> The next morning, teams of infantry and tanks approached the town only to fall under attack by mortars, bazookas, and small-arms fire. The tanks blasted the buildings while the infantry moved house-to-house and machine-gunned those enemy troops attempting to flee. By 1100 the town had cleared, with 328 prisoners taken.
> Two memorials appear just below the tower of the church. A large mountain stone flanked with flagpoles commemorates the liberation of the town by the 4th Armored Division. A second smaller stone bears a plaque dedicated to **Lt Robert M Lamar** of 355 Fighter Squadron, 354th Fighter Group. Lamar had flown a P-47D 'Thunderbolt' north of Bastogne on 2 January 1945 when his aircraft was hit by flak. He managed to reach an open plateau southwest of Bigonville before executing a belly landing and surviving his crash. The plaque was erected as a tribute to all of the men of the 8th and 9th USAAF.
> Location: 26 km south of Bastogne or 6 km east of Martelange in the center of the village near highway CR310. (49.850085, 5.792853)

[43]

> Follow the same route through Grandru and, after 3.3 km, stop at the fenced monument on the corner. (49.947361, 5.663952)

Battle of Assenois
26 December 1944

After four days of navigating landmines, shell craters, snow, fog, and iced roads, the 4th Armored Division had advanced to within only 8 kilometers (5 miles) from Bastogne. The division's CCR,[44] whose units were generally utilized as rest and replacement opportunities, left Neufchâteau shortly before noon on Christmas Day to approach Bastogne along that highway. The tanks and half-tracks raced through Vaux-les-Rosières with machine guns firing against a German engineering outpost. To avoid a potentially strong enemy force near Sibret, the unit commander, Colonel Wendell Blanchard, left the main road toward Nives in favor of secondary roads through Remioville, Clochimont, and Assenois.

---

43 Lt Robert M Lamar of Augusta, Georgia survived the war.

44 CCR, 4th Armored Division consisted of twenty Sherman tanks from the 37th Tank Battalion; the 53rd Armored Infantry Battalion; a platoon of SP-tank destroyers; the SP-guns of the 94th AFA Battalion; and a battery of 155-mm howitzers of 177th FA Battalion.

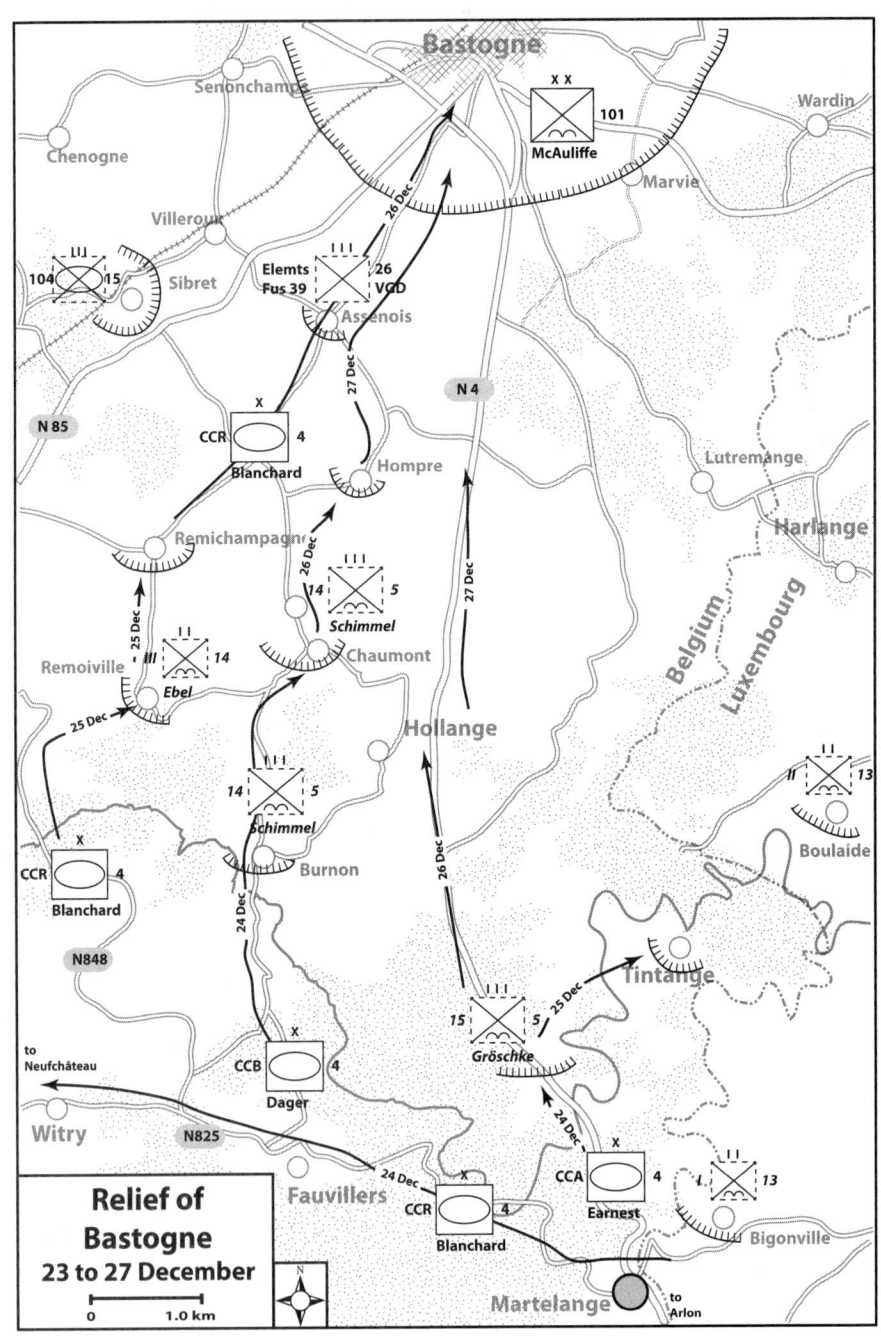

Relief of Bastogne
23 to 27 December

Chapter Seven

The Defense of Bastogne

AMERICAN OBJECTIVE	To break the German encirclement of Bastogne
FORCES	
American:	CCR (Colonel Wendell Blanchard), 4th Armored Division
German:	Fallschirmjäger Regiment 14 (Oberst Arno Schimmel) and 5th Fallschirmjäger Division
RESULT	American tanks opened and maintained a relief corridor
CASUALTIES	
American:	37th Tank Battalion: 5 killed, 22 wounded, 5 missing and 16 tanks knocked out
	53rd Armored Infantry Battalion: 30 killed and 180 wounded
German:	Estimated 150 killed and 380 taken prisoner
LOCATION	Assenois is 5 km south of Bastogne

Battle

Colonel Blanchard's Combat Command R, having encountered Major Ferdinand Ebel's III Battalion in Rémoiville, overran that unit with massed fire from four artillery battalions. The town, cleared by dusk, surrendered 327 prisoners. CCR then passed through Remichampagne on 26 December after P-47s cleared the way. At 1500, the leading tanks reached the road junction south of Clochimont. Ahead in front of Assenois, the terrain featured wide open, undulating hills. The enemy had positioned seven antitank guns in front of a rail line that ran along the creek bed southeast of the village.

After a brief conference, 29-year-old Lieutenant Colonel Creighton Abrams,[45] commander 37th Tank Battalion, and Lieutenant Colonel George L Jaques, commander 53rd Armored Infantry Battalion, made a 'damn the torpedoes' decision to take the direct route to Bastogne through Assenois and ignore the threat of strong enemy units on their left flank at Sibret. Abrams gave 1st Lieutenant Charles Boggess, of Greenville, Illinois, his instructions for the final push into Bastogne.

Artillery erupted from seven battalions of 105- and 155-mm guns onto the village and the forests beyond, keeping a depleted battalion from the 26th Volksgrenadier Division and some Fallschirmjägers sheltering in village cellars. The final shells were still falling when Boggess led Company C's seven tanks roaring into the village at full speed. Boggess's M4A3E2 Sherman tank 'Cobra King' fired straight ahead, the second tank in the column fired to the right, the third tank to the left, the fourth to the right, and so on.

---

45 Lieutenant Colonel Creighton Abrams was awarded his second Distinguished Service Cross for his intrepid leadership during the assault on Assenois. He received his first DSC reorganizing his outflanked companies and leading them in a frontal assault after they had been attacked by a superior armored force on 26 September 1944. Abrams also received two Silver Stars and the Legion of Merit. General Abrams served in the Korean War, commanded US armored forces during the 1961 Berlin Crisis, became the Commander US Forces in Vietnam, and Chief of Staff of the US Army, eventually achieving four-star rank. The Army's M1 main battle tank is named after the general. Abrams died in 1974 at age 59 and is buried in Arlington National Cemetery, Arlington, Virginia.

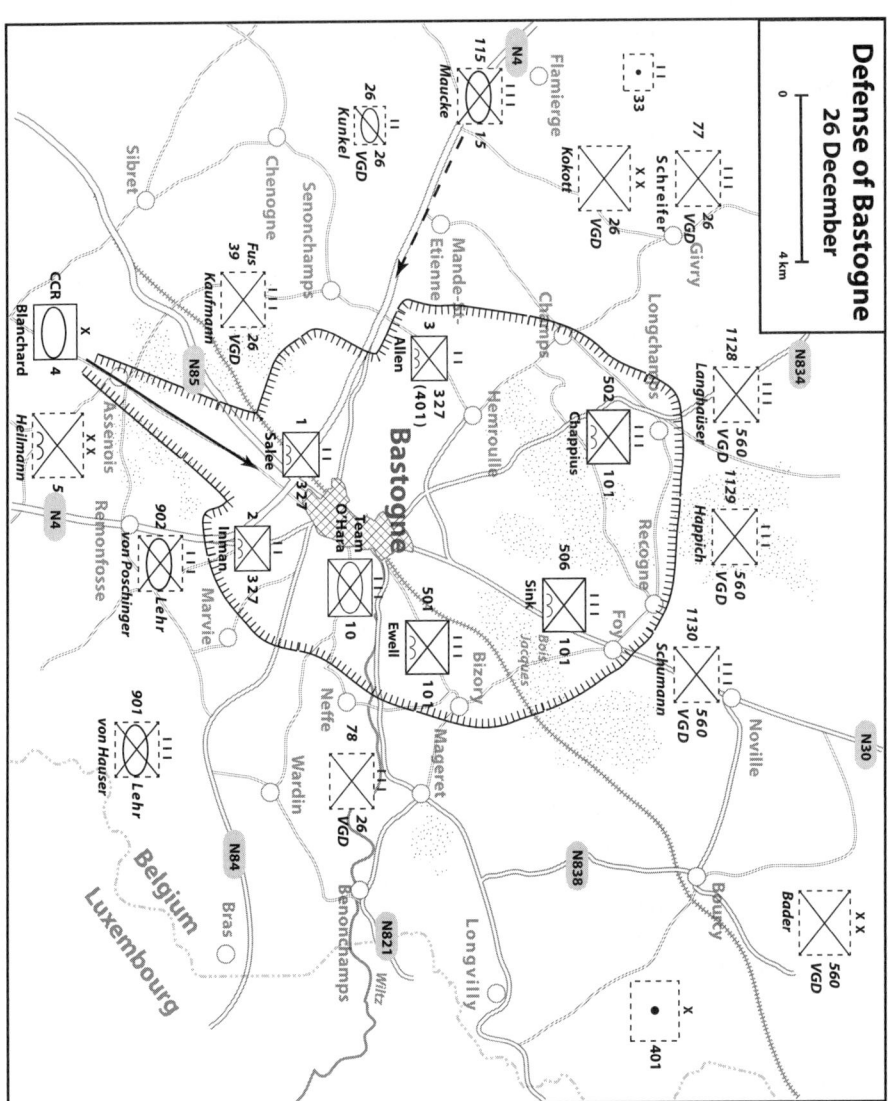

Assenois was nearly invisible hidden by smoke from burning buildings and dust raised by the artillery explosions. In the confusion and poor visibility, two of Boggess's tanks made a wrong turn and were momentarily lost. Three companies of armored infantry from 53rd Armored Infantry Battalion left their half-tracks to engage the German garrison of grenadiers and paratroopers streaming out of cellars in a melée. Buildings burned, half-tracks took shrapnel hits from their own artillery, and enemy poured out of their shelters. The tank battalion's Company B arrived to add its firepower as enemy resistance started to falter. Abrams command tank, nicknamed 'Thunderbolt,' personally eliminated one of the 88-mm antitank guns. By 1755, the battle for the village was over.

Boggess did not pause in his race through Assenois. His force, now reduced to three tanks and one half-track of infantry, continued through the village and the forests flanking the road. Several quick tank rounds disposed of a large concrete pillbox sited at the wood line north of the town. While the German defenders streamed onto the road, the tanks' machine gun opened fire and killed them all. In the field ahead, Boggess spotted the multicolored parachutes of an earlier airborne resupply. He slowed down and approached a line of foxholes each holding a helmeted figure behind a machine gun. Boggess shouted, 'Come on out, this is the 4th Armored.' After a moment of suspicious scrutiny, Lieutenant Duane Webster of the 326th Airborne Engineer Battalion emerged from a foxhole and reached up to shake Boggess's hand with a simple, 'Glad to see you.' At 1650 on 26 December, the siege of Bastogne was broken.[46]

Aftermath

In the pre-dawn hours of 27 December, forty supply trucks and seventy ambulances entered Bastogne, escorted through the narrow corridor by Abrams' tanks. The vehicles brought much-needed supplies, artillery ammunition, and doctors. Medics spent 27 December evacuating those able to be transported.

Lieutenant General George S Patton Jr had accomplished the impossible. On 20 December he had halted his attacking army of 350,000 men and pivoted it 90 degrees from facing east to the north to attack in a different direction in less than 72 hours. They then advanced 100 miles over ice-covered roadways to engage the enemy in one of the most remarkable events of the war.

Battlefield Tour

Colonels Abrams and Jaques had instructions to proceed northwest from this intersection toward Sibret and back to the Neufchâteau highway. After considering the possibility of a strong German presence in Sibret and witnessing aircraft dropping desperately needed supplies into Bastogne, the men decided upon taking the shorter route through Assenois.

The small park holds a **Belgian First World War monument** with a plaque added to name PoWs, political prisoners, and other patriots killed in the Second World War. To the right, a large granite stone bears a plaque in honor of the men of the **US Army** killed while fighting in the Vaux-lez-Rosières sector.

> Proceed north for 2.5 km. Turn left toward Villeroux and stop immediately past the church on the left. (49.966753, 5.679242)

Circuit Historique #10 stands immediately past the church. The sign depicts the Third Army's rush to relieve Bastogne with a few aerial photographs and scenes of snow-covered landscape.

---

46   In recognition of its relief of Bastogne, the 37th Tank Battalion was awarded the Presidential Unit Citation. The unit later penetrated the Siegfried Line, crossed the Rhine, and occupied areas of Czechoslovakia at war's end. Elements of Company C were detached to support the ill-fated attempt to rescue Americans from the Hammelburg PoW camp. Lt Boggess survived the war.

A large stone past the infosign bears a plaque commemorating the return of Sergeant James Hendrix to Assenois on 11 December 1999. Sergeant Hendrix was the oldest of fourteen children of a Lepanto, Arkansas sharecropper. Although he had left school after the third grade, the hunting skills he developed to forage food for the large family served him well after being drafted into the US Army. On 26 December, Hendrix, as a member of Company C, 53rd Armored Infantry Battalion, engaged the Assenois garrison during the assault upon the village. Hendrix dismounted from his half-track and captured two enemy 88-mm artillery gun crews with a volley of rifle fire. He suppressed the fire of two enemy machine guns with his M1 rifle while wounded comrades were being evacuated. Furthermore, Hendrix rescued a fellow soldier from a burning half-track despite enemy sniper fire, exploding mines, and the threat of detonating ammunition in the vehicle. Unfortunately the rescued soldier later died from his burns.[47] (49.966744, 5.679195)

> Reverse direction and turn left away from Hompré. Follow through Assenois for 2.5 km to the pillbox on the right. (49.984344, 5.699928)

The road from Assenois ran between two wooded areas, the Fosse de Sable to the west and the Bois Bechou to the east. The sudden appearance of American tanks surprised enemy infantry concealed in log-covered pillboxes in both forests. Uncertain as to who held the **Belgian Army bunker**, Boggess put two or three tank rounds into it as he approached. The resulting damage remains visible beside the gun embrasure.

Circuit Historique #9 stands beside the bunker. It describes the events of the breaking of the encirclement illustrated with period photographs. (49.984432, 5.699902)

> Continue northeast toward Bastogne. After 1.3 km, follow the roadway left (rue de la Wachenaule). Follow for 1.0 km (becomes rue d'Assenois). After 350 m, turn right onto avenue Albert Ier and, 150 m later, turn right onto rue Joseph-Renquin (unsigned, but N30 and N84). This is the same corner near the Général George Patton Memorial. At the roundabout, take the 1st exit and continue toward Arlon (N30). After 900 m, turn left onto rue de la Chapelle and stop near the small chapel. (49.990135, 5.722231)

The Arlon highway **Sherman tank turret** (model T34) sits amid the tree-shaded walkway in front of the dark gray Chapelle Notre-Dame de Bonne Conduite. This example carries a 76-mm gun and gun mantlet added to increase its frontal protection.

---

47 Sergeant James Richard Hendrix was awarded the Medal of Honor for his courage and gallantry. Hendrix became a paratrooper after the war and served in Korea. He died in 2002 at age 77 and is buried in Florida National Cemetery, Bushnell, Florida.

Surrender Demand
22 December

At 1205 on 22 December, two German officers and two enlisted men carrying a white flag approached a roadblock manned by Technical Sergeant Oswald Y Butler and Staff Sergeant Carl E Dickinson[48] of Company F, 327th GIR, and Private First Class Ernest D Premetz, 327th Medical Detachment. As it happened, Premetz spoke German. Leutnant Hellmuth Henke, General Fritz Bayerlein's personal adjutant, spoke English and asked to be taken to the American commander. Lt Henke was taken to the command post[49] of Lieutenant Leslie E Smith, Weapons Platoon, Company F, then to Captain James F Adams at Company F headquarters where he presented a surrender demand directly from von Lüttwitz. The glider regiment's S-3 carried the proposal to General McAuliffe. The note spelled out the tactical situation and threatened to unleash German artillery on Bastogne if not accepted within two hours. The missive ended with an accusation that civilian casualties resulting from German artillery would not 'correspond with the well-known American humanity.' The artillery threat was a bluff because the German units surrounding Bastogne lacked the ability to shell the city with any intensity.

McAuliffe was incredulous. Thus far, all German attempts on the city had been repelled. Still, the German commander wanted him to surrender! McAuliffe laughed and said, 'Aw, nuts.' He continued to conduct business until reminded by a staff officer that the German officers were still awaiting his reply. He looked at the divisional operations officer, Lieutenant Colonel Harry W Kinnard, and asked him to suggest an appropriate response. Kinnard answered, 'That first remark of yours would be hard to beat, General.' And thus McAuliffe delivered the most famous one-word retort in military history.

Colonel Harper, 327th GIR commander who happened to be in the headquarters at the time, volunteered to hand-deliver the reply to the awaiting Lt Henke. Harper arrived at the Company F command post and handed over the typed response:

> To the German Commander:
> NUTS
> — The American Commander

Puzzled by the short note, Henke asked if the reply was 'in the negative or affirmative.' Harper emphasized that it was decidedly not affirmative. After driving the apparently still uncertain Henke back to the front line, Harper added, 'If you don't know what "nuts" means, in plain English it is the same as "Go to Hell" … if you continue to attack we will kill every German that tries to break into this city.' Henke responded, 'We will kill many Americans. This is war.' As it turned out, both officers were true to their statements.

Leave the Chapelle Notre-Dame de Bonne Conduite south toward Lutrebois (chemin

---

48 Staff Sergeant Carl E Dickinson died in 2009 at age 95. He is buried in North Scriba Cemetery, Lycoming, New York.

49 The command post was in the farm house of Jean Kessler.

> du Swaiwet). Continue 1.3 km to the side road on the left. (49.979318, 5.726789)

Unfortunately, modern improvements to the heavily-traveled and high-speed N4 highway preclude a visit to the actual site of the American roadblock. Thus, views of **Jean Kessler's farm** are possible only from this country road. The farm buildings are partially visible amid a cluster of trees across the fields to the west. The American foxhole line had anchored in those fields to the south of the farm with the German parliamentarians approaching from the south along the Arlon highway (N4).

Other Points of Interest (southern sector)

> **Remoifosse**
> The exit to the Jean Kessler farm (49.978978, 5.719488) puts one near the actual site of the American roadblock that stood at a bridge over a small stream 200 meters south of the Kessler farm drive. (49.977307, 5.719000) Appropriately, a **Farthest Advance Stone** stands only 80 meters south of the Jean Kessler driveway. Location: 2.6 km south of Bastogne beside highway N4. (49.978310, 5.719275) Beware: this entire area can be especially dangerous because of the high-speed traffic.

The following side trips demonstrate the intense conflict that followed the opening of the corridor while German forces attempted to cut the corridor and American forces fought to maintain it. The tour route continues with the Battle of Longchamps below.

Side Trip: Battle of Senonchamps
21 to 22 December 1944

> Leave Bastogne east toward Namur / Marche (N84). After 350 m and, having crossed the rail line, turn left (unsigned, but toward Senonchamps). After 1.0 km, turn left to cross over highway N4 (Chaussée Romaine) and follow for 2.4 km. Turn left at the T-junction and continue 750 m into Senonchamps. (50.000607, 5.659295) Total one-way distance: 4.5 km.

Senonchamps is centered upon two secondary roads that ran from the Marche-en-Famenne highway to the Neufchâteau highway, both of considerable importance to the defense of Bastogne. To its east the Chaussée Romaine ran directly into Bastogne.

On 20 December, Kampfgruppe Kunkel skirted around Bastogne to the south and engaged Task Force Caraway, an ad hoc formation of remnants of General Norman Cota's 28th Infantry Division. The kampfgruppe joined Fallschirmjäger Regiment 14, 5th Fallschirmjäger Division to skirmish with Cota's stragglers. After six hours of bombardment and street fighting, American resistance collapsed. Cota and Caraway escaped to Vaux-les-Rosière and later Neufchâteau. The Germans had severed the main supply route from Neufchâteau.

Chapter Seven — The Defense of Bastogne

GERMAN OBJECTIVE	To enter Bastogne from the southwest	
FORCES		
American:	Team Pyle (Captain Howard Pyle) and Team Browne (Lieutenant Colonel Barry D Browne)	
German:	Kampfgruppe Kunkel (Major Rolf Kunkel) and Fallschirmjäger Regiment 14 (Oberst Arno Schimmel)	
RESULT	The German advance halted	
CASUALTIES		
American:	Unknown	
German:	Unknown	
LOCATION	Senonchamps is 5 km west of Bastogne	

Battle

Early on 21 December, Kunkel set out from Sibret for Villeroux, unknowingly threatening three American artillery battalions sited in that area. German troops overran the 771st Field Artillery Battalion and captured twelve 155-mm guns. A mobile defense force of fourteen tanks designated as Team Pyle appeared and attempted to block Kunkel. While the enemy slowly beat Pyle's force back toward Senonchamps, two other artillery battalions executed a hasty withdrawal.

Team Pyle made its stand outside Senonchamps and, with the assistance of the quad .50-caliber machine guns of Battery B, 796th AAA Battalion, beat off the kampfgruppe. Kunkel, reinforced by a battalion from Fusilier Regiment 39, renewed the assault the next morning, but Team Browne, a rag-tag collection of light and medium tanks and infantry stragglers commanded by Lieutenant Colonel Barry D Browne of the 420 AFA Battalion, successfully augmented the defense.

On 22 December, while Colonel Browne prepared to fire upon enemy occupied Sibret, a column of American vehicles with men in American uniforms left the village. When the column approached Senonchamps, it stopped, deployed, and fired with an M8 S-P gun, thus presenting dramatic proof that Germans disguised as Americans were using captured weapons. The enemy force slid sideways to shelter in the Bois de Fragotte, south of Senonchamps. Browne brought the fire of batteries from 420th and 755th FA Battalions and from Team Pyle upon the woods. Pyle's tanks and infantry moved into the woods only to be driven out by the high-velocity shells from a hidden gun. By nightfall, Browne and Pyle covered a four-kilometer front from south of Senonchamps to the Neufchâteau Road with 300 infantry, 19 tanks, and two battalions of artillery. That night McAuliffe added a company from the 327th GIR and one hundred men from Team Snafu.

Aftermath

American forces abandoned the village on 24 December during a general shortening of the defensive perimeter in this sector. On 2 January, Company F, 327th GIR, attached to Team Cherry for a limited objective attack against Senonchamps and the high ground to its north. The attack started at 0815 and, by 0845 Senonchamps was reoccupied against light opposition.

Battlefield Tour

The stone chapel in Senonchamps stands at the intersection of the roadways that gave rise to the importance of this location. **Circuit Historique #11** stands beside the chapel. Period photographs present the destruction brought by the combating artillery units. (50.000607, 5.659295)

> Leave the chapel toward Villeroux and follow for 1.3 km. (49.989427, 5.656956)

A **Belgian Army bunker** sits amid a small clump of trees off the highway. A large shell hole demonstrates its defenselessness against 1944 armaments.

> Continue south for 2.0 km through Villeroux. Turn left toward Bastogne (N85) and follow for 1.7 km to a minor crossroad. (49.980969, 5.683497)

The **Farthest Advance Stone** sits in the east corner of the intersection of highway N85 and a minor gravel road.

> Continue 3.1 km to return Bastogne.

50, 51

Side Trip: Battle of Lutrebois
30 December 1944 to 4 January 1945

> Leave Bastogne toward Arlon (N30). After 1.2 km, turn right onto chemin du Saiwet. After 2.3 km, turn right and then, after 1.1 km at the T-junction, turn left (unsigned, toward Lutrebois). Continue 800 m past the cemetery on the right. (49.959343, 5.729650) Total one-way distance: 8.5 km.

50   Kampfgruppe Kunkel consisted of Reconnaissance Battalion 26 of the 26th Volksgrenadier Division supplemented by twenty Sturmgeschütz.

Task Force Caraway mainly consisted of 1st and 2nd Battalions, 110th Infantry Regiment under Lieutenant Colonel Forrest Caraway.

Captain Howard Pyle, a tank company commander, led his small force from Neufchâteau toward Bastogne. The tanks, along with sixty armored infantrymen, formed the ad hoc Team Pyle.

Team Snafu consisted of approximately 600 stragglers from 28th Infantry Division designated as a centrally-located, rapid-response force.

51   Lieutenant Colonel Barry D Browne was severely wounded during the battle for Senonchamps. He was later killed when a bomb struck the building being used as a hospital. He was posthumously awarded the Distinguished Service Cross for his part in the defense of Bastogne.

Chapter Seven The Defense of Bastogne 363

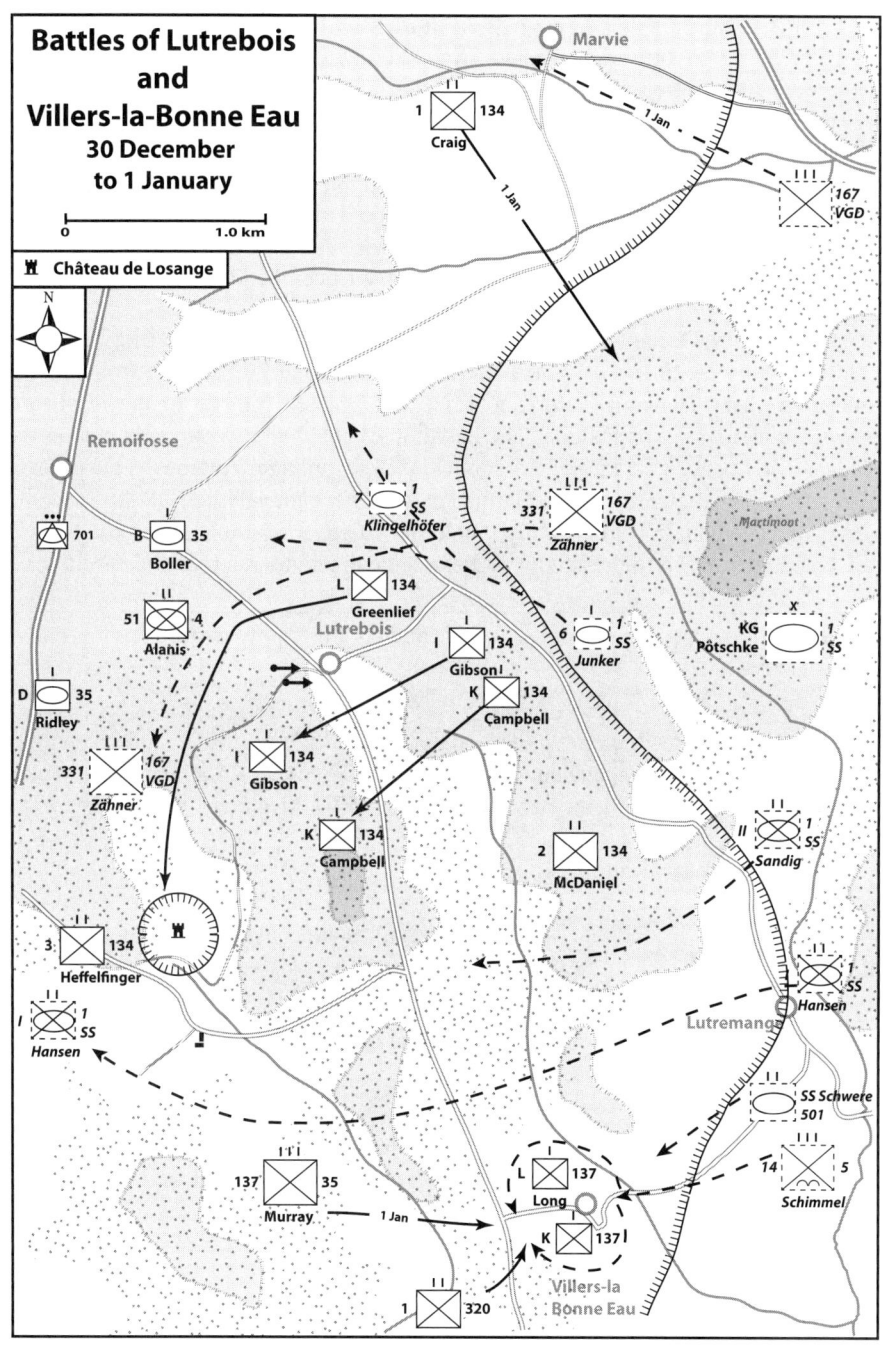

Under renewed orders to capture the city, von Lüttwitz sent newly-arriving units against the shoulders of the narrow lifeline while Patton sent his troops to widen it. As part of the newly created Army Group Lüttwitz, Kampfgruppe Pötschke was to capture Lutrebois and sever the Arlon highway near Remiofosse. Colonel Butler B Miltonberger's 134th Infantry Regiment arrived during the night of 28/29 December to relieve a battalion of 80th Infantry Division that had been attached to 4th Armored Division. Miltonberger was ordered to expand the corridor to the east.

The 35th Infantry Division had formed in 1940 from elements of the Kansas, Missouri, and Nebraska National Guards. The unit fought with distinction amid Normandy hedgerows and in Lorraine. By December 1944, it was a veteran organization.

On 29 December, Lieutenant Colonel Warren C Wood's 3rd Battalion, 134th Infantry Regiment occupied Lutrebois against light opposition from the 5th Fallschirmjäger Division. Efforts to seize the wooded hillside to the northeast, however, met strong opposition. The battalion established its command post in the Château de Losange 1.5 kilometers southwest of the village. Previously, the chateau had been the headquarters of the German paratroopers and later the US 4th Armored Division. The battalion's Company L held the village's few houses and established a CP on high ground to the southwest behind the machine-gun platoon's positions.

German Objective	To capture Lutrebois and cut the supply corridor
Forces	
American:	2nd Battalion (Major CF McDaniel) and 3rd Battalion (Lieutenant Colonel Warren Wood), 134th Infantry Regiment, 35th Infantry Division and 51st Armored Infantry Battalion (Major Dan C Alanis)
German:	Kampfgruppe Pötschke (SS-Major Werner Pötschke), 1st SS Panzer Division and Fallschirmjäger Regiment 14 (Oberst Arno Schimmel); later Grenadier Regiment 331 (Oberstleutnant Zähner), 167th Volksgrenadier Division (Generalleutnant Hans-Kurt Höcker)
Result	Although the village was occupied, the German advance was halted
Casualties	
American:	32 killed, 368 wounded or missing
German:	Estimated at 3,000 killed, wounded or missing
Location	Lutrebois is 5.5 km south of Bastogne

Battle

At 0430 on 30 December, panzers from 1st SS Panzer Division struck two front-line battalions of the 134th Infantry Division along a line from Lutrebois to Lutremange. American artillery concentrations slowed the German advance against

Companies I and K that held the woods southeast of Lutrebois. By 0515, grenadiers fired at troops of Company L holding the houses at the northeast end of the village. Three German columns formed: one bypassed the village to the northeast, another to the southeast, and the third pressed directly into the village. The southern column entered the woods and disorganized the advancing reserve Company E, cut off Company G, and attacked Company F from the rear.

Unable to withstand the force of the advancing grenadiers, Company L withdrew southwest through the forest to establish a perimeter defense around the Château de Losange. Grenadiers moved through the woods throwing 120-mm mortar shells and panzerfaust rockets against the chateau. The stubborn chateau defenders, later augmented by Companies I and K, fought off the attack with help from the 51st Armored Infantry Battalion.

Meanwhile, elements of Fallschirmjäger Regiment 14 and Panzer Regiment 1 added their power to the attack by advancing north on the Lutrebois–Lutremange road in front of Company I's positions. Although Company I had no weapons with which to attack the panzers, it did have an operational radio. Captain Lloyd D Gibson watched the panzers fan out to the northwest of Lutrebois when American 155-mm howitzer shells hit the German column. A platoon from the 701st Tank Destroyer Battalion added its fire from the road to Remiofosse, and then the tanks of Company B, 35th Tank Battalion hit the panzer column's flanks. Finally, at 1220, P-47 'Thunderbolts' strafed and rocketed the woods. Of the estimated forty panzers in the attack, twenty-five were destroyed.

Also during the morning, Grenadier Regiment 331 crossed the Martelange–Bastogne road to reach the edge of woods southeast of Remoifosse. The 51st Armored Infantry Battalion in half-tracks mounting .50-caliber machine guns met the grenadiers. The American infantry sprayed the exposed German troops with bullets while American batteries brought down shells, utilizing the pozit fuse, upon unsuspecting German troops. The combined effect was devastating and destroyed the lead battalion.

The next day witnessed small, but deadly, skirmishes. Company L made contact with the armored infantry near Remiofosse to trap one section of grenadiers in the forest. American artillery shells fell upon any detected German concentrations. The enemy attempted to strengthen its force in Lutrebois while Task Force Lagrew joined Colonel Wood's Battalion.

At 1330 on 1 January, American forces counterattacked, but German troops slowed their progress in the forest north of the chateau. Fighting resumed at 0630 the next day when Company K drove straight into Lutrebois while Company I, and the sorely diminished Company L, drove against the German pocket in the forest. By noon, the pocket had been eliminated and thirty PoW's taken. The day ended with possession of Lutrebois split between American and German forces. The small group of houses hosted two more days of fighting until Company K took complete possession of the ruins.

Aftermath

Repeated attempts to clear the forest to the northeast were defeated until a coordinated attack by an armored task force and five battalions of infantry drove through the woods. By 13 January the combined force achieved the Wiltz road (N84) west of Bras.

Battlefield Tour

Lieutenant William Shapiro's 2nd Machine Gun Platoon, Company M held a line barely within the wood line on the slopes above the cemetery west of the village. During the 30 December German attack, Lt Shapiro spotted dark figures approaching across the valley in the winter twilight, clearly outlined against the white background of fresh snowfall. The grenadiers fell to the coordinated fire of Shapiro's .30-caliber machine guns. For over one hour the platoon held off three successive assaults while headquarters troops withdrew through the woods toward the chateau. Finally, with the enemy moving against both flanks, the platoon executed its own orderly withdrawal without casualty and with all of its weapons intact.

Across the road and to the right, the single street of Lutrebois ran across a 1000 meters of open valley between wooded hillsides. The opposite hillside holds Bois Martaimont that American troops had so much difficulty taking from the enemy several weeks later during the American counterattack toward Bras.

Later in the battle, on 2 January, 2nd Lieutenant Walter Bomberger led an attack by Company I's Assault Platoon against the village. His men hesitated when they came under a mortar barrage, but Bomberger called upon his men to follow him across the open ground before the first houses. The men followed, but the young lieutenant was killed leading the assault.

> Continue southeast for 1.8 km. Turn right toward Losange and continue 1.1 km to the driveway on the left. (49.943142, 5.722431)

A German machine-gun team occupied the nose of the wooded hill across the road and brought its fire down upon the 81-mm mortar teams among the farm buildings located around this intersection. Private First Class Edward Lentz requested permission to leave his outpost and silence the enemy gun. Lentz stealthily crawled through the snow-covered forest, located the gun, and killed the three-man crew with his M-1 rifle. The American mortars then resumed firing.

> Continue forward 240 m to view the Château de Losange. Private property! (49.9448, 5.7204)

Nicolas de Losange first established the **Château de Losange** in 1420 in the area of the current large pond. The structure suffered damage during the local battle. The chateau remains a private estate of a Belgian nobleman, Patrick d'Udekem d'Acoz, father of the current Queen Mathilde of Belgium.

Lt Col Wood charged Lt Bomberger to establish a perimeter defense around the chateau with an odd collection of the Ammunition and Pioneer Platoon, Company L survivors (only about 28 men), the Antitank Platoon (who had lost its guns during the German advance), and members of 51st Armored Infantry Battalion who shared the chateau as a headquarters. The soldiers manned windows and shell holes in the chateau walls. One light and one medium tank and a half-track were situated to fully utilize their mounted .50-caliber machine guns. The Machine Gun Platoon and 81-mm mortars set up among the farm outbuildings and the woods to the southeast.

52, 53, 54, 55

Side Trip: Battle of Villers-la-Bonne-Eau
29 December 1944 to 10 January 1945

From the Château de Losange, reverse direction and proceed southeast for 1.4 km. Turn right toward Villers-la-Bonne-Eau and then turn left after 1.2 km. Follow for 500 m and stop 50 m past the church on the right. (49.933525, 5.748392)

Units of the 5th Fallschirmjäger Division first occupied the village on 19 December. As part of von Lüttwitz's effort to cut the American supply line, Kampfgruppe Hansen was to capture Villers-la-Bonne Eau and sever the Arlon highway after passing through Losange. Then it and Kampfgruppe Pötschke would link with the Führer Begleit Brigade and 3rd Panzergrenadier Division attacking from Senonchamps and Sibret.

GERMAN OBJECTIVE	To sever the American supply corridor west of Losange
FORCES	
American:	137th Infantry Regiment (Colonel William S Murray), 35th Infantry Division

---

52 Kampfgruppe Pötschke consisted of all available 1st SS Panzer Division tanks (quantity uncertain but probably less than fifty), two weak battalions of panzergrenadiers, and one engineer company. Recall, however, that these units were woefully undermanned after losses at La Gleize.

Task Force Lagrew, named after its commander Lieutenant Colonel Embry D Lagrew, was part of the 6th Armored Division and consisted of 15th Tank Battalion; 3rd Battalion, 134th Infantry Regiment; Company C, 603rd Tank Destroyer Battalion; Company A, 25th Armored Engineer Battalion; and two sections of Battery B, 777th Antiaircraft Battalion.

53 Remiofosse was known as Remonfosse in 1944 and appears as such on earlier maps.

54 In recognition of the 2nd Machine Gun Platoon's actions, each of its twenty-four members was awarded a Bronze Star.

Private First Class Edward Lentz of Indiana was awarded a Silver Star for gallantry.

Second Lieutenant Walter Bomberger was awarded a Silver Star for outstanding leadership and courage. Bomberger is buried in Wyuka Cemetery, Lincoln, Nebraska. He was 24 years old.

55 The M1917 Browning heavy machine gun, a .30-caliber, water-cooled, belt-fed weapon, weighed 103 pounds and was capable of firing 450 rounds per minute – not to be confused with the lighter M1919 air-cooled Browning which weighed 31 pounds and fired 400-to-600 rounds per minute. The M1919 also came in a .50-caliber model known as the M2 (heavy) machine gun, weighing 83 pounds and firing 1,200 rounds per minute.

German:	Kampfgruppe Hansen (SS-Colonel Max Hansen), 1st SS Panzer Division and Fallschirmjäger Regiment 15 (Oberst Kurt Gröschke)
Result	The assault was repulsed at significant loss to both armies
Casualties	
American:	31 killed, 286 wounded, and 274 missing
German:	Unknown number of killed or wounded, and 1,034 taken prisoner
Location	Villers-la-Bonne-Eau is 10 km south of Bastogne

Battle

The 137th Infantry Regiment's Companies K and L attacked Villers-la-Bonne-Eau on 29 December against strong resistance from a Fallschirmjäger engineer unit. By 0630 the next morning, the Americans held only four houses in the village and were under counterattack by seven Jagdpanzers and a battalion of panzergrenadiers from Kampfgruppe Hansen. German armor moved in close to blast the stone houses and set the village ablaze. After radioing that the companies needed bazooka ammunition and attempting to coordinate an artillery barrage around their own positions, communication ceased. Faced with complete destruction by the panzers and flamethrowers, the two companies surrendered on 31 December. Of the entire American force of 169 men, only Sergeant Webster Phillips escaped.

Attacks and counterattacks continued while both sides struggled to control the road junction west of the village. The 137th Regiment's companies were cycled in and out of the front line while the addition of Grenadier Regiment 339 strengthened the German resistance. Finally, late on 10 January, the 2nd Battalion captured the smoking ruins — the 13th day of the attack upon Villers-la-Bonne-Eau.

Aftermath

Villers-la-Bonne-Eau consisted of only seventeen houses in 1944. By the end of the battle for the small crossroad community, the village almost ceased to exist. During the battles for Lutrebois and Villers-la-Bonne-Eau, nighttime temperatures reached ten degrees below zero Fahrenheit, and snow drifts approached waist deep. The 35th Infantry Division suffered 1,432 battle casualties. Non-battle casualties, mostly trench foot and frost bite, outnumbered the killed and wounded.

Battlefield Tour

Circuit Historique #7 in Villers-la-Bonne-Eau describes the local fighting and in particular displays photographs of the destruction wrought by German and American artillery fire and bombings. The location of the infosign provides a viewpoint of the hillside overlooking the forests to the east and demonstrates the tactical importance of its position.

> Reverse direction and turn right at the church, following the curve to the left. Turn right and follow the road for 750 m to the copse on the right. (49.937444,5.756500) Total distance: 3.5 km.

Chapter Seven　　　　　　　　　　The Defense of Bastogne　369

A memorial stone flanked by American and Belgian flags bears a plaque 'dedicated to the soldiers and officers of the **US Third Army** commanded by General Patton and most particularly to the **35th Infantry Division** who suffered during terrible combat in this region during the winter of 1944-45 when they repulsed the German invader.'

A **Belgian Army bunker** shelters in the thin woods behind the memorial with its gun embrasure pointed over the valley to the east. The back portion of the bunker has been blasted off. The bunker walls hold metal plaques listing individual's names from 35th Division who were killed here. A French-only sign board describes the combat in the triangle formed by Lutrebois, Lutremange, and Villers-la-Bonne-Eau and the resultant destruction of the three villages.

> To return to Bastogne, continue forward following the roadway through Lutremange, Lutrebois, chemin du Saiwet and joining highway N30 back into the city.

56

Closing the Bulge
2 to 16 January 1945

On 2 January, 1st Battalion, 506th PIR left regimental reserve at Savy near Bastogne and relieved the regiment's 2nd Battalion along the Foy–Bizory road. The immediate objective was the Foy–Mageret road, little more than a farm and forest track that bisected the Bois Jacques and passed north of the swampy moors. The ultimate target was the high ground north of Noville. Weather conditions were the worst imaginable. Waist-deep snow and temperatures near zero limited infantry movement. Roads were coated with ice and covered with a snow blanket making tank progress difficult. Well-placed German antitank guns and minefields further hampered movement. The dense forest, dimmed by seasonally short days and limited sun, dulled the senses. Tree bursts were magnified by the narrow spacing of plantations of spruce and fir. The terrain was tailor-made for defense.

The German High Command needed to protect forces that were still west of the Houffalize road. It directed the 9th SS Panzer Division to attack from the north, the 12th SS Panzer Division from the northeast, and Führer Begleit Brigade from the northwest.

Battle of Longchamps
3 to 4 January 1945

By 3 January, Lt Col Steve Chappius's 502nd PIR held a 7-kilometer arc with its 1st Battalion at Champs, the 2nd Battalion covering from Longchamps to Monaville, and its 3rd Battalion from Somefontaine to Recogne. Only five 57-mm antitank guns and eight tank destroyers provided Chappius with anti-armor firepower.

56　Kampfgruppe Hansen consisted of SS Panzerjäger Battalion 1, an undetermined number of panzergrenadiers from Panzergrenadier Regiment 1, a reconnaissance platoon, and a pionier company.

German Objective	To break the Bastogne perimeter in the northwest sector
Forces	
American:	502nd Parachute Infantry Regiment (Colonel Steve Chappius)
German:	SS Panzergrenadier Regiment 19 (SS-Lieutenant Colonel F Geiger), 9th SS Panzer Division '*Hohenstaufen*' and Panzergrenadier Regiment 104 (Oberstleutnant Eberhard Nolte), 15th Panzergrenadier Division
Result	The last German effort to enter Bastogne was repulsed
Casualties	
American:	Company D: 72 killed or wounded and 47 missing Company B: 71 killed or wounded and 1 missing
German:	unknown
Location	Longchamps is 7 km north of Bastogne

Battle

At 1330 on 3 January, a force of 30-to-40 panzers and infantry from I Battalion, SS Panzergrenadier Regiment 19 approached Longchamps along the road from Compogne against Chappius's Company D. The panzers fanned out to form three attack columns. Six panzers targeted Monaville and eight against Longchamps while eleven others established a base of fire upon a ridge northwest of Longchamps. From that ridge, the panzers formed two lines and maintained ruinous fire against the antitank guns and machine guns defending the sector. Responding to the panzers striking Company D, Chappius ordered his reserve Company F to move forward. Enemy panzers caught the unit in the open while approaching Monaville, whereby it suffered forty-seven casualties including its commander, Captain Earl Hendricks.

General Taylor threw everything he could spare at the threat. Division artillery pounded enemy positions with some barrels displaced and used as antitank guns. Team Cherry deployed between Longchamps and Bastogne in case a breakthrough occurred. Tank destroyers from adjoining units relocated to intervene.

Although the panzers did penetrate into Longchamps and Monaville, the paratroopers held their ground throughout the three-hour battle, taking on German armor with bazookas. By 2200, the original line was restored.

Panzergrenadier Regiment 104 renewed the attack the next morning against 1st Battalion, 327th GIR at Champs. After a 90-minute artillery bombardment, the grenadiers supported by eleven panzers and SP-guns overran Company B's positions, which they had occupied in darkness only the previous night. At 0600, the panzers continued into the village and met a mixed Company C, the battalion's reserve. Two Panthers exploded when they ran over antitank mines set out the previous night. The remaining armor hesitated, but the infantry moved forward only to face automatic-weapon and 60-mm mortar fire from the company's Weapons Platoon. The German force threatened the battalion CP in Champs, but timely intervention by 1st Battalion, 502nd PIR, beat back the assault.

Chapter Seven　　　　　　　　　　The Defense of Bastogne　371

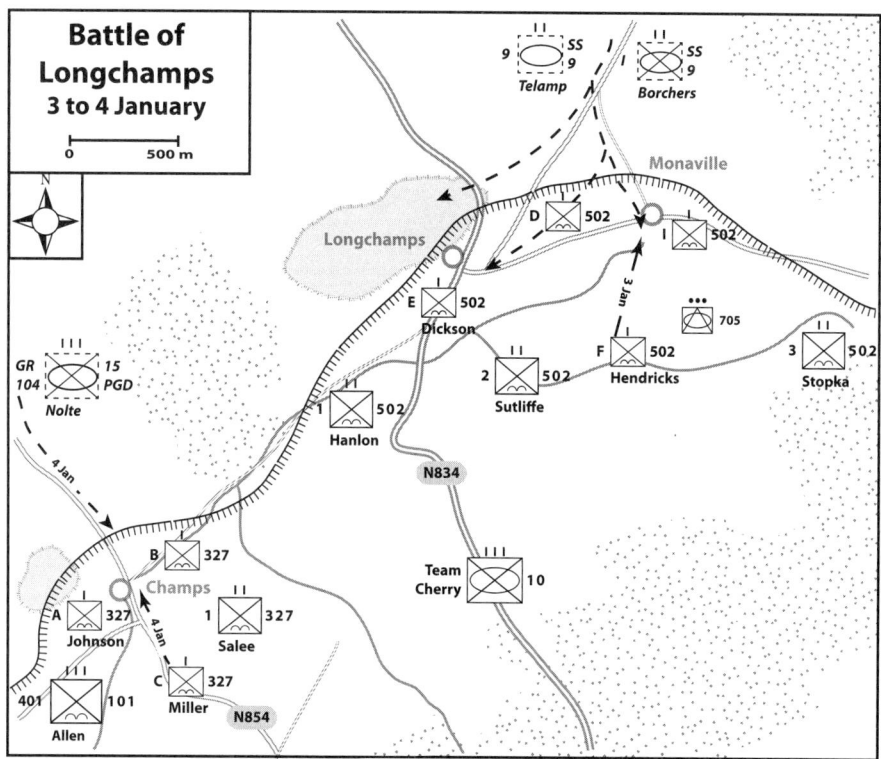

Battlefield Tour

Leave Bastogne north toward Houffalize (N30). At a roundabout, take 3rd exit toward La Roche (N834) and follow 6.2 km into Longchamps. At the cemetery, turn right toward Compogne and after 150 m, bear left to go up the hill. Stop at the park 100 m ahead on the right. (50.054061, 5.693277)

During the day-long engagement against the strong armored force, medic Technician Grade 5 Warren E Cobbett repeatedly risked his life rescuing wounded Company D paratroopers, frequently moving across a completely exposed snow-covered slope to give aid. At one point, he obtained an unmarked quarter-ton truck and drove among enemy tanks to reach wounded at overrun positions.[57]

Circuit Historique #13 presents the Battle of Longchamps, where the German attack met the paratrooper resistance. A rough stone block bears a brass plaque dedicated to the victors of the Battle of Longchamps. It reads (in French), 'Nearby, on the Longchamps–Monaville line, in December 1944, the **2nd Battalion , 502nd Parachute Infantry Regiment** joined by Antiaircraft Battalions of the 101st Airborne Division, courageously defended the perimeter of Bastogne'.

57　T/5 Warren E Cobbett was awarded the Distinguished Service Cross for intrepid actions and personal bravery while saving many lives.

> Continue for 1.0 km to a farm track on the left. (50.061416, 5.699367)

The German panzer column divided at this road junction where an intervening ridge hides the unit from view from Longchamps. However, at 1310, Sergeant Lawrence J Silva called his company CP from his nearby outpost to report fourteen approaching panzers .... then eighteen .... then twenty. His final report stated that a tank parked directly over his foxhole. [58]

> Proceed along the smaller roadway to the southeast, which the panzers used to attack Longchamps. The new houses on the right mark the location of the eleven German tanks that formed the gun line. Continue 750 m into Monaville. Turn right and proceed 1.2 km into Longchamps. With the cemetery on the left, turn right away from Bastogne (N834) and follow the road north for 750 m. (50.058084, 5.688721)

Farthest Advance Stone is slightly below the ridge summit, that is, on German side of the ridge where the panzers lined up on 3 January to attack Longchamps.

Battle of Bois Jacques (2)
2 to 3, 10, and 13 to 15 January 1945

On 2 January, 1st Battalion 506th PIR came out of reserve to move into 2nd Battalion's positions. The 2nd Battalion shifted its concentration onto the regiment's right flank to launch an attack across the Foy–Bizory road to clear the Bois Jacques. A battalion from 501st PIR paralleled the movement east of the rail line.

AMERICAN OBJECTIVE	To eliminate German pockets in Bois Jacques
FORCES	
American:	506th Parachute Infantry Regiment (Colonel Robert Sink), and 501st Parachute Infantry Regiment (Lieutenant Colonel Julian J Ewell, later Lieutenant Colonel Robert Ballard); later 502nd Parachute Infantry Regiment (Colonel Steve Chappius) and 327th Glider Infantry Regiment (Colonel Joseph H Harper)
German:	SS Panzergrenadier Regiment 26 (SS-Lieutenant Colonel Bernard Krause), 12th SS Panzer Division '*Hitlerjugend*'
RESULT	A series of achieved objectives resulted in the clearing of Bois Jacques
CASUALTIES	
American:	896 killed or wounded and 5 missing
German:	Unknown killed and wounded, 235 taken prisoner
LOCATION	Foy is 5 km north of Bastogne

---

58 Sergeant Lawrence J Silva was later found dead – still at his post. He is buried at Luxembourg American Cemetery, Luxembourg City, Luxembourg.

Battle

At 0930 on 2 January, 2nd Battalion, 506th PIR attacked across the road and along the rail line that had been so troublesome thirteen days earlier. The initial objective, the Foy–Mageret road, roughly paralleled the start line approximately 450 meters to the northeast. After initial stiff resistance, German troops abruptly fell back, leaving 20 dead and seven prisoners. By 1530, the first objective had been achieved, but the battle had just started.

On 3 January some of the most bitter fighting in the history of the 101st Airborne Division started in the contest for control of Bois Jacques. At noon, the 2nd and 3rd Battalions, 501st PIR, attacked north with the objective of the forest track that connected roads to Foy and Michamps. Temperatures hovered around zero and the few available roadways — mostly dirt forest tracks — were ice-coated. The weather conditions, when added to German antitank guns and mine fields, precluded much of 101st Division's armor and air support. It became an infantry battle fought in dense evergreen forests that dimmed the already winter-shortened daylight and amplified the shattering effect of German artillery tree bursts. The 3rd Battalion on the left met almost immediate resistance, but nevertheless continued forward 1.4 kilometers to achieve the targeted road. The 2nd Battalion on the right met almost no resistance in its 600-meter push through the forest and within an hour established a roadblock where the rail line crossed the Foy–Michamps road.

At 1430, SS Panzergrenadier Regiment 26 supported by Jagdpanzer IVs moved down the rail line and easily pushed aside a Company F roadblock. The battalion's reserve Company E, led by Lieutenant William P Heaton, deployed on the forest's eastern edge facing the rail line along with the displaced Company F. Together they met the enemy advancing across open ground west of Michamps. After suffering casualties, the German battalion shifted to the south but brought Heaton's line under intense mortar bombardment and artillery fire from four panzers and six half-tracks. A request by Major Homan, 2nd Battalion commander, for help against the armor brought the dispatch of Team O'Hara that deployed south of 2nd Battalion and broke up the enemy attack. Unfortunately on the right flank, the 50th Armored Infantry Battalion was driven back from Bourcy by SS Panzer Regiment 12 and the fully-exposed 501st PIR was forced to draw back just before dark, giving up all of the ground it had so costly gained.

A temporary period of relative quiet set in, wherein the 4th Armored Division relieved the 6th Armored Division on the paratroopers' right flank east of the rail line. On a bitterly cold 10 January, the 501st PIR advanced 1000 meters through Bois Jacques, once again reaching the Foy–Mageret road despite heavy small-arms fire into its right flank from the rail line. The 320th Infantry Regiment, attached to the 4th Armored Division, had failed to advance, whereby the paratroopers once again returned to their start line.[59]

Events finally broke loose on 13 January. The 506th PIR launched its successful attack upon Foy (see below). The 327th GIR and 502nd PIR attacked west

---

59 Lieutenant Colonel Julian Ewell was wounded by enemy artillery fragments on 9 January 1945 and Lt Col Ballard assumed command. Although Col Ewell survived his wounds, the military career of this highly regarded officer had ended.

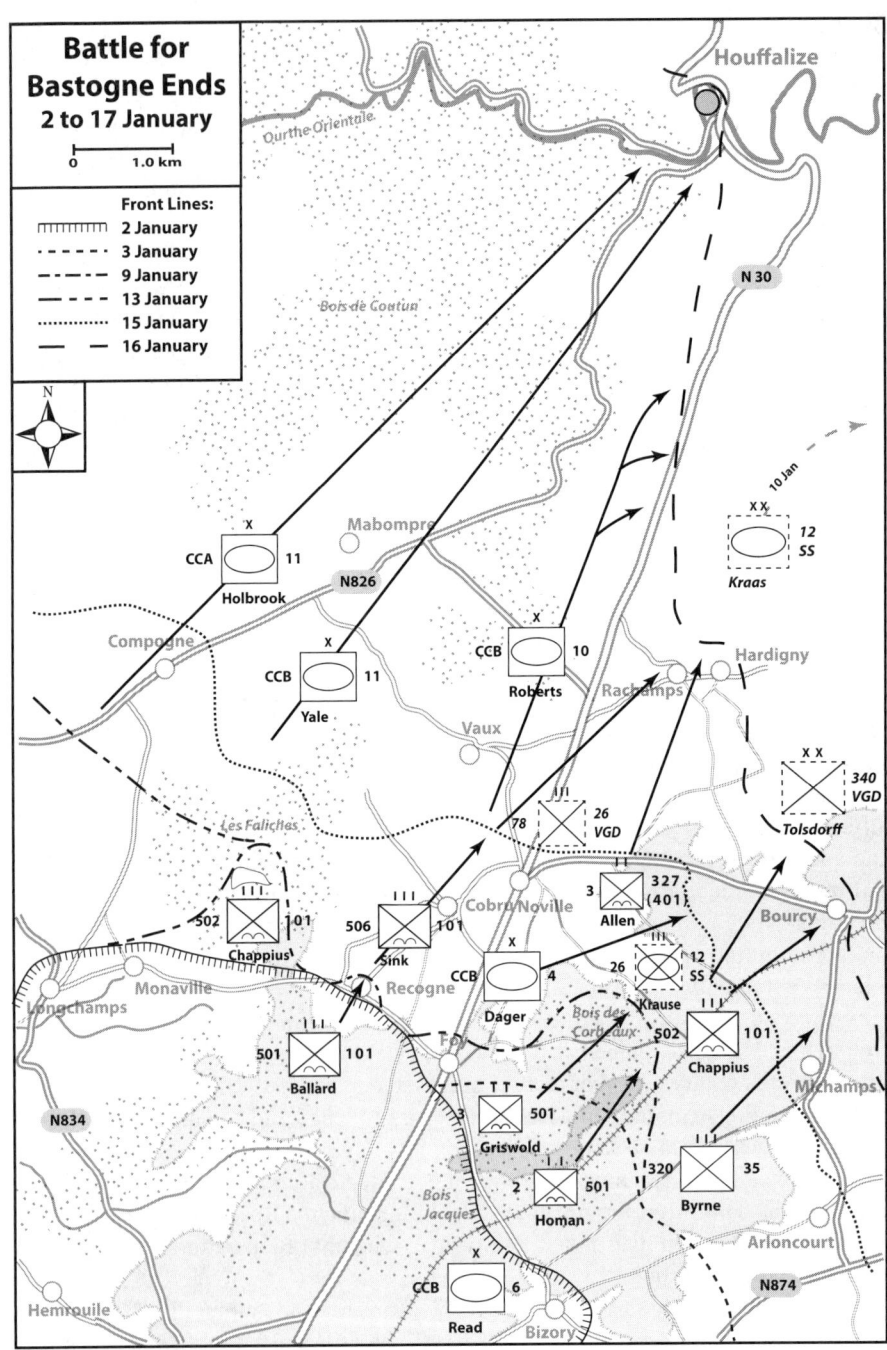

and east, respectively, of the troublesome rail line. At 0830, the 502nd PIR began what became a successful five-day assault to capture Bourcy, despite heavy enemy small-arms fire and well dug-in panzers. To the west of the rail line, the 327th GIR moved forward, capturing enemy dugouts and Nebelwerfer launchers while 'Ace' Company, a combination of depleted Companies A and C, achieved the northern edge of the Bois Jacques. However, its rapid advance opened a gap between it and the 502nd PIR — a gap infiltrated by a company of enemy troops. The reserve 3rd Battalion was committed and much of the next day in the dangerous process of clearing the woods. The 327th GIR completed its mission before dark of 15 January, establishing positions east of Noville.

Battlefield Tour
Battlefield sites in the northern sections of Bois Jacques are particularly difficult to locate due to the lack of paved roadways. The tour route circles around the northern limits of the forested area on narrow but paved roads. As an alternative, one can return to the site of the 506th PIR foxholes as described above.

> Leave the Longchamps Farthest Advance Stone southeast on highway N834. In Longchamps, turn left toward Compogne and follow the roadway for 4.8 km through Monaville, Recogne, and into Foy. Turn left toward Houffalize and continue into Noville. Turn right onto rue du général Desobry (N877). After 150 m, turn right onto a narrow side road. Cross over l'Ourthe Orientale and, after 200 m, turn left. Follow for 2.8 m, crossing the stream a second time. Turn right and follow for 1.0 km to a rural crossroad. (50.040144, 5.778631)

Shortly after noon on 3 January, Captain Arthur L Cady, commander Company F, 501st PIR, established a roadblock at this intersection of road and rail line. That day, Lieutenant Joseph C McGregor led his 26-man 1st Platoon, Company E around the left flank of the German attack and knocked out a panzer and two half-tracks with bazooka rockets. An antitank gun nailed three more panzers and two more half-tracks. The platoon captured the abandoned vehicles and used the enemy's machine guns on the retreating force.[60]

During the 3 January attack, Lieutenant James B McKearney's 2nd Platoon of the 501st PIR's Company G attacked a German position holding up the progress of the 3rd Battalion. The 33-man platoon and 11-man light machine-gun platoon came under fire of German automatic weapons, including at least one MG-42. In an incident reminiscent of the First World War's Alvin York, machine gunner Private First Class John M Fox, who could speak German, called out for the enemy to parley. A German medic came forward to hear Private Fox ask if they wanted to surrender. The medic returned to bring the message to his officer. The medic reappeared shortly with a counter proposal of a brief armistice to remove the wounded. Fox refused with a threat to bring up re-enforcements and wipe out the German force. Again, the medic reappeared accompanied by a German sergeant who surrendered his unit with the

---

60 Lieutenant Joseph C McGregor was killed one week later. McGregor is the recipient of a Silver Star, Bronze Star, and Purple Heart. He is buried in Henri-Chapelle American Cemetery, Henri-Chapelle, Belgium.

explanation that the officer had been seriously wounded. The American platoon, by this time reduced to twenty men, led its sixty-five captured enemy from the forest. An additional thirty enemy troops lay killed or wounded.

Battle of Foy (2)
13 to 14 January 1945

By 9 January, Foy had already changed hands four times when the 3rd Battalion, 506th PIR relieved the 401st GIR in positions in Bois Champay south of the hamlet. Due to the high number of casualties incurred during the previous weeks, rifle companies held less than one-half their normal complement. Therefore, 2nd Battalion's Company E was temporarily attached to the 3rd Battalion.

AMERICAN OBJECTIVE	To establish favorable position to continue attack toward Noville and Houffalize
FORCES	
American:	3rd Battalion with Company E attached (Lieutenant Colonel Lloyd E Patch), 506th Parachute Infantry Regiment
German:	Panzergrenadier Regiment 10 (Oberst Dingler), 9th Panzer Division (Generalmajor Harald Freiherr von Elverfeldt)
RESULT	Foy was liberated and held against counterattack
CASUALTIES	
American:	47 killed or wounded
German:	30 killed or wounded and 70 taken prisoner
LOCATION	Foy is 5 km north of Bastogne

Battle

At 0845 on 13 January, two platoons of Company E, 506th PIR spearheaded the assault across 250 meters of open ground (the forest is now much farther away from Foy than in was in 1944) along the western side of the Houffalize highway (N30) to the edge of the hamlet against increasing resistance. Companies G and H maintained the line of defense and the 81-mm mortar platoon suppressed German fire from three machine-guns positions on the high ground beyond the village.

At 1015, Captain Gene Brown led Company I along the eastern side of the highway only to discover that the highway was mined and to encounter dozens of booby traps along its shoulders. Intense machine-gun fire forced Brown's men to take cover in a house just recently abandoned by German troops. Bazooka man Private Al Cappelli moved forward to take on a panzer sheltering in a road depression near the German command post. Before he could secure his position, he was wounded in his left knee. He continued almost to the main intersection where he fired a rocket into the tank, leaving it immobilized. A German soldier then wounded Cappelli a second time,

Chapter Seven   The Defense of Bastogne   377

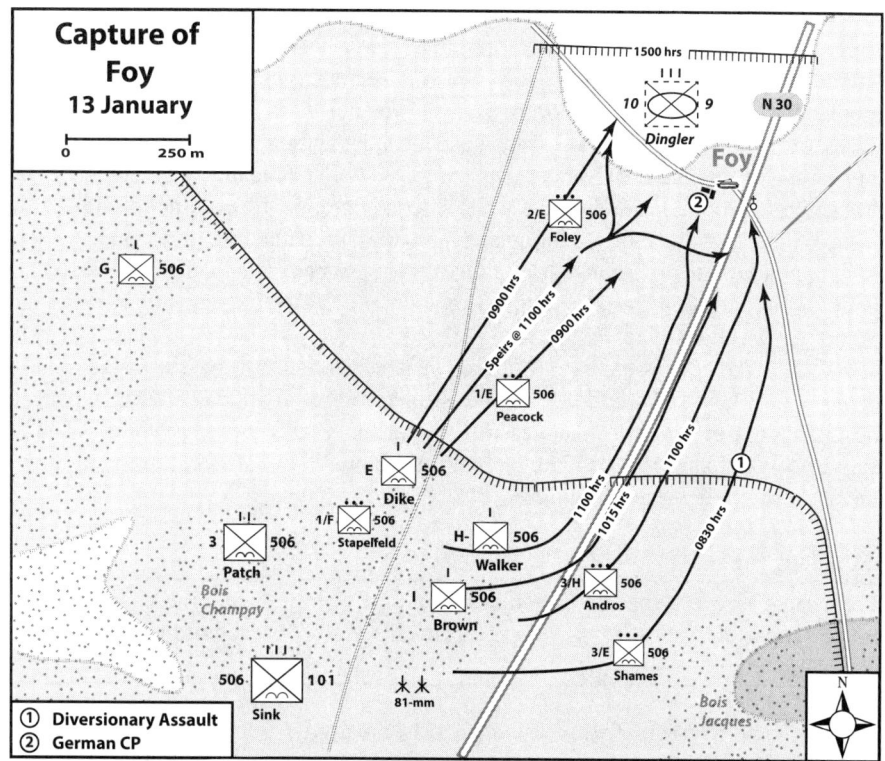

and he withdrew to the aid station. The panzer was eventually captured after it ran out of ammunition.[61]

With Company I halted and Company E's attack faltering because of poor leadership,[62] 1st Lieutenant Ronald Speirs, a platoon leader from Company D, assumed command of Company E. In rapid succession, Speirs re-directed the attacking platoons, selected targets for the mortar squad, and established suppressive fire from the company's machine guns.

---

61 Private Cappelli, from the Philadelphia area, survived his wounds. Cappelli had been wounded three times in Holland in addition to wounds and frostbite in Bastogne. While in training in England, he met and later married his wife of 65 years.

62 Company E commander Lieutenant Norman Dike was born to an elite New York family and graduated from Brown University in 1941. He received a Bronze Star for organizing the successful defense of a road junction in Holland despite being completely surrounded. He was awarded a second Bronze Star for rescuing three men while under intense small-arms fire. Dike assumed leadership of Company E in November 1944.

Lt Dike was relieved by Captain Richard Winters during the attack upon Foy when Dike apparently was unable to lead his men. Dike afterward became an aide to General Maxwell Taylor. He also served in Korea attaining the rank of lieutenant colonel. Dike received a law degree from Yale Law School and worked in the State Department and CIA before practicing law in New York City. He held several senior business positions, mainly in minerals exploration, before becoming a permanent resident of Switzerland. Dike died in 1989 at age 71.

At the same time, Company H joined the attack. Its 3rd Platoon advanced along the east side of highway N30 as far as the village church while 1st and 2nd Platoons crept along both shoulders. Meanwhile Headquarters Company and a platoon from Company F moved in support of Speirs. The three elements of the attack engaged in crossfire against the enemy machine guns but endangered their own men. Speirs then jumped up ran through the German line, conferred with Company I's commander, and ran back to continue leading his men.[63] The combined assault continued through the cluster of houses while the men threw handgrenades, fired machine guns and bazookas, and directed mortar fire on any strong German resistance. The hamlet, cleared of the enemy, then withstood a weak, nighttime counterattack by 6th Company, PGR 10 that in its effort was destroyed.

At 0415 on 14 January, a pre-dawn attack upon Foy by six panzers and a company of infantry sputtered. A second, stronger effort at 0600 by fourteen panzers and a battalion of infantry managed to recapture Foy, at least for a while. A much-diminished Company I re-took the hamlet for the final time later that morning after a concentrated artillery barrage.

Battlefield Tour

> From Bois Jacques, reverse direction and return to Foy. Leave the center of Foy toward Bastogne (N30). After 270 m, note the three-story brick building on the right. (50.042510, 5.747482)

Doctor Bernard Ryan[64] established Company I's **Forward Aide Station** in the Albert Koeune house during the second phase of the attack upon Foy. Unknown to the aide men, four grenadiers hid in the cellar. One German panicked when blood began to drip through the floorboards. The noise attracted paratrooper attention, and the four were captured. They became stretcher-bearers carrying American wounded to the rear. The structure still displays repairs to the battle-damage suffered during the engagement. The German minefield that crossed highway N30 lies a few meters farther south.

> After 1.9 km, turn right onto the forest road. Shortly after entering the forest road, note the large shell crater near the roadway on the right. The 3rd Battalion and Regimental Command Posts and the Battalion Aide Station were located farther ahead in the forest also on the right. Stop after 1.4 km at the crossing forest track. (50.040937, 5.740135)

---

63   Lieutenant Ronald Speirs, born in Edinburgh, Scotland, emigrated to the United States at age 4. He was awarded a Silver Star for his actions in Holland. Speirs later served in Korea, where he again commanded a rifle company. He became the American Governor of Spandau Prison in Berlin, eventually retiring as a lieutenant colonel. He died in 2007 at age 86.

64   Doctor Bernard J Ryan, a graduate of Harvard Medical School, became a casualty slightly later when he and two others were hit with a burst of machine-gun fire. Ryan received one bullet to the lung but survived. By the end of the war, Dr Ryan had received two Silver Stars and two Purple Hearts.

The paratroopers' lines had been established along this ridge-line after the withdrawal from Noville on 20 December. Company E began its final attack upon Foy from the edge of these woods. The slight rise between the start line and the incline into the hamlet resting in the bowl-like lower ground provided shelter from German direct fire. From various locations along the forest track, attainable by driving east to the intersection with the Houffalize road (N30), viewpoints dramatize the terrain of the attack from near the places where it actually occurred. The broad rise provides excellent observation to the north for probably 20 kilometers.

> Continue north for 850 m. Turn right and proceed 500 m toward Foy, noting the farm complex on the right. (50.045246, 5.748329)

Germans troops used the large brick and stone farm buildings belonging to the Jules Koeune's family as a strongpoint and command post. Several machine guns occupied the upper floor windows with uninterrupted views toward Company E positions. The slight dip in the roadway provided cover for a PzKpfw IV.

Later in the assault, troops in the cellar apparently directed German mortar fire. Men from Company F approached and fired submachine guns through the windows. The German troops moved back to a separate compartment, but when bullets tore through the wall and ricocheted across the ceiling, they surrendered. Twenty troops emerged and were marched rearward.

> Continue 120 m crossing highway N30 and stop past the housing complex on the right. (50.044350, 5.749264)

On 13 January, after Foy had been secured, a German sniper sheltering in this farmhouse wounded several 3rd Platoon paratroopers. Staff Sergeant Darrell C 'Shifty' Powers located and killed the enemy with a single shot.[65]

The side of the house around the upper floor window retains the **bullet scars** incurred during the capture of the village. The attic window revealed the hiding place of the sniper.

Battle of Noville (2)
14 to 15 January 1945

American Objective	To liberate Noville as the next step to cutting off the Bulge at Houffalize
Forces	
American:	506th Parachute Infantry Regiment (Colonel Robert Sink)

---

65 S/Sgt Darrel Powers from Clichco, Virginia, grew up hunting in the nearby woods and was an excellent shot. He was never wounded in combat but was seriously injured in a traffic accident during the trip to the airfield for his flight home. Powers, married for 60 years, died in 2009 at age 86 and is buried in Russel County, Virginia.

	German:	Elements 12th SS Panzer Division '*Hitlerjugend*' (SS-Colonel Hugo Kraas)
RESULT		The town was liberated
CASUALTIES		
	American:	296 killed or wounded
	German:	unknown
LOCATION		Noville is 8 km north of Bastogne

Battle

At 1220 on 14 January, 2nd Battalion, 506th PIR left the woods south of Foy to move against Noville via Recogne and Cobru while 1st Battalion cleared the woods farther west. Major Richard Winters, 2nd Battalion Executive Officer, felt that his men needed cover to survive the broad daylight assault over two kilometers of open, snow-covered fields. A deep shoulder ran southwest from near Recogne to Noville, and Winters selected it as the route against the town. German panzers in Noville spotted the 1st Battalion moving through the forest to the west paralleling Winter's unit and let loose with their 88-mm guns. Eventually, enemy machine gunners also spotted the 2nd Battalion when the troopers crossed a small stream between Cobru and Noville. The 2nd Battalion sheltered for the night along the shoulder, still 1000 meters from its objective.

The assault resumed at dawn. German resistance was strong but was overpowered with the help of Sherman tanks arriving from Foy. The panzers that did not succumb to bazookas exited to the north. Scattered around Noville, the paratroopers recovered the bodies of men from Team Desobry that had lain frozen in place since 20 December.

Battle of Bastogne Ends
16 January 1945

Battlefield Tour

From the center of Foy, proceed 10.8 km northeast toward Houffalize stopping at the memorial stone on the left near the entrance to the town. (50.127200, 5.794425)

The weather-worn stone bearing a plaque dedicated to **Lieutenant Alonzo P Francis**[66] and **Sergeant Ernest Arnold**, members of 3rd Platoon, Company C, 518th MP Battalion who, on 19 December, while returning from a patrol, fell under the guns of a German light panzer lying in ambush. The two soldiers were killed, but their wounded driver escaped. The stele was erected in 1994 under the auspices of Don Evans, a veteran of the US 2nd Armored Division, and the town of Houffalize.

Continue 350 m into Houffalize to the tank on the left. (50.128982, 5.790786)

---

66   Lieutenant Alonzo P Francis Jr, from Mississippi, is buried in Luxembourg American Cemetery, Luxembourg City, Luxembourg.

The **Panther Ausf G (PzKpfw V)** German tank belonged to the 116th Panzer Division that passed through Houffalize on 19 December. The tank crashed through the bridge into the Ourthe River, some say during a bombing raid, and became embedded in the river-bank mud. The armored vehicle lay where it fell until 1950 when it was removed, refurbished, and placed on display.

Houffalize

Houffalize, situated in a narrow valley of the Ourthe River, was the location of one of the few well-constructed Ourthe River bridge crossings.

Syndicat D'Initiative De Houffalize
Place du Crucifix 2
Tel: +32 (0)61 28 95 59
Website: http://www.houffalize.be

6660 Houffalize, Belgium
Email: info@houffalize.be

> Continue north 350 m on highway N30. Turn left onto place du Crucifix and shortly turn right into the place de l'Église and park.

Walk back to the memorials in place de Javier 1945. The small square next to the tourist office holds a stone stele bearing several memorials to the liberators of Houffalize, some erected during anniversary commemorations of the local battles. Units remembered are the **2nd, 3rd and 11th Armored Divisions**, and **17th Airborne Division**. One plaque recalls the junction between the **US First Army** and **US Third Army** that occurred nearby on 16 January 1945. (50.132589, 5.789595)

Walk back to the place de l'Église and continue to the church. (50.133366, 5.788696)

A stylized tombstone provides a fitting remembrance for the **189 civilian victims of the Battle of the Bulge** who died during fighting and bombing in and around Houffalize. On Christmas Day, the US Ninth Air Force bombed the town, targeting assembled German troops and vehicles. Bombing raids were repeated almost every day of the German occupation. The worst came on 6 January when, during a 35-minute period starting at 0325, US bombers killed 119 civilians. The ages of the civilian dead ranged from a three-year-old boy to an 85-year old woman. The entire 6-member Hoffman family — including all four children — was wiped out. Other civilians fled the town, but many had no place to go, caught between the competing armies. When the civil government returned in late January, only 130 people remained out of a pre-war population of 1,325.

> Leave the place de l'Église to the south on N860 toward La Roche-en-Ardenne and follow 7.3 km to a bridge on left. Turn left and cross the bridge to the rock escarpment 75 m ahead. (50.136767, 5.721540)

At 0845 on 16 January, a patrol from the First Army's 334th Infantry Regiment greeted a soldier from the Third Army's 11th Armored Division at this crossing of the Ourthe River. The junction of the two formidable armies had unofficially been accomplished. Three plaques on the rock mark the event. The larger upper plaque depicts three war-weary soldiers on the right speaking to one soldier on the left, the background appearing to be the scarred face of this rock escarpment. The other two plaques record the event in English and French.

> Reverse direction and return to highway N860. Turn right and return to Houffalize. Turn right onto rue de Schaerbeek (N30) and follow for 17.0 km to place du général McAuliffe in Bastogne.

On the morning of 18 January, in the center of what later became place McAuliffe, Major General Troy Middleton,[67] commander US VIII Corps, signed a 'Memorandum Receipt' as requested by General Maxwell Taylor. It stated:
Received from the 101st Airborne Division
The town of Bastogne, Luxembourg Province, Belgium.
Condition: Used but serviceable, Kraut disinfected.

This concludes the Bastogne tour.

---

67 Lieutenant General Troy Middleton became the President of Louisiana State University after the war. He died in Baton Rouge in 1976 at age 86.

Chapter Eight
Battle of the Sûre and Sauer Rivers
16 December 1944 to 28 January 1945

The Our River flows southeast through Belgium into northern Luxembourg, where it forms the border between the Grand Duchy of Luxembourg and Germany.[1] The Sûre River[2] snakes across northern Luxembourg in a generally easterly direction until it joins the Our River at Wallendorf, Germany to form the Sauer River, which in turn flows east and then south to join the Moselle River. The combination of these swiftly-flowing, deep-valley river courses forms a difficult-to-cross natural defensive barrier. In addition, smaller streams such the Ernz Blanche and Ernz Noire cut narrow defiles through the broad plateaus in an area of Luxembourg known as 'Little Switzerland.' Luxembourg roadways twist and curve down the steep shoulders of these defiles, presenting difficult routes for tracked vehicles. The broken terrain characterized by deep valleys and forested hilltops also played havoc with radio communications.

General der Panzertruppen Erich Brandenberger's German Seventh Army stood south of von Manteuffel's Fifth Panzer Army with the mission of protecting the southern flank of Operation HERBSTNEBEL by punching through the American front line to establish a defensive screen on the flank of the main advance and to tie down American reserves. Brandenberger's assignment presented a difficult challenge. Both Field Marshals von Rundstedt and Model argued that the Seventh Army was insufficiently manned to perform its assigned mission, but Hitler foresaw such Allied panic at the unexpected penetration by Fifth and Sixth Panzer Armies that the Americans would be unable to react before his *Schwerpunkt* crossed the Meuse River.

Brandenberger fielded two weak army corps at his disposal that together would barely equal a normal corps. The Seventh Army held only four divisions – three of which were newly-created Volksgrenadier Divisions (VGD) composed of young recruits, re-assigned naval or air force personnel, and older men swept from hospitals, farms, or factories across the shrinking German Reich. The infantry troops were supported by only 30 assault guns, 427 mostly horse-drawn artillery pieces, and no tanks. As a conservative and experienced commander, Brandenberger realized the impossibility of his instructions.

The Seventh Army front followed the Our and Sauer Rivers, requiring the initial infantry assault to cross the rivers and the construction of bridges to bring forward artillery, armor, and supplies. On the right, the LXXXV Corps consisted of the 5th Fallschirmjäger Division and the 352nd Volksgrenadier Division with the initial objective of the ridge line and road from Diekirch to Hosingen. On the left, LXXX Corps with 212th and 272nd Volksgrenadier Divisions was to cross the Sauer from Wallendorf to Echternach to turn south and southwest before adopting a mobile defensive posture.

---

1 Although the Our River generally traces the border, an area east of the river around Vianden is in fact within the Luxembourg canton of Vianden.

2 We will follow historian Trevor Dupuy's convention and label the river as Sûre, where it flows through Luxembourg and Sauer where it forms the Luxembourg – German border.

The 5th Fallschirmjäger Division was a parachute unit in name only. Originally commissioned as part of Luftwaffe ground combat forces in 1943, the unit had fought in Normandy and essentially was destroyed in the Falaise Pocket in August 1944. The Ardennes version was rebuilt around a few surviving veterans and employed largely excess Luftwaffe ground personnel. By December the division held 13,500 men with an additional 2,800 men in attached units. Luftwaffe Oberst Ludwig Heilmann assumed command only one week before the offensive, with no knowledge of his subordinates' or their capabilities.

The volksgrenadier divisions presented uneven quality, ranging from the adequate 212th VGD, reconstructed around a cadre of Eastern Front fighters, to the completely inexperienced 'cannon fodder' of the 276th VGD. The 352nd VGD was re-constituted from a similarly numbered infantry division after its destruction in Normandy. Its regiments held poorly trained naval personnel and lacked experienced leaders.[3]

The weak German forces still held an enormous initial numerical superiority over their American counterparts. Three experienced battalions of the 109th Regiment, 28th Infantry Division held isolated defensive strongpoints for 16.5 kilometers (10.3 miles) from Stolzembourg south along the wooded west bank of the Our River to Wallendorf, where the Our and Sûre Rivers joined.

The 60th Armored Infantry Battalion, an inexperienced unit of the 9th 'Phantom' Armored Division,[4] had assumed responsibility for a short segment of the front line from Wallendorf to the Ernz Noire valley south of Dillingen. The sector was so quiet that its commander expressed concern that the unit would achieve its objective of gaining combat experience.

Major General Raymond Barton's 4th 'Ivy Leaf' Infantry Division had lost nearly 5,000 men in the Hürtgen Forest. The division relocated to the quiet front to absorb and train replacements while holding a 56-kilometer (35-mile) stretch along the Sauer and Moselle Rivers, even though most rifle companies were still 20-to-25 percent undermanned. The division's 12th Infantry Regiment held the northern sector from the Ernz Noire valley southeast to Dickweiler.

GERMAN OBJECTIVE	To establish a firm defensive front against potential American counterattack from the south
FORCES	
American:	Two infantry regiments and one armored infantry battalion
German:	Four infantry divisions of Seventh Army (General der Panzertruppe Erich Brandenberger)

---

3 The 352nd Infantry Division defended Omaha Beach against landings by the US 29th Infantry Division, whose assistant division commander at that time was Brigadier General Norman Cota.

4 The 9th Armored Division earned its 'Phantom' nickname during the Battle of the Bulge when its three combat commands, operating in separate sectors of the battlefield, seemed to the Germans to be everywhere — like phantoms.

Chapter Eight Battle of the Sûre and Sauer Rivers

RESULT	Stubborn American defensive pockets delayed the German advance and inflicted a high level of casualties.
CASUALTIES American: German:	Period 16 December to 16 January: 649 killed, 3,277 wounded, and 2,158 missing in action 2,107 killed, 7,055 wounded, and 7,072 taken prisoner (includes Führer Grenadier Brigade and entire operations of 5th Fallschirmjäger Division)
LOCATION	Diekirch is 50 km southeast of Bastogne

Battle Summary

The initial bombardment specifically targeted command centers and artillery positions, thus essentially sparing the front-line troops. German fire was especially accurate, resulting from good observation from bunkers situated on high ground east of the Our River. Light rain, sleet, and a heavy ground fog obscured German infantry crossings of the river. By the end of the first day, four German divisions had penetrated the American front and had effectively isolated the units facing them. However, American artillery fire had prevented completion of bridges necessary to bring German artillery forward. By 19 December, a firm defensive line had been re-established on the southern flank while pockets of strong resistance remained at Osweiler, Dickweiler, Berdorf, Echternach, and Lauterborn (Lauterbur)— a fact recognized by the German LXXX Corps commander, General der Infanterie Franz Beyer, who switched to the defensive.

The high point of the Seventh Army occurred on 22 December when leading elements of 5th Fallschirmjäger Division cut the Bastogne–Martelange highway (N4) near Lutrebois whereby the division's Fallschirmjäger Regiment 13 entered Martelange. Motorized patrols advanced as far as the Libramont–Neufchâteau road (N40).

The same day, the 352nd VGD struck out from Ettelbruck toward Grosbous only to become the victim of a surprise counterattack by the 80th Infantry Division. Elements of the 10th Armored Division suddenly halted its advance and then surrounded and mauled Grenadier Regiment 985. Survivors fought back to the German bridgehead at Ettelbruck while its division assumed the defensive.

The next day, the hastily-redirected but veteran US 5th 'Red Diamond' Infantry Division drove northward across open fields on both sides of the Ernz Noire. By 25 December, despite bitter cold and falling snow, it reached the Sûre River at Reisdorf, threatening to cut off LXXX Corps. American artillery took over by laying aerial bursts upon German troops trying to re-cross the river into their homeland. The shattered 212th and 276th Volksgrenadier Divisions withdrew across bridges at Bollendorf and Dillingen, respectively, and took up positions in the Westwall defenses.

A stalemate ensued with opposing forces facing each other from Diekirch to Bettendorf until Bastogne was secure. On 18 January at 0300, the 5th Infantry Division, with the 4th Infantry Division to its right and 80th Infantry Division to its left, ferried

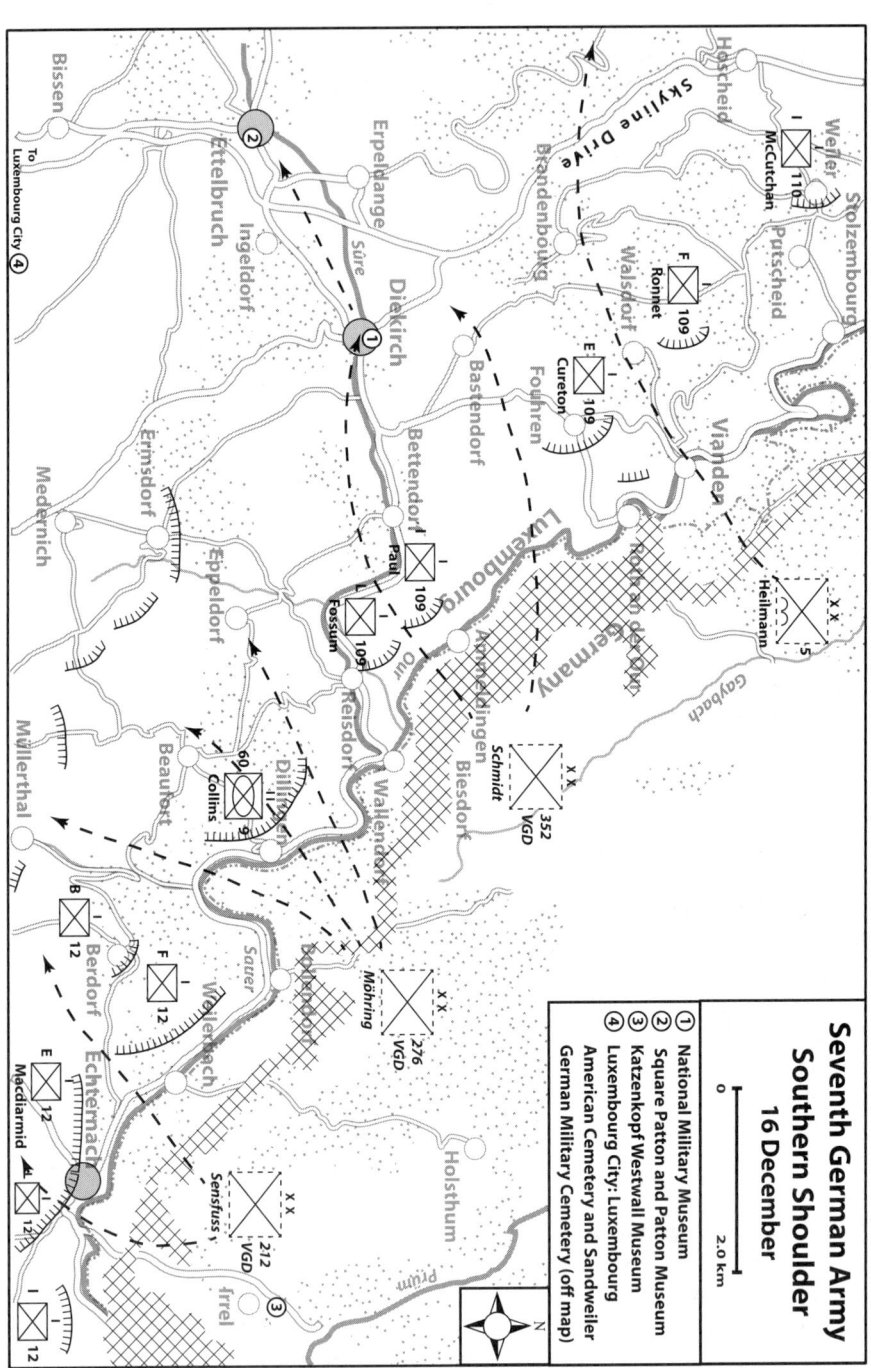

the Sûre River to attack scattered strongholds of the 212th and 352nd VGDs between Reisdorf and Ettelbruck. The attack took the defenders by surprise, and by nightfall the Americans had advanced four kilometers up Skyline Drive. The American north-south attack routes, especially along the Skyline Drive, were decidedly superior to the German east-west escape routes available to General von Manteuffel's Fifth Panzer Army that, by this point, attempted to withdraw into Germany.

The possibility of encirclement demanded a precipitous withdrawal by 20 January while light snowfall escalated into a full blizzard bringing most vehicular movement to a halt. After skies cleared in the afternoon of 22 January, Allied air power and American artillery wrought a great price upon the retreating enemy. Hitler withdrew units to face a threatened Russian Winter Offensive on the Eastern Front while a few small German rear-guard detachments held out until 28 January in a shriveled bridgehead between Dasburg and Vianden. The Battle of the Bulge was over.

Aftermath

The German inability to rapidly erect bridges for its heavy assault guns and artillery spelled the doom of the Seventh Army's operations. Once beyond range of its Westwall based artillery battalions, German infantry frequently faced American armor with only infantry-born panzerfausts. American artillery pounded enemy troop concentrations and bridge construction efforts until forced away from the border rivers by German infantry. Thus, instead of eight bridges available to German transport by late on 16 December as planned, the first two at Gentingen and Roth were completed one day late while the seventh and final bridge at Vianden was not completed until 28 December.

American casualties in the entire Battle of the Bulge from 16 December to 28 January totaled 80,987, with almost one-half occurring after 3 January when the Germans were on the defensive. The rapid and professionally-managed withdrawal did not result in unusually high German losses and was not a repeat of the Battle of Falaise Pocket. More remarkably, the rearward movement labored under harsh weather and terrain conditions with an acute shortage of gasoline and overwhelming Allied air superiority. German casualty estimates, for estimates are all they can be, range from a German low of 81,834 to an Allied estimate of 103,900.

The Allies launched the Rhineland Campaign on 7 February that culminated in the seizure of the Remagen Bridge across the Rhine River on 7 March 1945, thus passing the last natural barrier in front of heartland Germany.

Consequences

Hitler's Operation HERBSTNEBEL was doomed from the beginning. Despite the skillful and determined performance of German troops and commanders, the German Army lacked the resources to effect the anticipated Allied collapse. American commanders, especially Eisenhower, Bradley, and Patton at the highest levels, and a multitude of low level unit commanders, reacted rapidly and with determination. American ground troops, often outnumbered and outmaneuvered, resisted panic and doggedly fought the enemy to a standstill. Allied air power and superior American artillery firepower, especially use of the new 'Pozit' proximity fuse, stopped numerous German attacks.

Although the Germans had already lost the war, without squandering the men and matériel during the Ardennes Offensive, the Rhine River could have become an almost insurmountable barrier, and thereafter the bloodshed could have been prolonged for an additional six or nine months. In that case, one must wonder where the first atomic bomb would have been dropped.

Battlefield Tour Summary
The tour route breaks into three sectors corresponding to each of the three American units on the front line. Each sector tour begins at points of the German river crossings and follows their advance. A fourth sector presents sites in and around Luxembourg City — the capital and largest city in the Grand Duchy.

Highly Recommended Sites:
Diekirch: National Military Museum
Ettelbruck: Square Patton and General Patton Museum
Irrel: Katzenkopf Westwall Museum
Luxembourg City: Luxembourg American Cemetery and Sandweiler German Military Cemetery

109th Infantry Regiment Sector
The 5th Fallschirmjäger Division planned to advance along Panzer Lehr's left flank, bypass Wiltz, and form a blocking position south of Bastogne. Anticipating the difficult objectives of the LXXXV Corps, Brandenberger assigned two-thirds of his artillery to that unit. The 352nd VGD was to follow the Sûre River westward to capture Diekirch and Ettelbruck.

The 109th Regiment, commanded by Lieutenant Colonel James Rudder,[5] held a front line of more than 16 kilometers — too long a front for an infantry division, much less a single regiment.[6] In the rolling country west of the Our River, the regiment established strong points north of Walsdorf, and at Fouhren (Führen),[7] Longsdorf, Hoesdorf, and Reisdorf. Conifer forests covered the hilly terrain. Deep draws divided the landscape and made vehicular travel difficult except upon the roadways.

---

5 Lt Col James Rudder had commanded the 2nd Ranger Battalion and led it in the assault upon Pointe du Hoc during the D-Day Invasion. Twice wounded during that engagement, Rudder received the Distinguished Service Cross for his leadership of the attack. Major General Rudder retired in 1957 after commanding the 90th Infantry Division. After the war, he returned to teaching, eventually becoming the president of his alma mater, Texas A&M University. He died in 1970 at age 60 and is buried at College Station Cemetery, College Station, Texas.

6 The 109th Infantry Regiment was supported by a company of M4 Sherman tanks from 707th Tank Battalion; Company A, 630th Tank Destroyed Battalion with twelve towed guns; 107th and 108th Field Artillery Battalion with twelve towed 105-mm and 155-mm howitzers, respectively; Company A, 447th AAA Weapons Battalion; and Company A, 103rd Engineer Combat Battalion.

7 The people of Luxembourg speak a German dialect known as Lëtzebuergesch (most also speak a variety of other languages including French, German, English, and Dutch). Local map references frequently carry names in alternate languages requiring some interpretation by visitors. Alternate spellings are indicated in parentheses.

Chapter Eight — Battle of the Sûre and Sauer Rivers

GERMAN OBJECTIVE	To achieve the Meuse River at Givet
FORCES	
American:	109th Infantry Regiment (Lieutenant Colonel James Rudder)
German:	LXXXV Corps (General der Infanterie Baptist Kniess)
RESULT	The 5th Fallschirmjäger Division breached the American line and reached the Bastogne–Arlon highway. The 352nd VGD's advance was stopped west of Ettelbruck.
CASUALTIES	Period 16 to 31 December 1944
American:	98 killed, 313 wounded, 159 missing, 254 non-battle injuries, and 350 taken prisoner
German:	875 total casualties including 285 taken prisoner
LOCATION	Vianden is 11 km northeast of Diekirch

Battle

At 0545 the 109th Infantry Regiment's 2nd and 3rd Battalions reported receiving heavy concentrations of enemy artillery fire resulting in the almost complete destruction of communication between units and headquarters.

The entire 5th Fallschirmjäger Division crossed the Our near Vianden, its right flank Fallschirmjäger Regiment 14 proceeding west to capture Putscheid and Weiler and attack Wiltz (see Chapter Six). The I Battalion, Fallschirmjäger Regiment 15 had captured Vianden and passed through a gap between Company F north of Walsdorf and Company E in Fouhren. Colonel Rudder moved to fill the gap by sending Company G to the right of Company F and sending Company C of the regimental reserve's 1st Battalion from Diekirch to 2nd Battalion headquarters in Brandenburg.

Rudder's 3rd Battalion held a strong defensive position on the high bluffs above Hoesdorf overlooking the confluence of the two rivers. The 352nd VGD crossed the Our River in two prongs. To the north, Grenadier Regiment 915 crossed at Gentingen and advanced 4 kilometers to the Skyline Drive at Tandel, effectively cutting off Company E at Fouhren. On 17 December, the grenadiers continued to Bastendorf, where they forced displacement of the regiment's two field artillery battalions after a day-long fight.

To the south, Grenadier Regiment 916 effected a crossing of the Our unobserved but suffered heavy losses to well-placed American automatic weapons and artillery fire from Companies I and L on the Hoesdorf Plateau. The loss of Fouhren exposed the flank of those troops, but Company K advanced from Bettendorf to strengthen that flank.

Although starved for heavy weapons resulting from continuing issues in bridging the Our River, LXXXV Corps moved forward between and around American positions. By 18 December, Companies F and G had fallen back to Bastendorf, and Companies A and B barely held open the Wallendorf–Diekirch road near Bleesbeck to permit the escape of 3rd Battalion from Reisdorf. Rudder, recognizing the danger of his isolated units being destroyed one-by-one, ordered a withdrawal to Diekirch. The

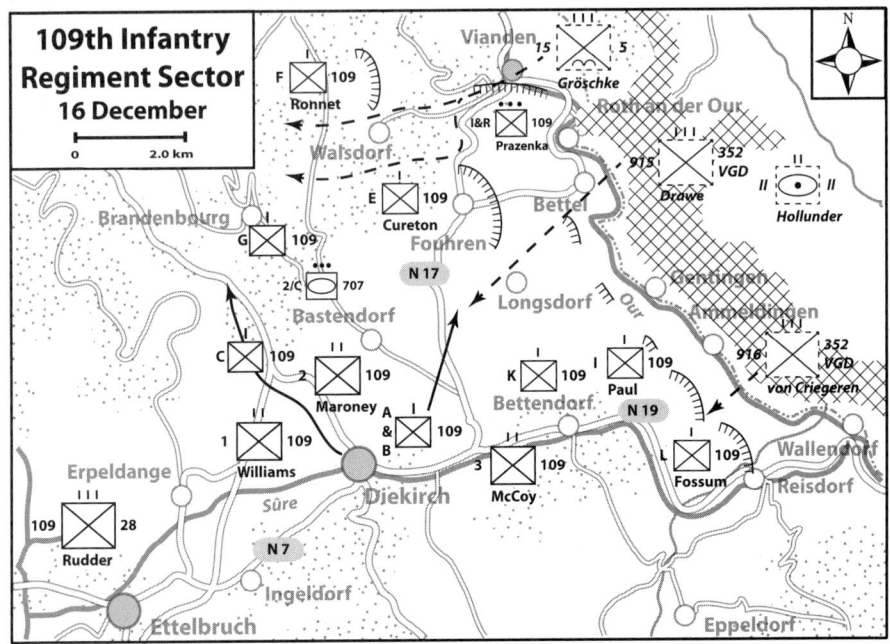

retrograde movement to the southwest opened a gap for Fallschirmjäger Regiment 15 to reach the Sûre at Bourscheid and push against Wiltz from the south.

Rudder's men were well-positioned on high ground east of Diekirch when German infantry struck on 19 December after finally getting its artillery forward. That night Rudder abandoned Diekirch to establish a new defense south and east of Ettelbruck along the Wark River on a line Grosbous–Mertzig–Feulen–Ettelbruck. The strong positions protected roadways northwest to Bastogne and south to Luxembourg City. Rudder's companies blew up the bridges over the Sûre River and, with the assistance of the 80th Infantry Division, halted further German advance.

Battlefield Tour

The tour begins in the Luxembourg city of Vianden, 53 km east of Bastogne, Belgium and 11 km northeast of Diekirch, Luxembourg.

Vianden

The charming old town occupies an extremely picturesque location on both banks of the fast-flowing Our River and holds numerous restaurants, cafes, hotels, and shops. Vianden's origins date to the Gallo-Roman age, but the first recorded mention was in 698. The Counts of Vianden monitored and controlled river traffic starting in 1090 through the 15th century. Their castle, built from the 11th-through-14th centuries in a Romanesque style, presents one of the largest castles west of the Rhine River. The family evolved a spectacular legacy as ancestors to William of Orange, the Netherlands royal family, and King William III of England. Other buildings include the 1248 Gothic parish church, one of the most significant religious buildings in the country, and the former Trinitarian cloister, which dates from 1250.

In the pre-dawn of 16 December, elements of Fallschirmjäger Regiment 15 crossed the Our River at Vianden over a damaged railway bridge while divisional engineers ferried other regimental troops across the Our River between Roth an der Our and Vianden. The 4th Company, Fallschirmjäger Pionier Battalion 5, commanded by Leutnant Hans Prigge, captured or killed the thirty-six men of Lieutenant Steve Prazenka's I&R platoon that had held positions in the Hotel Heintz. The fallschirmjäger sidestepped Company F, dug in west of Vianden, in its move toward Skyline Drive.

During the dark hours of 16/17 December, a few StuG IIIs managed to cross the Our on a weir at the base of rue Victor Hugo (49.935591, 6.205552). The assault guns' move up the road toward Hoscheid threatened to separate the 109th Regiment from the rest of the 4th Infantry Division.[8]

Tourist Office
1A rue du Vieux Marché
Grand Duchy of Luxembourg
Web: http://www.vianden-info.lu

L-9419 Vianden
Tel: +352 83 42 57

Château de Vianden
Montée du Château
Grand Duchy of Luxembourg
Email: caisse@castle-vianden.lu

9408 Vianden
Tel: +352 83 41 08 1
Web: http://www.castle-vianden.lu

Open daily January, February, November, and December from 10:00 to 16:00; March and October from 10:00 to 17:00; and April to September from 10:00 to 18:00; closed 1 January, 2 November, and 25 December. Guided visits on request.

> Leave the center of Vianden east on highway N17. After 260 m, pass Hotel Heintz where the I&R platoon manned its roadblock. (49.933314, 6.204085) After 1.2 km, turn right (CR322) and continue to the overlook on the right. (49.93234, 6.20166)

The overlook provides outstanding views of the chateau and holds a monument and explanatory signboard describing the recapture of the chateau on 12 February 1945 by **Company A, 1255th Engineer Combat Battalion**. The bronze plaque records the names of the eleven members of that unit who died in the effort.[9] The lower section of town across the river was not re-occupied until 10 days later, the last town in Luxembourg to be liberated.

Battle of Fouhren
16 to 17 December 1944

GERMAN OBJECTIVE	To eliminate by-passed American strongpoints that threatened transportation routes.

---

8   Lieutenant Stephen Prazenka was imprisoned at Stalag IVb in Muhlberg, Germany.

9   Of the eleven, only T/5 Cyrel N Evanow and Private William Tiff are buried in Europe in Luxembourg American Cemetery, Luxembourg City, Luxembourg. Fifty-one others were wounded in the engagement.

Forces	
American:	Company E (Captain Roy W Cureton), 2nd Battalion, (Major William J Maroney), 109th Infantry Regiment
German:	Grenadier Regiment 915 (Oberstleutnant Johannes Drawe)
Result	The town was taken
Casualties	
American:	1 killed, 60 taken prisoner
German:	uncertain
Location	Fouhren is 3.5 km south of Vianden; Vianden is 11 km northeast of Diekirch

Battle

Grenadier Regiment 915, commanded by Oberstleutnant Johannes Drawe,[10] crossed the Our near Bettel in the pre-dawn darkness with the first day's objective of reaching Ettelbruck. The German infantry's route passed through a 1.8 kilometer gap between 2nd Battalion's Company E stationed in Fouhren and 3rd Battalion's Company I in positions above Hoesdorf.

Captain RW Cureton's Company E sat astride highway N17 that led from Vianden south to the Sûre valley and the Echternach–Diekirch highway (N7). Company E held its ground against weak probes while providing heavy and accurate mortar fire to so severely retard bridging efforts at Roth an der Our that the bridge was not completed until 17 December.

Colonel Rudder dispatched Companies A and B from his reserve battalion supported by a platoon of medium tanks from Company C, 707th Tank Battalion toward Bastendorf to counter the German advance. Their progress was slow but not so the German pace. By nightfall, the Grenadier Regiment's II Battalion reached Bastendorf three kilometers southwest of Fouhren to completely isolate Company E.

Rudder strengthened his relief efforts by adding a platoon from Company A, 103rd Engineer Combat Battalion and a platoon from Company A, 630th Tank Destroyer Battalion to bolster Company A outside Longsdorf. He also sent another platoon of M4 Shermans to Company B outside Tandel while Company E became desperate for re-supply of food and ammunition.

The battlefield expanded when the reserve Fallschirmjäger Regiment 13 and I Battalion, Grenadier Regiment 914 threw their weight against Fouhren in repeated uncoordinated attacks broken up by artillery fire from the 107th and 108th Field Artillery Battalions.

Company A struggled to achieve Longsdorf against mortar and machine-gun fire from I Battalion, Grenadier Regiment 915. Company B took Tandel, but grenadiers swamped the ground north toward Fouhren, and enfilade fire forced American infantrymen to draw back. At that point, elements of the I Battalion supported by two Jagdpanzer 'Hetzers' found the gap between the two relief companies and pushed through. Although two Shermans were knocked out, American 40-mm Bofors guns

---

10   Oberstleutnant Drawe was wounded in action on 18 December while leading his troops at Tandel.

Chapter Eight   Battle of the Sûre and Sauer Rivers   393

caused heavy casualties, causing the Germans to abandon the attack. The Americans suffered also — Company A had been reduced to 26 men.

In the evening of 17 December, III Battalion, Grenadier Regiment 915 and I Battalion, Grenadier Regiment 914 launched coordinated attacks against Fouhren from two directions supported by three 'Hetzers.' German engineers of Pionier Battalion 352 used flamethrowers to herd the Americans in Fouhren into a large barn. The last radio message from Company E logged at 2300. At daylight on 18 December, a patrol from the I&R platoon approached the village to observe the house that had held the company CP had burned to the ground. The relief force withdrew back to Diekirch. Sixty survivors of Company E were taken prisoner.[11]

Battlefield Tour

> From the Vianden overlook, return to highway N17 and turn right. Follow for 2.8 km into Fouhren, then turn left toward Longsdorf (CR354). After 300 m, stop at the old barn on the right. (49.909824, 6.195190)

No marker or memorial exists to commemorate the fight for Fouhren or the fate of the men of Company E; however, the old barn, that held forward observers from 687th Field Artillery Battalion and was the last building taken, remains unchanged.

> Reverse direction and return 300 m to highway N17. Turn right and almost immediately turn right again (N17b). Follow the highway for 3.0 km joining highway N10 before turning right to cross the Our River into Germany. After 130 m, turn right onto Ourtalstraße (becomes K5) and follow south along the banks of the Our River for 2.8 km. In Gentingen, turn right on Dorfstraße and follow for 350 m to the footbridge. (49.899362, 6.235386)

Wallendorf Trail and Hoesdorf–Bettendorf Promenade du Souvenir

Local organizations have established two historical circuits related to the fighting in this area. Each of the seventeen tour stops presents an informational panel in English and German. In Germany the 8.0-kilometer **Wallendorf Trail** offers sites of the Westwall defenses, with various other locations accessible by motor vehicle. In Luxembourg, the 10.5-kilometer **Hoesdorf–Bettendorf Plateau circuit** presents sites of the American defense. The tour includes the most interesting and accessible of the sites.

While II Battalion, Grenadier Regiment 916 crossed the river in rubber boats, Pionier Battalion 352, commanded by Leutnant Günter Stottmeister, worked feverishly to complete a heavy infantry bridge capable of transporting armored cars, the lighter 'Hetzer' tank destroyers, horse-drawn artillery pieces, and supplies. Stottmeister described the efforts required to fell nearby trees and haul them to the river to augment the insufficient quantity of bridging materials available to his engineering troops. First efforts failed when the river current, swollen to four times its normal strength, tore the wooden construction apart. Construction resumed and continued all night under

---

11   Captain Roy W Cureton was held temporarily at Stalag XIIa, then transferred to Stalag IXb in Bad Orb, Germany.

artificial moonlight created by antiaircraft searchlight batteries. Harassed by American mortar and artillery fire, the bridge reached completion late on 17 December after which German artillery units began the race to catch up with the infantry. The appearance of the armored weapons sealed the fate of American troops on the Hoesdorf Plateau.

Promenade du Souvenir Panel #10 describes the river crossings where a modernized, rebuilt footbridge stands in front of a small white chapel encircled by a small cemetery. This relatively small bridge became the main supply route of the 352nd VGD.

> Return to highway K5 and turn right (southeast). Follow for 850 m to a bunker on the left. (49.897755, 6.246489)

In the sector near the Our River, Westwall installations provided overlapping fire for mutual self-support. Mine fields and barbed wire obstacles, moreover, were usually located in front of the bunkers' field of fire. Camouflage or vegetation unrealistically attempted concealment, but allied-friendly local citizens frequently revealed their locations.

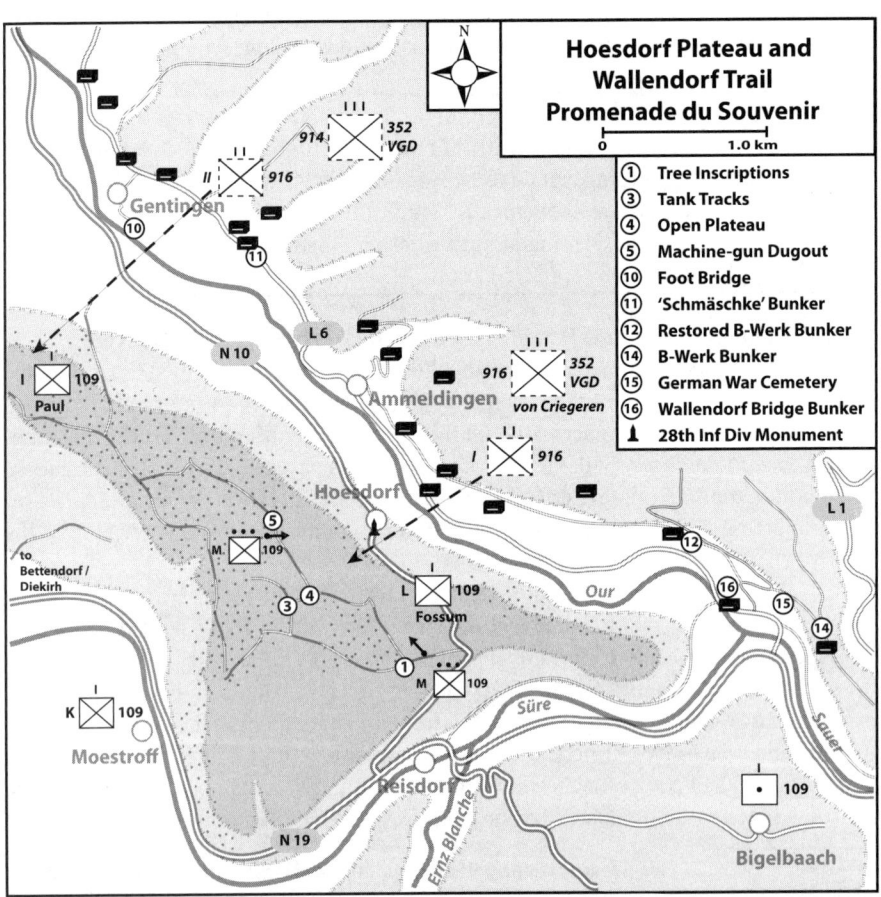

Chapter Eight   Battle of the Sûre and Sauer Rivers

In September 1944, when American forces first entered this area, they found most of the bunkers unoccupied. However, while the front line stagnated, German troops reoccupied the bunkers as observation posts, especially at night. In the vicinity of Wallendorf, Ammeldingen an der Our, and Gentingen, more than 300 concrete pillboxes, commando bunkers, observation posts, anti-tank bunkers, and underground ammunition depots posed a serious threat to any American river-crossing.

French engineers destroyed many of the bunkers during the post-war occupation period while locals stripped the bunkers of salvageable metal. Their ruins have become overgrown piles of rubble and are usually unobservable without knowledge of their location. The tour presents a few exceptions that are still easily accessible.

Promenade du Souvenir Panel #11 describes a **'B-Werk' Westwall bunker** that acted as a company command post for Grenadier Regiment 916. Originally designed to hold a 37-mm antitank gun, it became obsolete after the 1940 campaign in the west was over. The gun embrasure faces almost due south and overlooks a section of the Our where the flat valley widens considerably. The northern spur of the Hoesdorf Plateau (see below) is visible on the opposite side of the river.

On 16 December, this bunker housed grenadiers before the artillery bombardment that preceded the attack across the river. Seventeen-year-old Soldat Friedrich Schmäschke's recollections of the distribution of von Rundstadt's daily order to the soldiers, iron rations, extra small arms ammunition, fearful last 'hangman's meal,' and consumption of a liquor ration portray the sense of loneliness and despair of German soldiers who knew the war was lost but, nevertheless, fought on.[12]

Post-war demolition efforts collapsed the bunker.

Continue southeast for 4.2 km to the info sign on the left. (49.87722, 6.28500)

On 13 September 1944, CCR, 5th Armored Division probed the Westwall defenses at Wallendorf. Absent any response from German troops, Colonel Glen H Anderson, CCR commander, sent troops across the Sauer River, where they encountered only small-arms fire. By 15 September, despite an engagement against eight PzKpfw IVs, the Americans were well past the Westwall and six miles inside Germany. Although a bridgehead had been established, logistical problems in the face of increased German resistance and heavy artillery shelling led to a withdrawal back to the western banks.

Wallendorf served as the boundary between the 352nd and 276th Volksgrenadier Divisions during the Ardennes Offensive. Intense artillery fire and air force bombings struck during the German assault and again in February 1945 when allied troops launched their offensive into Germany. During that time, over ninety percent of the buildings in the area were destroyed.

Promenade du Souvenir Panel #16 describes a **'C-Werk' bunker** standing at the eastern end of the Wallendorf Bridge with its gun embrasure facing directly

---

12   Friedrick Schmäschke had been in a support unit of the Kriegsmarine before being transferred to the infantry. Schmäschke was wounded on 18 December in fighting near Longsdorf, only four kilometers away. He survived the war.

along the length of the bridge. The bunker's façade has been camouflaged to appear as a rock garden wall, but closer scrutiny reveals the armored embrasure. The 2- to 4-man enclosure used as an observation and listening post included an automatic weapon. The interior is much larger than appearances would indicate, as the interior space extends back into the hillside. It could be made quite comfortable with table, chairs, cots, drinking water, lighting, and communication equipment to report enemy troop movements to command bunkers farther from the front line. A heavy, steel, gas-tight access door opens into the backside of the bunker.

In February 1945, the 80th Infantry Division crossed at this location under intense fire from automatic weapons, mortars, and artillery.

> Continue southwest and, after 70 m, turn left onto Genovevastraße. After 180 m turn left onto Brunnenstraße and follow for 350 m. The location is only approximate, but a sign post along the roadway indicates the access point to the bunker. (49.880278, 6.283175)

Promenade du Souvenir Panel #12 states that this '*B-Werk*' bunker suffered little damage during the local fighting, despite its location being known to Allied troops from a Luxembourg engineer who provided a detailed map of this sector of the Westwall. American artillery fire stripped it of its natural vegetation camouflage, and a record of American and German patrols engaging in a firefight in the vicinity enriches the story.

Community volunteers from Wallendorf cleared the bunker's post-war debris to preserve a silent witness to the war. Its position and orientation indicate its function as an observation point overlooking the Our River. The rear-faced entrance door is protected by machine-gun ports and the steel tubes in the wall were such that hand grenades could be hurled against attackers. The bunker can be entered, but no lighting is provided, so flashlights are a must. Note the German military inscription still visible on the interior wall: *Feind hört mit* or 'the enemy is listening.'

> Reverse direction and proceed southeast on Brunnenstraße. After 370 m, turn left onto Bergstraße and follow for 290 m to the cemetery on the right. (49.877782, 6.290351)

The small **Wallendorf German War Cemetery** and **Promenade du Souvenir Panel #15** lies opposite the parking lot for Hotel Haus Wallstein. Established in 1954, the grounds hold the remains of 326 German soldiers killed in the local fighting and who were temporarily buried in emergency field graves in the Wallendorf sector during the September 1944 to February 1945 time frame. Their bodies were relocated here after identification. The grave plaques indicate that most of the German soldiers buried here were indeed young.

> Continue southeast for 350 m to the bunker on the right. (49.87555, 6.29387)

Chapter Eight   Battle of the Sûre and Sauer Rivers

Promenade du Souvenir Panel #14 stands near the squad-sized *'B-Werk'* **bunker** constructed in 1938 by Organization Todt. The 1.5-meter-thick walls offered greater protection against American artillery fire than the thinner *C-Werk* structures. With a wide observation and gun embrasure overlooking the confluence of the Sûre and Our Rivers, this bunker held 10-to-12 men and equipment for observation and communications powered by a self-contained generator. Armaments included machine guns, automatic grenade or mortar launchers, and a fixed-direction flamethrower.

During the 14 September 1944 American advance across the Our, 155-mm artillery shelled this bunker. The four-hour bombardment destroyed most of the buildings in Wallendorf and removed the bunker's vegetation camouflage. German troops re-occupied the site upon the American withdrawal across the Our and used it for counterbattery fire despite sporadic American shelling. The bunker became a key target on 7 February 1945 when Third Army troops launched their drive into Germany.

This bunker remains fairly intact by Westwall standards, although the rear-access doorway has been bricked to prevent entrance. Stairs lead to the bunker's roof, and views of the river junction and Hoesdorf Plateau in Luxembourg display the obvious importance of the position. The front of the bunker balances upon a dangerous cliff edge, and the gun embrasure has been crushed by artillery fire.

> Reverse direction and follow Bergstraße down the hillside for 900 m. Turn left onto Sauertalstraße for 720 m to cross the Wallendorf Pont into Luxembourg. After 160 m, turn right onto N10 / N19 and follow for 2.7 km. Turn right to follow highway N10 and ascend the hillside. Follow for 2.1 km and stop at the memorial on the left. (49.88047, 6.25625)

Battle of Hoesdorf Plateau
16 to 19 December 1944

GERMAN OBJECTIVE	To eliminate American troops from the commanding observation site.
FORCES	
American:	Company L (Captain Embert Fossum), 109th Infantry Regiment
German:	Grenadier Regiment 916 (Major Walter von Criegeren)
RESULT	American troops withdrew after inflicting numerous casualties.
CASUALTIES	
American:	uncertain
German:	estimated at 400
LOCATION	Hoesdorf is 8 km southeast of Vianden; Vianden is 11 km northeast of Diekirch

Battle

Company L, as the southern-most unit in the entire 28th Infantry Division, held positions along the west bank of the Our River around Hoesdorf from the river lowlands to the plateau heights to the west. The battalion's Company I held similar positions to the north. At dawn on 16 December, after the initial artillery bombardment, German Grenadier Regiment 916 crossed the river utilizing rafts, rubber boats, and hastily constructed footbridges in a futile assault on American foxholes.

American artillery targeted by observers from the Hoesdorf Plateau continued to sweep the Our River crossings from Gentingen to southeast of Wallendorf until a concentrated effort by II Battalion, Grenadier Regiment 915 forced the American batteries to displace.

At dawn on 18 December, a determined assault by Grenadier Regiment 916 overcame a platoon of Company K on the battalion's left flank. With the capture of Company E at Fouhren, the 3rd Battalion's positions became untenable. Shortly after noon, instructions received via radio ordered the unit to withdraw to Bettendorf. The movement faced considerable difficulty when enemy penetrations into Company I's sector permitted them to bring automatic weapons fire onto a critical roadway. After Company L took up positions around Bettendorf, the remainder of the battalion withdrew to high ground around Diekirch. The following night, Company L followed as well. As a final act at Bettendorf, they assisted Company A, 103rd Engineer Combat Battalion in blowing up bridges over the Sûre River.

Battlefield Tour

The **28th Infantry Division Memorial**, flanked by the Luxembourg and American flags, stands up the hillside above the entrance to the village. The stone bears a plaque attached in 1984 and 'Dedicated to the 109th Infantry Regiment from the city of Reisdorf.' Attached in 2014, a second, newer plaque in the shape of the 'Bloody Bucket' of the 28th Infantry Division commemorates the 70th anniversary of the battle. The site is one of the few places on the plateau where a break in the trees allows views over the Our river to the German-held opposite hillside.

> Reverse direction and proceed 1.0 km to the side road on the right. Park at a safe and convenient location. (49.874288, 6.263921)

Although motor vehicles are restricted on the hilltop plateau to farm vehicles, sites of the actual battle are but a 2.1-kilometer (one way) walk. See the map for locations.

Walk uphill following the farm track to the west. After 300 m, note the copse on the right. During the quiet time on this front, American soldiers carved initials into the birch trees in this forest. A few such carvings have been preserved and are still visible at the corner behind **Promenade du Souvenir Panel #1**.

Continue approximately 700 m and then turn right and walk along the edge of the forest for approximately 350 m. (49.877105, 6.249604)

Promenade du Souvenir Panel #3 describes earlier events on the plateau. On 14 September 1944, an American bombardment across the Our began. The dominating heights of the Hoesdorf Plateau offered excellent opportunity to place direct fire upon German pillboxes and bunkers from tank guns positioned at this site. The 32-ton

Chapter Eight   Battle of the Sûre and Sauer Rivers   399

Sherman M4A1 and M4A3 tanks left their **track impressions** in the rain-soaked soil during that bombardment, and they remain to this day.

Walk east along the farm track approximately 300 m. (49.87749, 6.25132)

Promenade du Souvenir Panel #4 describes how I Battalion, Grenadier Regiment 916 crossed the river, passed through empty Hoesdorf, and ascended the plateau under cover of darkness and fog. Upon reaching the barren plateau crest, the grenadiers were completely exposed to American small-arms fire from Captain Fossum's Company L and observer-directed artillery fire while the Germans turned southeast aiming for the Wallendorf–Diekirch highway (N19). After three attempts and enormous casualty rates, they abandoned the effort for the day. Bloody hand-to-hand fighting continued on this high ground until the early afternoon of 18 December when the outnumbered Americans withdrew. The panel stands at the intersection of farm tracks in the open plateau.

Proceed north along the farm track and into the forest across the field. (49.881715, 6.247973)

Promenade du Souvenir Panel #5 describes a dugout that held one of a line of three-man, .30 caliber water-cooled Browning 1917A1 machine-gun teams from Company M (Heavy Weapons). The depression would normally be covered by logs and loose dirt for artillery protection and branches and grass for camouflage. Night attacks were suppressed by pre-planned overlapping firing angles.

Walk into the forest. (49.8817, 6.24864)

Behind the panel, a short path leads into the wood where two large depressions mark the **actual dugout** barely within the current tree line. At the edge of the forest, a stone monument bears a plaque in the shape of a Bloody Bucket with the unusual inscription dedicated to both sides of the bloody conflict:

> In memory of the soldiers from the **109th Regiment, US 28th Infantry Division** and the **German Grenadier Regiment 916, 352nd VGD** who fought and died on this high ground above Hoesdorf on the opening day of the Battle of the Bulge 16 December 1944. May their sacrifices never be forgotten.

The field described on Panel #4 is viewed from a differing perspective that of a dark forest spitting machine-gun bullets at an enormous rate. The grenadiers, many in their first combat experience, blindly attempted to cross the open ground, never to achieve the opposite side.

Return to your vehicle and continue down the hillside on highway N10. At the bottom of the hill, turn right onto route de Diekirch (N19). After 6.2 km, enter a roundabout and take the 3rd exit (N17-a). After 2.4 km, turn right onto Bamerthal (N7) and follow 120 m to the museum entrance on the right. Signs in the city indicate directions to the Musée Militaire. A small number of parking spaces lie inside the gate. (49.870937, 6.158927)

Battle of Diekirch
17 to 19 December 1944 and 18 to 21 January 1945

German Objective	To capture the city and its bridge over the Sûre River.
Forces	
American:	Remnants of 109th Infantry Regiment (Lieutenant Colonel James Rudder); later 2nd Infantry Regiment (Colonel Worrell Roffe), 5th Infantry Division
German:	Elements of Grenadier Regiments 915 and 916, 352nd Volksgrenadier Division (Oberst Erich Schmidt, later Generalmajor Bätzing)
Result	The weakened American force could not hold the town, which was recaptured one month later after a perilous wintertime river assault.
Casualties	Period 17 to 19 December only
American:	34 casualties
German:	107 taken prisoner
Location	Diekirch is 50 km southeast of Bastogne

Battle

By 19 December, losses in manpower and heavy infantry weapons so weakened the 109th Infantry Regiment that it struggled to establish a defensive perimeter around Diekirch. By that afternoon, Volksartillery Regiment 352 began a bombardment of the town prior to Oberst Schmidt's [13] Grenadier Regiments 915 and 916 launching a series of piecemeal assaults of little consequence. Probing continued into the night while the enemy looked for gaps in the American line. Finally, at 2000, Colonel Rudder, fearful that his regiment would be cut off and surrounded, asked for and received permission from General Cota to withdraw to the west.

The American exodus from Diekirch was followed by three-thousand men, women, and children fleeing westward between the advancing and retreating forces. Four-hundred old or infirm were left behind. Grenadier Regiment 916 entered abandoned Diekirch on 20 December and captured the partially demolished bridge across the Sûre River.

After their defeat at Grosbous and Mertzig (see Battle of Ettelbruck, below), German troops retained control of Diekirch until mid January 1945 while a weeks-long static situation prevailed. At 0300 on 18 January, with 12 inches of new snow on the ground and temperatures of 16 degrees Fahrenheit, the 2nd Infantry Regiment, 5th Infantry Division moved along the southern banks of the Sûre River to cross two battalions on either side of Ingeldorf, southwest of Diekirch. West of Ingeldorf, the 1st Battalion was successful; the 2nd Battalion east of the town was not so fortunate when bridging attempts failed. Later, an assault-boat crossing succeeded with every gun literally blasting the enemy from the far-shore defenses. Despite heavy German

---

[13] Oberst Erich Schmidt was wounded on 18 December and replaced by Generalmajor Bätzing.

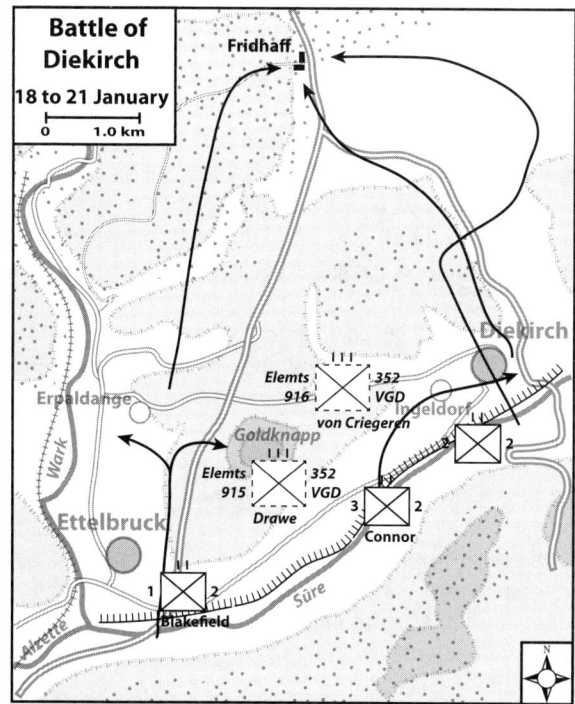

mining of the river bank, deep salients drove into the thin German lines, bypassing machine-gun and mortar positions blinded by a thick smoke screen. With Diekirch outflanked by the 1st and 2nd Battalions, the 3rd Battalion crossed and drove into the city from the southwest. By nightfall, Diekirch was surrounded.

Upon infiltrating American lines, the enemy counterattacked at dawn the next morning in the area of the Friedhof (Fridhaff) Farm. The Company A command post had become isolated when its commander, Captain Lennis Jones, having personally killed eleven enemy troops with his carbine and pistol, worked his way back to his men and led them in repulsing the attack.[14] The 3rd Battalion spent the next two days clearing Diekirch of enemy troops while the other two battalions continued ad-vancing to the north.

Battlefield Tour

Diekirch

The town and its name derive from an 8th century resettling of Anglo-Saxons by Charlemagne. The Holy Roman emperor built a Christian church for the pagan tribe whose town became known as *diet-kirch*, or people's church, in Old High German. The medieval walls built by King John of Bohemia were destroyed during a French occupation in the 19th century.

Almost sixty percent of the city's buildings were destroyed during the fighting. Local citizens could not return to their city until March 1945 after engineers had cleared mines from the area.

Tourist Office Diekirch
3, place de la Libération
L-9255 Diekirch
Tel: +352 80 30 23
Web: http://tourisme.diekirch.lu/

(pedestrian zone)
Grand Duchy of Luxembourg
E-mail: tourisme@diekirch.lu

---

14   Captain Lennis Jones from San Antonio, Texas was awarded the Distinguished Service Cross.

Musée Militaire (National Museum of Military History)
10 Bamertal   L-9209 Diekirch
Grand Duchy of Luxembourg   Tel: +352 80 89 08
E-mail: info@mnhm.lu   Web: https//www.mnhm.lu

The exterior grounds hold an excellent collection of American armor including a 155-mm 'Long Tom' gun, post-war Patton M-47 tank, Sherman M4A1 tank (identified as 'Blockbuster 3rd,' the lead tank of then Captain James Leach, commander, Company B, 37th Tank Battalion), and an 8-inch M1 howitzer. The weapons are visible even when the museum is closed because the grounds are not gated.

The museum comes loaded with artifacts and full-size dioramas of the Battle of the Bulge placed in the alcoves of this old brewery building, including the famous crossing of the Sûre River by the 2nd Infantry Regiment and 50th Field Artillery Battalion on 18 January 1945. The walls and rooms contain displays of various sizes and topics. Most, if not all, of the items are authentic and generally identified as to their original owner. Still, to complete the museum if one reads all of the trilingual explanation panels, would take days.

The second floor presents a surprise of heavy equipment (jeeps, trucks, smaller cannon) in a barn-like room packed with material. A display of German weaponry includes a 37-mm antitank gun, 80-mm mortars, a 'Hetzer' SP-gun, 20-mm Flakvierling 38,[15] and a couple light field howitzers. Only the larger items are labeled — but the small items add texture to the display.

Leave the museum and walk up the hillside behind to view an American M1 155-mm howitzer. In addition, a plaque on the exterior of the building presents a photo of damage the museum complex suffered in December and January when it was the Bamertal Diekirch brewery. A small section of the wall displays unrepaired battle damage.

Open daily from 10:00 to 18:00; closed 25 December and 1 January. Fee; not handicap accessible.

> Exit the museum parking area and turn left onto Bamerthal (N7). Follow the highway (N7, also becomes avenue de la Gare) for 800 m before seeking a convenient parking area. Walk south through the park and find the footbridge over the river. The memorial is below the bridge to the west. (49.864937, 6.158412)

A tree-and-shrub shrouded alcove in a park near the Hôtel de Ville on the banks of the river holds the **American Liberators Memorial** erected in gratitude by the citizens of Diekirch. The flat stone bears insignia of 5th, 9th, and 10th Armored Divisions and the 28th, 5th, and 4th Infantry Divisions topped with the five-pointed American star. The plinth holds a bronze plaque bearing the image of the footbridge across the river that stands a few feet from the memorial.

---

15   Flakvierling 38: a 20-mm antiaircraft gun that combined four Flak 38 guns onto a single carriage.

Chapter Eight   Battle of the Sûre and Sauer Rivers   403

> Retrieve you vehicle and continue southwest on avenue de la Gare for 180 m to the old train station. (49.864641, 6.154038)

The **old train station**, only a short distance west of the park, retains traces of small-arms fire on its façade.

> Continue southwest on avenue de la Gare (N7) for 3.8 km, following the highway through two roundabouts. After crossing the Sûre River and the rail tracks, find a convenient parking area 300 m past the memorial. (49.851633, 6.110433)

Battle of Ettelbruck
21 to 25 December 1944

Ettelbruck held a road-and-rail intersection at the confluence of the Sûre, Alzette, and Wark Rivers and was a transport node for east-west and north-south road systems.

AMERICAN OBJECTIVE	To halt the German westward advance and push against the southern flank of the Bulge.
FORCES	
American:	109th Infantry Regiment (Lieutenant Colonel James Rudder), later 80th Infantry Division (Major General Horace McBride)
German:	352nd Volksgrenadier Division (Generalmajor Bätzing)
RESULT	The town was lost but quickly regained
CASUALTIES	Period 22 to 27 December
American:	10 killed, 139 wounded, and 19 missing in action
German:	Killed and wounded described as heavy; 477 taken prisoner
LOCATION	Ettelbruck is 6.5 km southwest of Diekirch

Battle

After reaching the south bank of the river at Diekirch, General Bätzing's infantry advanced upon Ettelbruck from the north and south on 21 December. Faced with overwhelming odds, Rudder withdrew that night to establish blocking positions near Vichten, south of Mertzig. The next day, I and II Battalions, Grenadier Regiment 915 continued west past Mertzig toward Grosbous.

On 22 December, Third Army's 80th Infantry Division's two assault regiments moved rapidly forward toward Mertzig on a cold cloudy morning, tramping over a light blanket of snow that had fallen during the night. The 319th Infantry on the division's left reached Vichten to relieve Col Rudder's battered 109th Regiment. The 319th Infantry Regiment then moved north along a broad front while the 318th Infantry Regiment kept pace on the right flank in the Alzette River valley and the 26th Infantry Division's 104th Infantry Regiment paralleled the northward movement on the left flank. At the same time, Grenadier Regiment 915 moved west directly across the American line of march along the Ettelbruck–Mertzig highway. The unsuspecting

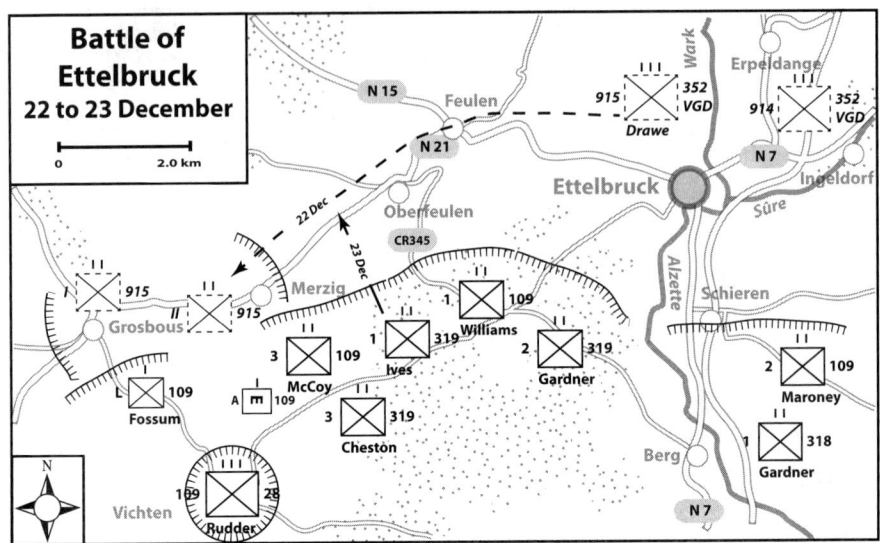

German troops were caught in enfilade and a devastating blow from tanks, tank destroyers, and antitank guns.

The grenadiers became isolated in defensive positions in Grosbous and Mertzig. As I Battalion ambushed the 104th Infantry Regiment's initial attack on Grosbous from woods southwest of the town, the Americans reeled back in disorder. American artillery fire drove the grenadiers to shelter in the woods while the bulk of American infantry passed through Grosbous, leaving one company to keep the enemy contained.

On 23 December, the 3rd Battalion, 319th Infantry Regiment attacked the weakened II Battalion at Mertzig and, at the same time, an additional company from 104th Infantry Regiment returned to the I Battalion in the woods. Both German battalions resisted until ammunition shortages forced their surrender on 24 December. A few survivors made their way east.

Grenadier Regiment 914 reached Ettelbruck before the Americans and German artillery fire repelled repeated efforts to enter the city. General McBride then chose to use his artillery and bombarded the town with 105- and 155-mm guns for 24 hours, thus forcing the German grenadiers to abandon the city during the night of 24/25 December.

Battlefield Tour

The impressive and beautifully maintained **Square Patton** occupies a park containing weeping willows, European and Japanese cherry trees, and arborvitae overlooking the main train line and the Sûre River. The 3-meter-high (9-foot) statue of Patton portrays the general in his tanker's jacket with his binoculars at the ready. The statue is identical to the one at West Point Military Academy.

The nearby monument to General Patton, erected in 1952, presents a red sandstone plinth bearing a military broadsword framed by olive branches to symbolize truce and peace. Above it, a bald eagle with a 2.1 meter wingspan — emblematic of the

United States — keeps watch. Two Luxembourg nationals crafted the sculpture: Pierre Droessart the sketches and Aurelio Sabbatini the sculpture.

A Sherman tank, originally a dozer tank of Headquarters Company, 5th Armored Division, has been restored as a standard M4A1 model. A bronze battle map honors the memory of General Patton and outlines the German offensive in Luxembourg and the US Third Army's counterattack. Other remembrances dot the park, including presentations from various American military units thanking the people of Luxembourg for their hospitality during unit reunions.

An international bicycle race named the Grand Prix Général Patton took place for the first time in 1947 and continues to be held each year. The 102-kilometer route starts in Ettelbruck and ends in Troisvierges.

> From Square Patton, continue southwest on highway N7 (now avenue J-F Kennedy) for 700 m. Turn right onto avenue Lucien Salentiny (CR348). After 190 m, turn right onto rue Prince Jean and right again after 95 m onto rue Dr Klein. The museum is ahead 170 m on the right. (49.84874, 6.104361)

General Patton Memorial Museum
5 rue Dr. Klein   L-9054 Ettelbruck
Grand Duchy of Luxembourg   Tel: +352 81 03 22
Web: http://www.patton.lu

The museum maintains photographs and documents detailing Luxembourg's participation in the Second World War from its invasion in May 1940 to the liberation by American forces. Also on display are numerous weapons and relics found on the Ardennes battlefields. A small, but interesting, section offers items relating to the air war in the skies over Luxembourg.

Open daily 1 June to 15 September from 10:00 to 17:00; Sundays only 16 September to 31 May from 13:00 to 17:00.

> Continue southeast on rue Dr Klein. Turn right onto highway N7 and then, after 160 m, left onto rue Prince Henri (N7). Continue to follow highway N7 as it returns toward Diekirch. In Diekirch turn left onto highway N17-A. After 2.1 km, take the 1st exit from the roundabout onto highway N19 and continue for 2.0 km into Bettendorf. Turn right onto rue du Pont (CR357) and, after 170 m, turn left, then right onto highway CR357. Cross the modern highway bridge and enter the intersection known as Breckinridge Square. (49.872352, 6.218091) The route retraces the important and scenic Echternach–Diekirch highway.

Battle of Bettendorf
16 to 18 December 1944 and 18 to 19 January 1945

GERMAN AND AMERICAN OBJECTIVE	To control the bridge over the Sûre River
FORCES	
American:	3rd Battalion, 109th Infantry Regiment, (Lieutenant Colonel Jim H. McCoy); later 10th Infantry Regiment (Colonel Robert P Bell)
German:	Grenadier Regiment 915 (Oberstleutnant Johannes Drawe), 352nd Volksgrenadier Division
RESULT	The town changed heads in two quick battles
CASUALTIES	uncertain
LOCATION	Bettendorf is 4 km northwest of Diekirch

Battle

On 16 December, Lieutenant Colonel James McCoy learned of Grenadier Regiment 915 at 1000 when the grenadiers fired upon Battery A, 108th Field Artillery Battalion positioned 4.0 kilometers to his rear east of Diekirch. The completion of an Our River bridge brought German assault guns into action and, by the morning of 18 December, with the artillery displaced farther west and Fouhren silent, Grenadier Regiment 916 launched its strongest attack yet against the 3rd Battalion on the Hoesdorf Plateau as described above. As part of the general withdrawal ordered by Col Rudder, 3rd Battalion headquarters abandoned Bettendorf for positions around Diekirch. The engineers, last troops out, blew the bridge over the Sûre River.

The 5th Infantry Division took up positions along the south bank opposite Bettendorf in late December while General Patton launched his counteroffensive against Bastogne and Wiltz. On 10 January, amid deteriorating weather conditions that brought heavy snowfall and plummeting temperatures, a six-man patrol crossed the river in Bettendorf and captured several German prisoners. An enemy NCO carried documents outlining the defenses in the town. At 0300 on 18 January, the 7th Engineer Combat Battalion ferried elements of the 10th Infantry Regiment across the icy floe-strewn river at Bettendorf and the 2nd Infantry Regiment at Diekirch. The detonation of non-metallic mines lining the river bank disclosed the attack. Automatic weapons and Nebelwerfer rockets stalled the attack, but the assault repeated the next day with ultimate success and cleared Bettendorf.

Battlefield Tour

The low stone wall on the left bears a plaque honoring **Lieutenant Colonel William M Breckinridge**, Executive Officer of the 10th Infantry Regiment, 5th

Infantry Division who planned the 1945 attack to recapture Bettendorf. The square has been renamed in his honor.[16]

Slightly farther ahead, a field stone framed in shrubs bears a diamond-shaped plaque to the **10th Infantry Regiment** in recognition of the unit's liberation of the town. The memorial was erected in gratitude by the citizens of Bettendorf. (49.872299, 6.218242)

Continue along the rue de la Gare where, on the right, a triangular fieldstone almost hidden in a grove of pine trees bears a plaque commemorating the liberation of Bettendorf by the **5th Infantry Division**. The upper section of the plaque bears the image of the **Sûre River crossing** — the same image as the diorama presented in the Diekirch Museum. The plaque states in part, '...crossed the Sûre River at sub-zero temperatures and liberated Bettendorf and its surroundings after murderous combat.' (49.872278, 6.219436)

Other Points of Interest near Diekirch

Bettendorf
A fieldstone niche in the embankment below a modern barn holds a stone and plaque dedicated to **Flying Officer Douglas A Cameron**, No 226 Squadron, RAF. Cameron piloted a British Fairy Battle aircraft on 10 May 1940, the first day of the German invasion of Luxembourg. Heavy flak struck his plane while making a low pass over Wallendorf. Cameron attempted an emergency landing near the Hitzenhaff farm south on highway CR357. He died that night in a Diekirch hospital, becoming the first Allied soldier to die in Luxembourg. Location: 6.5 km east of Diekirch and 2.4 km south of Bettendorf beside highway CR357.(49.86136, 6.22857)

[17]

Brandenbourg
The ruins of **Château de Brandenbourg** stand upon a rocky nub above the village. The castle, constructed in the 13th century upon the site of an earlier 9th century wooden fortress, was inhabited until the 18th century when it fell into disuse. Although once open to visitors, the site is now restricted. Brandenbourg served as command post for the 109th Infantry Regiment's reserve Company G. The infantry troops marched forward to protect the right flank of Company F after it was outflanked by Fallschirmjäger Regiment 15. Most of the villages on this tour occupied the knobs of hills for their observation potential. Brandenbourg is the exception because it lies in the valley. Blees Creek runs behind the houses of the one-street village. Across the creek, a

---

16   William M Breckinridge graduated from West Point in 1928. He retired in 1962 with the rank of major general after serving as the chief of the Army Security Agency as his last command. Breckinridge died in 1996 at 92 years of age and is buried in Arlington National Cemetery, Arlington, Virginia.

17   Flying Officer Douglas A Cameron is buried in the Diekirch Communal Cemetery. He was 25 years old.

bronze plaque in the shape of the bloody bucket adorns a large mountain stone and bears the simple words, '**Memorial to the 28th Infantry Division 1944.**'
Location: 7 km north of Diekirch near highway CR353. (49.911441, 6.136948)

Eschdorf

Through 24 and 25 December, recurrent counterattacks and stiff resistance delayed the progress of the attacking Third US Army. In Eschdorf, heavy fighting took place in the sector of the 26th Infantry Division against the defending Führer Grenadier Brigade. Both American and German commanders saw Eschdorf as the key road junction providing access to crossings of the Sûre River. The 328th Infantry, 26th Infantry Division attempted to clear Eschdorf of German troops on Christmas Eve when two companies became trapped inside the town's buildings while German armored vehicles roamed the village street firing through doors and windows. Captain Vaughn Swift, commanding officer of Company E, ran a gauntlet of bullets to reach American tanks gathering outside the town for an attack. Clinging to the side of the forward vehicle, Captain Swift directed the tanks into the strongly-held town while his company advanced in coordinated attack with the tanks. Despite being hurled from the side of the tank when it sustained a direct hit, the captain managed to crawl back to his third platoon where he killed twelve of the enemy with his rifle. Directing artillery fire by radio, Captain Swift subsequently organized a perimeter defense that held the enemy.

A memorial stands in a parking area on the north side of the church. A bronze plaque affixed to a stone cut in the shape of the Grand Duchy of Luxembourg pays homage to the men of the **26th Infantry Division** who fought in this sector during the Battle of the Bulge.
Location: 21 km west of Diekirch beside highway CR314. (49.885389, 5.935015)

[18]

Heiderscheid

Patton pushed his troops on and, by midnight, 319th Infantry Regiment approached Heiderscheid and the main Ettelbruck–Bastogne highway (N15). Lieutenant Colonel Paul Bandy's 2nd Battalion reached Heiderscheid at 0230 on 23 December, but concentrated assault-gun and machine-gun fire stopped the rifle companies near the edge of the town. A minefield likewise stopped two approaching tanks from the 702nd Tank Battalion. A German assault gun fired, revealing its position to the tankers who quickly set it afire. The explosions illuminated a path for riflemen to capture the village police station. Once the minefield had been crossed, by 1100 the town had been cleared.

One hour later, an assault by two enemy companies was driven off. Later still, eleven enemy tanks appeared. Company F bazooka teams led by 2nd Lieutenant Michael Hritsik crept forward and took out two enemy tanks. Tank destroyers appeared and accounted for five more before the enemy withdrew. The main crossing points of the Sûre River in this sector were now open to American traffic.

---

18   Captain Vaughn Swift was awarded the Distinguished Service Cross for his leadership and heroism.

Chapter Eight Battle of the Sûre and Sauer Rivers 409

> The **80th Infantry Division Monument** stands on an impressive ridge that overlooks the Sûre River. A rough stone bears a simple brass plaque that states, 'To the memory of the valiant soldiers of the 80th Infantry Division US who fought on these ridges during the Battle of the Ardennes.' (French only)
> Location: 19 km west of Diekirch beside highway N15 west of Heiderscheid. (49.888372, 5.965912)

19

> **Useldange**
> The 5th Armored Division liberated Useldange on 10 September 1944 when its CCR bypassed Arlon in a drive toward the German border. The unit engaged a column of German horse-drawn artillery attempting to escape to the northeast. The village later became the headquarters of 159th Engineer Combat Battalion.
> The center of Useldange holds a complex of parks, castle ruins, and cobblestone streets. The interior of the 12th-century **Château d'Useldange** is always accessible by a bridge over the 10-meter-wide moat. Ramps, steps, and even an elevator have been restored to permit touring its walls and the interior courtyard that now also holds the town hall. A second elevator accesses one of the towers.
> Location: 25 km southwest of Diekirch near highway N24 in the center of the village. (49.768139, 5.979926)
>
> Undoubtedly, the **German SK18 105-mm heavy field gun** on display at the southern edge of the town was captured during the German retreat.
> Location: beside highway N24 700 m southwest of the village. (49.76365, 5.9757)

60th Armored Infantry Battalion Sector
16 to 20 December 1944

The 60th Armored Infantry Battalion held a 6.5-kilometer front along a high plateau between the Sauer River on the north and a meandering stream that flowed through a deep gorge known as the Ernz Noire on the south.

Lieutenant Colonel Kenneth Collins sited his headquarters in the 12th century castle at Beaufort across from a small creek that defined the edges of a broad, flat, treeless plateau to the east. Although a fairly weak force in itself, the 60th Armored Infantry Battalion drew support from much of CCA, 9th Armored Division deployed 6.5 kilometers to the rear between Ermsdorf and Waldbillig.

GERMAN OBJECTIVE	To displace the Americans and form a blocking force against possible American movements from the south
FORCES	
American:	60th Armored Infantry Battalion (Lieutenant Colonel Kenneth Collins); later elements of CCA, 9th Armored Division (Colonel Thomas L Harrold)

---

19 Second Lieutenant Michael Hritsik of Beaver County, Pennsylvania was awarded a Distinguished Service Cross for his bravery. He died in 1975 at age 64.

German:	276th Volksgrenadier Division (Generalmajor Kurt Möhring; then Oberst Hugo Dempwolff)
Result	After presenting determined resistance, the Americans withdrew
Casualties	Period 1 to 31 December 1944:
American:	65 killed, 160 wounded, 145 missing, and 2 taken prisoner
German:	578 killed, 327 wounded, and 518 taken prisoner
Location	Beaufort is 15 km southeast of Diekirch

Battle

A relatively light initial barrage succeeded in cutting all telephone lines connecting the battalion units with artillery farther to the rear. The immediate German objectives – the 3rd Armored Field Artillery Battalion positions behind Haller – interdicted the river crossing points of both LXXX Corps' divisions. The first assault companies crossed the river in rubber boats at 0630 and flooded up the draws approaching the plateau.

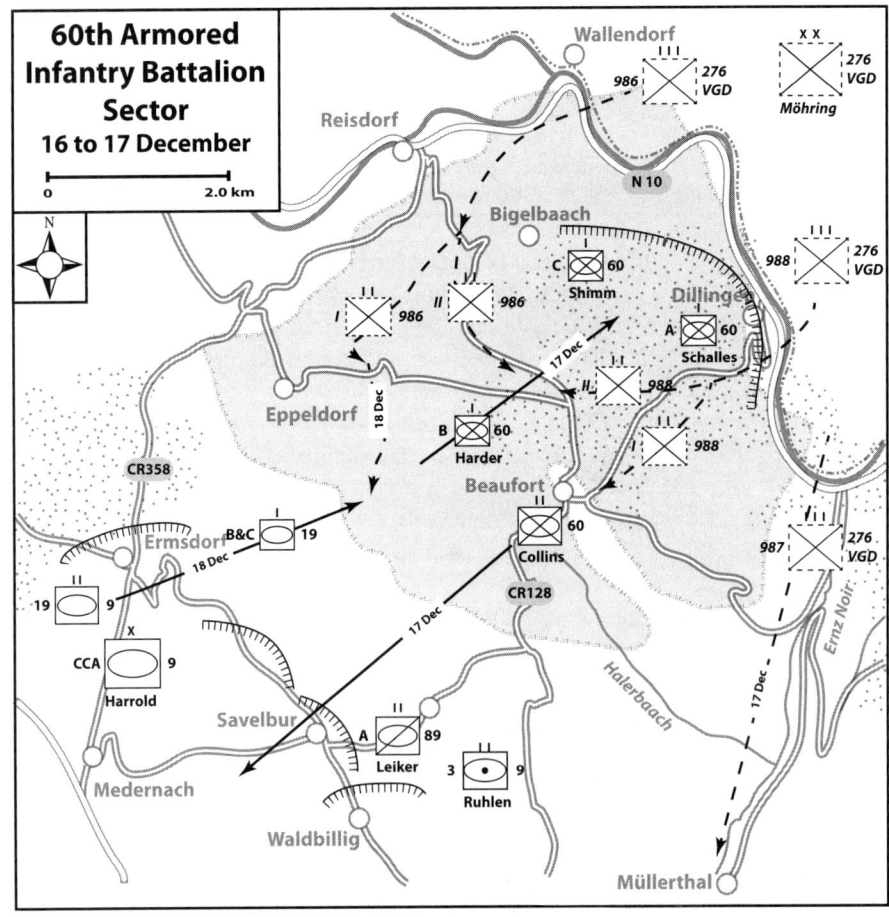

Chapter Eight Battle of the Sûre and Sauer Rivers 411

Grenadier Regiment 986 quickly occupied the tip of the plateau above Wallendorf while Grenadier Regiment 988 crossed the Sauer River south of Dillingen to attack 150 men of Company A in the village. By midday, the grenadiers had infiltrated the thick pine woods to the heights behind Company A. Colonel Collins released his only reserve, Company B, to fill the gap between Companies A and C. During its advance, it engaged grenadiers who had already broached the American front-line's rear. Although the 60th Armored Infantry Battalion retained control of the heights, the forward companies became isolated with both flanks open.

On 17 December, CCA, 9th Armored Division moved to protect the armored infantry from attack by General Möhring's Grenadier Regiment 987 that had advanced through the undefended Ernz Noire gorge as far as Müllerthal and threatened the 3rd Armored Field Artillery Battalion at Haller. Meanwhile, Colonel Collins' headquarters at Beaufort displaced under threat from the grenadiers.

On 18 December, Colonel Harrold struck his blow along a line along Waldbillig–Savelborn–Ermsdorf directly into General Möhring's planned advance also centered on Savelborn. The leading Companies B and C of 19th Tank Battalion entered Esselbur Forest north of Savelborn to be hit by panzerfausts that destroyed six Sherman tanks in minutes and wiped out the 60th Armored Infantry's I&R Platoon. The American rescue died before it began, but the engagement had also shaken the armor-less German infantry that withdrew to Beaufort. During the nights of 18 to 20 December, the 60th Armored Infantry Battalion exfiltrated from its exposed forward positions after almost one-half of the 800-man force had been killed or captured.

Battlefield Tour

Leave Bettendorf east toward Echternach (N19) and follow along the river for 4.9 km. In Reisdorf, turn right onto place de l'Église (CR358) and, after 200 m, turn left onto rue de l'Ernz (CR128) and then almost immediately onto highway CR128. Follow highway CR128 for 1.8 km to a memorial on the left. (49.856562, 6.274881)

Two platoons of Company C, 60th Armored Infantry Battalion defended the ridge known locally as Scheidberg (Scheed) overlooking the Sûre River valley. When the battalion CP withdrew, the platoons remained to defend the sector. After four days of resisting German attacks, forty survivors of the original eighty-man force retreated during the night of 19/20 December. In the inky darkness, the men passed single file through enemy territory, maintaining contact by holding the belt of the man before him. T/Sgt Robert N Hebert[20] was the last man in that line.

An yellow stone bears a plaque to 'the men of **Company C, 60th Armored Infantry Battalion**, who defended this position 16 to 19 December.' The plaque sits on the opposite side of the stone and is not visible from the road. The gravel road that circles behind the rest stop ascends the ridge where their foxholes dot the forest.

Continue south on highway CR128 for 2.7 km into Beaufort. (49.843713, 6.288953)

---

20 T/Sgt Robert N Hebert survived the war. He died in 2010 at age 90. He is buried in Riverside Cemetery, Ontogonan, Michigan.

Colonel Collins headquarters in Hotel Meyer in Beaufort came under threat of attack on 17 December by the advancing I Battalion, Grenadier Regiment 988. During daylight, American howitzers around Savelborn literally blew away the attackers. At nightfall, however, the grenadiers slowly infiltrated into the town from nearby woods and successfully overran the 81-mm mortar platoon on the eastern edge. Soon house-to-house fighting erupted against the defending Headquarters Company. Collins withdrew the battalion headquarters to Savelborn while Captain Victor Leiker's Troop A, 89th Cavalry Squadron fought a rearguard action that cost the unit forty-three casualties. By 2030 the town was in grenadier hands.

> Continue south 700 m into Beaufort. In the center of the town, continue straight on Grand-rue toward Grundhof (becomes CR364) and follow for 1.3 km to the side road on the right. (49.830576, 6.302598)

General Brandenberger, unhappy with the speed of **Generalleutnant der Infanterie Kurt Möhring's** advance, ordered his replacement. General Möhring proceeded to a last conference with his unit commanders when he was killed at this rural lane outside Beaufort on 18 December. American troops supposedly ambushed his car; however, local historians doubt the veracity of that claim. The Luxembourgers are convinced that General Möhring was a victim of friendly fire from a German squad near the intersection, believing that German sentries had heard the sound of the captured jeep Möhring was using and assumed the occupants were American because almost no Germans had vehicles.[21]

Other Points of Interest near Beaufort

> **Dillingen**
> At 0300 on 7 February, the US XII Corps began its assault on Germany with a crossing of the Sauer River. XII Corps commander Major General Manton Eddy sent the 80th Infantry Division to cross between Wallendorf and Bollendorf. Engineers and riflemen approached the river bank in a light snow during the night of 6/7 February. Smoke from 80th Infantry chemical mortars drew enemy fire to phony crossing sites while Company F, 318th Infantry Regiment executed an unopposed crossing. Later units did not fare as well. Alerted German troops responded with machine-gun and small-arms fire supported by mortars and artillery. Bullets ripped holes in the rubber assault boats while the 10- to 17-mile-per-hour current swept away others. Small groups forged across against punishing enemy fire. Three days later and after repeated failed attempts, with the first bridge was finally in place and the flow of men and materiel increased.
> A field stone positioned in a highway rest stop along the banks of the Sauer River forms a memorial to the **80th Infantry Division**. The bronze plaque inscrip-

---

21 General Kurt Möhring was a participant of all of the large battles during the war, starting with the Invasion of Poland and concluding with the Battle of the Bulge. He received his final promotion posthumously. Möhring is buried in Kriegsgräberstätte Holsthum, Holsthum, Rheinland-Pfalz, Germany. He was 44 years old.

tion reads in part, 'In honor of units of this division that crossed the flooded Sauer River here on 7 February 1945, despite adverse weather and intense enemy fire.'
Location: 4.5 km northeast of Beaufort beside highway N10. (49.857206, 6.315797)

Haller

On 16 December, 480 men of the 9th Armored Division's 3rd Armored Field Artillery Battalion manned three batteries in Haller, each holding six M-7 105-mm self-propelled guns. The initial German artillery bombardment targeted the batteries who continued to receive shelling through 17 December while gradually becoming encircled by the 276th VGD. At 0200 on 18 December, the batteries escaped west to Savelborn, where they immediately resumed action against the advancing enemy. On Christmas Day, amid heavy fighting, the 11th Regiment, 5th Infantry Division reoccupied Haller before driving German forces back across the Sauer River.

A field stone wall along the main highway below the village church bears the local war memorial. To the right a plaque commemorates the soldiers of the **5th US Infantry Division** who had fought here at Christmastime 1944. Special mention commends Private Louis F Schwall of the division's Company G, 11th Infantry Regiment, who was killed in action outside of Haller on 25 December 1944.
Location: 3 km southwest of Beaufort in the center of the village beside highway CR358. (49.819873, 6.281451)

[22]

Medernach

In a park shaded by weeping willows and birches, a memorial column erected in 1983 commemorates the actions of the **9th Armored Division** during the Battle of the Bulge. A bronze battlefield map indicates the routes and widely-separated defensive positions of the division's three combat commands around Medernach, Bastogne, and St Vith. Plaques on the sides of the column celebrate the unit's various achievements, including not only the Bulge defense — for which all three commands were awarded Presidential Unit Citations — but also the division's capture of the Ludendorff Bridge over the Rhine River at Remagen, Germany on 7 March 1945. Combat Command A is also acclaimed for stopping German forces along the Ermsdorf–Waldbillig line on 20 December 1944.
Location: 9.6 km southwest of Beaufort at the intersection of highways N14 and CR358. (49.806340, 6.213546)

Ermsdorf

On 16 December, Company D (light tanks) of the 19th Tank Battalion maneuvered past this point to the north to protect the left flank of the 60th Armored Infantry Battalion. The next day those tanks pushed II Battalion, Grenadier Regiment 986 from its occupation of Eppeldorf 2.5 kilometers to the northeast. The German

---

22 Private Louis Schwall, a son of German immigrants from Bay City, Michigan, was 23 years old when he died; he had been with his unit just 15 days. His son was born the day after his death.

absence of artillery and antitank guns again became apparent the next day when elements of the Grenadier Regiment's I Battalion attacked Ermsdorf, supported only by mortar fire, but the light tanks beat them off again.

A small pathway leads from the road to a large mountain rock bearing a plaque dedicated to the units of **Combat Command A, 9th Armored Division** who stopped the German Ardennes advance along the Medernach–Savelborn–Waldbillig–Christnach line. The plaque lists the individual units. The opposite face of the rock bears an inscription to the memory of the victims of the war. (French only)

Location: 8 km west of Beaufort beside highway CR358. (49.829020, 6.223128)

12th Infantry Regiment, 4th Infantry Division Sector
16 to 25 December 1944

GERMAN OBJECTIVE	To displace the Americans and form a blocking force against possible American movements from the south
FORCES	
American:	12th Infantry Regiment (Colonel Robert H Chance), 4th Infantry Division
German:	212th Volksgrenadier Division (Generalleutnant Franz Heinrich Otto Sensfuss)
RESULT	The regiment, heavily supported by other divisional units, held the southern corner of the Bulge battlefield
CASUALTIES	Period 16 to 23 December
American:	113 killed, 478 wounded, and 717 missing in action
German:	123 killed, 486 wounded, and 418 missing in action

Battle Summary

After a short artillery preparation, grenadiers crossed the Sauer River at Weilerbach and on both sides of Echternach camouflaged by the early morning fog. Although the assault started at 0530 as elsewhere, not until 1000 did contact with American outposts take place. By 1250, Company E in Echternach, Company G in Lauterborn, and Company I in Dickweiler were surrounded. Receiving reports of the incursions, 4th Infantry Division commander Major General Raymond O Barton ordered '…no retrograde movement.' By dusk, the 12th Infantry still held Dickweiler, Osweiler, Echternach, Lauterborn, and Berdorf, but each location braced for attacks by superior forces.

By 17 December, General Barton sent a make-shift Task Force Luckett[23] to seal the Ernz Noire gorge east of Müllerthal. Meanwhile, Col Chance, with three companies of 1st Battalion under his temporary command, sent Company B, supported by light tanks from 70th Tank Battalion, to rescue Company F, still holding out at the Parc

---

23 Task Force Luckett, commanded by Colonel James S Luckett, consisted of 4th Reconnaissance Troop; 4th Engineer Combat Battalion; eight Shermans of Company B, 70th Tank Battalion; and Lieutenant Colonel George Mabry's 2nd Battalion, 8th Infantry Regiment.

Chapter Eight   Battle of the Sûre and Sauer Rivers   415

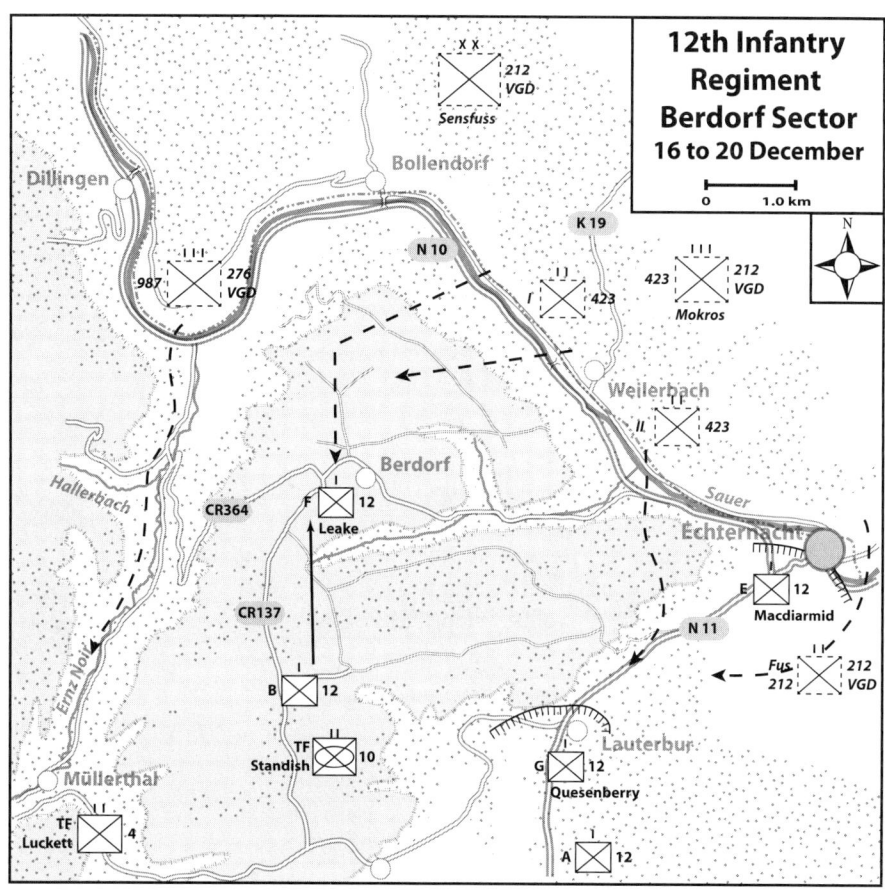

Hotel in Berdorf but they could only achieve the edge of the forest south of the village before encountering German gunners. Company A attempted to rescue Company E in Echternach, but only advanced as far as Lauterborn. Company C reinforced the troops in Osweiler and Dickweiler holding the river line. In mid-morning, Barton also dispatched Lieutenant Colonel Thomas A Kenan's 2nd Battalion, 22nd Infantry Regiment and a company of tanks routing a company of German infantry west of Osweiler. The two villages were then firmly defended.

On 18 December, Brigadier General Edwin W Pilburn's CCA, 10th Armored Division divided into task forces to clear the Ernz Noire gorge and halt Grenadier Regiment 987's assumed drive south toward Luxembourg City. Grenadiers firing numerous panzerfausts at armored vehicles stopped one force driving west toward Müllerthal. Company C, 11th Tank Battalion, with a company of 61st Armored Infantry, drove into Berdorf but withdrew under heavy panzerfaust attack. The third force, Task Force Riley, aborted its move against Lauterborn. Finally, on 19 December, General Pilburn halted the attacks in favor of sealing the German troops in the gorge.

Battle of Ernz Noire
17 to 25 December 1944

Infantry Battalion to the west and 12th Infantry Regiment to the east. The undefended gorge presented a natural path to cut through American defenses. On 17 December, General Möhring, under pressure from Brandenberger, released his Grenadier Regiment 987 to cross the Sauer at the broad river loop near Grundhof. By later that morning, the unopposed lead battalion entered Müllerthal, where the gorge splayed in three directions offering routes behind the American forces threatening the 4th Infantry Division's rear.

GERMAN OBJECTIVE	To isolate American forward positions
FORCES	
American:	Elements of 4th Infantry Division (Major General Raymond Barton) and 5th Infantry Division (Major General Stanford Leroy Irwin)
German:	Grenadier Regiments 987 and 988, 276th Volksgrenadier Division (Generalmajor Kurt Möhring) and Grenadier Regiment 423, 212th Volksgrenadier Division (Generalmajor Franz Sensfuss)
RESULT	German forces became themselves isolated in the narrow gorge
CASUALTIES	
American:	Uncertain
German:	200 taken prisoner
LOCATION	Müllerthal is 18 km southeast of Diekirch

Battle

At 1330, Colonel Thomas L Harrold, commander CCA, 9th Armored Division, sent Troop B, 89th Cavalry Reconnaissance Squadron, supported by four M18s from 811th Tank Destroyer Battalion, to halt the German advance. A panzerfaust disabled the leading M18, blocking the narrow road and sealing the exit to the west toward Waldbillig. Enemy infantry subjected the dismounted cavalry to intense small-arms fire from positions hidden among the huge boulders and tree-shrouded slopes to stop the American advance into the gorge.

After the dispatch of Task Force Luckett, elements of CCA, 10th Armored Division moved forward as reinforcements. In an event never explained, Grenadier Regiment 987 made no attempt on 17 December to leave the gorge and press its advantage against the flank of the American defense.

Well-camouflaged grenadiers hidden among the rocky outcrops and canyons defeated repeated attempts to surge up the gorge. The narrow, winding trail through the valley afforded the grenadiers excellent defensive positions and forced advancing armor to move single file. German artillery, that had finally crossed the bridges at Dillingen, broke up infantry attempts to outflank the grenadiers.

Chapter Eight — Battle of the Sûre and Sauer Rivers

A stalemate ensued until 24 December when the US 5th Infantry Division arrived and attacked along both sides of the gorge. On Christmas Day, a battalion swung ahead by entering the gorge from the west along Hallerbach creek and 2nd Regiment entered Berdorf after an all-night American artillery bombardment. Grenadier Regiment 987 became increasingly exposed in a salient while German units to its east and west were slowly driven back. By 26 December, the German line had been exposed whereby units were rapidly ferrying men east across the Sauer.

Battlefield Tour

> Continue southeast on highway CR364 for 2.7 km. Turn right onto rue de l'Ernz Noire (CR121). Follow through the gorge for 4.1 km to the Hotel des Cascades du Müllerthal. (49.790385, 6.307467)
> The profusion of huge boulders and rock formations presents the difficulties American forces faced when attempting to push German troops from the gorge.

Although no actual battlefield sites or memorials are identified, the drive along the Ernz Noire River is in itself a pleasant experience. Local tourist offices advertise the region as the **Little Switzerland of Luxembourg**, despite the absence of mountain peaks. The 112-kilometer Müllerthal hiking trail, divided into three circular routes, is considered one of the best in Europe. Tour information is available at the Echternach Tourist Office (see below).

> Return north and continue straight onto rue du Grundhof (CR364), follow the curving highway where it climbs out of the Ernz Noire gorge for 2.7 km to the Priedegtstull Viewpoint. (49.817455, 6.332451)

The stairs up the **Priedegtstull** (literally: priest's pulpit) rock formation leads to a boulder, where highway CR364 leaves the gorge to access the flat plateau.

> Continue 1.2 km on rue de Grundhof to the intersection with An der Ruetsbech, the site of the Hotel du Parc. (49.823185, 6.347459)

Battle of Berdorf
16 to 21 December 1944

The Berdorf sector rests on top of a large plateau whose boundaries are the steep gradients into the bordering river valleys. The position provided observation and control over a wide area in this part of Luxembourg.

GERMAN OBJECTIVE	To clear the Berdorf Plateau of American forces
FORCES	
American:	Company F (1st Lieutenant John L Leake), 12th Infantry Regiment; later Company C (Captain Steve Lang), 11th Tank Battalion

	German:	I Battalion, Grenadier Regiment 423, 212th Volksgrenadier Division (Generalleutnant Franz Sensfuss)
Result		American forces held for five days against overwhelming opposition
Casualties		
	American:	4 killed and 20 wounded
	German:	350 killed
Location		Berdorf is 24 km southeast of Diekirch

Battle

Company F, 12th Infantry Regiment maintained its command post in the Hôtel du Parc on the northwestern outskirts of Berdorf. The majority of the company's men were stationed two kilometers forward at four outposts overlooking the Sauer River. A well-coordinated attack by I Battalion, Grenadier Regiment 423 overwhelmed three of the four platoon outposts and captured the company's mortars, machine guns, and antitank guns. The three-story, reinforced concrete Hôtel du Parc became a bastion where outpost survivors straggled in over the next few days to join 1st Lieutenant John Leake eventually totaling sixty men. Twenty-two men of the 2nd Platoon sought shelter in the stone buildings of Birkelt Farm 2.2 kilometers east of the town center. Two accompanying forward observers radioed target coordinates to American artillery for the next four days while enemy attempts to take the well-fortified position failed. Finally, the appearance of heavy assault weapons ended their resistance on 20 December.

General Barton dispatched reserve Company B with five Sherman and five Stuart tanks from 70th Tank Battalion toward Berdorf. The relief force was ambushed at the town's southern entrance and fought to a standstill. The next day, the tanks prepared to fire on American troops in the hotel, believing it to be German-held, until an American flag appeared on the roof. Lt Leake and his men held against repeated assaults and tested their marksmanship by dropping German soldiers who carelessly showed themselves in the town's buildings hundreds of meters away.

On 18 December, another relief force from Task Force Standish comprised of two platoons of tanks from Company C, 11th Tank Battalion and the 61st Armored Infantry, CCA, 10th Armored Division under Captain Steve Lang of Chicago, Illinois arrived in Berdorf by midday and succeeded in clearing most of the village. House-to-house fighting filled the next 72 hours while possession of the town repeatedly changed hands. Leake's infantry and Lang's tanks beat off repeated German assaults against their positions aided by a remaining telephone connection in the hotel that allowed Leake to call in artillery support.

Finally, on 21 December, after five days of resisting every enemy effort to overcome the positions, Lang and Leake received permission to withdraw. That night, fifty-four survivors made their way 800 meters to awaiting tanks and half-tracks to

Chapter Eight   Battle of the Sûre and Sauer Rivers   419

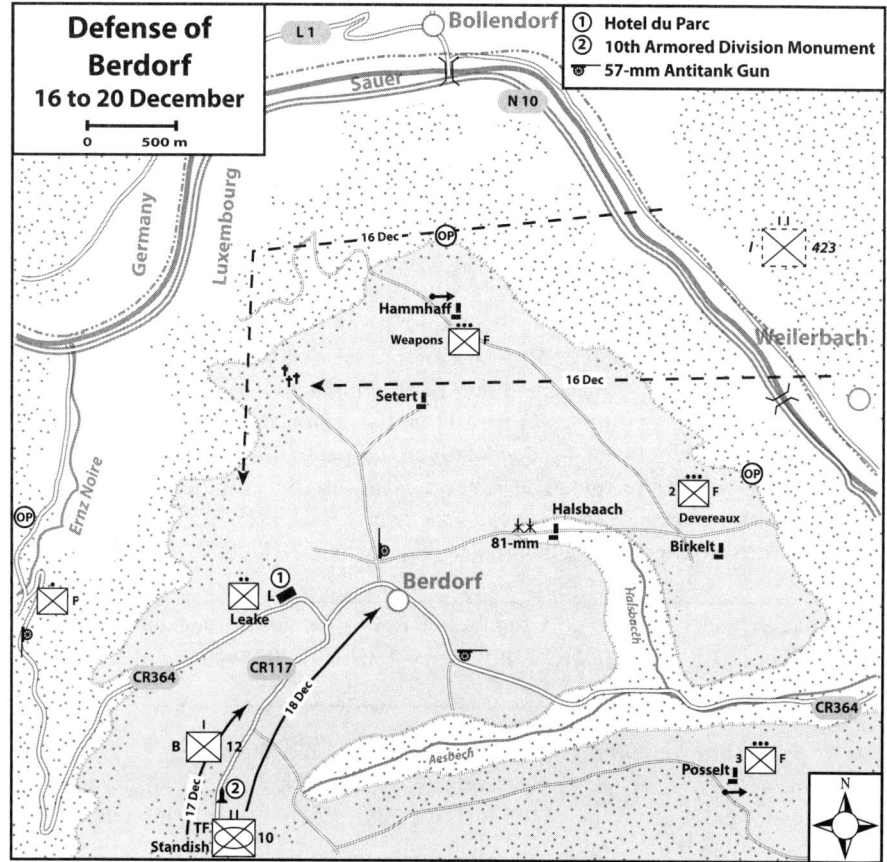

escape back to Consdorf.[24] On 26 December, 2nd Infantry Regiment, 5th Infantry Division re-occupied Berdorf after a short fight.

Battlefield Tour

On 16 December, Lieutenant William McConnell[25] sped to Consdorf to report the German attack but was captured on his return trip while carrying the company's $5600 payroll. McConnell's driver, T/5 John Mandichiak of Cresson, Pennsylvania, escaped capture and spent the next seven days behind enemy lines before rejoining American forces. McConnell, escorted by thirty-three German soldiers led by a sergeant, approached the hotel with instructions to demand an American surrender. Because none of the German soldiers understood English, McConnell and Leake pretended to discuss the surrender while actually planning to free McConnell. Leake

---

24 Upon his return to regimental headquarters in Consdorf, Lt Leake and twenty-one of his men were assigned to that town's defense. The men spent the next three days in foxholes half filled with icy water before being relieved. Lieutenant John Louis Leake received a Silver Star for his leadership. He died in 1992 at age 75 and is buried in Keokuk National Cemetery, Keokuk, Iowa.

25 Lt William McConnell of Utica, New York survived the war.

instructed his men to each pick a target and shoot upon command. McConnell yelled, 'Don't shoot! And don't miss!' before he turned and smiled at the German sergeant. In an instant, firing erupted from the hotel's doors and windows and the German troops, fully exposed on the open ground, started to fall. McConnell raced for the safety of the building from where 1st Sergeant Gervis Willis[26] and Sergeant Norman Finan dropped twenty enemy soldiers between them. The only German survivor was the sergeant who was taken prisoner into the hotel.[27]

Hôtel du Parc was reduced by repeated shelling from German artillery, which literally blew the top floors off the structure. During a 19 December German night attack a demolition charge blew a hole in the wall but attacking enemy troops were repelled with volley of hand grenades.

In 1944, the hotel lay on the outskirts of Berdorf surrounded by open fields and farms. After the war, the structure was rehabilitated and again became a hotel specializing in servicing tourists to the Müllerthal scenic trail. In 2009, the building was completely derelict with windows broken, shutters pulled down, and the breeze blowing through the structure. The Hôtel du Parc has recently been demolished to construct apartments on the same space. Nonetheless, the hotel's location demonstrates its defensive potential commanding routes from Berdorf to the Ernz Noire gorge.

Continue southeast on rue de Grundhof (CR364) for 230 m and turn right onto rue de Consdorf (becomes CR137). Proceed 1.1 km to the memorial on the right. (49.813090, 6.341191)

The **10th Armored Division Memorial** is a mountain stone inscribed with the outline of the Grand Duchy of Luxembourg placed amid a small landscaped setting at the edge of the forest south of Berdorf. A small bronze plaque in its center honors the division in the Battle of the Bulge. The 10th Armored Division, much like the 9th Armored Division, did not fight as a consolidated unit, but instead its three combat commands fought independently: CCA was the mobile defense force in the Ernz Noire gorge area; CCB entered Bastogne on 18 December and fought in the early defense of that city; CCR joined CCA, 9th Armored Division on 21 December 1944 in a vain effort to recover Waldbillig.

Reverse direction and return to Berdorf. Turn right onto rue d'Echternach (CR364) and follow for 4.3 km before turning toward Diekirch (N10). After 2.2 km, stop at the memorial on the right. (49.833733, 6.383604)

Upon leaving Berdorf toward Echternach pass the Hotel Pérékop that was used as an observation post. After 1.3 km, note the parking area on the left (49.817929, 6.375846) where the 5th Infantry Division established a medical station

---

26 1st Sergeant Gervis Willis of Augusta, Georgia was awarded the Distinguished Service Cross for this and other actions during the defense of the company CP at Berdorf.

27 The surviving sergeant was Feldwebel Franz Krüger from the free city of Danzig – now Gdansk, Poland.

Chapter Eight　　　　Battle of the Sûre and Sauer Rivers　　421

> after advancing into the area. Continue to the Bel Air Hotel on the left. The large building housed at first a German military hospital and later an American hospital prior to the battle.

Crossing the Sauer River
7 to 17 February 1945

While not part of the Battle of the Bulge, the Sauer River crossing completes the story of combat in this area.

AMERICAN OBJECTIVE	To launch the invasion of Germany
FORCES	
American:	5th Infantry Division (Major General Stafford Irwin)
German:	212th Volksgrenadier Division (Generalleutnant Franz Sensfuss)
RESULT	The river line was breached at great cost
CASUALTIES	
American:	Uncertain
German:	Undetermined
LOCATION	Weilerbach is 24 km southeast of Diekirch

Battle

At 0100 on 7 February 1945, the first rubber boats pushed from the banks into the river's swollen and turbulent waters when the 5th Infantry Division launched the invasion of Germany. The water's churn immediately capsized a handful of boats while others ran wildly downstream driven by the 10- to 17-mile-per-hour current. The few surviving boats reached midstream before the entire east bank of the river became alive with enemy fire. Only one eight-man boat of each of the two assault regiments reached the far shore. Division commander Major General Stafford Irwin directed all available artillery batteries to target territory beyond the small beachhead. Tanks, tank destroyers, and 155-mm self-propelled guns lined the river's edge to take enemy positions under direct fire, especially the dreaded pillboxes and bunkers. However, by nightfall, still only sixteen men held the perilous beachhead. The attached 417th Infantry Regiment, 76th Infantry Division crossing at Echternach and the 80th Infantry Division crossing farther west (see Dillingen, above), fared slightly better.

The river current and enemy fire denied repeated engineer efforts to support the stranded men by bridging efforts. The next day the 10th Infantry Regiment manhandled a boat across to rescue its eight-man team. Meanwhile, in the 11th Infantry Regiment's sector, six boatloads of Company F riflemen and a heavy machine-gun team from Company K successfully crossed. The 417th Infantry Regiment added riflemen and machine gun crews to its meager holdings around Echternach. So it continued for three days while American strength on the east bank gradually increased. Fortunately, the depleted 212th VGD lacked the resources to launch a counterattack.

Supporting the beachhead by boat proved a near-impossible assignment. Engineers continued their bridging efforts against incredible natural obstacles of terrain, current, muddy supply roads, and enemy fire. Within the entire XII Corps' sector, one dozen bridges were swept away while under construction. On 11 February, the engineers successfully pushed the first bridge across the swirling waters. It was not until 17 February that XII Corps established a unified beachhead.

Battlefield Tour

The text on the diamond-shaped stone reads, 'In honor of the 5th Infantry Division that crossed the Sauer River here on 7 February 1945 under heavy enemy fire and adverse weather conditions. Their sacrifices helped to bring freedom again to our country. We shall remember.'

Walk across the Alfred Töpfer Bridge to the east bank of the river. (49.833725, 6.384038)

On 16 December, the 212th VGD crossed the Sauer River on an engineering bridge constructed upon the piers of a previously-destroyed railroad bridge. By the start of the assault, the bridge had been only partially finished such that German troops had to use ladders to descend from the completed section down to the west bank of the river. American artillery failed in its attempts to destroy the bridge, but it did hamper construction efforts by repeatedly interrupting construction and causing casualties to the German pionier troops. The bridge was finally completed in the evening of 18 December. The current **Alfred Töpfer footbridge** now occupies the same location.

Continue forward approximately 10 meters. (49.83403, 6.38474)

This destroyed pillbox had been part of the Westwall. Its appearance suggests that it had actually been two constructions, and local lore relates stories of Russian PoWs working in a concrete sheltered factory on the site, but its actual purpose remains mystery.

> Return to your vehicle and reverse direction (it may be necessary to continue north before making a U-turn). At the entrance to Echternach, turn left onto rue de la Gare and enter a parking area. (49.816130, 6.416645)

Battle of Echternach
16 to 19 December 1944

GERMAN OBJECTIVE	To eliminate forward American positions	
FORCES		
American:	Company E (1st Lieutenant Morton A Macdiarmid), 12th Infantry Regiment	
German:	I Battalion, Grenadier Regiment 320, 212th Volksgrenadier Division (Generalleutnant Franz Sensfuss)	
RESULT	The defending company was captured	

CASUALTIES	
American:	130 taken prisoner
German:	Over 150 killed
LOCATION	Echternach is 27 km southeast of Diekirch

Battle

General Franz Sensfuss's Grenadier Regiment 320 intended to cross the Sauer directly into Echternach, but the recent heavy rainfall had so swollen the river that a rubber-boat crossing against the swift current became impossible. Instead, the regiment crossed at Edigen, 5 kilometers downstream. The I Battalion circled back behind Echternach while the II Battalion struck against American forces at Osweiler and Dickweiler.

Echternach was occupied by only Company E and, while isolated, it did not immediately come under enemy fire. First Lieutenant Morton A Macdiarmid's company headquarters on the southwestern edge of town along rue de Luxembourg was not threatened, but three squad-sized outposts in the town were cut-off.

Meanwhile, two tanks from 10th Armored Division's Task Force Riley entered Echternach and brought Company E's 1st Platoon back to the company CP at a hat factory and adjacent Hotel Luxembourg. However, Lt Macdiarmid believed General Barton's last command of 'no retrograde movement' remained in effect and refused to leave Echternach. The tanks returned to Lauterborn at dusk.

As darkness fell, the German attack fell upon Company E. First Lieutenant Richard L Cook, accompanied by S/Sergeant Michael J Siscock, raced a jeep up the rue de Luxembourg to seek help from American tanks in Lauterborn. The task-force commander was reluctant to commit his tanks to the narrow town streets at night in an increasingly dense fog. Company E was therefore on its own.

German control of the LXXX Corps area had consolidated with the exception of Lt Macdiarmid's small band still holding out in Echternach. General Sensfuss was determined to eliminate them. American artillery fire defeated German attempts to place bridging spans across the piers of the old stone bridge. A later attempt at a pontoon bridge met the same fate, but on 19 December a bridge suitable for armor was completed at Edingen while a platoon of StuGs along with Fusilier Battalion 212 made for Echternach. At 1400 on 20 December, the Fusilier Battalion slipped into buildings facing those held by Company E to bring a barrage of machine-gun, panzerfaust, and Sturmgeschütz fire upon the hotel and its outbuildings, blowing holes in the hotel's façade. Eventually the survivors, 20 men from (Heavy Weapons) Company H and 110 from Company E, surrendered.[28]

Battlefield Tour

Echternach

The eldest town in Luxembourg, Echternach is one of Europe's earliest centers of culture and Christianity. Saint Willibrord from Northumberland founded a

---

[28] Lieutenant Morton (or Martin) A Macdiarmid was held at Stalag XIIa before transferring to Stalag IXb at Limburg, Germany.

Benedictine abbey here in 698, which became an artistically-refined writing school in the 10th and 11th centuries. Echternach displays an impressive architectural history, including a 5th-century Roman Villa, the Merovingian, Gothic and Romanesque Peter and Paul parish church, an 11th-century Romanesque Basilica with its 8th-century crypt, and the ancient patrician houses on the 15th-century market square. The abbey town had been a prime destination for pre-war tourism. The basilica was destroyed during the battle presumably by a purposeful detonation by retreating German troops. A graceful stone bridge connects Luxembourg Echternach with German Echternacherbrück.

Tourist Office
9-10 Parvis de la Basilique   L-6486 Echternach
Grand Duchy of Luxembourg   Tel: +352 72 02 30.
Web: http://www.echternach-tourist.lu
For information of the Müllerthal region: Web: http://www.mullerthal.lu

At the rear of the parking area, a large field stone bears a plaque dedicated to the American troops that twice liberated Echternach. The text reads:
In gratitude to the valiant soldiers of the **83rd, 4th and 5th U.S Infantry Divisions**, who liberated the city of Echternach, October – December 1944, and to the 76th US Infantry Division, who crossed the river Sauer here on 7 February 1945, ending the Nazi oppression of our country. [29]

Reverse direction back to highway N10 and turn left (south). After 500 m, turn left onto rue Andre Duchscher and stop 25 m ahead. (49.812120, 6.417443)

Company E, 12th Infantry Regiment and elements of Company M (Heavy Weapons) made its last stand among the buildings that included this restaurant (then the **Hôtel du Luxembourg**), a garage, and a hat factory that occupied the half block from rue Andre Duchscher to route de Luxembourg. At the time, this marked the southwest edge of the town and highway N10 now traces what once were the town's medieval walls. The bronze plaque on the wall of Le Vesuve Brasserie commemorates the sacrifices of the members of the two companies in holding back the enemy advance. Note the smooth new stone of the repaired façade that had been destroyed by German StuGs. Patched areas on the wall and especially the chipped window sill stones are also a result of shell damage.

Reverse direction and turn south on rue Maximilien (N10). After 90 m, turn left

---

29   American author Sergeant JD Salinger was a member of the US 4th Counter Intelligence Corps attached to the 12th Infantry Regiment. Salinger, stationed in the Echternach area on 16 December, was not captured or believed to have been involved in the fighting. Salinger landed on Utah Beach on D-Day, experienced the Battles of the Hürtgen Forest and the Ardennes, and was one of the first soldiers to enter a satellite concentration camp near Dachau. His wartime experiences impacted his later writings.

> onto route de Luxembourg and note the driving school on the right. (49.811409, 6.418004)

On the morning of 20 December, 3rd Company, Fusilier Battalion 212 proceeded along a minor street behind the former city walls. The group took up positions in what is now a building occupied by a driving school across the route de Luxembourg from the Americans. After firing a panzerfaust at the American-held garage, the German troops established a machine gun in a first-floor window while riflemen took up positions in the upper windows. The clanging treads of an approaching assault gun encouraged the 50 - 60 Americans in the hat factory to surrender.

Side Trip: Westwallmuseum Panzerwerk Katzenkopf

> Follow rue du Pont to cross the Echternacher bridge into Germany and remain on Bitburgerstraße for 1.6 km passing through the roundabout. Turn right to merge onto highway B257 toward Bitburg / Irrel. Exit the highway after 4.3 km turning right onto Niederweiser Straße. Turn right onto Heidstraße and follow to the museum on the left. The town of Irrel presents several brown tourist signs indicating directions to the museum. (49.85195, 6.45417) Total distance 7.7 km

Westwallmuseum Panzerwerk Katzenkopf

Katzenkopf 54666 Irrel, Germany
Tel: +49 (0) 6525 492 E-Mail: info@westwallmuseum-irrel.de
Web: http://www.westwallmuseum-irrel.de/en/

The museum is one of the few preserved and open Westwall bunkers in Germany and one of only thirty-two fortifications of its type built. The site overlooks the valley and town of Irrel below. After entering the bunker the first rooms present posters and diagrams describing the design and construction of this particular installation that include forty-five separate rooms holding a garrison of eighty-four men. The self-guided tour allows access to several levels of the bunker where signs identify each room's special purpose. However, the bunker has been stripped of most of its metal, including blast doors, circular staircases, and most of its 60 electric motors and diesel generators. Little besides the dampness now remains. Down the stairs, one reaches the main corridor and the 100-meter-long 'hollow' corridor leading to the separate tank turret. Unfortunately, the six-port gun turret is not accessible. The main corridor displays large photos of the construction and destruction of the installation. The floor is slick with condensation, and the air is heavy with moisture. The bunker, built into a hillside, permits the surviving rooftop armored observation cupolas to be plainly visible. The exterior bears monuments to German soldiers who once manned the installation including one to the men of Fusilier Regiment 39 of whom 4,000 did not return.

Open daily April to 3 October from 14:00 to 17:00. Fee; not handicap accessible.

Battle of Lauterborn (Lauterbur)
16 to 21 December 1944

German Objective	To take command of the Echternach–Luxembourg City highway
Forces	
American:	Company G and Company A, 12th Infantry Regiment (Colonel Robert H Chance); later 159th Engineer Combat Battalion (Lieutenant Colonel Dick Staeffler)
German:	II Battalion, Grenadier Regiment 423, 212th Volksgrenadier Division (Generalleutnant Franz Sensfuss)
Result	The positions was held for five days
Casualties	Unknown
Location	Lauterborn is 3 km southwest of Echternach; Echternach is 27 km southeast of Diekirch

Battle

While events unraveled in Echternach, Grenadier Regiment 423 pushed forward to cut off Company G at Specksmillen northeast of Lauterborn and, by midday, surrounded the Americans still fighting at the mill north of the village while a platoon from Company H held a few buildings to the southwest.

On 17 December, Colonel Chance sent Company A from his reserve battalion, along with light tanks from Company D, 70th Tank Battalion, to reinforce positions at Lauterborn with the intent of moving to rescue the men in Echternach. The effort to reach Lauterborn took most of the day against German troops holding the high ground on either side of the highway. Darkness ended the approach with Company A in Lauterborn. Meanwhile, troops from Grenadier Regiment 320 circled around Lauterborn intent on cutting highway N11 south of Lauterborn.

By the next day, Task Force Riley,[30] 10th Armored Division was making itself felt. By early afternoon it re-occupied Scheidgen against a German rear guard left by German troops pushing farther south. A relief force of medium tanks from 21st Tank Battalion, and Companies B and C, 159th Engineer Combat Battalion, launched a surprise attack upon Hill 313. Five tanks silently coasted down highway CR118 to catch German troops unaware. Other elements of the task force advanced to the Company G CP at the mill while two infantry squads with two tanks reached the hat factory in Echternach, as described above. On the night of 20 December, Riley, forty survivors of Company G, and Company A left Lauterborn to establish a new main line of resistance at a road junction at Michelshaff, a hamlet of a few buildings directly on the Echternach–Luxembourg City road.

On 21 December, Fusilier Battalion 212 moved through abandoned Lauterborn and advanced down draws towards Michelshaff, Scheidgen, and Consdorf. The engineer battalion's Company C, now joined by Company A, held Hill 313 with

---

30 Task Force Riley held a company from 61st Armored Infantry Battalion and a company of medium tanks from 21st Tank Battalion, under the command of Lieutenant Colonel John R Riley.

Chapter Eight   Battle of the Sûre and Sauer Rivers   427

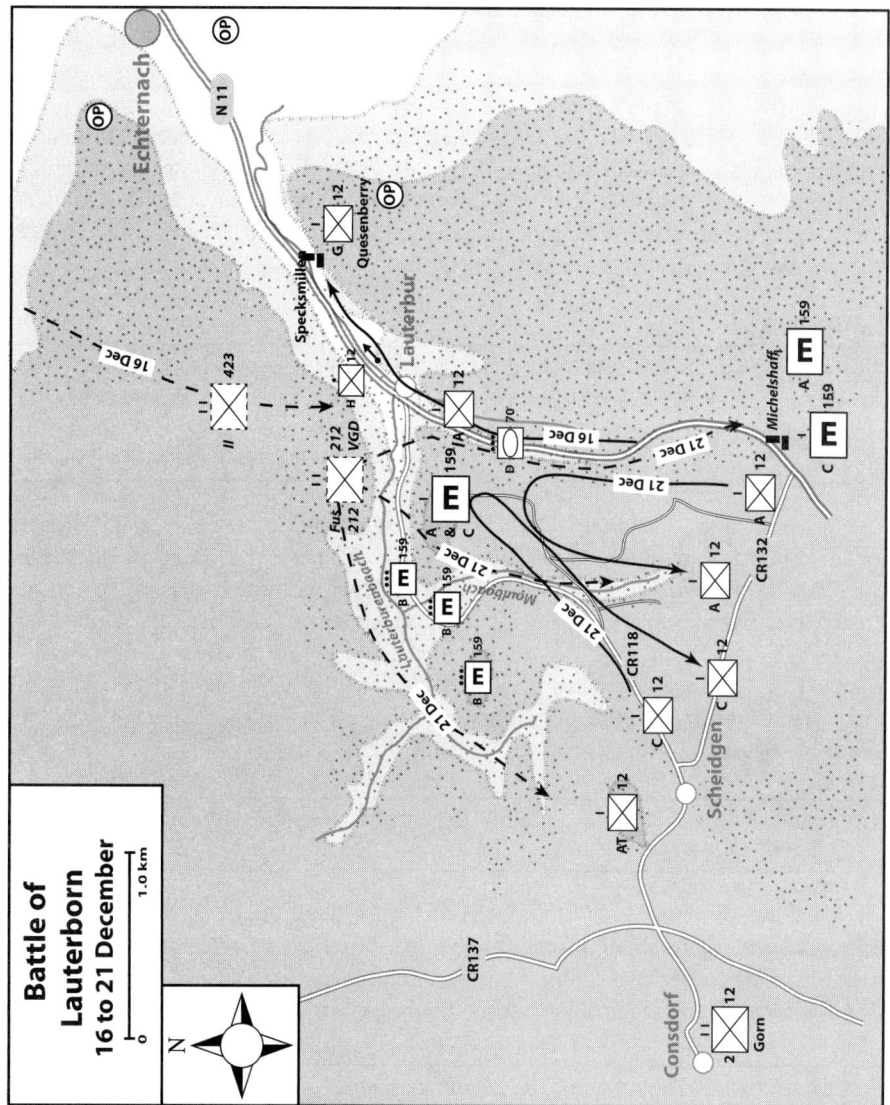

Company B on a smaller rise to the west, but the Americans' flanks were wide open. One platoon of Company B's engineers was annihilated defending the hilltop to the west of Hill 313 forcing the other two platoons to fall back to Scheidgen while company commander Captain Anthony B Chapek remained behind to cover the withdrawal. His men saw him last when he stood alone, pinning down the enemy with rapid and accurate fire from his carbine.[31] Companies A and C likewise withdrew southeast to Michelshaff.

---

31 Captain Anthony B Chapek of Omaha, Nebraska, was awarded a Distinguished Service Cross posthumously for his sacrifice in allowing his men to escape. Captain Chapek is buried in Luxembourg

American efforts to retake Lauterborn on 21 December utilizing infantry Companies A and C were defeated by well-entrenched German troops on Hill 313.

Aftermath

The 12th Infantry Regiment continued to hold the southern shoulder until relieved on 24 December. Of the five strategic towns that they defended, Echternach, Lauterborn, Osweiler, Dickweiler, and Berdorf, only Echternach was captured by force. The various outposts held their ground despite frequently being surrounded. They fought off enemy attacks for three or four days without resupply and generally without heavy infantry weapons.

Battlefield Tour

> Leave Echternach southwest toward Luxembourg City on rue de Luxembourg (E29/N11). Approximately 1.8 km southwest of Echternach, note the industrial complex on the left and in particular the stone wall lining the highway. Company G command post was sited in the two story building beside the highway. (49.802367, 6.397122)

At about 1400 on 16 December, a large group of German and American soldiers appeared marching along the road from Echternach. Major Glenn Zarger, 2nd Battalion Executive Officer who had arrived that morning to access the German assault, ordered his men to open fire. The fifteen American prisoners jumped into ditches behind the stone wall while a fire fight erupted with the forty or fifty German troops. The exchange continued all afternoon until the arrival of a platoon of light tanks from Company D, 70th Tank Battalion drove off the attackers to the relief of the fifteen prisoners still sheltering in the roadside ditch.

> Continue 1.0 km and stop in Lauterborn at the junction with highway CR118. (49.796244, 6.387023)

Lauterborn consists of little more than a hotel-restaurant complex, a few scattered farms, and a small residence known as the Villa de René Deltgen that stands on the east side of the intersection.[32] Fusilier Battalion 212 established its headquarters in the cellar of the ruined chateau during its occupation of the area.

> Turn right toward Larochette (CR118 and stop at the side of the road after 150 m. Walk up the forest steps. (49.795773, 6.384141)

A monument in memory of the men who fought on this hill against the German offensive stands upon Hill 313. The bronze plaque affixed to a large boulder commends **Company A, 12th Infantry Regiment, 159th Combat Engineer (sic)**

American Cemetery, Luxembourg City, Luxembourg. He was 29 years old and had never met his only child.

32 Deltgen was a Luxembourger actor who performed in many 1930s and 1940s movies produced in Berlin. He continued doing so during the Nazi occupation and was tried for treason after the war. He received a mild sentence, regained his Luxembourg citizenship, and returned to acting.

Chapter Eight   Battle of the Sûre and Sauer Rivers   429

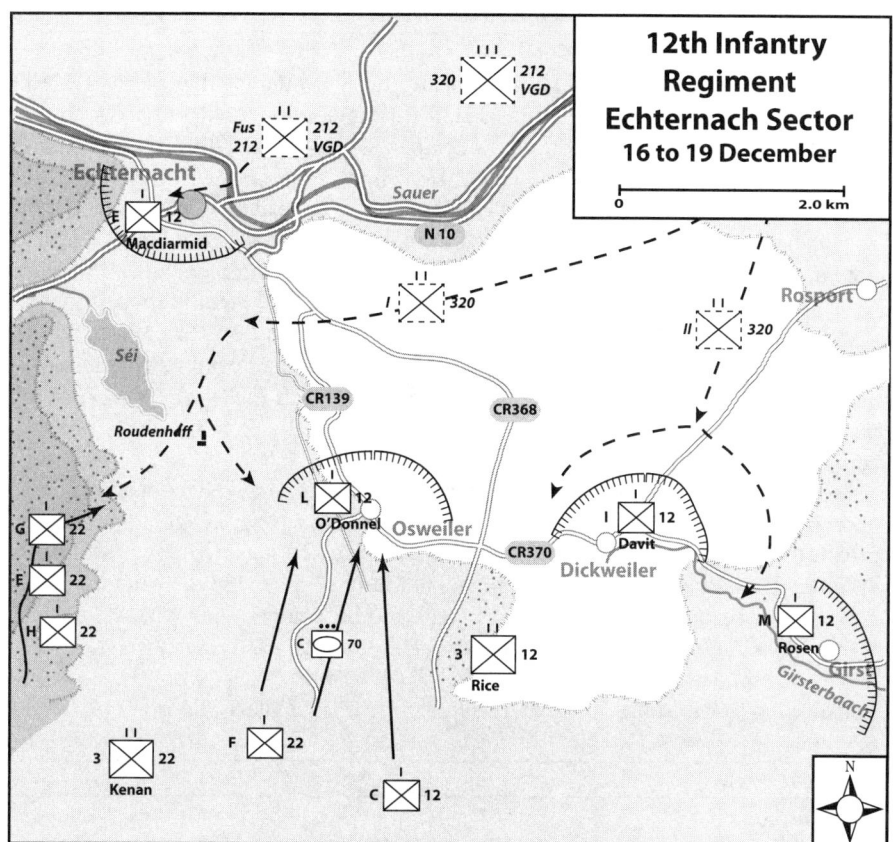

Battalion, and **10th Regiment, 5th Infantry Division**. The heights overlooking highway N11 toward Echternach retain foxholes dug during the engagement.

Return to highway E29 and turn right toward Altrier (E29). Stop at the road junction after 2.4 km. (49.775052, 6.381866)

On 22 December, 212th VGD made its last concentrated attack. At 1330, 158 grenadiers advanced across an open field toward the Michelshaff farm complex where Companies A and G – supported by tanks, tank destroyers, and two companies of engineers – awaited. The Americans held their fire until the enemy approached to within 100 meters of their foxholes. The fusillade dropped the unsuspecting German troops where they stood. Three wounded German survivors were killed while attempting to surrender and one survivor walked to American lines amid 154 dead. The 212th VGD began its withdrawal from the salient later that night.

Other Points of Interest between Echternach and Luxembourg City

Osweiler

Osweiler was defended by Company L, 12th Infantry Regiment. By 1100 on 16 December, Grenadier Regiment 320 surrounded the town, but the stubborn defenders held on. At 1500 on 19 December, Company C, 70th Tank Battalion passed through Osweiler and took up positions north of the town.

On 21 December, Grenadier Regiment 320 gathered in the woods at Roudenhaff (Rodenhof) Farm to launch a final assault upon Osweiler at the same time that two companies from re-enforcing 22nd Infantry Regiment moved forward to clear those woods. The two forces met with neither side gaining the advantage. The Americans dug in for the night south of the farm. By 24 December, the 5th Infantry Division had passed through the 4th Division and began its counterattack along a line from Osweiler on the east to Savelborn on the west. Enemy troops yielded terrain reluctantly but, by 26 December, the 212th VGD was streaming across the Bollendorf bridge back into Germany.

Osweiler commemorates its liberation with a flag-flanked mountain boulder upon which numerous American units have affixed their insignia, including the **5th and 9th Armored Divisions** and the **4th, 5th, 28th, 76th, 83rd, and 87th Infantry Divisions**. From September 1944 to March 1945, the soldiers of these units defended or reconquered the area. A plaque on the boulder ends with the tribute, 'Many gave their lives so that we can live in freedom. We the living must ensure that they have not died in vain.'

Location: 4.5 km south of Echternach on rue Principale (CR139). (49.78508, 6.43868)

Grevenmacher

The 83rd Infantry Division captured Grevenmacher and Echternach on 7 October 1944 and spent the next month on defensive patrols along the west bank of the Moselle River. The unit moved to the Hürtgen Forest before entering the Battle of the Bulge on 27 December 1944 to fight against the tip of the Bulge.

A simple rough stone standing below the *Mosellebrücke* comprises a memorial to the members of the **331st Infantry Combat Team, 83rd Infantry Division**, 'whose sacrifices and suffering during the conflict will be remembered forever.'

Location: 20 km south of Echternach or 30 km east of Luxembourg City beside highway N10 almost immediately below the bridge across the Moselle River. (49.676148, 6.442636)

Continue southwest toward Luxembourg (E29). After 21 km, exit toward Bruxelles / Metz / Luxembourg (E44 / A7). After 1.2 km, use left lane to merge toward Aéroport (A1 / E44). After 2.4 km, exit toward Aéroport. Merge onto highway N1 and take the 3d exit from the roundabout making three left turns to approach the monument. Near the large roundabout outside the airport terminal, a small access drive past the monument allows for parking. (49.6363, 6.21722)

Luxembourg City

The impressive polished rose-granite columns of the **4th Infantry Division Monument** pay tribute to the leadership and men of the 4th Infantry Division, US Army, who halted the left shoulder of the German thrust into the American lines during the Battle of the Bulge and thereby saved the city of Luxembourg.

> Leave the monument by returning to the large roundabout and take the 4th exit toward Sandweiler (N1, becomes N1-A after 2.2 km and N2-B after an additional 1.5 km). At the roundabout, take the 5th exit toward Sandweiler (E29). After 750 m, take the 1st roundabout exit (CR234) and proceed 650 m to the cemetery entrance path on the left. (49.60815, 6.20304)

Volksbund Deutsche Kriegsgräberfürsorge e. V.
Werner-Hilpert-Str. 2   34112 Kassel, Germany
Tel.: +49 (0)5 61 70 09 1 39   E-Mail: presse@volksbund.de
Web: https://www.volksbund.de/en/volksbund.html

Signs at the edge of the parking area provide directions to the Cimetière Militaire Allemand / Deutschen Soldaten Friedhof sited in dense woods. A long path leads to a gray stone portico through which one enters the **Sandweiler German War Cemetery** containing the graves of 10,913 German soldiers — 4,829 of whom were buried in 'comrades' graves. Almost all of the deaths occurred during the Battle of the Bulge during which American Graves Registration buried over one-half that number. The additional bodies were re-interred from more than 150 burial plots from all over Luxembourg. The names of those Luxembourg locations are inscribed on eight plaques hanging in the portico in alphabetical order, starting with Allerborn and ending with Wormeldingen.

Admission to the cemetery is never restricted. No admission fee.

> Reverse direction and proceed northwest (CR234). After 160 m, turn left onto rue de Sandweiler (CR159) and shortly right onto Val du Scheid. Follow for 1.0 km to the American Cemetery parking area.
> Alternatively, approach the Luxemburg American Cemetery via highway A1; exit at E27 and follow the signs toward Cimetières Militaire. (49.612796, 6.185676)

Luxembourg American Cemetery
50, Val du Scheid   2517 Luxembourg City
Grand Duchy of Luxembourg   Tel: +352 43 17 27
Web: https://www.abmc.gov/cemeteries-memorials/europe/luxembourg-american-cemetery#

The **Luxembourg American Cemetery**, located in the Hamm district of Luxembourg City, was originally designated as the burial location for soldiers of the US Third Army who had died in the Battle of the Bulge or the following advance to the Rhine River. The cemetery's 17 acres of grave plots form a gentle fan and now contain the graves of 5,076 service personnel, including 22 pairs of brothers buried side by side. The plots are separated by four water courses. The names of 371 missing are inscribed of the reverse sides of the battle maps. Contrary to his specific burial wishes, the grave of Lieutenant General George S Patton Jr occupies a place of prominence at the front center of the plots.[33]

The courtyard in front of the American chapel and between the two large battle maps bears a metal inscription of a quotation from President Dwight Eisenhower:

> All who shall hereafter live in freedom will be here reminded that to these men and their comrades we owe a debt to be paid with grateful remembrance of their sacrifice and with the high resolve that the cause for which they died shall live eternally.

The cemetery is open daily from 9:00 to 17:00; closed December 25 and January 1. No admission fee.

Other Points of Interest in or near Luxembourg City

A tree-shaded vale below street level contains the **German War Cemetery Luxembourg-Clausen** with graves from the two world wars. Proceed down the stairway to find four tablets listing the names of the 205 German soldiers from the First World War in a mass grave immediately on the right, as no individual graves from that conflict exist. The grave plot containing 262 soldiers from the Second World War is ahead and down additional steps.
Location: Along rue Jules Wilhelm south of Parc des Trois Glands (49.615173, 6.140103)

Monument national de la solidarité (National Memorial of Solidarity)
Plateau du Saint Esprit   L-1475 Luxembourg City
Grand Duchy of Luxembourg

Opened in 1971, this stark monument venerates those who lost their lives in the Second World War and recalls the resistance to Nazi occupation. The paved interior suggests the concentration camps, prisons, and barracks where Luxembourg people suffered. A small chapel contains a symbolic tombstone representing the victims of the war.
Location: Near Boulevard Franklin Delano Roosevelt (N50 / N57) (49.607046, 6.134132)

Cimetière-Notre-Dame
allée des Résistants et des Déportés   2450 Lëtzeburg
Luxembourg City   Grand Duchy of Luxembourg

A newer section in the left front of Notre-Dame Cemetery contains a small square of granite tiles framed by sharply-trimmed yews, which forms the **National Monument to the Resistance and Deportation 1940 - 1945**. In the center, a polished black granite modernist sculpture depicts an individual with hands tied be-

---

[33] On 21 December 1945, Lieutenant General George S Patton Jr, who became legendary for having commanded the American Third Army during the Second World War, was killed in a highway accident in the vicinity of Mannheim, Germany.

Chapter Eight   Battle of the Sûre and Sauer Rivers   433

hind its back to commemorate murdered political prisoners. (49.61504, 6.11942)

An additional sandstone building in the middle rear of the cemetery adjoins columns that form three porticos around a central space. A memorial to the French soldiers of the *Grand Guerre (First World War)*, who died in the Grand Duchy, appears to the left. The tomb of an **Unknown Luxembourgeois Legionnaire** lies in the center. The tomb's cover bears bronze palm fronds and flower bouquets.
Location: Cemetery entrance along rue Jean-Pierre Probst which is best accessed from intersection of highways N6 and N51. (49.616524, 6.118413)

RAF Graves

West of the city, the **Hollerich Communal Cemetery** contains the graves of nine RAF airmen of the Second World War. Seven of the victims died in a crash on 11 April 1943, one 15 May 1940, and an earlier victim on 10 May 1940. The RAF graves are flanked on the right by two French soldiers killed in 1945, one of whom is unknown, and on the left by three stone crosses marking the graves of French soldiers killed in 1945, one of whom is unknown.
Location: Along rue de Bouillon (CR230). (49.59874, 6.11333)

Villa Pauly
57, boulevard de la Pétrusse   Luxembourg City
Grand Duchy of Luxembourg   Tel: +352 47 82 280
Email: Paul.Dostert@cnr.etat.lu

After the general strike of 1942 (see entry for Wiltz), a state of emergency was declared whereby German authorities imposed arrests, deportations to concentration camps, resettlement of whole families to German-occupied territories in the east, and a prohibition on using the French language or the Lëtzebuergesch dialect.

This mansion, built in 1923 in an upscale district of Luxembourg City, became the headquarters of the German *Geheime Staatspolizei*, or **Gestapo**. The structure's brooding medieval architecture and the suspicion that interrogations and torture took place in its cellar make it a fitting symbol of Nazi oppression. The building is now a documentation center on the Resistance Movement in Luxembourg
Location: South of the city center and crossing the Adolphe Bridge. (49.606091, 6.124991).

Musée national de la Résistance (National Resistance Museum of Luxembourg)
place de la Résistance   L-4041 Esch-sur-Alzette
Grand Duchy of Luxembourg   Tel: +352 54 84 72
Email: musee@villeesch.lu   Web: http:/www.esch.lu/culture/musee

Carved stone monoliths in front of the museum depict the struggles of the Luxembourg people under German occupation that ended with the arrival of American soldiers. The interior holds permanent and special exhibits on the history of the war from the eyes of the Luxembourg people. The captions are mostly in French and German.

The balcony bears permanent displays on German concentration camps including Hinzert, Mauthausen, Ravensbruck, Auschwitz, Buchenwald, and Dachau. These artfully-designed panels bear three languages and describe the fate of Luxembourger citizens persecuted by the Nazis.

The entrance-hall alcove holds urns of unique design that contain ashes from different concentration camps. A duplicate of the sculpture in the National Monument to the Resistance and Deportation stands in the center of the space. Open Wednesday through Sunday from 14:00 to 18:00; no admission fee.

Location: In southern Esch-sur-Alzette near the intersection of highway N4 and rue Louis Pasteur, 23 km southwest of Luxembourg City. (49.492437, 5.976177)

This completes the tour of the Bulge battlefields.

Acknowledgments

Any author who generates historical content stands upon the shoulders of those who went before. In the case of the Ardennes Offensive, two seminal works stand out: Dr Hugh Cole's *The Ardennes: Battle of the Bulge. Unites States Army in World War II. The European Theater of Operation.* Washington DC, 1965 and Charles A McDonald's *A Time for Trumpets: The Untold Story of the Battle of the Bulge.* New York, 1985. The post-war writings (published or otherwise) of the participants provide valuable detail and insights. Unsung contributors have digitized After Action Reports, units histories, and personal recollections.

Travel guides require extensive field research, which could not have been possible without aide by numerous local citizens who offered advice and located particularly hard-to-find memorials. Primary among them Jean-Marie Castermans guided us on our first tour of the battlefield and offered his expert opinions on events, locations, and personalities.

Research institutions provide guidance often provide new directions of investigation. The professionals and volunteers at the United States Army Heritage and Education Center and the United States National Archives stand among those who added to the richness of the work. Pritzker Military Library and Arlington Heights Public Library offer their services and use of Interlibrary Loan agreements to provide additional, and usually hard to find, materials. Mr James O'Loughlin again did heroic work in converting the author's draft to readable and coherent text and my wife, Nancy, admirably corrected the final manuscript.

The superintendents of the American military cemeteries in Europe and the employees of the American Battle Monuments Commission have been singularly helpful in relating local history or suggesting important sights to be reviewed. Finally and of course, I thank the people of Belgium and the Grand Duchy of Luxembourg who, 72 years after the events, continue to honor the American soldiers who fought for their liberation by maintaining memorials, flying flags, and organizing commemorations.

Appendices

Appendix A: Farthest Advance Stones

The Belgian Touring Club erected twenty-six small, rough-cut stones to mark the limits of the German advance during the Ardennes Offensive. Each Farthest Advance Stone carries an inscription of a tank and the words (in French) 'Here, the invader was stopped – winter 1944 - 45.' Not all markers have survived the years of weather, vehicular traffic, and road construction. The locations of the remaining stones are listed below (locality: unit: GPS co-ordinates):

Farthest Advance Stones mentioned in the text:
Baugnez: Kampfgruppe Peiper: (50.403910, 6.065781)
Bure: Panzer Lehr Division: (50.086996, 5.250829)
Briscol: 12th SS Panzer Division: (50.292929, 5.593172)
Creppe: Kampfgruppe Peiper: (50.46334, 5.87209)
Foy Notre-Dame: 2nd Panzer Division: (50.247857, 4.989193)
Foy: 2nd Panzer Division: (50.04069 5.74633)
Habiémont: Kampfgruppe Peiper: (50.368172, 5.719864)
Hampteau: Führer Beliet Brigade: (50.255593, 5.476327)
Hans-sur-Lesse: Panzer Lehr Division: (50.125744, 5.181893)
Hotton: 116th Panzer Division (50.268279, 5.44746)
Leignon: 2nd Panzer Division: (50.267853, 5.106496)
Longchamps: 9th SS Panzer Division: (50.058084, 5.688721)
Malmédy: 150th Panzer Brigade (50.416881, 5.997979)
Manhay: 2nd SS Panzer Division: (50.296137, 5.672159)
Neffe: Panzer Lehr Division: (50.007311, 5.746388)
Reharmont: 9th SS Panzer Division: (50.340463, 5.807276)
Remoifosse: 26th Volksgrenadier Division: (49.978457, 5.719308)
Stavelot: Kampfgruppe Peiper: (50.39458, 5.93009)
Stoumont Station: Kampfgruppe Peiper: (50.417265, 5.76418)
Villeroux: 26th Volksgrenadier Division: (49.980969, 5.683497)
Waha: 9th Panzer Division: (50.209819, 5.367562)

Farthest Advance Stones not described in the text:
Eupen: Kampfgruppe von der Heydte: (50.609826, 6.048517)
Libramont: Panzer Lehr Division (49.982449, 5.459043)
Witry: 5th Fallschirmjäger Division: (49.859133, 5.609491)

Missing Farthest Advance Stones:
Martelange: 5th Fallschirmjäger Division
Senonchamps: 26th Volksgrenadier Division (once was along N4)

Appendix

Circuit Historique Informational Panels are place in and around Bastogne describing important events that occurred during the battle for the city. A complete list of the panels is below (town and GPS co-ordinates):

#1 Bastogne: place McAuliffe (50.000779, 5.715130)
#2 Noville: (50.062845, 5.760347)
#3 Recogne: German Cemetery (50.049214, 5.741350)
#4 Mageret: (50.014442, 5.784964)
#5 Neffe: (50.005709, 5.763951)
#6 Marvie: (49.987032, 5.746730)
#7 Villers-la-Bonne-Eau: (49.933525, 5.748392)
#8 Bastogne: place du Général Patton (49.99811, 5.71555)
#9 Bastogne: Belgian Army bunker (49.984432, 5.699902)
#10 Assenois: (49.966753, 5.679242)
#11 Senonchamps: (50.000607, 5.659295)
#12 Champs: (50.039804, 5.668904)
#13 Longchamps: (50.054120, 5.693237)
#14 Hemroulle: (50.022491, 5.688893)
#15 Bastogne: Heintz Barracks (50.009138, 5.717070)

Appendix B: Comparison of Ranks

American	British	French	German (Army)	German (SS)
			Soldat	SS-Mann
Private	Private	Soldat de deuxième classe	Obersoldat	Sturmmann
Private First Class	Lance Corporal	Soldat 1e classe	Gefreiter Stabsgefreiter or Obergefreiter	Rottenführer
Corporal	Corporal	Caporal	Unterofficier	Unterscharführer
		Caporal-chef		
		Caporal-chef (1e classe)		
		Élève sous-officier		
Specialist				
Sergeant	Sergeant	Sergent	Unterfeldwebel	Scharführer
Staff Sergeant	Staff Sergeant or Color Sergeant	Sergent-chef	Feldwebel	Oberscharführer
Technical Sergeant			Oberfeldwebel	Hauptscharführer
Master Sergeant		Adjudant	Stabsfeldwebel	Sturmscharführer
First Sergeant				
Sergeant Major		Adjudant-chef		
Command Sergeant Major				
Sergeant Major of the Army				
Second Lieutenant	Second Lieutenant	Sous- lieutenant	Leutnant	Untersturmführer
First Lieutenant	Lieutenant	Lieutenant	Oberleutnant	Obersturmführer
Captain	Captain	Capitaine	Hauptmann / Rittmeister	Hauptsturmführer
Major	Major	Commandant	Major	Sturmbannführer
Lieutenant Colonel	Lieutenant-Colonel	Lieutenant-colonel	Oberstleutnant	Obersturmbannführer
Colonel	Colonel	Colonel	Oberst	Standartenführer
				Oberführer
Brigadier General	Brigadier	Général de brigade	Generalmajor	Brigadeführer
Major General	Major-General	Général de division	Generalleutnant	Gruppenführer
Lieutenant General	Lieutenant-General	Général de corps d'armée	General der... (Infanterie, Artillerie, Panzertruppen, etc)	Obergruppenführer
General	General	Général d'Armée	Generaloberst	Oberstgruppenführer
General of the Army	Field Marshal	Maréchal de France	Generalfeldmarschall	Reichsführer-SS

Appendix C: Unit compositions

Divisional Composition (typical and at full deployment)[1,2,3]

	Personnel	Description
American		
Infantry Division	14,253	(3) infantry regiments, artillery regiment, and cavalry reconnaissance troop
Airborne Division	12,900	(3) parachute regiments and (1) glider regiment, (2) parachute artillery battalions, (2) glider artillery battalions, and antitank, engineer and AA battalions, and a reconnaissance platoon
Light Armored Division	10,734	(3) combat commands lettered A,B, and R each with a tank battalion and armored infantry battalion, (3) artillery battalions, also cavalry reconnaissance squadron and an engineer battalion
Heavy Armored Division	14,664	(2) armored regiments, (1) armored infantry regiment, (3) armored artillery battalions, also engineer and armored reconnaissance battalion
German		
Infanterie (old)	17,000	(3) infantry regiments with (3) battalions per regiment
Infanterie (1944)	12,500	(3) infantry regiments with (2) battalions per regiment
Infanterie (2 Regiment type)	10,000	(2) infantry regiments with (3) battalions per regiment
Volksgrenadier	10,000	(3) infantry regiments with (3) battalions per regiment
Jäger	13,000	(2) infantry regiments with (3) battalions per regiment
Panzergrenadier	14,000	(2) infantry regiments and tank and AA battalions
SS-Panzergrenadier	15,000	(2) infantry regiments and a tank or assault gun battalion and AA battalion,
Panzer	14,000	(2) infantry regiments and a tank regiment and AA battalion,
SS-Panzer	17,000	(2) infantry regiments and SS tank regiment, SS rocket and SS AA battalions, less the artillery regiment
Fallschirmjäger	16,000	(3) parachute regiments and a parachute AA battalion and parachute heavy mortar battalion,
Luftwaffenfeld	12,500	absorbed into army as 1944 type infantry division

Regimental Composition (typical and at full deployment)

American	
Infantry	(3) infantry battalions each with (4) companies (lettered A-M skipping J), a cannon company with (2) SP 105-mm howitzers and (6) SP 75-mm howitzers, and a HQ company with an Intelligence & Reconnaissance Platoon,
Armored	(1) light tank battalion, (2) heavy tank battalions, and a reconnaissance company
Armored Infantry	(3) armored infantry battalions with HQ, assault gun, and reconnaissance companies
Airborne (parachute and glider)	(3) parachute battalions each with (3) companies (lettered A-I)
Artillery	(3) artillery battalions each with (12) 105-mm guns (1) artillery battalion with (12) 155-mm guns,

1 Over the course of the war, changes to unit organizations were common, during an engagement support units were frequently attached or detached as the situation warranted.

2 The fighting strength of a division was considerably lower, for example an American armored Division had 5,000 combat soldiers, British armoured division approximately 7,000, but a German Waffen SS division could be as high as 12,000.

3 A division also included medical, signal, service, ordinance and military police units.

German	
Infanterie (old type)	(3) infantry battalions of (4) companies
Infanterie 1944	(2) infantry battalions of (4) companies
Volksgrenadier	(2) infantry battalions each of (3) grenadier companies and a heavy weapons company
SS-Infanterie	(2) infantry battalions of (4) companies with howitzer and antitank companies
Grenadier (mot)	(3) motorized infantry battalions with SP heavy infantry howitzer and antitank companies
Panzergrenadier	(2) motorized infantry battalions with SP heavy infantry howitzer and engineer companies
SS-Panzergrenadier	(1) armored battalion and (2) motorized infantry battalions with SP heavy infantry howitzer, half-track engineer, and AA companies
Panzer	(1) Panzer Battalion with (22) PzKpfw IV and (1) Battalion with (22) PzKpfw V; also (1) Flak platoon
SS Panzer	(2) Panzer Battalions
Fallschirmjäger	(3) parachute battalions and 120-mm gun and antitank companies
Artillerie in 1944 Infantry Div	(3) battalions with 105-mm howitzers and (1) battalion of 150-mm howitzers
Artillery Regiment in Volksgrenadier Divisions	(1) battalion with 75-mm antitank guns, (2) battalions with 105-mm howitzers, and (1) battalion with 150-mm howitzers
Artillery Regiment in Panzer & Panzergrenadier Divisions	(1) battalion of SP 105-mm and 150-mm howitzers, (1) battalion with 105-mm howitzers, and (1) battalion of 150-mm howitzers
Heeresküsten-artillerie	Army Coast Artillery with (2) or (3) coast artillery battalions and any number of independent batteries

Battalion Composition (typical and at full deployment)

American	
Infantry	(4) companies lettered A-M, fourth company in each battalion was heavy weapons company with machine guns and mortars; HQ Company with antitank platoon initially with (4) 37-mm and later with (3) 57-mm antitank guns, 871 men total
Armored Infantry	(3) rifle companies each with antitank platoon and a HQ company with mortar, reconnaissance, assault gun, and machine gun platoons, 1001 men total
Armored Infantry (Heavy Division)	(3) rifle companies and a HQ company with mortar, reconnaissance, assault gun, and machine gun platoons, 700 men total
Armored (Light Division)	(1) light tank company, (3) medium tank companies with a HQ company with a HQ, mortar, reconnaissance, and assault gun platoons
Armored, (Heavy Division)	(3) light tank companies with a HQ company with a HQ, mortar, reconnaissance, and assault gun platoons or (2) medium tank companies and armored reconnaissance platoon
Parachute / Glider	(3) rifle companies each with mortar squad and a HQ company with mortar and light machine gun platoons, 706 men total / 658 men total
Tank	Headquarters and Headquarters Company, Service Company, (3) medium tank companies and a light tank company with HQ and Service Companies.
Tank Destroyer	(3) companies each with (12) guns and a mechanized cavalry troop
Artillery	(3) batteries each with (4) 105-mm SP howitzers
Armored Artillery	(3) batteries each with (6) 105-mm SP howitzers
Armored Reconnaissance	(4) cavalry troops, lettered A to D, each equipped with (13) M8 armored cars and jeeps and a assault gun troop; E company with (8) M8 SP howitzers and light tank company with (17) M5 Stuart, or later M24, tanks

Cavalry Reconnaissance Squadron,	(3) cavalry troops, lettered A to C, each equipped with (13) M8 armored cars and jeeps and an assault gun troop
Ranger	(6) rifle companies and a HQ company, 504 men total
German	
Infantry	(4) infantry companies
Maschinegewehr	(machine gun battalion): (3) companies of heavy machine guns and panzerfausts plus a heavy weapons company
Schwere Granatenwerfer	(heavy mortar battalion): (3) companies each with (12) 120-mm mortars
Panzerjäger	(antitank battalion): (1) company of (12) towed 75-mm AT guns, (1) company of (14) SP 75-mm AT guns, and (1) company of (12) 20-mm AT guns
Panzer	(tank battalion): (3) companies each of (3) platoons each with (4) tanks, (2) tanks in company HQ, (6) tanks in battalion HQ, frequently also a fourth assault gun company
SS-Panzer	(SS-tank battalion): similar to tank battalion with (1) additional tank per platoon and (2) additional tanks in battalion HQ
HQ PzKpfw VI (Tiger)	(tank battalion assigned to corps): (14) Tiger tanks per company and (3) in battalion reserve
HQ PzKpfw V (Panther)	(tank battalion assigned to corps): with (17) Panther tanks per company and (3) in Bn reserve

Appendix D: German Military Units

	Commander	Allied army equivalent	Composition
Trupp			a small group dedicated to a specific task
Gruppe	Obergefreiter or Unteroffizier	British section or US squad	the smallest permanent unit in an infantry formation, usually 8-12 men
Zug	Unteroffizier, Haupt Feldwebel or Leutnant	infantry platoon	(3) gruppen and a HQ trupp
Zug, artillerie	same		a trupp with two guns
Zug, panzer	same	armored platoon	(5) tanks
Kompanie (numbered sequentially in a regiment with Arabic numerals, 1st, 2nd, 3rd, 4th company in I Batallion, etc,	Oberleutnant or Hauptmann	infantry company	(3) platoons and a kompanietrupp HQ;
Kompanie, panzer	Oberleutnant or Hauptmann	armored company	(4) panzer Zug plus a HQ
Batterie, artillery	Oberleutnant or Hauptmann	artillery battery	two zug with four guns
Schwadron, cavalry	Rittmeister	squadron	

Unit	Commander	Type	Composition
Batallion (numbered consecutively in a regiment with Roman numerals)	Major or Oberstleutnant	infantry battalion	(3) infantry companies and a support company
Abteilung, artillery	Major	artillery battalion	three batteries totaling 12 guns
Abteilung, panzer	Major or Oberstleutnant	armored battalion	(3) light kompanie (PzKpfw III) and one heavy kompanie (PzKpfw IV)
Regiment infantry panzer,	Oberstleutnant or Oberst	infantry regiment	(3) battalions, mortar kompanie, anti-tank kompanie, support and HQ kompanie; a regiment frequently had a 13th kompanie (mortar and light artillery), a 14th kompanie (antitank) and sometimes even a 15th kompanie (engineers)
Regiment, artillery	same	artillery regiment	(4) artillery abteilungen (3 light and 1 heavy)
Regiment, panzer	same	armored regiment	(2) panzer abteilungen and a support services company
Brigade (not frequently used)	Oberst or Generalmajor		(2) motorized infantry regiments in a panzer division
Division	Generalmajor or General-leutnant	infantry division	(3) infantry regiments, (1) artillery regiment and anti-tank, reconnaissance, and engineer battalions with support troops
Panzer Division	Generalmajor or General-leutnant	armored division	varied but generally (2) motorized infantry regiments with (2) battalions each; (1) panzer regiment with (1) battalion PzKpfw IV and (1) battalion with PzKpfw V; (1) artillery abteilung with mix light and heavy SP guns; (1) antitank battalion
Korps	General-leutnant	corps	2 to 4 divisions
Panzergruppe	varied		armored corps command reporting to army group
Artillerie-kommandeur or Arko	varied	corps artillery	command with large assets to support korps or armee
Armee	General der ... Infanterie or Generaloberst	Army	2 or more korps
Panzerarmee	General der ... Panzertruppen or Generaloberst		armored force with weak or strong armored elements
Heerestruppen			independent battalions for specialized support functions
Kampfgruppe	assumed the name of its commander	battlegroup	ad-hoc combat formation usually for identified purpose

Appendix E: Glossary of German Military Terms

	Abbreviation, acronym, nickname or literal translation	Description
Abteilung	Abt	Detachment or section, or battalion-sized unit of armor, artillery of cavalry
Abwehr		Counter-espionage service of the German High Command
Allgemeine SS	General SS	Full-time administrative, security, intelligence and police branches of the Schutzstaffel
Armeekorps		Infantry corps
Armeeoberkommando		Field Army Command
Aufklärungs Abteilung		Reconnaissance unit or battalion
Drang nach Osten	Drive to the east	Historic German desire to expand eastward
Einsatzkommando		Company-sized subunits which killed Jews, Communists and others in the Soviet Union
Eisernes Kreuz	Iron Cross	Medal awarded for valorous service
Fall Gelb	Case Yellow	Plan for invasion of the Netherlands, Belgium and France
Fall Grün	Case Green	Plan for intended invasion of Czechoslovakia
Fall Rot	Case Red	Plan for counterstrike against France in the event of an attack from the West
Fall Weiß	Case White	Plan for invasion of Poland
Fallschirmjäger		Parachute trooper
Festung		Fortress
Flakpanzer		Armored self-propelled antiaircraft gun
Flugabwehrkanone	FlaK	Anti-aircraft artillery gun
Freya radar		First operational radar in the Kriegsmarine
Führerhauptquartiere	FHQ	Official headquarters especially constructed for use by the führer
Füsilier		Light infantry, given to reconnaissance formations when the Germans reduced the number of standard infantry battalions in their divisions from 9 to 6
Gebirgsjäger		Mountain troops
Gefallen	Fallen	Killed in action
Geheime Staatspolizei	Gestapo	Secret State Police
Generalkommando		Headquarters of an army corps
Generalstab des Heeres	Gen. St.d. H.	German Army General Staff
Geschwader		Luftwaffe squadron
Granatwerfer		Mortar
Hakenkreuz	hooked cross	Swastika used by the Nazi Party
Haubitze		Howitzer
Heeresgruppen-kommando	HGr.Kdo	Army Group Command
Höckerlinie		Antitank defenses, Dragon's Teeth
Jagdbomber	Jabo	Fighter-bomber
Jagdgeschwader	JG	Single-engine fighter wing/group, literally: hunting squadron
Kampfgeschwader	KG	Bomber wing/group
Kampfgruppe		Army battle group usually an ad hoc task force
Kampfwagenkanone	KwK	Turret-mounted main cannon of a battle tank
Kanone		Gun as opposed to a howitzer
Kaserne		Barracks
Kübelwagen	Kübel	Open-topped military utility cars

German	Abbreviation	English
Landsturm		Infantry of non-professional soldiers or militia
Landwehr		Territorial Army: a type of militia
Maultier	SdKfz 4	Half-track truck
Nachtjagdgeschwader	NJG	Night-fighter wing/group
Nationalsozialistische Deutsche Arbeiterpartei	NSDAP	National Socialist German Worker's Party or Nazi Party
Nebelwerfer	Nb. W, fog thrower	Multi-barrel rocket launchers used for smoke or high-explosive projectiles
Oberbefehlshaber des Heeres	Ob.d.H.	Commander-in-Chief of the Army
Oberfehlshaber West	OB West	Commander-in-Chief West
Oberkommando der Luftwaffe	OKL	High Command of the Air Force
Oberkommando der Marine	OKM	High Command of the Navy
Oberkommando der Wehrmacht	OKW	High Command of the Armed Forces
Oberkommando des Heeres	OKH	High Command of the Army and Army General Staff
Organisation Todt		Civil and military engineering group named after its founder, Fritz Todt, which built the Autobahns, Westwall (Siegfried Line), Wolfsschanze, and Atlantic Wall, notorious for its use of conscript and slave labor
Panzer-abwehrkanone	PaK	Antitank gun
Panzerfaust	tank fist	Disposable portable antitank weapon
Panzergrenadier		Mechanized infantry or a soldier belonging to a mechanized infantry unit
Panzerjäger		Tank destroyer or antitank unit fielding a variety of antitank weapons
Panzerkampfwagen	PzKpfw	Armored fighting vehicle (tank)
Panzerschreck	tank terror	Reloadable portable antitank weapon
Pionier (pl. Pioniere)		Combat engineer
Reichskanzlei	Reich Chancellery	Office of the German Chancellor (Reichskanzler).
Reichs-sicherheitshaupt-amt	RSHA	Reich Main Security Office or Reich Security Head Office created by Himmler to combine all German security and police departments, including the Gestapo, Kripo and SD
Ritterkreuz des Eisernen Kreuzes	Knight's Cross of the Iron Cross	Highest award for bravery
Sanität		Medical unit or medical personnel
Schützen-panzerwagen	SPW	Armored half-track or self propelled weapon
Schutzstaffel	SS	Nazi organization that grew from Hitler's personal body guard into a fourth branch of the Wehrmacht
Sicherheitsdienst der SS	SD	Security service of the SS and Nazi Party, main intelligence and counter-espionage section of the RSHA
SS-Totenkopf verbände	SS-TV	SS responsible for the concentration camps, Death's Head units
Stammlager	Stalag	German prisoner-of-war camp
Sturmabteilung	SA	Storm troopers, originally Hitler's praetorian guard (bodyguard) of Brown Shirts, disbanded
Sturmgeschütz	StuG	Self-propelled assault gun

Sturz-kampfflugzeug	Stuka		Any dive-bombing aircraft but generally associated with the Ju-87 dive bomber
Tommy			German slang for a British soldier
Unterseeboot	U-boot		Submarine
Vergeltungs-waffen-1	V1		First German vengeance weapon, pilotless, cruise missile powered by a pulse-jet engine
Vergeltungs-waffen-2	V2 or A4		Supersonic long-range rocket
Vergeltungs-waffen-3	V3		Long-range, smooth-bore gun
Volksgrenadier			Honorary title given to mostly low-grade infantry divisions formed late in the war
Volkssturm			People's defense force, mostly of boys and older men
Wacht am Rhein	Guard on the Rhine		December 1944 Ardennes Offensive, known by Americans as the Battle of the Bulge
Waffen-SS			Armed SS, military combat branch of the SS
Walküre	Valkyrie		(1) officially a Reserve Army contingency plan in the event of a breakdown in law and order, (2) failed 20 July 1944 Plot to arrest SS and Nazi officials and seize control of the German government
Wannsee Conference			Meeting held on January 20, 1942 near Lake Wannsee in Berlin in which it was made official Nazi policy to totally annihilate European Jews and other ethnic groups
Wehrmacht			Combined three branches of German armed forces
Wolfsschanze	Wolf's Lair		Hitler's Eastern Front military headquarters
Würzburg radar			German air defense radar
Zyklon-B			Commercial name for the prussic acid (hydrocyanic acid) gas used in German extermination camps

Appendix F: Armor Comparison

Tanks

	Model	Crew	Front Armor (mm)	Vehicle weight (tons)	Road Speed (kph)	Main Gun	Description, auxiliary guns
American	M26 Pershing	5	102	41.2	48	90-mm	Heavy tank, (1) 12.7-mm and (2) 7.62-mm MG
American	M3A1 Stuart III	4	38	12.7	57	37-mm	Light tank, (3) 7.62-mm MG
American	M4A4 Sherman	5	81	33	36.8	75-mm	Medium tank, (1) 7.62-mm MG
British	A22 Mark IV Churchill	5	102	38.5	27	76-mm & 40-mm	(1) 7.92-mm Besa MG, up-gunned in succeeding marks
British	A27L Cruiser Mark VIII Centaur	5	76	28.4	43	6-pounder	(2) 7.92-mm Besa MG,
British	A27M Cruiser Mark VIII Cromwell	5	76	27.5	51	6-pounder	(2) 7.92-mm Besa MG, upgunned with 75-mm
British	A30 Cruiser Challenger	5	101	32	51	76.2-mm	(1) 7.62-mm MG
British	A34 Cruiser Comet	5	101	35	46	77-mm	(2) 7.92-mm Besa MG

British	Crusader I	5	40	18.5	43	40-mm	(2) MG
British	Firefly	4	81	33	40	17-pounder	up-gunned American Sherman
French	Char B-bis	4	60	32	28	75-mm & 47-mm	(2) 7.5-mm MG
French	Hotchkiss H-35	2	40	10.43	27	37-mm	(1) 7.5-mm MG
French	Hotchkiss H-39	2	40	11.9	36	37-mm	(1) 7.5-mm MG
French	Renault R-35	3	45	14.3	41	37-mm	(1) 7.5-mm MG
French	Souma (S-35)	3	40	19.2	40	47-mm	(1) 7.5-mm MG
German	PzKpfw 38(t)	4	25	9.25	42	37-mm KwK L/40	Czech Skoda LT-38, (2) 7.92-mm MG
German	PzKpfw III J	5	77	22	40	50-mm Kwk	Medium Tank, up-gunned, (2) MG 34
German	PzKpfw IV Model H	5	60	22	32	75-mm KwK 40 (L/43)	Medium Tank, (2) 7.92-mm MG 34
German	PzKpfw V (Panther) G	5	100	45.5	48	75-mm KwK 42 (L/40)	Heavy Tank, (2) 7.92-mm MG 34
German	PzKpfw VI (Tiger I)	5	100	56	36	88-mm KwK 36 L/56	Heavy Tank, (2) 7.92-mm MG 34
German	PzKpfw VI (Tiger II or Königstiger)	5	150	68	39	88-mm KwK 43 (L/71)	Heavy Tank (2) 7.92-mm MG 34

Tank Destroyers

	Model	Gun	Max Armor (mm)	Description / armament
American	M-10 Wolverine	76-mm	37	(1) 12.7-mm MG, later up-gunned with 90-mm gun
American	M-18 Hellcat	76-mm	12	(1) 12.7-mm MG
American	M-36	90-mm	50	(1) 12.7-mm MG
British	A30 Avenger	17-pounder	101	(1) 7.7-mm Bren MG on AA mount
British	M10 Achilles	17-pounder	37	Upgunned American M10
German	Elephant	88-mm Stu K 43 (L/71) or 88-mm Pak 43/2	185	Formerly known as Ferdinand, mounted on Pz Jäger Tiger P chassis
German	Jagdpanther	88-mm Pak 43/3 or 43/4	100	Mounted on Pz Jäger Panther chassis, (2) 7.92-mm MG
German	Jagdpanzer IV	75-mm Pak39 L/48	100	Mounted on Pz Kpfw IV chassis
German	Jagdtiger	128-mm Pak 44 (L/55)	150	Mounted on Pz Jäger Tiger B chassis, (2) 7.92-mm MG
German	Nashorn (Rhinoceros)	88-mm Pak 43	30	On hybrid Pz Kpfw III and IV chassis

Index

A
Aachen 4, 8, 20, 84, 133, 215, 222, 230
Abraham, Sgt Lincoln 95
Abrams, Lt Col Creighton 353–355
Adams, 1st Lt George 66–67
Afst 135
Aiken, Capt John 252
Aircraft
  British Hudson 255
  Spitfire Mk XIV 229
Alanis, Major Dan C 362
Alexander, S/Sgt Wallace 296
Allen, Lt Col Ray C 335–336, 340
Allen, Lt Col William H 236
Allerborn 284–285, 429
Ammeldingen an der Our 394
Anderson, Col Glen H 394
Andler 134, 136, 140, 142, 152–153
Andrus, Maj Gen Clift 70
Antitank Guns. See Artillery Pieces
Antoniushaff Crossroad 283–287
Antwerp 1, 2, 4, 6, 14, 15, 207
Arlington National Cemetery 61, 65, 136, 146, 214, 288, 296, 353, 405
Armée secrète 207, 220
Armstrong, PFC Mason 114
Arn, Capt Edward 114–115
Artillery Pieces
  British 25-pounder 115
  German 20-mm Flakvierling 38 401
  German 37-mm antitank 401
  German 75-mm Pak 40 154, 185, 277
  German 75-mm Pak 40: definition 155
  German 88-mm Pak 43 241, 252, 256, 272
  German 88-mm Pak43 351
  German 105-mm FH18/40 272
  German 105-mm SK18 408
  German 150-mm sFH 18 206, 351
  US 105-mm M2A1 howitzer 181, 241, 304
  US 155-mm 'Long Tom' 400
Assenois 352–358
Auw 140, 141
Axelson, Col Oscar 21

B
Bader, Gen Rudolf 235, 236
Bahe, Major Gordon A 217–218
Ballard, Lt Col Robert 371
Bande 220
Bandy, Lt Col Paul 407
Barcellona, 1st Lt Gaetano R 58
Barkmann, Sr Sgt Ernst 185
Barrère Hinck 332–335
Barton, Maj Gen Raymond 383, 413–414, 417, 421
Bastendorf 388, 391
Bastogne 3, 8–14, 105, 154, 175, 215, 230–234, 251, 253, 256, 258–259, 267–268, 273, 279–280, 284–287, 288–381
Bastogne Circuit Historique. See Information Panels - Circuit Historique
Bastogne-Liège highway 181, 197, 294
Bastogne Surrender Demand 358–359
Bätzing, Gen 399, 402
Baugnez 84–85
Bayerlein, Gen Fritz 215–218, 258, 266, 282, 289–290, 303–311, 358
Bayer, Oberst Johannes 193, 197
Bayliss, T/Sgt James L 60–61
Beauloup 117–118
Belgian Army Units
  5th Belgian Fusilier Battalion 103
  Chasseurs Ardennes 132
Belgian Croix de Guerre
  99th Infantry Battalion (Separate) 94
  168th Engineering Combat Battalion 162
  291st Engineer Combat 113
  589th Fields Artillery Battalion 181
  Prior, Dr John 324
Bell, Col Robert P 404
Belle Haie 181
Benonchamps 256, 303, 305, 314
Berdorf 384, 416–419
Bérismenil 205
Berlé 278
Berry, Capt James D 120, 123
Bertogne 345–346
Bertruck, 1st Lt Hugh T 170
Bettendorf 397, 404–406
Beyer, Gen Franz 384
Biddle, PFC Melvin 191
Bielcki, S/Sgt Bernard C 24
Bigonville 352
Bihain 173
Bittrick, Gen Willi 176
Bizory 290, 293–294, 306–310, 314, 332
Blanchard, Col Wendell 353
Bleialf 142, 149–150
Bodarwé, Adèle 86, 88
Boggess, 1st Lt Charles 353–357
Bois
  de Chardonne 212
  Jacques 276, 294, 325, 329–332, 368, 371–376
Bolling, Brig Gen Alexander 207–209, 214–215, 217
Bomberger, 2nd Lt Walter 365
Bone, S/Sgt Odis 59
Boos, Col Francis 63, 68
Booth, Lt Col Robert M 283, 285
Bottomly, Major Raymond V Jr 310–312

Bouck, Lt Lyle J, Jr 45–47
Boudinot, Gen Truman E 110, 122
Boulaide 351
Bourcy 256, 285, 290, 294, 302, 309, 314, 320–321, 321, 329, 332, 372–373
Bowles, Capt Howard G 338–339
Boyle, Lt Col William J 191
Bra 126, 183
Bradley, Gen Omar 1, 3, 8–14, 125, 288, 289, 386
Brandenberger, Gen Erich 4, 382–383, 387, 410, 414
Brandenbourg 406
Bremm, Oberstlt 52
Brewster, Major Olin 181, 183
Bridges
  Alfred Töpfer 420
  Amblève 104
  Bailey Bridge Mark II 265
  Cheneux 112
  Dasburg 243–244
  Dreiherrenwald 56
  Han-sur-Lesse 218
  Hotton 195
  Malmédy 93
  Meuse. See Rivers, Meuse
  Neufmoulin 114
  Ouren 239–240
  Petit Spai 106
  Pont de Menufontaine 349
  Salmchâteau 169
  Schoenberg 142, 152
  Trois-Ponts 104
  Warche 93
British Military Units
  3rd Royal Tank Regiment 226
  6th Airborne Division 218, 220
  9th Parachute Battalion 220
  21st Army Group 1–2, 289, 313, 424–425
  29th Armoured Brigade 218–219
  51st (Highland) Division 203–204
  161 Squadron 255
  Imperial General Staff 1
  Northamptonshire Yeomanry 203
  Second Army 1
Bronze Star
  Bryson, Lt Charles K 197
  Consiglio, Sgt Vincent 94
  Fleig, Lt Raymond 251
  Fraser, Lt Col Harvey 195
  Goldstein, Major Elliot 181
  Harper, Lt Col Ralph S 285
  Myers, PFC Thomas R 263
  Rosenthal, PFC Paul 237
  Wallace Jr, Capt Claude D 315
Brooke, Field Marshall Alan 1
Brookins, Cpl Richard 271

Brown, Capt Gene 375
Browne, Lt Col Barry D 360–361
Browning M1917 Machine Gun: definition 366
Brummbär: definition 75
Buchanan, PFC Dallas 107
Buchholz Station 37, 42, 44, 46, 47–50
Buissonville 207, 215, 223–224
Büllingen 18, 29, 31, 40, 44, 50, 70–72, 76, 82–83
Bunkers
  Fuhrtsbachal or Bunker #121 30
  Hollerath 35
  Perlenbach 30
  Wahlerscheid 34
Bunkers, Belgian Army
  Assenois 357
  Bastogne 299
  Bra 126
  Cheneux 113
  Habiémont 114
  Senonchamps 361
  Villers-la-Bonne-Eau 368
Bunkers, German Westwall
  'B-Werk' bunker 394, 395
  'C-Werk' bunker 394
  Dasburger underground 245
  Schnee Eifel S4 148
  Schnee Eifel S5 148
  Schnee Eifel S7 148
  Schnee Eifel S8 148
  Weilerbach 420
Bure 218
Burg Reuland 156, 230
Burtonville 166–167
Bütgenbach 18, 29
Bütgenbach, Domaine 13, 18, 70–77
Butler, Lt Col McClernand 26, 29, 318, 358

C

Cady, Capt Arthur L 373
Café Schincker 266
Café Schumann 278, 279
Canadian Military Units
  1st Canadian Parachute Battalion 218, 220
  First Canadian Army 1
Cappelli, Pvt Al 375–376
Caraway, Lt Col Forrest 361
Carrefour du 1.517th Parachute Inf Regt 192
Carson, Lt Kit 246
Casemate. See Bunkers
Cavender, Col Charles C 142, 144, 147, 150, 152
Celles 11, 125, 176, 215, 223–226, 292
Celles Pocket 222–226
Cemeteries, Military
  American
    Ardennes 76, 100, 188, 220, 221
    Epinal 255

Index

Henri-Chapelle 18–20, 48, 54, 61, 70, 100, 107, 108, 132, 138, 155, 166, 189, 202, 315, 328, 351, 373
Lorraine 67, 206, 259
Luxembourg 282, 306, 328, 336, 342, 348, 371, 379, 390, 425, 430
Netherlands 183, 237
British
  Hollerich Communal Cemetery 431
  Hotton 196
German
  Auw Communal Cemetery 141
  Bleialf Communal Cemetery 149
  Daleiden 245
  Lommel 19, 213
  Luxembourg-Clausen 430
  Ormont 141
  Recogne 328
  Sandweiler 429
  Vossenack 175
  Wallendorf 395
Champs 296, 337–345
Chance, Col Robert H 412, 424
Chapek, Capt Anthony B 425
Chapin, Cpl Fred 113
Chappius, Col Steve 291, 327, 343, 368–371
Château
  de Brandenbourg 406
  de Clervaux 249–252
  de Froidcoeur 84, 110, 118, 124
  de Losange 362–365
  de Neffe 312
  de Rolle 340, 343–344
  de Verdenne 213
  de Vianden 390
  d'Useldange 407
  Remy 308
  Wiltz 270
Chaumont 347–350
Cheneux 116–118
Cherain 206
Cherry, Col Henry T 303–304, 306, 312
Chiwy, Augusta 297, 298
Churchill, Winston 14
Cierreux 170
Cinqfontaines 256
Citadel de Dinant 228
Civilian Victims
  Bande 220
  Büllingen 82
  Cinqfontaines 256
  Clervaux 250
  Érezée 190
  Givry 345
  Gouvy 206
  Houffalize 380

La Gleize 111
La Roche-en-Ardenne 204
Ligneuville 95
Malmédy 84–88
Maulusmühle 255
Noville 326
Parfondruy 109
Stavelot 99, 101
Trois-Ponts 107
Troisvierges 256
Clarke, Brig Gen Bruce C 156, 159–160, 167
Clervaux 8, 232–234, 234, 242–257, 267, 284, 287, 299, 303, 305, 307, 311
Cobbett, T/5 Warren E 370
Cody, Capt George R 339, 342
Cohen, Col Harold 350
Collier, S/Sgt Noah 75, 76
Collins, Gen J Lawton 12, 13, 175, 181, 207, 222–223, 408–410
Combat Command: definition 84
Composition C: definition 168
Concentration Camp
  Mauthausen 95
Condroz Plateau 186, 193, 207–209, 228
Conneux 223
Consiglio, Sgt Vincent 93–94
Cooper, Lt Col John 339, 345
Copeland, Capt Carrol 248
Cota, Gen Norman 3, 9, 14, 230–234, 246, 249, 258, 261, 266–269, 271, 359, 383, 399
Cowan, Capt William 240
Cowan, PFC Richard 55
Creeks. See Rivers
Crossroads
  88-corner 150, 152
  Antoniushaff. See Antoniushaff
  Baugnez 87–88
  Féitsch. See Féitsch Crossroad
  Lausdell. See Lausdell Crossroads
  Losheimergraben. See Losheimergraben Crossroads
  Morsheck 70–74
  Parker's. See Parker's Crossroad
  Purple Heart Corner 150
  Rocherath Baracken 70
Crossroads X. See Barrère Hinck
Cureton, Capt Roy W 390–392
Currey, Sgt Francis A 93

D

Dager, Brig Gen Holmes 347–348
Dahl 274, 279–281
Dairomont 131
Daleiden 245
Damon, Lt Col William F, Jr 136
D'Angelo, Sgt Anthony 342–343

Daniel, Lt Col Derrill 70, 71, 74, 75
Dasburg 8, 231, 240–241, 243–245, 386
D-Day 30, 58, 67, 172, 387, 422
Dec, Capt Stanley 237
de Gaulle, Lt Charles 228
Deluga, Cpl Leonard A 255
Dempwolff, Oberst Hugo 408
Descheneaux, Col George L 142–147, 153–154
Desobry, Major William 321–326
Detroz, Lt Albert 103
Devers, Jacob L 1, 10, 289
de Villenfagne, Baron Jacques 225
Devine, Col Mark A 135, 136
Dickweiler 384, 413, 421
Diefenthal, SS-Major Josef 119
Diekirch 10, 275, 296, 382, 384, 388–389, 392, 397–402, 405–408, 419, 424
Dietrich, General Joseph 4, 6, 8, 154
Dike, Lt Norman 376
Dillard, Col Douglas 132
Dillingen 383, 411
Dinant 10, 207, 218, 222–229
Dingler, Oberst 375
Distinguished Flying Cross
  Aageberg, Capt James B 166
  Helfer, Flt Lt Anthony 255
Distinguished Service Cross
  Abrams, Lt Col Creighton 353
  Armstrong, PFC Mason 114
  Bayliss, T/Sergeant James L 61
  Bouck, Lt Lyle J 47
  Boyle, Lt Col William J 192
  Browne, Lt Col Barry D 361
  Chapek, Capt Anthony B 425
  Cobbett, T/5 Warren E 370
  Cota, Brig Gen Norman 234
  Del Grippo, PFC Daniel 117
  Gniot, Lt Charles R 348
  Hill, Sergeant Robert H 132
  Houston, S/Sgt Robert 314
  Hritsik, Second Lt Michael 407
  Huempfner, PFC Milo 222
  Jones, Capt Lennis 400
  Lamm, Lt George 168
  McAuliffe, Brig Gen Anthony 296
  Mendez, Lt Col Louis G 173
  Metz, PFC Edwin W 188
  Mills, 1st Lieutenant AL 141
  Mills, 1st Lieutenant Aubrey 138
  Morrow, Lt Jesse 69
  Mullins, Sgt Oscar M 188
  Parker, 1st Lt Robert A 68
  Piersall, Sgt Thornton E 29
  Reeves, S/Sgt Woodrow 141, 165
  Robertson, Maj Gen Robert 65
  Rudder, Lt Col James 387
  Sirovica, S/Sgt Frank 173
  Skaggs, Lt Col Robert N 67
  Statler, Corporal CE 141
  Stopka, Major John P 328
  Swift, Capt Vaughn 407
  Vandervoort, Lt Col Benjamin 172
  Walsh, S/Sgt William 117
  Willis , 1st Sgt Gervis 417
  Withee, Corporal Edward S 140
  Wood, 1st Lt Eric Fisher, Jr 155
Distinguished Unit Citation. See Presidential Unit Citation
  7th Armored Div, Combat Command B 159
  168th Engineering Combat Battalion 162
Dochamps 197–198
Douglas, Lt Col Robert H 41, 100, 186
Dragon's teeth 50
  Großkampenberg 236
  Imgenbroich 24, 25
  Rollbahn A 38
  Stolzembourg 264
  Udenbreth 40
Drauffelt 257
Drawe, Oberstlt Johannes 391, 404
Dreiherrenwald 38, 55
Dresden 146
Dugan, Lt Col Augustine 165
Duncan, Lt Col William D 119
Durkee, Lt Richard 131

E

Eastern Front 13, 41, 79, 87, 133, 135, 210, 230, 294, 383, 386
Echternach 382, 384, 413, 421–423
Echternach-Diekirch highway 391, 404
Echternach-Luxembourg City highway 424
Edelstein, Lt Alvin 113
Eisenhower, Dwight D 1–3, 7–14, 115, 125, 271, 288–289, 293, 386, 430
Eisler, Lt Walter 52
Ekman, Col William E 105
Elsenborn 175
Elsenborn, Camp 9, 15, 18, 31, 55, 61, 64, 70
Elsenborn Ridge 7, 10, 15–78, 83
Ennal 132
Enseling, Lt Col Rudolf 182, 186
Érezée 186
Ermsdorf 412
Erpeldange 267, 268, 272
Erria 126–128
Ettelbruck 384, 389, 402–404
Ettelbruck-Bastogne highway 267, 278
Eupen 15, 21, 70, 89
Ewell, Lt Col Julian J 290, 311, 313–314, 329, 371–372

Index

F
Fanzel 186
Farrell, Pvt Grover C 69
Farrens, 1st Lt Kenneth 137, 138, 139
Farthest Advance Stones
  Baugnez 88
  Bristol 190
  Bure 219
  Creppe 124
  Dinant 227
  Foy 332
  Foy-Notre-Dame 227
  Habiémont 115
  Hampteau 197
  Han-sur-Lesse 218
  Hotton 195
  Leignon 221
  Longchamps 371
  Malmédy 94
  Manhay 185
  Neffe 312
  Rèhârmont 130
  Remoifosse 359
  Senonchamps 361
  Stavelot 102
  Stoumont Station 122
Feiker, Capt Frederick 257
Féitsch Crossroad 283, 287
Fell, Capt Donald 120
Ferme de Mahenne 226
Fickessen, Major Jack 193
Fieger, Oberst i.G. 52
Finan, Sgt Norman 417
First World War 4, 9, 15, 30, 91, 133, 139, 162, 167, 175, 210, 217, 273, 300, 324, 356, 373, 430, 431
Fisher, PFC John T 65
Fitzgerald, Lt Col Roy G, Jr 118
Flakvierling 38: definition 401
Flamierge 292, 335–339, 341
Fleig, 1st Lt Raymond E 251
Fleps, SS-Pvt George 85, 87
Forests
  Bois Bechou 357
  Bois Champay 375
  Bois de Lambaichenet 349
  Bois de la Paix 332
  Bütgenbacher Heck 73, 76–77
  Fosse de Sable 357
  Les Bresses 344
Fortified Goose Egg 167
Fosse 126, 130
Fossum, Capt Embert 396, 398
Fouhren 387–392, 397, 405
Fowler, Cpl Willis 344
Foxholes
  Bettendorf 410
  Dreiherrenwald 56
  Hasselpat Trail 62
  Hoesdorf Plateau 398
  Jansbach 55
  Losheimergraben 50
  Nothum Trail 276
  Prümerberg Heights 162
  Rollbahn A 38
Fox, PFC John M 373, 374
Foy 291, 321–332, 368, 371–372, 375–379
Foy-Notre-Dame 176, 223, 225–227
Frankland, Lt Col Robert 98
Fraser, Lt Col Harvey R 195
Fraser, Major Donald 191
Friendly Fire 187
Fuller, Col Hurley E 161, 242–243, 246–250, 254, 285
Fuller, Lt Col William 161

G
Gaffey, Maj Gen Hugh J 12, 346, 352
Galbraieth, Major RB 316, 317
Gardner, Col Glenn 349
Garlow, Major William J Cody 146
Garvey, Capt Jack J 60
Gauthier, Pvt Wilbrod 315
Gavin, Gen James 179, 181, 294
Gavin, Maj Gen James 11, 114, 125–126, 131
Geiger, Lt Col F 369
Gemünd 231, 243, 262, 265–266, 288
Gentingen 394
Gerhardt, Oberst Rudolph 316
German High Command 4, 14, 79, 288, 368
German, Major Edgar P 279
German Military Units
  Armies
    Fifth Panzer 4, 7, 8, 10, 14, 18, 130, 175, 176, 195, 212, 231, 234, 382, 386
    Seventh 1, 4, 8, 14, 280, 382–386
    Sixth Panzer 4, 5, 6, 8, 10–14, 46, 59, 107, 124, 154, 175, 200–201, 293–294, 382
  Army Groups
    B 3, 175
  Battalions
    84th Armored Flak 116
    Fallschirmjäger Pionier Battalion 5: 390
    Fusilier Battalion 212: 422–423, 425–427
    Fusilier Battalion 277: 40
    Panzerartillery Bn 130: 258
    Panzer Battalion 115: 339
    Panzer Battalion 501: 79
    Panzerjäger Battalion 9: 274
    Panzerjäger Battalion 103: 64
    Panzerjäger Battalion 130: 258, 303
    Panzerjäger Battalion 277: 62

Panzerjäger Battalion 560: 71, 73
Panzer Pioneer Battalion 277: 37
Panzer Pionier Battalion 600: 243
Panzer Reconnaissance Bn 2: 176, 284, 332
Panzer Reconnaissance Bn 116: 209, 241
Reconnaissance Bn 26: 335, 361
Reconnaissance Bn 130: 258, 266, 268, 282
Replacement Training Bn 26: 258
SS Flak Battalion 12: 37
SS Panzer Battalion 1: 87
SS Panzerjäger Battalion 1: 368
SS Panzerjäger Battalion 12: 37, 57
SS Panzer Pionier Battalion 12: 37
SS Panzer Reconnaissance Bn 1: 79, 154
SS Panzer Reconnaissance Bn 12: 71
Brigade
  Führer Begleit 10, 146, 156, 170, 194, 208, 293, 296, 366, 368
  Führer Grenadier 273–275, 280, 293, 352, 384, 406
  Panzer Brigade 150 6, 7, 89–94, 222, 227
  Sturmartillery Brigade 911 274
  Sturmgeschütz Brigade 244 140, 153
Corps
  II SS Panzer 6, 176, 190
  I SS Panzer 6, 7, 15, 74, 79
  LIII 8, 264
  LVIII 7, 9–10, 176, 194, 215, 230–231, 264
  LXVI 8, 134
  LXVII 6
  LXXX 8, 382, 384, 408, 421
  LXXXV 8, 382, 387–388
  XLVII Panzer 8, 215, 231, 288, 292
Divisions
  1st SS Panzer 5–6, 15, 18, 79, 106, 114, 124, 130, 154, 159, 275, 293, 362, 366
  2nd Panzer 8, 10, 125, 159, 176, 207, 212, 215–225, 231–232, 243–246, 254, 258, 283–285, 288–292, 302, 321, 324–325, 327, 333, 337
  2nd SS Panzer 5–6, 10, 169, 176–181, 188, 198
  3rd Fallschirmjäger 5–6, 45, 136
  3rd Panzergrenadier 10, 18, 64, 293, 366
  5th Fallschirmjäger 12, 242, 260–261, 268, 275, 347, 353, 359, 362, 366, 382–388
  9th Panzer 209, 215–216, 375
  9th SS Panzer 5–6, 10, 85, 87, 125–126, 130, 169, 176, 208, 293, 368, 369
  9th Volksgrenadier 273–276
  12th SS Panzer 5–6, 16, 18, 35, 37, 63, 71, 79, 83, 176, 198, 201, 293, 368, 371, 378
  12th Volksgrenadier 5–6, 16, 41, 48, 81
  15th Panzergrenadier 337, 351, 369
  18th Volksgrenadier 8, 10, 134, 136, 141, 156, 161
  26th Volksgrenadier 8, 231–234, 242, 257–258, 265, 268, 288–293, 304, 308–309, 332, 335, 347, 353, 361
  62nd Volksgrenadier 8, 10, 125, 131, 135, 156
  116th Panzer 7, 10, 125, 159, 176, 193–197, 203, 205, 207, 209–212, 230, 232, 235–236, 239–241, 244, 379
  167th Volksgrenadier 293, 362
  212th Volksgrenadier 12, 382–384, 413–416, 419–421, 424, 427
  246th Volksgrenadier 6
  272nd Volksgrenadier 382
  276th Volksgrenadier 12, 280, 383–384, 394, 408, 411, 414
  277th Volksgrenadier 6, 16, 31, 35–37, 62–63
  322nd Volksgrenadier 6
  326th Volksgrenadier 16, 21–22, 26–28
  352nd Volksgrenadier 12, 382–385, 387–388, 393–394, 398–401, 404
  560th Volksgrenadier 7, 156, 159, 179, 182, 191–194, 230, 232, 235–240, 242
  Panzer Lehr 8, 10–11, 207, 215–218, 231–232, 257, 263, 266, 268, 282, 288–293, 302–306, 313, 387
Kampfgruppe
  Bayer 193, 197, 205, 210–214
  Hansen 106, 124, 164, 366–368
  Kaufmann 265–266
  Knittel 98, 154
  Krag 190, 198, 200
  Kühlmann 71–72
  Müller 37, 52–53
  Peiper 6, 10, 18, 47, 49, 50, 71, 79–132, 177, 187, 288
  Sandig 98–99
  von Böhm 176, 222–226
  von Cochenhausen 223
  von Fallois 257–259, 305, 310–311
  von Pötschke 362, 366
OB West 4
Regiments
  Artillery Regiment 130: 304
  Fallschirmjäger Regiment 5: 137–138
  Fallschirmjäger Regiment 9: 45, 47, 82, 98
  Fallschirmjäger Regiment 13: 352, 384, 391
  Fallschirmjäger Regiment 14: 260–262, 264, 268–269, 278, 347, 353, 359–364, 388
  Fallschirmjäger Regiment 15: 268, 272–273, 366, 388–389, 406
  Fusilier Regiment 27: 42, 44, 48
  Fusilier Regiment 39: 243, 261, 266–269, 272, 335, 347, 360, 424
  Fusilier Regiment 49: 51
  Fusilier Regiment 89: 40
  Grenadier Regiment 36: 274–275
  Grenadier Regiment 48: 41–42

Index 453

Grenadier Regiment 77: 243, 257, 302–304, 329, 337–344
Grenadier Regiment 78: 258, 267, 308, 309
Grenadier Regiment 164: 171
Grenadier Regiment 183: 131
Grenadier Regiment 293: 134
Grenadier Regiment 294: 140, 159
Grenadier Regiment 295: 134, 140
Grenadier Regiment 320: 421, 424, 427
Grenadier Regiment 331: 362, 364
Grenadier Regiment 423: 414, 416, 424
Grenadier Regiment 751: 22–27
Grenadier Regiment 752: 27
Grenadier Regiment 753: 27
Grenadier Regiment 914: 391–392, 403
Grenadier Regiment 915: 388–392, 397, 399, 402–405
Grenadier Regiment 916: 388, 392–394, 396–399, 405
Grenadier Regiment 986: 408, 412
Grenadier Regiment 987: 414
Grenadier Regiment 988: 408, 410, 414
Grenadier Regiment 989: 16, 37, 52, 61
Grenadier Regiment 990: 39, 52
Grenadier Regiment 991: 16, 39
Grenadier Regiment 1129: 191
Grenadier Regiment 1130: 182, 236–240
Grenadier Regiments 294: 134
Panzergrenadier Regiment 2: 79–81, 99, 114, 116, 122, 157, 249, 321
Panzergrenadier Regiment 10: 375
Panzergrenadier Regiment 60: 193
Panzergrenadier Regiment 104: 351, 369–370
Panzergrenadier Regiment 115: 293, 339, 341
Panzergrenadier Regiment 156: 194, 210–212, 236
Panzergrenadier Regiment 304: 223, 243, 245–246, 326–327
Panzergrenadier Regiment 901: 265–266, 292, 302, 313–316
Panzergrenadier Regiment 902: 217–218, 282, 306
Panzer Regiment 1: 364
Panzer Regiment 3: 176, 223, 231, 237, 249, 284, 321
Panzer Regiment 16: 193
Panzer Regiment 130: 258, 316
SS Panzer Artillery Regiment 12: 37, 71
SS Panzergrenadier 19: 126
SS Panzergrenadier Regiment 1: 79, 104, 164
SS Panzergrenadier Regiment 2: 79, 81, 99, 114, 116, 119, 122
SS Panzergrenadier Regiment 3: 182, 186–187
SS Panzergrenadier Regiment 4: 179–183
SS Panzergrenadier Regiment 12: 71–72
SS Panzergrenadier Regiment 19: 369
SS Panzergrenadier Regiment 25: 37, 38, 53, 57, 60, 198
SS Panzergrenadier Regiment 26: 71–76, 371, 372
SS Panzerjäger Regiment 12: 57
SS Panzer Regiment 1: 101, 119
SS Panzer Regiment 2: 180, 182, 184
SS Panzer Regiment 12: 64, 68, 71, 72, 372
Volksartillery Regiment 352: 399
Gerow, Gen Leonard T 9, 18, 33
Gestapo 250–251, 255–256, 325–326, 431
  HQ (Villa Pauly) 431
Gibson, Capt Lloyd D 364
Gilbreth, Col Joseph H 249, 283, 284, 290, 302–304
Gniot, Lt Charles R 348
Goffigon, 1st Lt Long H 54
Gold, Lt Col David 332–333
Goldstein, Major Elliot 179–180
Goldstein, Pvt Bernie 97
Goolkasian, PFC Jerry 325
Gouvy 206
Grandmenil 186–188
Green, Capt Seymour 95
Gregg, Capt Frank 308
Griswold, Lt Col George M 311
Grosbous 399, 402–403
Gröschke, Oberstlt Kurt 272, 366
Großkampenberg 133, 135, 232–237
Grzonka, Lt Hans-Joachim 213
Guderian, Heinz 133
Guenther, 1st Lt Carl R 86
Guttmann, Oberst Joachim 249

H

Habiémont 13, 114–115
Haid-Hits 190–192
Haller 411
Hampteau 193, 194
Hanlon, Major John 345
Hansen, Lt Col Harold D 89
Hansen, SS-Col Max 79, 89–90, 104, 124, 366
Han-sur-Lesse 218
Happich, Oberstlt 191
Harlange Pocket 275
Harmon, Capt Harold M 140
Harper, Col Joseph H 291, 358, 371
Harper, Lt Col Ralph 283
Harris, Cpl Joseph 75
Harrison, Lt Col William E 116
Harrold, Col Thomas L 408–409, 415
Hartford, Capt James 226
Harwick, Major Robert 321
Hasbrouck, Brig Gen Robert W 165
Hasselpat Trail 19, 61, 276

Havrenne 215–216
Heaton, Lt William P 372
Hebert, T/Sgt Robert N 410
Heiderscheid 407
Heilmann, Oberst Ludwig 242, 383
Heinerscheid 241
Heintz Barracks 230, 288, 298–299
Hendrix, Sgt James 357
Henkem Lt Hellmuth 358
Hensel, Sgt Charles 96–97
Herdrick, Lt lorenz 140
Herlong, Lt Col Robert 120
Hetzer: definition 40
Higgins, Lt Col Walter 34
Higgins, PFC James L 107
Hightower, Lt Col John M 51
Hildoer, PFC Delmer 325
Hilliard, Sgt John 43
Hills
  Hill 336 (Au Spen) 212
  Hill 490 274
  Hill 500 320
  Hill 504 153
  Hill 510 309
  Hill 536 144
  Hill 539 238
  Hill 546 144
  Hill 575 144, 150
  Hill 576 151
  Hill 664 41, 42
  Höfen 21
  Monschau 21
  Mützenich 21
  Steinmauer 257, 258
  Thier du Mont 170–171
Himmler, Reichsführer-SS Heinrich 79
Hirschfelder, Col Chester 32
Hitler, Adolf 2, 4, 12–14, 79, 288, 293–294, 298, 305, 382, 386
Hitzfeld, Gen Otto 6
Hoban, Lt Col Thomas L 267–268
Hobbs, Maj Gen Leland 109–110
Höcker, Gen Lt Hans-Kurt 362
Höckerlinie. See dragon's teeth
Hodges, Capt Preston 193
Hodges, Courtney H 1, 9, 142, 175
Hoesdorf 387–388, 391, 396, 398, 405
Hoesdorf-Bettendorf Plateau circuit 392, 397–398
Hoesdorf Plateau 394, 396–398
Höfen 9, 15, 16, 22, 23, 26–31, 30
Hoffmann-Schönbrun, Oberst Günther 134, 136, 141, 156
Hoge, Brig Gen William H 156
Höhes Venn 6, 15, 16, 18, 22, 26, 28
Hollenbeck, PFC Donald 107
Hollerath 6, 19, 35

Holzinger, Sgt Warner W 264
Holzthum 243, 265–267
Homan, Major Sammie 308–310, 372
Hompré 347–348
Honsfeld 45, 47–50, 81, 82
Horrocks, Lt-Gen Brian C 215
Hoscheid 242, 258, 260–264, 266, 390
Hosingen 232, 242–243, 257–262, 266, 382
Hotel Claravallis 249, 252–254
Hôtel du Luxembourg 423
Hôtel du Parc 418
Hotton 10–11, 176–177, 181, 187, 192–197, 202, 209–210, 219, 293
Hotton-Marche highway 207
Houffalize 7, 12, 13, 175–176, 284–285, 294, 320–321, 325, 333, 368, 370, 373, 375, 379–381
Houffalize-Manhay highway 181
Howze, Col Robert, Jr 190, 193
Hoy, Col Charles 210
Hritsik, 2nd Lt Michael 407
Huempfner, PFC Milo 222
Huett, Capt John B 153
Humain 11, 215–216
Hünningen 40, 51, 81, 157
Hürtgen Forest 1, 3, 31, 70, 102, 173, 175, 209, 230, 251, 261, 285, 383, 422, 428
Hustead, Major Charles 321, 326
Hyduke, 1st Lt Edward P 303–304, 306

I

Imgenbroich 25
Information Panels
  Celles Pocket 224–226
  Cheneux, La Bataille de 113, 117–118
  Circuit Historique (Bastogne) 296, 297, 299, 307, 311, 319, 325, 328, 343, 345, 356–357, 361, 367, 368, 370
  Monschau - Bütgenbach Route of Commemoration 29, 30, 33, 61, 65, 68, 69, 78
  Promenade du Souvenir (Hoesdorf) 392, 393, 394, 395, 397, 398
  Promenade du Souvenir, Schumann's Eck 276
  Remember US 244, 251, 252, 253, 263, 264, 276, 277, 281
Inman, Lt Col Roy 316–317
International Highway 15, 35–41, 62, 139
Irwin, Maj Gen Stanford Leroy 414, 419–420
Irzyk, Major Albin 347–350

J

Jackson, Sgt Schuyler 343
Jaques, Lt Col George L 353, 355
Joerg, Lt Col Wood 128, 131
Jones, Capt Lennis 400
Jones, Maj Gen Alan W, Jr 141–142, 146, 156

Index

Jordan, Capt John 188
Jurgensen, SS-Major Arnold 64
Jüttner, Oberst Arthur 170

K

Kampfgruppe: definition 6
Karpac, Pvt George 333
Kaschner, Gen Erwin 21, 22, 25–27
Kaufmann, Oberstlt Walter 265–268, 335
Kaundorf 282
Kautenbach 265
Kean, Gen William 9
Kelley, Lt Col Thomas P Jr 152
Kenan, Lt Col Thomas A 413
Kichka, Henry 174
Kimbro, T/4 Truman 70
Kinnard, Lt Col Harry W 358
Kirkbride, Pvt William P 42
Kittel, Oberst Friedrich 125, 141
Kjeldseth, Lt Col Clarion 267–268, 268
Klinck, Lt Col Earl F 144
Kline, Capt Robert R 217
Klug, 1st Sgt Elmer P 48
Kniess, Gen Baptist 8, 388
Knight's Cross
    Barkmann, SS-Senior Sgt Ernst 185
    Druke, Major Wilhelm 159
    Heilmann, Oberst Ludwig 242
    Müller, SS-Major Siegfried 57
    Osterhold, Oberstlt Wilhelm 44
Knittel, SS-Major Gustav 79, 98–99, 113
Kobscheid 135, 140
Koch, Gen Oscar 8
Kokott, Oberst Heinz 242–243, 258, 290–293, 308, 329, 337–338, 347–348
Kolar, S/Sgt Anthony 75
Kolb, Oberst Werner 273
Korecki, Pvt Eddie 212
Kraas, Col Hugo 378
Kraas, Colonel Hugo 63
Krag, Major Ernst-August 200
Krause, SS-Lt Col Bernard 71, 371
Krewinkel 135–136
Krinkelt. See Rocherath
Krinkelter Wald 40, 50
Krüger, Gen Walther 7, 176, 194, 209, 230, 232, 418
Kuchenbach, Hauptmann 213
Kühlmann, SS-Major Herbert 71
Kunkel, Major Rolf 335–336, 359–361
Kursk 175

L

La Chapelle 128
La Gleize 11, 18, 81, 84, 104, 106, 110–112, 123–125, 288, 366
Lagrew, Lt Col Embry D 366
Lamm, 1st Lt George D 168
Lammerding, Gen Heinz 176, 182, 184, 186, 188, 242
Lander, Pvt Hugh 193
Lang, Capt Steve 416
Langhäuser, Oberst Rudolf 193
Lanzerath 3, 14, 15, 18, 44–47, 82, 135
LaPrade, Lt Col James 321–322, 325–326
La Roche-en-Ardenne 10, 170
Lary, Lt Virgil 85–86
Lauer, Maj Gen Walter E 3, 15, 17, 38
Lausdell Crossroads 38, 53–60
Lauterborn 384, 413, 424–427
La Vaulx Richard 96–97
Leake, 1st Lt John L 416–417
Legler, Major Matthew 38
Leignon 221–222
Leiker, Capt Victor 410
Leinbaugh, 1st Lt Harold P 213–214
Lemaire, Renée 297, 298
Lemm, Oberstlt George 44, 48
Lennon, Capt Harlow 68
Lentz, Pfc Edward 365
Liège 1, 2, 10, 14, 21, 166, 177
Lieler 241
Ligneuville 95–96
Longchamps 291, 327, 344, 359, 368–371
Long, Lt Ivan H 152
Long, Pvt Ted B 278
Longvilly 256, 284–285, 290, 302–307, 311
Loopey, S/Sgt Charles 122
Lopez, PFC Jose 54
Losheim 15, 41–42, 44–78, 48–50, 81, 133–134, 176
Losheimergraben 36, 40, 44, 48, 50, 71, 81
Losheimergraben Crossroads 41–44
Losheim Gap 3, 4, 6, 9, 15, 79, 133, 176
Love, Capt James 65–66
Love, Sgt Clyde J 341
Lucht, Gen Walther 8
Lutrebois 361–366
Lützkampen 7, 234–238
Luxembourg City 8, 125, 282, 379, 413, 425, 427, 428, 429–432
Luxembourg General Strike 271
Luxembourg, Grand Duchy of 239–287, 382–432
Lybarger, Capt Robert 249

M

M18 Tank Destroyer: definition 196
Macdiarmid, 1st Lt Morton A 421–422
MacDonald, Capt Charles B 52–56, 60
MacDonald, Capt Robert J 333
MacDonald, Col John C 216
Macht, 1st Lt Walter D 120

456 The Bulge Battlefields

Mackey, Capt Claude B 251–252
Maddox, Lt Kenneth 254
Mageret 256, 294, 303, 305–309, 311–312
Maher, Lt John 248
Malempré 182, 185
Malmédy 6, 9, 71, 89–92, 116
Malmédy Massacre 4, 84–88
Manderfeld 45, 135–136, 153
Mande St-Etienne 288, 293–294, 336–341
Manhay 11, 12, 102, 125, 130, 176, 181–187, 190, 294
Manhay-Hotton highway 186, 190, 197
Marche-en-Famenne 9, 175, 214–216, 220–221, 333, 337, 339
Marcouray 205
Marnach 243, 245–248, 251, 256, 266
Maroney, Major William J 391
Marshall, Capt James 198
Marvie 290–291, 314–320
Mass, Cpl Joseph P 95
Maucke, Oberst Wolfgang 339, 345
Maulusmühle 255
Mayes, Major James L 164
McArtor, Capt William Stein 66
McAuliffe, Gen Anthony 14, 288–292, 296–299, 314, 327, 337, 358, 360
McBride, Maj Gen Horace L 280, 402–403
McCarty, M/Sgt Ralph 93
McConnell, Lt William 417
McCoy, Lt Col Jim H 404–405
McCullom, PFC Lillard 107
McCutchan, Capt Floyd K 260–261
McDaniel, Major CF 362
McDonald, 1st Lt Robert L 350, 351
McGarity, Sgt Vernon L 56
McGee, Capt Robert 40
McGeorge, Major Kenneth 186
McGregor, Lt Joseph C 373
McKearney, Lt James B 373
McKinley, Lt Col William Dawes 38, 56–61
McPheeters, Capt Archibald A 130
Medal of Honor
  Biddle, PFC Melvin 191
  Cowan, PFC Richard 55
  Currey, Sgt Francis A 93
  Hendrix, Sgt James Richard 357
  Kimbro, T/4 Truman Carol 70
  Lopez, PFC Jose M 54
  McGarity, S/Sgt Vernon L 56
  Soderman, PFC William A 60
  Turner, Sgt Day G 281
  Warner, Cpl Henry F 75
  Wiedorfer, Sgt Paul J 350
Meddaugh, Lt William 106
Medernach 412
Melines 191, 201–202

Mendez, Lt Col Louis 171–172
Mergenthaler, Pvt George 282–283
Mertzig 399, 402–403
Meuse River 107. See Rivers, Meuse
Michamps 256, 372
Michelshaff 425, 427
Michin, Pvt Bernard 311
Middleton, Gen Troy 3, 10
Middleton, Major Gen Troy 230, 232, 268, 284, 288, 290, 298, 346, 381
Mildren, Lt Col Frank 63, 66–69
Miller, 1st Lt Victor 54
Millikin, Maj Gen John 12
Millikin, Major Gen John 273
Mills, 1st Lt Aubrey 138
Mills, Capt Roger 85
Miltonberger, Col Butler B 362
Milton, Major Harold F 273
Minier, Cpl Howard 239
Model, Gen Walter 3, 4, 18, 23, 175, 176, 382
Mohnke, Senior Col Wilhelm 6, 79, 96, 120
Möhring, Gen Kurt 408–411, 414
Monaville 370–371
Monceau 117–118
Monschau 3, 6, 15, 16, 18, 21–29, 249
Montgomery, Field Marshal Bernard Law 1–3, 10–14, 21, 125, 130, 157, 175, 223
Monuments / Memorials
  1st Canadian Parachute Battalion 218
  1st Infantry Division 20
  2nd, 3rd and 11th Armored Divisions 380
  2nd and 99th Infantry Divisions 68
  2nd Armored Division 216
  2nd Bn , 502nd Parachute Inf Regt 370
  2nd Infantry Division 164
  3rd and 6th Regts Chasseurs Ardennais 167
  3rd Armored Division 112, 186, 189
  3rd Bn, 112th Inf Regt 169
  3rd Bn, 517th Parachute Inf Regt 185
  4th Armored Division 350, 352
  4th Infantry Division Monument 429
  5th & 9th Armored & 4th, 5th, 28th, 76th, 83rd, and 87th Inf Div 428
  5th US Infantry Division 411
  6th Armored Division 241, 256
  7th Armored Division 163, 167, 169
  9th Armored Div, CCA 412
  9th Armored Division 412
  9th Armored Division, CCB 169
  10th Armored Division 419
  10th Infantry Regiment 405
  12th Inf Regt (Co A), 159th ECB, & 10th Reg 427
  17th Airborne Division 260, 380
  26th Infantry Division 407
  28th Infantry Division 169, 247, 270, 397

Index

28th Infantry Division 1944 406
35th Infantry Division 351
51st Engineer Combat Battalion 195
53rd (Welsh) Infantry Division 194
60th Armored Inf Bn, Co C 410
75th Infantry Division 189
80th Airborne Antiaircraft Bn 108, 111
80th Infantry Division 282, 407, 411
82nd Airborne Division Park 115
83rd, 4th and 5th U.S Infantry Divisions 422
83rd Infanty Division 185
84th Infantry Division 207
87 Mortar Battalion, Company C 201
90th Infantry Division 241, 278
99th Infantry Battalion (Separate) 94
101st Airborne Division 300
103rd Engineer Combat Bn, Co B 260
106th Infantry Division 163, 169
110th Infantry Regiment 267
110th Infantry Regiment, Co K 260
110th Infantry Regiment, HQ Co 253
116th Inf Div - Lost 500 151
168th Engineering Combat Battalion 162
238th Engineer Combat Battalion 186
249th Engineer Combat Battalion 244
289th Infantry Regiment 201
290th Infantry Regiment 166
291st Combat Engineer Bn 114
307th Engineer Combat Battalion 111
317 Regiment 283
325th Glider Infantry Regiment 185
326th Airborne Medical Company 335
331st Infantry Combat Team 428
335th Infantry Regiment 201
424th Infantry Regiment 132
463rd Parachute Field Artillery Bn 345
465th Parachute Field Artillery Bn 111
505th Parachute Infantry Regiment 108, 131
505th PIR, 82nd Airborne Division, Co I 130
505th Regimental Combat Team 111
506th Parachute Infantry Regiment 331
506th PIR, 101st Airborne Div, Co E 331
508th Parachute Infantry Regiment 172
509th Parachute Infantry Battalion 201
513th Parachute Infantry Regiment 337
517th Parachute Infantry Regiment 109, 131, 192
526th Armored Infantry Bn 100, 103
551st Battalion Memorial Park 131
551st Parachute Inf Bn, Co A 131
596th Airborne Engineer Company 101
702nd Tank Battalion 260
707th Tank Battalion 247
712th Tank Battalion 241
740th Tank Battalion 111
750th Tank Battalion 186

825th Tank Destroyer Battalion 100, 103
951st Field Artillery Battalion 189
1255th Engineer Combat Bn, Co A 390
1944 - 1945 Liberation Memorial 277
American / British Meeting Plaque 204
American Liberators Memorial 401
American Temporary Cemetery 328
Armée secrète 168, 184
B-17 medium bomber 206
Belgian Chasseurs Ardennais 299
Belgian SOE 255
Belgian Special Air Service 169, 219
Bertogne Remembers 343
Bois Jacques 330
Bomb Monument 282
Borne #1147 300
Breckinridge, Lt Col William M 405
British 51st Infantry Division 202
Brookins, Cpl Richard 271
Bryson, 1st Lt Charles K 196
Cameron, Flying Officer Douglas A 406
Chasseurs Ardennes 132
Civilian Victims - Malmédy 91
Civilian Victims - Parfondruy 109
Civilian Victims - Stavelot 100, 102
Civilian Victims - Trois-Ponts 107
Civilian Victims (Troisvierges) 256
Cohen, rue du Colonel H 350
Connealy, Lt George C 201
Croix Renkin 219
Desobry, Gen William R 324
Durkee, Lt Richard 131
Enclos des Fusillés 326
Enrôlés de Force 251
Europa Denkmal 240–241
First Allied Soldiers to Enter Germany 264
Francis, Lt & Arnold, Sgt 379
Francorchamps Gas Depot 103
GI Statue 253
Glessener, Ernest 301
Griffin, Lt Ray 241
Houffalize Civilian Victims 380
Howze Jr, Col Daniel B 190
Huempfner, PFC Milo 222
Hünningen War Memorial 51
Irzyk, place du général 350
Lamar, Lt Robert M 352
Lemaire, Renée 297
Ligneuville Atrocity 96
Malmédy Cenotaph 91
Malmédy Massacre 88
Mardasson Memorial 300–301
Mendez, Lt Col Louis 172
Mergenthaler, Pvt George 282
Monument Auschwitz 256
Monument des Fusillés 345

National Memorial of Solidarity 430
National Monument of Strike 271
National Monument to the Resistance and Deportation 1940 - 1945 431
Rollbahn A 38
Roth War Memorial 139
Royal Air Force 320 Squadron 169
Shields, Cpl John 202
Soldiers' Memorial 47
Square Patton 403–404
Strickler, Col Daniel B 267
Tannenbaum Memorial 173
The Parachute Regiment, British 6th Airborne Div 219
Tom Myers Square 263
Two B-17 'Flying Fortresses' 351
Unknown Luxembourgeois Legionnaire 431
US 109th Regt & German Gren Regt 916 398
US Army 356
US First Army 91
US First & Third Army Junction 380
US Third Army 367
Verdenne Pocket 214
Wereth Massacre 154
Wiegand, Cpl Richard F 189
Wood, 1st Lt Eric F 155
Zulli, Lieutenant Philip 196
Moon, Major William P, Jr 151
Mormont 188
Morrison, Lt Stanley 320
Morrow, Lt Jesse 69
Morsheck Crossroads 71
Moscow 175
Müller, SS-Major Siegfried 37, 52, 57, 200
Müllerthal 409, 413–414
Munshausen 242, 245, 248, 256
Mürringen 38, 40, 42
Museums
   Ars Tecnica 50
   Bastogne Ardennes 44 316
   Bastogne War Museum 300
   Bataille de Salm et du Saillant (Dec 44 - Jan 45) 132
   Bataille des Ardennes 203–204
   Battle of the Bulge 253
   Battle of the Bulge 1944/1945 270
   Baugnez 44 Historical Center 89
   Bulge Relics Museum 172
   Décembre 1944 111–112
   General Patton Memorial Museum 404
   Heintz Barracks 298
   l'ASBL 83rd 'Thunderbolt Division' Museum 174
   Le Mess 297
   Museum 1944 205
   National Museum of Military History 400–401

National Resistance Museum of Luxembourg 432
Remember Museum 39-45 19–20
Sadzot Museum 44 201
Spitfire 229
Truschbaum Museum 77
Westwallmuseum Panzerwerk Katzenkopf 423
WW II 385th Bombardment Group (Heavy) Memorial Museum 351
Mützenich 21, 22, 25, 27
Myers, PFC Thomas 263

N

Namur 2, 7, 8, 11, 230, 231, 335
Neffe 290, 294, 303, 306–312, 314, 330
Nelson, Col Gustin M 169, 235, 239
Nelson, PFC Carl 193
Neufchâteau 234, 288, 292, 293, 297, 309, 324, 337, 352, 359, 360, 361, 384
Neufmoulin Bridge 114
Niederwampach 302–303
Night Vision Devices 285
Nocher 274
Noirefontaine 126, 128
Nolte, Oberstlt Eberhard 369
Norris, Lt Col Jack K 63
Nothum 274–278
Nothum Trail 276–277
Novak, Hauptmann Heinz 248
Noville 10, 13, 285, 288, 290–292, 320–328, 330–332, 368, 373, 377–380

O

O'Brien, Lt Col Robert 22, 25
Ochmann, SS-Sgt Paul 95–96
Odeigne 182
O'Hara, Lt Col James 313, 316, 318
Operation
   Bodenplatte 12
   Greif 6, 89
   Herbstnebel 2, 23, 230, 288, 382, 386
   Lüttich 109
   Market Garden 1, 288
   Wacht am Rhein 2, 124, 133
Oradour-sur-Glane 176
Organization Todt 229, 395
Ormont 141
Orr, Lt Col William Orr 197
Osterhold, Oberstlt Wilhelm 41, 42, 44
Osweiler 384, 413, 421, 427–428
Ouellette, Major Albert 151
Ouren 230, 234–241, 244
Ourthe 207

P

Panzer: definition 37
Panzerfaust: definition 24

Index

Parfondruy 99
Parker, 1st Lt Robert A 68
Parker III, Major Arthur C 152, 178–180
Parker, Lt Harry C 39
Parker's Crossroad 294
Parker's Crossroad 12, 176–181, 184
Patch, Lt Col Lloyd E 326–327, 375
Patterson, Sgt Carl G 67
Patton, 2nd Lt Oliver 151–152
Patton, George S, Jr 1, 9, 10, 12–14, 151, 222, 258, 273, 289, 293–294, 297, 325, 346, 349, 355, 361, 368, 386, 403–405, 407, 430
Paul, Maj Gen Willard S 273
Paulsen, Unterfeldwebel Hans Hermann 62
Payne, 1st Lt Robert 258
Pedley, Col Timothy A 210
Peiper, SS-Lt Col Joachim 18, 47, 79, 98, 110, 130
Pergrin, Lt Col David 84–86, 89–90, 96–97, 104, 113
Perlé 350–351
Phelps, Sgt Don 213–214
Phillips, Pvt David J 328
Phillips, Sgt Webster 367
Piersall, Sgt Thornton E 29
Pigg, S/Sgt Edwin 113
Pilburn, Brig Gen Edwin W 413
Pintsch 283
Pionier: definition 79
Plankers, Lt Dewey 42
Plume, Capt Stephen B 37
Popp, Cpl Phillip 193
Porché, Capt Stanley E 139
Poteau 136, 164
Poteau de Harlange 278–279
Pötschke, SS-Major Werner 87, 120, 164, 362, 366
PoW Camps
  Oflag 13B 37
  Oflag 64 250, 333
  Oflag 73 58, 66
  Oflag 79 285
  Oflag 113B 285
  Stalag IVb 151, 257, 263, 390
  Stalag IXb 144, 146, 252, 392, 422
  Stalag IXc 152
  Stalag VIg 95
  Stalag XIb 326
  Stalag XIIa 392, 422
  Stalag XIIIb 252, 320
  Stalag XIIIc 42, 44, 140
  Stalag XIIId 60, 139
Powers, 2nd Lt Charles D 122, 123
Powers, S/Sgt Darrell C 378
Pozit Fuse: definition 90
Prazenka, Lt Steve 390
Presidential Unit Citation

3rd Bn, 9th Infantry Regiment 59
9th Armored Div, CCA, CCB & CCR 412
10th Armored Div, CCB 299
37th Tank Battalion 355
38th Cavalry Reconnaissance Squad 22
51st Engineer Combat Battalion 108, 195
110th Infantry Regiment 243
112th Infantry Regiment 235
291st Engineer Combat Battalion 113
307th Airborne Eng Bn, 1st Pl, Co C 117
394th Infantry Regiment 42
394th Inf Regt, I&R Platoon 47
504th Parachute Inf Regt, Co B and C 117
509th Parachute Infantry Battalion 201
517th Parachute Inf Regt, 1st Bn 192
551st Parachute Infantry Battalion 132
741st Tank Battalion 67
Priess, Gen Hermann 6, 15, 18
Prigge, Lt Hans 390
Prior, Dr John 297, 324
Probert, Sgt F 'Geordie' 226
Pruett, Lt Col Joseph F 144, 151–152
Prümerberg Heights 157–163
Purdue, Col Branner 89, 90
Putscheid 263, 388

R

Read, PFC David A 62
Recht 157
Recogne 291, 327–328
Reeves, Lt Gerald 165
Reeves, S/Sgt Woodrow 165
Rèhârmont 126, 128, 130
Reid, Capt Charles B 149
Reid, Col Alexander D 135
Reisdorf 384, 387
Remagen 13, 386, 412
Remer, Oberst Otto 156, 193, 194
Remoifosse 359, 364
Rettlinger, SS-Major Karl 164
Reuler 232, 249, 254
Richardson, Lt Col Walter B 187
Ridgway, Maj Gen Matthew B 177, 181
Riggs, Lt Col Thomas J, Jr 157–159, 161
Riley, Col Don 37, 47, 413, 421, 424–425
Riley, Lt Col John R 424
Rinehardt, Capt LeVoe 241
Rivas, Pvt Manuel 342
Rivers
  Alzette 402–403
  Amblève 3, 6, 10, 94, 96–101, 103, 106–108, 110, 112, 115, 118, 124, 175
  Clerf 232, 239, 242, 246, 249–250, 253, 257, 260, 264–265, 268, 282
  Durenbach 144
  Ernz Blanche 382

Ernz Noire 382–384, 408–409, 413–419
Ihrenbach 144, 146
Jansbach 39, 52–56, 54
Kyll Creek 43, 50
Lienne 114–115
Linnebach 144, 146, 153
Meuse 2, 6, 8, 10, 11, 15, 18, 103, 106, 133, 175, 176, 207, 223, 224, 227, 228, 230, 231, 292, 293, 324, 327, 382
Moselle 133, 383
Olef 32, 34, 38, 56
Our 3, 7, 134, 230–287, 288, 382–385, 387–390, 392–393, 395–397, 405
Ourthe 3, 7, 9, 10, 175–177, 186, 192–196, 202–204, 206, 207–209, 327, 332, 380
Ourthe Occidentale 175
Ourthe Orientale 175
Rhine 8, 13, 133
Roer 1, 2, 21–24, 30, 133
Salm 3, 9–11, 103–106, 108–109, 124, 125–127, 131–132, 157, 165, 167–171, 175, 177, 294
Sauer 382–383, 394, 402, 408, 411, 413–416, 419–423
Semois 2
Sûre 10, 230, 273, 275, 280, 282, 347, 349, 351, 382–384, 387–389, 391, 396–400, 402–407, 410
Warche 15, 51, 90, 93–94
Wark 389, 402–403
Robbins, Capt Dean D 130
Roberts, Col William 290, 303
Robertson, Gen Walter 14, 30–33, 51, 65, 83
Roberts, Sgt Charles 59
Robinson, Lt James 344
Roche-en-Ardenne, La 202–205
Rochefort vi, 11, 196, 207, 215–219, 223, 224
Rochelinval 130–132
Rocherath 52–70
Rocher Bayard 177, 227
Roffe, Col Worrell 399
Rohren 27
Rollbahn A 19, 35–41, 48, 52, 54–57, 63–65, 79, 83
Rollbahn B 39, 52–53, 64
Rollbahn C 40–41, 64, 71, 90
Rollbahn D 41, 47–48, 79, 81, 83
Rollbahn E 79
Rombaugh, Lt Warren 96
Rommel, Gen Erwin 15, 107, 228
Röppenvenn. See Ruppenven
Rosebaum, Col Dwight A 165, 181–182
Rose, Capt Lawrence K 283–284
Rose, Maj Gen Maurice 183, 197
Rosenthal, PFC Paul 237
Roth an der Our 390–391

Roth an der Prüm 136
Rouzie, Lt Col Thomas 318
Rubel, Lt Col George K 119
Rudder, Lt Col James 387–389, 391, 399, 402, 405
Ruhr 1–2, 13, 175, 210, 237
Rumpf, SS-Lt Erich 85, 87
Ruppenvenn 19, 52, 54, 57, 59
Rupp, Rupp 96
Ryan, Dr Bernard 377
Ryerson, Capt William 303, 305–307, 309

S
Salazar, Pvt Isabel 67
Salmchâteau 130, 157, 167, 169–170, 177
Salmchâteau-La Roche-en-Ardenne highway 170, 176
Samrée 10, 197, 198
Sandig, SS-Lt Col Rudolf 79, 98–99
Sandoz 198–201
Sauer River Crossing 411, 419–420
Savelborn 410
Saymon, Lt Vert 265–266
Scarborough, Capt Leon T 84
Scheidgen 425
Scheuber, Capt Samuel 108
Schimmel, Oberst Arno 260, 268, 347, 353, 360, 362
Schlausenbach 142
Schmäschke, Soldat Friedrich 394
Schmidt, Oberst Erich 399
Schmidt, Sgt George 312, 342
Schnee Eifel 8, 15, 133–174
Schoenberg 134
Schriefer, Oberstlt Martin 257, 302–304, 329, 339
Schulze-Kossen, SS-Lt Col Richard 53
Schumann, Oberstlt 239
Schumann's Eck 272–276
Schwartz, Cpl Irwin 76
Schwarze Mann 133
Schwarzenbruch Trail 38, 53, 57
Schwarzenbüchel 72, 74, 76
Schweiker, Lt Joseph B 329–332
Scott, Lt-Col Jean O 37
SdKfz 251: definition 71
Seeley, Col Theodore 285
Senonchamps 294, 359–361, 366
Sensfuss, Gen Franz 413–414, 416, 419, 421, 424
Sergent, Sgt Vern 193
Sevenig 234–235, 239
Shapiro, Lt William 365
Sherman Ecke 54
Sibret 233–234, 268, 334, 353, 355, 360, 366
Sicherheitsdienst 220, 251
Siegfried Line. See Westwall
Silva, Sgt Lawrence J 371

Silver Star
  Bahe, Major Gordon A 218
  Bomberger, Second Lt Walter 366
  Bouch, Lt Lyle J 47
  Collier, S/Sgt Noah G 76
  Dec, Capt Stanley 237
  Fowler, Cpl Willis 344
  Jackson, Sgt Schuyler 343
  Jahr, PFC Marco L 33
  Leake, Lt John Louis 417
  Lentz, PFC Edward 366
  Loopey, S/Sgt Charles 122
  McGregor, Lt Joseph C 373
  McKinley, Lt Col William D 59
  Parker III, Major Arthur C 181
  Powers, 2nd Lt Charles D 122
  Prior, Dr John 324
  Roberts, Sgt Charles 59
  Ryan, Dr Bernard J 377
  Scheuber, Captain Samuel 108
  Schmidt, Sgt George 342
  Strickler, Lt Col Daniel 273
  Travalini, S/Sgt Savino 49
  Vetland, T/Sgt Theodore 322
  Wiegand, Cpl Richard F 189
  Yates, Major Robert 105
Sink, Col Robert F 322, 327, 371, 378
Siptrott, SS-Sgt Hans 87
Sirovica, S/Sgt Frank 171–172
Skaggs, Lt Col Robert L 67
Skorzeny, Lt Col Otto 6–7, 89–90, 92, 94
Skorzeny, Lt-Col Otto 222, 227
Skyline Drive 134, 140, 144, 230–287, 385
Smith, Col Douglas B 186
Soderman, PFC William 59, 60
Solis, Major Paul J 97, 98
Soviet Winter Offensive 13, 294
Spa 6, 9, 84, 92, 98
Speirs, 1st Lt Ronald 376
Stadler, SS-Gen Sylvester 125
Staeffler, Lt Col Dick 424
Stavelot 6, 9, 10, 92, 96–103, 109, 113, 166
Steinebrück 135, 156
Sternebeck, SS-1st Lt Werner 81–83, 87
St-Hubert 10, 207, 218, 333
St-Jacques 130–131
Stockell, Lt Charles W 51
Stolzembourg 264
Stopka, Lt Col John P 328
Stottmeister, Lt Günter 392
Stoumont 118–124
Stoumont Sanatorium 122–124
Stoumont Station 120–124
Strickler, Col Daniel 266–268, 272–273
Strong, Gen Kenneth 8
StuG III: definition 41

Stumpf, S/Sgt Delbert 42
St-Vith 8–14, 12, 83–84, 91, 140, 156–164, 167, 175, 183, 230, 235, 287
Sûre River Crossing 401, 405
Sutherland, Col Edwin M 110, 119, 122
Swanson, Capt Wallace 338, 342–343
Sweat, Lt Jesse P 255
Swift, Capt Vaughn 406–407

T
Tanks
  British 'Achilles' Tank Destroyer 203
  British Sherman Firefly 194
  German Jagdpanzer 'Hetzer' SP-gun 401
  German King Tiger 111
  German Panther Ausf G 188, 224, 379
  US Patton M-47 400
  US Sherman M4A1 167, 203, 400, 403
  US Sherman M4A3 205, 206, 252, 272, 296, 300
  US Sherman M4 'Absentee' 300
  US Sherman tank turrets 194, 299, 301, 307, 319, 320, 344, 357
Tannenbaum, Pvt Henry I 173
Targnon 125
Task Force: definition 85
Taylor, Col William 280
Taylor, Maj Gen Maxwell 288, 293, 304, 376, 381
Tebbe, Major Gerhard 210, 212
Timberlake, Gen Edward W 95
Tobruk
  Wahlerscheid 33
Tomasik, Major Edmund 198
Tourist Offices
  Bastogne 295
  Cantons De L'Est 163
  Clervaux 250
  Dasburg 244
  Diekirch 400
  Dinant 228
  Echternach 422
  Hotton 194
  Houffalize 380
  La Roche-en-Ardenne 203
  Malmédy 90
  Monschau 22
  Stavelot 99
  St-Vith 163
  Trois-Ponts 107
  Vianden 390
  Vielsalm 167
  Wiltz 270
Towns, Capt Preston 336
Travalini, S/Sgt Savino 48
Treaty of Versailles 15, 22, 30, 91, 162
Trenches. See Foxholes

Trent, Sgt John 44
Trois-Ponts 6, 11, 13, 84, 98, 100, 103–109, 126, 177, 181
Trois-Ponts-Hotton highway 181, 198
Troisvierges 251, 256, 404
Truppner, 1st Lt Stephen 58
Tsakanikas, Pvt William 45, 46
Turner, Sgt Day G 280–282
Tuttle, Lt-Col Paul V 52

U
Udenbreth 50
Useldange 407
US Military Units
  Air Force
    307th Fighter Group 226, 229
    385th Bombardment Group (Heavy) 350
    406th Fighter Group 296
    474th Fighter Group 229
    IX Tactical Air Command 112
    IX Troop-Carrier Command 293
    XIX Tactical Air Command 292, 348
  Armies
    First 1–2, 4, 9–13, 18, 84, 99, 101, 109, 125, 142, 175, 380
    Ninth 1, 2, 4, 10, 12, 125, 210, 380
    Seventh 1
    Sixth 1, 10, 289
    Third 1, 2, 8, 12, 13, 244, 258, 277, 289, 293, 297, 300, 356, 367, 380, 396, 402, 403, 430
  Army Groups
    12th 1–2
  Battalions
    2nd Engineer Combat 70
    2nd Tank 232, 249, 251, 254, 283
    3rd Armored Field Artillery 408
    3rd Tank 303, 313, 320, 322
    4th Engineer Combat 413
    8th Tank 347, 349
    9th Armored Engineer 283
    11th Tank 413, 416, 417
    14th Tank 95
    15th Tank 366
    19th Tank 409, 412
    20th Armored Infantry 297, 303, 320, 324
    22nd Armored Artillery 349
    22nd Armored Field Artillery 348
    23rd Armored Infantry 193
    23rd Engineer Combat 187
    25th Armored Engineer 366
    31st Tank 161
    33rd Reconnaissance 187
    35th Engineer Combat 308
    35th Tank 364
    37th Field Artillery 51
    37th Tank 352, 353, 355, 401
    38th Armored Infantry 161
    40th Tank 165, 182
    41st Armored Infantry 294
    41st Tank 296
    44th Engineer Combat 267, 268
    48th Armored Infantry 182
    50th Field Artillery 401
    51st Armored Infantry 362, 364, 365
    51st Engineer Combat 103–104, 107, 192–193, 217
    52nd Armored Infantry 232, 283
    53rd Armored Infantry 352, 353, 355, 357
    54th Armored Infantry 313
    55th Armored Engineer 303, 313, 320
    58th Armored Field Artillery 304
    60th Armored Infantry 8, 383, 408–412
    61st Armored Infantry 417
    62nd Field Artillery 22
    70th Tank 413, 417, 424, 426, 427
    73rd Field Artillery 232
    73rd Armored Field Artillery 284
    80th Airborne Antiaircraft 108
    81st Airborne Antiaircraft 317
    81st Engineer Combat 140, 149, 157
    82nd Reconnaissance 226
    87th Chemical Mortar 198, 200, 211
    99th Infantry (Separate) 89, 92
    103rd Engineer Combat 257, 260, 387, 391, 397
    107th Field Artillery 387
    108th Field Artillery 387, 391, 405
    109th Field Artillery 242, 246, 258
    146th Engineer Combat 25
    158th Engineer Combat 305, 308, 311
    159th Engineer Combat 407, 424, 425
    168th Engineer Combat 157, 159
    193rd Glider Infantry 337
    196th Field Artillery 28
    203rd Antiaircraft Artillery 179
    254th Engineer Combat 83
    275th Field Artillery 138
    285th Field Artillery Observation 84, 85, 88
    291st Engineer Combat 84, 90, 93, 96, 104, 113, 116
    307th Airborne Engineer 106, 117, 169
    319th Glider Field Artillery 169
    321st Parachute Field Artillery 289
    324th Engineer Combat 61
    326th Airborne Engineer 320, 355
    333rd Field Artillery 154, 289
    371st Field Artillery 44
    377th Parachute Field Artillery 289, 344
    420th Armored Field Artillery 290, 360
    447th Antiaircraft 242, 267
    463rd Parachute Field Artillery 289, 339,

Index

340, 345
482nd Antiaircraft Artillery 304
509th Parachute Infantry 181, 198
526th Armored Infantry 89, 90, 98, 100
551st Parachute Infantry (Independent) 126, 128, 131
589th Field Artillery 140, 142, 151, 152, 179
590th Field Artillery 149, 150, 151
591st Field Artillery 135
592nd Field Artillery 140, 142
603rd Tank Destroyer 366
609th Tank Destroyer 303, 320, 322, 325
612th Tank Destroyer 26, 27, 71, 81, 82
613th Tank Destroyer 74
629th Tank Destroyer 188
630th Tank Destroyer 242, 245, 246, 250, 267, 391
638th Tank Destroyer 193, 196, 197, 217
644th Tank Destroyer 57, 68, 70
687th Field Artillery 242, 265, 267, 278, 279, 392
701st Tank Destroyer 364
702nd Tank 407
705th Tank Destroyer 292, 293, 312, 325, 327, 328, 335, 339
707th Tank 232, 247, 249, 258, 267, 268, 387, 391
712th Tank 241, 278
737th Tank 263
740th Tank 119, 120, 128
741st Tank 54, 58, 63, 67, 68, 70
743rd Tank 119, 120
771st Tank 209, 210
773rd Tank Destroyer 278
796th Antiaircraft Artillery 360
801st Tank Destroyer 81
811st Tank Destroyer 232
811th Tank Destroyer 283, 304, 415
814th Tank Destroyer 170
820th Tank Destroyer 45, 135, 137, 142, 149, 157, 164, 237
823rd Tank Destroyer 114, 118
825th Tank Destroyer 89, 90, 92, 97, 100
863rd Field Artillery 28
907th Glider Field Artillery 289, 307, 311
969th Field Artillery 289
Brigade
  49th Antiaircraft 95
Corps
  III 12, 13, 273–275
  V 1, 2, 9, 15, 17, 18, 33, 379, 429
  VII 2, 9, 12–13, 175, 181, 186, 209, 294
  VIII 2–3, 8, 13, 154, 230, 288, 298, 381
  XVIII Airborne 181, 184, 188
  XX 275
Divisions

1st Infantry 9, 18–20, 58, 67, 70, 71, 89
2nd Armored 176, 198, 207, 215–216, 222–226, 294, 379
2nd Infantry 14, 30–34, 51, 64, 83, 133, 399, 401, 405, 417
3rd Armored 9, 12, 110, 122, 175, 177, 180–181, 185–187, 193, 197, 200–202, 205, 409, 411
4th Armored 11–13, 251, 273, 289, 293–294, 346–347, 350, 352–355, 362, 372
4th Infantry 8, 230, 383, 384
5th Armored 26, 264, 394, 403, 407
5th Infantry 144, 263–264, 384, 399, 405, 411, 414–415, 417–420, 427
6th Armored 241, 244, 253, 256, 275, 293, 294, 366, 372
7th Armored 9, 13, 84, 98, 142, 156–159, 165, 170, 176–179, 181–183
9th Armored 8, 95, 142, 156, 169, 185, 232, 241, 249, 251–252, 283–287, 290–291, 293–294, 302–303, 321, 383, 408–409, 411–412, 415, 419, 428
9th Infantry 15, 18, 23, 31, 33, 57
10th Armored 9, 10, 230, 268, 290–292, 295–297, 299, 303, 311, 324, 347–348, 350, 384, 401, 413–415, 417–419, 421, 424
11th Armored 237, 293, 294, 296, 325, 380
17th Airborne 294, 337, 380
26th Infantry 11, 231, 270, 273–275, 290, 293, 346, 402, 406, 407
28th Infantry 3, 7–8, 133, 169, 176, 209, 230–231, 234, 241–273, 282, 302, 321, 359, 361, 383, 396–398, 406
30th Infantry 9, 18, 90, 101, 109–111, 118, 125, 177
35th Infantry 256, 293, 351, 362, 366–368
75th Infantry 176, 186
76th Infantry 420
78th Infantry 31
80th Infantry 11, 273, 280–281, 283, 290, 293, 346, 348, 362, 384, 389, 395, 402, 407, 411, 420
82nd Airborne 9, 11, 105, 108, 110–116, 125–132, 157, 167–170, 177–179, 183–186, 288, 294
83rd Infantry 173, 428
84th Infantry 9, 175, 193, 201–204, 207–218
90th Infantry 13, 241, 273–278, 294, 387
99th Infantry 3, 15–17, 26, 32, 33, 35–70, 78, 81–82, 90, 94
101st Airborne 9, 10, 13–14, 274, 288–290, 294, 296–298, 300, 325, 328, 331–335, 370–372, 381
106th Infantry 3, 8, 10, 133–162, 170, 177, 181, 230, 235

Heavy Armored: definition 175
Light Armored: definition 175
Groups
  405th Field Artillery 21
  1111th Engineer Combat 84, 103
Misc
  4th Reconnaissance Troop 413
  14th Cavalry Group 45, 51, 133, 135, 136, 164, 165
  102nd Cavalry Group 21
  106th Reconnaissance Troop 135
  395th Regimental Combat Team 31, 61
  728th Reconnaissance Troop 282
Regiments
  2nd Infantry 415
  8th Infantry 413
  9th Infantry 18
  10th Infantry 263, 404–405, 420
  12th Infantry 8, 383, 412–413, 416, 421–427
  18th Infantry 74
  22nd Infantry 413, 427
  23rd Infantry 17–18, 33, 38, 51–54, 60, 63
  26th Infantry 18, 70–77
  32nd Armored 181, 187–188
  33rd Armored 187
  36th Armored Infantry 187, 194
  38th Infantry 18, 33, 58, 63–69
  66th Armored Infantry 216
  67th Armored Infantry 216
  104th Infantry 402–403
  109th Infantry 8, 10, 230, 246, 258, 261, 264, 383, 387–392, 396–400, 402–406
  110th Infantry 230–234, 242–254, 257–263, 265–272, 285, 361
  112th Infantry 169–170, 183, 200–201, 230–240, 242
  117th Infantry 98–99, 110
  119th Infantry 109–110, 114, 118–123
  120th Infantry 89, 90, 93
  134th Infantry 362, 366
  137th Infantry 351, 366–367
  289th Infantry 176, 186–188, 200
  290th Infantry 181
  317th Infantry 283
  318th Infantry 347
  319th Infantry 280, 402–403, 407
  325th Glider Infantry 126, 179, 184–185, 292
  327th Glider Infantry 291–292, 294, 314–319, 358, 360, 370–371, 373
  328th Infantry 274, 406
  331st Infantry 173
  333rd Infantry 210–213
  334th Infantry 193, 207–212, 380
  335th Infantry 201, 207, 209, 217
  357th Infantry 241, 274, 278
  393rd Infantry 15–18, 31, 33, 35–40, 48, 52–57
  394th Infantry 15–17, 36–51, 81
  395th Infantry 15–18, 21, 26–31, 61–62
  401st Glider Infantry 292–293, 333–336, 338–341, 375
  417th Infantry Regiment 420
  422nd Infantry 141–154
  423rd Infantry 135, 142–154
  424th Infantry 132, 156, 177, 183, 230, 235, 237
  501st Parachute Infantry 290–291, 294, 301, 306–314, 329–330, 371–373
  502nd Parachute Infantry 291–293, 323, 327–328, 335, 338–343, 345, 368–371, 373
  504th Parachute Infantry 116–118
  505th Parachute Infantry 105, 126–132, 170
  506th Parachute Infantry 290, 294, 309, 321–323, 325–332, 368–379
  508th Parachute Infantry 168–171
  509th Parachute Infantry 200
  517th Parachute Infantry 184, 191–192
Sixth Army 10
Squadrons
  18th Cavalry 135–142, 164
  24th Cavalry 215
  32nd Cavalry 135, 153, 164
  32nd Reconnaissance 81
  38th Cavalry 16, 21, 28
  38th Reconnaissance 22
  87th Reconnaissance 160
  87th Reconnaissance Cavalry 179
  89th Cavalry 410
  89th Reconnaissance 415
  90th Cavalry 303
  90th Reconnaissance 313, 320
Task Forces
  Booth 283, 285
  Brewster 181–183
  Caraway 359, 361
  Harper 283, 285, 290, 291, 302
  Hoban 267–268
  Hogan 197
  Kane 197
  Lagrew 364, 366
  Luckett 413, 415
  Mayes 164
  McGeorge 186–187
  Orr 176–177, 197–198
  Richardson 187
  Riley 424
  Rose 283–284
  Standish 417
  Team Browne 360
  Team Cherry 290, 294–295, 303–307, 310, 317, 360, 370

Index

Team Desobry 290, 320–328, 379
Team O'Hara 290, 311, 313–318, 372
Team Pyle 360
Team Snafu 360–361

V

V-2 Rockets 1
Vaccaro, Tony 174
Vallitta, Sgt Lawrence 342–343
Vandervoort, Col Benjamin H 104, 106, 128, 171–172
van Fleet, Maj Gen James 273
Vaux-Chavanne 182, 184
Verdenne 213
Verdenne Pocket 209–214
Vetland, Sgt Ted 322
Vianden 8, 382, 386, 388–390
Viebig, Gen Wilhelm 31, 37, 40, 63
Vielsalm 6, 103, 126, 135, 157, 165, 167–169, 177
Vielsalm-La Roche-en-Ardenne highway 198
Villers-la-Bonne-Eau 296, 366–368
Voboril, Lt Rudolph 335–336
Voie de la Liberté 296, 300, 301
Voightsberger, Oberst Heinrich 236
von Böhm, Hauptmann 176, 222–227, 284, 332
von Cochenhausen, Major Ernst 223–226, 246, 327
von Courbière, Major 273, 280
von Criegeren, Major Walter 396
von der Heydte, Oberstlt Friedrich 6
von Elverfeldt, Gen Harald Freiherr 375
von Fallois, Major Gerd 257–259, 268, 304–305, 310–311
von Hauser, Oberst Paul Freiherr 265, 302, 313, 316
von Hoffman, Oberst Helmut 45, 81
von Lauchert, Oberst Meinrad 207, 223, 231, 245, 284, 321, 327, 334
von Lüttwitz, Gen Heinrich 8, 231, 258, 267, 288, 292, 302, 327, 358, 361, 362, 366
von Manteuffel, Gen Hasso 4, 10–11, 13, 18, 133–134, 139, 159, 175–177, 207–209, 224, 231, 236, 288, 292–294, 310, 341, 382, 386
Vonnegut, PFC Kurt, Jr 146
von Poschinger, Oberstlt Joachim 217, 306
von Rundstedt, Gen Gerd 4, 12, 18, 101, 382
von Wagner, Oberstlt Carl 249, 284
von Waldenburg, Gen Siegfried 176, 209–211, 230, 235–236, 239

W

Wadehn, Gen Karl 136
Waha 215
Wahlerscheid Crossroads 30–34, 133
Waimes 9, 18, 29

Walker, 2nd Lt LR 151
Wallace, Capt Claude D 313–314
Wallendorf 382–383, 394–395
Wallendorf Trail 392–396
Wallerode 156–157, 161
Wardin 256, 290, 294, 311, 313–316
Warner, Cpl Henry F 74–75
Watson, Major Jack 219
Webster, Lt Duane 355
Weckerath 136
Weidinger, Lt Col Otto 179, 182, 183
Weidner, Sgt Mel 42
Weiler 243, 260–264, 388
Weisserstein Trail 39
Welc, Sgt Jacob 261
Werbomont 84, 103, 105, 110, 114–115, 128, 288
Westwall 19, 20, 24–25, 30–34, 61, 65, 133, 141, 147–148, 231, 236–237, 244–245, 264, 282, 289, 392–396, 420, 423
White, Brig Gen Isaac D 223
Wibrin 206
Wiedorfer, Pvt Paul 350
Wiegand, Cpl Richard F 189
Willis, 1st Sgt Gervis 417
Wiltz 232–234, 243, 246, 261, 265, 267–273, 276–280, 282–283, 311, 316–317, 388, 431
Winters, Capt (later Major) Richard 376, 379
Winterscheid 142
Winterspelt 156
Wirbelwind: definition 112
Wirtzfeld 18, 38–40, 64, 67, 70
Wisliceny, Lt Col Günther 182, 186
Withee, Cpl Edward S 140
Wood, Lt Col Warren C 362, 365
Wood, Lt Eric Fisher, Jr 140, 152, 155
Woodruff, Capt Junior R 179

Y

Yates, Major Robert B 104–105
Young, LT Harold E 320

Z

Zähner, Oberstlt 362
Zarger, Major Glenn 425
Zeiner, SS-Lt Helmut 53, 57–59, 63, 63–67